Sixth Edition

Accounting Information Systems

Ulric J. Gelinas, Jr.
Bentley College

Steve G. Sutton
University of Connecticut

James E. Hunton
Bentley College

THOMSON
SOUTH-WESTERN

Australia · Canada · Mexico · Singapore · Spain · United Kingdom · United States

THOMSON

SOUTH-WESTERN

Accounting Information Systems, 6e

Ulric J. Gelinas, Jr., Steve G. Sutton, and James E. Hunton

VP/Editorial Director:
Jack W. Calhoun

VP/Editor-in-Chief:
George Werthman

Publisher:
Rob Dewey

Acquisitions Editor:
Sharon Oblinger

Developmental Editor:
Carol Bennett

Marketing Manager:
Chip Kislack

Production Editor:
Chris Sears

Manufacturing Coordinator:
Doug Wilke

Technology Project Editor:
Amy Wilson

Media Editor:
Kelly Reid

Design Project Manager:
Bethany Casey

Production House:
Cover to Cover Publishing, Inc.

Cover Designer:
Bethany Casey

Cover Images:
© Getty Images, Inc.
Photographer: Jason Reed

Internal Designer:
Bethany Casey

Printer:
QuebecorWorld
Versailles, KY

Welcome to the beginning of a journey through the exciting field of accounting information systems. We are very pleased that you have chosen to become another member of our international community of students, accounting professionals, and educators who make this book an integral part of their library as a text and reference. We promise to make the journey through this complex, challenging, and exciting topic as easy and pleasant as possible. While tackling these demanding topics, a conversational and relaxed tone was adopted, rather than stilted, technical language. At the same time, the text fully explores the integrated nature of the topic with all of its foundations in information technology, business processes, strategic management, security, and internal control. Thank you for the opportunity to serve as your guide on this journey.

Before beginning, let's discuss two key ideas that inspire the story in the text. First, the accountant is defined as an information management and business measurement professional. Second, information systems are in essence the wheels that drive an organization—wheels that allow the organization to progress and move forward. These two philosophies are briefly attended to before moving on to addressing the most frequently asked questions (FAQs) by users of this book.

ACCOUNTANT AS AN INFORMATION MANAGEMENT AND BUSINESS MEASUREMENT PROFESSIONAL

There is no doubt that the long-standing image of the accountant as a conservative, green eye shaded, non-social employee who is tucked in the backroom of an organization has been forever shattered. Today's accounting professional is relied upon by owners and managers to identify and monitor enterprise risks (events that may cause an entity to fail to achieve its objectives); assure the reliability of information systems used to gather, store, and disseminate key information for decision making; and possess the requisite general business knowledge, coupled with business process measurement and assessment skills, to evaluate the state of the business enterprise and its supporting operations. In a post-Enron and WorldCom era, the primary focus of organizations is on enterprise risk management, and the accounting professional (as external auditor, internal auditor, corporate accountant or manager) is increasingly expected to take the leadership role in identifying and mitigating enterprise risks. Accordingly, the accounting professional must arrive on the job armed with a solid understanding of (1) key information qualities, (2) critical information technologies that drive the information systems, (3) core business processes that allow an organization to operate effectively and efficiently, (4) common documentation tools used to diagram and assess business processes, and (5) vital corporate governance/internal control concepts that can be applied to mitigate risks. Each of these fundamental knowledge requirements is addressed throughout this book.

INFORMATION SYSTEMS: THE WHEELS DRIVING THE ORGANIZATION

In today's information-technology-centric world, organizations clearly can neither operate nor survive without information systems. The quality of the information systems and the reliability of the information available through such systems dictate, to a large degree, the effectiveness of decision making within the organization. Without good information, managers cannot make sound decisions. It is imperative that all pieces of the information system are in sync and operating effectively if the enterprise as a whole is to operate effectively and efficiently, and move forward in a positive direction. Figure P.1 shows the integrated nature of information systems components like a wheel on a race car.[1] The wheels and tires must be in good shape across all dimensions for the race car to safely, yet quickly, move forward and win the trophy. Any weakness in the wheel or tire puts the driver, vehicle, and outcome at risk. In an analogous fashion, the enterprise is similar to the race car in its level of dependence on safe and secure information systems that allow the organization to move forward at a controlled yet competitive pace.

Figure P.1 Information Systems—"The Wheels Driving the Organization"

The wheel representing an information system consists of six integral components. Those six components include:

- An *enterprise database* that stores the data related to an enterprise's business activities and resources.
- *Database controls* that safeguard the data in the enterprise database from illicit access, destruction, and corruption.

---

[1] Even though a car has four wheels, we are talking about one integrated information system.

- Database *views* that allow decision makers to aggregate related data from the enterprise database in a form that supports effective decision making and allows the enterprise to conduct its business activities.

- *Business processes* that reflect the core activities completed by an organization in achieving its business objectives. These processes include such activities as selling goods or services, collecting payment, purchasing materials or inventory, paying for those items, hiring and retaining a quality set of employees, and producing goods or services for sale. All of these processes both use and generate data that is stored in the enterprise database.

- *Process controls* are the procedures put in place within each business process to identify specific business risks, prevent identified risks from disrupting operations or corrupting data, detect failures that get past preventive measures, and correct for detected errors and irregularities that slip past the control boundary.

- *Pervasive controls* represent the overall corporate governance structure and related control procedures that are designed to create a regulated organization that can face the challenges of the external business environment, keep the enterprise on track and moving forward in a controlled manner, and beat its competitors to ultimately win the race!

Each of these components is explored in detail while progressing through the book. After completing the study of the concepts presented in this text, you should have a strong grounding in the critical knowledge necessary to help an organization create and manage effective information systems that minimize related enterprise risks.

FREQUENTLY ASKED QUESTIONS (FAQS)

When examining a book and considering how to most effectively acquire the information with which you are particularly interested, several questions may arise that need answered to help make the journey more efficient. In the remainder of this preface, the focus will be on the most frequently asked questions by previous adopters and readers of this book. Hopefully, the answers to your most pressing questions can be found in the following sections.

FAQ #1: What Are the Core Themes of This Book?

The book's focus is on providing the skills necessary for a foundation in enterprise risk management—particularly as these risks pertain to business processes and their information systems components. Fundamental to an enterprise risk management orientation, from an information systems perspective, are the underlying *enterprise systems, e-Business systems,* and *controls* for maintaining these systems. The emphasis on these core themes is apparent even by reviewing the table of contents. Chapters 2 and 3 immediately focus on *enterprise systems* and *e-Business* in the introductory section of the text. *Controls* are the focus of three chapters (Chapters 7, 8, and 9). More importantly, however, these themes are carried out throughout the remainder of the text in the integrative fashion for which the previous five editions of this book have been known. Icons have been added in the margins throughout the book to help emphasize the coverage of these core themes in their integrated state and to facilitate absorption of the material by the reader. Given the critical nature of these three themes, the following paragraphs provide brief explanations for each.

ENTERPRISE SYSTEMS

Enterprise systems integrate the business process functionality and information from all of an organization's functional areas, such as marketing and sales, cash receipts, purchasing, cash disbursements, human resources, production and logistics, and business reporting (including financial reporting). They make possible the coordinated operation of these functions and provide a central information resource for the organization. The concept of enterprise systems can be realized in various ways. For instance, an organization might develop its own separate business process systems and tie them together in an integrated manner. Or, an organization could purchase an enterprise system from a vendor. Such externally acquired systems are commonly called **enterprise resource planning (ERP) systems**—software packages that can be used for the core systems necessary to support enterprise systems. A number of ERP systems are commercially available with SAP R/3, Oracle Applications, PeopleSoft, and J.D. Edwards dominating the large- and medium-sized enterprise markets. Microsoft Business Solutions also has become a major player in the small- and medium-sized enterprise market with its relatively recent acquisitions of Great Plains and Navision. Many organizations use a combination of ERP systems, externally purchased sub-systems, and internally developed sub-systems to create their overall enterprise systems.

E-BUSINESS

E-Business (electronic business) is the application of electronic networks (including the Internet) to exchange information and link business processes among organizations and/or individuals. These processes include interaction between back-office (i.e., internal) processes, such as distribution, manufacturing, and accounting, and front-office (i.e., external) processes, such as those that connect an organization to its customers and suppliers. Traditionally, e-Business has been driven in business-to-business (B2B) environments through *electronic data interchange (EDI)*. The most familiar form of e-Business is the business-to-consumer (B2C) model where interactions are largely driven by browser-based applications on the Internet. This communication medium has spilled over into the (B2B) arena, replacing EDI in some cases, while also providing opportunities for new B2B interaction in this rapidly changing environment.

CONTROLS

Internal control is a system of integrated elements—people, structure, processes, and procedures—acting in concert to provide reasonable assurance that an organization achieves its business process goals. These goals include efficiency and effectiveness of operations, reliable financial reporting to stakeholders, compliance with applicable laws and regulations, and the safeguarding of valuable organizational resources. A strong system of internal controls is imperative to effective enterprise risk management, and is of great interest to top management, auditors, and external stakeholders.

FAQ #2: How Does This Book Present Accounting Information Systems?

This book is organized into four parts and a supplement. The core text has been reduced to 16 chapters. A supplement on the selection and development of accounting information systems includes the related chapters from the fifth edition of the text, updated for a contemporary environment where off-the-shelf software dominates (if one considers enterprise systems software as off-the-shelf equivalents for bigger organizations). The following paragraphs discuss briefly each of the components of this book.

Part I: Understanding Information Systems consists of three chapters. Chapter 1 provides an overview of basic information systems concepts that are of interest to the accounting professional and explores the critical characteristics of information that must be considered in systems design and evaluation. Chapter 2 introduces the concept of *en-*

terprise systems and the key role that these systems play in the successful and timely operation of contemporary enterprises. Chapter 3 addresses the extended enterprise environment, the *e-Business* relationships that an organization forms when linking its organization with the individuals or other organizations that represent their customers and vendors, and other stakeholders.

Part II: Organizing and Managing Information includes the following three chapters. Chapter 4 provides the basic tools necessary for diagrammatically documenting organizational data flows (*data flow diagrams—DFDs*) and business processes (*systems flowcharts*). This chapter is divided into sections focusing first on reading documentation and then on creating documentation to meet the varied needs of our readers and users. Chapter 5 provides a more comprehensive exploration of data storage methods, the role of databases in *data management*, and the various business intelligence tools that are available for making sense out of the vast enterprise databases in order to enhance strategic decision making. Chapter 5 also includes sections on reading and understanding *entity relationship (E-R) diagrams* (used to model database structures). Chapter 6 takes a deeper look at modeling information systems using the REA (Resources, Events, and Agents) method, creating E-R diagrams, mapping these diagrams to *relational databases*, and using *SQL query language* to manipulate and retrieve data from relational databases.

Part III: Enterprise Risk Management consists of three chapters exploring the various dimensions of corporate governance and associated effective internal control systems. Chapter 7 begins this section with an overview of internal control frameworks, general corporate governance guidelines, and the changes effected by the Sarbanes-Oxley Act of 2002. Chapter 8, designed around CoBIT, an internationally recognized framework for IT control, then focuses in on the risks that specifically exude from information systems and can put an enterprise in a stage of acute risk if not properly monitored and controlled. Chapter 9 focuses on the control procedures applicable to minimizing such risk and presents a methodology for comprehensively evaluating the risks and controls within a defined business process. This framework is subsequently demonstrated and applied across the business processes presented in Chapters 10 through 14.

Part IV: Business Processes examines the various business processes that are necessary for an enterprise to successfully operate. These chapters focus on applications supported by ERP system implementations (including exhibits of screens from SAP R/3 and J.D. Edwards software), the key controls for maintaining successful business processes, and application of the methodology for evaluating risks and controls within the given business process. The order-to-cash (revenue) flows are captured in Chapter 10—The Order Entry/Sales (OE/S) Process and Chapter 11—The Billing/Accounts Receivable/Cash Receipts (B/AR/CR) Process. The purchase-to-pay (expense) flows are captured in Chapter 12—The Purchasing Process and Chapter 13—The Accounts Payable/Cash Disbursements (AP/CD) Process. Chapter 14—The Human Resources (HR) Management and Payroll Processes, Chapter 15—Integrated Production Processes (IPP), and Chapter 16—General Ledger and Business Reporting (GL/BR) Process round out coverage of the core business processes.

Accounting Information Systems Supplement: Acquiring, Developing, and Implementing Accounting Information Systems provides an extensive overview on the selection of accounting information systems—including the buy versus build decision. With the extensive use of off-the-shelf software, including ERP software, that can be modified to fit an enterprise's business needs, we take a look at the issues that should be considered in selecting the right software and knowing when to internally develop software when the "right" solution is not available from external sources. The supplement includes a fully working version of *The Accounting Library*, a software system designed specifically to assist organizations in identifying externally available software with the best fit for their organization. The supplement then proceeds through steps that should be systematically taken to either modify purchased software, adjust business processes to mesh with the software, or to build information systems that support existing business processes. This includes the AIS acquisition cycle (Chapter S1), the analysis phase (Chapter S2), the selection and design phases (Chapter S3), and the implementation and operation phases (Chapter S4).

FAQ #3: What Are the Major Changes from the Fifth Edition?

An increase in emphasis on enterprise systems and e-Business, which is symbolized by their movement to the front of the text in Chapters 2 and 3. Chapter 2 provides extended coverage of enterprise systems and the software used to implement them, including a focused look at SAP R/3 ERP software as a case in point. Chapter 3 builds on the enterprise systems focus of Chapter 2 with a strengthening of the coverage for business-to-business (B2B) e-Business as a core component of exploring extended-enterprise systems relationships. At the same time, the strong business-to-consumer (B2C) orientation of the fifth edition is retained to provide a comprehensive view of contemporary e-Business. Placing these chapters at the front end of the text facilitates the depth of coverage that can be provided in subsequent chapters as enterprise systems and e-Business concepts and applications are integrated throughout the remaining chapters. Key enabling technologies and ERP functionality also are discussed within the context of enterprise risk management and effective business processes.

An extension of internal control focus to enhance coverage of enterprise risk management, a highly critical area as businesses struggle to meet the requirements of the Sarbanes-Oxley Act of 2002 in the United States and parallel pressures across the globe. Enterprise risk management has become a primary focus of CEOs, CFOs, and CIOs as they struggle to limit personal liability, calm external stakeholders, and ensure the continued growth of their enterprises. As in past editions, this text maintains a strong focus on corporate governance, IT controls, and the framework for assessing risk and controls across the business processes of an enterprise. Chapter 9 presents a simplified and more structured process for preparing the control matrix and for identifying present and missing controls.

Introduction to the Sarbanes-Oxley Act of 2002 including the overall implications for the accountant as an information management and business measurement professional (Chapter 1, Sections 404 and 409 of Sarbanes-Oxley), documenting business processes and key controls (Chapter 4, Section 404 of Sarbanes-Oxley), the effect on corporate governance and enterprise risk management (Chapter 7, Sections 210, 302, and 404 of Sarbanes-Oxley), and the effect on internal control reporting and financial reporting (Chapter 16, Sections 302, 401, 404, and 409 of Sarbanes-Oxley).

Use of enterprise systems-driven processes to discuss an extended set of business processes in recognition that such systems predominate at the large-, medium-, and small-enterprise levels. With the large ERP software players such as SAP, Oracle, PeopleSoft, and J.D. Edwards (now a subsidiary of PeopleSoft) pushing further down into the small- and medium-sized enterprise markets, coupled with Microsoft Business Solution's relatively recent acquisitions of Great Plains and Navision, and a decision on their part to push upward into the large enterprise market, it seems clear that all market segments are increasingly becoming saturated with enterprise systems implementations. Consistent with this market movement, all of the business processes discussed in the body of the text emphasize business processes in enterprise systems environments, the value of integrated business process information to management decision making, and business process risk and control analysis in enterprise systems environments. The business processes coverage has been extended to provide a more comprehensive examination of the primary business processes supported by enterprise systems:

- Order Entry/Sales Process (Chapter 10)
- Billing/Accounts Receivable/Cash Receipts Process (Chapter 11)
- Purchasing Process (Chapter 12)
- Accounts Payable/Cash Disbursements Process (Chapter 13)
- Human Resources Management and Payroll Processes (Chapter 14)
- Integrated Production Processes (Chapter 15)
- General Ledger and Business Reporting Process (Chapter 16)

Extended coverage of the REA (Resources, Events, and Agents) Model for developing REA models of accounting information systems. Chapter 5 introduces the REA model and Chapter 6 describes how to develop REA models. Chapters 10 through 13 contain E-R diagrams, based on the REA model, of the business processes depicted in those chapters.

Revamping of systems analysis and design segment and division into a separate supplement to facilitate the many adopters who use this section of the text in a second AIS course either at the undergraduate or graduate level. The supplement maintains its seamless integration with the text presentation of concepts, but provides a separate and lighter text to carry when the entire AIS text is not needed for class and study. At the same time, the supplement is a stand-alone module that can be used in conjunction with software development or project-oriented courses. A major addition to the systems analysis and design module is the inclusion of *The Accounting Library* that is identical to the software used in practice to facilitate selection of off-the-shelf software. This wonderful tool helps in the understanding of key concepts underlying software selection all the way from big ERP software packages to smaller accounting packages for family businesses. While using the software, an understanding is gained of the key issues that should be considered during the systems survey and systems analysis stages of the systems development life cycle, for either the build or buy situation. In short, a user can learn about selecting pre-packaged software versus building a system, and then progress on through the life cycle to understand all of the steps in modifying pre-packaged systems and/or building systems tailored to the organization.

FAQ #4: How Can This Text Be Adapted to Meet a User's Desired Content Coverage?

Learning from an Enterprise Risk Management Approach,[2] a user would want to focus on three key components of the text: (1) documentation tools for diagramming and analyzing business processes, (2) enterprise risk management and component internal control concepts, and (3) core business processes enabling enterprises to successfully complete order-to-cash (revenue) and purchase-to-pay (expenditure) activities. An enterprise risk management focus also necessitates the consideration of enterprise systems

---

[2] This approach also might be called the *business process approach*, the *accounting applications approach*, or the *accounting cycles approach*.

and e-Business concepts. But, given that those are fundamental threads running throughout the text, those should be covered with any approach. Coverage of ancillary topics related to database management systems and other key business processes is recommended (e.g., human resources management and payroll processes, integrated production processes, and the general ledger and business reporting process). Depending on a specific user's interests, exploring relational databases in detail and/or covering the foundations of the systems development process may be necessary. Recommendations and options are graphically depicted in Figure P.2 to assist in the decision process.

Learning from a database and/or REA approach, a user would want to focus on two key components of the text: (1) documentation and modeling skills for relational databases and (2) core business processes that must be integrated in enterprise-level databases. Additionally, the user would want to confer with appropriate external support specifically focused on REA modeling techniques if extended coverage is desired. A database approach can be used with the text without these additional materials, if REA models are not necessarily a preference. Again, a database approach also would necessitate the consideration of enterprise systems concepts, which are a fundamental thread running throughout the text. A database approach may focus on only a limited core set of chapters combined with an outside database software text or may be supplemented with other key AIS topics, such as documentation development tools for systems flowcharts and data flow diagrams, additional business processes, corporate governance, and IT controls. Our recommendations and options are graphically depicted in Figure P.2 to assist you in your decision process.

Learning from a systems development approach, a user would want to focus on three key components of the text: (1) documentation tools for diagramming and analyzing business processes, (2) structured systems analysis and design (text supplement), and (3) core business processes enabling enterprises to successfully complete order-to-cash (revenue) and purchase-to-pay (expenditure) activities. A systems development approach also necessitates the consideration of enterprise systems—a fundamental thread running throughout the text. Coverage is recommended of ancillary topics related to database management systems, enterprise risk management, and general ledger and business reporting. Depending on a specific user's interests, it may be necessary to explore relational databases in detail and to cover human resources management and payroll and integrated production processes. Recommendations and options for this approach also are depicted graphically in Figure P.2.

FAQ #5: How Does This Book Facilitate Coverage of IFAC International Education Guideline 11 on IT for Professional Accountants?

The International Federation of Accountants (IFAC) International Education Guideline 11 (IEG-11) on Information Technology for Professional Accountants was revised for a second time and re-released in January 2003.[3] In October 2003, IFAC released International Education Standard for Professional Accountants, IES 1–6.[4] One of those standards, IES 2, Content of Professional Education Programs, highlights three areas that upper-division university education should cover: (1) organizational and business

---

[3] IFAC Education Committee, *International Education Guideline 11: Information Technology for Professional Accountants*, International Federation of Accountants, http://www.ifac.org, January 2003.
[4] IFAC Education Committee, *International Education Standard for Professional IES 1–6*, International Federation of Accountants, http://www.ifac.org, October 2003.

Figure P.2 Selecting Chapters to Meet Selected Pedagogical Objectives

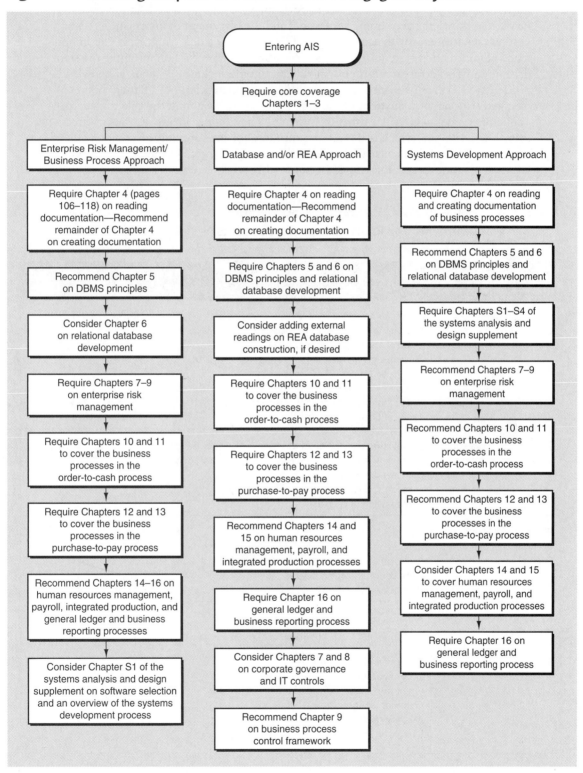

Note: Systems analysis and design supplement is *Acquiring, Developing, and Implementing Accounting Information Systems*.

knowledge; (2) information technology knowledge; and (3) accounting, finance, and related knowledge. The proposed standard emphasizes the broad education needs for new entrants into the accounting profession, and the placement of information technology on equal footing with accounting and finance knowledge emphasizes the importance of information systems to today's accounting professional. Importantly, the standard notes that information systems knowledge should include: (1) general knowledge of IT; (2) IT control knowledge; (3) IT control competencies; (4) IT user competencies; and (5) one, or a mixture, of the competencies for assuming the role of manager, evaluator, or designer of information systems. These components are taken directly from IFAC IEG-11, which is the reference source for interpreting the components of the knowledge requirements. Table P.1 outlines in detail the coverage of IFAC IEG-11 knowledge requirements that are addressed in this book.

Table P.1 Coverage of IFAC Prescribed Knowledge Requirements for Professional Accountants*

Broad Knowledge/ Skill Area	Main Topic Coverage	Chapters Directly Addressing Topic	Chapters Containing Related Information
General Systems Concepts	Nature and types of systems	1, 5	10–16
	Information systems architectures	3, 5, 6, 7, 8	
	Control and feedback in systems	8	SA&D*(4)
	Systems development life cycle	SA&D(1–4)	
	Nature and types of information	5, 16	
	Attributes of information	1, 8	
	Role of information within business	10–16	1–3
	Types of business systems	1, 5	10–16
Transaction Processing in Business Systems	Transaction processing phases	1, 5, 8, 9, 10–13	4, 14–16
	Processing modes	2, 3, 8, 9	10–13
	Business documents, accounting records, databases, control/ management reports	10–16	
Physical and Hardware Components of a System	Facilities	7, 8	
	Processing units		3
	Input/output devices		10–13
	Data communication devices		3
	Physical storage devices		8
Networks and Electronic Data Transfer	Network components, configurations, and designs		3, 8
Software	Components of a software configuration		2, 8
	Operating systems		3, 5
	Communication systems		8
	Security software	8	9
	Utility software		8

*SA&D refers to the systems analysis and design supplement, *Acquiring, Developing, and Implementing Accounting Information Systems*.

Table P.1 Coverage of IFAC Prescribed Knowledge
Requirements for Professional Accountants (*continued*)

Broad Knowledge/ Skill Area	Main Topic Coverage	Chapters Directly Addressing Topic	Chapters Containing Related Information
	Programming languages/compilers		8, 16
	Programming aids, interactive programming software	SA&D(1)	SA&D(2, 3)
	Library management systems		8
	Data management systems	5, 6	
	General application software	2, 3, 16, SA&D(1)	10–13, SA&D(2–4)
	E-Business enabling software	2, 3, 10–16	
	Software for profession use		5, 6, 16
Protocols, Standards, Enabling Technologies	Common standards	3	
	Internet protocols	3, 16	
	Standard-setting organizations		SA&D(1)
Data Organization and Access Methods	Data structures and file organization	5, 6	10–13
	Access methods	5	
	Types of data files	1, 5, 8, 9	16
	Database management systems		4, 5
	Database administration	5, 6, 8	
	Document management	2	10–14
IT Professionals and Career Paths in IT Organizations	Job functions	8, SA&D(1)	
	Recruiting/developing IT human resources	8	
	Organization	8	
System Acquisition/ Development Life Cycle Phases, Tasks	Approaches	SA&D(1)	
	Acquisition/development phases	SA&D(1–4)	
	Standards, methods, and controls	4, SA&D(1–4)	7, 8
Investigation and Feasibility Study	Investigation	2, 10–15, SA&D(1, 2)	
	Feasibility study	SA&D(1, 2)	
Requirements Analysis and Initial Design	User requirements elicitation	SA&D(1–4)	
	Systems analysis/design tools & techniques	3, 5, SA&D(1–4)	
	Process design, data organization, software requirements	SA&D(1–3)	
	Control requirements	7, 8, 9	10–14, SA&D(4)
System Design, Selection, Acquisition/ Development	Infrastructure and software services	SA&D(1–3)	
	Developed software	2, SA&D(1–4)	
	System design	SA&D(3)	
	Documentation	SA&D(1–3)	

(*continued*)

Table P.1 Coverage of IFAC Prescribed Knowledge
Requirements for Professional Accountants (*continued*)

Broad Knowledge/ Skill Area	Main Topic Coverage	Chapters Directly Addressing Topic	Chapters Containing Related Information
System Implementation	System implementation plan Install/deploy system Acceptance testing System conversion/changeover Post-implementation review Maintenance standards Change controls	SA&D(1, 3, 4) SA&D(3, 4) SA&D(4) SA&D(3, 4) SA&D(4) 7, SA&D(4) 7, 8, SA&D(4)	8
Systems Maintenance and Program Changes	Initiate the project Plan the project Risk management approach on the project Execute the project plan, ensuring (objectives achievement) Control the project Complete the project	SA&D(1) SA&D(1–4) SA&D(1) SA&D(3, 4) SA&D(1–4) SA&D(4)	
IT Organization	IT policies, procedures, and methodologies IT human resource (HR) policies	8 8	
Management of IT Operations, Effectiveness, and Efficiency	HR management for effectiveness Relationship of infrastructure to applications and user requirements Monitoring service provider activities	8 7, SA&D(1) 3, 8, SA&D(3)	14 8
Asset Management	Asset life cycle Asset management and control	8	SA&D(2, 3) SA&D(3)
Management of System Change and Problem Resolution	Change control techniques Problem management Management of end-user computing	8 7, 8	SA&D(1, 4) 7, 8
Performance Monitoring and Financial Control Over IT Resources	Performance metrics IT cost controls IT control objectives	7–9	8 7, 8 10–14
Enterprise Strategy and Vision	Internal and external business issues Factors that impact IT	. 2, 10–13, 15 2, 3, 7, 8, 10–13, 15	3 SA&D(1)
Assess Current and Future IT Environment	Current status of entity's use of IT to support business processes IT risks and opportunities	2, 3, 8, 10–16 2, 3, 8, 10–16	

(*continued*)

Table P.1 Coverage of IFAC Prescribed Knowledge
Requirements for Professional Accountants (*continued*)

Broad Knowledge/ Skill Area	Main Topic Coverage	Chapters Directly Addressing Topic	Chapters Containing Related Information
IT Strategic Planning	Envision future status of the entity's system Align future IT strategy with business strategy	8 8	
Ongoing Governance and Outcome Monitoring Process	Framework for IT governance Outcome measurement	7, 8 7, 8	
Stakeholders and Their Requirements	Monitoring service-level performance against service-level agreements		8
The Entity's Business Models	Business models Effectiveness of entity business processes	2, 3, 7, 10–13, 15 10–16	
Risk and Opportunities	Barriers and enablers	1, 7, 8, 10–15	SA&D(1)
Impact of IT on the Entity's Business Models, Processes, and Solutions	Applications of Internet-commerce Enterprise systems	3, 10–13, 15 2, 10–16	
Control Frameworks	Risks and exposures in computer-based information systems IT control frameworks	7–9, 10–16 7–9	10–13
Control Objectives	Operations effectiveness/efficiency/economy Reliability of financial reporting Effectiveness of controls IT asset safeguarding Compliance with applicable laws and regulations System reliability Data integrity	7–9, 10–14 1, 7, 9, 10–16 9, 10–13 7–9, 10–16 7, 9, 10–16 8, 9 1, 9, 10–14	15–16
Layers of Control	Societal, organizational environment, technology infrastructure, business process	7–9	
Responsibility for Control	Roles and responsibilities of key parties	7–9	

(continued)

Table P.1 Coverage of IFAC Prescribed Knowledge Requirements for Professional Accountants (*continued*)

Broad Knowledge/ Skill Area	Main Topic Coverage	Chapters Directly Addressing Topic	Chapters Containing Related Information
Control Environment	External regulatory controls		7, 9, 14, 16
	Board/audit committee governance	7, 8	
	Management philosophy & operating style	7, 8	
	Plan/structure of organization	7, 8	
	Methods to communicate the assignment of authority and responsibility	7	
	Management control methods	7–9, 16	SA&D(1, 4)
	Human resource policies and practices	8, 14	
	Financial policies and practices		8
Risk Assessment	Risk categories	7–9, 10–13, SA&D(1)	
	Probability of loss	7	8
	Consequences	7–9, 10–16	
Control Activities	Control design	7–9, 10–15	
	Control procedures	9, 10–15	
	Control over data integrity, privacy, and security	3, 7–9, 10–14	
	Availability/continuity of processing, disaster recovery planning, and control	7, 8	
	IS processing/operations	7, 8	
Information and Communications	Information processing system	10–14	
	Communication of authority/ responsibilities	4, 7, 8	
Monitoring of Control Compliance	Roles of management users/auditors	7, 8	
	Computer-assisted audit techniques	4	SA&D(4)

FAQ #6: Does the Book Fit the Core Competencies Guidelines of the AICPA Vision Project?

Several professional bodies across the globe have undertaken projects to better understand how the environment of professional accounting is changing and how these changes impact the required competencies for skilled professionals. While responding to all of the reports being generated by accounting bodies around the globe is not possible in this preface, we will briefly review how the text facilitates the preparation of new professionals based on the results of one such report—the American Institute of Certified Public Accountants (AICPA) CPA Vision Project. Let's take a look at how this book supports the knowledge prerequisites for attaining each of the AICPA CPA Vision Project's five identified core competencies:

Communications and Leadership Skills. Development of communication and leadership comes largely through practice. The AIS course of study provides great opportunities for students to participate in written and oral presentations of detailed analyses of problems. Additionally, throughout the text a host of documentation tools are covered and applied including flowcharts, data flow diagrams, narratives, entity-relationship diagrams, and control matrices. The text's supplement describes a variety of reports for use in the systems analysis and design process. Mastery in use of these tools can aid in effective communication and the synthesis of complex information in a form that can be easily explained.

Strategic and Critical Thinking Skills. The documentation tools noted under the communication section further enhance the student's ability to link data, knowledge, and insight related to information technology, internal control, and business processes to solve complex problems. Numerous short and long cases along with briefer problems are provided throughout the book to provide ample opportunity to practice and self-test the mastery of skills in strategically and critically analyzing and synthesizing information related to business environments.

Focus on the Customer, Client, and Market. While the early segments of the book are oriented toward assembling a set of foundation skills related to documentation, systems environments, enterprise systems, e-Business, and internal control assessment, the business process chapters bring all the information together to analyze the business processes of an entity. This analysis of business processes integrates the information for management decision making—the aggregation and processing of information, key controls, and business process objectives—that allows the student to better understand the full scope of an organization's business processes—not just the accounting aspects. This prepares the student to enter different business environments, analyze business activities, and identify areas for strategic improvement.

Interpretation of Converging Information. As noted under the prior competency statement on customer, client, and markets, this text's core chapters address the integration of financial and non-financial information to solve problems. The addressing of non-financial information is usually the weakest point for accounting graduates, and as such the strategies used in the text should help counteract this weakness.

Technologically Adept. Throughout the text, emerging technologies that are reshaping the business environment are described and demonstrated within the context of a business process. This focus on emerging technologies helps prepare the student for understanding how new technologies can be utilized to improve business efficiency and effectiveness, and to leverage competitive advantage.

FAQ #7: How Does the Text Help Prepare Students for the Revised U.S. CPA Exam?

In the United States, the new CPA Examination has become an interest for those about to enter the accounting profession. Quite frankly, the change in the exam has not affected this book much because the philosophy has long been consistent with the exam's new content. Students need to have a broad understanding of the business environment, how information is used by business decision makers, and the organizational control structures that should be in place to minimize risk to the enterprise. Thus, this book is an excellent source for helping students prepare for the two major segments of the exam that are changing and for the changes in testing methods. Let's consider the latter issue first. The change in testing methods requires use of certain software tools, but also uses a host of case studies, called "simulations," to provide information that must be critically examined and synthesized. The extensive use of small and large cases in this book should help students prepare for these simulation problems. This book's approach has always emphasized several skills being tested by the revised exam: communication, research, analysis, judgments, and comprehension.

As for the two big content changes on the exam, this book is also well-positioned to help. The auditing and attestation section of the exam will require examinees to have a better understanding of enterprise-level controls and the technology-based environments in which auditing is conducted. This book emphasizes enterprise systems, e-Business, database environments, control frameworks, IT controls, and business process environments—all of which should be helpful in the changing exam environment. This content is even more critical in preparing for the changes in the new "business environment and concepts" portion of the exam where 20 percent will be on business structure (an item addressed within the context of each business process in the text); 10 percent on measurement (i.e., managerial), which is addressed in the text at the level expected by the exam; and 70 percent on general business environment and concepts. As to this latter section, the detail in the business processes chapters (Chapters 10–16) describe the overall business context and then how information flows from the transaction side through to use by key management decision makers. This presentation should aid in understanding how contemporary business environments operate. The focus in the book on enterprise systems and e-Business should further aid in preparing for anticipated focus in the exam on state-of-the-art technologically enabled business environments.

FAQ #8: Does the Text Provide a Foundation for ISACA's CISA Exam?

Another question that frequently arises is whether the foundation-level skills for the Information Systems Audit and Control Association's (ISACA) Certified Information Systems Auditor (CISA) Exam are covered. These skills are also commonly required for several other global accounting organizations' certification processes for IT specialization. Let's take a brief look at the seven areas covered by the CISA Exam:

Management, Planning, and Organization of IS (11%): Chapter 8 on controlling IT processes provides a foundation for understanding how policies and standards should be established and maintained. This information is at a foundation level of knowledge.

Technical Infrastructure and Operational Practices (13%): Chapter 9 lays out a control matrix approach for assessing risk and controls in IT-based environments. Chapters 10 through 14 subsequently apply this matrix approach to analyzing IT-based systems for assurance of data and information processing reliability. Chapter 8 is based on the COBIT framework and describes the processes used to strategically guide IT selection and operation.

Protection of Information Assets (25%): Chapters 7 through 9 focus on the control structures that should be in place at the environmental, physical, and logical level to provide both pervasive and specific controls over IT systems.

Disaster Recovery and Business Continuity (10%): Chapter 8 provides an overview of the core concepts underlying disaster recovery and business continuity in business environments. While the knowledge is at a foundation level, the concepts are easily extended as the business process environments are explored later in the text.

Business Application System Development, Acquisition, Implementation, and Maintenance (16%): The supplement text on systems analysis and design provides a four chapter extensive look at the processes and controls that should be in place when selecting available software or when building tailored software systems.

Business Process Evaluation and Risk Management (15%): This area of the exam is at the core of the book's focus and the overlap is very strong. Early chapters (2 and 3) on enterprise systems and e-Business lay the foundation. The enterprise risk management chapters (7 through 9) provide the tools for assessing risk from an IT standpoint. The business process chapters—particularly those on the order-to-cash processes (revenue cycle, Chapters 10 and 11) and the purchase-to-pay processes (expenditure cycle, Chapters 12 and 13) match the IT risks analysis with parallel business process risks and controls to create an overall framework for evaluation. Coverage is particularly strong for this area of the exam.

The IS Audit Process (10%): While this book provides the foundation for understanding how to assess the risks that must be considered in contemporary risk-based audit approaches, the actual audit procedures that would be applied are beyond the scope of this text.

INSTRUCTIONAL SUPPLEMENTS

This book includes the following supplemental materials to assist the student and the instructor:

- *Supplement Text*, **Acquiring, Developing, and Implementing Accounting Information Systems**, describes the systems analysis and design process. It includes *The Accounting Library*, software that gives students the opportunity to experience software selection using state-of-the-art software used by business and consultants.

- The *Instructors Resource Manual*, revised by David Dearman, University of Arkansas, includes chapter overview, outline, and teaching suggestions.

- The *Test Bank*, revised by Charles Russo, Bloomberg University, includes a variety of types of questions including true/false, multiple-choice, short-answer, and problems. An electronic test bank also is available to simplify the customization of tests by instructors.

- A *Solutions Manual*, verified by Donald Saftner, University of Toledo, providing all answers to in-text Discussion Questions and Problems is available to instructors. NOTE TO INSTRUCTORS: The electronic solutions (available at the text Web site or on the Instructors Resource CD) allow you to tailor the way you assign problems and give out solutions. For example, a control matrix solution can be modified so as to hand out a partially completed solution. Or, a flowchart solution can be handed out, or posted on a course Web site, with the requirement that students analyze the system for efficiency and effectiveness, or complete a control matrix.

- *PowerPoint* slides cover all major concepts and key terms and are presented in an appealing way designed to hold the student's interest and effectively communicate lecture material.

- A *Web site* for this book also is available at http://gelinas.swlearning.com/ with additional materials (including those previously mentioned) to facilitate the student and instructor.

ACKNOWLEDGMENTS

In closing, we must acknowledge that the pronoun "we" as used in this text extends far beyond the three authors. We owe so much to so many people who have helped us in this project that to name them all would leave little space for any AIS material. However, special thanks must first go to three authors who contributed to the text by revising some chapters. They are Richard Dull, Clemson University; Stacy Kovar, Kansas State University; and Gary Schneider, University of San Diego.

We also want to thank the graduate assistants, secretaries, and work-study students who helped us all along the way. To the countless AIS students who have obliged us by letting us class-test our materials on them, we owe a special debt of gratitude.

Thanks also go to the current users of the first five editions, several of whom have provided us with feedback. These include our colleagues at Bentley College: Professors John Beveridge, Jane Fedorowicz, Janis Gogan, Karen Osterheld, and Vincent Owhoso; and our former colleagues at Oklahoma State University (Pat Dorr), Bryant College (Saeed Roohani), and Texas Tech (Ron Daigle and David Malone). Other adopters and reviewers who deserve our thanks for providing helpful comments include Professors Mary Callahan Hill, Kennesaw State University; Stan Lewis, University of Southern Mississippi; Donald Saftner, University of Toledo; Christine Schalow and Curt Westbrook, California State University, San Bernardino; Jim Yardley, Virginia Tech; and Stewart Leech, University of Melbourne.

We would also like to thank the editorial staff from Thomson Business and Professional Publishing, including George Werthman, editor-in-chief; Rob Dewey, publisher; Sharon Oblinger, acquisition editor; Carol Bennett, developmental editor; Chris Sears, production editor; Kelly Reid, media editor; and Amy Wilson, technology production editor.

We greatly appreciate the work of the reviewers and/or verifiers for this edition. Thanks to Georgia Smedley, University of Nevada; Paul Sheldon Foote, California State University, Fullerton; David Dearman, Arkansas State University; Carol Strand, Virginia Commonwealth University; Karen Bammel, East Texas Baptist University; Michael Emerson, Harding University; Mary Sheets, University of Central Oklahoma; Jane Findlay, Belmont University; Roger Luli, Balwin-Wallace College; Joan Holloway, Champlain College; Amelia Baldwin, University of Alabama, Culverhouse; Erwin Goodwin, Rogers State University; Daniel Hraber, SUNY Brockport; George Weinberger, SW Texas State University; Raouf Moussa, California National University; Rebecca Rosner, Long Island University; Wallace Wood, University of Cincinnati; and Andreas Nicolaou, Bowling Green University.

Our thanks also go to the supplement authors and verifiers, Donald Saftner, University of Toledo; David Dearman, Arkansas State University; and Charles Russo, Bloomberg University.

We extend a special thanks to Charles Chewning for TAL The Accounting Library software for the supplement. We also would like to thank SAP for their numerous screen shots and PeopleSoft for the J.D. Edwards screen shots.

Finally, to our wives, to whom we dedicate this book, we thank you for your infinite patience throughout this project. Without your support and encouragement, this sixth edition would not have been possible.

Ulric J. Gelinas, Jr.
Steve G. Sutton
James E. Hunton

DEDICATION

We dedicate this sixth edition to our wives, Roxanne, Vicky, and Betty with grateful appreciation for their patience and support throughout this project.

About the Authors

Ulric J. (Joe) Gelinas, Jr., Ph.D., is Associate Professor of Accountancy at Bentley College, Waltham, Massachusetts. He received his A.B. in Economics from St. Michael's College, Winooski, Vermont, and his M.B.A. and Ph.D. from the University of Massachusetts, Amherst. Professor Gelinas has also taught at the University of Tennessee and at Vesalius College, Vrije Universtiteit Brussel in Brussels, Belgium. As a Captain in the United States Air Force, he was Officer-in-Charge of IT Operations. Professor Gelinas was the founding editor of the *Journal of Accounting and Computers* (formerly the *Kent/Bentley Journal of Accounting and Computers* and the *Kent/Bentley Review*). Professor Gelinas has published articles on interorganizational collaboration and coordination infrastructures, accounting information systems, using technology in business education, technical communications, and information privacy. In 2003, Professor Gelinas received the Innovation in Auditing and Assurance Education Award from the American Accounting Association. In 2000, he received the John W. Beveridge Achievement Award from the New England Chapter of the Information Systems Audit and Control Association for outstanding contributions to the IS Audit and Control profession. He has made presentations and conducted workshops at the International Conference of the Information Systems Audit and Control Association (ISACA); ISACA's Computer Audit, Control and Security (CACS) conferences; as well as other professional groups. He is a member of the American Accounting Association, the Information Systems Audit and Control Association, Beta Alpha Psi, and Beta Gamma Sigma. Professor Gelinas was a member of the U.S. expert panel that reviewed *Control Objectives for Information and Related Technology* (COBIT) and has conducted COBIT workshops throughout the world. He was the author of *Implementation Tool Set*, a volume that accompanies the second and third editions of COBIT. In his spare time, Professor Gelinas is engaged in his favorite activities: sailing, hiking, and bird-watching.

Steve G. Sutton, Ph.D., CPA, is Professor of Accounting Information Systems in the Department of Accounting at the University of Connecticut, Storrs, Connecticut. He is also a Professorial Fellow in Business Information Systems with the Department of Accounting and Business Information Systems at the University of Melbourne, Victoria, Australia. He received his BSA, MA, and Ph.D. from the University of Missouri—Columbia. Professor Sutton also has taught at the University of Calgary, Texas Tech University, Oklahoma State University, Arizona State University West, and Bryant College. His audit and information systems consulting experience with Mayer Hoffman McCann, CPAs, and KPMG Peat Marwick (and a pre-merger KMG Main Hurdman), along with experience as a computer operator with Deere & Co., support his teaching and research interests in accounting information systems, auditing, and accounting education. Professor Sutton is the founding and continuing editor of the *International Journal of Accounting Information Systems* and its predecessor publication—*Advances in Accounting Information Systems*. He is also a founding and continuing co-chair of the annual Accounting Information Systems Research Symposium now in its twelfth year and organizing chair for the International Research Symposium on Accounting Information Systems now in its fifth year. In addition, he formally served as a departmental editor for the journal, *Database of Advances in Information Systems*. Professor Sutton is a co-author of the monograph, *Productivity and Quality Measurement Systems for Inter-*

nal Auditing (Institute of Internal Auditors Research Foundation) and co-editor of two other monographs, *Behavioral Accounting Research: Foundations and Frontiers* and *Researching Accounting as an Information Systems Discipline* (both with the American Accounting Association). Professor Sutton has published over 80 journal articles and made over 80 conference presentations on accounting information systems, auditing, and computers in accounting education. He has made continuing education presentations for both the international association and Phoenix Chapter of the Institute of Internal Auditors and the American Public Power Association, as well as several public accounting firms. Professor Sutton is the first President of the Association for Information Systems Special Interest Group on Accounting Information Systems, and a member of the American Accounting Association, Canadian Academic Accounting Association, Accounting and Finance Association of Australia and New Zealand, European Accounting Association, American Institute of CPAs, Decision Sciences Institute, Beta Alpha Psi, and Beta Gamma Sigma. He is also a past chair of the Information Systems Section of the American Accounting Association. Among Professor Sutton's hobbies are 3-on-3 basketball tournaments, travel, and hiking.

James (Jim) Hunton, CPA, Ph.D., is the Trustee Professor of Accounting at Bentley College in Waltham, Massachusetts. Dr. Hunton's primary teaching interests include accounting information systems, corporate fraud, forensic accounting, management accounting and control, electronic commerce, information systems audit and control, enterprise modeling, assurance services, database design, and behavioral research methods. He has taught courses of this nature at the undergraduate, graduate, and Ph.D. levels since 1990. Due to his extensive experience as an auditor, controller, and consultant, Dr. Hunton communicates very effectively with business students who possess considerable business experience in a wide variety of domains. Dr. Hunton has published articles in top-tier journals in the domains of accounting (for example, *The Accounting Review; Journal of Accounting Research; Accounting, Organizations and Society; Auditing: A Journal of Practice & Theory; Journal of Management Accounting Research; Behavioral Research in Accounting; Journal of Information Systems*), information systems (for example, *MIS Quarterly, Management Science, Decision Sciences*), and psychology (for example, *Organizational Behavior and Human Decision Processes, Journal of Applied Psychology, Personality and Social Psychology Bulletin, Journal of Behavioral Decision Making*). The underlying theme of most of his research projects focuses on behavioral experimentation, although he has published theoretical and archival articles as well. Additionally, he actively publishes in professional journals, such as *The Journal of Accountancy* and *Information Systems Auditing & Control Journal.* Dr. Hunton is past-editor of *Advances in Accounting Behavioral Research.* He often presents technology-based topics at local CPE forums. He is actively involved in the Information Systems, Auditing, and Accounting Behavioral Organization sections of the American Accounting Association, and the Accounting Systems special interest group of the Association for Information Systems. He served as president of the Information Systems section for the 2002/2003 year. In his spare time, Jim enjoys rebuilding his 1930 Pontiac and taking leisurely cruises around the coast of Maine in his 34-foot Mainship.

Brief Contents

Contents

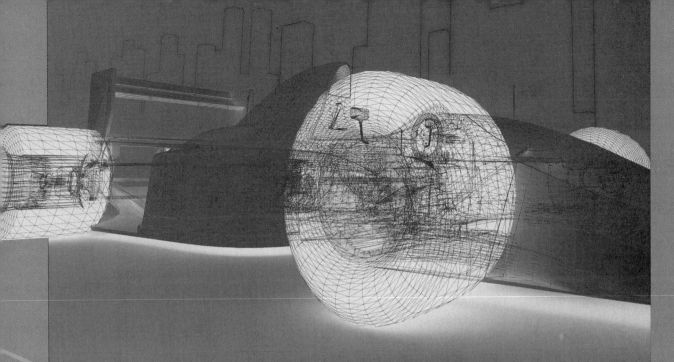

Understanding
Information Systems

Part One

Introduction to Accounting Information Systems

We start each chapter in this text with a real-life story, a vignette, describing a situation that introduces and emphasizes the importance and relevance of the material in the chapter. In this chapter, however, we take a slightly different approach. We describe in our own words three recent developments that will affect your role as accountants in a rapidly changing business world. First, the Sarbanes-Oxley Act of 2002 (SOA) has changed the daily work of financial accountants, auditors, and others. Second, the blackout in the northeastern part of the United States and portions of Canada in August 2003 has once again demonstrated the vulnerability of our information technology resources. Third, the new format and content of the Uniform CPA Examination reflects a radically changed work environment for practicing accountants. Let's expand, briefly, on these three developments.

Section 404 of the Sarbanes-Oxley Act means changes for both auditors and the companies that they audit. To comply with SOA management must identify, document, and evaluate significant internal controls. Auditors must then audit and report on managements' assertions about the organizations' systems of internal control. Section 409 of the SOA requires disclosure to the public on a "rapid and current basis" of material changes in an organization's financial condition.

In August 2003 a massive power failure left major portions of the eastern United States and Canada without electricity. Power was not restored in some areas for days. Many businesses were unable to operate during the blackout because their backup facilities were located within the blackout area. What happens to a business if it has no operating backup facilities? Entire supply chains may be interrupted. A business may not be able to enter customer orders, make purchases, manufacture products, ship goods, bill customers, and receive payments.

As noted in the Preface, the Uniform CPA Examination changed in April 2004 and became a computer-based test with new sections and content. The content changes require that CPA candidates be able to answer questions in such areas as internal control in manual and computerized environments and the technology-based environments in which business processes and accounting systems operate.

Learning Objectives

· To appreciate the complex, dynamic environment in which accounting is practiced.

· To know the AIS and its relationship to the organization's business processes.

· To know the attributes of information.

· To understand decision making.

· To recognize how information is used for different types of decisions and at various levels in the organization.

· To recognize how the information system supports the management function.

· To appreciate the influence of strategic planning to the ongoing success of the organization.

· To understand the importance of the information system's strategic plan and to recognize the relationship of that plan to the organization's strategic plan.

· To recognize the accountant's role in relation to the current environment for the AIS.

· To understand how to use this textbook effectively to learn AIS.

At this point in each chapter of this text we present the AIS wheel introduced in the Preface and describe the part(s) of the wheel addressed by
that chapter. In this chapter we introduce you to the study of accounting
information systems. The topics are broad and provide a foundation for the
remainder of the text and for all parts of the wheel.

Read on to learn how these developments will affect your career and how this text will
help prepare you for a success in that career.

SYNOPSIS

In this chapter, we introduce you to the subject of accounting information systems
(AIS), describe the importance of AIS to your future success, and lay out some important terms and concepts that we will use throughout the text. We begin by presenting a
view of the practice of accounting. We will see that accountants today are shifting their
focus from being business accountants and auditors to being information management
and business measurement professionals, providing value-added services to their organizations and clients. This view, rooted in changes in information technology and changes
in a volatile business environment, reflects the practice of accounting for those on the
leading edge of their profession. Next, we define and explain AIS and its relationship to
the organization. Then, we describe the qualities that information must possess to drive
the organization and enable the performance of key management functions. We also discuss organization-wide and information systems-specific strategic plans and how these
must be coordinated to ensure that the organizations' and the information systems' objectives are in sync. Finally, we summarize the role of the accountant in today's business
environment.

Throughout the text we will present three themes to connect our discussions to topics that are currently of great interest to accountants. These themes are enterprise
systems and enterprise resource planning (ERP) systems—such as those sold by SAP,

Oracle, and PeopleSoft; e-Business—including retail e-Business such as Amazon.com and B2B marketplaces such as Covisint.com (operated by the Big Three and other auto manufacturers); and internal control—those business practices that keep an organization out of trouble and heading toward achievement of its objectives. We introduced these in the Preface and discuss them further later in this chapter.

INTRODUCTION

At the start of this chapter three developments were introduced that will affect your role as an accountant. Here, each development will be discussed in turn. First, the requirements of Section 404 of the Sarbanes-Oxley Act (SOA) represent significant expansions of the internal control-related roles of management and auditors. These responsibilities are increasing at the same time that computer-based systems are becoming more sophisticated, thus adding to the complexity of the systems of internal control. Compliance with Section 409 of the SOA will require the application of legal, financial, and technical expertise to ensure that the organization's accounting information systems are able to produce financial data in a timely and accurate manner. Who else but the accountant, armed with the latest knowledge of accounting and information technology, can ensure compliance with these provisions of the SOA?

Second, the blackout of August 2003—and many other natural disasters in the past—has motivated organizations to develop plans to respond to these events and to be able to continue operations once they have occurred. At one point in our past, organizations could use information technology to create a competitive advantage. In many industries this is no longer true. Organizations now create an advantage by installing information technology that has functionality equal to or better than their competitors, and is more secure and reliable. For example, it is no longer an advantage to interact with business partners via the Internet. Everyone does that. Rather, it is the successful organization that ensures that their Internet connections are reliable and secure, even when faced with a disaster. An accountant's knowledge of the business, information technology, and the costs and benefits of internal controls, makes them uniquely qualified to design contingency plans to mitigate the results of such disasters.

Third, the revised content of the Uniform CPA exam reflects the knowledge required for the accountant's role as an information management and business measurement professional. To address these issues, this textbook takes you on a journey through a set of elements broader than that introduced in a typical accounting course. Becoming reasonably comfortable in dealing with these elements will probably require a substantial effort that can bring handsome rewards in terms of your professional success and the competitive edge you can gain in the marketplace. We begin by presenting a view of accountants at work. You will see that the accountants' success is closely linked to their conceptual knowledge of and ability to effectively utilize the available information technology (IT). We ask you to consider the opportunities—and, yes, the challenges—of the future accountant's environment.

We continue our introduction to AIS with some background material and definitions. First, we define and describe AIS, depict it as a major part of business processes and an organization, and describe the critical functions that an AIS performs in an organization. Then we describe the qualities that information must possess to support management and drive the organization. We also discuss the organization and information systems strategic plans that ensure that the information system effectively supports organization objectives. Finally, we indicate the accountant's critically important AIS roles.

Some of the terms in this chapter may not be familiar to you. Don't let that worry you at this point. We will define and illustrate these terms later in the book.

THE TEXTBOOK'S THREE THEMES

Before we embark on our journey, we want to describe for you the importance of our three themes and how they will be included in our discussions throughout this text. The three themes were introduced and defined in the Preface. *Enterprise systems* integrate the business process functionality and information from all of an organization's functional areas, such as marketing and sales, cash receipts, purchasing, cash disbursements, human resources, production and logistics, and business reporting (including financial reporting). *Enterprise resource planning (ERP) systems* are software packages that can be used for the core systems necessary to support enterprise systems. It is critical that accountants understand these systems because they will be members of the teams that will install and operate them in their organizations. To install an enterprise system, the business processes of an organization must be understood and documented. If necessary, the business processes must be changed and then mapped to the enterprise system. A major part of the installation project is the configuration of the enterprise system to tailor it to the business processes. As consultants, business process owners, system users, or auditors, we must understand these systems and be able to install, use, and audit them. Enterprise systems are described more fully in Chapter 2 and are discussed throughout the remainder of the book.

ENTERPRISE SYSTEMS

E-Business is the application of electronic networks (including the Internet) to undertake business processes between individuals and organizations. These processes include interaction between back-office (i.e., internal) processes, such as distribution, manufacturing, and accounting, and front-office (i.e., external) processes, such as those that connect an organization to its customers and suppliers. The electronic networks include the Internet and electronic data interchange (EDI), both described in Chapter 3. E-Business has created entirely new ways of working within and across organizations. For example, organizations are buying and selling goods and services at virtual marketplaces. This changes how organizations identify customers and select vendors. It should change how they determine what it costs to acquire goods from a vendor and what price(s) they should charge their customers for their products. Obviously, accountants should be aware of the opportunities and risks associated with this new way of doing business. E-Business is explained more fully in Chapter 3 and discussed throughout the remainder of the book.

E-BUSINESS

Internal control is a system of integrated elements—people, structure, processes, and procedures—in concert to provide reasonable assurance that an organization achieves its *business process* goals. These goals include efficiency and effectiveness of operations, reliable financial reporting to stakeholders, compliance with applicable laws and regulations, and the safeguarding of valuable organizational resources. For example, controls ensure that an organization's products (its inventory) are not stolen and that the organization does not have too much inventory (perhaps a waste of resources), or too little inventory (leading, perhaps, to a lost opportunity to sell the product). Compliance with laws and regulations includes the SOA that, as noted earlier, requires that management identify, document, and evaluate significant internal controls and that auditors report on managements' assertions about the system of internal control. While management has the responsibility for an organization's system of internal control, it is the accountant and other business process owners who are given the responsibility to effect the system

CONTROLS

of control. Therefore, it is incumbent on all managers and accountants to know how to use controls to ensure achievement of the organization's goals. In Chapter 7 we introduce internal control and then apply it throughout the remainder of the book.

BEYOND DEBITS AND CREDITS

CONTROLS   Have your accounting studies to date convinced you that the most serious problem you may face in your career is that your trial balance doesn't balance? If so, here are a couple of examples that might persuade you otherwise. It wasn't too long ago that the procedures used to process credit card sales were completely manual. A sales clerk would prepare the credit card slip by hand, run it through a machine to imprint your name and account number, and—to reduce the possibility of credit card fraud—look up your credit card number in a book that listed stolen credit cards. But, this printed book was printed only periodically and could never be up-to-date. Soon a procedure was developed whereby clerks would call the credit card companies for approval for a purchase. While this took longer, the selling merchants were able to assure themselves that the credit card had not been reported stolen and that sufficient credit was available on the customer's account. Finally, we evolved to the system that we have today: approvals are obtained automatically by connecting directly (i.e., online) to the credit card company. Why do we do this? The merchant and the credit card company want to make sure that they will get paid for the sale. As you will learn in Chapter 10, an accountant can't book a sale unless it is likely that they will get paid for the sale.

E-BUSINESS   Many of you are familiar with a different control problem that exists today—the purchase of items using credit cards on the Internet. You can read the statistics about individuals who do not want to buy on the Internet because they fear that their private information, especially their credit card number, is not secure. Controls have been put in place to protect the consumer, merchant, and credit card company (we'll read about them in Chapters 3, 8, and 9). Still, fraudulent transactions occur and millions of dollars are lost. Again, we see controls protecting the assets of the organization and assuring effectiveness of operations. After all, if customers aren't confident in the security of a merchant's Web site they will go elsewhere with their purchases.

ENTERPRISE SYSTEMS   Another example is demonstrated with a large multinational company in the health care industry. It acquired a new, large division after having just installed an ERP system in all of its worldwide operations. After installing the ERP system in the new division, the data related to the previous year's purchases and sales for the entire company, including the new division, were exported from the ERP system into a separate database (i.e., a data warehouse, as will be explained in Chapter 5). The cost accountants were then asked to analyze the costs and selling prices for a line of products and to suggest a new pricing structure that would make sense in light of the incorporation of the products from the new division. To accomplish this task, the cost accountants needed to know how the data was defined and stored in the ERP systems, how it had been exported, and finally how to get it out of the data warehouse in a form that they could use. What seemed like a simple analysis, one that would be performed all the time by a staff accountant, became something quite different!

As much as we think we know how to effectively utilize computers, these examples demonstrate that we do not know—or do not or cannot apply—everything that we have learned. These examples indicate challenges for you, while offering opportunities to those who learn in this course to be effective information management and business measurement professionals.

Challenges and Opportunities for the Accountant

Are you preparing yourself to be effective in the future? Will you be able to adapt to advances in technology, and will you look ahead and prepare yourself to take advantage of technology improvements? Could you perform the analysis of the cost and price data described in the previous section? Could you help assess the risks and benefits related to an organization's e-Business and develop the controls necessary to ensure a secure and reliable Web presence? Could you help consult with management to comply with SOA Section 404 or audit managements' internal control assertions? We intend to help you prepare yourself to utilize the available technology and to participate in planning for and growing with the technology.

The business consulting units of the Big Four public accounting firms have accounted for a significant percentage of the firms' business and were growing faster than are the accounting, auditing, and tax portions of their businesses. The consulting units of three of these firms have been split off from the "accounting" portions of the firms (Ernst & Young Consulting became Cap Gemini Ernst & Young, KPMG Consulting became BearingPoint, and the consulting division of PricewaterhouseCoopers was sold to IBM). Still, the growth portion of the remaining "accounting" firms will remain in their value-added, business advising lines. For example, a major line of business for these firms has been to assist their clients in complying with SOA Section 404.[1] Also, the new consulting firms will be recruiting personnel with accounting and technology skills. If you aspire to a career in public accounting, your success in the consulting segment of public practice will depend on your knowledge and experience in relatively technical areas that, at first glance, are far afield from the practice of accounting.

The story is the same in other accounting positions. Management accountants and internal auditors find themselves buying, using, and evaluating complex computer-based information systems. Financial accountants must be sure that their accounting information systems can produce financial statements to comply with the SOA Section 409. The management accountant must be sure that a new information system has the necessary features, such as controls and the ability to access data and to trace data from input to output. Also, these information systems must be protected from fraud and other abuses. How effectively you use technology to perform these functions will determine how well you can do your job. That may decide the very survival of your company in a competitive, international marketplace.

A survey sponsored by the Institute of Management Accountants asked some 800 CPAs and other finance professionals about the nature of the work they perform today and what they anticipate they will be doing in the future. Asked to rank in order of importance the professional activities that will be most valued by employers in two or three years, respondents named the following as their top five (the chapter numbers in parentheses indicate where aspects of these topics are discussed in this text):

1. Customer and product profitability (Chapters 10 and 15).
2. Process improvement (*Acquiring, Developing, and Implementing Accounting Information Systems*, the supplement that accompanies this text).

---

[1] The type of service performed depends on whether the work is performed for an audit client.

3. **Performance evaluation** (Chapters 7–8 and the text supplement *Acquiring, Developing, and Implementing Accounting Information Systems*).

4. **Long-term strategic planning** (Chapters 1 and 8, and the text supplement *Acquiring, Developing, and Implementing Accounting Information Systems*).

5. **Computer systems and operations** (Chapters 2–3, 5-6, and 8–16).[2]

Independent auditors are faced with deciding on the "reasonableness" of financial statements produced from data contained in the information system. As an auditor, you will be asked to execute your audit tasks and to provide additional "value-added" service to the client. You will, for example, provide your client with advice on improving operations and will alert your firm to potential consulting engagements. Successful public accounting firms will be those that provide cost-effective audits along with broader, high-quality service to the client.

These conclusions were confirmed by the report of a project sponsored by the American Accounting Association, the American Institute of Certified Public Accountants, the Institute of Management Accountants, and the Big Five (there were five at the time) public accounting firms. Practitioners surveyed reported that accounting graduates would need to be able to provide services in the areas of financial analysis, financial planning, financial reporting, strategic consulting, and systems consulting.[3]

Historically, the accountant has performed an *attest function* to determine the reliability of financial information presented in printed financial statements. This role is expanding to include the following:

- **Non-financial information.** For example, accountants might help sports teams determine whether their stadiums are located in the best places to generate income and whether they operate efficiently.[4]

- **Use of information technology** to create or summarize information from databases.

- **An *assurance service*** whereby the accountant will interpret information to determine the quality and relevance of information to be used for decision making.[5]

A special committee of the American Institute of Certified Public Accountants (**AICPA**) has identified six assurance services[6] that will be offered by accountants. These services are:

- **Risk assessment** (CPA Risk Advisory Services).
- **Business performance measurement** (CPA Performance View).
- **Information systems reliability** (SysTrust, see Chapter 3).
- **Electronic commerce** (WebTrust, see Chapter 8).
- **Health care performance measurement.**
- **ElderCare Services** (now called PrimePlus Services).

---

[2] Gary Siegel, C. S. Kulesza, and James E. Sorensen, "Are You Ready for the New Accounting?" *Journal of Accountancy* (August 1997): 42–46.

[3] W. Steve Albrecht and Robert J. Sack, *Accounting Education: Charting the Course Through a Perilous Future* (Sarasota, FL: American Accounting Association, 2000): 15.

[4] Lee Burton, "Accountants Expand Scope of Audit Work," *The Wall Street Journal* (June 17, 1996).

[5] See Robert K. Elliott, "Assurance Services and the Audit Heritage," *Auditing: A Journal of Practice and Theory* (Supplement 1998): 1–7.

[6] See http://www.aicpa.org/assurance/index.htm for a description of the assurance services and other services being defined by the AICPA. See http://www.cica.ca/ for those services being defined by the Canadian Institute of Chartered Accountants (CICA).

Development of these services has been a joint effort between the AICPA and the Canadian Institute of Chartered Accountants (CICA). In addition to the development of these assurance services, the AICPA has, in cooperation with CPAs across the United States and other professional organizations, proposed a vision of the profession's future. Called the "CPA Vision project,"[7] it proposes five core services. Three of those five address or apply information technology. They are "assurance and information integrity," "management consulting and performance measurement," and "technology services." Among the core competencies that will be required of those performing these services are "interpretation of converging information" (able to interpret and provide a broader context using financial and non-financial information) and "technology adept" (able to utilize and leverage technology in ways that add value to clients, customers, and employers).

Finally, the AICPA has created a new credential, the certified information technology professional (CITP), to recognize CPAs who can provide skilled advice on using IT to implement business strategy.[8] Skills necessary to obtain this accreditation include (chapter coverage in this text is shown in parentheses) the following:

- An understanding of project management (the text supplement *Acquiring, Developing, and Implementing Accounting Information Systems*).
- Familiarity with IT and business processes (IT throughout the text, business processes in Chapters 10–16).
- Competence in technology (throughout the text).[9]

Components of the Study of AIS

Figure 1.1 (page 10) depicts the elements central to our study of AIS. Many should be familiar to you, and many have been introduced earlier in this chapter. Let's briefly discuss each element, with special emphasis on how the accountant is affected. Before beginning, let us tell you two things. First, the *study* of AIS is our *broad view*, while the accounting information system itself is our *narrow view*. Second, you shouldn't assign any meaning to the placement of the elements in Figure 1.1. The figure just tells you that there are 10 elements.

Technology. Our ability to plan and manage business operations depends partly on our knowledge of the technology available. For instance, can we manage production without knowledge of robotics? It goes without saying that technological developments have a profound effect on information systems; enterprise systems, ERP systems, e-Business, databases, and intelligent systems are but a few examples. Technology provides the foundation on which AIS and business operations rest, and knowledge of technology is critically important to our complete understanding of the AIS discipline. Exhibit 1.1 (page 11) describes the 10 most important technological challenges and opportunities facing CPAs in 2003. These technologies were selected by a group of CPAs and other professionals recognized as technology leaders. The AICPA's Top Technologies Task Force sponsored this group and published the results. The exhibit indicates where these technologies are discussed in this text.

Databases. Your other accounting courses have emphasized accounting as a reporting function. The full accounting cycle, however, includes data collection and

---

[7] See http://www.aicpa.org/vision/index.htm for a description of the CPA Vision project.

[8] See http://citp.aicpa.org/ for a description of the CITP designation.

[9] "IT Credential to Help CPAs Make Business Sense Out of Technology," *Journal of Accountancy* (July 2000): 95–96.

Figure 1.1 Elements in the Study of Accounting Information Systems

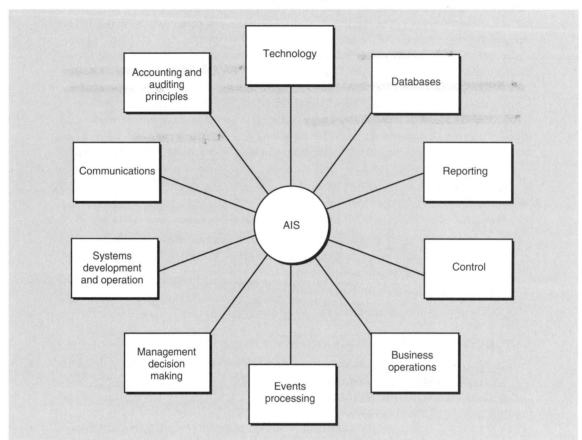

storage, and these aspects must become part of your knowledge base. In addition, important to a complete understanding of AIS are the variety of databases, both private and public; the quantity and type of data available in these databases; and methods of retrieving those data. To perform analysis, to prepare information for management decision making, and to audit a firm's financial records, an accountant must be able to access and use data from public and private databases. Chapters 5 and 6 explore the design and use of an organization's own databases. Chapter 3 examines the use of public databases.

Reporting. To design reports generated by an information system, the accountant must know what outputs are required or are desirable. Often, the user will prepare a report on an ad hoc basis using powerful report-generating tools or a database query language (discussed in Chapters 5 and 6). These reports often support management decisions as well as fulfill certain reporting obligations. GAAP-based financial statements are but one example of reporting that will be considered in our study of AIS.

Control. Traditionally, accountants have been experts on controlling business processes. As a practicing accountant, you will probably spend much of your time providing such expertise. Consider how much more difficult it will be to control modern, complex business processes. You must develop an understanding of con-

Exhibit 1.1 **American Association of Certified Public Accountants (AICPA) Top Ten Technology List for 2003**

1. *Information security:* The hardware, software, processes, and procedures in place to protect an organization's information systems from internal and external threats. They include firewalls, anti-virus, password management, patches, locked facilities, Internet protocol strategy, and perimeter control. Discussed throughout the text but especially in Chapters 7–16.

2. *Business information management:* The process of capturing, indexing, storing, retrieving, searching, and managing documents electronically, including knowledge and database management (XML, PDF, and other formats). Business information management brings to fruition the promise of the "paperless office." Discussed throughout the text but especially in Chapters 2–6.

3. *Application integration:* The ability of different operating systems, applications, and databases to "talk" to each other and for information to flow freely regardless of application, language, or platform. Discussed throughout the text but especially in Chapter 2.

4. *Web services:* Applications that use the Internet as their infrastructure and access tool, including both Web-enabled and Web-based applications. Examples include Java applications, Microsoft's .Net initiative, and today's application service providers (ASP) and business portals. Discussed in Chapter 10.

5. *Disaster recovery planning:* The development, monitoring, and updating of the process by which organizations plan for continuity of their business in the event of a loss of business information resources due to impairments such as theft, virus in-festation, weather damage, accidents, or other malicious destruction. Discussed in Chapter 8.

6. *Wireless technologies:* The transfer of voice or data from one machine to another via the airwaves without physical connectivity. Examples include cellular, satellite, infrared, Bluetooth, wireless (WiFi), 3G, and 2-way paging. Discussed in Chapter 3.

7. *Intrusion detection:* Software or hardware solutions that list and track successful and unsuccessful login attempts on a network such as Tripwire. Intrusion detection capabilities are being built into many of today's firewall applications. Discussed in Chapter 8.

8. *Remote connectivity:* Technology that allows a user to connect to a computer from a distant location outside of the office. Examples would include RAS (Remote Access Services), WTS (Windows Terminal Server), Citrix, MangoMind, and PCAnywhere. Discussed in Chapter 3.

9. *Customer relationship management:* Managing all customer touch points, including call center technologies, e-commerce, data warehousing, and all other technologies used to facilitate communications with customers and prospects. Discussed in Chapters 2 and 10.

10. *Privacy:* Today, more and more personal information is being collected and converted to digital formats. This information must be protected from unauthorized use by those with access to the data. Privacy is a business issue, as well as a technology issue, because of state, federal, and international regulations. Discussed in Chapters 3 and 7–9.

Source: See http://www.toptentechs.com/ for the list of top ten technology issues, technologies, technology applications, and emerging technologies. This list was obtained from the Web site in October 2003.

trol that is specific to the situation at hand, yet is adaptable for the future. Control—the means by which we make sure the intended actually happens—will be introduced in Chapter 7 and explored in detail in Chapters 8 and 9 and in the business process chapters, Chapters 10 through 16.

The next three elements—business operations, events processing, and management decision making—comprise a major focus of this text, *business processes.* The logical components of business processes are described later in this chapter. Knowledge of these processes is essential for success as an accountant, consultant, business process owner, or IT specialist.

Business operations. Organizations engage in activities or operations, such as hiring employees, purchasing inventory, and collecting cash from customers. An AIS operates in concert with these business operations. Many AIS inputs are prepared by operating departments—the *action* or *work* centers of the organization—and many AIS outputs are used to manage these operations. Therefore, we must analyze and manage an AIS in light of the work being performed by the organization. For example, to advise management and to prepare reports for management decision making, a management accountant must understand the organization's business.

Events processing. As organizations undertake their business operations, events, such as sales and purchases, occur. Data about these events must be captured and recorded to mirror and monitor the business operations. The events have operational and AIS aspects. To design and use the AIS, an accountant must know what event data are processed and how they are processed.

Management decision making. The information used for a decision must be tailored to the type of decision under consideration. Furthermore, the information is more useful if it recognizes the personal management styles and preferences of the decision maker. For instance, the manager of department A prefers to receive a monthly cash flow statement that groups receipts and payments into broad categories. The manager of department B, on the other hand, wants to see more detailed information in the form of an analysis of payments by vendors. Beyond the information available to managers, many decision makers now use *intelligent systems* to help them make decisions. Later in this chapter we introduce management decision making and then discuss management's use of the data collected by each business process (Chapters 10–16). In Chapter 5 we examine intelligent systems.

Systems development and operation. The information systems that process business events and provide information for management decision making must be designed, implemented, and effectively operated. An accountant often participates in systems development projects. He or she may be a user or business process owner contributing requests for certain functions or an auditor advancing controls for the new system. Choosing the data for a report and designing that report or configuring an enterprise system are examples of systems development tasks that can be accomplished by an accountant. In the text supplement *Acquiring, Developing, and Implementing Accounting Information Systems,* we examine systems development and operation and the accountant's role in those processes.

Communications. To present the results of their endeavors effectively, accountants must possess strong oral and written communication skills. Have your professors been drumming this message into you? If not, you'll become acutely aware of its importance when you enter the job market. Unlike in other accounting courses, there are few right or wrong answers in the study of AIS. Throughout this course, you will be required to evaluate alternatives, to choose a solution, and to defend your choice. Technical knowledge won't be enough for the last task.

Accounting and auditing principles. To design and operate the accounting system, an accountant must know the proper accounting procedures and must understand the audits to which the accounting information will be subjected. As an illustration, suppose you were designing an AIS for the billing function at XYZ, Inc. Would you invoice a customer at the time the customer's purchase order was received, or would you wait until XYZ's shipping department notified you that the goods had been shipped? We're confident that you chose the second alternative.

WHAT IS AN ACCOUNTING INFORMATION SYSTEM?

In this section, we suggest a definition for AIS (this is our *narrow view* of AIS) and discuss related terms to help you understand the subject matter of this textbook. Because these definitions establish a background for later study, you should read this section carefully. We begin with a definition of a system and then define and discuss an accounting information system. We conclude this section by discussing how the accountant interacts with the AIS and with the current business environment.

Systems and Subsystems

A **system** is a set of interdependent elements that together accomplish specific objectives. A system must have organization, interrelationships, integration, and central objectives. Using Figure 1.2 (page 14), we can discuss this definition. Figure 1.2(a) depicts a system consisting of four *interrelated* parts that have come together, or *integrated*, as a single system, which we have named System 1.0. Each part of a system—in this case, parts 1.1, 1.2, 1.3, and 1.4—is known as a **subsystem**. Within limits, any subsystem can be further divided into its component parts or subsystems. Figure 1.2(b) depicts subsystem 1.2 as a system consisting of three subsystems. Notice that we use the term *system* (versus *subsystem*) to describe our area of current interest. For example, in a typical university, the College of Business and the College of Engineering are subsystems of the university system, whereas the School/Department of Accountancy and the Marketing Department are subsystems of the College of Business system.

In Figure 1.2, parts (a) and (b) depict the *interrelationships* (A through H) in a system; part (c) depicts the hierarchical *organization* structure inherent in any system. Again, picture system 1.0 as a university and system 1.2 as the College of Business. Interrelationship F might be a finance student being sent by the Finance Department (1.2.1) to the School/Department of Accountancy (1.2.2) for a minor in accounting.

A system's *basic objectives* depend on its type—natural, biological, or man-made—and on the particular system. For example, the human circulatory system is a biological system (a subsystem of the human body) whose purpose is to carry blood containing oxygen and carbon dioxide to and from the organs and extremities of the body.

Determination of the purpose of man-made systems—such as governments, schools, and business organizations—is a matter we must discuss and understand. Disagreement over the basic functions of the government of the United States has always led to spirited debate among political parties. For example, is the U. S. government the "employer of last resort" and therefore responsible for providing jobs for every citizen? Even when we agree on what the objectives should be, we may disagree on how they should be attained. For example, we might all agree that the objective of a municipal school system is to "educate the young citizens of the city." However, if you attend a meeting of a local school board, you probably won't discover consensus over how to meet that objective.

Business organizations usually have more straightforward purposes that are normally related to the "bottom line." However, many businesses establish goals other than financial return to the owners. For example, a business might strive to improve the quality of life of its employees, or to use its natural resources responsibly. Here is our own bottom line: We must know a business organization's objectives to understand that business as a system and to understand the actions and interactions of that business components or subsystems. This is a central theme of our study of AIS.

Figure 1.2 Systems and Subsystems

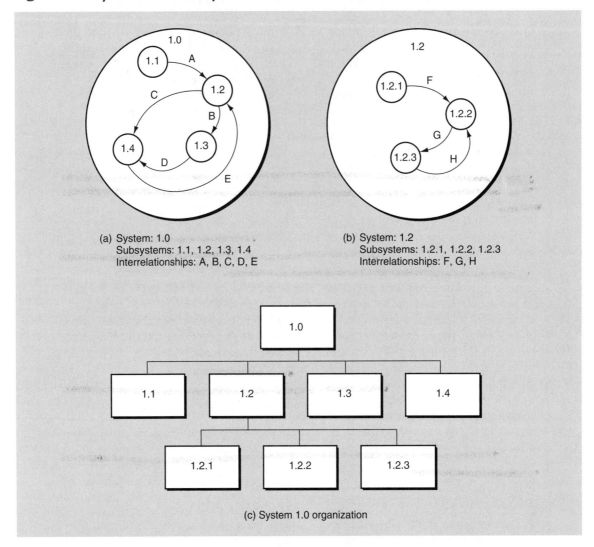

(a) System: 1.0
Subsystems: 1.1, 1.2, 1.3, 1.4
Interrelationships: A, B, C, D, E

(b) System: 1.2
Subsystems: 1.2.1, 1.2.2, 1.2.3
Interrelationships: F, G, H

(c) System 1.0 organization

The Information System

An **information system (IS)** (or **management information system [MIS]**) is a man-made system that generally consists of an integrated set of computer-based and manual components established to collect, store, and manage data and to provide output information to users. Figure 1.3 depicts the functional components of an information system. Imagine a simple information system used to maintain inventory balances for a shoe store. The inputs for such a system might be receipts of new shoes or sales of shoes; the processing might be to update (in storage) the inventory records for the particular shoe; and the output might be a listing of all the kinds and sizes of shoes and their respective recorded balances. That is, a simple information system is directed at the processing of business events.

The IS facilitates these operational functions and supports management decision making by providing information that managers can use to plan and control the activi-

Figure 1.3 Functional Model of an Information System

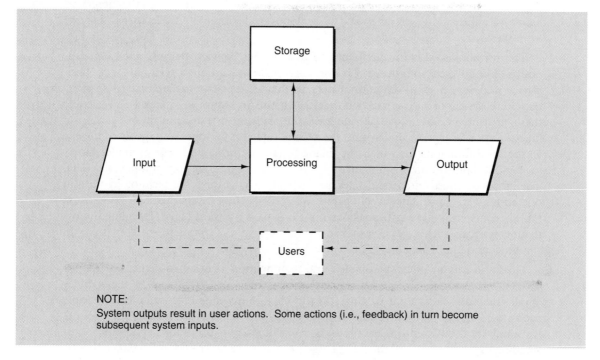

NOTE:
System outputs result in user actions. Some actions (i.e., feedback) in turn become
subsequent system inputs.

ties of the firm. The IS may have advanced elements, such as a database for storage, and
use decision models to present output information for decision making. For example,
assume that, while entering data about shoe sales, we also enter data about who purchased the shoes, how they paid for the shoes, and why they decided to buy their shoes
at our store. We might store those data and periodically print reports useful in making
decisions about advertising effectiveness. Or we might decide, on the basis of analysis of
the sales data, to engage in joint advertising campaigns with a credit card company
whose cards are often used in the store.

The Accounting Information System

The IS used in our shoe store might have components designed specifically for the organizational function being supported. For example, the IS in our shoe store supports
inventory control (a logistics function) by maintaining records for each shoe stocked in
the store. The shoe store IS also supports a sales and marketing function by analyzing
sales in a variety of ways. Other typical IS components include personnel, production,
finance, and accounting. However, integrated IS processing, such as that in an *enterprise
system,* has allowed the distinctions among these separate systems to become blurred.[10]

So it is that historically an IS incorporated a separate **accounting information system (AIS),** a specialized subsystem of the IS. The purpose of this separate AIS was to
collect, process, and report information related to the financial aspects of business events.
For example, the input to our AIS might be a sale, such as the shoe sale in our earlier example. We process our sale by recording the sales data in the sales journal, classifying the

**ENTERPRISE
SYSTEMS**

[10] These separate IS components and their related business processes are often referred to as "stovepipes" to
emphasize that they are separated and may not communicate with each other.

data using our chart of accounts, and posting the data to the general ledger. Periodically, the AIS will output trial balances and financial statements. However, given the integrated nature of information systems today, we seldom can distinguish an AIS that is separate from the IS.

This textbook studies the discipline of AIS and takes the view that the AIS often cannot be distinguished from the IS. This view is consistent with our assertion that contemporary accountants are information management and business measurement professionals. Our coverage of AIS is based on the 10 elements of Figure 1.1 (page 10). We cover these elements because, as an accountant, your skills must transcend the processing of financial data. You must understand the technology and the operating goals of the organizational functions for which the financial data are processed. For example, supermarket checkout scanners simultaneously collect accounting and operational sales data. Therefore, we must understand sales and marketing goals and the technology used in operations if we are to effectively operate, analyze, or audit a supermarket's AIS. These skills become even more critical as organizations evolve toward highly integrated information systems, such as *enterprise systems*. In summary, a complete study of the AIS should consider all 10 elements of Figure 1.1.

Finally, just as an IS can be divided into its functional components, the AIS may be divided into components based on the operational functions supported. In the sales example, the sales data might originate in the billing/accounts receivable/cash receipts subsystem. We call these AIS components the *AIS processes* or *AIS subsystems*. In this text we subdivide the AIS into these processes to facilitate our discussions and your understanding of the elements of the AIS. These processes are described in Chapters 10–16.

Comparison of Manual and Automated Accounting Information Systems

Table 1.1 (page 18) compares portions of a manual AIS with an automated AIS. The business events described in the table are for Waltham Company for the month of June 20X1, the first month of operations. The left column of the table describes portions of a manual accounting cycle, while the middle column describes the equivalent steps that would be performed in a computerized accounting system. Figure 1.4 (page 19) depicts the journal, ledgers, and trial balance described in Table 1.1. You should be familiar with the terms and concepts in column 1 and the terms *input, process(ing), storage, output, and update* that we introduced with Figure 1.3 (page 15). In this section we define and discuss the other terms in the middle column of Table 1.1.

First, we look at terms related to the input stage. **Input data** are data received by the information system from the external environment or from another area within the information system. Data input includes *capturing* data (for example, completing a source document such as a sales order or preparing batch totals) and, if necessary, *conversion of the data to machine-readable form*.[11] Input data, such as the sales event data in Table 1.1 (page 18), are normally recorded in business event data. **Business event data** represent the "books of original entry" used for recording most business events.[12] These business

---

[11] When inputs are keyed into a computer directly without the use of a source document, the capture and conversion steps are combined. For instance, order entry clerks might key in a customer order without first transcribing it onto an order form. This might be done with catalog sales. When inputs are received electronically, such as when an order is sent from a customer via the Internet, the capture and conversion steps do not involve any keying within the capturing organization.

[12] As we will discuss later in this chapter, business event data and master data represent the relevant portions (or *views*) of the *enterprise database* being used for a particular application.

events comprise the activities of the organization, such as purchasing goods from vendors and collecting cash from customers. The general and special journals used in manual accounting systems are examples of business event data. Business event data reflect the business events for a certain time period, such as one day.

Next, we examine the terms related to the two process stages in Table 1.1. Business event data are used often as a key source of data to *update* various master data. **A master data update** can be defined as an information processing activity whose function is to incorporate new master data into existing master data. Updating includes adding, deleting, and replacing master data and/or records. For example, in Table 1.1, the sales event data are used to update the accounts receivable master data by adding new accounts receivable records.

Master data updates are recorded on master data. **Master data** are repositories of relatively permanent data maintained over an extended period of time.[13] Master data contain data related to *entities*—persons (e.g., employees, customers), places (e.g., buildings), and things (e.g., accounts receivable, inventory). Master data include such data as the accounts receivable master data (that is, the accounts receivable subsidiary ledger), the customer master data, and the general ledger master data (that is, the general ledger).

Two types of updates can be made to master data: information processing and data maintenance. **Information processing** includes data processing functions related to economic events such as accounting events, internal operations such as manufacturing, and financial statement preparation such as adjusting entries. The updates in Table 1.1 are information processing updates related to a sales event. **Data maintenance**, on the other hand, includes activities related to adding, deleting, or replacing the *standing data* portions of master data. Master data **standing data** include relatively permanent portions of master data, such as the credit limit on customer master data and the selling price and warehouse location on inventory master data. In this textbook, we emphasize information processing, and our analysis of the internal controls related to master data updates is restricted to master data updates from information processing. However, at appropriate points in the text, we refer to controls related to data maintenance.

Let's summarize. A computerized accounting information system automates the manual accounting cycle with which you are already quite familiar. When we computerize an AIS, we merely change *how* the data are processed; we do not change *what* tasks are performed. As you undertake your study of AIS, keep that thought in mind; it should facilitate your study.

LOGICAL COMPONENTS OF A BUSINESS PROCESS

Figure 1.5 (page 20) depicts the three logical components of a business process; the information process is that portion of the overall IS (introduced earlier and depicted in Figure 1.3 on page 15) related to a particular business process.[14] In this section, we define the other two processes, describe how the three processes work together, and emphasize the critical role that the management information process plays.

---

[13] See footnote 10.

[14] Many would use the terms information *process* and information *system* interchangeably. But, we ask you to think of an information process as the portion of the information system that is related to a particular business process.

Table 1.1 Comparison of Manual and Automated Accounting Cycles

Manual Accounting Cycle[a]	Automated Accounting Cycle	Impact Analysis[b]
Journalize—Record sales data in a sales journal.	**Input**—Record the sales data (*input data*) in the sales event data (input to storage).	Two entries are made in the book of original entry, one for the Smith sale and one for the Jones sale.
Post—Post each entry from the sales journal to the customer subsidiary ledger.	**Process**—Record each sale in the accounts receivable (AR) master data (**update** *storage*).	Smith's AR balance is increased by $75 and Jones' AR balance is increased by $50.
Post—Total the sales journal and post to the general ledger (GL).	**Process**—Total the sales event data and record in the GL master data (**update** *storage*).	The sales account and the AR control account are each increased by $125.
Summarize[c]—Prepare a trial balance.	**Output**—Retrieve (a *process*) the general ledger master data (from *storage*) and print the trial balance.	The debit and credit balances in each general ledger account are listed (Sales = CR $125, AR = DR $125).

[a] Some types of financial events may be journalized in the general journal (i.e., no special journal) and posted only to the general ledger (i.e., no subsidiary ledgers).
[b] Assume two sales, one to Stan Smith for $75 on June 5, 20X1 (Invoice 601) and one to Julie Jones for $50 on June 16, 20X1 (Invoice 602). Assume further that these are the first and only sales to these customers and the only sales for this period (June) to any customers.
[c] The accounting cycle continues after the preparation of the general ledger trial balance. Additional steps usually include adjusting entries, preparation of financial statements and closing entries, and reconciling subsidiary ledger balances to general ledger control account balances.

The **operations process** is a man-made system consisting of the people, equipment, organization, policies, and procedures whose objective is to accomplish the work of the organization. Operations processes typically include production, personnel, marketing and sales, accounting, finance, warehousing, and distribution.

The **management process** is a man-made system consisting of the people, authority, organization, policies, and procedures whose objective is to plan and control the operations of the organization. The three most prominent management activities are planning, controlling, and decision making. These are discussed in the next section of this chapter.

If we follow the flows connecting the three processes of Figure 1.5, we can gain an understanding of how these processes work together to accomplish the business process'—and therefore the organization's—objectives. To focus our discussion, we chose a customer order/sales event to illustrate Figure 1.5. Stay with us as we discuss each of the numbered flows in the figure.

- *Flow 1.* Management hires personnel and establishes the means for accomplishing the work of the organization. For example, management would design the procedures used to warehouse inventory and then to ship those goods to the customers.
- *Flow 2.* Management establishes broad marketing objectives and assigns specific sales quotas by which progress toward the long-run objectives can be measured. In addition, management designs the information system's procedures for facilitating operations, such as the procedures used to pick and ship goods to the customer.

Figure 1.4 Journalizing, Posting, and Summarizing in a Manual Accounting System

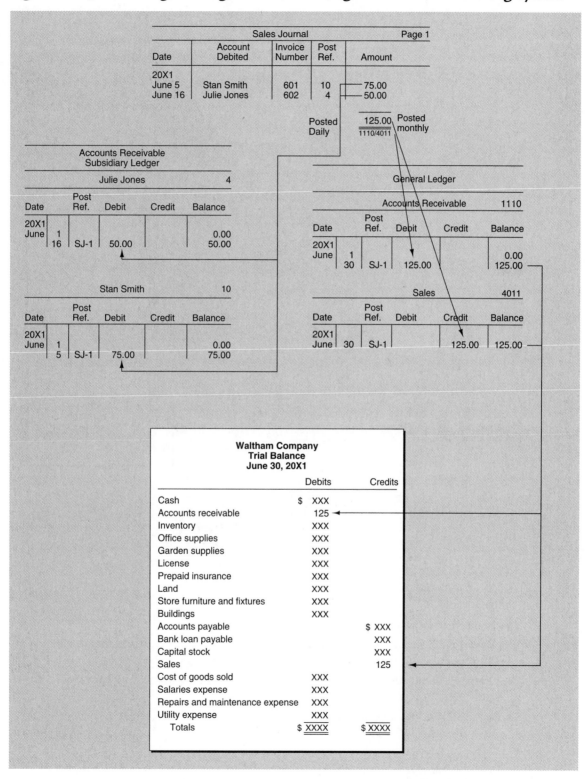

Figure 1.5 A Logical Model of a Business Process

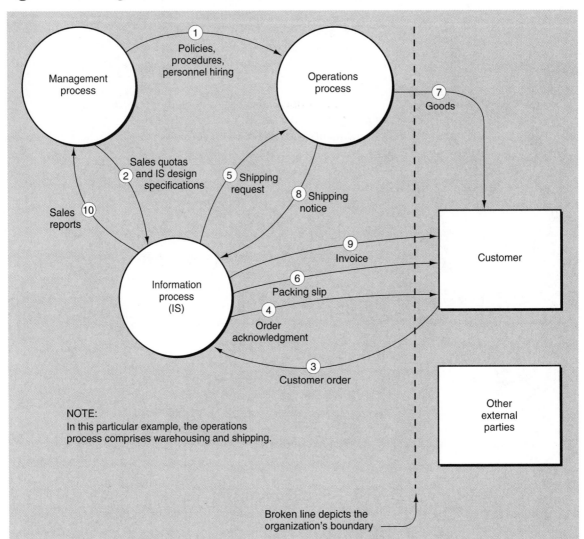

NOTE:
In this particular example, the operations
process comprises warehousing and shipping.

- *Flow 3.* Normal operations begin with the IS receiving a customer's order to purchase goods.
- *Flow 4.* The IS acknowledges the customer's purchase order.
- *Flow 5.* The IS sends to the warehouse a request to ship goods to the customer. This request identifies the goods and their location in the warehouse.
- *Flow 6.* A document (i.e., a packing slip) identifying the customer and the goods is attached to the goods.
- *Flow 7.* The goods are shipped to the customer.[15]

---

[15] Note that flow 6 is shown as coming from the IS, whereas flow 7 emanates from the operations process. Physically, the two flows are really inseparable; logically, however, they are separate. In later chapters, we will have more to say about the difference between logical and physical system features.

- *Flow 8.* The shipping department reports to the IS that the goods have been shipped.
- *Flow 9.* The IS prepares an invoice and sends it to the customer.
- *Flow 10.* The IS sends management a report comparing actual sales to previously established sales quotas.

These 10 flows highlight several important concepts that we need to discuss.

- The information process facilitates operations by maintaining inventory and customer data and by providing electronic signals (such as those used in automated warehouses) and paper documents with which to execute business events, such as shipments to customers.
- The information process provides the means by which management monitors the operations process. For example, management "learns" sales results only from the sales report.
- Operations-related and accounting-related processes are integrated. For example, the shipping notice triggers the accounting process of updating the sales and accounts receivable data in conjunction with preparing the invoice, an operational activity.
- Management designs the operations and information processes and establishes these processes by providing people, equipment, other physical components, and policies.
- Information process users include operations personnel, management, and people outside the organization, such as the customer.

Our discussion of Figure 1.5 should make it clear that the IS can be crucial to an organization's success by facilitating the day-to-day operations processes and by providing useful information for the organization's management. Let's examine the attributes that make information useful to a decision maker and how management can make use of that information to drive the organization toward achievement of its strategic objectives.

MANAGEMENT USES OF INFORMATION

An information system serves two important functions within an organization. First, the information system mirrors and monitors actions in the operations system by processing, recording, and reporting business events. For example, the information system processes customer orders; records sales to customers by updating sales, accounts receivable, and inventory data; and produces invoices and sales event summaries.

The second major function of the information system is to support managerial activities, including management decision making. How do managers use this information? First, they monitor current operations to keep their "ship" on course. For example, managers need to know if enough inventory is being produced each day to meet expected demand. Managers' second use of information is to help them achieve satisfactory results for all their stakeholders (e.g., customers, stockholders). For example, information can measure attainment of goals regarding product quality, timely deliveries, cash flow, and operating income. Finally, managers use the information system to recognize and adapt in a timely manner to trends in the organization's environment. For example, managers need answers to questions such as: "How does the time it takes us to introduce a new product compare to our competitors?" "Does our unit cost to manufacture compare to our competitors?"[16] Because information systems provide critical support to such management activities, we must understand these activities, including decision making, to understand the required design features of good information systems. In this section we discuss, in general terms, management uses of information.

Data Versus Information

Our definitions of *data* and *information* are a bit circular. **Information** is data presented in a form that is useful in a decision-making activity. The information has value to the decision maker because it reduces uncertainty and increases knowledge about a particular area of concern. **Data** are facts or figures in raw form. Data represent the measurements or observations of objects and events. To become useful to a decision maker, data must be transformed into information. Figure 1.6 illustrates the transformation process. Notice that part (a) repeats the functional model of an *information system* that we saw in Figure 1.3 (page 15), whereas part (b) uses the same symbols with different labels. Might you conclude, then, that the function of the information system is to transform data into information? Absolutely.

We said, however, that *information* must be *useful* in decision making. What attributes give information its utility value? Let's answer this question next.

Qualities of Information

To provide output useful for assisting managers and other users of information, an information system must collect data and convert them into information that possesses important qualities. In this section, we examine some of the elements of information quality that allow us to design and control the collection and processing of data. Exhibit 1.2 (page 24) describes qualities of information that, if attained, will help an organization achieve its business objectives. Figure 1.7 (page 25) presents an overview of information qualities depicted as a hierarchy. In the following paragraphs we discuss and expand upon these various information qualities.

You can see from the exhibit that the *effectiveness* quality overlaps with other qualities as it includes such measures as "timely" (i.e., availability) and "correct" (i.e., integrity). The effectiveness of information must be evaluated in relation to the purpose to be served—decision making. Effective information is information that is useful for the decision to be made. Effectiveness, then, is a function of the decisions to be made, the method of decision making to be used, the information already possessed by the decision maker, and the decision maker's capacity to process information. The superior factors in Figure 1.7, such as "users of information" and "overall quality (decision usefulness)," provide additional emphasis for these points. Our examples should make these points clear.[17]

Understandability enables users to perceive the information's significance. Valued from the user's point of view, understandable information is presented in a form that permits its application by the user in the decision-making situation at hand. For example, information must be in a language understood by the decision maker. By language,

---

[16] To read more about measures of performance, see Robert S. Kaplan and David P. Norton, "The Balanced Scorecard Measures That Drive Performance," *Harvard Business Review* (January–February 1992): 71–79, as well as subsequent articles that have appeared in the *Harvard Business Review*.

[17] The descriptions of many of these terms are adapted from *Statement of Financial Accounting Concepts No. 2: Qualitative Characteristics of Accounting Information*, Financial Accounting Standards Board (FASB), May 1980.

Figure 1.6 Transforming Data into Information

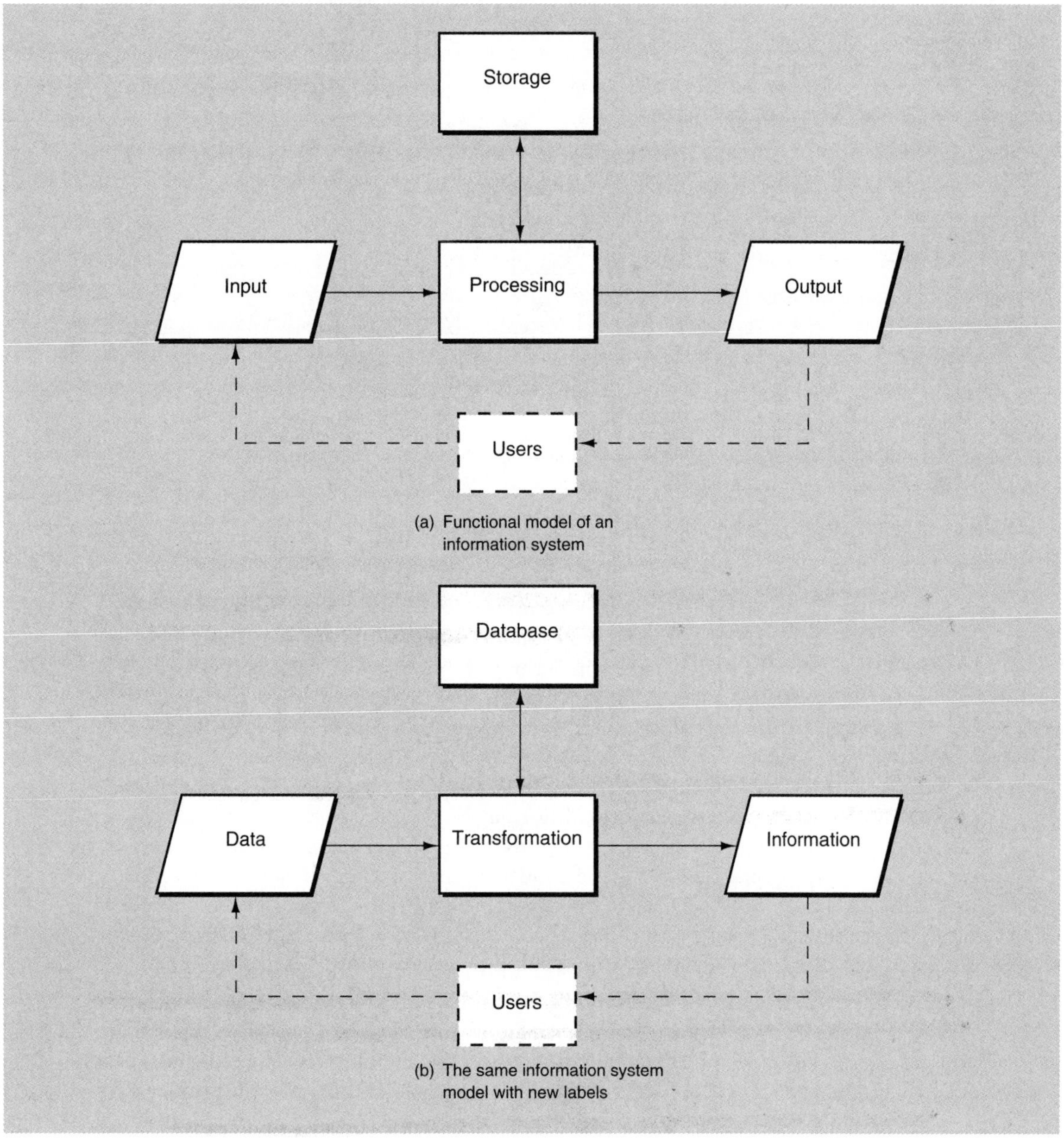

(a) Functional model of an information system

(b) The same information system model with new labels

we mean native language, such as English or French, as well as technical language, such as those used in physics or computer science. Also, information that makes excessive use of codes and acronyms may not be understandable to some decision makers.

Information capable of making a difference in a decision-making situation by reducing uncertainty or increasing knowledge for that particular decision has **relevance**. For example, a credit manager making a decision about whether to grant credit to a customer might use the customer's financial statements and credit history because that information could be relevant to the credit-granting decision. The customer's organization chart

Exhibit 1.2 Qualities of Information

Effectiveness: deals with information being relevant and pertinent to the business process as well as being delivered in a timely, correct, consistent, usable, and complete manner.

Efficiency: concerns the provision of information through the optimal (most productive and economical) usage of resources.

Confidentiality: concerns the protection of sensitive information from unauthorized disclosure.

Integrity: relates to the accuracy and completeness of information as well as its validity in accordance with a business's set of values and expectations.

Availability: relates to information being available when required by the business process, and hence also concerns the safeguarding of resources.

Compliance: deals with complying with those laws, regulations, and contractual obligations to which the business process is subject, that is, externally imposed business criteria.

Reliability of information: relates to systems providing management with appropriate information for both to use in operating the entity, in providing financial reporting to users of the financial information, and in providing information to regulatory bodies with regard to compliance with laws and regulations.

Source: Reprinted with permission from *COBIT: Control Objectives for Information and Related Technology—Framework*, 3rd ed. (Rolling Meadows, IL: The Information Systems Audit and Control Foundation, 2000): 14.

would not be relevant. The description of *reliability of information* in Exhibit 1.2 uses the term "appropriate." Relevance is a primary component of appropriateness.

Information that is available to a decision maker before it loses its capacity to influence a decision has **timeliness**. Lack of timeliness can make information irrelevant. For example, the credit manager must receive the customer's credit history before making the credit-granting decision. If the decision must be made without the information, the credit history becomes irrelevant. Exhibit 1.2 describes *availability* as "being available when required." Thus, availability can increase timeliness.

Predictive value and **feedback value** improve a decision maker's capacity to predict, confirm, or correct earlier expectations. Information can have both types of value, since knowledge of the outcomes of actions already taken will generally improve a decision maker's abilities to predict the results of similar future actions. A buyer for a retail store might use a sales forecast—a prediction—to establish inventory levels. As the buyer continues to use these sales forecasts and to review past inventory shortages and overages—feedback—he or she can refine decision making concerning inventory.

If there is a high degree of consensus about the information among independent measurers using the same measurement methods, the information has **verifiability**. In accounting, we record assets at their historical cost. Why? Because evidence of the assets' cost will permit several people to arrive at a similar estimate of the book value of the asset.

Neutrality or **freedom from bias** means that the information is not biased. Bias is the tendency of information to fall more often on one side than on the other of the object or event that it represents. For example, an accounts receivable balance that is usually higher than what can be collected is biased. Notice that verifiability addresses the reliability of the measurement method (e.g., historical cost, market value), and neutrality addresses the reliability of the person doing the measuring.

Comparability is the information quality that enables users to identify similarities and differences in two pieces of information. If we can compare information about two similar objects or events, the information is comparable. For example, in either your financial or managerial accounting course you probably studied ratio analysis of financial statements. You also learned that one of the "yardsticks" against which you might evaluate

Figure 1.7 A Hierarchy of Information Qualities

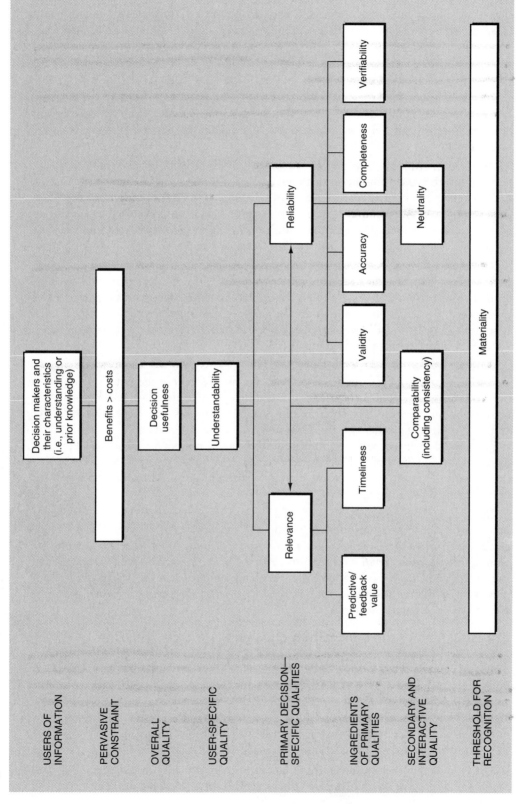

Source: Adapted from *Statement of Financial Accounting Concepts No. 2: Qualitative Characteristics of Accounting Information*, Financial Accounting Standards Board (FASB), May 1980, p. 15. Copyright by Financial Accounting Standards Board, 401 Merritt 7, P.O. Box 5116, Norwalk, CT 06856-5116. Reprinted with permission. Copies of complete documentation are available from the FASB.

the ratios of company A would be similar ratios for competitor company B or for the industry as a whole. But how good is your comparison of two companies if one uses FIFO (first in, first out) inventory costing, and the other uses LIFO (last in, first out) costing? Generally accepted accounting principles strive to make accounting information as comparable as possible across firms by establishing common practices for accounting for inventory, fixed assets, leases, and so on.

If, on the other hand, we can compare information about the same object or event collected at two points in time, the information is **consistent**. Again, in doing ratio analysis, you probably performed horizontal or trend analysis for two or more years for one company.

As noted in Exhibit 1.2 (page 24), *integrity* is an information quality that can be expanded into three very important qualities: validity, accuracy, and completeness. In Figure 1.7 (page 25) these are components of reliability. Information about actual events and actual objects has **validity**. For example, suppose that the IS records a sale and an account receivable for a shipment that didn't occur. The *recorded* information describes a fictitious event; therefore, the information lacks validity.

Accuracy is the correspondence or agreement between the information and the actual events or objects that the information represents. For example, we would have inaccurate information if the quantity on hand in an inventory report was reported as 51 units, when the actual physical quantity on hand was 15 units (note the transposition). Inaccurate information also would result if, for instance, 15 units were actually on hand, yet the inventory report indicated only 10 units.

Completeness is the degree to which information includes data about every relevant object or event necessary to make a decision. We use *relevant* in the sense of all objects or events that we *intended* to include. For example, in Chapter 7 we will learn that an accountant must ensure that an accounting system captures and records all *valid* accounting event data, otherwise the accounting database is not complete. For instance, suppose the shipping department prepared 50 shipping notices for 50 actual shipments made for the day. Two of the notices were accidentally blown to the floor and were discarded with the trash. As a result, the billing department prepared customer invoices for only 48 shipments, not 50.

In summary, the *effectiveness* of information can be measured in many ways. Those previously discussed and included in Exhibit 1.2 and Figure 1.7 (pages 24 and 25) include *understandability, relevance* (or *reliability*), *timeliness* (or *availability*), *predictive value, feedback value, verifiability, neutrality* (or *freedom from bias*), and *comparability, consistency,* and *integrity* (or *validity, accuracy,* and *completeness*). We will see these qualities again, in addition to those not discussed here (*efficiency, confidentiality,* and *compliance*) in subsequent chapters.

Conflicts Among the Information Qualities

It is virtually impossible to simultaneously achieve a *maximum* level for all the qualities of information. In fact, for some of the qualities, an increased level of one requires a reduced level of another. In one instance, obtaining *complete* information for a decision may require delaying use of the information until all events related to the decision have taken place. That delay may sacrifice the *timeliness* of the information. For example, to determine all the merchandise shipments made in November, an organization may have to wait until several days into December to make sure that all shipments get posted.

CONTROLS

Let's look at another example. To obtain *accurate* information, we may carefully and methodically prepare the information, thus sacrificing the *timeliness* of the information.

For example, to ensure the accuracy of a customer invoice, billing clerks might check the invoice for accuracy several times and then get their supervisor to initial the invoice, indicating that he or she also has checked the invoice for accuracy. These procedures certainly delay the mailing of the invoice.

Management Decision Making

We have asserted that the purpose of an IS is to facilitate an organization's business processes and to support management *decision making* by providing information that managers can use to plan and control the activities of the firm. Let's pursue the meaning and importance of decision making. Very simply, **decision making is the process of making choices.** It is the central activity of all management. Managers make decisions or choices, such as what products to sell, in which markets to sell those products, what organizational structure to use, and how to direct and motivate employees. Herbert A. Simon, a Nobel-prize-winning economist, describes decision making as a three-step process:

1. *Intelligence*: Searching the environment for conditions calling for a decision.
2. *Design*: Inventing, developing, and analyzing possible courses of action.
3. *Choice*: Selecting a course of action.[18]

Figure 1.8 (page 28) depicts these three steps. Analyze the figure to see what information is required for each step. Information from and about the environment and the organization is needed to recognize situations or problems requiring decisions. For example, information about economic trends, marketing intelligence, and likely competitor actions should help management to recognize opportunities for new markets and products. Information about inefficient or overworked processes in the organization should focus management's attention on problems in the organization. Managers use information from inside and outside the organization to design courses of action. For example, information about personnel resources, production capacity, and available distribution channels should help management to develop alternative methods for producing and distributing a new product. Finally, a manager requires information about the possible outcomes from alternative courses of action. For example, to choose from among alternative production options, a manager needs information about the costs and benefits of the alternatives or about the probability of success of each option.

The pyramid on the left side of Figure 1.9 (page 28) represents data flows related to the processing of business events. It emphasizes that operations and information flows are both horizontal and vertical, and that there are several levels of management.[19] At the level of operations and business events processing, the flows are horizontal as the information moves through operational units such as sales, the warehouse, and accounting. In the sales example of Figure 1.5 (page 20), the operational documents and records are the outputs of these horizontal flows.

For example, horizontal flows relate to specific business events, such as one shipment, or to individual inventory items. This information is narrow in scope, detailed, accurate, and comes largely from within the organization. The data captured at the operations and business event processing level constitute the foundation for the vertical information flows that service a multilevel management function.

---

[18] Herbert A. Simon, *The New Science of Management Decision* (New York: Harper & Row, 1960): 2.

[19] Because Figure 1.9 depicts data from business events, the vertical information flows upward. Other data, such as budgets, would flow downward.

Figure 1.8 Steps in Decision Making

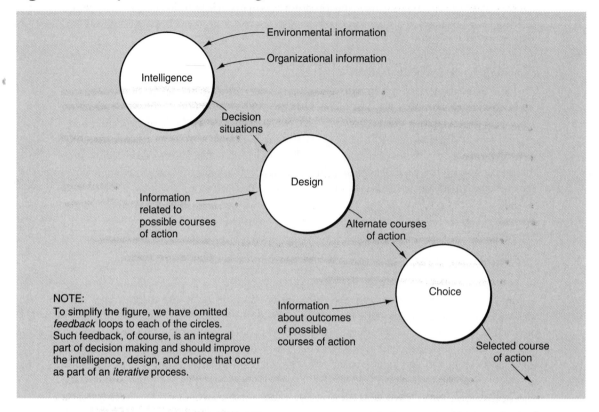

Figure 1.9 Management Problem Structure and Information Requirements

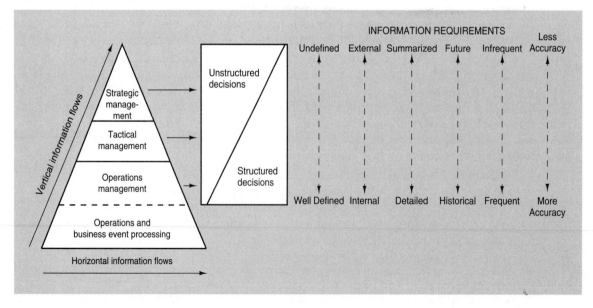

On the other hand, information useful to operations management personnel is often an aggregate of data related to several business events. For example, a report summarizing shipments made each day might be useful to the shipping manager. At the operations management level, supervisors use this type information to monitor the daily functioning of their operating units. The vertical information useful to operations management is a summarized and tailored version of the information that flows horizontally.

Tactical management requires information that focuses on relevant operational units and is more summarized, broader in scope, and need not be as accurate as the information used by operations management. Some external information may be required. For example, a warehousing and distribution manager might want information about the timeliness of shipments each month.

Finally, strategic management requires information to assess the environment and to project future events and conditions. Information is even more summarized, broader in scope, and comes from outside the organization more than does the information used by tactical management. To be useful to division managers, chief financial officers (CFOs), and chief executive officers (CEOs), information must relate to longer time periods, be sufficiently broad in scope, and be summarized to provide a means for judging the long-term effectiveness of management policies. External financial statements, annual sales reports, and division income statements are but a few examples of strategic-level information. We should note, however, that current computer technology facilitates access to detailed data at all management levels.

The decision's structure, or lack thereof, also heavily influences the kind of information required to make a decision. *Structure* is the degree of repetition and routine in the decision. Structure implies that we have seen this very decision before and have developed procedures for making the decision. We can use the degree of structure inherent in each decision-making step to categorize the decisions as structured or unstructured. We define **structured decisions** as those for which all three decision phases (intelligence, design, and choice) are relatively routine or repetitive. In fact, some decisions are so routine that a computer can be programmed to make them. For example, many organizations have automated the decision of when and how much credit to grant a customer when an order is received. At the time the customer's order is entered, the computer compares the amount of the order to the customer's credit limit, credit history, and outstanding balances. Using this information the computer may grant credit, deny credit, or suggest a review by the credit department. These procedures are described in more detail in Chapter 10.

CONTROLS

Consider, on the other hand, managers' decision-making process when choosing what research and development projects to undertake in the next year. This is only one example of what we classify as an **unstructured decision**, one for which none of the decision phases (intelligence, design, or choice) are routine or repetitive.

Look again at Figure 1.9 and see that it summarizes several concepts introduced in this section and also helps us to understand the nature of the characteristics associated with information used by the three levels of management for decision making. Further, this figure indicates the proportion of structured and unstructured decisions handled by the three management levels.

Information Qualities and Decision-Making Level

The level of the decision maker and the type of decision to be made will determine the preeminence of certain information qualities. For example, strategic management may require information high in predictive value. Information used for strategic planning should help managers "see" the future and thereby assist them in formulating long-term plans. The strategic manager may not be as concerned with timeliness or accuracy and would therefore prefer a quarterly sales report to a daily report. Operations management must make frequent decisions, with shorter lead times, and may therefore require a daily sales report to be able to react in a timely manner to changes in sales patterns. Operations management may require timely and accurate information and may not be concerned about the predictive value of the information.

Conclusions About Management Decision Making

From Figures 1.8 and 1.9 (page 28) and their related discussions, we can reach the following conclusions. Information needed for decision making can differ in degree of aggregation and detail, in source, and in fundamental character. We have also seen that the required qualities of information will differ by decision type and level of management.

Within the organization, managers can secure inputs to their decisions directly, from the environment or from direct observation of business processes. Managers can also receive information indirectly through the IS, which retrieves and presents operational and environmental information. As we understand more about the decisions to be made and can better anticipate the data needed to make those decisions, the information system can be designed to provide more of the required information. For example, in ever-increasing numbers, organizations' information systems are obtaining information about economic trends and indicators that is available in public databases.

Because data requirements for structured decisions are well defined, we strive to improve our understanding of decisions so that we can make more decisions structured, anticipate the data needed for those decisions, and regularly provide those data through the information system.

ENTERPRISE SYSTEMS   Let's conclude this section by asking: How does the IS support the multiple information uses suggested by the preceding discussions? For example, how does the IS support such users as the organization's operations units, the organization's management, and people outside the organization? How does the IS supply the information needed by three levels of management? One key component enabling the IS to meet the needs of this diverse constituency is the enterprise database. As noted in the Preface, the enterprise database is the central repository for all the data related to the enterprise's business activities and resources. IS processes, such as order entry, billing, and inventory, update the database. Output can be obtained by other IS processes and by other users, such as management. When processes or other users access the enterprise database, they are given a *view* of the database appropriate for their needs. For example, when entering the customer order in Figure 1.5 (page 20), the IS was given access to that *portion* of the database that was required, such as the applicable customer and inventory data.

STRATEGIC PLANNING AND INFORMATION SYSTEMS

Strategic planning is the process of selecting the organization's long-term objectives and of setting the strategies for achieving those objectives. This planning process is the responsibility of strategic management and is concerned with the overriding issues facing the organization, such as product lines and profitability. Given the international, competitive, and dynamic environment confronted by an organization, strategic planning is crucial to the survival of that organization. Figure 1.10 depicts the strategic planning process.

Figure 1.10 Organizational Strategic Planning Process

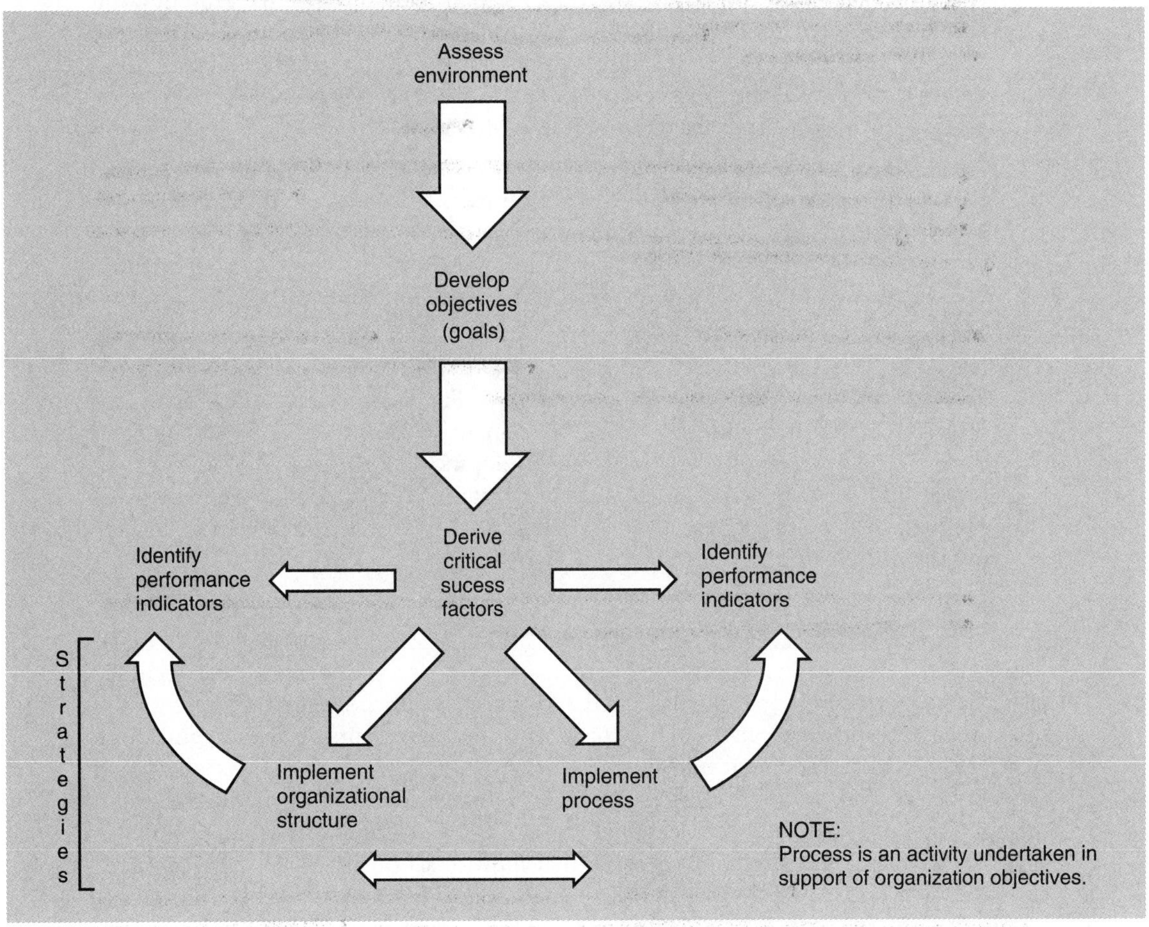

The strategic planning process addresses such questions as:

1. What business are we in and who are our customers?
2. What knowledge advantage do we have in our business?
3. How should our products be perceived?
4. What rate of return on assets, earnings, or cash flow are we trying to achieve?
5. What are our social responsibilities?

The strategic plan includes answers to these questions. In this section, we summarize organizational strategic planning and suggest the critical importance of that planning process and the information system to the long-term success of an organization.

Organizational Strategic Planning

As shown in Figure 1.10, the strategic planning process includes the following steps:

1. Assess the environment for factors suggesting opportunities and threats. Figure 1.10 depicts the importance of the environment in selecting the organization's objectives. That is, the environment is the only independent variable.

2. Assess the organization's strengths and weaknesses and develop objectives that match the organization's strengths and weaknesses with the opportunities and threats in the environment. An **objective** is an intention; it is a desired state or condition being sought. For example, an organization may want to be the biggest, the most profitable, the most respected, or the firm with the broadest product line in its industry. We also refer to an objective as a **goal**.

3. Derive the factors that are central to the accomplishment of the objectives and to the survival of the organization—the critical success factors. **Critical success factors (CSFs)** are events, circumstances, conditions, and activities that are essential to the survival of the organization. Examples include cost control, product pricing, product styling, and close ties with high-quality franchisees.

4. Develop corporate strategy (also referred to as a **plan**). A **strategy** is the means (organizational structure and processes) by which an organization has chosen to achieve its objectives and critical success factors. For example, a strategy for achieving prominence in an industry might be to increase research and development to achieve a higher level of new-product development. Or as an alternative to research and development, an organization might choose to copy competitors' products. Strategies apply to a variety of functions within the organization, including the information systems function.

5. Identify the *performance indicators* that will demonstrate achievement of the organization's strategies and critical success factors.

Recall from our earlier discussions of management decision making that strategic planning decisions are largely unstructured and that the source of much of the information needed for the strategic planning process comes from outside the organization. Also, lower-level management must convert the strategic plan to plans directed at each organizational level and unit. During this process, management must ensure that goals are not in conflict between organizational levels or between functions at the same level. That is, the planning process must ensure that individuals or functions work toward a common objective. An organization strives to establish *goal congruence* for individuals and functions so as to attain optimal output for the organization. Without goal congruence, individuals will strive to maximize their own output.

Information Systems for Aiding the Strategic Planner

The information system can play an important role in the *development of the strategic plan* and in monitoring ongoing operations to *measure attainment of the plan*. In this section we discuss the upfront and ongoing assistance that the strategic planner obtains from the information system.

ENTERPRISE SYSTEMS

During the strategic planning process, data from the *enterprise database* can be compared to data about the competition to determine an organization's relative strengths and weaknesses. For example, these data might include sales trends, gross margin on sales, age of capital assets, skills of existing personnel, debt/equity ratio, and so on. These data can be presented in reports from the existing information systems applications, such as sales/marketing, human resources management, fixed assets, finance and inventory, or via decision models incorporated in the IS. Strategic planners can combine the environmental data with those obtained internally to assess the organization's competitive position. The demand for such information has been a major driver in the move to *enterprise systems*, which bring all of the organization's information together into a single *enterprise database* and generally provide the associated tools for strategic analysis and decision support.

In addition to assisting in the planning phase, the IS can be used to follow up by reporting certain *performance indicators* that illustrate the status of processes and critical success factors. For example, the number of franchises along with the level of sales and number of customer complaints for each should indicate the status of an organization's franchise network. Other performance indicators might be the number of new products, the cost to manufacture the products, and their selling price. If the *enterprise database* is developed in light of the strategic plan, many of the data for the performance indicators should be readily available.

Strategic Uses of Information Technology

In addition to an organizational strategic planning process, there must be a strategic planning process for the information systems function (discussed in Chapter 8). That process must be coordinated with the organization's strategic planning process to ensure that the *organization's* strategic plan is supported and that information technology is used to the best advantage of the organization. For example, during the strategic planning process, organizations should seek to achieve strategic advantage over their competitors by utilizing available information technology. This is particularly observable as companies ponder how to deal with the rapidly evolving world of e-Business. If the organization regards its information system as useful only for supporting operations-level processes, however, it will soon find itself at a competitive disadvantage.

CONTROLS

E-BUSINESS

As you study AIS, reflect on the implications that the strategic use of information technology will have on the organization structure and process of the AIS. Also, consider the impact that the strategic application of information technology will have on your career as a user and developer of information technology.

Strategic Planning and the Financial Specialist

Let's review what we have learned in the last three sections. Superior strategic planning efforts can enhance the long-term success of an organization. Successful strategic use of information technology is another determinant of an organization's success.

Before concluding our coverage of strategic planning, let's discuss the important relationship that exists between the financial manager and the strategic planning process of the organization and the information system. First, the financial manager should participate in the planning process. One function of the financial manager in this process is to analyze the financial structure of the organization and its competitors to determine relative strengths and weaknesses. For example, information about the mix of fixed and variable costs and the proportion of short- and long-term debt to total equity may indicate relative advantages of one firm over another. Also, the financial specialist could assist in the design of the reporting system established to monitor achievement of planning goals. For example, the financial specialist could establish some of the financial *performance indicators*.

Second, the financial manager should approve the output of the planning process—the organizational strategic plan and the information systems strategic plan. A financial manager is in a unique position to sign off on the plans' feasibility and financial viability (discussed in greater detail in Chapter 8).

Finally, the planning process will have a significant impact on the information system. Recall the elements of the study of AIS introduced in Figure 1.1 (page 10) and note that the information systems strategic planning process must address many of those elements. For example, the organizational planning process should explore plans for new business operations, and the information systems strategic planning process should address the technology requirements for those new operations. Any changes in operations or technology mean changes in events processing, control, and so on. To illustrate, suppose that a department store chain is planning to install new point-of-sale (POS) equipment in its retail outlets. The information systems strategic plans must include strategies for the interface of the new POS technology with the existing information systems structure.

Be prepared to participate in the strategic planning process. A financial specialist conversant in the organizational and information systems strategic planning will have an advantage in management and operation of the AIS. A financial specialist knowledgeable in the elements of the AIS will be better able to participate in strategic planning efforts in the organization.

THE ACCOUNTANT'S ROLE IN THE CURRENT BUSINESS ENVIRONMENT

Let's return to a discussion of the accountant as an information management and business measurement specialist that we began in the Preface and examine the accountant's role in and for the modern business and the AIS. Regarding the AIS, the accountant can assume three roles: designer, user, and auditor.

As a *designer* of an AIS, the accountant brings a knowledge of accounting principles, auditing principles, information systems techniques, and systems development methods. In designing the AIS, the accountant might answer such questions as:

- What will be recorded (i.e., what is a recordable business event)?
- How will the event be recorded (i.e., what data elements will be captured and where will they be stored? For example, what ledger accounts will be used)?
- When will the event be recorded (i.e., before or after occurrence)?
- What controls will be necessary to provide valid, accurate, and complete records; to protect assets; and to ensure that the AIS can be audited?
- What reports will be produced, and when will they be produced?
- How much detail will the reports include?

In short, the accountant often participates in designing and implementing the AIS. Bookkeepers, clerks, and computers operate the AIS.

Accountants perform a number of functions within organizations, including those of controller, treasurer, tax specialist, financial analyst, cost accountant, general accountant, and information systems and budgeting specialist. In all cases, the accountant *uses* the AIS to perform his or her functions. The accountant's effectiveness depends on how well he or she knows the AIS and the technology used to implement it. For instance, to be able to analyze financial information (e.g., to function as a financial analyst or managerial accountant), an accountant must know what data are stored in the AIS, how to access those data, what analysis tools exist and how to use them, and how to present the information using available report-writing facilities.

As a *user*, the accountant may also be called on to participate in the AIS design process. In fact, an information system user should insist on being involved to make sure that a new system contains required features. To be effective in the design process, the user must know how systems are developed, the techniques used to develop a system, and the technology that will be used in a new system.

As internal and external auditors, accountants *audit* the AIS or provide the assurance *services* mentioned earlier in this chapter. Auditors are interested in the reliability of the accounting data and of the reports produced by the system. They may test the system's controls, assess the system's efficiency and effectiveness, and participate in the system design process. To be effective, the auditor must possess knowledge of systems development techniques, of controls, of the technology used in the information systems, and of the design and operation of the AIS.

SUMMARY

In February 2003, the International Federation of Accountants (IFAC) published a revised version of Education Guideline 11, Information Technology for Professional Accountants,[20] "to assist member bodies to prepare professional accountants to work in the information technology environment" (page 1). In 1996, one of those member bodies of IFAC, the American Institute of Certified Public Accountants (AICPA), published its own report in response to a previous version of Guideline 11, *Information Technology Competencies in the Accounting Profession: AICPA Implementation Strategies for IFAC International Education Guideline No. 11*,[21] to encourage implementation of the guideline in the United States. Several passages in the AICPA report serve to emphasize the importance of the AIS course in your studies, as well as validate the approach that we take in presenting the AIS material to you.

Regarding the importance of information technology to an accounting career, the AICPA concludes, ". . . professional accounting has merged and developed with IT to such an extent that one can hardly conceive of accounting independent from IT" (page 5). The AICPA goes on to describe three important challenges currently facing the accounting profession. Information technologies are (1) affecting the way in which organizations operate, (2) changing the nature and economies of accounting activity, and (3) changing the competitive environment in which accountants operate (page 6).

In discussing the teaching of technology concepts, the AICPA report reads ". . . it is important to emphasize the need for strategic, conceptual understanding of information technology as a resource to enable achievement of business objectives. A *strategic, conceptual understanding* of information technology focuses on the functions of each information component, the objectives of technology achievements for each information technology component, the potential business impact of new technology. . . . understanding the concepts behind the technology helps students to learn to use, evaluate, and control technology more effectively. . . . encourages students and professionals to concentrate on applying and using technology to achieve business purposes" (page 7).

It is our hope that when you have completed your journey through AIS with us that you will confirm that we have followed that philosophy in this text. Further, it is our firm belief that years from now you will conclude that the knowledge and skills developed in the AIS course will have been central to your career success.

---

[20] International Education Guideline 11: Information Technologies for Professional Accountants, International Federation of Accountants (IFAC), February 2003. See http://www.ifac.org.

[21] The material in the remainder of this section is taken from *Information Technology Competencies in the Accounting Profession: AICPA Implementation Strategies for IFAC International Education Guideline No. 11* (New York: AICPA, 1996). Page numbers in parentheses in this section refer to that report.

REVIEW QUESTIONS

RQ 1-1 Describe this textbook's three themes.

RQ 1-2 What 10 elements are included in the study of AIS?

RQ 1-3 A system must have organization, interrelationships, integration, and central objectives. Why must each of these four components be present in a system?

RQ 1-4 Are the terms *system* and *subsystem* synonymous? Explain your answer.

RQ 1-5 What is the relationship between an AIS and an IS?

RQ 1-6 Compare the elements of a manual accounting cycle and an automated accounting cycle.

RQ 1-7 What are three logical components of a business process? Define the functions of each. How do the components interact with one another?

RQ 1-8 Why is the information system important to the organization?

RQ 1-9 What are the two major functions of an information system?

RQ 1-10 What factors distinguish *data* from *information*?

RQ 1-11 What are the qualities of information presented in this chapter? Explain each quality in your own words and give an example of each.

RQ 1-12 What are the three steps in decision making?

RQ 1-13 Refer to Figure 1.9 (page 28). Characterize the horizontal information flows and the vertical information flows.

RQ 1-14 What factors distinguish the types of information required by strategic managers, by tactical managers, and by operational managers?

RQ 1-15 In your own words, explain *structure* as it relates to decisions.

RQ 1-16 Why do we coordinate the organizational and the information systems strategic plans?

RQ 1-17 What three roles can an accountant fill in relation to the AIS? Describe them.

DISCUSSION QUESTIONS

DQ 1-1 "I don't want to learn about technology; I just want to be a good accountant." Comment.

DQ 1-2 Examine Figure 1.1 (page 10). Based on your college education to date, with which elements are you most comfortable? With which are you least comfortable? Discuss your answers.

DQ 1-3 Examine Figure 1.1 (page 10). Based on any practical experience that you have had, with which elements are you most comfortable? With which are you least comfortable? Discuss your answers.

DQ 1-4 Why might we have more trouble assessing the success of a federal government entitlement program than we would have judging the success of a business organization?

DQ 1-5 Why must we have knowledge of a system's objectives to study that system?

DQ 1-6 Do you think your accounting education is preparing you effectively to practice accounting? Why or why not? Discuss, from both a short-term (i.e., immediately on graduation) and a long-term (i.e., 5 to 10 years after beginning your career) standpoint.

DQ 1-7 Examine Figure 1.9 (page 28). Discuss the relative importance of horizontal information flows and vertical information flows to the accountant.

DQ 1-8 "When we computerize an AIS, we merely change how the data are processed; we don't change what tasks are performed." Do you agree? Give examples to support your position.

DQ 1-9 Give several examples not mentioned in the chapter of potential conflicts between pairs of information qualities.

DQ 1-10 Regarding financial reporting, which quality of information do you think should be superior to all other qualities? Discuss your answer.

DQ 1-11 What information quality is most important—relevance or reliability? Discuss your answer.

DQ 1-12 Describe a few structured decisions and a few unstructured decisions. Discuss the relative amount of structure in each decision.

DQ 1-13 "To be of any value, a modern information system must assist all levels of management." Discuss.

DQ 1-14 "We don't need an information system strategic planning process. We can just respond to user requests for information system applications." Discuss.

DQ 1-15 Describe some factors critical to your success in college (i.e., your college *critical success factors*).

PROBLEMS

P 1-1 In his first address as Chairman of the Board of the American Institute of Certified Public Accountants (AICPA), Robert K. Elliott said:

> "Knowledge leveraging will shape a wide range of CPA services. CPAs will be able to identify relevant information and its sources, perform modeling, devise and apply performance measures of all kinds, design systems to obtain needed information, advise on controls and security and otherwise ensure relevance and reliability. CPAs will identify and deploy knowledge needed for strategic planning and investments, for marketing decisions, for monitoring internal and external conditions, for conducting daily operations, for maximizing the productivity of employee behavior and for measuring the effectiveness of operations, personnel and processes. All this and more."[22]

Write a paper (your professor will tell you how long the paper should be) to discuss ways in which this chapter agrees with this quote. Discuss any disagreements. Do you think that the CPA should be performing these services? Why or why not?

P 1-2 Conduct research on the expansion of the role of the accountant into areas such as non-financial information, assurance services, and similar functions. Write a paper (your professor will tell you how long the paper should be) to discuss the pluses and minuses of this expansion.

---

[22] Robert K. Elliott, "Who Are We As a Profession—and What Must We Become?" *Journal of Accountancy* (February 2000): 84.

P 1-3 Conduct research on the implementation of Section 404 of the Sarbanes-Oxley Act of 2002. Write a paper (your professor will tell you how long the paper should be) to discuss how accountants within an organization are involved in helping their organizations comply with this section. Describe also how accountants in public accounting and consulting are affected by this section of the SOA.

P 1-4 Assume that a manager can obtain information from the organization's database in three ways: by direct inquiry using a computer, by a daily printout, and by a monthly report. Using the qualities of information discussed in this chapter (*understandability, relevance, timeliness, predictive value/ feedback value, neutrality/freedom from bias, comparability, consistency, validity, accuracy,* and *completeness*), compare and contrast these three sources of information.

KEY TERMS

system

subsystem

information system (IS)

management information
  system (MIS)

accounting information
  system (AIS)

input data

business event data

master data update

master data

information processing

data maintenance

standing data

operations process

management process

information

data

understandability

relevance

timeliness

predictive value

feedback value

verifiability

neutrality

freedom from bias

comparability

consistent

validity

accuracy

completeness

decision making

structured decisions

unstructured decision

enterprise database

strategic planning

objective

goal

critical success factors
  (CSFs)

plan

strategy

effectiveness

efficiency

confidentiality

integrity

availability

compliance

reliability of information

chapter
2

Learning Objectives

Enterprise Systems

At the time that Nestlé SA, the Switzerland-based consumer goods company, embarked on a worldwide implementation of SAP's R/3 enterprise resource planning (ERP) software, they had 200 operating companies in 80 countries. Nestlé USA, the $8.1 billion U.S. subsidiary, had nine autonomous divisions that did not have common processes, systems, or organization structures. They even had 29 different names for the ingredient vanilla, and were paying 29 different prices for that vanilla, from the same vendor! Each division and factory was allowed to name, and develop specifications for, vanilla and all of their other raw material purchases.

One of the purposes for the worldwide SAP implementation was to standardize processes and systems across the organization. The fact that Nestlé USA had 9 different general ledgers and 28 points of customer entry gives one some idea of the problems they faced. To achieve common practices, divisional functions, such as manufacturing, purchasing, marketing, sales, and accounting, Nestlé would need to give up their old approaches to doing business.

The Nestlé SAP project was not without its problems. The project team learned, for example, that this was not a software project nor was it an IT project. Because this project changed the way people worked, it required that the team focus their attention on change management. As a result the project took several years longer and cost millions of dollars more than had been planned.[1] Personnel resisted the changes in business practices that were taking place. For example, as a result of employees' unwillingness to adapt to new supply chain tools, turnover of personnel who forecasted demand for Nestlé products reached 77 percent.

In the end Nestlé implemented six SAP modules—purchasing, financials, sales and distribution, accounts payable, accounts receivable, and advanced planning and optimization (APO)—as well as parts of Manugistics' supply chain module.[2] Business practices were standardized across divisions and operating companies. For example, the purchasing group for confections used the same best practices as the purchasing group for beverages. We'll have one vanilla, thank you! Also, as a result of using one common database, discount terms offered by the salesperson were honored by

---

[1] The project was started in 1997 and restarted in 2000 with the signing of a $280 million contract with SAP. The last rollout of the SAP system took place in 2003.

[2] Manugistics (http://www.manugistics.com) is a software vendor providing software to implement an organization's supply chain. Supply chain, APO, and the other software modules are described later in the text.

In this chapter, we highlight most of our AIS wheel by exploring the enterprise systems that assist in the operation of all of an organization's business processes and integrate, in the enterprise database, all of the data related to those business processes. In addition, functionality within the enterprise system protects the database from unauthorized use, change, or disclosure (i.e., database controls). Finally, business rules within the enterprise system ensure the proper functioning of each business process (i.e., process controls).

accounts receivable. Previously, with separate databases, communicating these terms proved difficult.

As of May 2002 the SAP project had saved Nestlé USA $325 million, the majority of savings arising from improved demand forecasting. In the past, the salesforce, demand planners, and factories all had separate databases. With the new business processes and ERP system, forecasts are more accurate resulting in reduced inventory and costs to redistribute inventory that had resulted from too much product being sent to one place and not enough to another.[3]

SYNOPSIS

Nestlé SA undertook their SAP project to take advantage of the benefits, including the competitive advantage, that can accrue for organizations that integrate business processes and implement ERP systems. But, as Nestlé learned, significant costs and business disruptions may be endured before the benefits are realized. To function effectively in any modern organization, you will need to understand the benefits and costs of organization-wide integration of information systems and the ERP software used in the integration process.

---

[3] Ben Worthen, "Nestlé's ERP Odyssey," *CIO Magazine* (May 15, 2002): 62–70.

In this chapter we describe these systems and the functionality they provide. We broadly introduce the business processes that ERP systems support. What you learn here, while it is important in its own right, will provide important background for your study in later chapters of the text.

INTRODUCTION

We place the enterprise systems icon here to indicate that this entire chapter is entirely about enterprise systems. The other two icons, controls and e-Business, will be placed at appropriate places throughout the remainder of the chapter.

ENTERPRISE SYSTEMS

As defined in the Preface and Chapter 1, **enterprise systems** (also known as **enterprise-wide information systems** and **enterprise information systems**) integrate the business process functionality and information from all of an organization's functional areas, such as marketing and sales, cash receipts, purchasing, cash disbursements, human resources, production and logistics, and business reporting (including financial reporting). They make possible the coordinated operation of these functions and provide a central information resource for the organization. For example, the enterprise system might facilitate the purchase of some office equipment by:

- Providing an electronic order form (a purchase requisition).
- Applying business rules to ensure that complete information and proper approvals have been obtained. For instance, the system might need to connect to accounting processes and data to determine that the purchase is within the requester's budget.
- Routing the order to appropriate authorities for specific approvals. The system may need to connect to human resource processes and data to determine appropriate approvers.
- Sending the order to a buyer in purchasing for preparation of a purchase order to be sent to a vendor. The system may assist the buyer with selection of an appropriate vendor.
- Being connected to the enterprise systems of business partners, such as the vendor that will sell us the office equipment. **E-BUSINESS**
- Completing the business process by making data available for ongoing management and analysis of the purchase and subsequent related events. For example, data would be available for (1) receiving the equipment and enabling routing of it to the purchasing party, (2) projecting funding requirements to pay for purchases, (3) analyzing the vendor's performance (e.g., timeliness, quality, and price), and (4) comparing the purchasing party's budget and actual expenditures.

Notice that there are several points during this purchase process where controls might be implemented by the enterprise system. For example, by ensuring that proper approvals are obtained and that the purchase is within the purchaser's budget, the enterprise system reduces the risk that unauthorized purchases will be made. **CONTROLS**

Organizations install enterprise systems to differentiate themselves from their competitors. For example, with an enterprise system an organization should be able to conduct business in a timelier and less costly manner and provide services to its customers that would otherwise not be possible. Also, as previously noted, the enterprise system collects data about each business event, as well as data about an organization's business partners and other aspects of the business, such as inventory, manufacturing, and human resources. This data contains nuggets of gold that management can mine and use to monitor the organization's operations, improve performance, and create additional business opportunities. We'll discuss more about the advantages, and disadvantages, of enterprise systems as our discussion continues.

Enterprise Resource Planning (ERP) Systems

Enterprise resource planning (ERP) systems are software packages that can be used for the core systems necessary to support enterprise systems. Think of the relationship between enterprise systems and ERP this way: an organization's enterprise system might comprise customer relationship management software from one vendor, warehouse and shipping software that was developed internally by the company's information systems function, and an ERP system from a second vendor. Any combinations like this are possible.

The point is that a company might adopt all modules offered by an ERP system vendor. In that particular case the ERP system and the ES are, for all practical matters, one in the same. For example, the Walt Disney Corporation is engaged in a four-year, £240 million project to implement SAP worldwide to replace ERP systems from multiple vendors.[4] Or, the ERP system might be one of many software solutions that comprise the enterprise system. It might be helpful for you to think about ES as the general phenomenon and ERP systems as a specific instance of the phenomenon. A number of ERP systems are commercially available. The dominant player is SAP whose R/3 product commands the largest percentage of the Fortune 500 market. Table 2.1 lists some of the other ERP vendors, their market share, and number and type of customers.

ERP products are designed to offer integration of virtually all of an organization's major business functions. Figure 2.1 (page 44) depicts this integration in the SAP R/3 system. The large diamond in the center depicts the core of the R/3 system, including the centralized database. The smaller boxes surrounding the center represent the basic SAP R/3 modules that an organization might adopt. The empty boxes represent third-party add-on modules that could be implemented to extend the R/3 system's functionality.

E-BUSINESS   The third-party modules in Figure 2.1 complement an ERP system such as R/3 to provide the full range of functionality required for support of an *enterprise system*. Some of these modules, such as Web interfaces for customers and business partners, may be required to engage in e-Business. The most common add-on modules include:

- **Customer relationship management (CRM) software**, such as that from Seibel Systems, Inc., builds and maintains an organization's customer-related data. This data is collected from multiple customer interactions, such as Web, call centers, field sales, and service calls. The data is aggregated, managed, and coordinated across the entire organization to support identification, acquisition, and retention of customers and to maximize the benefits of those relationships. You have experienced the functionality of a CRM system if you have set up an account with Amazon.com or other Web vendors. These vendors keep track of such things as your name, address, and purchases. In this way they can personalize your shopping experience and increase their business by making the experience pleasant and more efficient for you and by offering to sell you products that are consistent with your buying habits.

---

[4] Mike Simons, "Disney Keeps Global SAP Roll-out on Track by Making Local Executives Responsible," *ComputerWeekly.com* (July 1, 2003).

Table 2.1 Selected[a] ERP Vendors

Company Name	Revenue, 2001 ($M)[b]	Revenue Share, 2001[b]	Number of Customers[c]	Market[d]
SAP	6,600	33%	19,600	Large
Oracle[f]	2,843	14%	13,000	Large
PeopleSoft[e, f]	2,069	10%	5,100	Large
J. D. Edwards[e]	858	4%	6,600	SME
Sage Group	769	4%	3,100,000	Large, SME, Small
GEAC	499	3%	18,000	Large, SME
Lawson Software	326	2%	2,200	Large, SME
Intentia	392	2%	3,500	Large, SME
Baan[h]	326	2%	6,500	Large
SCT	325	2%	2,750	Large
Great Plains[g]	265	1%	130,000	SME
Navision[g]	196	1%	130,000	SME, Small
SSA Global Technologies[h]	131	1%	7,500	SME, Small

Notes:
[a] Table contains top-10 companies and selected companies in the 1 percent market-share category.
[b] Bob Kraus and Jim Shepherd, "The Enterprise Resource Planning Report, 2001–2006," *AMR Research* (July 2002).
[c] Company Web sites.
[d] Large: Sells mostly to large enterprises (>$1b revenue). SME: Sells mostly to small- and medium-sized enterprises ($30m–$1b revenues). Small: Sells mostly to enterprises with <$30m in revenues.
[e] On July 18, 2003, PeopleSoft completed the acquisition of J.D. Edwards & Company.
[f] On June 6, 2003, Oracle Corp. announced a hostile takeover of PeopleSoft, Inc.
[g] Great Plains and Navision are owned by Microsoft.
[h] On June 3, 2003, Baan announced that it was to be sold and combined with SSA Global Technologies.

- **Customer self-service (CSS) software,** often an extension of *CRM software*, allows an organization's customers to complete an inquiry or perform a task (including sales) without the aid of an organization's employees. These integrate with ERP systems to allow customers to check the status of their orders, review inventory availability, and even check production plans. Again, you have experienced such software when making purchases on the Internet.

- **Sales force automation (SFA) software** is another extension of *CRM software* that automates sales tasks such as order processing and tracking.

- **Supply chain management (SCM) software,** such as that from Manugistics, Inc. and i2 Technologies, Inc., helps plan and execute the steps in an organization's supply chain including demand planning; acquiring inventory; and manufacturing, distributing, and selling the product. You may recall that Nestlé implemented Manugistics supply chain software.

- **Product lifecycle management (PLM) software** manages product data during a product's life, beginning with the design of the product, continuing through

Figure 2.1 SAP R/3 Modular Integration

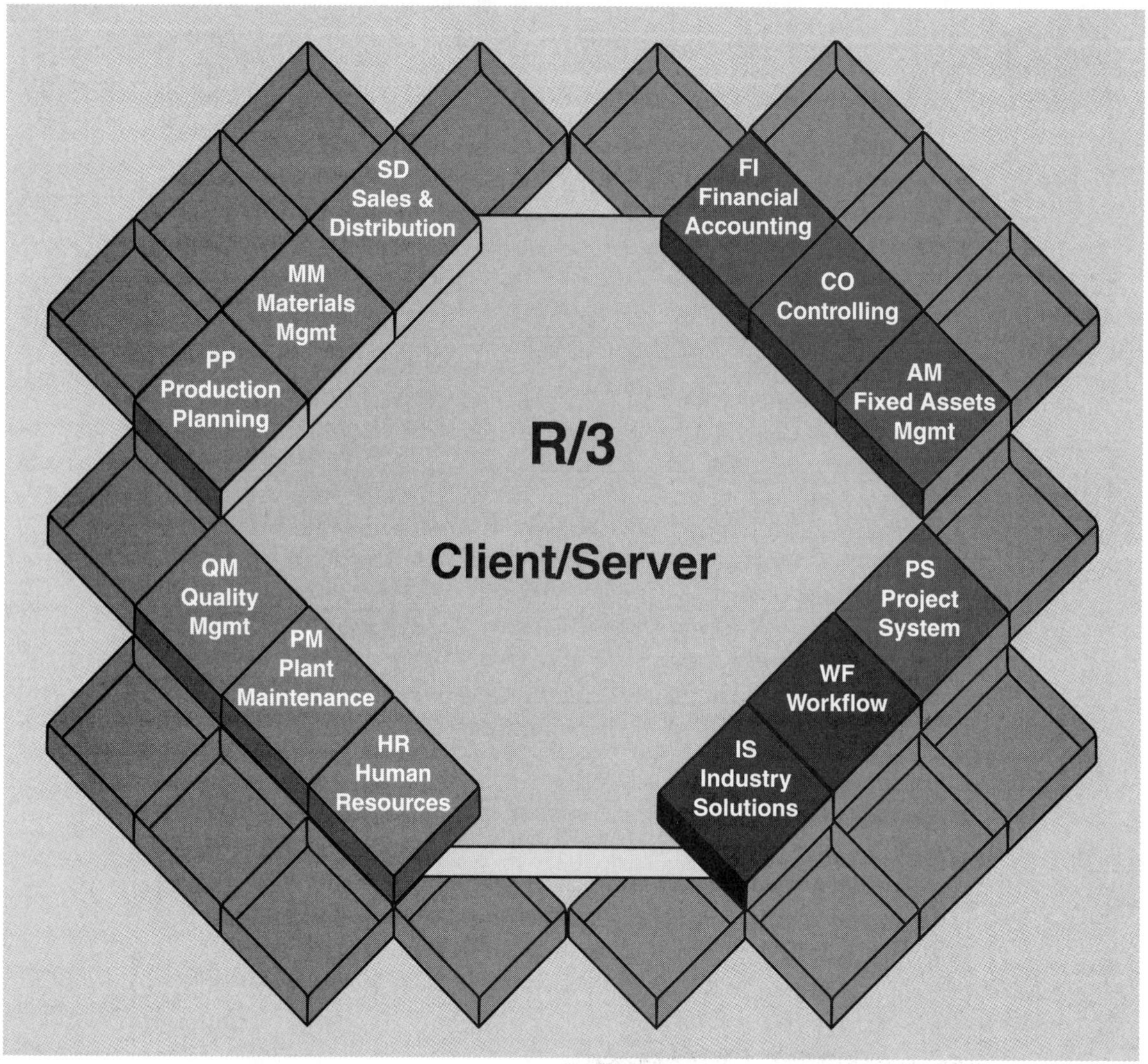

SD Sales & Distribution
MM Materials Mgmt
PP Production Planning
QM Quality Mgmt
PM Plant Maintenance
HR Human Resources

R/3 Client/Server

FI Financial Accounting
CO Controlling
AM Fixed Assets Mgmt
PS Project System
WF Workflow
IS Industry Solutions

Source: Reprinted with permission from SAP.

manufacture, and culminating in the disposal of the product at the end of its life. PLM software integrates data across many units of an organization, such as engineering, logistics, and marketing, and data from partner organizations, such as vendors, contract manufacturers, and distributors. PLM software is offered by vendors of engineering software, ERP vendors, and specialized providers such as Arena Solutions and Agile Software.

• Other third-party modules extract data from ERP systems and from legacy systems that may still exist within an organization (or subsidiary of the organization). For instance, Hyperion Software focuses on financial and accounting applications, but is very effective at executing consolidations of financial information for multinationals.

SAP R/3 and other similar products reflect large, monolithic ERP systems made up of a number of modules that can be selected for implementation. Third-party add-ons selected by the organization must be connected (or "bolted on") to the ERP system through an interfacing facility provided by the ERP vendor or a third party. Technology Summary 2.1 describes *enterprise application integration (EAI)*, an approach to connecting together multiple pieces of an enterprise system. Technology Application 2.1 describes a few EAI examples. Notice that EAI is also an approach to connecting the enterprise systems of different organizations, such as would be needed for B2B integrations.

Technology Summary 2.2 describes an alternative approach that very well could be adopted in the near future whereby an organization may select software modules from a variety of vendors. Rather than being connected together, the modules would communicate and coordinate activities through middleware.[5] *Web services,* another method used for systems integration is described in Chapter 10.

Originally, the implementation of ERP systems was targeted to large multinational manufacturers such as General Motors, Goodyear, and General Mills. Such early adoptions made sense, as companies like these would be expected to see the greatest benefits from ERP systems: that is, large multilocation and multidivision companies often present the greatest challenges to managers who want to coordinate worldwide activities and mine data from corporate databases to improve overall organizational decision making. Plus, ERP systems arose from early manufacturing requirement planning (MRP) applications, which were specifically designed for manufacturing companies; hence, it is no surprise that the early adopters were in the business of making products.

ERP systems have seen many improvements over time. Most ERP system vendors now offer solutions for a wide variety of industries, such as retail, banking, financial,

---

T e c h n o l o g y   S u m m a r y   2 . 1

Enterprise Application Integration (EAI)

Enterprise application entegration (EAI) combines processes, software, standards, and hardware to link together two or more systems allowing them to operate as one. Originally developed to link together systems within an organization, EAI is now used to connect together the enterprise systems of different organizations. EAI systems are characterized by integration of business processes, applications, databases, data standards (e.g., EDI, XML), and platforms (e.g., NT, UNIX). Examples of EAI integration include:

· ERP and CRM systems.
· ERP and legacy systems.

· Legacy or ERP systems with a data warehouse.
· Applications from different vendors such as a manufacturing package with a general ledger package.
· Enterprise systems in two or more organizations such as with supply chain collaborations between buyers and suppliers of goods and services.

Companies offering EAI services and products include IBM, Microsoft, BEA Systems, webMethods, and Vitria Technology. IDC Research expects the EAI market to grow to $21 billion by 2005.

Source: "EAI Overview," http://eai.ittoolbox.com/pub/eai_overview.htm, May 19, 2003.

---

[5] Middleware is a software product that connects two or more separate applications or software modules.

Technology Application 2.1

Examples of Enterprise Application Integration (EAI)

Case 1

Mennonite Mutual Aid Association (MMAA) is using tools from Vitria Technology Inc. to integrate core insurance applications running on IBM AS/400s with applications running on Windows NT servers. They have also integrated databases from a Windows NT SQL Server with a DB2 database running on an AS/400. Finally, MMAA is using the Vitria tools to coordinate the exchange of data with health care providers.

Case 2

Corporate Express Inc., is using tools from Web-Methods, Inc., to build interfaces with more than 200 business partners. This has cut inter-nal and customer costs and allowed them to remain attractive as a preferred supplier. They also have integrated their PeopleSoft ERP system and their warehouse management system.

Case 3

Southern Co., is using tools from Vitria Technology, IBM, and Microsoft to optimize parts of their supply chain. For example, they have used Vitria's BusinessWare tools to provide real-time exchanges of purchasing data with business partners. They are also integrating internal procurement, work-order, and accounting applications.

Sources: Maria Trombly, "Piecing It All Together," *Computerworld* (July 7, 2003): 40; Thomas Hoffman, "Utility Turns to EAI Tools to Revamp Sully Chain," *Computerworld* (March 10, 2003): 16.

entertainment, construction, and so on. ERP systems allow companies to standardize systems across multiple locations and multiple divisions in order to link business processes and data in a consistent fashion and provide organization-wide data accessibility. This is what we saw with the Disney example cited previously. Another reason that Disney was able to implement one ERP package worldwide is the ability of a single package to provide the needed capacity—to scale sufficiently—for the scope of Disney's operations.[6]

Not only were early adopters primarily involved with manufacturing, but they were also very large enterprises, primarily because implementation costs were so enormous that smaller companies simply could not withstand the economic burden. These systems typically took a year or more to implement at a cost of up to hundreds of millions of dollars, necessitating a similarly significant return in benefits. As advances in the technology underlying these systems have evolved, small- and medium-sized enterprises (SMEs) have driven the new implementation base. You can see in Table 2.1 (page 43) that there are some major players in the market for ERP systems for SMEs. For instance, Microsoft's acquisition of Great Plains in 2001 and Navision in 2002 would be one indicator of the importance of this market segment.

Enterprise Systems Value Chain

To examine the role that enterprise systems play in the success of an organization, we might look at the activities performed by the organization as a **value chain**, a chain of activities performed by the organization to transform inputs into outputs valued by the customer. An organization creates a competitive advantage by creating more value for

[6] Simons, "Disney Keeps Global SAP Roll-out on Track."

Technology Summary 2.2

Event-Driven Architecture (EDA)

Event-driven architecture (EDA) is an approach to designing and building enterprise systems in which business events[a] trigger messages to be sent by middleware between independent software modules that are completely unaware of each other. This differs from the traditional, internally driven, enterprise architectures. Event-driven processes operate in the following manner.

1. Each business event is handled individually as it appears, rather than waiting for a batch of events to accumulate. Business events are then processed in a timely manner.
2. The business unit that experiences a business event "pushes" the event to the recipient rather than waiting for the recipient to request, or "pull," the event to them. Recipients learn immediately about relevant business events.
3. Business events are pushed immediately and simultaneously to all interested parties. For example, when a vendor sends a notice that a shipment will be delayed, interested parties such as purchasing, receiving, manufacturing, sales, and the customer would be notified.
4. The meaning and attributes of each business event is documented, as a process is developed, and is shared across multiple processes within the system.

5. Event notifications are managed in a systematic way to ensure that event data is sent to the correct recipient at the right time and that there is appropriate follow-up.

These technical-level design aspects of an EDA generate two business-level opportunities that enable the enterprise to operate in real-time and to choose the best available modules for the enterprise system, the so-called "best of breed" approach to software selection. A "real-time enterprise" driven by an EDA experiences reduced delays and business processing overhead resulting in more responsive and flexible business units. For example, senders and receivers can operate asynchronously and the sender is not tied up waiting for the receiver to respond or to process the event. And, not being restricted to software modules provided by the ERP vendor, or those that can be connected to existing ERP and legacy systems, the organization can put together an enterprise system that is more closely tailored to the needs of each business unit and business process. These modules need not know about the existence or location of any other modules. When a business event occurs, they send an event notification to the middleware (also known as a "publish" or "send") and the middleware notifies those modules that have asked to receive this type of event (also known as "subscribe").

---

[a] A **business event** is a meaningful change in the state of the enterprise such as creating a new employee record, submitting a purchase order to a vendor, receiving a payment from a customer, picking goods from the warehouse and delivering to the shipping department, and revaluing inventory.
Sources: Carol Sliwa, "Event-Driven Architecture Poised for Wide Adoption," *Computerworld* (May 12, 2003): 8; Roy Schulte, "A Real-Time Enterprise is Event-Driven," Gartner, Inc. Research Note T-18-2037, September 26, 2002.

its customers than does its competition. Value is created by performing the activities at lower costs and by enhancing differentiation of its products or services.[7] Differentiation is created through production of superior quality, with innovative products and services,

---

[7] M. E. Porter and V. E. Millar, "How Information Gives You Competitive Advantage," *Harvard Business Review* (July–August 1985): 149–160.

and by responsiveness to customer requirements for such features as product design and customization, and quality of service during and after the completion of a sale.

You may be familiar with Dell, Inc. (http://www.dell.com), the online seller of computers, printers, software, and related goods and services. The company has a reputation as an extremely efficient manufacturer and distributor. Indeed, Dell's value chain is one of the best in the world. It takes raw materials, manufactures computers and other products, and delivers them to customers in a timely manner at an attractive price. The keys to Dell's success are its business processes (Dell holds 550 patents for them) and the application of IT to drive those processes and to integrate its suppliers, customers, manufacturing, shipping, and after-sales support (i.e., the value chain). In this section we describe some ways that enterprise systems play a key role in creating the value customers seek.

Figure 2.2 depicts a generic organization value chain and value system. The activities in the value chain, the value activities, may be divided into two categories, primary and support activities.[8] The primary activities are depicted in the figure and are those directly involved in marketing, selling, producing, and delivering the good or service to the customer, and include functions such as moving raw materials into and around the organization, producing and delivering goods to the customer, and performing services such as installation and after-sales support. The secondary activities are those that provide the supporting infrastructure to enable the primary activities and include functions such as procurement, information technology (IT), human resources and accounting. Note that we depict the value chain as overlaying the functional activities of an organization. To efficiently and effectively serve the customer, the value chain must traverse these traditionally independent activities, often referred to as "silos,"[9] and join these activities together into an end-to-end business process (often called cross-functional integration).

IT has been able to assist in creating additional value by reducing the cost or improving quality in the performance of these activities. For example, IT has been successfully applied to optimize the cost and quality of raw materials by providing information to help select the right material at the right cost from the right vendor. Also, IT has been applied to the production scheduling process to balance the cost and timeliness of manufacturing. Notice that in both of these examples, IT assisted in creating value by lowering costs and differentiating the product. In the first case quality differentiates the product in that we obtain the materials that allow us to manufacture a product that is consistent with our quality objectives. In the second case the timelines of availability of the product was the differentiating factor.

E-BUSINESS   In these two examples, IT assisted in value creation within individual activities. However, value activities are interdependent and need to be closely coordinated to be most effective in creating value for the customer. As described in the next section, enterprise systems are required to provide the necessary interactivity (and interbusiness process) communication and coordination. For example, to really optimize value to the customer (e.g., Dell), the activities related to marketing the product, receiving the customer order, scheduling the order into production, delivering and installing the product, and providing after-sales support, must all be coordinated to ensure the delivery of the product at the cost, and with the quality, the customer expects.

---

[8] *Ibid.*

[9] The term *silo* is used to refer to organization functions—such as product development, marketing, and manufacturing—that stand alone, disconnected, and often unaware of activities taking place in the other functions.

Figure 2.2 Value Chain and Value System

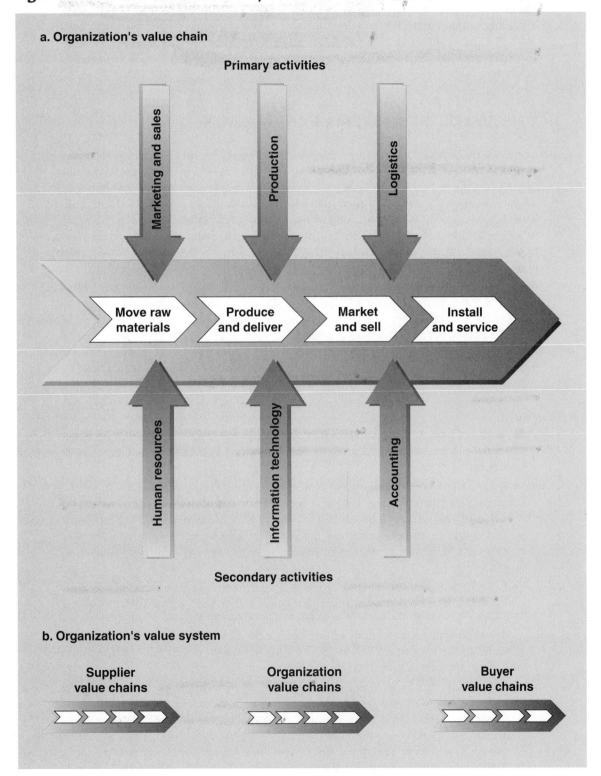

Finally, an organization's value chain is but one component in a value system that extends back (upstream) to the organization's suppliers—each with their own value chain and value system—and forward (downstream) to the customers—each with their own value chain and value system. Value optimization in the value system requires interorganizational information sharing and coordination in the supply chain, a subject discussed in Chapter 10.

THE VALUE OF SYSTEMS INTEGRATION

As previously discussed, one of the values provided by an enterprise system is the coordination of value activities in the value chain. The system performs this coordination by sharing data across business processes. In this section we describe what life would be like without integrated systems and then how enterprise systems solve some of those problems. Figure 2.3 depicts the processing of a customer order in the Customer Service Department at Sudbury, Inc., a hypothetical company that manufactures and sells electronic subassemblies. As you can see in the figure, Sally the Sudbury customer sales representative (CSR) needs to have access to information from a variety of sources in order to tell customers when and if they can expect to receive their order and how much that order will cost.

The Problem

Imagine first, that Sudbury's information processes are completely disaggregated and follow along as we describe the problems that it would cause for Sally. First (see flow 1), Sally needs to know if this is an existing customer in good standing (i.e., that they have good credit). Let's assume that Sally can key in the customer's name and obtain this data.

Second (see flow 2), Sally needs to be able to tell the customer when he would receive the item. This date, known as "available to promise" or ATP, may be a function of several elements of data:

- If the item is on the shelf in one of Sudbury's warehouses, and is not committed to another customer, the item would be available after it has been picked from the shelf, packed for shipment, and delivered to the customer. With no automated link to current inventory data, Sally would need to examine computer printouts of inventory balances or call the warehouses to ask someone to look on the shelf.

- If the item is not on the shelf (see flow 3), the item would be available when released from manufacturing, unless that quantity has been committed to another customer. Sally could review production schedules to determine when the item would be available and would add to that the time normally required to pick, pack, and ship the item to this customer. This would not, however, tell her if the item had already been allocated to another customer.

- In the event that the item must be scheduled for manufacturing, Sally would need to know when it could be scheduled, and how long the manufacturing process would take. This would depend on the availability of the production line and personnel, as well as the required raw materials (see flow 4). This latter piece of information may require contacting the vendors that supply these materials to determine when they can promise delivery (see flow 5). This is the ATP from Sudbury's vendors.

Figure 2.3 Sudbury Customer Service Process

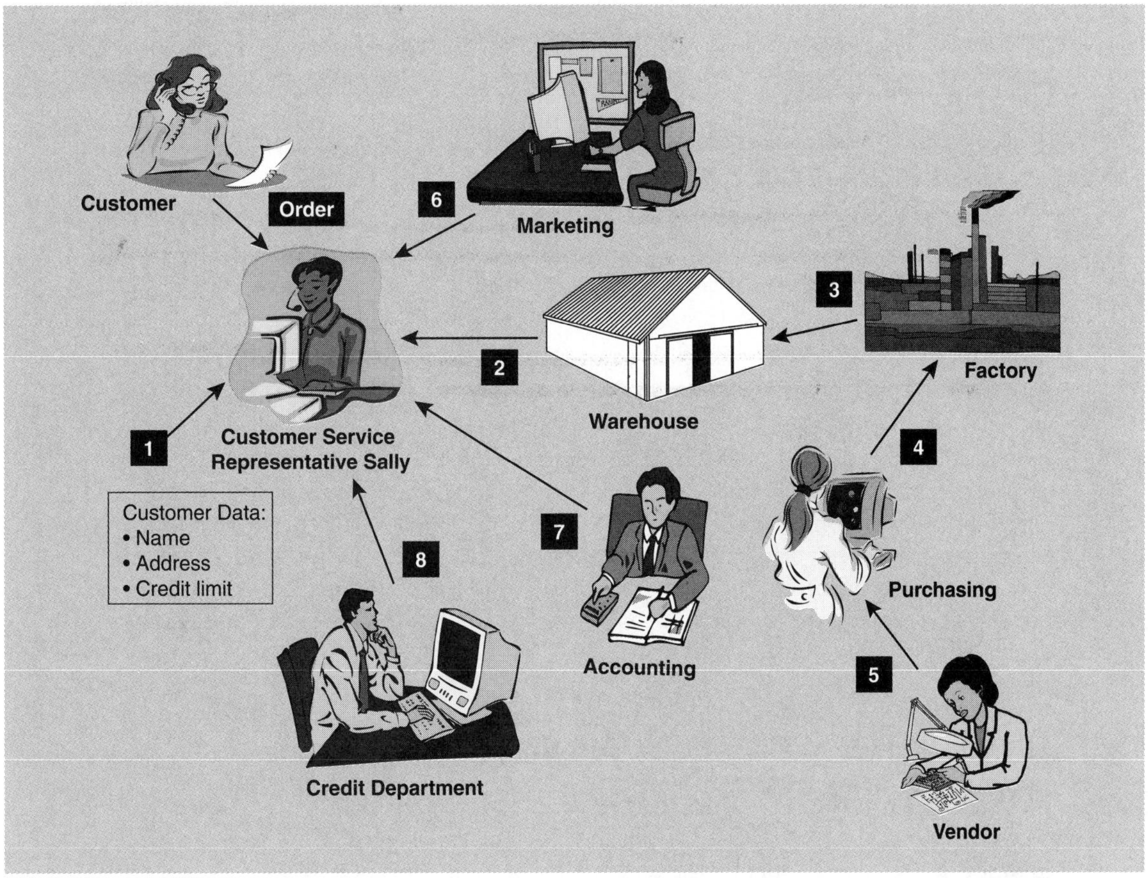

- Let's assume that Sally has determined when the item will be available to ship to the customer. What price will be charged to this customer for this order? This price may be found on a static price list that Sally keeps near the phone. However, prices may be dynamically determined by the marketing department (see flow 6), and this determination may be based on customer status, market conditions, quantity being purchased, and current manufacturing costs. This implies multiple flows into the marketing process not depicted in Figure 2.3.

- Once pricing has been determined, Sally needs to know if the amount of the order **CONTROLS** falls within this customer's credit limit. Now, we assume that Sally has obtained the credit limit from the customer data that she has (flow 1), But, let's assume that the amount of money that the customer already owes Sudbury must be considered (see flow 7). Without direct access to the open accounts receivable data, Sally will need to call accounting to approve this order.

- Finally, let's assume that it is Sudbury policy not to turn down an order for insufficient credit without first checking with the credit department (see flow 8). Without an integrated system, this would require that Sally call the credit department.

Do you think that Sally wants to keep the customer on the phone throughout this process? Not likely. Would you consider this to be good customer service? We hope not. What does Sudbury need to do?

The Solution

The solution, as we are sure you have surmised, is to integrate the disaggregated processes of Figure 2.3 (page 51) into an enterprise system. Look again at Figure 2.3 and let's see how the process would change if the pieces of the customer service process were integrated.

- As before, input of the customer name or number would give Sally access to the customer data (flow 1).
- Upon entering the number of the requested item, the enterprise system would establish the ATP date by determining if the item is available in any of Sudbury's worldwide warehouses (flow 2), or is scheduled to be manufactured (flow 3), and if scheduled for manufacture, when it would be available (flows 4 and 5).
- Once the source of the item is known, the system will automatically determine the price (flow 6) and the customer's credit worthiness (flows 7 and 8).

So, Sally does not need to keep the customer on the phone forever! With an integrated system, all of the previous steps would be determined in a matter of seconds. Should the item not be available in a time consistent with the customer's request, the system can provide data with which management can make decisions to allocate available items from other customers; plan increased production; streamline warehouse and factory logistics to reduce manufacturing, picking, packing, and shipping time; and other such decisions. This process, called "capable to promise (CTP)," and ATP will be discussed further in Chapter 12.

ENTERPRISE SYSTEMS SUPPORT FOR ORGANIZATIONAL PROCESSES

An information system supports the functioning of an organization in several ways. First, it facilitates the functioning of the organization's operations as *business events* occur by, for example, providing data as required to complete the event, applying business rules to ensure that the event is handled properly, and communicating the need for action to business units. Second, the information system retains records about business events that have occurred. Third, the information system stores data that is useful for decision making. In the sections that follow we describe how the information system provides this support and how that support is more robust when an enterprise system provides the support. First, however, we provide an overview of the capturing of data during the execution of business processes.

Capturing Data During Business Processes

The data captured as business processes unfold should be sufficient for someone who was not a party to the business event to reconstruct every aspect of what happened—whether he or she is in accounting, marketing, human resources, financial management, manufacturing, or any other part of the organization. Typically, this mandates that data be collected and stored related to the four Ws:

- The *who* relates to all individuals and/or organizations that are involved in the event (sometimes called agents to the event).
- The *what* relates to all resources that are exchanged as a result of the event.

- The *where* relates to the locations in which (1) the event takes place, (2) exchanged resources reside before and after the event, and (3) the agents are during the event.
- The *when* relates to the time periods involved in completion of the event—including future exchanges of resources (e.g., payment of cash for an account receivable) arising from the event.

Once the details of the four Ws (i.e., the event data) are collected and recorded, the data can be aggregated and summarized in any manner that a given user chooses. Aggregations and summarizations are temporary and for the user's application only, but the event data remain available to other users in their original form. For routine applications such as the generation of accounting reports, programmed procedures can be developed to generate such reports automatically.

Enterprise Systems Facilitate Functioning of the Organization's Business

In Chapter 1 we introduced you to two types of data, master data (entity-type data) and business event data (event-type data). Normally, a business event processing system operates with one or more data tables (often called "files"). Some of these tables are used to obtain reference information, such as the warehouse location of an item of merchandise. Other tables are used to organize and store the data that are being collected, such as sales order or inventory data. We hope that the hierarchy of data pictured in the table on the right side of Figure 2.4 is familiar to you from your computer programming or management information systems courses. Let's quickly review. A character is a basic unit of data such as a letter, number, or special character. A field (a single cell in a table) is a collection of related characters that comprise an attribute, such as a customer

Figure 2.4 Data Maintenance: Create Customer Record

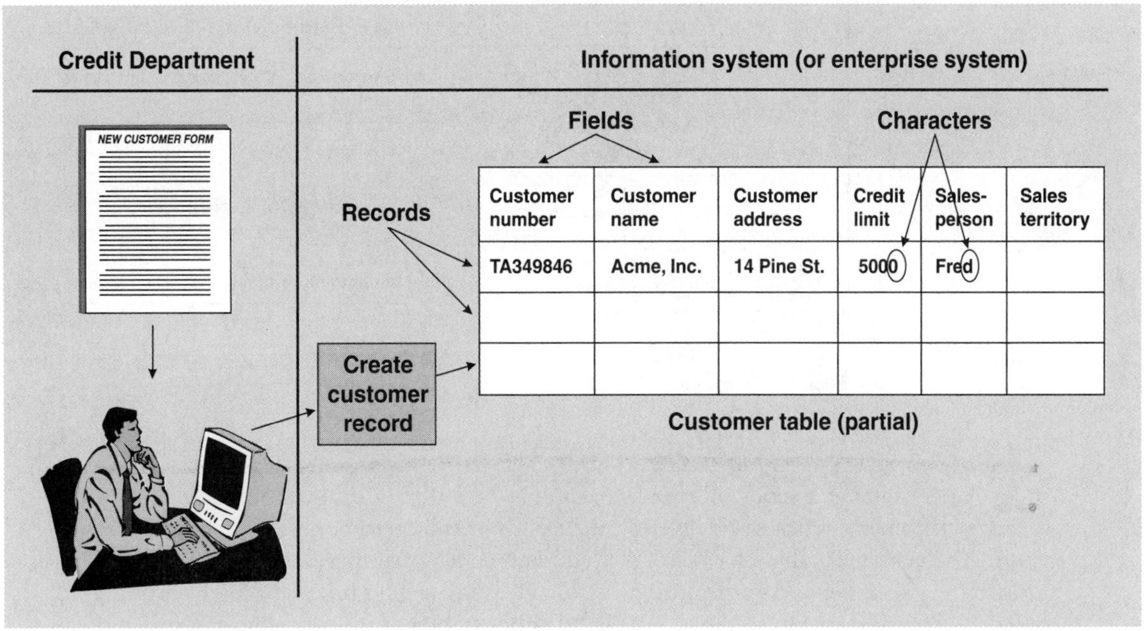

Customer number	Customer name	Customer address	Credit limit	Sales-person	Sales territory
TA349846	Acme, Inc.	14 Pine St.	5000	Fred	

Customer table (partial)

number or a customer name. A record (a row in a table) is a collection of related data fields (attributes) pertaining to a particular entity (person, place, or thing, such as a customer record) or event (sale, hiring of a new employee, and so on). A table (or file) is a collection of related records (sometimes called entity/event instances), such as a customer table or a sales order table.

Figure 2.4 depicts a typical data maintenance activity for a single table—the addition of a new customer record to the customer table—and provides us with an example of how an information system can facilitate the functioning of the organization's business processes. For example, the name and the address fields will be used to address monthly invoices. Figure 2.5 depicts how the existence of the customer record—including the credit limit—provides the basic authorization required to enter the customer's order. Without the customer record, the computer would reject the customer order in Figure 2.5. Thus, it is important to separate authorizations for data maintenance activities from authorizations for business event processing activities. This separation between, for example, the Credit Department in Figure 2.4 and the Sales Department in Figure 2.5, provides an important control, *segregation of duties*, a topic explored in greater detail in Chapters 8 and 9.

Figure 2.5 Business Event Data Processing: Enter Customer Order

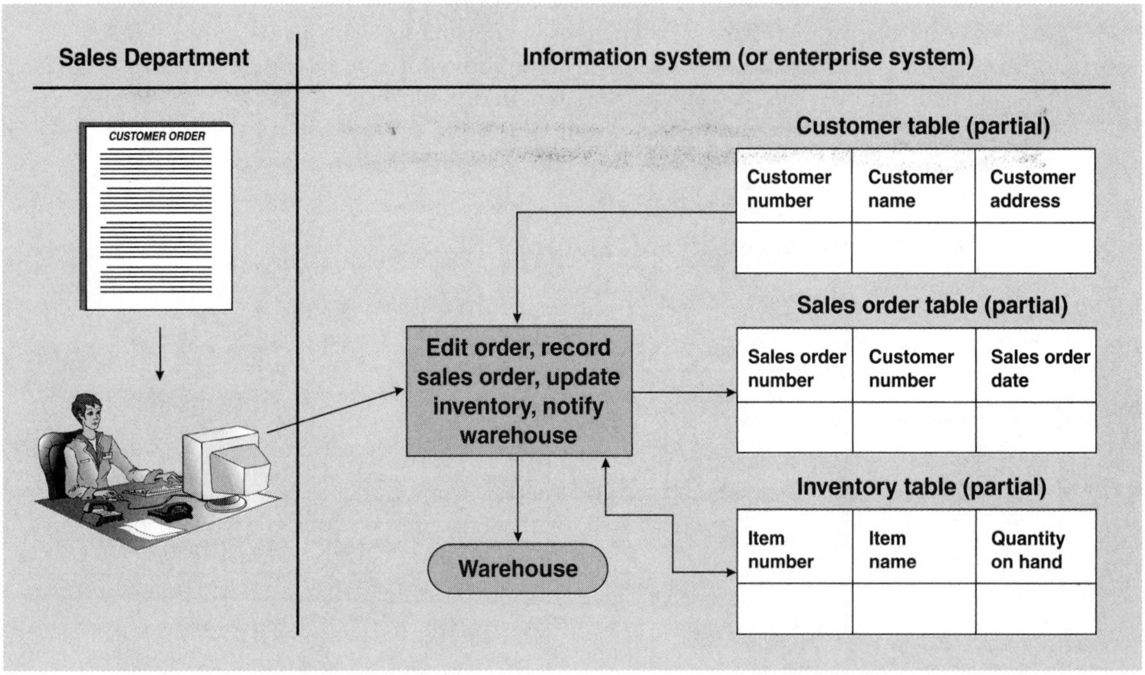

Figure 2.5 depicts a typical business event processing activity—entering a customer's order. Let's examine a series of events that might take place during the course of capturing a customer's order and delivering the goods to the customer. First, as noted previously the customer table provides the credit and other customer data required to authorize the order. Next, data regarding the quantity and selling price of the inventory is obtained from the inventory table. Finally, an order to pick, pack, and ship the ordered

goods (including the inventory location obtained from the inventory table) would be sent to the warehouse.[10]

In enterprise systems there should be only one version of each of the tables depicted in Figure 2.5 and that central database would be used by all functions in the organization, such as marketing, accounting, and logistics. For example, there will be only one record for each customer and one credit limit, worldwide. All of the inventory data worldwide would be available (often called "visible") during the processing of customer orders. The centralization of the data permits an organization to have accurate and reliable data and to operate their business processes in a consistent manner throughout the organization.

In addition, the communication across functions is enhanced in enterprise systems. For example, in Figure 2.5 we see that data related to the inventory is readily available during entry of the customer order. And, we see that a request for shipment is sent directly to the warehouse. (We don't see any document here because the transmission to the warehouse is electronic.) Finally, although not shown in the diagram, the purchasing function could be informed immediately that merchandise has been sold and may need to be replenished. Thus, the enterprise system with a centralized database and communication among the organization business functions provides a higher level of support for the functioning of the business than would be possible by less-integrated approaches to the information system.

Enterprise Systems Record That Business Events Have Occurred

As the business event progresses, the information system must capture the multifaceted data to track the progression of the process. To capture the sales event, we need to record data related to the customer and the salesperson (the who), the goods ordered (the what), the delivery location (the where), and the date of sale and promised delivery (the when). This information would then be linked with information already stored that relates to, for example, the supplier of goods that were not available. Based on the combined information, a purchase order might be sent to the supplier. For the purchase order we record the supplier (the who), the goods (the what), the location to which the goods will be delivered (the where), and the delivery date from the supplier to our company (the when) and link the purchase order to the order from our customer.

All of the data in our example that is required for the sales, billing, purchasing, and general ledger functions are all captured and available in a typical information system. But with an enterprise system the data is linked together. Thus, if the delivery date is changed by the supplier, the salesperson has immediate access to the change and can notify the customer. To accomplish this, the salesperson pulls together the necessary data by utilizing links between the changed order information, the sales order, and the customer, and narrows the search to only the sales that he or she is handling. Very quickly, the salesperson has the information needed to notify the customer of any delay in shipment.

Notice how this discussion relates to the event-driven architecture in Technology Summary 2.2 (page 47) If there was an event-driven architecture, the notice from the

---

[10] Notice the direction of the flows into and out of the tables. We obtain data *from* the customer and inventory tables and send data *to* the sales order (i.e., a new sales order record) and inventory (i.e., a changed quantity on hand) tables.

supplier about a changed delivery date would cause the "pushing" of notices to the salesperson, the customer, and other interested parties.

Enterprise Systems Store Data for Decision Making

Figure 2.6 depicts a manager using the data collected and stored by the organization's information system. We show only those data tables that we had in Figure 2.5. Hundreds, indeed thousands, of tables of data are available in a typical information system.

Figure 2.6 Using Stored Data for Decision Making

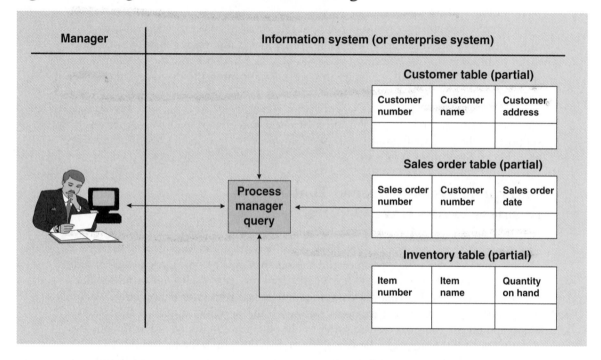

Some simple examples follow of how our manager might use the data to make decisions. A warehouse manager might look at sales orders that have not yet been shipped to follow-up and find out why. An inventory manager might look at the inventory data to follow-up on those items with low balances on hand.

With an enterprise system, potential queries can be complex and yield results that are more significant. For example, a marketing manager might want to have a list of those customers who have not made a purchase in a month. To obtain this information, the manager would need to combine the customer and sales tables. Or, the credit manager might want to compare customer credit limits, sales, billing data, and payment data to determine if credit limits need to be adjusted for customers with high sales or late payments. Finally, a logistics manager might want to examine the time of the day that orders are received and delays in shipping those orders to determine if staffing in the warehouse needs to be scheduled at different times. All of these queries assume that data can be shared across multiple functional areas, a common situation with enterprise systems.

MAJOR ERP MODULES

To give you an appreciation for the typical, core modules in an ERP system we will describe here five modules in the SAP R/3 system: (1) sales and distribution, (2) materials management, (3) financial accounting, (4) controlling and profitability analysis, and (5) human resources. These modules are included in Figure 2.1 on page 44. Most ERP systems have similar modules with comparable functionality.

Sales and Distribution

The Sales and Distribution Module (SD) of the SAP R/3 system contains the functions related to the sale of goods to customers and includes recording a customer order, shipping goods to the customers, and billing the customer. There are connections to the Materials Management module to check the availability of inventory and to record the issue of the goods, to the Financial Accounting module to post the sale, and to the Controlling module for profitability analysis related to the sale. The three major steps in the SD process (order entry, shipment, and billing) are briefly outlined here.

The SD order entry process might start with receiving and recording an inquiry from a customer and preparing and recording a sales quotation. Should the customer choose to place an order, the process continues with the receipt and entry of a customer order. Upon entering the order, the R/3 system would check the customer's credit, determine availability of the goods ordered, and record the order (now called a sales order). If this is a new customer, the customer data would be added to the database using a data maintenance activity similar to that in Figure 2.4 (page 53).

The SD shipment process includes scheduling the shipment, picking the goods from the shelf, packing the goods for shipment, and recording the shipment. Organizations often choose to record each of these steps as they occur to keep a complete record of the sale as it progresses. Once the post shipment event has been entered, the inventory quantity-on-hand is reduced and the sale is scheduled for billing.

The SD billing process creates invoices for all shipments that are ready to be billed. The billing process may be automatically triggered by each shipment or may be executed periodically by an action taken by a billing clerk. In this latter case, multiple shipments to a customer might be consolidated and placed on a single invoice.

Materials Management

The Materials Management (MM) module of the SAP R/3 system contains the functions related to the acquisition of goods from vendors and management of the goods while they are in stock. The module includes preparing and recording a purchase order, receiving the goods from the vendor, and recording the vendor's invoice. The MM module interacts with the SD module during the processing of customer orders, with the Financial Accounting module to post the receipt of the goods and the vendor invoice, and with the Controlling module for analysis of the costs associated with the purchases. The three major steps in the MM process (creating a purchase order, receiving the goods, and recording the vendor invoice) are briefly outlined here.

The MM purchase order process might start with the preparation of a purchase requisition by a person or function within the organization and sending a request for quotation (RFQ) to one or more vendors. Once responses to the RFQ have been processed and a vendor selected, the purchase process continues with the creation and recording of a purchase order and communication of that purchase order to the vendor. Should this be a new vendor, the vendor data would be added to the database using a data maintenance activity similar to that in Figure 2.4 (page 53).

The MM goods receipt process includes comparing the received and ordered quantities, recording the receipt, and increasing the quantity-on-hand. When the vendor invoice is received and entered, the R/3 system performs a three-way match between the purchase order, the receipt, and the invoice. If these agree, the invoice is recorded.

Financial Accounting

The Financial Accounting (FI) module plays a central role in the SAP R/3 system. Business events from other modules, such as SD and MM, are incorporated by the FI module into the general ledger accounts and included in the external account statements, the balance sheet, profit and loss statement, and statement of cash flows. The FI module also includes accounts receivable and accounts payable functions to record and manage that data directly and to complete events begun in the SD and MM modules. Some specific examples follow.

After a customer is billed in the SD module, the accounts receivable portion of the FI module manages that receivable until paid (e.g., aging of open receivable, dunning for late payments) and records the customer payment. Also, in the absence of the SD module and for special circumstances, such as one-time sales of non-merchandise items, invoices may be directly entered in the FI module.

Once a vendor invoice has been entered in the MM module, the accounts payable portion of the FI module schedules the invoice for payment and executes that payment at the appropriate time.

Controlling and Profitability Analysis

The Controlling (CO) module of SAP R/3, often called Controlling and Profitability Analysis (CO/PA), handles internal accounting, including cost center accounting, profitability analysis for sales, activity-based accounting, and budgeting. For example, the CO module can produce internal profit and loss statements for portions of an organization's business.

Human Resources

The Human Resources (HR) module of SAP R/3 includes functions related to the recruitment, management, and administration of personnel, payroll processing, and personnel training and travel. For example, when a new employee is hired, it is from within the HR module that the human resources department would add the personnel data to the database using a data maintenance activity similar to that in Figure 2.4 (page 53). The HR module is also used to maintain data related to benefits, training, and work shifts. Finally, the payroll function facilitates the processing of payroll for countries throughout the world and to prepare payroll reports in accordance with the jurisdictions of those countries.

ENTERPRISE SYSTEMS SUPPORT FOR MAJOR BUSINESS EVENT PROCESSES

Most organizations group their major business events into two processes, the order-to-cash process and the purchase-to-pay process. For ease of presentation, this text divides these further into processes comprised of a few closely related events. For example, we describe the process employed to enter a customer's order and to ship the goods to the customer as the order entry/sales process, while the management of the accounts receivable and the billing of the customers are included in the accounts receivable/billing/cash receipts process. In the sections that follow, we describe the two major processes, order-to-cash and purchase-to-pay, describe how an enterprise system supports those business processes, and map those processes into the chapters where they are covered in this text. Our discussion is limited to the purchase of goods, not services, and to goods acquired for resale, not goods acquired as raw material inputs to a manufacturing process.

Order-to-Cash

Figure 2.7 (page 60) depicts the **order-to-cash process**, which includes the events surrounding the sale of goods to a customer, the recognition of the revenue, and the collection of the customer payment. The order-to-cash process comprises all activities in the order entry/sales process (Chapter 10), the billing/accounts receivable/cash receipts process (Chapter 11), and the applicable parts of the general ledger process (Chapter 16). Follow along with us as we describe the numbered steps in Figure 2.7 and how an enterprise system supports the business activities in those steps. The order-to-cash process includes:

- Step 1, pre-sales activities, includes responding to customer inquiries and requests for quotes (RFQs). Organizations may choose to collect and retain a rich assortment of customer-related data about prospective and active customers. This data is recorded in an ERP system and can be analyzed to determine what goods are being requested by customers and the RFQs that do, and do not, result in customer orders. Some organizations purchase separate *CRM* packages to supplement the customer-related features in standard ERP systems.

- Step 2, sales order processing, includes capturing and recording customer orders. At this point in the process an enterprise system would link together customer, inventory, purchasing, and vendor data to determine if the customer is in good standing and likely to pay the bill (i.e., using customer credit and inventory pricing data) and where and when inventory will be available to send to the customer (i.e., using worldwide inventory quantity-on-hand, on-order, and vendor data). At the conclusion of step 2 the enterprise system sends a picking request to the appropriate warehouse. If goods are not available within the organization, a purchase order would be sent to a vendor.

- Step 3, pick and pack, includes picking the goods from the shelf in the warehouse and packing the goods for shipment. Each of these events may be recorded in the enterprise system to maintain a record of the progress and to retain control over the location of the goods.

- Step 4, shipping, include transferring the goods to the organization's transportation function, or to a third-party carrier, for shipment to the customer. The enterprise system would choose the appropriate routing and carrier, record the reduction in the inventory quantity-on-hand, calculate and record the cost of goods sold and inventory reduction in the general ledger, and record data to be used in the billing process. Some enterprise systems are configured to immediately trigger the billing process when a shipment takes place.

- Step 5, billing, includes preparing the customer invoice and recording sales and accounts receivable data in the general ledger. The enterprise system links together

Figure 2.7 Order-to-Cash Process

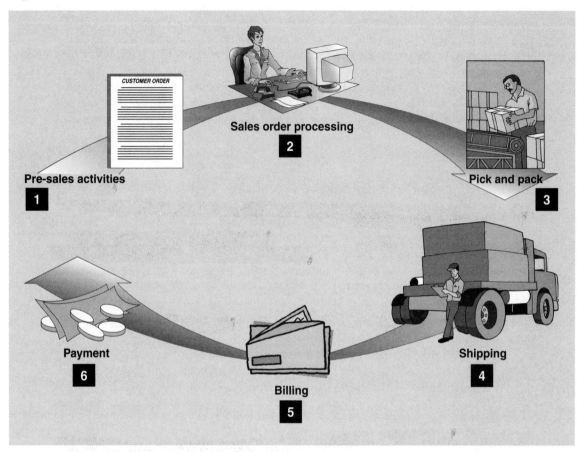

sales, customer, and inventory data to ensure that the invoice contains correct quantities, prices, terms, addresses, etc. It is at this point that the enterprise system can be used to analyze sales profitability by comparing product costs to selling price.

- Step 6, payment, includes capturing and recording cash receipts and updating cash and accounts receivable amounts in the general ledger. Data in the enterprise system will be used to manage customer credit and invest available cash.

Figure 2.8 depicts the SD menu from the R/3 system and points to the SD options described previously. Figure 2.9 shows the audit trail that the R/3 system retains to document the completion of the steps in the sales process.

Purchase-to-Pay

Figure 2.10 (page 62) depicts the **purchase-to-pay process**, which includes the events surrounding the purchase of goods from a vendor, the recognition of the cost of those goods, and the payment to the vendor. The purchase-to-pay process comprises all of the activities in the purchasing process (Chapter 12), the accounts payable/cash disbursements process (Chapter 13), and the applicable parts of the general ledger process

Figure 2.8 SD Menu Options in the R/3 System

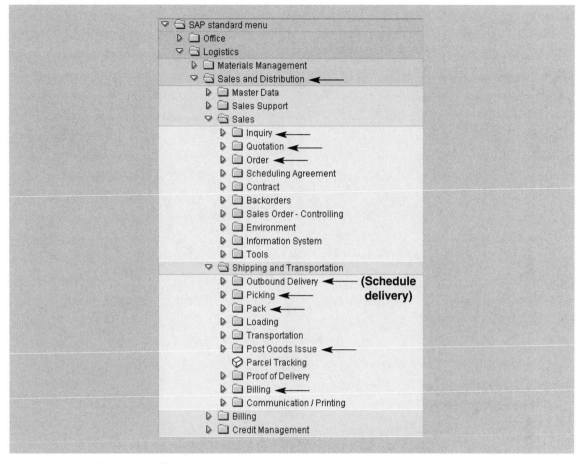

Figure 2.9 SD Audit Trail for Completion of Steps in the R/3 Sales Process

Document	Date	Overall processing status
. Quotation 20000011	09/15/03	Completed
Standard Order 6325	09/15/03	Completed
. Delivery 80006049 **(Schedule delivery)**	09/15/03	Completed
.. WMS transfer order 31 **(Picking ticket)**	09/15/03	Completed
.. GD goods issue:delvy 13	09/15/03	complete
.. Invoice 90015520	09/15/03	Completed
... Accounting document 100000001	09/15/03	Cleared

Figure 2.10 Purchase-to-Pay Process

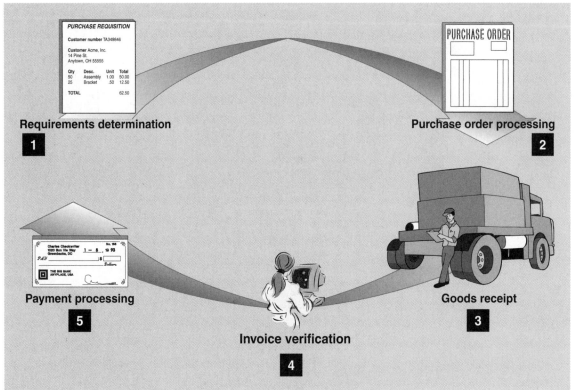

(Chapter 16). Follow along with us as we describe the numbered steps in Figure 2.10 and how an enterprise system supports the business activities in those steps. The purchase-to-pay process includes:

- Step 1, requirements determination, includes preparing a purchase requisition to request the purchase of goods from a vendor. An enterprise system may automatically generate the purchase requisition on the basis of data such as quantity-on-hand, quantity-on-order, and expected demand. Ad-hoc requests may be entered by authorized individuals within the organization. An enterprise system will review purchase requests to determine that they are authorized and within budget.

- Step 2, purchase order processing, includes preparing and recording purchase orders. An enterprise system assists the buyer in identifying sources of supply for the requested item, preparing RFQs to be sent to vendors, analyzing vendor quotations, and selecting vendors by comparing vendor prices, terms, and past performance (e.g., timely, accurate deliveries).

- Step 3, goods receipt, includes comparing the on-order quantity and the quantity received, increasing the quantity-on-hand, creating a record of the receipt, and recording the cost of inventory in the general ledger. If the two-way match fails, the enterprise system notifies the proper personnel to ensure timely reconciliation of differences. The enterprise system also ensures timely availability of the goods by routing them to the function that requested them or directing that they be placed on the shelf in the warehouse and made available for immediate sale. Finally, the enterprise system records data related to the vendor's performance (e.g., delivery accuracy and timeliness) to be used in future purchase decisions.

- Step 4, invoice verification, includes receiving vendor invoices; three-way matching of the purchase order, receipt, and vendor invoice; and recording accounts payable in the general ledger. An enterprise system links this data together to make the three-way match possible and provides the interface to the general ledger. If the three-way match fails, the enterprise system notifies the proper personnel to ensure timely reconciliation of differences.

- Step 5, payment processing, includes preparing and recording cash disbursements and updating cash and accounts payable amounts in the general ledger. An enterprise system facilitates this process by using vendor and accounts payable data to schedule payments in accordance with vendor terms and to receive discounts, as appropriate.

Figure 2.11 depicts the MM menu from the R/3 system and points to the options described previously. Figure 2.12 (page 64) shows the audit trail that the R/3 system retains to document the completion of the steps in the purchase process.

Figure 2.11 MM Menu Options in the SAP R/3 System

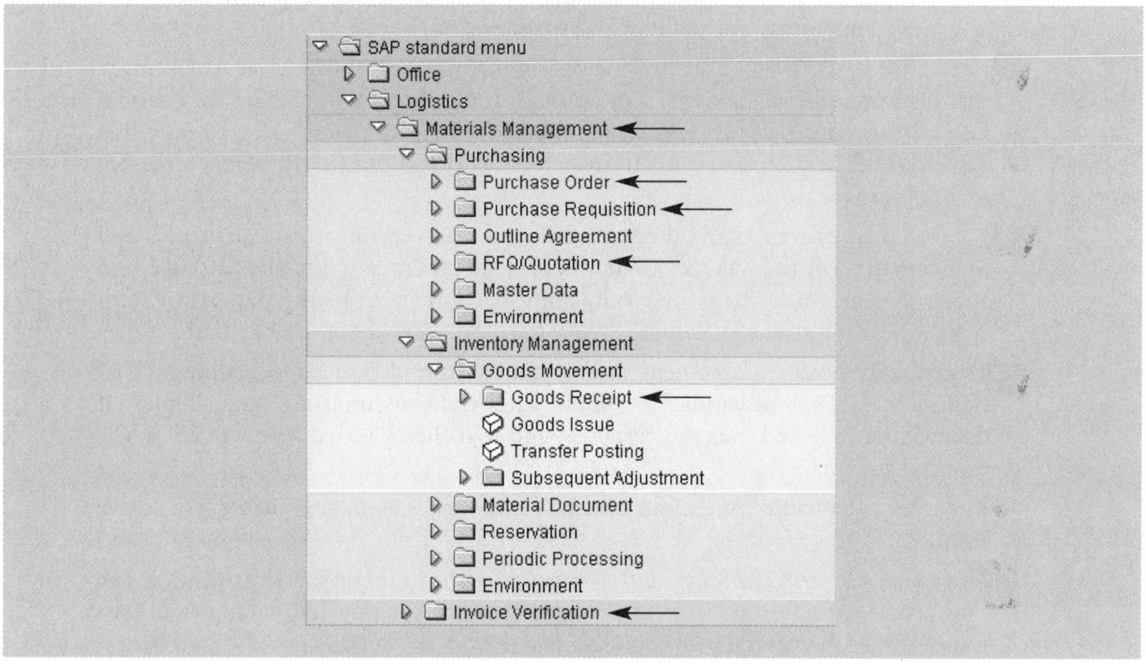

Source: Reprinted with permission from SAP.

Figure 2.12 Audit Trail for Completion of Steps in the R/3 Purchase Process

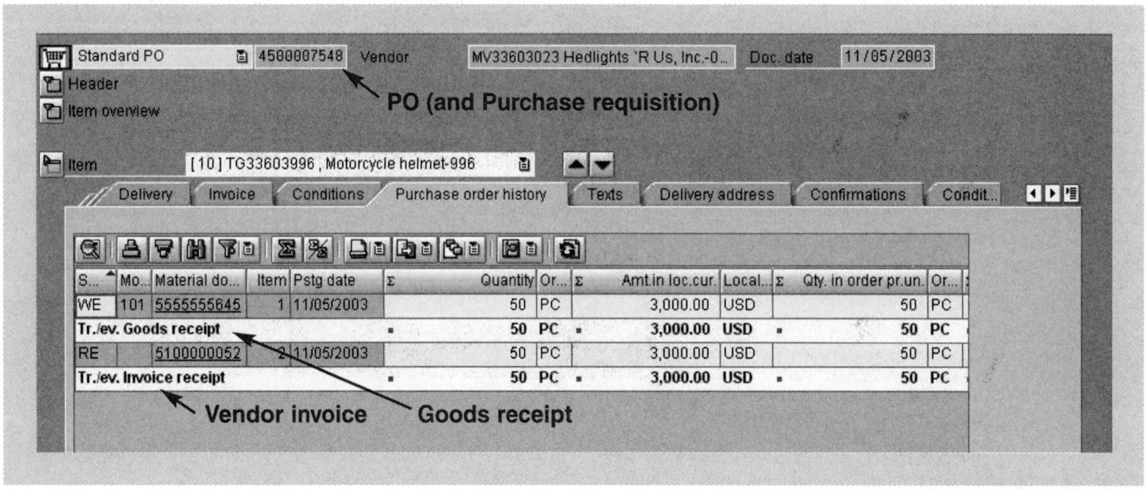

Source: Reprinted with permission from SAP.

SUMMARY

In Chapter 1 we introduced the qualities of information (see Exhibit 1.2 on page 24 and Figure 1.7 on page 25) that should be the goals of any information system. Enterprise systems achieve these goals in the following manner:

- Enterprise systems can collect a wide variety of data about *business events* and make that data available for use by all of an organization's personnel. The data should help all users (i.e., *relevance, understandability*) make decisions (i.e., *decision usefulness*), and analyze past events to make predictions about future events (i.e., *predictive/feedback value*).

- An enterprise system's central database retains one version of data elements, uses that data to verify the accuracy of new data elements entered into the database, and applies business rules to permit only authorized changes to the database. Combined, these improve the *reliability, validity,* and *accuracy* of the database.

- Organization-wide enforcement of data standards and business rules means that business events will be handled *consistently* across the organization, that all relevant data will be collected (i.e., *completeness*) and that the collected data will be *verifiable* and *neutral*.

- The integrated nature of the enterprise system makes all data available in a *timely* manner.

- Shared services for efficiency and consistency. For example, an organization can ship products to customers from multiple shipping points while billing their customers from one central location.

The following table summarizes some of the advantages and disadvantages of enterprise systems for an organization. Notice that some of the advantages and disadvantages relate to the ERP systems that are used to support the core systems of the enterprise system.

Pros/Benefits and Cons/Disadvantages of Enterprise Systems

Pros
Of Enterprise Systems

· Single database
· Integrated system (e.g., visibility to do ATP)
· Process orientation (vs. function)
· Standardization of business processes and data, easier to understand across the organization
· Faster business processes (e.g., customer fulfillment, product development)
· Timely information
· Better financial management (partly due to integration)
· One face to the customer
· Reduced inventory
· Improved cash management
· Productivity improvements, reduced personnel
· Full and accurate financial disclosures
· Improved budgeting, forecasting, and decision support
· Seamless integration and accessibility of information across the organization
· Catalyst for reengineering old, inefficient business processes

Of ERP Packages

· One package across many functions (if one ERP)
· "Best practices"
· Modular structure (buy what you need)
· No development needed
· Configurable
· Reduced errors (i.e., business rules, enter data once)

Cons
Of Enterprise Systems

· Centralized control vs. decentralized empowerment
· Inability to support traditional business processes that may be best practices for that organization
· Loss of flexibility in rapidly adapting to desired new business processes in the post-implementation period
· Increased complexity of maintaining security, control and access permissions for specific information embedded in central database
· The rigidity of "standardization" can impede creative thinking related to ongoing business process improvements

Of ERP Packages

· Complex and inflexible
· Implementation horror stories
· Best practices are shared by all who buy
· Difficult to configure
· Long implementation
· Best of breed might be better (than single ERP package)
· Can't meet all needs (i.e., developed for many user types)

REVIEW QUESTIONS

RQ 2-1 Describe the key features of an enterprise system.

RQ 2-2 Describe the key features of an enterprise resource planning (ERP) system.

RQ 2-3 What is a value chain?

RQ 2-4 What is the relationship of the organizational value chain and an enterprise system?

RQ 2-5 Describe the problems caused by lack of information systems integration.

RQ 2-6 Describe the four ways that an enterprise system supports the functioning of an organization's processes.

RQ 2-7 Explain why it is important to capture the who, what, where, and when in describing business events.

RQ 2-8 Describe four modules of the SAP R/3 system.

RQ 2-9 Describe the 6 steps in the order-to-cash process.

RQ 2-10 How does an enterprise system support the order-to-cash process?

RQ 2-11 Describe the 6 steps in the order-to-cash process.

RQ 2-12 How does an enterprise system support the purchase-to-pay process?

RQ 2-13 List the advantages and disadvantages of an enterprise system.

DISCUSSION QUESTIONS

DQ 2-1 Once the core of an ERP system has been implemented, any of the modules may then be implemented separately. What is the implication of being able to implement an ERP system on a piece-by-piece basis?

DQ 2-2 Dover Company is considering taking customers' orders on their Web site.

   a. What information would Dover collect from the customer during this process?

   b. What information would need to come from Dover's system to complete the order?

   c. How would an enterprise system facilitate this exchange of information?

DQ 2-3 Discuss the pros and cons of consolidation of the ERP software industry.

DQ 2-4 Refer to Figure 2.5 (page 54) and identify the key business event data (who, what, where, and when) you would want to capture.

DQ 2-5 Describe how an enterprise system can assist an organization in optimizing its value system.

DQ 2-6 Consider a business process that you have experienced at work, as a customer, or as a student. Examples might include any process in a work setting such as payroll and purchasing, or any process with which you have interacted, such as ordering from a Web site, obtaining a loan, eating at a restaurant, or registering for classes at your college or university. Describe the degree to which the steps in the process are integrated. What is/was the impact of that integration on you and on the organization?

DQ 2-7 Describe a situation in which information would be shared between two of the "silos" in Figure 2.2 (page 49). What data would be shared? Why would the data be shared? (*Hint:* You might refer to Figures 2.3, 2.7, or 2.10.)

DQ 2-8 Why might a firm decide to implement only certain modules in an enterprise resource planning system rather than a complete implementation?

PROBLEMS

P 2-1 Conduct research on successful and unsuccessful ERP implementations. What seem to be the key elements of a successful implementation? What seem to be the key elements of an unsuccessful implementation? What conclusions can be reached?

P 2-2 Conduct research on an ERP package other than SAP and compare the modules that it has to those described within this chapter for the SAP R/3 system.

P 2-3 Conduct research on an ERP package, such as Great Plains or Navision, intended for small- to medium-sized (SME) organizations. Compare that package for available modules, functionality, etc. to the SAP R/3 system.

P 2-4 Choose a Web site with which you are familiar, such as Dell, Amazon, etc. Illustrate the order-to-cash process, from the customer's perspective, illustrated by that site.

P 2-5 Conduct research on the Web sites of either *CIO Magazine* or *CFO Magazine* for stories about ERP implementation successes and failures. Using specific examples, describe the reasons for the successes and failures.

KEY TERMS

enterprise systems

enterprise-wide information systems

enterprise information systems

enterprise resource planning (ERP) systems

customer relationship management (CRM) software

customer self-service (CSS) software

sales force automation (SFA) software

supply chain management (SCM) software

product lifecycle management (PLM) software

enterprise application integration (EAI)

event-driven architecture (EDA)

business event

value chain

order-to-cash process

purchase-to-pay process

Electronic Business (E-Business) Systems

Some say that e-Business was born in 1910 when several florists formed the Florists' Telegraph Delivery group (FTD Inc.) to exchange out-of-town orders.[1] While electronic transmission of orders may have helped the florists incrementally improve their businesses, more recent technological advances have supported major changes in the way existing businesses operate and enabled the creation of new e-Businesses such as Amazon.com. Amazon.com began business with only a few workstations and no physical sales locations (i.e., no "bricks and mortar"). Because it began early in the era of business-to-consumer (B2C) e-Business, many customers were skeptical of providing credit card information online. To provide comfort to these customers, Amazon.com processed credit card orders by receiving orders on one computer, writing the information to a floppy disk and physically walking the order to a separate computer. Amazon.com could not have grown to nearly $4 billion in annual sales[2] on such primitive systems. Instead, Amazon.com grew by developing and implementing secure transaction software, online shopping carts, and sophisticated data analysis programs.

Amazon.com's e-Business model would not be feasible without this software. The model is based on Amazon.com's "almost-in-time" inventory concept. It supplements the B2C interface that you see as a customer with an innovative B2B interface for quick acquisition and shipment of non-stocked items. That is, if the item that you order is not in stock, the company gets it from its supplier for shipment to you, the customer.

Through the development of technology, Amazon.com has been able to develop its e-Business model as well as use its technology to provide similar services to companies such as Borders, Inc., and Toys"R"Us, Inc., which traditionally would have been its competitors. Amazon.com's future may revolve around its B2C and B2B technology capabilities, rather than its ability to sell books.[3]

Learning Objectives

- To appreciate the possible changes to organizational processes that occur when electronic business is introduced.

- To understand the major approaches used to transfer electronic data during business events processing.

- To recognize the complexities that are introduced as electronic document management moves us steadily toward the paperless office.

- To understand the complexities surrounding electronic data interchange that are introduced when linking two different organizations' computer systems for joint business event data processing.

- To appreciate the challenges faced by organizations when they pursue direct business links with customers via the Internet or other networks.

- To appreciate the business advantages gained through effective use of electronic business.

---

[1] Frank Hayes, "The Story So Far: FTD's flowers-by-wire network planted the seeds of e-Commerce a century ago," *Computerworld* (June 17, 2002): 24

[2] Taken from the company's 2002 income statement at http://www.amazon.com.

[3] A primary source for this vignette is Stacy Collett, "The Web's Best Seller: Amazon.com drew consumers to the Web in droves and forever changed inventory control," *Computerworld* (September 30, 2002): 40, 42.

In this chapter, we highlight our entire AIS wheel by exploring the systems that support the electronic interaction of an organization's business processes and information systems with those if its customers and vendors. These e-Business systems allow external access and interaction with the enterprise database and therefore require sophisticated controls to safeguard the database. Process controls must be in place to ensure that the business processes achieve their goals. Pervasive controls must be in place to ensure these systems are secure, are not interrupted, and maintain the course charted by management.

SYNOPSIS

This chapter introduces the concept of **electronic business (e-Business)**, which was defined in the Preface and Chapter 1 as the application of electronic networks (including the Internet) to exchange information and link business processes among organizations and/or individuals. These processes include interaction between back-office (i.e., internal) processes, such as distribution, manufacturing, and accounting; and front-office (i.e., external) processes, such as those that connect an organization to its customers and suppliers.[4] We also explore how communications technology is revolutionizing the way individuals and organizations conduct business.

E-BUSINESS

As organizations venture down this trail of electronic communications-driven business processes, the trail of paper including invoices, check payments, and so forth quickly disappears by capturing business event data at the e-Business connection with a customer or supplier and by using *enterprise systems* to store data and make it accessible. The evolution to e-Business has been slow in the past, but advances in Internet communication have switched the evolution into high gear. As you read and study this chapter, you will learn about the underlying technologies that facilitate e-Business, the complexities

ENTERPRISE SYSTEMS

CONTROLS

---

[4] Some would distinguish the terms e-Business, the comprehensive concept we have defined, and e-Commerce, the external e-Business processes (i.e., the buying and selling of products and services electronically, typically on the Internet). For simplicity, we do not distinguish the terms e-Business and e-Commerce in this text.

of displacing paper records with electronic ones, the challenges faced in overcoming differences in technology and accounting systems design in order to link two companies' computer systems, and finally the barriers that must be overcome for successful execution of secure business events over the Internet. All these technologies, along with the flexible processes they allow to exist, are fundamental to providing traditional companies with the capability to implement new streamlined processes and new services for their customers. These new technologies also have enabled e-Businesses like Amazon.com to exist and prosper. Amazon.com's business processes are dependent on technology to provide efficient processing and the analysis of information to support product sales and delivery and the acquisition of replacement products—virtually all of the company's value chain.

INTRODUCTION

The power of computers in transforming society is perhaps most obvious today in the way communications have changed. Our society has evolved from one that relied on face-to-face communication, to one in which phones became the primary medium, to a contemporary society that is increasingly dependent on electronic messages (i.e., e-mail and instant messaging). In essence, the richness of the media has been sacrificed for efficiency and effectiveness. In other words, the phone took away the ability to detect emotions through an individual's appearance, including smiles, frowns or other facial expressions. E-mail went a step beyond the phone and also took away the ability to detect emotions through voice inflection and context sounds such as a chuckle. For example, you may have chosen in the past to send a family member or friend a voice mail, e-mail, or fax when you wanted to get them a message quickly, but didn't really have time to talk beyond what you could deliver in the message. In effect, you used technology to make the delivery of the message more efficient. Through these actions, you made the completion of the necessary activities a more efficient process—much like the objectives of most business organizations in today's heavily competitive business environment.

E-BUSINESS

ENTERPRISE SYSTEMS

CONTROLS

From a business perspective, the shift toward increasingly automated business processes and communications based on the transfer of electronic data is designed to achieve greater efficiencies in business processing. When an organization engages in *e-Business,* they complete electronic-based business events (i.e., the partial or complete elimination of paper documentation during business processes in favor of more efficient electronic-based communication). These electronic-based business events entail the interconnection of the underlying back-office processes of both organizations, effectively eliminating the errors associated with a paper-driven process. A by-product of e-Business is often the elimination of the sales staff that would normally serve as the intermediary between the two parties to the business event. Bypassing the sales staff speeds up the business event by eliminating the interaction with a salesperson, establishing a direct and therefore immediate linkage to the vendor's computerized information system (which for many organizations participating in e-Business today will be their *enterprise systems*) for faster communication of an order, and facilitating the electronic transfer of funds for immediate payment. The business event is completed more quickly. Additionally, the purchaser will normally electronically solicit pricing and quickly determine the best price—increasing price efficiency as well. Even price checking may be done automatically by the computer, eliminating the waste of the purchaser's time on such activities.

Amazon.com's success is not solely driven by its B2C sales systems. As we mentioned earlier, sophisticated B2B systems that are integrated with Amazon.com's suppliers' systems must exist to support acquiring products that consumers want. When Amazon.com needs to obtain a book or other item, it electronically sends a purchase order to the manufacturer or distributor of the item. The vendor will provide Amazon.com with the product (a physical flow) and also the expected warehouse delivery time—information that is ultimately used to provide the expected shipping and delivery dates to its customer.

B2B systems are not limited to companies that sell predominately over the Internet. Using processes similar to Amazon.com, companies such as Wal-Mart, which sell most of their merchandise in retail stores, also rely heavily on B2B. When the cashier at Wal-Mart scans an item, not only are sales recorded, but the inventory balance in the warehouse is updated. Wal-Mart's vendors read that data and, if the warehouse quantities fall below the desired reorder point for the item, the vendor ships replenishment stock to Wal-Mart automatically.[5] Today, the majority of e-Business volume is conducted between business trading partners rather than consumers and businesses. That is, B2B is much bigger than B2C.

It is not just big organizations that are using such technologies to quicken the process. For instance, your favorite pizza joint or sandwich shop may accept e-mail or online ordering—basically allowing you to avoid being put on hold when you place your order and the risk of the phone answerer getting the wrong ingredients on your pizza or sandwich. You simply create the order yourself and ship it off, reducing the business' need for people to answer the phones and take orders.

With the Internet, many organizations have the opportunity to directly reach customers through electronic communication. The potential in this market has led to the explosion of e-Business over the Internet. Airlines had such success with ticket sales over the Internet, that they discontinued paying commissions to travel agents. In this chapter, we will explore a variety of technologies that enable e-Business. We also will learn about the various forms of e-Business that are used by organizations in today's business environment.

Throughout this text the discussion of e-Business is highlighted as it relates to various business processes, controls, and systems development issues. Since this chapter is specifically on e-Business, we will reserve use of the e-Business icon to those places in the chapter where a particularly critical e-Business technology or concept is discussed.

APPLYING E-BUSINESS TO THE VALUE CHAIN

Amazon.com has grown because it has used technology to enhance the company's value chain and satisfy customer needs. The basic function of providing a book to a customer is not new; for centuries booksellers have been in existence. Historically, booksellers have stocked books that are consistent with their target customers. The customers personally visited the store for their selection, or perhaps in the case of a specialty store, corresponded by mail. Amazon.com's primary innovation was to offer a vast selection of books that were not necessarily in stock, and to have the systems in place to acquire the nonstocked items quickly and relatively inexpensively. This concept allows a customer to

---

[5] This process, called Vendor Managed Inventory (VMI), is described in Chapter 12.

shop at one "location" (although it may not be a physical location) for many different items, without burdening Amazon.com with the inventory carrying expenses of traditional retailers.

A second major innovation from Amazon.com is the collection and analysis of customer purchase data. The analysis uses sophisticated software to identify patterns and trends in customer preferences. When such information is identified, Amazon.com suggests items that customers with similar buying patterns have purchased; in other words, items that the customer has not purchased, but might want. This process can obviously benefit Amazon.com through increased sales but may also increase the customer's satisfaction by offering to them additional products they may enjoy.

Amazon.com has used each of these technology innovations to enhance its value chain and value system. By offering a wide variety of books (and ultimately other products) online, and having the procurement and delivery systems in place to satisfy orders in a timely manner, Amazon.com has been able to grow substantially. This growth has come without having a physical retail presence or vast numbers of items in inventory.[6] Another major component of Amazon.com's value chain is the ability to market and sell items to customers based on customer interest. Each of these items has provided Amazon.com a competitive advantage in the online retailers' marketplace—an advantage that has persuaded some competitors (such as Borders and Toys"R"Us) to outsource their online operations to Amazon.com.

If you have purchased a book or other item from Amazon.com (or read or heard about the process), you are familiar with the process that we have described here. This has been an example of B2C (business-to-consumer) e-Business. While much is written about B2C e-Business and it is probably familiar to you, it is a small part of the overall e-Business picture. The U.S. Census Bureau estimated that in 2001 only 7 percent of e-Business is B2C. The remaining 93 percent falls under B2B (business-to-business) categories. B2B e-Business includes Amazon.com's book purchases from its suppliers. It also includes raw materials purchased electronically for manufacturing concerns and electronic purchases by retailers, such as Wal-Mart and Kohl's. It follows that the cost saving and decrease in delivery time when the purchasing process is automated yields a more efficient organization and improves the value chain.

THE CHANGING WORLD OF BUSINESS PROCESSING

For centuries, the basic manner in which commerce transpired changed very little. In the past, a merchant would meet with a customer or another merchant and form an agreement to provide goods to customers in exchange for cash or other goods and services. The merchant would then record these exchanges in books of accounts, and periodically consolidate the entries recorded in the books to determine how much various individuals owed the merchant, how much the merchant owed other people, and the excess cash and assets that the merchant owned.

ENTERPRISE SYSTEMS   Over the past three decades, the relative change in commercial practices has been exponential. At the leading edge of technological advance, cottage industries now are springing up on the *Internet* where personal contacts and face-to-face negotiations do not occur. *Online* catalogs can be viewed through an *Internet browser*, and orders can immediately be placed and paid for over the Internet. Of course, the bookkeeping func-

---

[6] In recent years, Amazon.com has increased the items stocked in inventory.

tions may be done in much the same way as the ancient merchant did them, but in many cases the system will automatically trigger collection from the credit card company, automatically record the business event in the electronic database, and automatically update all of the related accounts. Indeed, many companies are using Web development tools from their ERP vendors to build web sites that are linked to the ERP system's processing and central database.

While it may appear that companies have switched from an old way of doing commerce to a brand new way, both methods are actually used by many organizations. The evolution of information technology has simply provided for alternative forms of business processes and business event data processing that enable some organizations to become more efficient and effective by altering the traditional means by which they have done business. To fully understand how technology can enable an organization to *reengineer* its business processes and more effectively enter into commerce activities, you first must have a solid understanding of how business event data processing can be completed. Once you understand how processing is done, then the exploration of the technologies that enable improved efficiencies in business event data processing will be more meaningful.

In this chapter, the evolution of business event data processing is examined. This will help in understanding and appreciating the evolution of business, including the different stages of e-Business.

Automating Manual Systems

Since the earliest days of accounting when fairly primitive manual approaches were the only available accounting information systems, accountants recognized that the cheapest and most efficient way to do data processing on large volumes of similar business event data was to aggregate (i.e., batch) several events together and then periodically complete the processing on all the event data at once. The **periodic mode** is the processing mode in which a delay exists between the various data processing steps. Although technically not the same, the *periodic mode* is heavily dependent on the use of *batch processing*, and the two terms are often used interchangeably. **Batch processing** is the aggregation of several business events over some period of time with the subsequent processing of these data as a group by the information system.

Almost all manual systems use the *periodic mode*. If you think about how you learned the basics of financial accounting and financial statement development, you likely started by recording a set of journal entries that represented the business activities that had occurred. These journal entries were then transferred as a group (posted) to the general ledger and then to the trial balance. Executing the journal entry transfers as a *batch* was a more efficient way of maintaining the financial statements than transferring each business event individually to create a complete set of financial statements after each event was recorded (i.e., after each journal entry you would have to post to the general ledger and recreate the trial balance). In a computerized environment, the easiest approach to automating the accounting process has been to simply mirror these manual batch processing systems, which are relatively simple to develop, and provide for the most efficient use of employees and computer hardware.

Batch processing systems typically require four basic subprocesses to be completed before an event is converted into information reports that can be used by decision makers. Follow along with Figure 3.1 (page 74) as we explain how each of these four subprocesses is typically completed.

Figure 3.1 Automated Equivalent to a Manual System

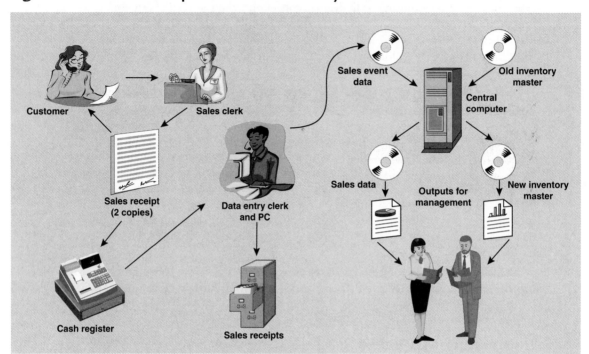

- *Business event occurs.* At the point of occurrence for the business event, the information for the event will be recorded on a source document (by the sales clerk in Figure 3.1). For example, if you think of one of the small businesses you might frequent, such as a used books and CDs shop, they often will have you bring the books and CDs you wish to purchase to a clerk at the front of the store. The clerk will then write a description of the items purchased on a sales slip (prepared in duplicate) and total the sale. The clerk will return one copy to you (often a white copy) and stuff the other copy (generally a yellow or pink copy) into the cash register drawer.

- *Record business event data.* A batch of source documents will be transferred (taken out of the cash register and sent) to a data entry operator who will take the information from the source documents and enter the data in a computerized format. The business event data are usually entered using an **offline** device (i.e., one, such as the PC in Figure 3.1, that is not directly connected to a central computer or network). The resulting computerized format becomes the sales event data store. In our used books and CDs store, the owner-manager or the employee closing up at the end of the day may take responsibility for keying all the sales slips into a personal computer for storage on a disk. The PC becomes simply a data entry device for keying in the sales data. Upon completing the entry, the copies of the sales receipts will be clipped together and stored in a file cabinet for possible future reference.

- *Update master data.* After all the data have been entered into the system, the sales event data store is brought to the computer (using a disk or CD) to be processed, and any calculations and summarizations completed (represented by the central computer symbol in Figure 3.1). This information is used to update the master data. In the sales example, this might include taking prior inventory totals and subtracting out the items sold to derive the new inventory levels. The new inventory levels are accordingly written to an updated master data store. The sales event data also would be stored in a more permanent data store, such as the sales data store. It would not be uncommon for the owner-manager of our used books and CDs store to either take the data stores home and process them on a computer at home or, perhaps even more likely, to take the information to a public accountant for processing.

- *Generate outputs.* After all the calculations have been completed and the data updated, the system will periodically generate the applicable reports (the report generator program in Figure 3.1). For our used books and CDs store, this might include such documents as a sales report and an inventory update report. For our small store, both reports would probably go to the owner-manager.

Note that between each step is a time delay before the next step occurs. We might think of this form of automated system as a *pure* periodic system in that the entire process uses a *periodic mode* for processing. For instance, in our used books and CDs store, the day's sales documents are collected before being passed on for keying. After keying, the sales data are held until the data can be transferred to the location and person where the data can be used to update the master data. After the data are updated each day, the reports still may not be generated until later—perhaps on a weekly or monthly basis.

A disadvantage of *periodic mode* systems is that the only time the master data are up to date is right after the processing has been completed. As soon as the next business event occurs, the master data are no longer up to date. As a result, little reason exists to provide a query capability (as discussed in Chapters 5 and 6) for data that are used in a *periodic mode* system. Usually, systems users will simply get a copy of the reports generated at the end of a processing run and use this information to make their decisions until the next processing run and a new set of reports is available. Only in rare situations will a query capability be provided, and then only to eliminate the needless printing of reports for occasional users of the information generated by the system.

Online Transaction Entry (OLTE)

Information technology improvements in recent years have provided a low-cost means for improving the efficiency of these traditional automated equivalents to manual accounting systems. The most prevalent change has been the increasing use of *online transaction entry* to reduce redundancies in pure *periodic mode* processing (see Figure 3.2, page 76). In an **online transaction entry (OLTE)** system, use of data entry devices allows business event data to be entered directly into the information system at the time and place that the business event occurs. These systems merge the traditional subprocesses of *business event occurs* (which includes completion of the source document) and *record business event data* into a single operation. At the point of the business event, a computer input device is used to enter the event data into the data entry system rather than onto a source document. Generally, prices are automatically generated by the system as the computer retrieves the data from the system data stores. Such a system is considered **online** because the data entry device is connected to the computer. The input system usually also will serve as a printer that will then print document copies to serve the still-needed role of source documents. As business events occur, they are usually accumulated either on magnetic tape or on disk.

Figure 3.2 Online Transaction Entry (Batch Processing Environment)

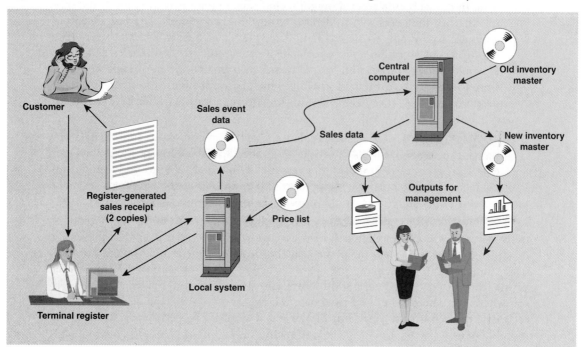

If we go back to our used books and CDs store scenario, it may be that you prefer to buy your books and CDs at one of the chain stores such as those found in shopping malls. When you take your books and CDs to the clerk at the counter in these types of stores, the clerk generally keys the purchase straight into the cash register. As noted in Figure 3.2, what is occurring at this point is that the sales items are being entered into a terminal that is creating (recording) a log of the sales event (the sales event data store), retrieving price list information, and generating duplicate copies of the sales receipt. One copy of the sales receipt is given to you (the customer) and the other is placed in the cash register drawer (for filing in the audit file). Note the differences between Figures 3.1 (page 74) and 3.2. The manual recording process (in Figure 3.1) by the sales clerk becomes a terminal entry process (in Figure 3.2), and the record input (i.e., data entry) process in Figure 3.1 becomes part of process sales in Figure 3.2. Other than these changes, the two processes are the same.

The use of OLTE eliminates the need to have one person enter business event data on a source document and then have a second person perform the data entry to convert the business event data to a computer-ready form. In an OLTE system, one person performs both operations. In many contemporary systems, this data entry will be completed using *bar code readers, scanners,* (see Chapter 10), or *RFID (Radio-Frequency Identification) readers* (see Chapter 12). The use of such technologies eliminates the human error that can result from entering the data manually. Thus, in many OLTE systems the only human impact on the accuracy of the input data is the necessity to properly scan items into the system. Various control procedures that are used to ensure data accuracy are discussed in detail in Chapter 9.

It should be noted that the processing of the data in Figure 3.2 is still completed on a batch of event data at a later point in time. In the case of many sophisticated systems in use by businesses today, sales event data are aggregated by cash register terminals for the entire day; after the store has closed, the data is electronically transferred over phone lines to the computer system where the business event data are processed. This is reflected in Figure 3.2 by the communications line connecting the sales event data in the local system to the central computer. The processing is typically completed overnight while all stores in a region are closed, and updated reports are periodically generated to reflect the sales event updates to the master data.

Note that the use of electronic communication technology does not change the traditional periodic approach, but rather makes the approach more efficient. Hence, we encounter one of the first steps in the evolution toward advanced-level e-Business systems.

Periodic mode systems traditionally have been the most common method for completing business event data processing. Nonetheless, with accounting information systems being transferred almost exclusively to computerized systems, and given the rapid improvements in information technologies, *periodic mode* systems are becoming less common for most activities. However, for some applications *periodic mode* processing is the preferred approach. For instance, payroll systems are a natural match with the batching of business event data, since all employees are generally paid on a periodic basis and at the same time. It is unrealistic to think that such an application will eventually be processed using systems other than *periodic mode*.

Online Real-Time (OLRT) Processing

Among the many clichés that one hears in today's rather harried business environment is the phrase "time is money." While the cliché tends to be somewhat worn out, it is descriptive of the current demands on information systems. Traditional *periodic mode* systems that provide information primarily through periodic reports that are hours, days, or weeks out of date can put an organization's decision makers at a disadvantage if its competitors are using up-to-date information to make the same decisions (e.g., recall the importance placed on *timeliness* and *relevance* in Chapter 1). The pressures for timely information flows coupled with significant advances in available information technologies have led to a rapid migration toward *online real-time systems*. **Online real-time (OLRT) systems** gather business event data at the time of occurrence, update the master data essentially instantaneously, and provide the results arising from the business event within a very short amount of time—that is, in *real-time*. *OLRT* systems complete all stages of business event data processing in *immediate mode*. **Immediate mode** is the data processing mode in which little or no delay occurs between any two data processing steps (as opposed to *periodic mode* where a significant delay occurs between two or more data processing steps).

OLRT systems typically require three basic subprocesses to be completed before an event is converted into information that can be used by decision makers. Follow along with Figure 3.3 (page 78) as we discuss each of these subprocesses.

- *Business event occurrence and recording of event data.* At the time of the business event, the related data are entered directly into the system. Source documents are almost never used, as they significantly slow the process and remove some of the advantages of nonredundant data entry. Notice that the data entry process where the sale is entered into the system is the same as in Figure 3.2 (other than the absence of the filed copy of the sales receipt). This is consistent with the use of *online transaction entry (OLTE)* for *OLRT* systems.

- *Update master data.* Each business event that has been entered into the system is processed individually and any calculations and summarizations completed. This

Figure 3.3 Online Real-Time Processing

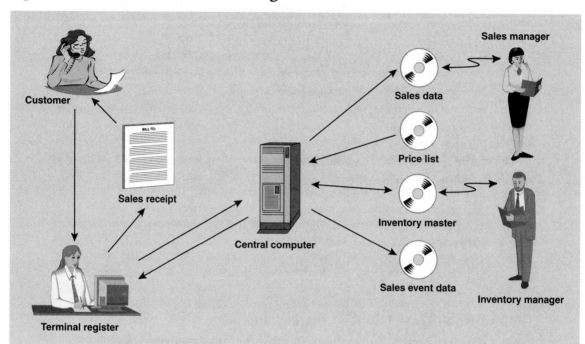

information is then used to update the master data. Note in Figure 3.3 that the processing is now being done on-site where the sales event data are entered.[7] Because each business event is processed independently and immediately, the master data at any given point in time will be within minutes or seconds of being up to date. When your books and CDs store is entering your information into the terminal, it may actually be using an *OLRT* system if it is important to the store to know whether a given book or CD title is in stock at a given point in time—perhaps to answer a customer's question.

- *Generate reports and support queries.* It is neither practical nor desirable that reports be generated after each business event is recorded and master data have been updated. Typically, applicable reports will still be generated by the system on a periodic basis. At the same time, however, these reports will usually be instantaneously available through access of the system on an as-needed basis, as demonstrated in Figure 3.3 with the communications links to the sales and inventory managers. One of the main advantages provided by many *OLRT* systems is an ability to check the current status of master data items at any given point in time. In the books and CDs store, it would allow the sales staff to quickly check whether a given book or CD is in stock. In many cases, rather than using pre-specified reports that may not necessarily provide the information that decision makers need, these information systems users will use a query language (as discussed in Chap-

---

[7] This is one method of accomplishing *OLRT* that uses expensive, continuous direct communications to a remotely located central computer. Many organizations use a distributed processing mode that places the computer locally to avoid the costs associated with the continuous communications line; however, as in the case shown here, the need to centrally process information for multiple locations may warrant the communications line costs of continuous direct communication.

ters 5 and 6) to dynamically create unique reports that provide the one-time information they need to make key decisions. For instance, the store manager may want to run a report on the inventory stock for the top-10 selling CDs and books.

While another cliché says that "you cannot buy time," *OLRT* systems allow users to nearly eliminate the delay in accessing up-to-date information. However, the primary disadvantage of *real-time* systems is clearly the cost. To efficiently operate an *OLRT* system, it is imperative that the point of the business event be linked directly with the computer system—that is, *online*. Accordingly, to operate an OLRT system, *online transaction entry* (OLTE) methods must also be used.

It was noted previously that OLTE systems are increasingly being used with systems that primarily use the *periodic mode*. While the data entry performed in all OLTE systems is essentially the same, the mode of processing may vary. While a pure *periodic mode* system still processes business event data in batches, an *OLRT* system using *OLTE* will process each recorded business event in real time. In a *real-time* system, business event data cannot be aggregated on a local computer to be transferred later to the data processing center. Rather, each business event must be communicated for processing at the time the event occurs. This results in a more expensive approach to *OLTE*. In essence, rather than creating a temporary electronic communications connection to download the data to the central computer, an *OLRT* system generally requires a continuous electronic communication connection that will usually necessitate the use of some form of *network*. This will be addressed later in this chapter.

It should be noted here that automated systems that model manual systems and *OLRT* systems are the two extremes in business event data processing. The systems that mimic manual systems are what we might term pure *periodic mode* systems in that a delay occurs between every step of the processing. On the other hand, *OLRT* systems represent pure *immediate mode* systems in that little or no delay occurs between any steps in the processing. We note these as the extremes because many systems lie somewhere between these two extremes, exhibiting a mix of *periodic* and *immediate mode* processes at various stages. For example, *OLTE* used with batch processing results in an *immediate mode* approach for combining the *business event occurrence* and *record event data* steps, while *periodic mode* processing might be used for the remainder of the steps.

Online Transaction Processing (OLTP)

In an effort to reduce both the expense and time delay resulting from the need to communicate business event data over what are sometimes great distances to complete business event data processing in real time, many entities are turning to **online transaction processing (OLTP)** systems. An OLTP system is a real-time system that performs all or part of the processing activities at the data entry terminal location. These systems use business event data processing terminals that have the capability to manage data, run applications, and control communications with the central processing computer and data stores. Hence, by performing most of the processing at the terminal location, the delays caused from electronic communications between the terminal and the central computer are reduced or eliminated (see Figure 3.4) as is the cost associated with communicating to the central processing location *during* the processing of the business event. Only the results need be communicated. The most common applications for these systems to date have been automatic teller machines (ATMs) and computerized reservation systems. Note in Figure 3.4 that the electronic communication network in an OLTP system becomes even more complex as processing occurs at the terminal end, but then data must be updated at all terminals. For instance, in the case of an ATM, once an individual has

Figure 3.4 Alternative Approaches to Real-Time Processing

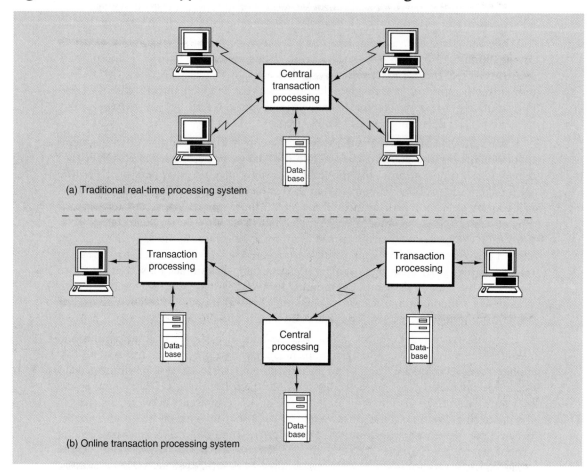

(a) Traditional real-time processing system

(b) Online transaction processing system

withdrawn money from his or her account, the system needs to update the balance at all ATMs before additional withdrawals may be made.

CONTROLS   It should be noted that most banks have converted to OLTP technology, with only a few not yet using this advanced processing method. Microprocessor technology only recently has become powerful enough to make this approach feasible for banks. You should also note that in an OLTP system, the immediate updating of balances at the central processing unit and the terminal locations is done with shadow data (e.g., copies of the master data used for real-time processing) that are duplicated at each site, but for control purposes the actual master data are usually updated once a day using batch processing.

While *immediate mode*-dominated systems are becoming the most prevalent method for new business event data processing applications, they are not necessarily the end-all solution for all applications. Both *periodic mode* and *immediate mode* approaches have distinctive characteristics that make each a preferable option for certain types of applications. While primarily *periodic mode* systems, as noted earlier, are preferable for most payroll systems, you would certainly use an *immediate mode* system for maintaining working balances for ATM event data. If *periodic* processing was used, a person might withdraw the entire balance out of his or her account multiple times before the system processed the event data and updated the accounts—a significant losing proposition for a bank. Clearly, any given application should be matched with the best or most applicable processing method.

Each of the described processing methods requires data communications pathways among PCs, terminals, and/or other systems. Technology Summary 3.1 describes the interconnectivity of such systems.

Technology Summary 3.1

Communication Networks

The key component for electronic communication systems is the network that provides the pathways for transfer of the electronic data. Communication networks range from those designed to link a few computers together to the Internet, where the goal can almost be perceived as linking all computers in the world together.

Within organizations, a major focus of network computing has been on client server technology. **Client server technology** is the physical and logical division between user-oriented application programs that are run at the client level (i.e., user level) and the shared data that must be available through the server (i.e., a separate computer that handles centrally shared activities—such as databases and printing queues—between multiple users). The enabling networks underlying client server technologies are **local area networks (LANs)** and **wide area networks (WANs)**. LANs are communication networks that link several different local user machines with printers, databases, and other shared devices. WANs are communication networks that link distributed users and local networks into an integrated communications network. Such systems have traditionally been the backbone of enterprise systems technology, but recent advances in communications technology are rapidly changing the underlying infrastructure models.

These emerging network technologies are driving the future of e-Business. These technologies allow for more simplified user interaction with networks and empower users to access broad arrays of data for supplementing management decision making as well as opening new avenues for direct commerce linkages. The leading technology in this arena is the Internet. The **Internet** is a massive interconnection of computer networks worldwide that enables communication between dissimilar technology platforms. The Internet is the network that connects all the WANs to which organizations choose to allow access. With the expansion of the Internet also has come increased accessibility to public databases that provide rich information sources, searchable on a for-fee basis (see Technology Summary 3.2, page 83).

Web browsers are software programs designed specifically to allow users to easily browse various documents and data sources available on the Internet. The advent of this easy-to-use software has rippled through organizations and caused a rethinking of how companies can set up their own internal networks to be more accessible to decision makers. The result has been the growing development of intranets, which are essentially mini-internal equivalents to the Internet that link an organization's internal documents and databases into a system that is accessible through Web browsers or, increasingly, through internally developed software designed to maximize the benefits from utilization of organizational information resources.

By combining the benefits of the Internet and intranets, many organizations have begun to allow customers, vendors, and other members of their value system access to the company's intranet. This type of intranet, which has been extended to limited external access, is referred to as an **extranet**.

The by-product of the expansion in intranets, extranets, and the Internet is a rich medium for e-Business. These networks provide the foundation for what likely will be exponential growth in e-Business—both at the resale level and in supplier-buyer relationships.

Methods for Conducting E-Business

To this point the discussion has focused on the modes of business event data processing and related communication technologies that underlie the ability of organizations to enter into e-Business. In this segment of the chapter, we redirect the discussion to specific methods for conducting e-Business and how these methods utilize alternative modes of business event data processing and available electronic communication technologies.

The four methods of e-Business that we will discuss are fairly diverse. First, we provide an overview of the role of *electronic mail* (e-mail) in e-Business—a lesser-used, but more directed approach. Second, we discuss *electronic document management* (EDM). Many would not include EDM as part of e-Business since the majority of such applications support non-e-Business events. We chose to include it in this section because of the integral role it has in supporting the last two stages. *Electronic data interchange* (EDI) is the third area we discuss. It currently represents the predominant form of e-Business. The fourth method is *Internet commerce*, which represents the fastest-growing segment of e-Business. Concurrent with the development of Internet businesses that sell physical products, new organizations have surfaced existing solely to provide data through the Internet. Technology Summary 3.2 describes some businesses focused on Internet commerce, providing information in the form of public databases.

Commerce Through E-Mail

Electronic mail (e-mail) is the electronic transmission of non-standardized messages between two individuals who are linked via a communications network (usually an *intranet* or the *Internet*). *E-mail* represents a weak form for e-Business because of the non-standardized format by which messages are transmitted. Before exploring the use of *e-mail* as a mode for e-Business, let's briefly examine the limitations of using a non-standardized format.

If you think back to our earlier discussions in this chapter related to various technologies that can be used to automate the data entry process, all the technologies relied on a standardized format for the data (e.g., a bar code or a printed response such as *amount paid* written on the transmittal document). This is almost the antithesis of *e-mail*. *E-mail* tends to be a very free-form mode of expression and, for the most part, a fairly casual and informal mode of communication. This unstructured nature of the communication mode makes data capturing more difficult and generally requires human translation and entry of the data. This increases the likelihood of error and requires more stringent data control procedures to be in place. The e-mail essentially becomes a *source document* for use in the business event data processing. Organizations using e-mail as source documents also must have in place a mechanism to deal with unsolicited, non-document mail (SPAM).

Despite the limitations, *e-mail* does have several characteristics that make it tolerable for some e-Business events. From a sales standpoint, a targeted market can often be identified by locating an appropriate *e-mail* list. Much like their mailing list counterparts that are used for postal delivery, lists of *e-mail* addresses for individuals that are likely to be interested in a given product can be useful. Generally, if the marketing medium is *e-mail*, then the purchase request also will be transmitted in this manner.

As a means of getting around the unstructured nature of *e-mail* transmissions, marketers will frequently provide an electronic order form that adds structure to the information content of the message. However, even with the electronic order form, entry of the data into the system generally requires some keying by data entry personnel. Thus,

---

Technology Summary 3.2

Public Databases

A **public database service** can be called by many names, including *online database service*, *electronic reference service*, *electronic retrieval service*, and *third-party electronic databases*. Through your personal computer, you already may have experienced working with such reference services (e.g., CompuServe®, America Online®, or the like). Common to *most* such services is that they allow subscribers, for a fee, to access and search an external database, usually through the Internet or a direct telephone line connection. Fees typically include set-up charges, monthly subscription charges, and occasionally fees for actual online connect time.

The difference among services generally lies in the kinds of data stored in the available database. For instance, much of the research for this book involved doing computer searches of periodical literature databases using an online search service available through our college library. Public accounting firms commonly access electronic databases to obtain information on client industries, corporate files, ratio analysis, tax laws and regulations, and authoritative accounting pronouncements—through services such as Total On-Line Tax and Accounting Library (TOTAL) or LEXIS/NEXIS and other materials—to help manage their accounting practices

and to assist in rendering management advisory and computer consulting services. Other databases can range in content from profiles of persons seeking the "love connection" (computer-assisted dating arranged from your living room) to stock quotations, to business and economic news, to travel and leisure directories, to just about anything. Two factors that electronic reference services have in common, however, are that they are big business, and they are growing.

One recently developed Internet-based service is EDGAR Online at http://www.edgar-online.com. This subscription-based service takes regulatory filings of public companies and puts them in a database for easy access. The service provides users the ability to research the financial statements, footnotes, and auditors' reports and other filings of publicly traded companies for *each of several years*. Imagine having hard copies of all those annual reports at your disposal. What a wealth of valuable information! But where would you store it, and how would you even begin to search it for the information you need? The database facilitates document retrieval by providing subscribers several tools to confine their searches to the specific topics desired.

---

the general objectives of e-Business—to avoid the need for a salesperson to make the contact and to avoid the business event recording activities during business event data processing—are not achieved.

Electronic Document Management

Electronic document management (EDM) is the capturing, storage, management, and control of electronic document images for the purpose of supporting management decision making and facilitating business event data processing. The capturing and storage of document images typically relies on the *digital image processing* approaches (see Chapter 10). The added dimensions of management and control are critical to maintaining the physical security of the documents while at the same time assuring timely distribution to users requiring the information. Technology Application 3.1 (page 84) discusses some general uses of EDM.

In general, business applications of EDM fall into two categories:

1. *Document storage and retrieval*. For example, mortgages, deeds, and liens are archived and made available to the public for such uses as title searches. Other documents in this category include birth certificates, death certificates, marriage

---

Technology Application 3.1

General Uses of Electronic Document Management Systems

Case 1

The need to organize client files for quick access and processing leads many accounting firms to adopt document management systems. One such system was developed by Integrated Computer Management (ICM). The Electronic Compliance File (ECF) created for Ernst & Young LLP lets thousands of tax professionals in 100 cities manage their documents and images in one structured folder. In addition to eliminating the loss of critical paper-based information, the folder provides secure, distributed, online access, regardless of a staff member's location. The program reduced shipping costs, cut paperwork, and increased overall efficiency.

Case 2

A new law, Check 21 was recently enacted to allow banks to substitute electronic images for paper checks in the check clearing and settlement process. The legislation is expected to save the banking industry billions of dollars. Although the law calls for "electronic replacement documents" to be in use within a year, industry experts caution that it will take years for the clearance process to include the entire financial industry. One of the main issues that will determine the success of the electronic processes is the attitude of consumers. Consumers willing to accept copies, rather than their original checks, will be one determining factor for the success of the implementation of the new processes. The success of technology, such as document processing, is heavily dependent on the acceptance those receiving outputs.

Sources: "Microsoft Names Solution Provider Award Winners," Microsoft press release, http://www.microsoft.com/presspass, May 5, 1997; Lucas Mearian, "Check 21 Becomes Law: Allows Speedier Electronic Settlements," *Computerworld Online* (November 3, 2003).

---

licenses, banking-account signature cards, user manuals, price lists, and catalogs. An EDM system stores the images (e.g., pdf files) of these items and displays or prints a copy of them upon request. Document storage and retrieval also could be implemented using *micrographic-based* image processing systems (i.e., microfilm).

2. *Business event data processing.* For example, loan and insurance applications must pass through several stages, such as origination, underwriting, and closing. The EDM system can manage the workflow and route the documents to the appropriate people—even if these people are geographically dispersed. *Electronic-based* image processing systems must be used for this type of application. An organization's communications networks also must be interconnected in a manner that facilitates access and transmission of document images.

EDM systems provide a relatively inexpensive alternative to paper documentation. Although computer storage and processing requirements are much greater than for key-entered documents, the ability to access and manipulate real images of business documents offers great opportunities for improving the efficiency and effectiveness of many business applications and can create significant competitive advantages for an organization. For instance, fast access to imaged documents often translates into faster and better customer service and results in increased customer loyalty—themes we explore in some depth in Chapter 10. The typical benefits include:

- Reduced cost of handling and storing paper.
- Improved staff productivity.
- Superior customer service.

- Enhanced management of operational workflow.
- Faster processing.

However, as with any technology, the applications selected for EDM should be chosen wisely. Applications with a high chance of success might be those in which:

- A large amount of paper is produced and stored. We know of an organization that adopted EDM because they had no more room to store paper within their existing office space. In fact, the engineers told them that the floor could not support another file cabinet! Imaging systems also can produce economies in situations where paper documents are not abandoned altogether, but are moved from storage in expensive office locations to cheaper off-site warehouse storage.

- Data, such as signatures, must be scanned. For example, banks use image processing for signature verification cards.

CONTROLS

- Frequent access to the stored data from geographically dispersed locations is needed. For example, clerks at every branch of a bank must be able to view signature verification cards.

- Processing of the stored data are extensive and complex and takes place from multiple locations, as in the case of loan and insurance applications that must be processed, reviewed, and approved by many people.

EDM also is becoming an increasingly important component of *electronic data interchange (EDI)*. In many cases, organizations are requiring document and image support for *EDI* data. Most notable are manufacturing- and engineering-related event data where specifications may need to be more clearly defined with computer-aided design/ computer-aided manufacturing drawings.

Electronic Data Interchange

Computer and communications technology have been successfully applied by organizations to improve accuracy and control and to eliminate paper *within* their information systems applications. However, direct, paperless, business communication *between* organizations has been slowed by the lack of transmission and presentation standards. What this often means is that an organization uses its computer technology to prepare a purchase order (PO), for example, completely without paper and human intervention—efficient, fast, and accurate process. But the PO must then be printed and mailed to the vendor. Then, at the vendor, the PO must be sorted from other mail in the mailroom, routed to the appropriate clerk, and entered in the vendor's computer. The efficiency, timeliness, and accuracy gained by the automated purchasing process at the originating organization are lost through the mailing and reentry of the data at the vendor.

One technology that has had a significant impact on streamlining data communication among organizations is that of *electronic data interchange (EDI)*. **Electronic data interchange (EDI)** is the computer-to-computer exchange of business data (i.e., documents) in structured formats that allow direct processing of those electronic documents by the receiving computer system. Figure 3.5 (page 86) depicts the typical EDI components. Follow along with us as we describe those components; the numbers in circles are cross-references to corresponding locations in the narrative description.

Application Software (Circles 1 and 7)

An originating application prepares an electronic business document, such as a purchase order (PO). At the destination organization, an application processes the business data. For example, the originating application's PO would be processed as a customer order by the destination organization's order entry/sales (OE/S) process.

Figure 3.5 Electronic Data Interchange Components

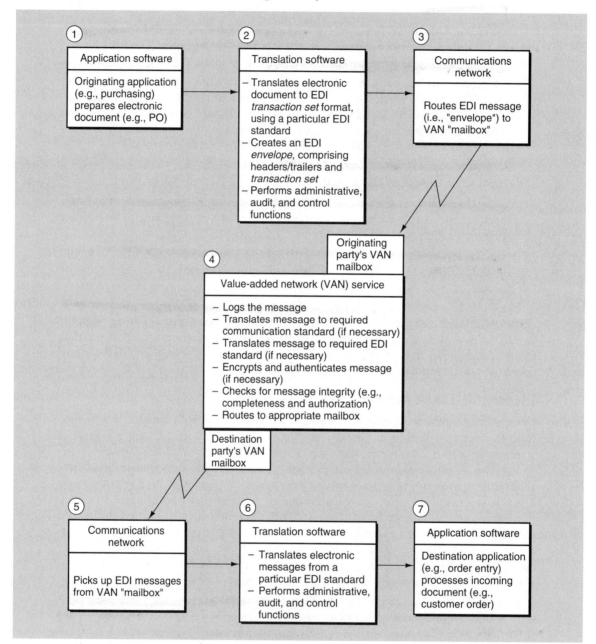

Translation Software (Circles 2 and 6)

An application's electronic business document must be translated to the structured EDI format that will be recognized by the receiving computer. Presently, two major, nonproprietary, public translation standards exist:

1. In the United States and Canada, the American National Standards Institute (ANSI) X12 standard has been used.

2. EDIFACT (EDI for Administration, Commerce, and Transport) is the predominant standard for international EDI transactions. Actively promoted by the United Nations for member nations, this standard includes some aspects of ANSI X12 and permits global communication between trading partners.

In addition, several standards are specific to particular industries, such as the Automotive Industry Action Group (AIAG), Transportation Data Coordinating Committee (TDCC), and Chemical Industry Data eXchange (CIDX). Some of these industry standards are compatible with the public, interindustry standards (e.g., ANSI X12); some are not compatible.

Translation standards include formats and codes for each transmission type, called a *transaction set*, as well as standards for combining several transaction sets for transmission. For example, under the ANSI X12 standard, a purchase order (PO) is a transaction set "850," a shipping notice is a transaction set "856," an invoice is a transaction set "810,"and so forth. The ANSI *data dictionary* for transaction set 850 defines the length, type, and acceptable coding for each data element in an EDI purchase order. For example, ANSI X12 describes the format and location within the message of the customer name and address, the part numbers and quantities ordered, the unit of measure of the items ordered (e.g., each, dozen, ton), and so on. Figure 3.6 (page 88) depicts the translation process. The figure shows a sample PO as it might appear as a conventional paper document and then illustrates how the PO is transformed into EDI transaction set 850.

Besides purchase orders, other typical EDI transaction sets include (the ANSI X12 transaction set number appears in parentheses):

- Purchase order acknowledgment (855).
- Advance shipping notice (ASN) (856). From supplier to customer, advising that the goods are on the way.
- Receiving advice (861). From customer to supplier to report late, incomplete, or incorrect shipments.
- Invoice (810).
- Payment order/remittance advice (820). From customer to supplier for payment.
- Functional acknowledgment (FA) (997). A message is sent from receiver to sender to acknowledge receipt of *each and every one* of the previous transaction sets. For instance, when the seller receives a purchase order (850) from the buyer, the seller sends back an FA (997) to indicate the message was received. Then, when the buyer receives a purchase order acknowledgment (855), the buyer acknowledges that the message was received by sending the seller an FA (997).

Translation software translates outgoing messages so that they are in the standard message format (e.g., ANSI X12) and translates the incoming messages from the standard message format into the form understood by the application system. This intermediate translation to/from the EDI format precludes the need for an organization to reprogram its application so that it can communicate with *each* trading partner's application.

The translation software also performs administrative, audit, and control functions.   **CONTROLS**
For example, the software inserts identification and control information in front of (header) and after (trailer):

- Each transaction set, such as one purchase order.
- Each *functional group* (e.g., a group of purchase orders, a group of receiving advices, and so forth) so that several groups may be sent in one transmission.
- All components comprising one transmission.

Figure 3.6 Electronic Data Interchange Transaction Set

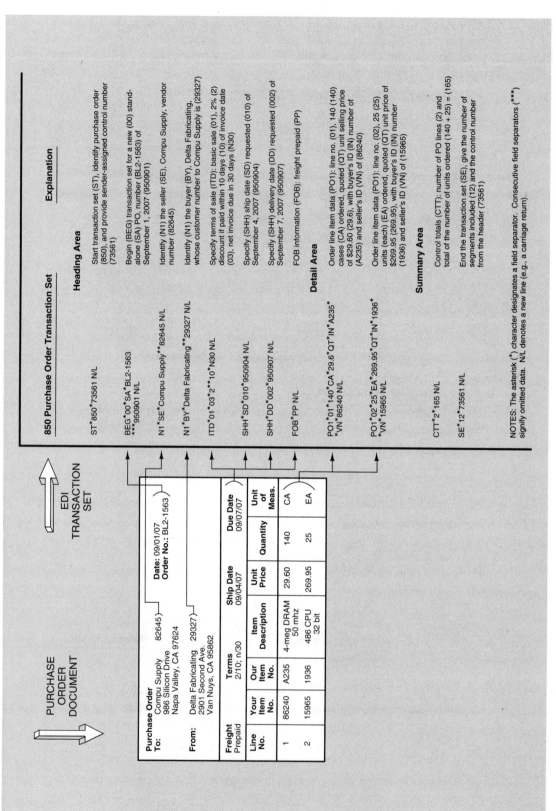

Source: Adapted with permission from A. Faye Borthick and Harold P. Roth, "EDI for Reengineering Business Processes," *Management Accounting* (October 1993): 35–36.

In EDI lingo, the data sets and the headers/trailers are called "envelopes." In addition to assembling and disassembling the EDI envelopes, the translation software may log incoming and outgoing messages and route the messages from and to the proper application.

Communications Network (Circles 3 and 5)

The two trading partners must have a method of communicating the electronic messages to each other. One procedure is for the originating organization to put its messages on a computer disk or CD and deliver the disk/CD to the receiving organization. But this approach offsets some of the time and cost benefits that an organization can accrue by adopting EDI.

A second method is to establish a direct computer-to-computer link between the origination computer and one or more destination computers. This interface is accomplished through a leased or dedicated communication line with each trading partner, or through a communications network in which one of the partners—let's say a large manufacturer—serves as the "hub" of the network, and its suppliers and other trading partners are the network "spokes." The modem and communications software in your PC exemplifies such a communications system. However, communications system incompatibilities may require that one partner or the other purchase communications hardware or software, making this a costly option. Further, agreeing on such details as what time of day to send and receive data from trading partners makes this option difficult to manage.

To overcome some of the shortcomings of these direct connections, organizations may use either EDI service bureaus or the Internet. The EDI *service bureau* is an organization that acts as an intermediary between a large hub company and its suppliers. The EDI service bureau generally works with smaller suppliers that are reluctant to acquire in-house translation and communications software. In such a case, the *translation software* and *communications software* reside on the service bureau's computer system. For a fee, the service bureau takes EDI messages from the hub, translates the messages into formats that are usable by the suppliers' computer applications, and forwards them to the suppliers. In the other direction, the bureau translates suppliers' *paper* documents—such as shipping notices or invoices—into EDI format and sends the electronic documents to the hub. The Internet provides organizations with a modern network infrastructure to accomplish direct communications and has increasingly become the communication method of choice for EDI transmissions. (We discuss Internet connections later in this chapter.)

Value-Added Network (VAN) Service (Circle 4)

Rather than connecting to *each* trading partner, an organization can connect to a **value-added network (VAN)** service. A *VAN* service acts as the EDI "postman." An organization can connect to the *VAN* when it wants, leave its outgoing messages and, at the same time, pick up incoming messages from its "mailbox." A *VAN* is a packet-switched network service that provides communications capabilities for organizations not wishing to obtain their own packet-switched or dedicated communications links.

As shown in Figure 3.5 (page 86), one of the several functions that the *VAN* will perform is to translate the message from one communications protocol to another, if necessary. Presently, two protocols are used for much of the EDI traffic: the ITU Telecommunication Standardization Sector (formerly the Consultative Committee for International Telegraph and Telephone, or CCITT) X.400 and the X25 protocols. X.400 is generally the preferred method as it can accommodate multiple message formats in a single transmission. For example, an EDI document and an e-mail message or an electronic document image could all be sent in the same "envelope."

Technology Summary 3.3 presents some management, operational, and control issues associated with EDI, and Technology Application 3.2 (page 92) describes some general uses of EDI.

Technology Summary 3.3

EDI Management, Operational, and Control Considerations

Benefits of EDI include the following:

- Many organizations have survived by being "forced" to implement EDI if they wished to continue doing business with certain customers. For instance, Wal-Mart Stores and Kmart Corporation have told all their suppliers to establish EDI capability by a specified deadline if they wished to continue doing business with these retail giants.
- Responsiveness to customers' needs has improved. In many cases, trading partners have discovered that the cooperation engendered by EDI has reduced conflicts between them, improved communication, and fostered trust. In some cases, EDI has led to what are known as "quick response" replenishment systems. In such systems, a large customer—Sears Roebuck, for instance—gives its suppliers access (through EDI communication links) to real-time, *point of sale (POS)* information about what is and is not selling at its various retail outlets. With that information available, the suppliers can forecast customer demand more accurately, fine-tune their production schedules accordingly, and meet that demand in a highly responsive manner. This is discussed further in Chapter 12.
- By not reentering data at the receiving organization, processing costs are reduced and accuracy is improved. To better appreciate the potential impact of this benefit, consider the fact that, according to one estimate, 70 percent of the data processed by a typical company's mainframe computer had been output by another computer system.

- Mailroom and other document preparation and handling costs are eliminated. For example, in the automobile industry, it is estimated that $200 of the cost of each car is incurred because of the amount of paper shuffling that has to be done.
- By providing timely and accurate data, forecasting and analysis and cash flow are improved, and the occurrence of stock-outs is reduced.
- In the course of implementing EDI, an organization has the chance to rethink and redesign existing processes and controls.

Costs of EDI include:

- Modifying trading relationships and negotiating contracts.
- Buying or leasing hardware and software.
- Establishing relationships with VANs and negotiating contracts.
- Training employees.
- Reengineering affected applications.
- Implementing security, audit, and control procedures.

Control considerations:

- Since signatures will no longer evidence authorizations, controls must ensure proper authorization. And, at some point during the process, we must authenticate that the message is sent to—and received from—the party intended and is authorized by someone having the proper authority.
- Without external, visual review, some business event data can be significantly in error. For example, a payment could

be off by one decimal point! Therefore, controls must *prevent* rather than *detect* such errors.

- Given that the computer will initiate and authenticate messages, controls over the computer programs and data—*program change controls* and *physical security* (see Chapter 8)—become even more important than in non-EDI systems.
- If a VAN is used for communicating between partners, security procedures must prevent compromise of sensitive data, and controls must ensure correct translation and routing of messages.

Therefore, *controls* must be in place to ensure that:

- All transaction sets are received from the trading partners.
- All transaction sets are received by the trading partners.
- All recorded business event data are recorded once and only once.
- Data are accurately received (sent).
- Data are accurately translated.
- Data are accurately passed through the application interface (EDI translator).
- Business event data are received from authorized senders.
- Senders are authorized to send the transaction type.
- Messages are not intercepted or altered during transmission.
- The log of business event data is protected.
- Unauthorized messages are prevented from being sent.

To attain these control goals, organizations have implemented the following control plans, among others:

- Some control plans are inherent in the very nature of the way that EDI is implemented. As we noted, the EDI headers and trailers accompanying transaction sets contain important control data. For example, the next to last line in Figure 3.6 (page 88) contains an item/

line count and a *hash* total of the number of units ordered. The last line includes a control total of the number of segments comprising the transaction set (12) and a control number (73561) that should agree with the corresponding number from the header on line one of the table. Functional acknowledgments (FAs) also help to ensure the integrity of EDI messages (i.e., that data have not been lost or garbled in transmission).

- *Expert systems* (see Chapter 5) may be used to determine that incoming messages are reasonable—consistent with normal message patterns—to authenticate the source and authorization for the message.
- Access to EDI applications may require a *biometric security system*, a *smartcard*, or a physical key as well as a *password* (see Chapter 8).
- *Data encryption* (see Chapter 9) may be employed to protect data during transmission.
- *Digital signatures* (see Chapter 9) may be used. Much like a password or other access code, the digital signature uniquely identifies who approved a business event and also helps to ensure that the EDI message was not altered during transmission.
- "Continuous auditing" may be implemented through the use of *integrated test facilities (ITF)* or *imbedded audit modules*. An ITF creates dummy corporations or branches in the system data and processes test data for these dummy entities at the same time that live data are being processed for real entities. An imbedded audit module acts like an audit "alarm" that is programmed to alert the auditor—by printing an audit log—to suspect data (e.g., business event data of an unusually high dollar amount) or to unauthorized attempts to access the system.

Finally, contracts between trading partners and with the VANs must specify responsibility for controls and for erroneous transmissions. For

(continued)

example, who is responsible for authenticating the source and destination of messages? If a message is garbled by the VAN, who is responsible for any resulting financial loss—the sender, the receiver, or the VAN? Contracts might address the following issues:

- When is a message considered received: When it is sent, when it is transmitted, when it gets to the mailbox, or when it is picked up? The answers to such questions are important in establishing the point at which an agreement, such as a purchase, legally exists between trading partners. Resolving such questions also is critical in situations where the message is a bid with a time deadline.
- Who is responsible for data integrity, audit trails, security, and so on?
- What are the penalties for failing to perform as required?

Technology Application 3.2

General Uses of Electronic Data Interchange

Case 1

The cost of processing a purchase order can reach $150, due to manual processes and paperwork. Saks Department Store Group purchases over $900 million of product per year, from over 5,000 vendors. Such a volume of purchases executed in a manual environment can lead to a costly and inefficient process. In addition to experiencing significant savings on purchases, management is able to identify and monitor purchasing and spending patterns across stores, regions, and nationally, uncovering opportunities for additional savings or purchase consolidation. The system also facilitates the procurement cycle, speeding up the process and reducing the risk of running out of items or requiring expensive, last-minute shipments.

Case 2

Perhaps the biggest change in EDI in recent years is being driven by the Internet. Recently, Wal-Mart announced that it would move its EDI purchases from VANs to the Internet. The use of the Internet for EDI is a sign of confidence in the stability of the environment. The use of the Internet is relatively free of transaction cost, providing significant cost savings over the old VAN processes for Wal-Mart and its vendors. Until recently, to implement EDI over the Internet, software on each side of the transaction had to be provided from the same vendor. This lack of standardization meant that frequently, companies had to purchase and support several different EDI software packages to deal with multiple customers/vendors. Today, using the Electronic Data Interchange Internet Integration Applicability Statement 2 protocol (AS2) standard, interoperability of EDI software is becoming a reality.

Sources: IBM Case Studies, "Saks Incorporated," http://www-5.ibm.com/services/uk/ondemand/saks.html (November 2003); Robert Scheier, "Internet EDI Grows Up," *Computerworld* (January 20, 2003).

EDI and Business Event Data Processing

If we consider the implications of EDI to business event data processing, one of the main advantages is the significant reduction in need for interaction between purchasers and salespeople, coupled with the standard implementation of *online transaction entry (OLTE)*. You should recall from our earlier discussion in this chapter that OLTE eliminates the redundancy between source document capture of business event data and subsequent keying in of the source document. With EDI, both activities are eliminated for the selling organization as OLTE activities are initiated and completed by the linking purchaser. This eliminates any risk of erroneous data entry from within the selling organization. As we go forward, you should keep in mind that EDI may be completed through traditional modes using dedicated communications lines, but EDI is increasingly moving to the Internet as was demonstrated in Technology Application 3.2.

You should be careful, however, not to draw any assumptions as to the mode of business event data processing. You will recall from our earlier discussion that OLTE can be used with both *periodic* and *immediate* modes of processing. The same holds true for the core business processing activities in an EDI environment. The business event data are frequently processed using an *online real-time* system, but many organizations also choose to do the bulk of the processing steps using *periodic mode* as well—particularly with batching of business event data for more efficient processing. It is worth noting also that particularly when *batch* processing is being used, the need may exist to use *online transaction processing (OLTP)* approaches to handle order and payment confirmation activities during acceptance of the externally generated OLTE transmission—in other words, the customer may need an *immediate* confirmation that the order has been accepted and that the business event will be completed by the vendor.

Let us offer one additional comment before we move on. When trading partners communicate with each other electronically, they also discover that they have to communicate *internally* in new ways to achieve the full benefit of EDI. That is, EDI forces an organization to assume that all information flows—both internally and externally—are instantaneous. Accordingly, for many, EDI—along with other enabling technologies such as electronic document management—has been the catalyst for change in a firm's basic business processes. In other words, EDI has been the forerunner to *business process reengineering (BPR)* for those companies.

Internet Commerce

To date, EDI has clearly been the dominant domain in e-Business. In fact, a mere decade or so ago, e-Business was basically EDI. The *Internet* is radically changing the nature of e-Business to the point that in the not-too-distant future, the *Internet* will become the dominant platform for not only e-Business, but EDI as well. Does this mean EDI is dying? Well, not exactly. Many experts believe EDI is here to stay and currently EDI volume continues to grow at a rate of about 15 percent per year. Still, the *Internet* shows far more potential growth—primarily from the potential seen in the emerging replacement language for HTML on the Web, XML (eXtensible Markup Language).[8]

Internet commerce is the computer-to-computer exchange of business event data in structured or semi-structured formats via *Internet* communication that allows the initiation and consummation of business events. In many cases, the goods or services that are contracted for through the *Internet* are immediately (or soon thereafter) forwarded back to the consumer via the *Internet* as well (i.e., when the goods or services can be provided in electronic format, such as the case with software and music). *Internet commerce* radically simplifies e-Business by allowing the organization that is receiving and processing business event data to project template formats across the Internet to business partners for easy data entry and data transmission. For instance, if you connect across the Internet with Lands' End (a direct merchandiser of clothing) it has what it refers to as the "catalog quick order" form. With this form, you are provided an entry

---

[8] Carol Sliwa, "Firms Wait on XML, Increase Use of EDI," *Computerworld Online* (May 1, 2000).

box to key the product number for the item you want to order. The Web page automatically takes the number and identifies what additional information is needed (e.g., for most clothing, it will be size, color, and quantity). The additional information is presented in menu form for you to select from the options that are available (e.g., for color, the menu might show red, navy, black, white, and green). As you enter the responses on your computer, the data are automatically captured and recorded on the Lands' End computer. Technology Summary 3.4 provides some management, operational, and control issues associated with *Internet commerce*, while Technology Application 3.3 (page 96) provides some examples of ventures into *Internet commerce*.

Two primary categories of e-Business exist over the Web: (1) business to consumer, or B2C (e.g., Lands' End), and (2) business to business (B2B). *Internet commerce* has traditionally referred to the first category, business to consumer linkage although recently more B2B commerce is taking place over the Internet. Figure 3.7 (page 97) depicts a typical secure *Internet commerce* arrangement. Follow along with us as we describe the components in the commerce relationship. Note that the numbers in the circles are cross-references to corresponding locations in the narrative description.

Client-Server Relationship (Circles 1 and 7)

The connection created between the customer and the vendor is an extended form of *client-server* applications. The customer (circle 1) is the client node—dictating that during connection, the customer computer environment should be secure and essentially nonaccessible via the network. The vendor (circle 7) is the server node and therefore must have the capability to receive the customer's transmission and translate that transmission into processable data for use in the vendor's application programs. This translation is made through *common gateway interface (CGI)* software. The vendor, acting as the server part of the relationship, then provides the necessary correspondence back to the customer (client) in an understandable format (i.e., *Internet*-based language). To use the Lands' End example again, this means that when you place your order, your computer should be nonaccessible (i.e., secure) over the Internet, and the type of computer and software you are using will be unknown on the system. The Lands' End computer will receive your order and use CGI to translate your message into a form its program can understand and process. Similar to EDI environments, once the business event data have been collected by the vendor, the applications can be completed through any of the modes of business event data processing. For instance, Lands' End uses a *perpetual mode* approach to process sales events immediately upon receipt.[9]

Network Providers (Circles 2 and 5)

Much like the examples discussed with EDI, to participate in Internet commerce both parties to the business event must have the capability to communicate. For *Internet commerce*, this means being connected to the *Internet*. For many companies and organizations (as well as some individuals), this access will be obtained through a direct connection between the entity's computer networks (or a single server) and the Internet. For other companies and organizations, as well as the vast majority of individuals, it will be more desirable to gain access through a *network provider*.

Network providers are companies that provide a link to the Internet by making their directly connected networks available for access by fee-paying customers. From the customer side, this connection is made in Figure 3.7 by using a modem to dial in over

---

[9] Lands' End, "Security on the Lands' End Web Site," http://www.landsend.com, November 2003.

Technology Summary 3.4

Internet Commerce Management and Operations Considerations

Benefits of Internet commerce include the following:

- Many organizations have survived by being "forced" to implement Internet commerce to compete in the changing nature of their industry. If they wish to remain competitive with other industry companies that may be taking advantage of the cost savings accruing from use of the Internet for commerce, they may need to venture to the Web.
- Responsiveness to customers' needs has improved. Increasingly, customers are expecting immediate feedback and easy availability of information and help. The Internet can be a useful tool for servicing customer and client needs—forming the communications medium for distributing information and support services.
- Many organizations have achieved global penetration. The Internet is generally the easiest and least expensive way to reach global customers that an organization may never have been able to reach before. The Internet commerce marketplace is truly global.
- By not reentering data at the organization receiving the electronic transmission, processing costs are reduced and accuracy is improved. Customers now provide most of the data entry themselves, removing the need for the selling organization to key most of the business event data.
- Mailroom and other document preparation and handling costs are eliminated. The business event data processing side of a business can operate with virtually no human intervention until it is time to prepare and deliver goods.
- In the course of implementing Internet commerce, an organization has the opportunity to rethink and redesign existing business processes and controls.

Costs of Internet commerce include:

- Organizational change to a completely different way of doing business.
- Buying equipment and maintaining connection to the Internet (or leasing through a network provider).
- Establishing connections with a new set of customers.
- Staffing and training employees to work in a technology-driven environment.
- Reengineering application systems to process data acquired through the Internet.
- Maintaining security of the Internet site.

Risks of Internet commerce include:

- Hackers attempting to access sensitive information such as customer lists or customer credit card information.
- Denial of service attacks. Denial of service attacks are expected to escalate over the next few years as individuals or organizations attempt to knock out Web sites by overloading them with site visits and preventing customers or other users from gaining access. These attacks may occur simply for the challenge or frequently due to a political or other difference with the organization that hosts the site.
- Trust. Increasingly, the success of B2B Internet commerce relationships necessitate the identification of business partners that are allowed to gain access to sensitive internal information. Trust must be placed with these business partners, but certainly a breakdown of that trust can have grave consequences to the organization making its information available.

Technology Application 3.3

General Uses of Internet Commerce

Case 1

One type of business that is particularly compatible with Internet commerce is one where the goods or services can be delivered across the Internet instantaneously, much the same as the payment is provided by the customer. TheStreet.com is one company that has implemented such a business plan. TheStreet.com is in the business of providing financial information that is valuable, unique, and timely. The company philosophy is that if it fails in any of these three attributes for the information it delivers, customers will stop coming. The only appropriate medium for delivery was the Internet, and that is where the company set up shop. Despite the many business publications on the market, TheStreet.com has quickly risen as a leading provider of financial information by being both cheaper and more timely. It is one of the few information providers that have been able to provide subscription service solely through the Internet. This is one form of the so-called Internet cottage industry whereby new businesses are springing up on the net to provide unique services.

Case 2

Wal-Mart is one of many retailers setting up electronic store fronts on the Internet to sell its goods directly to customers. Wal-Mart takes the customer's order and credit card number over the Internet, electronically processes the business event, and sends the order directly to the manufacturer, who ships the product to the customer. Hence, the company's Web site becomes little more than a for-fee electronic interface between the customer and the manufacturer. In an effort to broaden the scope of products offered via the Web site, Wal-Mart shut down its site during the fall of 2000 to completely overhaul it. Wal-Mart re-opened the site on October 31, 2000, in hopes of enlarging its share of online Christmas season sales.

Sources: Linda Rosencrance, "TheStreet.com Looks for Road to Profitability," *Computerworld Online* (November 16, 2000); Todd R. Weiss, "Walmart.com Site Back Online After 28-day Overhaul," *Computerworld Online* (October 31, 2000).

phone lines and connect with the *network provider's* network (examples of phone connection providers include AOL, MSN, Earthlink, as well as many local phone companies). A variety of alternatives to phone line connections are available for linking with *network providers*. While phone linkage is the most common contemporary approach, access using high-speed phone connections (DSL) as well as service over cable television lines is quickly overtaking traditional phone connections. Service is also available using mini-satellite dishes (similar to those used for satellite television!), and cellular technologies are also eating into the phone-based market share. Some companies and other organizations are also using high-speed direct lines (referred to as "Trunk Level 1" or T1 lines) to maintain continuous access.

Most *network providers* bring a host of other benefits along with Internet access. Common benefits include e-mail access, electronic mail boxes, space allocation for personal Web pages, and remote connection to other computer sites (e.g., telnet and FTP connection). Many organizations also will use *network providers* to run their Internet servers for them, thus hosting their Web presence. In Figure 3.7, circle 5 denotes a *network provider* that is providing server management services for the CPA or CA firm denoted by circle 6. Hence, when the business event is being completed between the customer and the vendor, information from the accounting firm would be acquired from a server operated by the firm's *network provider*.

Figure 3.7 Typical Electronic Communications Connection for Internet Commerce

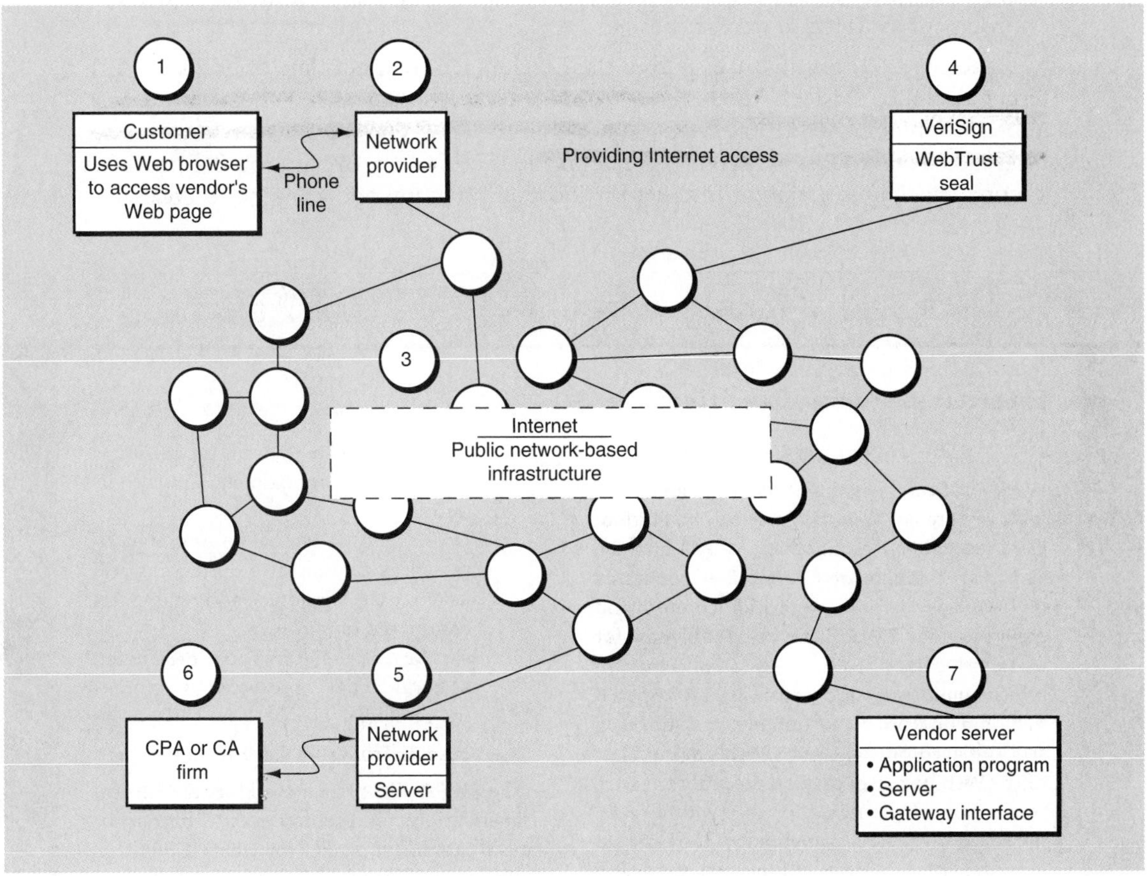

Assurance Providers (Circles 4 and 6)

A major concern with participating in *Internet commerce* for most organizations and individuals has been Internet security. This is the single most critical factor that has hampered the growth of Internet commerce to date. One early survey showed that 90 percent of Internet users felt increased security was necessary before they should transmit personal information (e.g., credit card information) across the Internet.[10] As security technology has increased, so has the public's willingness to participate in Internet commerce. A recent survey indicates 52 percent of Internet users feel comfortable providing their credit card numbers to a *secure* Web site.[11] Many stories exist about credit card numbers being stolen from Internet computers, including one incident involving the unauthorized access to *8 million* accounts![12] Additionally, the Internet has spawned a whole array of cottage industries that have no physical store fronts, but rather are operated completely from Internet server-supported Web pages. Many Internet users are rightfully concerned about the possibility that a company may be fictitious, with the electronic store front merely being a means by which to gather credit card and debit

[10] J. Walker Smith, "Who Are the New, Interactive Consumers?" *Commerce in Cyberspace: A Conference Report* (The Conference Board, New York, 1996): 13–15.
[11] The 2002 Privacy Values Survey, http://www.theprivacyplace.org, April 2003.
[12] "Root of massive credit card theft found," http://www.cnn.com, February 20, 2003.

card information for illicit use. In Chapter 9, you will be introduced to technologies such as encryption and SSL that provide organizations and their customers a protected environment in which to transact business.

Concerns over security have spurred the development of a new line of business—Internet assurance services. **Internet assurance** is a service provided for a fee to vendors in order to provide limited assurance to users of the vendor's Web site that the site is in fact reliable and event data security is reasonable. Technology Application 3.4 provides a more detailed discussion of Internet certification programs and assurance services.

Technology Application 3.4

Internet Security Certification

Case 1: WebTrust Certification

WebTrust Seal of Assurance is the product of a joint venture between the American Institute of Certified Public Accountants (AICPA) and the Canadian Institute of Chartered Accountants (CICA). It is designed to provide comfort and assurance that a Web site is reasonably safe for users participating in business-to-consumer Internet commerce. Upon receiving an unqualified opinion from an accounting practitioner, a seal is placed on the client's Web page. A user of the Web page can click on the seal to receive verification of the rights for the symbol to be displayed on the given Web page. If a user selects the link provided with the seal, he or she can view the practitioners' actual report on the client's Web site. The WebTrust seal provides assurances that a CA or CPA has evaluated the business practices and controls of the given client to determine whether its Web page is in accordance with WebTrust criteria. Once a site receives WebTrust certification, it should be reviewed periodically by the practitioner to assure adequate standards have remained in place and the site remains reasonably secure. Basically, a Web site must meet the following principles:

- *Security*. The system is protected against unauthorized access (both physical and logical).
- *Availability*. The system is available for operation and use as committed or agreed.
- *Processing integrity*. System processing is complete, accurate, timely, and authorized.
- *Online privacy*. Personal information obtained as a result of e-Business is collected, used, disclosed, and retained as committed or agreed.
- *Confidentiality*. Information designated as confidential is protected as committed or agreed.

Case 2: TruSecure Certification

As the AICPA/CICA has moved forward on recommendations for alternative areas beyond financial statement audits for which CPAs/CAs could provide assurance services, they have often noted that these other areas would not be protected from competition by non-CPA organizations. Web certification is certainly one of these areas where non-CPA competition already exists. TruSecure Certification is designed to provide reduced risk to both the customer and the vendor by providing, verifying, and improving the use of appropriate security standards. The TruSecure standards revolve around six primary concerns: electronic threats and vulnerabilities, malicious code, privacy, human factors, physical environment, and downtime, standards that overlap with the goals and objectives to the WebTrust certification. Similar to WebTrust, TruSecure certification is also displayed through a seal, the TruSecure Certified Seal, placed on the client's Web page.

Sources: AICPA/CICA, "CPA/CA WebTrust[SM] Version 2.0," http://www.cica.ca, August 2000; AICPA/CICA, "Suitable Trust Services Criteria and Illustrations for Security, Availability, Processing Integrity, Online Privacy, and Confidentiality (Including WebTrust® and SysTrust®)," http://www.aicpa.org/download/trust_services/final-Trust-Services.pdf, November 2003; TruSecure, "Security Certification," http://www.trusecure.com, November 2003.

In Figure 3.7 (page 97) we demonstrate how one common type of assurance provider operates using the WebTrust program as discussed in Technology Application 3.4. The vendor (circle 7) will display the WebTrust certification seal and a reference to the assurance provider on its server Web page. When the customer accesses the vendor's Web page, he or she can click on the WebTrust symbol to determine that it continues to be applicable. Clicking on the WebTrust symbol executes a link to the VeriSign server (circle 4) for verification of the authorized use of the symbol. VeriSign, which simply operates as a verification company, will verify the symbol's appropriate use by sending a message to the customer (circle 1). The customer also can get a report on the level of assurance provided with the certification by clicking on the Web link (contained on the vendor's Web page) for the accounting firm. Clicking on this link will connect the customer with the accounting firm's (circle 6) server—provided by its network provider in this case (circle 5)—and the auditor's Internet assurance report for the vendor will be displayed on the customer's computer (circle 1).

In addition to concerns regarding event data, many customers have apprehensions over the protection and use of their personal information. To address this issue, the AICPA/CICA Privacy Framework has recently been issued.[13] The framework includes the AICPA/CICA Trust Services Privacy Principle and Criteria to be used in all assurance engagements.

Internet Connection (Circle 3)

We briefly note here how the *Internet connection* is provided between two or more entities. The network diagram displayed at circle 3 pictorially presents a representation of how the *Internet* operates. First, you must have a link to one of the network providers that are connected to the Internet (as discussed earlier). The client machine provides an Internet address indicating the Internet site with which the client wants to connect. A connection is then made between the *client* and the desired site—the *server*. This connection is made by working a path between the *network provider* (circle 2) and the *server* connection (circle 7). The path chosen will differ from one time to the next based on what links in the Internet may not be working at a given time and based on how busy the "traffic" is on various network connections between the *client* and the *server*. The amount of "traffic" also influences the speed of connection and is the reason why the Internet is slower than at other times.

A couple of other issues related to the organization of the *Internet* and its impact on such commerce should be noted. First, by the nature of the Internet being a "public network-based infrastructure," it has greatly leveled the field in *e-Business*. With traditional EDI, only fairly large businesses could afford the communications hardware and software to effectively use e-Business as a competitive weapon. The creation of a public network and the subsequent creation of relatively inexpensive (or even free) software for using the network have brought the costs of e-Business within the threshold of economic feasibility for most small- and medium-sized entities. This change in cost structure and ease of use are the two forces driving the strong growth in *Internet commerce*.

The other phenomenon that has arisen from the new economic feasibility of e-Business is an explosion in cottage industries and electronic store fronts. These cottage industries that have sprung up to support Internet commerce include companies that provide one or more of the following: Internet access, Web page development, interface software for linking between Web pages and application programs, e-mail, and related goods and services. **Electronic store fronts** represent the creation of Internet-located

---

[13] Available for download at http://www.aicpa.org.

resources for displaying goods and services for sale and for conducting related sales events. For many emerging small companies, these *electronic store fronts* are the only store fronts and no sales staff or physical store fronts need to be maintained. Even better, you can run your operation from that ski chalet in Vermont or the beach condominium in Florida regardless of where your potential customers live. Further, the world is now your marketplace!

Other Internet Uses for E-Business

Before leaving this chapter on *e-Business*, we should discuss other ways in which the Internet is being used to support commerce. While we have focused in this chapter on the most common forms of Internet commerce and the direct linkages between customer and vendor, a number of intermediaries are evolving that promise to reduce costs for organizations. The two forms that seem most likely to have long-term success are *auction markets* and *market exchanges*. These are explained in greater detail in Technology Summaries 3.5 and 3.6.

ENTERPRISE SYSTEMS   The Internet is not only a place for completing sales, but is also an environment for improving customer support for non-Internet-based commerce. Probably the biggest use for the Internet at this point in time is to support the providing of goods and services for customers. In its simplest form, a Web page may simply be one more venue in which to advertise and market an organization's goods and services. At the next level, it may be an arena for providing ongoing customer support. For instance, Symantec is one of many companies that provide software upgrades over the Internet—in this case, providing monthly updates for their anti-virus software. For many courier companies (such as Federal Express), the Internet has become a means for allowing customers to instantly access information to track their packages at any given point and to know when they have reached their destination. These latter examples of customer support have become a huge new market for major software vendors. These systems fall under the broader category of *customer relationship management (CRM)* and *customer self-service (CSS)* systems, both introduced in Chapter 2. These systems provide customer self-service capabilities (i.e., let the customer inspect his or her account or get product help through a Web interface rather than through interaction with a support person), electronic catalogues, and shipment update information. They aid the salesperson by storing an ana-

---

Technology Summary 3.5

Internet Auction Markets

Internet auction markets provide an Internet base for companies to place products up for bid or for buyers to put proposed purchases up for bid. In the first case, a scenario common to the eBay exchange, a market participant puts an item up for bid, sets a minimum bid price, and awaits completion of the bidding process. While this market is fairly successful for business-to-consumer Internet commerce, it is not so effective for business-to-business Internet commerce. For business-to-business Internet commerce, a company may put specifications for a product out on the marketplace as a request for proposals (RFPs). Participating organizations in the market can then bid on the sales by providing a proposal that includes details on product specifications, costs, availability (i.e., timing of delivery), and logistics. The buying organization can then select the proposal that seems most desirable for meeting the organization's needs at a minimal cost and risk.

Technology Summary 3.6

Internet Market Exchanges

Internet market exchanges bring together a variety of suppliers in a given industry with one or more buyers in the same industry to provide Internet commerce through organized markets. Suppliers can put their products online, generally feeding into electronic catalogs that allow the buyer(s) to sort through alternatives from different suppliers and electronically place an order. Often, only one supplier will carry a certain item, but efficiencies are still gained by avoiding the purchase order process (described in detail in Chapter 12) and executing an order through selection from a Web catalog. In some cases, buyers make their needs known on the marketplace and suppliers review the needs and determine whether to fill the orders. The key is to make sure the market is efficient enough to assure that the buyer will get the product purchased on a timely basis for when it is needed— often meaning that the purchased goods arrive at an assembly line within an hour of when the goods will be needed for production. This part can be quite tricky and the exchange must be set up carefully.

Internet market exchanges can be either private or public. Private exchanges restrict the buyers and suppliers that can participate in the market. Public exchanges bring together suppliers and buyers and allow essentially any organization to participate, subject sometimes to credit approval and background checks. Private exchanges that have been planned or are currently operating outnumber such public exchanges 30,000 to 600.[a] However, private exchanges have drawn the watchful eye of the Federal Trade Commission (FTC), which maintains concerns over fair trade practices and potential anti-competitive practices that evolve from restricting participation in the market exchange.

[a] Steve Ulfelder, "Members Only Exchanges," *Computerworld Online* (October 23, 2000).

---

lyzable history of the customer and the customer's past business interactions. One of the bigger challenges has been to get the CRM systems to interact with the ERP system to share data between the two systems and enhance the power and capability. In an effort to improve the integration, all the major software firms are involved in initiatives to further empower CRM extensions to their ERP systems.

SUMMARY

The future of e-Business will see an increased merging of technologies as the lines between EDI and Internet commerce become less defined. The major impediment to most organizations (and individuals) conducting business over the Internet is the concern about security. However, advances in Internet security have been significant in the past few years, with the potential major benefactors of Internet commerce pushing the charge. For instance, software companies such as Microsoft and Netscape along with financial providers MasterCard and Visa have been on the forefront of development efforts to assure safe use of the Internet in commerce.

The evolution of EDI practices toward the Internet will initially be facilitated by increased use of corporate *extranets*. Moving EDI applications to an extranet environment can help simplify the processing while maintaining higher levels of control and security. These extranets will be open to business partners using programs that limit access to selected business partners—hence the corporate networks will not be accessible by unintended Internet users. As Internet security increases, extranets will lose their appeal and the Internet will increasingly become a viable alternative as the communication infrastructure of choice.

These same increases in security will help fuel the growth of Internet commerce. As Internet commerce becomes an increasingly acceptable way of doing business, companies will experience newfound opportunities for reaching customers; for many companies, a new globalization of their customer base will occur. On the other hand, new competition also will arise from distant companies that now have access to the same customers.

Entering the e-Business domain is not simply a matter of switching on the connection. E-Business is nothing less than a fundamental change in the way organizations do business and, as such, is a driver of organizational change. To succeed in an e-Business environment, an organization must recognize the need to embrace change and must effectively plan and manage change. Management must take a proactive stance and lead the change.

It is thought to be an ancient curse to wish upon someone "may you live in interesting times." We are certainly not wishing this upon you, but the reality is that we are all living in interesting times. Success will rely heavily on your understanding of how to manage and control change. In Chapters 7 through 9 you will learn about ways in which to implement and maintain effective organizational and information systems control structures. While these are interesting times, they are also exciting times.

REVIEW QUESTIONS

RQ 3-1 Briefly define e-Business.

RQ 3-2 Explain the relationship between the periodic mode and batch processing.

RQ 3-3 List and describe the four basic subprocesses completed in processing business event data using batch processing.

RQ 3-4 Explain how the use of online transaction entry (OLTE) can increase efficiency when using batch processing.

RQ 3-5 Explain the relationship between online real-time (OLRT) and immediate mode processing.

RQ 3-6 List and describe the three basic subprocesses completed in processing business event data using online real-time processing.

RQ 3-7 How does the use of online transaction processing (OLTP) improve the timeliness of online real-time processing?

RQ 3-8 Describe how technology has supported Amazon.com's growth.

RQ 3-9 Explain the concept of Internet assurance services.

RQ 3-10 Explain the difference between wide area networks and local area networks.

RQ 3-11 How can e-mail be adapted to a more structured form to aid in capturing business event data?

RQ 3-12 Explain the advantages of using electronic document management rather than traditional paper-based document systems.

RQ 3-13 Explain how electronic data interchange is used to link two companies' business processes together.

RQ 3-14 Explain how value-added networks (VANs) are used to simplify electronic data interchange between two or more companies.

RQ 3-15 How does Internet commerce simplify the world of e-Business?

RQ 3-16 What role do network providers play in the Internet commerce environment?

RQ 3-17 What types of assurances are provided by Internet assurance services?

DISCUSSION QUESTIONS

DQ 3-1 The business environment is increasingly demanding the use of online real-time systems for more up-to-date information. Identify one business process, and the environment in which it would be used, as an example of why immediate mode processing is so critical. Be prepared to explain your answer to the class.

DQ 3-2 Consider your favorite fast food chain restaurant. How do you think this restaurant might use online transaction entry to improve its business event data processing activities? Explain.

DQ 3-3 We noted during the chapter discussion that banks are one of the earliest adopters of online transaction processing systems. Discuss why OLTP would be desirable for use in ATM systems.

DQ 3-4 How could (and/or is) your university bookstore use technology to improve customer interactions with students, faculty, and staff?

DQ 3-5 What do you perceive to be the advantages and disadvantages of conducting business on the Internet? Be prepared to explain your answer.

DQ 3-6 Why has the Internet caused such an explosion in e-Business when electronic data interchange has been available for decades?

DQ 3-7 One of Amazon.com's marketing strengths is the ability to collect and analyze customer purchase data. How does this add value to the company? From the customer's perspective, is value added?

DQ 3-8 Some potential e-Business customers have security concerns regarding online purchases. How do Internet security certifications attempt to address these concerns?

PROBLEMS

P 3-1 Find a merchandising business on the Internet (other than the Lands' End or Amazon.com examples used in this chapter). Explore its Web page and how the order processing system works.

    a. Is there any information provided on how secure the Web page is? What level of comfort do you feel with its security? Explain.

    b. Does the business provide information regarding delivery time/stockouts on purchases?

    c. What methods of payment does it accept?

    d. Analyze the design of the Web page in terms of usability and completeness of information content. Write a brief critique of your company's page.

P 3-2 Think about a business you might want to start on the Internet using e-mail to communicate with customers and capture business data. Explain why e-mail would be a good approach for your business. Draft a brief business plan evaluating the advantages and disadvantages of e-mail-based commerce in your business, and how you plan to get your business rolling (your professor will tell you how long the report should be).

P 3-3 Identify a business venture that you believe could be successful using only Internet commerce. Explain how you would design your Web page, how you would capture business event data, and the mode of processing you would use. Provide a report detailing support for your design decisions (your professor will tell you how long the report should be).

P 3-4 Develop a research paper on the emerging use of the Internet to support electronic data interchange (EDI) between companies. Your paper should consider how companies set up communications over the Internet to maintain the same security and standardization that are achieved using value-added networks for non-Internet EDI (your professor will tell you how long the paper should be).

P 3-5 Explain how electronic document management could be used in your accounting information systems class to eliminate all paper flow between the students and professor. Include in your explanation what technologies would be necessary to facilitate your plan (your professor will tell you how long the paper should be).

P 3-6 Using the Internet, find and describe an *Internet market exchange* or *Internet auction market*. Your discussion should include the products and/or services available and the type buyers and sellers you expect to participate. If you choose a *private market*, also identify the owner/sponsor of the exchange.

P 3-7 Use the Internet to locate http://www.cia.gov and http://www.Amazon.com. Find the privacy and security policies for each. Compare and contrast the use of privacy statements, encryption, SSL, and cookie policies.

KEY TERMS

electronic business (e-Business)

periodic mode

batch processing

offline

online transaction entry (OLTE)

online

online real-time (OLRT) systems

immediate mode

online transaction processing (OLTP)

client server technology

local area networks (LANs)

wide area networks (WANs)

Internet

Web browsers

extranet

electronic mail (e-mail)

public database service

electronic document management (EDM)

electronic data interchange (EDI)

value-added network (VAN)

Internet commerce

network providers

Internet assurance

electronic store fronts

Internet auction markets

Internet market exchanges

Organizing and Managing Information

Part Two

chapter

4

Documenting Information Systems

We wanted to know what impact the Sarbanes-Oxley Act of 2002 (SOA) has had on the process of documenting business processes and internal controls. We spoke with a senior manager at PricewaterhouseCoopers LLP and asked her how she was using flowcharting in SOA and other related work. Her response follows:

> Auditors and business advisors at Pricewaterhouse-Coopers LLP have used flowcharts and systems narratives in a variety of engagements, including financial audits, business process reengineering, and security reviews. To document a process, the auditor conducts interviews with the process owner, writes a narrative, and prepares accompanying flowcharts. These documents allow an auditor to design the audit approach and identify areas where controls may be needed.
>
> The passage of Sarbanes-Oxley has reemphasized the importance of documenting business processes and internal controls. For example, Sarbanes-Oxley Section 404 requires that organizations document internal controls over their financial reporting processes. This mandate will require more extensive documentation than has been prepared in the past. Various people may be involved in preparing this documentation, including financial managers, business process owners, internal auditors, external auditors and others. Once documented, the client uses the documentation to identify gaps in their processes and to define and implement new controls.
>
> To comply with Sarbanes-Oxley, the auditors will conduct walkthroughs of their clients' systems to understand the process flows and to evaluate the controls over financial reporting. One of my clients has over 3,000 relevant controls. We cannot gain an adequate understanding of how these controls operate without having good documentation; detailed workflows will be a key element of these discussions. Obviously the level of effort put into the first year review would be difficult to sustain. Clients will benefit from a central, electronic repository of their documentation that they can go to each year to record changes to the processes and controls so that the auditor can perform an ongoing analysis of those controls. For this purpose there are many tools available on the market.[1]

---

[1] Sally Bernstein, senior manager, PricewaterhouseCoopers LLP, assisted us in the preparation of this section.

Learning Objectives

- To read and evaluate data flow diagrams.
- To read and evaluate systems flowcharts.
- To prepare data flow diagrams from a narrative.
- To prepare systems flowcharts from a narrative.

In this chapter, you will learn to read and prepare documentation that depicts business processes and the process controls within those processes. You will learn that data flow diagrams portray a business processes' activities, stores of data, and flows of data among those elements. Systems flowcharts, on the other hand, present a comprehensive picture of the management, operations, information systems, and process controls embodied in business processes.

SYNOPSIS

This chapter teaches you to read and prepare documentation to portray aspects of business processes including their operations and information processes. We show you how to read and prepare data flow diagrams and systems flowcharts. In Chapters 5 and 6 we show you how to read and prepare entity-relationship diagrams. Proficiency with these tools will help you to understand and evaluate business processes, information systems, and internal controls.

Auditors, systems analysts, students, and others use documentation to understand, explain, evaluate, and improve complex business processes, information systems, and internal controls. Let's consider, for example, the order-to-cash process described in Chapter 2. Recall, that this process includes all of the activities associated with receiving a customer order, picking the goods off a warehouse shelf, packing and shipping the goods, billing the customer, and receiving and depositing the customer's payment. Further, the information system supporting this business process is likely an *enterprise system*, has a number of PCs connected to it via telecommunications links, is used by dozens of people within and outside the organization, has one or more *ERP systems* with many modules and perhaps hundreds of programs, and performs functions for virtually every department in the organization. This system processes thousands of business events and hundreds of requests for management information, and has people throughout the organization preparing inputs and receiving system outputs. In an *e-Business* environment this system might be accessed directly, perhaps automatically, by systems and individuals in the organization's supply chain.

ENTERPRISE SYSTEMS

E-BUSINESS

CONTROLS

For such a system, we require "pictures," rather than a narrative description, to "see" and analyze all the activities, inputs, and outputs. Being able to draw these diagrams demonstrates that we understand the system and can explain the system to someone else. For example, with a systems flowchart we can understand and analyze document flows (electronic and paper) through the operations, management, and information processes. Perhaps our analysis will lead to system improvements. We are convinced that, after preparing and using systems documentation, you will agree that data flow diagrams, systems flowcharts, and entity-relationship diagrams are much more efficient (and effective) than narratives for working with complex systems. The application of these tools, even to the relatively simple systems depicted in this textbook, should convince you of this.

CONTROLS   In addition to using documentation to understand and improve a system, an organization can use it for other important purposes. For example, documentation is used to explain systems and to train personnel. Also, auditors use documentation to describe systems so as to understand the systems and to evaluate the systems' controls. Management, internal auditors, consultants, and independent auditors have recently all become more engaged in this last activity to comply with Section 404 of the Sarbanes-Oxley Act of 2002.

INTRODUCTION

We will begin by showing you how to read data flow diagrams and flowcharts. Next, we will show you how to prepare those diagrams and flowcharts. These documentation tools will be used throughout the remainder of the textbook. If you invest time now to study and practice using these tools, your improved understanding of the following chapters will reward your effort. You cannot achieve this chapter's learning objectives with traditional study methods; you cannot be a passive observer in these proceedings. You must work along with us as we demonstrate these tools. Further, you must practice these tools to develop your skills.

READING SYSTEMS DOCUMENTATION

We will look at two types of systems documentation, data flow diagrams and systems flowcharts. In the following section we will show you how to read and interpret this documentation. First, we will look at data flow diagrams.

Reading Data Flow Diagrams

A **data flow diagram (DFD)** is a graphical representation of a system. A DFD depicts a system's components; the data flows among the components; and the sources, destinations, and storage of data. Figure 4.1 shows the four symbols used in a DFD. Study these symbols and their definitions before reading on.

Context Diagram

Figure 4.2 is an example of our first type of DFD, the context diagram. A **context diagram** is a top-level, or least detailed, diagram of an information system that depicts the system and all of its activities as a single bubble, and shows the data flows into and out of the system and into and out of the external entities. **External entities** are those

Figure 4.1 Data Flow Diagram (DFD) Symbols

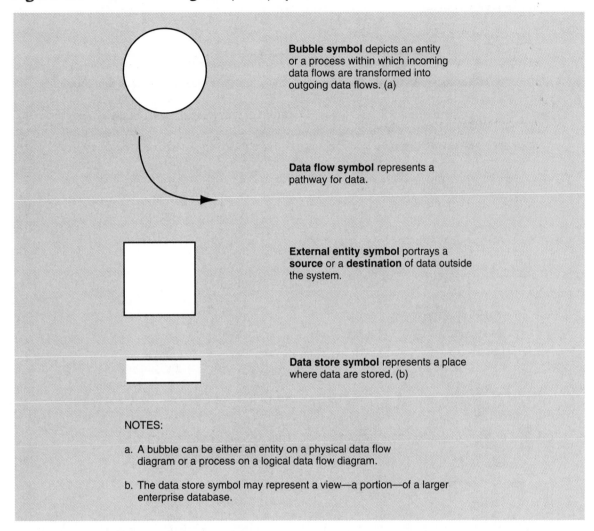

Bubble symbol depicts an entity or a process within which incoming data flows are transformed into outgoing data flows. (a)

Data flow symbol represents a pathway for data.

External entity symbol portrays a **source** or a **destination** of data outside the system.

Data store symbol represents a place where data are stored. (b)

NOTES:

a. A bubble can be either an entity on a physical data flow diagram or a process on a logical data flow diagram.

b. The data store symbol may represent a view—a portion—of a larger enterprise database.

Figure 4.2 A Context Diagram

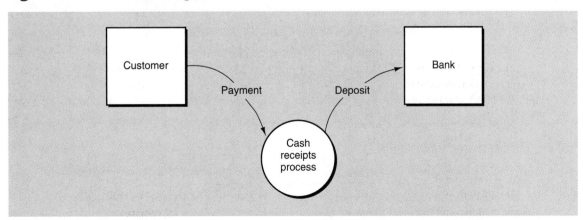

entities (i.e., persons, places, or things) outside the system that send data to, or receive data from, the system.[2]

Physical Data Flow Diagram

A **physical data flow diagram** is a graphical representation of a system showing the system's internal and external entities, and the flows of data into and out of these entities. An **internal entity** is an *entity* (i.e., person, place, or thing) within the system that transforms data.[3] Internal entities include, for example, accounting clerks (persons), departments (places), and computers (things). Therefore, physical DFDs specify *where, how*, and by *whom* a system's processes are accomplished. A physical DFD does not tell us *what* is being accomplished. For example, in Figure 4.3 we see that the sales clerk receives cash from the customer and sends cash, along with a register tape, to the cashier. So, we see *where* the cash goes and *how* the cash receipts data are captured (that is, on the register tape), but we don't know exactly *what* was done by the sales clerk.

Figure 4.3 A Physical Data Flow Diagram

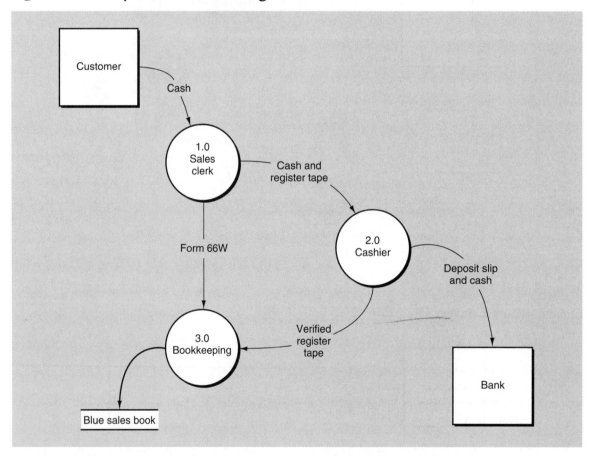

---

[2] Used in this manner, *entities* is a narrower concept than that used in Chapter 1 where they were all persons, places, and things. *External* entities must be able to send or receive data.

[3] Used in this manner, *entities* is a narrower concept than that used in Chapter 1 where they were all persons, places, and things. *Internal* entities must be able to transform data.

Note that the physical DFD's bubbles are labeled with *nouns* and that the data flows are labeled so as to indicate *how* data are transmitted between bubbles. For example, the sales clerk sends Form 66W to bookkeeping. Note that a data store's location indicates exactly *where* (in bookkeeping) and a data store's label indicates *how* (in a blue sales book) a system maintains sales records. Finally, whereas the entity boxes on the context diagram define the external entities in the relevant environment, the bubbles in the physical DFD define the internal entities.

Logical Data Flow Diagram

A **logical data flow diagram** is a graphical representation of a system showing the system's processes (as bubbles), data stores, and the flows of data into and out of the processes and data stores. We use logical DFDs to document information systems because we can represent the logical nature of a system—*what* tasks the system is doing—without having to specify *how*, *where*, or by *whom* the tasks are accomplished. What a system is doing will change less over time than will how it is doing it. For example, a cash receipts system will typically receive customer payments and post them to the customer's account. Over time, however, the form of the payment—cash, check, or electronic funds—and the method of recording—manual or computer—may change.

The advantage of a *logical* DFD (versus a *physical* DFD) is that we can concentrate on the functions that a system performs. See, for example, Figure 4.4 (page 112), where the labels on the data flows describe the nature of the data, rather than *how* the data are transmitted. Is the payment in the form of a check, cash, credit card, or debit card? We don't know. Is the sales journal a book, card, or electronic file? Again, we don't know. We do know that customer payments are received, verified for accuracy, recorded in a sales journal, and deposited in the bank. So, a logical DFD portrays a system's activities, whereas a physical DFD depicts a system's infrastructure. We need both pictures to understand a system completely.

Finally, note that the processes in Figure 4.4 are labeled with *verbs* that describe the actions being performed, rather than with the nouns as we saw in the physical DFD.

Figure 4.4 is a top-level view of the single bubble in Figure 4.2, the context diagram. Because all of the bubbles in Figure 4.4 contain numbers followed by a decimal point and a zero, this diagram is often called a "level 0" diagram.[4] Notice that each of the data that flows into and out of the context bubble in Figure 4.2 (page 109) also flows into and out of the bubbles in Figure 4.4 (except for the flows between bubbles, such as "Sales record," which were contained *within* the bubble in Figure 4.2). When two DFDs—in this case, the context and the level 0—have equivalent external data flows, we say that the DFDs are **balanced**. Only balanced sets of DFDs (that is, a context diagram, a logical DFD, and a physical DFD) are correct.

To derive Figure 4.4, we have "exploded" the context diagram in Figure 4.2 into its top-level components. We have looked inside the context diagram bubble to see the major subdivisions of the cash receipts process. The successive subdividing, or "exploding," of logical DFDs is called **top-down partitioning** and, when properly performed, leads to a set of balanced DFDs.

We will use Figure 4.5 (page 113), which depicts a generic set of balanced DFDs, to study partitioning and balancing. Notice that the level 0 DFD (part b) has the same input "A" and the same output "B" as the context diagram (part a). Now look at part c, an explosion of bubble 1.0. Part c has the same input "A" and the same outputs "C"

---

[4] Even though physical DFDs are similarly numbered, we do not use the term "level 0" when referring to a physical DFD because there are no lower-level DFDs.

Figure 4.4 A Logical Data Flow Diagram (Level 0 Diagram)

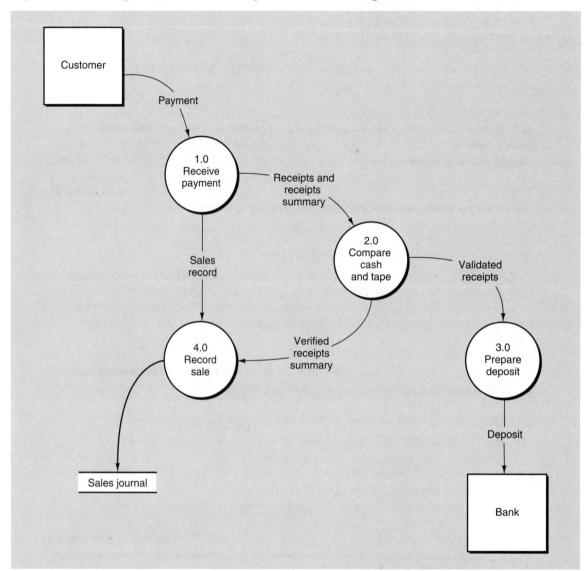

and "D" as part b. This relationship must exist because diagram 1.0 (part c) is an explosion of bubble 1.0 in part b. The same can be said for part d, the partitioning of bubble 3.0. Finally, part e shows diagram 3.1, a partitioning of bubble 3.1 in part d. Study Figure 4.5 and make sure you understand the relationships among levels in this set of DFDs. While you are studying the figure, you might also note the convention used to number the bubbles at each level. Also, note that the entity boxes that appear in the context and level 0 diagrams do not usually appear in diagrams below level 0.

Reading Systems Flowcharts

A **systems flowchart** is a graphical representation of *information processes* (activities, logic flows, inputs, outputs, and data storage), as well as the related *operations processes* (entities, physical flows, and operations activities). Containing manual and computer ac-

Figure 4.5 A Set of Balanced DFDs

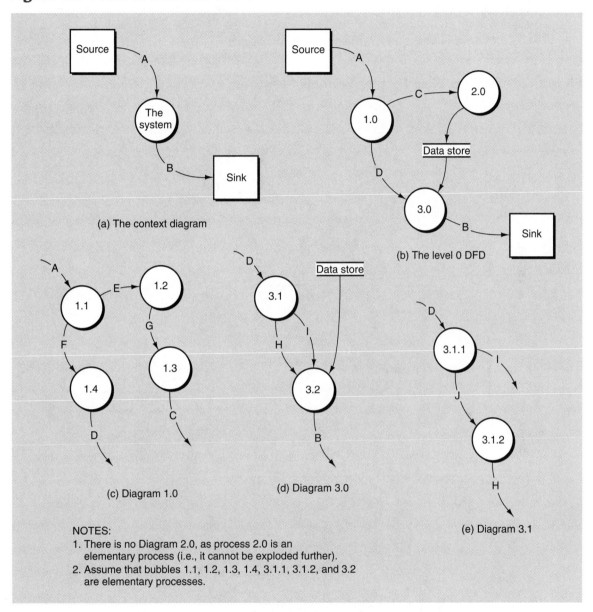

(a) The context diagram

(b) The level 0 DFD

(c) Diagram 1.0

(d) Diagram 3.0

(e) Diagram 3.1

NOTES:
1. There is no Diagram 2.0, as process 2.0 is an elementary process (i.e., it cannot be exploded further).
2. Assume that bubbles 1.1, 1.2, 1.3, 1.4, 3.1.1, 3.1.2, and 3.2 are elementary processes.

tivities, the systems flowchart presents a logical and physical rendering of the *who, what, how,* and *where* of operations and information processes.

The systems flowchart gives us a complete picture of a system by combining the physical and logical aspects of the system. Physical and logical DFDs each depict different aspects of a system. In addition, the systems flowchart includes the operations process and management context for a system. These aspects are ignored in the DFDs. In addition to DFDs, auditors and management use systems flowcharts to understand a system and to analyze a system's controls. In this text, we use systems flowcharts for a similar purpose. Taken together, DFDs and flowcharts provide us with multiple, complementary methods for describing a system.

CONTROLS

Systems Flowcharting Symbols

Figure 4.6 shows the systems flowcharting symbols that we will use in this textbook. We have intentionally limited this set to reduce your work in learning the symbols. You should take some time now to study the symbols in Figure 4.6.

Figure 4.6 Systems Flowcharting Symbols

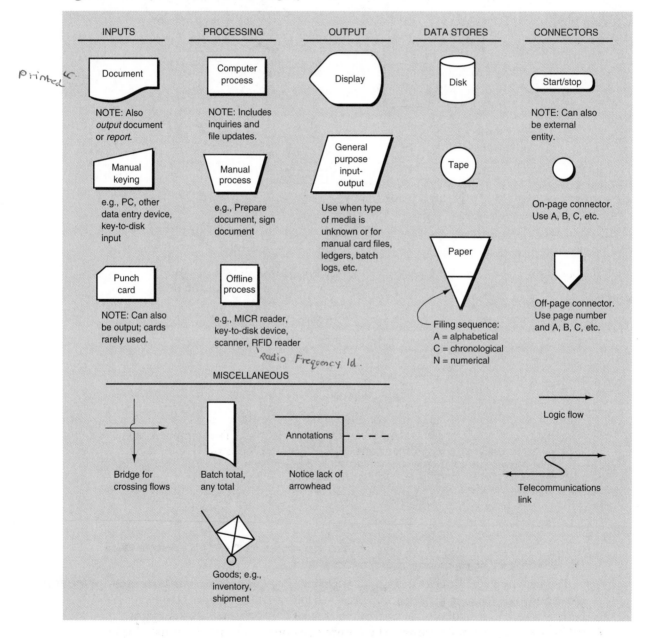

Common Systems Flowcharting Routines

Figure 4.7 (pages 116–117) contains routines often found on systems flowcharts. Follow along with us as we describe each of these routines.

Figure 4.7, part a, depicts a typical two-step data entry process that might be described as follows:

> The data entry clerk keys an input document into a computer. The computer accesses data in data store 1 (perhaps a table of valid codes, such as customer codes) and in data store 2 (perhaps a table of open sales orders) to edit/validate the input. The computer displays the input, including any errors. The clerk compares the input document to the display, keys corrections as necessary, and accepts the input. The computer updates the table in data store 2 and notifies the clerk that the input has been recorded.

CONTROLS

Notice the following about Figure 4.7, part a:

* The edit or validate step may be performed with one or more data stores.
* The display is implied with most, if not all, data entry processes.
* By combining the "Edit/validate input" rectangle with the "Record input" rectangle, we could depict this input process in one step without losing much detail about the activities being performed.
* The manual processes undertaken by the clerk are isolated in a separate column to distinguish them from the automated processes undertaken by the computer.
* We show the input document at the bottom of the column to indicate that the document "flows" through the input process.

Figure 4.7, part b, depicts a typical computer query, which might be described as follows:

> A user keys a query request into a computer. The computer accesses the table(s) in one or more data stores and presents a response to the user.

Notice the following about Figure 4.7, part b:

* The user and computer activities are again isolated in separate columns.
* The display is an implied element of the data entry device.

Figure 4.7, part c, depicts the update of master data stored in a sequential data store and might be described as follows:

> Inputs (cash receipts, for example) that had previously been recorded on a magnetic disk are input to the computer, along with the existing (old) master data (accounts receivable master data, for example). The computer updates the existing master data and creates a new version of the master data.

Notice the following about Figure 4.7, part c:

* When sequential master data are updated, we show two data store symbols on a flowchart. One symbol represents the existing (old) version and the other represents the new version.
* A dashed line connects the new with the old master data version to show that the new *becomes* the old version during the next update process.

Figure 4.7, part d, depicts the input and reconciliation of computer inputs and might be described as follows:

CONTROLS

> The user batches the input documents, prepares batch totals, and keys the documents into the computer. The computer records the inputs on a disk and notifies the user as each input is accepted. The user files the input documents in numerical sequence. At the end of the batch, the computer prepares an exception and summary report that includes batch totals. The user compares the computer batch totals to those prepared prior to entry of the documents.

Figure 4.7 Common Systems Flowcharting Routines

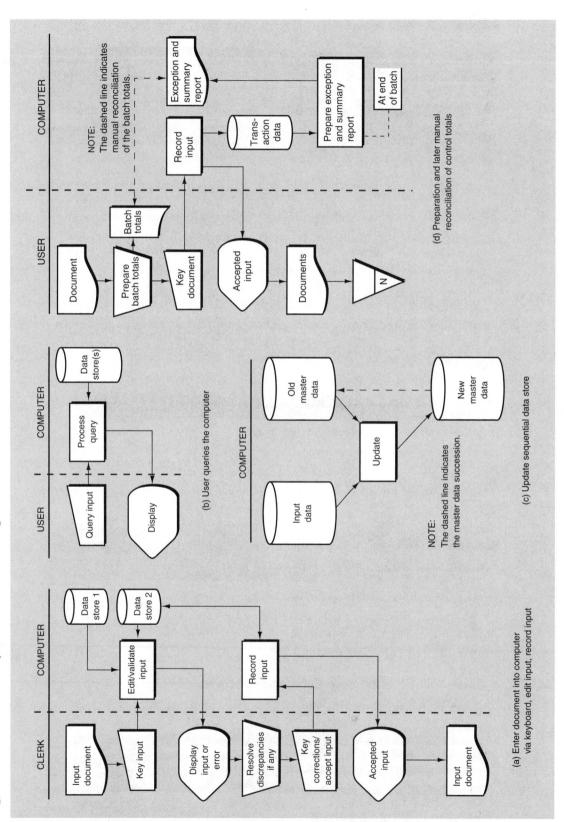

Figure 4.7 Common Systems Flowcharting Routines (*continued*)

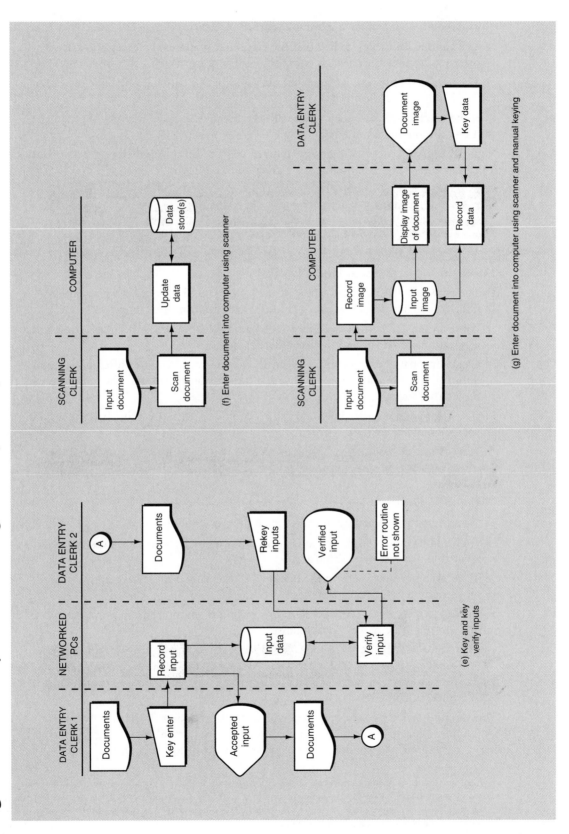

Notice the following about Figure 4.7, part d:

- The annotation makes it clear that the computer prepares the exception and summary report after the user has completed entry of the batch.
- The user's comparison of the batch totals is depicted with a dashed line instead of the manual process symbol.
- If the batch totals had been input with the batch, the computer—rather than the user—could compare the batch totals.

CONTROLS   Figure 4.7, part e, depicts the entry and key verification of inputs into a networked personal computers system and might be described as follows:

> A data entry clerk (perhaps clerk 1) enters documents into a networked PC system. The system records the inputs on a disk and notifies the user of the acceptance of each input. The documents are then forwarded to a *different* clerk (say clerk 2) who keys the documents *again*.[5] Differences are resolved and the event data are updated to reflect the verifications and corrections.

Notice the following about Figure 4.7, part e:

- The networked PCs are an offline device and should be depicted with a square—rather than a rectangle—and in a column separate from the computer.
- We show the data entry clerks in two columns to emphasize that the keying and verification are performed by two different clerks.
- Clerk 2 probably follows an established procedure to reconcile differences found during the verification step. We use the annotation to suggest the existence of these procedures.

Figure 4.7, part f, depicts the entry and recording of an input using a scanner and might be described as follows:

> A clerk scans a document into the computer. Using the data from the scanned document, the computer updates the data located on one or more data stores.

Notice the following about Figure 4.7, part f:

- We represent the scanner with the offline process symbol.
- We could include a display coming from the scanner, showing the clerk the document that had just been scanned.
- To be able to read data from the document, the scanner must have optical character recognition (OCR) capabilities.[6]

Figure 4.7, part g, depicts the entry and recording of an input using a scanner and a keyboard and might be described as follows:

> A clerk scans a document into the computer. The computer routes an image of the scanned input to a data entry clerk, who keys data from the document's image into the computer. The computer records the keyed data with the scanned document.

You should quickly become reasonably proficient in reading flowcharts if you learn these routines. You may encounter many different flowcharting methods during your career, but the principles you learn here will carry over to those techniques.

---

[5] The majority of data processing errors occur at the data entry stage and the majority of those errors can be attributed to misreading or miskeying the input. Because it is unlikely that two different clerks will make the same reading or keying mistake, the re-keying by a different clerk will discover the majority of these errors.
[6] Document scanning and OCR are discussed in Chapter 10.

PREPARING SYSTEMS DOCUMENTATION

In this section we show you how to prepare data flow diagrams and systems flowcharts. The DFDs we will be creating are context diagrams, physical DFDs, and logical DFDs. We also will give you our own tried and true guidelines for creating DFDs and systems flowcharts. As we mentioned earlier in this chapter, you will learn these concepts best by studying and practicing these steps as you go along.

Preparing Data Flow Diagrams

We use DFDs in two main ways. We may draw them to document an existing system, or we may create them from scratch when developing a new system. Construction of DFDs for new systems is described in the supplement that accompanies this text, *Acquiring, Developing, and Implementing Accounting Information Systems*. In this section, we explain a process for deriving a set of DFDs from a narrative that describes an existing system.

The Narrative

Figure 4.8 (page 120) contains a narrative describing the cash receipts system for Causeway Company. The first column indicates the paragraph number; the second column contains the line number for the text of the narrative. We describe here an orderly method for drawing the DFDs for the Causeway system. You will get the most benefit from this section if you follow the instructions carefully, perform each step as directed, and don't read ahead. As you follow along with us, you may want to draw your diagrams by hand or use the software package of your choice.

Table of Entities and Activities

Our first step is to create a table of entities and activities. In the long run, this list will lead to quicker and more accurate preparation of DFDs and a systems flowchart because it clarifies the information contained in a narrative and helps us to document the system correctly.

To begin your table, go through the narrative line by line and *circle* each activity being performed. An **activity** is any action being performed by an *internal* or *external entity*. Activities can include actions related to data (originate, transform, file, or receive) or to an operations process. Operations process activities might include picking goods in the warehouse, inspecting goods at the receiving dock, or counting cash. For each activity there must be an entity that performs the activity. As you circle each activity, put a *box* around the entity that performs the activity.

Now you are ready to prepare your table. List each activity *in the order that it is performed, regardless of the sequence in which it appears in the narrative*. List the activity, along with the name of the entity that performs the activity and the paragraph number indicating the location of the activity in the narrative. *After* you have listed all activities, consecutively number each activity.

Compare your table to Table 4.1 (page 121). Notice that the narrative refers to some entities in more than one way. For example, we have "accounts receivable" and the "clerk" on line 15. Notice that we listed both activity 7 and activity 8. It might be that activity 7 describes activity 8 and does not need to be listed itself. However, it is better to list doubtful activities than to miss an activity. See how we listed activity 11, found on lines 22 and 23. We changed to the active form of the verb "notify" so that we could show the activity next to the entity that performs the action. Before reading on, resolve any differences between your list of entities and activities and those in Table 4.1.

Figure 4.8 Narrative of the Causeway Cash Receipts System

Para	Line	Text
1	1	Causeway Company uses the following
	2	procedures to process the cash received from
	3	credit sales. Customers send checks and
	4	remittance advices to Causeway. The
	5	mailroom clerk at Causeway endorses the
	6	checks and writes the amount paid and the
	7	check number on the remittance advice.
	8	Periodically, the mailroom clerk prepares a
	9	batch total of the remittance advices and
	10	sends the batch of remittance advices to
	11	accounts receivable, along with a copy of
	12	the batch total. At the same time, the
	13	clerk sends the corresponding batch of
	14	checks to the cashier.
2	15	In accounts receivable, a clerk enters
	16	the batch into the computer by keying
	17	the batch total, the customer number, the
	18	invoice number, the amount paid, and the
	19	check number. After verifying that the
	20	invoice is open and that the correct amount
	21	is being paid, the computer updates the
	22	accounts receivable master data. If there
	23	are any discrepancies, the clerk is notified.
3	24	At the end of each batch (or at the
	25	end of the day), the computer prints a
	26	deposit slip in duplicate on the printer
	27	in the cashier's office. The cashier
	28	compares the deposit slip to the
	29	corresponding batch of checks and then
	30	takes the deposit to the bank.
4	31	As they are entered, the check number
	32	and the amount paid for each receipt are
	33	logged on disk. This event data is used to
	34	create a cash receipts listing at the end of
	35	each day. A summary of customer accounts
	36	paid that day is also printed at this time. The
	37	accounts receivable clerk compares these
	38	reports to the remittance advices and batch
	39	totals and sends the total of the cash
	40	receipts to the general ledger office.

Drawing the Context Diagram

We are now ready to draw the context diagram. Since a context diagram consists of only one circle, we begin our context diagram by drawing one circle in the center of our page (paper or computer). Next, we must draw the external entity boxes. To do this, we must decide which of the entities in Table 4.1 are external and which are internal to the system.

DFD guideline 1:

Include *within* the system context (bubble) any entity that performs one or more information processing activities.

Table 4.1 Table of Entities and Activities for Causeway Cash Receipts System

Entities	Para	Activities
Customers	1	1. Send checks and remittance advices.
Mailroom (clerk)	1	2. Endorse checks.
Mailroom (clerk)	1	3. Write the amount paid and the check number on the remittance advice.
Mailroom (clerk)	1	4. Prepare a batch total of the remittance advices.
Mailroom (clerk)	1	5. Send the batch of remittance advices and a copy of the batch total to the accounts receivable clerk.
Mailroom (clerk)	1	6. Send the batch of checks to the cashier.
Accounts receivable (clerk)	2	7. Enter the batch into the computer.
Accounts receivable (clerk)	2	8. Key the batch total, the customer number, the invoice number, the amount paid, and the check number.
Computer	2	9. Verify that the invoice is open and that the correct amount is being paid.
Computer	2	10. Update the accounts receivable master data.
Computer	2	11. Notify the clerk of errors.
Computer	4	12. Log events.
Computer	3	13. Print a deposit slip.
Cashier	3	14. Compare the deposit slip with the batch of checks.
Cashier	3	15. Take the deposit to the bank.
Computer	4	16. Create a cash receipts listing.
Computer	4	17. Print a summary of customer accounts paid.
Accounts receivable (clerk)	4	18. Compare the computer reports with the remittance advices and batch totals.
Accounts receivable (clerk)	4	19. Send the total of cash receipts to the general ledger office.

Information processing activities are those activities that retrieve data from storage, transform data, or file data. Information processing activities include document preparation, data entry, verification, classification, arrangement or sorting, calculation, summarization, and filing—both manual and automated. The sending and receiving of data between entities are not information processing activities because they do not transform data. If we send data to another entity, we do not process data. If, however, we file data, we do perform an information processing activity. Likewise, if we receive data from another entity, we do not perform an information processing activity. However, if we retrieve data from a file or table, we do perform an information processing activity. Operations process activities are not information processing activities.

To discover which entities perform no information processing activities, we must inspect the table of entities and activities and mark those activities that are not information processing activities. Any entities that do not perform any information processing activities will be *external* entities; the remaining entities will be *internal*. Review your table of entities and activities and mark all activities that do not perform information processing activities. These marked activities—mostly sends and receives—indicate your data flows.

You should have indicated activities 1, 5, 6, 15, and 19 because these activities only send or receive data. As we mentioned earlier, activity 7 only describes activity 8 and can also be marked. Finally, activity 11 can be marked because of the following guideline:

DFD guideline 2:

For now, include only *normal* processing routines, *not* exception routines or error routines, on context diagrams, physical DFDs, and level 0 logical DFDs.

Because activity 11 occurs only when the payment data contain an error, we will not consider this activity *for now*.

Your table of entities and activities, with certain noninformation processing activities marked, should indicate that the mailroom, accounts receivable, cashier, and computer perform information processing activities and will be included in our diagrams as *internal* entities. The customer, on the other hand, does not perform any such activities and will be an *external* entity.

Are there other external entities to be included in our diagrams? To answer this question you must go through the narrative one more time and put a box around those entities not yet marked. You should find that the bank (line 30) and the general ledger office (line 40), in *this* system, do not perform information processing activities. These entities, along with the customer, are external entities and are included in the context diagram as sources or destinations of data. We now have 3 external entities, 4 internal entities, and 19 activities. *No other entities or activities are to be added* because of the following guideline:

DFD guideline 3:

Include in the systems documentation all (and only) activities and entities described in the systems narrative—no more, no less.

When we say narrative, we are talking about the narratives that you will find as problem material in this book. You are to assume, in those cases, that the narrative is complete and accurate. However, when you prepare a narrative to document a real-world case, you cannot assume that your narrative is perfect. When you have verified that your narrative is complete and that it accurately reflects reality, you must then follow DFD guideline 3.

Because there are three entities external to the Causeway cash receipts system—the customer, the bank, and the general ledger office—you must draw on your page three boxes surrounding the one context bubble. Next, draw and label the data flows that connect the external entities with the bubble. Since logical (versus physical) labels are normally used on a context diagram, you should do your best to derive logical labels for the flows. The final step is to label the context bubble. Write a descriptive label that encompasses the processing taking place within the system. Our label in Figure 4.9 indicates the scope of the Causeway system—namely, cash receipts from charge customers. The Causeway system does not include cash receipts from any other source.

Figure 4.9 is the completed Causeway context diagram. Compare it to your context diagram and resolve any differences. Notice that we include a single square for many

Figure 4.9 Causeway Context Diagram

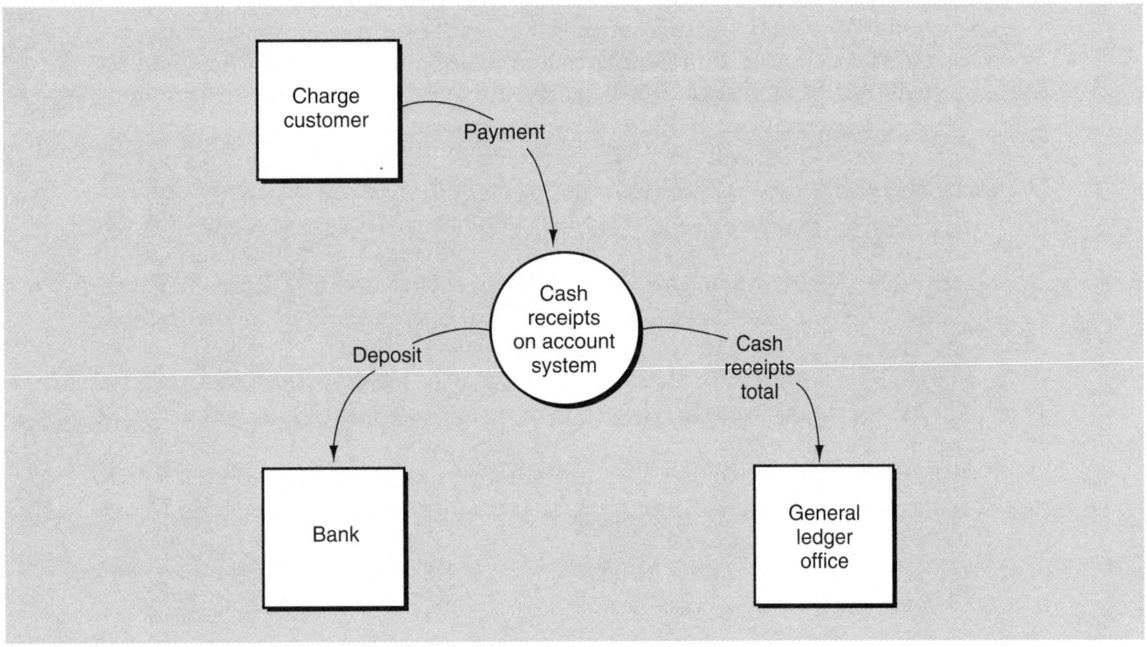

customers. Likewise, although we may use several banks, we have a single bank square. The following guideline applies:

DFD guideline 4:

When multiple entities operate identically, depict only one to represent all.

Drawing the Current Physical Data Flow Diagram

To keep the current physical DFD balanced with the context diagram, start your current physical DFD by drawing the three external entities from the context diagram near the edges of a page. Next, draw and label each data flow going into the two destinations and coming out of the single source. Leave the center of the page, into which we will sketch the rest of the diagram, blank. Since this is a physical DFD, the data flows should have labels that describe the means by which the flow is accomplished. For example, the "Payment" from the customer should now be labeled "Checks and remittance advices," and the "Deposit" should now be labeled "Deposit slip and checks."

Because each *internal* entity listed in Table 4.1 (page 121) becomes a bubble in our physical DFD, we know that our current physical DFD will contain four bubbles: one each for the mailroom, cashier, accounts receivable, and computer. We will add these four bubbles by first drawing the bubbles on our diagram that are connected to the sources and destinations. During this process, you must consider all send and receive activities and the implied reciprocal activities. (Many of these were marked earlier to indicate that they were not data processing activities.) For example, activity 1 indicates that the customer sends the checks and remittance advices. Draw and label a mailroom bubble, an accounts receivable bubble, and a cashier bubble. Use a data flow symbol (i.e., a curved line with an arrowhead) to connect these bubbles to their related external entities.

To complete the physical DFD, we must go through the table of entities and activities once again and draw all the remaining entities and flows. Follow along with us as we complete the diagram. Activity 5 indicates a connection between the mailroom and accounts receivable. Activity 6 indicates a connection between the mailroom and the cashier. Activity 8 tells us that the accounts receivable clerk enters data into the computer. Draw the computer bubble, label it "4.0," and connect it to accounts receivable. To perform activity 18, accounts receivable must receive the reports from the computer. Draw and label one or two flows (we chose two flows) from the computer to accounts receivable. To perform activity 14, the cashier must receive the deposit slip from the computer. Activity 16 implies that the table of accounts receivable master data must be read so that the open invoice record can be retrieved. Draw the data store for the accounts receivable master table and a flow from the data store to the computer bubble. Notice that the label on the data store shows that the *physical* storage medium is a disk. We draw a flow only from the data store because a data *request* is not a flow of data. Therefore, we do not show the request for the open invoice record. The movement of the record out of the data store in response to this request *is* a flow of data and is shown. Notice that we did not show a flow from the accounts receivable data store directly to the accounts receivable bubble. Because the accounts receivable data store is on a computer disk, only the computer can read from or write to that disk. This also excludes any direct connection between computerized data stores. To update the data on one computerized data store from another, you must go through a computer bubble.

Because the open invoice record must be read into the computer, updated, and then written back to the accounts receivable master table, activity 10 requires a data flow from *and* a data flow to the accounts receivable data store. Because we already drew a flow from the data store for activity 9, we need only draw a flow back to the data store. Activity 12 requires that we draw a data store for the cash receipts log and that we draw a data flow from the computer into that data store, whereas activity 13 requires that we draw a flow from the data store. Finally, to depict the flow of data required to print the reports indicated in activities 16 and 17, we need to draw flows from both data stores into the computer. You may think that all the flows into and out of the data stores aren't necessary. We offer a suggestion in the form of a guideline:

DFD guideline 5:

For clarity, draw a data flow for each flow into and out of a data store. You may, also for clarity and to help you determine that you have included all necessary flows, label each flow with the activity number that gives rise to the flow or with a description of the flow (e.g., "retrieve accounts receivable master data").

Figure 4.10 is the completed Causeway current physical DFD. Compare it to your diagram and, before reading on, resolve any differences. You should notice that there is a data store of endorsed checks connected to the cashier. This file, not mentioned in the narrative, was added to show that the cashier must retain batches of checks until the deposit slip is printed on the computer terminal. We offer the following guideline:

DFD guideline 6:

If a data store is logically necessary (that is, because of a delay between processes), include a data store in the diagrams, whether it is mentioned in the narrative.

Should we draw a data store to show that the remittance advice batches and batch totals are retained in accounts receivable until the computer reports are received? We could. You must use DFD guideline 6 carefully, however, so that you don't draw DFDs that are cluttered with data stores and are therefore difficult to read. You will need to

Figure 4.10 Causeway Current Physical DFD

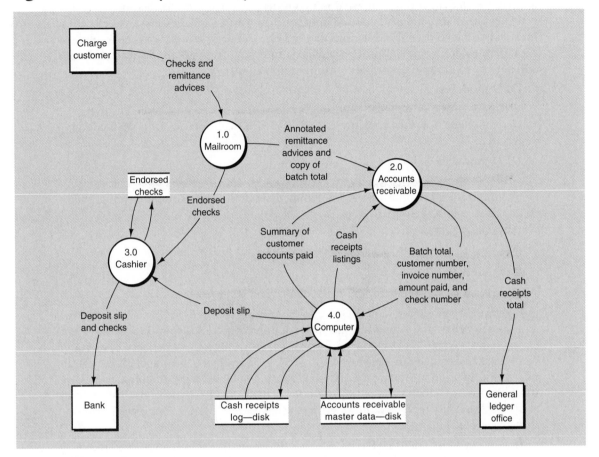

use your judgment. Does this guideline contradict DFD guideline 3? No. DFD guideline 3 tells you to include in your diagrams only those activities included in your narrative, while DFD guideline 6 tells you to completely describe those activities. So, if the narrative implies an activity or data store, include it in the diagrams. How about an example that would violate DFD guideline 6? Because they are *outside the context* of this particular system, the following activities are not described in the narrative (Figure 4.8, page 120) and should not be included in the diagrams:

- The actual update of the general ledger data
- Cash receipts from cash sales
- Customer billing

Drawing the Current Logical Data Flow Diagram

The current logical DFD portrays the logical activities performed within the system. Level 0 DFDs depict a particular grouping of the logical activities, so we start the level 0 DFD by enumerating the activities in the system and then group those activities. If you have been following along with us, you already have a list of the activities to be included in the level 0 DFD. Do you know what that list is? The activities to be included in the level 0 DFD are the *unmarked* activities on the table of entities and activities,

Table 4.1 (page 121). Our list includes activities 2, 3, 4, 8, 9, 10, 12, 13, 14, 16, 17, and 18. Recall that, at this time, we don't consider any other activities because the other activities either are actions performed in other-than-normal situations and therefore not included on a level 0 DFD, are actions that merely send or receive data rather than transform data, or are operations process activities, such as picking goods. Several guidelines will help us to group the activities remaining in our list:

DFD guideline 7:

Group activities if they occur in the same place and at the same time. For example, the clerk performs activities 2 and 3 in the mailroom as each payment is received.

DFD guideline 8:

Group activities if they occur at the same time but in different places. For example, the cashier performs activity 14 "immediately" after the computer prints the deposit slip in activity 13.

DFD guideline 9:

Group activities that seem to be logically related.

DFD guideline 10:

To make the DFD readable, use between five and seven bubbles.[7]

To start preparing your logical DFD, try bracketing the activities in Table 4.1 (page 121) as you believe they should be grouped (do not consider the marked activities). For example, if we apply DFD guideline 7 (that is, same time *and* same place), we could combine activities 2 and 3; activities 9, 10, and 12; and activities 16 and 17. Although this would provide a satisfactory solution, there would be eight bubbles, and there would be several bubbles containing only one activity. Since we prefer not to have too many single-activity bubbles until we get to the lowest-level DFDs, we proceed with further groupings.

If we apply DFD guideline 8 (that is, same time but different place) to the preceding grouping, we could combine activity 8 with 9, 10, and 12; 13 with 14; and 16 and 17 with 18. This solution is also fine, and is better than our first solution because we now have five bubbles and only one single-activity bubble.

If we apply DFD guideline 9 (that is, logically related activities), we can combine activities 2, 3, and 4. Although this leaves us with only four bubbles, this solution is superior to the first two because we have no single-activity bubbles.

In summary, our groups are:

- Group 1: activities 2, 3, 4
- Group 2: activities 8, 9, 10, 12
- Group 3: activities 13, 14
- Group 4: activities 16, 17, 18

After we choose our groupings, we must give each group a name that describes the logical activities within the group. For Causeway, we chose the following labels:

- Group 1 (activities 2, 3, 4) is bubble 1.0 and is labeled "Capture cash receipts" because that bubble comprises all the activities after the payment is sent by the customer until the payment is keyed into the computer.

---

[7] For very simple systems, such as those described in the narratives in this textbook, your solutions may have fewer than five bubbles.

- Group 2 (activities 8, 9, 10, 12) is bubble 2.0 and is labeled "Record customer collections" because the activities in bubble 2.0 record the payment in the cash receipts events table and the accounts receivable master table.
- Group 3 (activities 13 and 14) is bubble 3.0 and is labeled "Prepare deposit" because the activities generate a deposit slip and send the deposit to the bank.
- Group 4 (activities 16, 17, 18) is bubble 4.0 and is labeled "Prepare cash receipts total" because that is the main purpose of the reporting and comparison that takes place.

Mark these groups and labels on Table 4.1 (page 121).

Table 4.2 demonstrates how you should annotate your table of entities and activities. (Notice that we have not carried forward from Table 4.1 the marked activities.) Follow along with us now as we draw the current logical DFD for Causeway. You'll need paper and pencil (or your computer), the Causeway context diagram (Figure 4.9, page 123), the Causeway current physical DFD (Figure 4.10, page 125), your annotated table of entities and activities (Table 4.2), and your original table of entities and activities (Table 4.1, page 121). To draw the logical DFD, you should begin in the same manner that you began to draw the current physical DFD. Draw the external entities near the edges of a page. Draw and label flows to and from the external entities, while leaving the center of the page blank to receive the remainder of the diagram. Because this is a *logical* DFD, the data flows to and from the entities must have logical descriptions (for example, the descriptions used on the context diagram).

Table 4.2 Entities and Activities for Causeway Cash Receipts System (Annotated)

Entities	Para	Activities	
Mailroom (clerk)	1	2. Endorse checks.	
	1	3. Write the amount paid and the check number on the remittance advice.	*1.0 Capture cash receipts*
	1	4. Prepare a batch total of the remittance advices.	
Accounts receivable (clerk)	2	8. Key the batch total, the customer number, the invoice number, the amount paid, and the check number.	
Computer	2	9. Verify that the invoice is open and that the correct amount is being paid.	*2.0 Record Customer Collections*
	2	10. Update the accounts receivable master data.	
	4	12. Log events.	
Computer	3	13. Print a deposit slip.	*3.0 Prepare deposits*
Cashier	3	14. Compare the deposit slip with the batch of checks.	
Computer	4	16. Create a cash receipts listing.	
	4	17. Print a summary of customer accounts paid.	*4.0 Prepare cash receipts total*
Accounts receivable (clerk)	4	18. Compare the computer reports with remittance advices and batch totals.	

After we have completed the external flows, we can begin to draw the internal bubbles and flows. The "Payment" from the "Charge customer" is the input to bubble 1.0. Activities 2, 3, and 4 happen within the bubble. What are the outputs? The endorsed checks leave bubble 1.0 (see activity 6 in Table 4.1, page 121). For the logical DFD, we'll call this flow "Monetary transfers." The other data flow out from bubble 1.0 was called "Annotated remittance advices and copy of batch total" (see activity 5 in Table 4.1, page 121). For the logical DFD, let's call it "Batched customer receipts." Before moving on, compare your drawing to bubble 1.0 in Figure 4.11.

Figure 4.11 Causeway Current Logical DFD (Level 0)

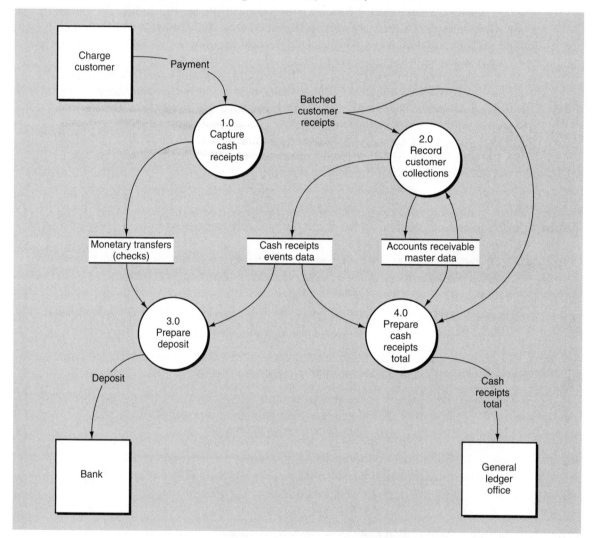

The batched customer receipts are the input to bubble 2.0. In response to the keying action (activity 8), a record is read from the accounts receivable master table. Draw the data store for this table (remember, use a logical label) and a flow *from* the data store into bubble 2.0. Activity 9 occurs within the bubble. What are the outputs? Activity 10 indicates a flow *to* the accounts receivable master table, and activity 12 indicates a flow *to* the cash receipts events table. Draw the data store for the events data and the flows into that data store and into the accounts receivable data store. Before moving on, compare your drawing to bubble 2.0, Figure 4.11.

Now we must draw bubble 3.0. To accomplish activity 13, bubble 3.0 must obtain the records contained in the cash receipts events table. Draw a flow from that table's data store into bubble 3.0. To perform activity 14, bubble 3.0 must obtain the records stored in the monetary transfers data store. Draw a flow from that data store into bubble 3.0. What are the outputs from bubble 3.0? Activity 15 in Table 4.1 (page 121) indicates that bubble 3.0 should be connected to the flow "Deposit" going into the bank. Before moving on, compare your drawing to bubble 3.0 in Figure 4.11.

Finally, let's draw bubble 4.0. To create a cash receipts listing (activity 16), bubble 4.0 must obtain the records contained in the cash receipts events table. Draw a flow *from* that table's data store into bubble 4.0. To print a summary of customer accounts paid (activity 17), bubble 4.0 must obtain the records stored in the accounts receivable master table. Draw a flow *from* that table's data store into bubble 4.0. To perform activity 18, bubble 4.0 must obtain the data contained on the remittance advices and batch totals. Where are those data? They are in the flow "Batched customer receipts" that went into bubble 2.0. Since bubble 4.0 must also obtain those data, we must split that flow and connect it to both bubble 2.0 and to bubble 4.0.

We have finished drawing the Causeway current logical DFD. Compare your diagram to the solution in Figure 4.11. Resolve any discrepancies. Your diagram should look like that in Figure 4.11 *if you use the groupings we described.* Many other groupings are possible within the guidelines. Each different grouping should lead to a different logical DFD.

Summary of Drawing Data Flow Diagrams

First and foremost, don't let the rigor of the documentation get in the way of using the diagrams to understand the system. We have presented many guidelines, hints, and instructions to help you draw DFDs. Use your judgment in applying this information.

There will be times when an *operations process* function performs information processing activities. Here are a few new DFD guidelines and examples that didn't come up when we drew the Causeway DFDs. For example, when the receiving department (primarily an operations process unit) prepares a document indicating how many widgets have been received, it is performing an information processing activity. The warehouse and the shipping department are other operations process units that often perform information processing activities. The following guideline applies:

DFD guideline 11:

A data flow should go to an operations process entity *square* only when operations process functions (that is, work-related functions such as storing goods, picking goods from the shelves, packaging the customer's order, and so on) are to be performed by that entity. A data flow should enter an entity *bubble* if the operations process entity is to perform an information processing activity.

For example, when an operations process entity is receiving goods, a physical DFD could show either a "receiving" box or a "receiving" bubble, whereas the logical DFD might show either a receiving department box or a "Complete receiving report" bubble.

DFD guideline 12:

On a physical DFD, reading computer data stores and writing to computer data stores must go through a computer bubble.

DFD guideline 13:

On a logical DFD, data flows cannot go from higher- to lower-numbered bubbles.

If on a logical DFD you have a data flow going back to a previous processing point (that is, to a lower-numbered bubble), you have a physical representation of the flow or process. Flows may, however, flow backwards to a data store.

Aren't there occasions when processing can't proceed as planned? Yes, there are—in such cases processes called **exception routines** or **error routines** handle the required actions. These are processes for out-of-the-ordinary (exceptional) or erroneous events data. Processing that is performed in other-than-normal situations should be documented *below the level 0 DFD* with reject stubs that indicate that exceptional processing must be performed. A **reject stub** is a data flow assigned the label "Reject" that leaves a bubble but does not go to any other bubble or data store. These reject stubs, *which are shown only in lower-level diagrams*, may be added without bringing the set of diagrams out of balance.

Preparing Systems Flowcharts

In this section we describe the steps for preparing a systems flowchart. The following guidelines outline our basic flowcharting technique. Study each guideline before proceeding.

Systems flowcharting guideline 1:

Divide the flowchart into columns: one column for each internal entity and one for each external entity. Label each column.

Systems flowcharting guideline 2:

Flowchart columns should be laid out so that the flowchart activities flow from left to right, but you should locate columns so as to minimize crossed lines and connectors.

Systems flowcharting guideline 3:

Flowchart logic should flow from top to bottom and from left to right. For clarity, put arrows on all flow lines.

Systems flowcharting guideline 4:

Keep the flowchart on one page. If you can't, use multiple pages and connect the pages with off-page connectors.

To use an off-page connector, draw the symbol shown in Figure 4.6 (page 114) at the point where you leave one page *and* at the corresponding point where you begin again on the next page. If you leave page 1 for the first time and you are going to page 2, then the code inside the symbol on page 1 should be "P. 2, A" and on page 2 the code inside the symbol should be "P. 1, A." That is, you point to page 2 from page 1 and you point back to page 1 from page 2. Disciplining yourself to draw flowcharts on pages of limited size is essential when you must draw flowcharts on standardized forms for workpapers and systems documentation. Also, as you might expect, computerized flowcharting packages will print your flowcharts only on paper that will fit in your printer!

Systems flowcharting guideline 5:

Within each column, there must be at least one manual process, keying operation, or data store between documents. That is, do not directly connect documents within the same column.

This guideline suggests that you show all the processing that is taking place. For example, if two documents are being attached, include a manual process to show the matching and attaching activities.

Systems flowcharting guideline 6:

When crossing organizational lines (i.e., moving from one column to another), show a document at both ends of the flow line unless the connection is so short that the intent is unambiguous.

Systems flowcharting guideline 7:

Documents or reports printed in a computer facility should be shown in that facility's column first. You can then show the document or report going to the destination unit.

Systems flowcharting guideline 8:

Documents or reports printed by a centralized computer facility on equipment located in another organizational unit (e.g., a warehouse or a shipping department) should not be shown within the computer facility.

Systems flowcharting guideline 9:

Processing within an organizational unit on devices such as a PC or computerized cash register should be shown within the unit or as a separate column next to that unit, but *not* in the central computer facility column.

Systems flowcharting guideline 10:

Sequential processing steps (either computerized or manual) with no delay between them (and resulting from the same input) can be shown as one process or as a sequence of processes.

Systems flowcharting guideline 11:

The only way to get data into or out of a computer data storage unit is through a computer processing rectangle.

For example, if you key data from a source document, you must show a manual keying symbol, a rectangle or square, and then a computer storage unit (see, for example part a of Figure 4.7, page 116).

Systems flowcharting guideline 12:

A manual process is not needed to show the sending of a document. The sending should be apparent from the movement of the document itself.

Systems flowcharting guideline 13:

Do not use a manual process to file a document. Just show the document going into the file.

Drawing Systems Flowcharts

We are now ready to draw the Causeway flowchart. Get some paper (or your computer) and follow along with us. The entities in our current physical DFD (Figure 4.10, page 125) should help us to set up and label our columns. Although we set up columns for each entity (systems flowcharting guideline 1), we do not have to include columns for the customer, bank, or general ledger office because these entities do not perform any information processing activities. Because accounts receivable and the cashier both interact with the computer, let's locate them on either side of the "Computer" column (see systems flowcharting guideline 2). So, from left to right, your columns should be "Mailroom," "Accounts Receivable," "Computer," and "Cashier."

We usually start a flowchart in the top left corner with a start symbol. Because we have eliminated the Customer column, we must start the flowchart with a start symbol labeled "Customer," followed by two documents labeled "Remittance advices" (RAs) and "Checks." To show that they are together, we can place the RAs and the checks on top of each other with the back document a little above and to the right of the front document. We place all these symbols in the Mailroom column because lines 3 and 4 of the narrative tell us that the customer sends checks and remittance advices. This technique makes it clear where the flowchart starts and the source of the document that starts the process. Draw this portion of your flowchart.

Lines 5 and 6 of the narrative tell us that the mailroom clerk endorses the checks, and lines 6 and 7 tell us that the clerk writes the amount paid and the check number on the RA. "Endorse" and "write" are manual processes that, being performed by the mailroom clerk, should be documented with a *manual process symbol* (or two symbols) placed in the Mailroom column. Systems flowcharting guideline 10 tells us that sequential processes may be documented in one or more process symbols. Because one action is directed at the checks and the other action at the RAs (and because our description of the actions would not fit in one process symbol), we'll use two processes. Draw these processes.

In lines 8 and 9, we find a process—preparing the batch total—that is performed periodically by the mailroom clerk. So, still working in the Mailroom column, draw another manual process for the batch total preparation. Find the *annotation* symbol on Figure 4.6 (page 114) and annotate the batch total preparation process to describe the periodic nature of the process.

Lines 10 through 14 describe the three items exiting the mailroom and their destination. All three items should exit the batch total preparation process. Because the RAs and the batch total are going to the next column, they can exit from either the right side or the bottom of the process. Systems flowcharting guideline 6 tells us that we do not need to show the RAs and the batch total in both the Mailroom and the Accounts Receivable columns. Since you'll probably have more room in the Accounts Receivable column, draw these items at the top of that column. Your flow line will require arrows because your logic flow has gone up, rather than down! Did you find the symbol for batch totals in Figure 4.6?

Send the endorsed checks to the cashier using an on-page connector. Systems flowcharting guideline 6 dictates showing the endorsed checks in the sending and receiving columns. In the Cashier column, the endorsed checks must be filed awaiting the receipt of the deposit slip. We introduced this file when we described the current physical DFD (Figure 4.10, page 125). Notice that the on-page connector is shown where the process ends and again where the process begins. The same letter is shown in both places. Use letters, starting with the letter "A," and restart with A on each page. Review the Mailroom column of Figure 4.12 and compare it to your solution. Resolve any discrepancies.

Let's return now to drawing Figure 4.12. Narrative paragraph 2 describes the process by which the RAs are entered into the computer by the accounts receivable clerk and are edited and posted to the accounts receivable master table. Figure 4.7 part a on page 116 depicts a method for documenting such a process. Notice that the keying symbols, the manual process symbols, and the display symbols are located in the Clerk column, whereas the computer process and storage devices are located in the Computer column. Figure 4.7 part a, indicates a two-step process in which input errors are displayed on the display screen and a clerk corrects the errors and notifies the computer that the input is acceptable. Because paragraph 2 of the Causeway narrative implies, but does not directly

Figure 4.12 Causeway Systems Flowchart

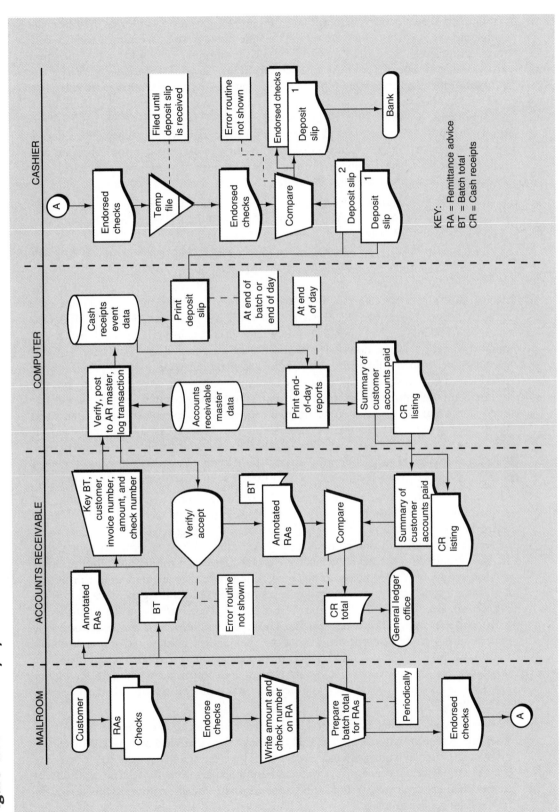

require, a two-step process such as that in Figure 4.7 part a, we can draw the flowchart with a one-step process. Draw the activity included in narrative paragraph 2 using a one-step input process. Send the RAs and the batch total out of the "bottom" of the input process, that is, out of the bottom of the screen, as shown in Figure 4.7 part a. If the computer does not accept the input, we can assume that the accounts receivable clerk will correct and rekey the erroneous RA. To show this, connect—with a dashed line—an annotation symbol to the display screen. Include the phrase "Error routine not shown" within the symbol. Lines 31 through 33 (paragraph 4) tell us that the events are logged as they are input. Include a disk symbol for this data store in the computer column of your flowchart. Connect it to the same computer process block with which you updated the accounts receivable data store.

We have completed flowcharting the accounts receivable clerk's activities *for now*. Review the upper portion of the Accounts Receivable column in Figure 4.12 and compare it to your solution. Resolve any discrepancies.

Let's return once again to drawing Figure 4.12. Narrative paragraph 3, lines 24 through 27, describes the process by which the computer prints the deposit slip on a printer in the cashier's office. What data must be accessed to get the information for the deposit slip? The cash receipts log has the check number and the amount, and is the only table that contains the most recent payments—the accounts receivable master table summarizes *all* billings and payments. Read systems flowcharting guidelines 7 and 8 and draw this section of the flowchart. We have used an annotation to indicate that this process is performed only periodically. If you have laid out your flowchart well, the file of endorsed checks—previously sent from the mailroom—and the deposit slip printed by the computer should be near each other in the Cashier column. Now, to flowchart lines 28 through 30 we need only a manual process for comparing these two items and then, coming out of the process, we have the endorsed checks and a copy of the deposit slip going to the bank. If we had a Bank column these items would go to that column. Because we have no such column, we send these items to a *start/stop* symbol labeled "Bank." Complete your own flowchart and then review these sections of Figure 4.12.

To complete our flowchart, we need to chart the end-of-day report generation described on lines 33 through 36 and the use of these reports in accounts receivable described on lines 37 through 40. Because both reports are generated at the same time, we can depict this with one computer process symbol. Access to both computer data stores is required for the report generation, and the reports must be shown in the Computer column and then go to accounts receivable where they are compared to the RAs and to the batch total. A total of cash receipts must be sent to the general ledger office. Figure 4.6 (page 114) shows that the symbol used for batch totals can be used for any total. However, since the narrative is not clear, you would not be wrong in using the general-purpose input-output file symbol (parallelogram). Because we're not sure how the total is prepared, just send the total to the general ledger office directly from the process where the batch totals, RAs, and reports are compared. Again, without a General Ledger column we send the cash receipts total to a stop symbol labeled "General ledger office."

We have now completed the flowchart. Verify your work by checking the table of entities and activities (Table 4.1, page 121) to make sure that each activity has been diagrammed. Compare your flowchart to the narrative (Figure 4.8, page 120) to see that the system has been accurately documented and compare your flowchart to the DFDs to see whether the flowchart and DFDs are consistent. Finally, compare your flowchart to the solution in Figure 4.12 (page 133). Resolve any discrepancies.

Summary of Systems Flowcharting

Drawing flowcharts requires judgment, which you can develop through practice. We have provided you with a number of guidelines that we hope will help you as you learn how to draw flowcharts. Before you get locked into the guidelines and the details of flowcharting, or of drawing DFDs, remember that the purpose of creating this documentation is to simplify and clarify a narrative. We draw these diagrams so that we can better analyze and understand a system. Because we want to portray a system's logic and implementation *accurately*, there can be many correct solutions. With practice, you can learn to use these techniques to create many correct solutions.

We leave you with the following flowcharting hints, which should help you to develop your flowcharting skills:

- Strike a balance between clarity and clutter by using annotation judiciously and by using on-page connectors whenever flow lines might create clutter.
- Avoid crossing lines wherever possible. If you must cross lines, use a "bridge."
- Flowchart normal routines and leave exception routines for another page of the flowchart.

DOCUMENTING ENTERPRISE SYSTEMS

In Chapter 2 we described *enterprise systems* and how they integrate the business processes from all of an organization's functional areas. With an enterprise system we will have a central enterprise database, such as the one we see at the center of the AIS Wheel. How else will an enterprise system manifest itself? The answer is "it depends." It depends on how the organization chooses to reengineer its business processes when it installs the enterprise system. Let's look at Figure 4.12 (page 133), the Causeway systems flowchart, and see what would definitely change. As mentioned previously, we would have one data store/disk symbol that would be labeled "Enterprise database," not the two data stores that are in Figure 4.12.

What else *might* change if we had an enterprise system? First, the customer payments could be sent directly to the bank where the checks would be entered into the bank's enterprise system, a deposit made to Causeway's account, and an electronic notice sent to Causeway via a direct link between Causeway's enterprise system and that of Causeway's bank. This would eliminate, or significantly alter, much of the activity in the Accounts Receivable and Cashier columns. Second, the paper reports and listings could be replaced by "electronic reports" that could be viewed online. Finally, many of the comparisons conducted by staff in accounts receivable and the cashier would be replaced by business rules inside of the enterprise system.

How will this affect our systems documentation, the DFDs and flowcharts? Figure 4.13 (page 136) depicts the Causeway system with the only change that *must* be made if they install an enterprise system—the data stores have been replaced by an enterprise database. Other changes *could* be made if we knew how else the business processes would be changed if Causeway installed an enterprise system.

How would the DFDs change? The data stores connected to the computer in the physical DFD (see Figure 4.10 on page 125) would be replaced by one data store labeled "Enterprise database." The context diagram and the logical DFD would not change, unless there were changes to the business processes. For example, if the customer payments were to be sent to the bank, the "Payment" flow would enter the sys-

Figure 4.13 Causeway Systems Flowchart with an Enterprise Database

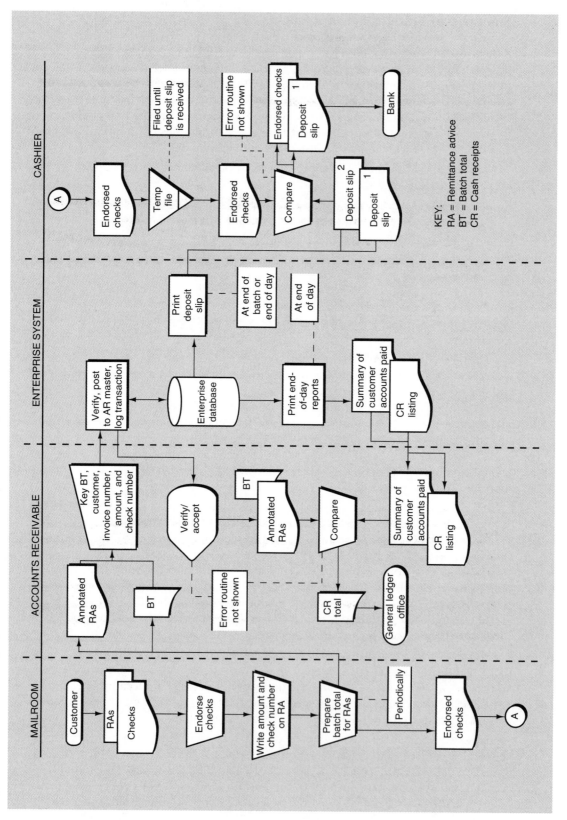

tem from a "Bank" entity instead of from the customer. The data stores would not change. In a logical DFD we want to see each table of data that is part of the process.

In conclusion let us repeat DFD guideline 3: "Include in the systems documentation all (and only) activities and entities described in the systems narrative." So, don't be tempted to depict improvements to a system as you document its existing processes and data flows. Document what is there! Only after you have done that can you move on to analysis and improvements. So, the Causeway system, as it is described in Figure 4.8 (page 120), is documented in Figure 4.9 (the context diagram on page 123), Figure 4.10 (the physical DFD on page 125), Figure 4.11 (the logical DFD on page 128), and Figure 4.12 (the systems flowchart on page 133). The discussion here, and the proposed changes and systems flowchart in Figure 4.13, are just that, proposed changes.

SUMMARY

The diagramming tools introduced in this chapter illustrate common techniques business professionals encounter when seeking a pictorial representation of business processes. Each technique has its own purpose, strengths, and weaknesses. The chapters that follow include many examples of each technique to help you understand how to read them, when to use them, and how to create them yourself. If ever there was a good example of "practice makes perfect," this is one. The more you use the techniques, the better prepared you will be to work with them later in your professional career.

REVIEW QUESTIONS

RQ 4-1 Why do we need to document an information system?

RQ 4-2 What is a data flow diagram (DFD)?

RQ 4-3 What are the symbols used in constructing data flow diagrams? Describe each of them.

RQ 4-4 Distinguish internal and external entities.

RQ 4-5 What is the difference between a context diagram, a logical DFD, and a physical DFD?

RQ 4-6 When is a set of DFDs balanced?

RQ 4-7 What is a systems flowchart?

RQ 4-8 What is a table of entities and activities? What uses does it serve?

RQ 4-9 Which activities can be included in the logical processes on a logical DFD?

RQ 4-10 Why are some entities found in a narrative included in the context diagram as external entities, whereas others are included as internal entities?

RQ 4-11 What are the guidelines for grouping logical activities for a logical DFD?

RQ 4-12 Where are error and exception routines shown on DFDs?

RQ 4-13 Where are error and exception routines shown on systems flowcharts?

DISCUSSION QUESTIONS

DQ 4-1 "Data flow diagrams and flowcharts provide redundant pictures of an information system. We don't need both." Discuss.

DQ 4-2 "It is easier to learn to prepare data flow diagrams, which use only a few symbols, than it is to learn to prepare flowcharts, which use a number of different symbols." Discuss.

DQ 4-3 Describe the *who, what, where,* and *how* of the following scenario: A customer gives his purchase to a sales clerk, who enters the sale in a cash register and puts the money in the register drawer. At the end of the day, the sales clerk gives the cash and the register tape to the cashier.

DQ 4-4 Why are there *many* correct logical DFD solutions? Why is there only one correct physical DFD solution?

DQ 4-5 Explain why a flow from a higher- to a lower-numbered bubble on a logical DFD is a physical manifestation of the system. Give an example.

DQ 4-6 Compare and contrast the purpose of and techniques used in drawing physical DFDs and logical DFDs.

DQ 4-7 "If we document a system with a systems flowchart and data flow diagrams we have overdocumented the system." Discuss.

DQ 4-8 "Preparing a table of entities and activities as the first step in documenting systems seems to be unnecessary and unduly cumbersome. It would be a lot easier to bypass this step and get right to the necessary business of actually drawing the diagrams." Do you agree? Discuss fully.

DQ 4-9 "In terms of the sequence used in documenting systems, it would be easier to prepare a systems flowchart *before* we prepare a data flow diagram." Do you agree? Discuss fully.

DQ 4-10 "Since there are computer-based documentation products that can draw data flow diagrams and systems flowcharts, learning to draw them manually is a waste of time." Do you agree? Discuss fully.

PROBLEMS

P 4-1 Prepare a narrative to describe the system depicted in the physical DFD in Figure 4.14.

P 4-2 Prepare a narrative to describe the system depicted in the logical DFD in Figure 4.15.

P 4-3 Prepare a narrative to describe the system depicted in the flowchart in Figure 4.16 (page 140).

Problems 4 through 7 are based on the following two narratives. Lincoln Company describes sales and credit card billing systems. Bono Insurance describes an automobile insurance order entry and billing system. For those who wish to test their documentation skills beyond these problems, there are narratives at the end of Chapters 10 through 14. Note that for the Lincoln case we do not discuss, and you should ignore, the handling of cash received at the time of a sale.

Lincoln Company

Lincoln Company operates pet supply stores at many locations throughout New England. The company's headquarters are in Boston. The company

Figure 4.14 Physical DFD for Problem 4-1

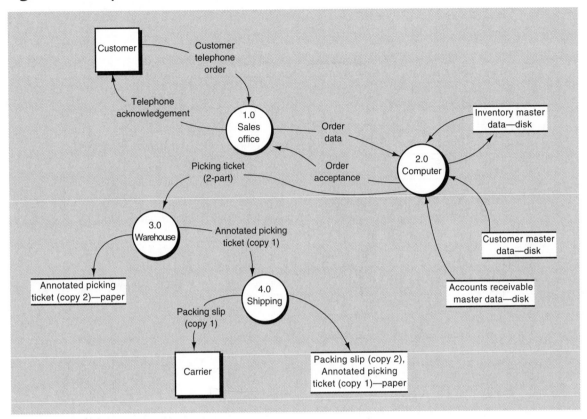

Figure 4.15 Logical DFD for Problem 4-2

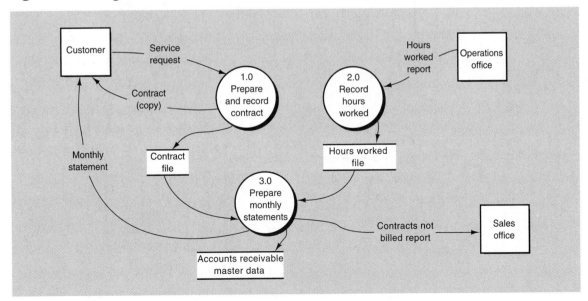

Figure 4.16 Flowchart for Problem 4-3

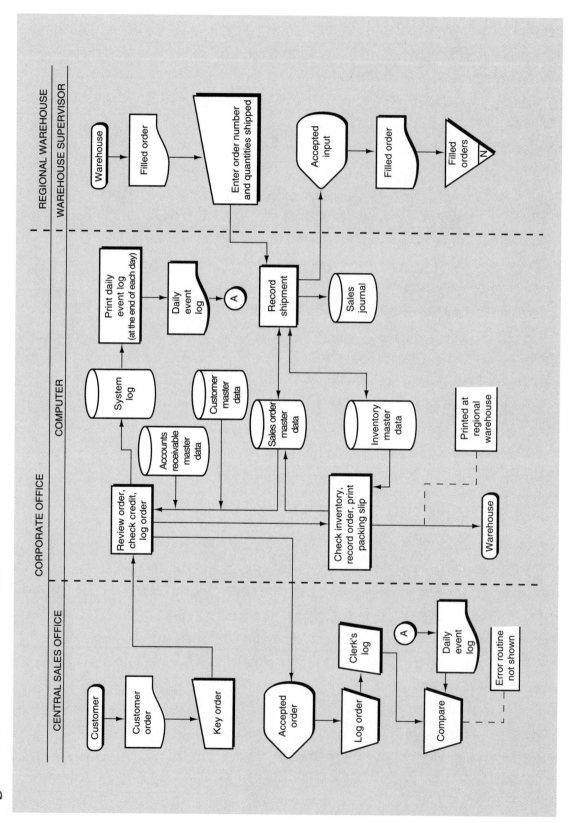

accepts cash and its own Lincoln charge card (LCC). LCC billing and the treasury functions are located at headquarters.

At each store a customer presents the item(s) to be purchased along with cash or an LCC. Sales clerks prepare LCC slips and then all sales, cash and charge, are keyed into the cash register. At the end of the shift, the clerk forwards the LCC slips to the store cashier (again, as noted previously, ignore the handling of the cash). The store cashier batches the LCC slips and sends the batches to the cash receipts section in Boston at 5:00 P.M. each day.

As each sale is keyed by the sales clerks, Lincoln's central computer system captures the sales data and stores them on a disk ("sales events data"). Each night, the computer prints a sales report summarizing each store's sales events data. On the following morning, the sales report is sent to the cash receipts section, where the LCC slips for each store are reconciled to the line on the sales report that totals LCC sales for that store. The LCC slips are then sent to Lincoln's IT division, where data preparation clerks scan the LCC slips to record the charges on a disk ("credit sales data"). At 9:00 each evening the disk containing the Credit sales data is sent to the computer room, where it is used to record the accounts receivable master data (also on disk). Each month, the computer prepares customer statements that summarize the LCC charges, and sends the statements to the customers.

Bono Insurance

Bono Insurance Company of Needham, Massachusetts, processes its automobile insurance policies on a batch-oriented computer system with magnetic disk storage. Customers send requests for auto insurance into the Needham sales office where sales clerks prepare policy request forms. They file a copy of the form and forward the original to the input preparation section where data entry clerks use networked PCs to key and key-verify the data contained on the documents to a disk ("policy events").

Each evening, computer operations retrieves the policy events data from the network and edits the data on the computer and then sorts the data in policy number sequence. Events data that do not pass the edits are deleted from the events data disk and printed on an error report. The error report is sent to the sales office where sales clerks review the report, correct the errors (contacting the customer, if necessary), and prepare another policy request form. These forms are submitted to data preparation each day along with other policy request forms.

In addition to the error report, the computer also prints a summary report listing the good events data. This report is sent to the sales office where the sales clerks compare the report to the copy of the policy request form that they previously filed. If everything checks out, they notify computer operations to go ahead with processing. When notified, computer operations processes the correct events data against the policyholder master data to create a new policy record. Each evening, a disk, which was created during the processing run, is used to print premium notices that are sent to the customer.

P 4-4 a. Prepare a table of entities and activities based on either the Lincoln Company or the Bono Insurance narrative.

   b. Construct a context diagram based on the table you prepared in part a.

P 4-5 Prepare a physical DFD based on the output from Problem 4.

P 4-6 a. Prepare an annotated table of entities and activities based on the output from Problems 4 and 5. Indicate on this table the groupings, bubble numbers, and bubble titles to be used in preparing a level 0 logical DFD.

  b. Prepare a logical DFD (level 0 only) based on the table you prepared in part a.

P 4-7 Construct a systems flowchart based on the narrative and the output from Problems 4 through 6.

P 4-8 A description of 14 typical information processing routines is given here, along with 10 numbered excerpts from systems flowcharts (see Figure 4.17).

  Match the flowcharting segments with the descriptions to which they correspond. Four descriptions will be left blank.

  a. Data on source documents are keyed to an offline disk.

  b. A deposit slip and check are sent to a bank.

  c. A printed output document is filed.

  d. Output is provided to a display device at a remote location.

  e. A clerk manually posts sales invoices to the accounts receivable ledger.

  f. A report is printed from the contents of a disk.

  g. Data stored on a disk is sorted and placed on another disk.

  (10) h. Data on a magnetic tape are printed during an offline operation.

  i. Data are keyed from a terminal at a remote location.

  j. A batch total of input documents is compared to the total reflected on an error and summary report produced after the documents were recorded.

  (5) k. Magnetic tape input is used to update master data kept on a disk.

  l. The computer prepares a cash receipts summary report which is sent to the general ledger bookkeeper.

  m. Input stored on two magnetic disks is merged.

  n. Programmed edits are performed on key input, the data entry clerk investigates exceptions and keys in corrections, then data on the disk are updated.

P 4-9 Refer to Figure 4.11 (page 128), the level 0 DFD of Causeway's cash receipts system.

  a. Construct a diagram 1, which "explodes" process 1.0, "Capture cash receipts," down to the next level.

  b. Construct a diagram 2, which "explodes" process 2.0, "Record customer collections," down to the next level.

  c. Construct a diagram 3, which "explodes" process 3.0, "Prepare deposit," down to the next level.

  d. Construct a diagram 4, which "explodes" process 4.0, "Prepare cash receipts total," down to the next level.

Figure 4.17 Flowchart Segments for Problem 4-8

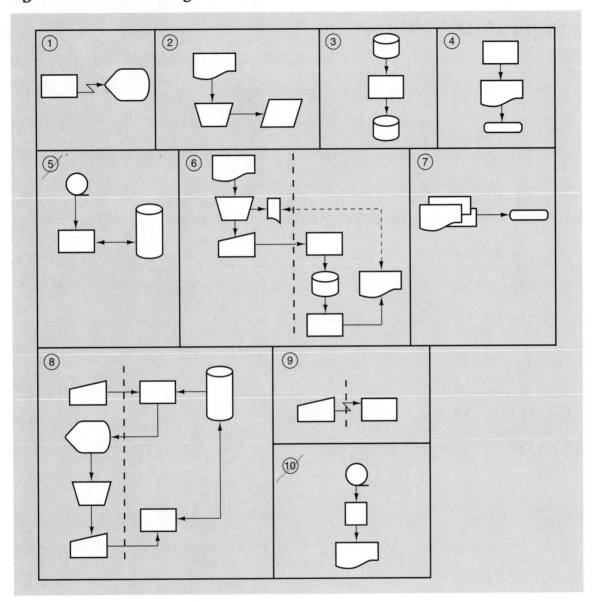

KEY TERMS

data flow diagram (DFD)

bubble symbol

data flow symbol

external entity symbol

source

destination

data store symbol

context diagram

external entities

physical data flow diagram

internal entity

logical data flow diagram

balanced

top-down partitioning

systems flowchart

activity

information processing
  activities

exception routines

error routines

reject stub

Database Management Systems

The fall 2000 massive recall of Firestone tires, particularly those on Ford Explorer SUVs, produced a major financial impact on both Firestone (including its parent Bridgestone) and Ford Motor Co. The recall occurred as tire blowouts and related vehicle rollovers were reported at alarming rates. Basically, the tread on certain brands and sizes of Firestone tires had a tendency to separate—particularly if the tires were underinflated, driven at high speeds in hot climates, and carrying a heavy load. Numerous lawsuits were filed against both Bridgestone/Firestone and Ford Motor Co.

The burning question is why did Ford and/or Firestone not discover the problem earlier? Quite simply, Ford "lack[ed] a database it could use to determine whether incident reports on one type or brand of tire represented a deviation from those of other tires on Ford vehicles."[1] As a result, Ford did not identify the problem until the public relations damage was severe and then only after organizing a team to pore over the documentation on hand in the offices of Firestone. If a *database* of information related to tire problems had been available, standard *data mining* techniques likely would have detected the information much earlier. In this chapter, we will explore the advantages of *database management systems* and the related analysis tools that can improve the decision support required for timely decision making.

chapter 5

Learning Objectives

- To describe the limitations of traditional application approaches to managing data.
- To analyze the advantages gained by using the database approach to managing data.
- To learn how to create normalized tables in a relational database.
- To know how entity-relationship diagrams are used in database design and implementation.
- To explain the importance of advanced database applications in decision support and knowledge management.

[1] R. L. Simison, K. Lundegaard, N. Shirouzu, and J. Heller, "How the Tire Problem Turned into a Crisis for Firestone and Ford—Lack of a Database Masked the Pattern that Led To Yesterday's Big Recall," *The Wall Street Journal* (August 10, 2000): A1 and A12.

In this chapter, we highlight the enterprise database and the database controls including how organizations use databases to store information about business events such as sales, purchases, cash receipts, and cash disbursements. The chapter discusses the major types of databases that are available and how organizations undertake database design for accounting information systems. Larger organizations store information in data warehouses in ways that let managers analyze it to gain important insights. Many companies combine their data resources with decision support systems, executive information systems, group decision systems, and other advanced technology-based systems to improve decision making and operations.

SYNOPSIS

In this chapter you will learn about the approaches that organizations use to process business event data. These events, as you learned in Chapter 2, include sales, purchases, cash receipts, and cash disbursements. In this chapter, you will learn how data from these events are recorded and processed using differing accounting systems designs. As business events are processed, accounting data are recorded. In a manual accounting system, or in automated systems designed in the format of manual accounting systems, the accounting data are recorded in journals and classified in ledgers. Increasingly, however, accounting systems are built on underlying databases of business event data. In these databases, accounting information (along with other business information) is stored in database tables. Accounting reports, such as financial statements, and traditional accounting records, such as journals and ledgers are generated from the information stored in these database tables. In a database accounting system, data management is broken into two functions, the recording of event data (see Figure 2.5 on page 54) and the maintenance of that data (see Figure 2.4 on page 53). You will learn the basic elements of database design and implementation that organizations use when they create databases for their accounting information. In some larger organizations, the business event data is copied periodically into a separate database (often called a *data mart* or *data warehouse*) where it is stored. Managers can gain important insights by analyzing this collected historical data with multidimensional analytic tools and exploratory techniques (called *data mining*). In some companies, these data warehouses are combined with business event databases to create sophisticated reporting systems that help managers make better decisions. These systems include decision support systems, executive information systems, group support systems, and expert systems. Many of these advanced systems use software tools called *intelligent agents*. Finally, you will learn about knowledge management systems that combine event processing databases, data warehouses, and decision support systems and make the combined knowledge contained in these systems available across the organization.

INTRODUCTION

Organizations engage in various business processes, such as hiring employees, purchasing inventory, making sales, and collecting cash from customers. As you learned in Chapters 1 and 2, the activities that occur during the execution of these business processes are called *events*. Among the most important elements in any organization's information systems, whether those systems deal with accounting information or other information that managers use to make decisions, are the data describing these events that are stored in those systems. This is the *business event data* first described in Chapter 1.

As an aspiring accountant, you should know that data and databases will become an integral part of your day-to-day work. In this chapter, the major approaches used to manage data are described and compared. You will learn about the benefits and costs of alternative methods for collecting, storing, and using business data.

TWO APPROACHES TO BUSINESS EVENT PROCESSING

Before we begin, let's summarize what we have described about the processing of this business event data. First, we know that as organizations engage in business processes, such as purchasing inventory, several business events, such as preparing a purchase order and receiving the goods, will occur. Second, as these business events occur business event data is captured to describe the *who, what, where,* and *when* about that event. In this section we will learn about the two major approaches to capturing and storing that business event data.

The Applications Approach to Business Event Processing

Figure 5.1 compares the applications approach (discussed in this section) with the database approach to business event processing (discussed in the next section). Figure 5.2 (page 148) contains the record layouts for the files in Figure 5.1, part (a).

Before databases became widely used in business information systems, organizations tended to view their data as a subordinate element to the program that used the data. As you can see in part (a) of Figure 5.1, this traditional **applications approach to business event processing** view concentrates on the process being performed. In this case, data play a secondary or supportive role to the programs that run in each application

Figure 5.1 Two Approaches to Business Event Processing

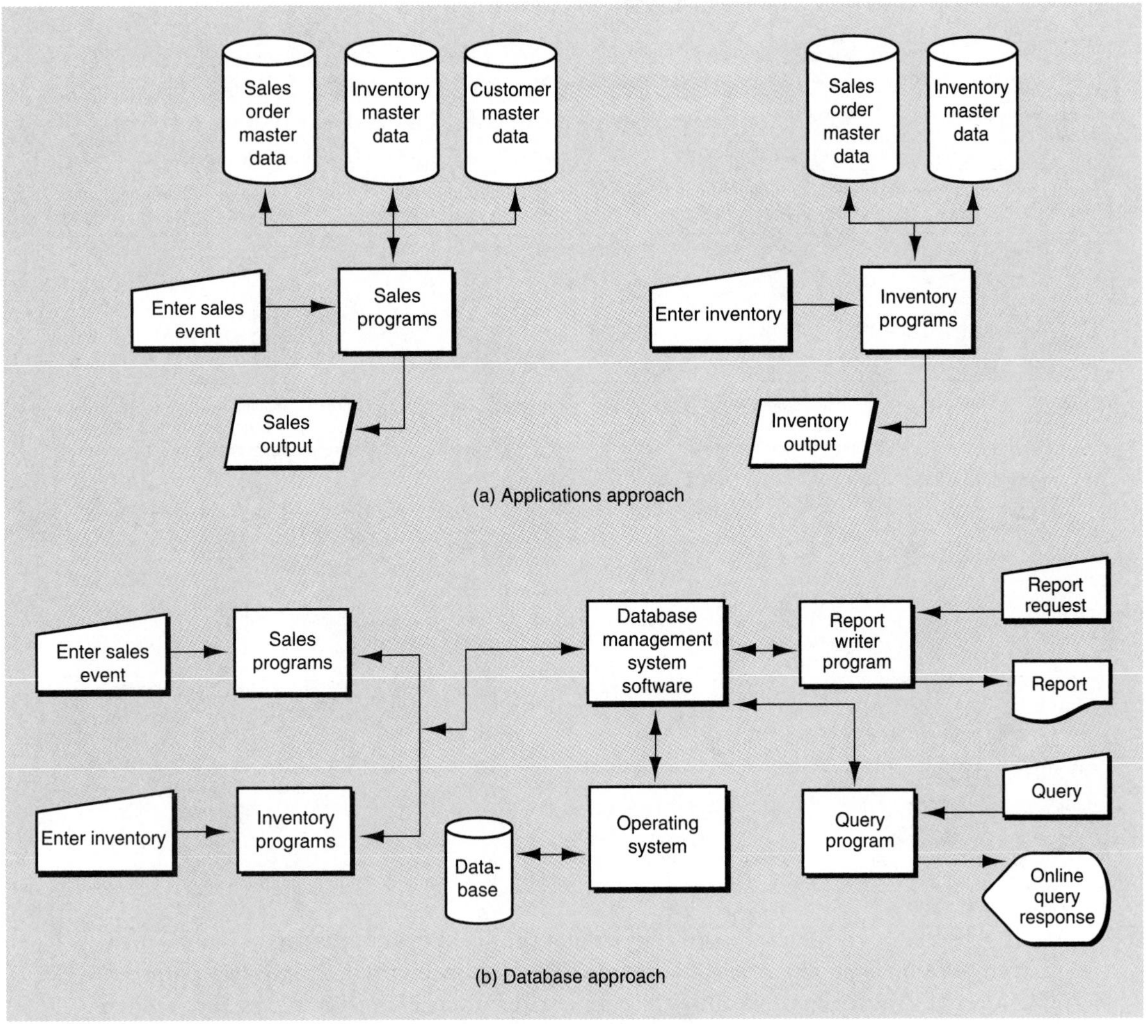

(a) Applications approach

(b) Database approach

system. Under this approach, each application collects and manages its own data, generally in dedicated, separate, physically distinguishable files for each application.

Data Redundancy

An important consequence of the applications approach is the *data redundancy* that occurs among the various files. For example, notice the redundancies (indicated by double-ended arrows) depicted in the record layouts in Figure 5.2. Data redundancy can cause inconsistencies among the same data in different files. This redundancy increases storage costs because the system must store and maintain multiple versions of the same data in different files. In addition, data residing in separate files are not shareable among applications. The worst consequence of using an applications approach is that the redundant data stored in multiple files can become inconsistent when information is updated in one file and not in other files where it also resides.

Figure 5.2 Record Layouts Under an Applications Approach to Business Event Processing

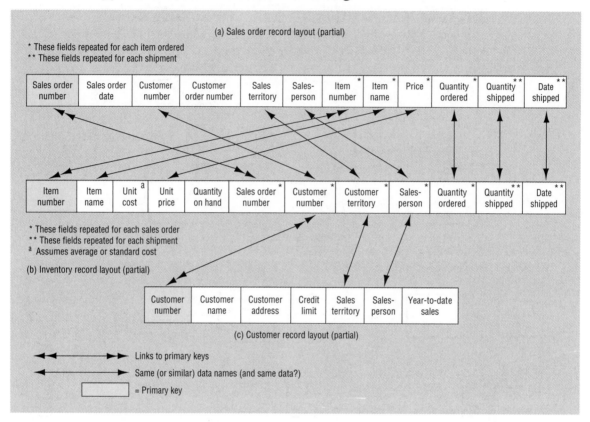

In Chapter 1, you learned about horizontal (business operations) and vertical (managerial decision support) information flows. The data in Figure 5.2 have two purposes. The data (1) mirror and monitor the business operations (the *horizontal information flows*), and (2) provide the basis for managerial decisions (the *vertical information flows*). In addition to data derived from the horizontal flows, managers use information unrelated to event data processing. These data would be collected and stored with the business event related data.

Suppose that a manager asked that the sales application be designed to perform sales analysis and generate reports such as product sales by territory, by customer, or by salesperson. To do this, the sales application would store data for sales territory and salesperson in the sales order record shown in part (a) of Figure 5.2. Next, assume that a different manager asked to have the inventory application conduct similar analyses. To do this, the inventory application would store similar (and redundant) data about territory and salesperson such as that depicted in part (b) of Figure 5.2. As implied by Figure 5.1, part (a) (page 147) the sales data in the inventory file—including customer territory and salesperson—could be updated by the sales application or updated separately by the inventory application. This would create a condition in which different information about the same fact is stored in different files. This condition violates the *integrity* of the data. As a second example, consider a feature in the sales application that allowed managers to find the current amount of sales for a particular customer. The summary data in the customer master file (in the year-to-date sales field) could be stored as shown in part (c) of Figure 5.2. Alternatively, the information could be obtained as needed by summarizing data on the sales order or in the inventory data. As a final sales example, assume that a sales manager would like to know all the products that a particular customer has purchased (perhaps so the company can promote those products that the customer is no longer buying). Given the record layouts depicted in Figure 5.2, the information could be obtained by sorting the inventory or sales order data by customer number. Alternatively, the company could have collected these data in the customer master data. In all of these examples, the data are difficult and expensive to obtain. Also, if the applications were not originally designed to yield these data, the applications approach to business event processing makes it difficult to add this access after the fact.

The Database Approach to Business Event Processing

The preceding examples have all involved business event data related to the selling of merchandise. The applications approach leaves us with similar problems for *standing data*. In Figure 5.2 you can see the redundancies among the three files with respect to master file standing data such as customer number, territory, and salesperson. These fields could easily take on different values for the same facts over time as changes are made in one file and not all files in which the data is stored. The **database approach to business event processing**, in which facts about events are stored in relational database tables instead of separate files, solves many of the problems caused by data redundancy. You will learn about the database approach in the next section, then you can return to Figure 5.2 and see how these data are handled in a database approach, rather than an application approach.

Databases and Business Events

Earlier in this book, you learned that traditional file management approaches that focus on an applications approach to data management are often sufficient to support a traditional applications approach to processing business event data. The use of databases has improved the efficiency of processing business event data by eliminating data redundancies and improving data integrity. However, the big change that databases have helped make possible are the creation of integrated business information systems that include data about all of a company's operations in one massive collection of relational tables (in one database or in a set of databases that are linked to each other). Multiple users from throughout the organization can view and aggregate *event* data in a manner most conducive to their needs.

At the heart of this movement is a fundamental shift in the view of information processing in business organizations. Traditionally, organizational information systems have been focused on capturing data for the purpose of generating reports, and using the reporting function to support decision making. Increasingly, management's view is shifting to one of viewing information systems processing as a decision support activity first and a reporting function second. This perspective leads to a focus on aggregating and maintaining data in an original form from which reports can be derived, but users also can access and manipulate data using their own models and their own data aggregations. In Chapter 2 you learned about strategic shifts in information design, including the trend toward the use of *enterprise systems* that might include one or more *ERP systems*, *CRM systems*, and other special-purpose systems. Some of these systems include their own databases, but most are built on existing relational databases.

ENTERPRISE SYSTEMS

DATABASE MANAGEMENT SYSTEMS

A **database management system (DBMS)** is a set of integrated programs designed to simplify the tasks of creating, accessing, and managing data. *Database management systems* integrate a collection of files that are independent of application programs and are available to satisfy a number of different processing needs. Organizations use *DBMSs* to coordinate the activities of their many functional areas. The database management system, containing data related to all an organization's applications, supports normal data processing needs and enhances the organization's management activities by providing data useful to managers. Although in its strictest sense a database is a collection of files, we will use the term *enterprise database* synonymously with *database management system* or DBMS. This use is consistent with the meaning intended by most computer users and developers.

Logical versus Physical Database Models

The concept underlying the *database approach to business event processing* is to decouple the data from the system applications (that is, to make the data independent of the application or other users). This decoupling is called **data independence** and it is a major difference between the database approach and the applications approach. Recall that in the applications approach the data is subordinate to, or dependent upon, the application program that uses the data. Therefore, as reflected in part (b) of Figure 5.1 (page 147), the data become the focus of attention. Several other aspects of the database approach are noteworthy:

- The database is now shared by multiple system applications that support related business processes, as shown at the left of Figure 5.1, part (b).

- In addition to being used by application programs, the data can be accessed through two other user interfaces that are built in to most database management software: (1) *report generation*, the creation of on-screen or printed summaries of specific data as shown in the upper-right portion of part (b), and (2) ad hoc user inquiries, also called *queries*, that allow users to ask questions about the data in the database handled through *query language* software, depicted in the lower-right portion of part (b).

- Two layers of software are needed to translate user views (as shown in the AIS wheel at the beginning of this chapter) into instructions for retrieving the data from the physical location in which it is stored (for example, a computer's disk drive). The distinction between the way a user thinks of the data in a database, which is called a user's *logical view*, and the way the data is actually stored on the computer hardware, which is called the *physical view* of the data, is important for computer scientists who develop database software, but it is not very important for accountants and managers who use the software because the DBMS includes the software that handles this translation automatically. Some of the more technical design issues of database management systems are described in Technology Summary 5.1.

Figure 5.3 (page 152) depicts how a database might look to us if the data from Figure 5.2 (page 148) were stored in a database that used a relational structure, which is the most common type of database structure used in businesses today. The data from our three files are now stored in four tables: CUSTOMERS (instead of the customer master data file), INVENTORY_ITEMS (instead of the inventory master data file), SALES_ORDERS and SALES_LINES (these two tables replace the sales order master

Technology Summary 5.1

Database Management Systems (DBMSs)

A database management system (DBMS) is a set of integrated programs designed to simplify the tasks of creating, accessing, and managing a database. The DBMS performs several functions, such as:

- Defining the data.
- Defining the relations among data.
- Interfacing with the *operating system* for storage of the data on the *physical* media.
- Mapping each user's view of the data.

In the language of DBMS, a **schema** is a complete description of the configuration of record types and data items and the relationships among them. The schema defines the *log-* *ical* structure of the database. The schema, therefore, defines the organizational view of the data. A **subschema** is a description of a *portion* of a schema. These are the views shown in the AIS Wheel. The DBMS maps each user's view of the data from subschemas to the schema. In this way the DBMS provides flexibility in identifying and selecting records. Each of the many database users may want to access records in his or her own way. For example, the accounts receivable manager might want to access customer records by invoice number, whereas a marketing manager may want to access the customer records by geographic location. The following figure portrays the schema-subschema relationship.

Customer number	Customer name	Customer address	Credit limit	Sales-person	Sales territory	Year-to-date sales

(a) Schema

Customer number	Customer name	Credit limit

(b) Credit department subschema

Customer number	Customer name	Sales-person	Sales territory	Year-to-date sales

(c) Sales manager subschema

A chief advantage of a DBMS is that it contains a **query language** (also called a **data manipulation language**, or **DML**), which is a language much like ordinary language. A query language is used to access a database and to produce inquiry reports. These languages allow non-technical users to bypass the programmer and to access the database directly. Deriving data from the database using a query does not replace applications programs, which are still required to perform routine data processing tasks. However, when information is needed quickly, or when a manager wishes to browse through the database, combining data in a variety of ways, the query facility of a DBMS is a vast improvement over the traditional method of requesting that a program be written to gen-erate a report. Later in this chapter and in Chapter 6 you will see examples of *SQL* (*structured query language*), the de facto standard for DBMS query languages.

A DBMS normally contains a number of security controls to protect the data from access by unauthorized users as well as from accidental or deliberate alteration or destruction. A DBMS also includes software that allows the data to be simultaneously shared by multiple users. This software often allows managers to manage access rights for specific users. For example, all employees might be able to view employee names and addresses, but only specific authorized users would be able to view employee's pay rates.

data file). These tables are *logical views* of data that are *physically* stored in a database. The **logical database view** is how the data appear to the user to be stored. This view represents the structure that the user must use to extract data from the database. The

Figure 5.3 Record Layouts as Tables

Shaded_Attribute(s) = Primary Key

CUSTOMERS

Cust_Code	Cust_Name	Cust_City	Credit_Limit	Sales_YTD
ETC	Bikes Et Cetera	Elgin	10000.00	9561.55
IBS	Inter. Bicycle Sales	New York	5000.00	4191.18
RODEBYKE	Rodebyke Bic. & Mopeds	San Jose	2000.00	1142.50
STANS	Stan's Cyclery	Hawthorne	10000.00	8330.00
WHEEL	Wheelaway Cycle Center	Campbell	10000.00	6854.00

INVENTORY_ITEMS

Item_Number	Item_Name	Qty_On_Hand	Unit_Cost	Unit_Price
1000-1	20 in. Bicycle	247	55.00	137.50
1001-1	26 in. Bicycle	103	60.00	150.00
1002-1	24 in. Bicycle	484	60.00	150.00
1003-1	20 in. Bicycle	4	24.37	60.93
1280-054	Kickstand	72	6.50	16.25
2010-0050	Formed Handlebar	90	4.47	11.25
3050-2197	Pedal	23	0.75	1.88
3961-1010	Tire, 26 in.	42	1.45	3.13
3961-1041	Tire Tube, 26 in.	19	1.25	3.13
3965-1050	Spoke Reflector	232	0.29	0.63
3970-1011	Wheel, 26 in.	211	10.50	25.00

SALES_ORDERS

SO_Number	Cust_Code	Cust_Order_Number	SO_Date
1010	WHEEL	453	061205
1011	ETC	347	061205
1012	WHEEL	56-6	061205
1013	IBS	3422	061205
1014	ETC	778	061205
1015	WHEEL	5673	061206
1016	ETC	3345	061206

SALES_LINES

SO_Number	Item_Number	Qty_Ordered	Sales_Price	Qty_Shipped
1010	1000-1	5	137.50	0
1010	2010-0050	2	11.25	0
1011	1001-1	10	127.50	8
1011	1002-1	5	150.00	4
1012	1003-1	5	60.93	0
1012	1001-1	10	127.50	5
1013	1001-1	50	78.30	0
1014	1003-1	25	37.42	0
1015	1003-1	25	37.42	0
1016	1003-1	5	60.93	0
1016	3965-1050	50	33.00	0
1016	3961-1041	5	3.13	0
1016	1000-1	4	137.50	0

physical database storage is how the data are actually physically stored on the storage medium used in the database management system. The physical storage of the data often have little relation to the logical view. Thus, accountants and other business users of DBMSs do not need to worry about the details of the physical storage of the data. Users can access the data in the tables by:

1. Formulating a query.
2. Preparing a report using a report writer.
3. Including a request for data within an application program.

These three methods are depicted in the flowchart in Figure 5.1, part (b) (page 147). The following two examples can help you see how easily data can be obtained from the tables in Figure 5.3. These examples use the database query language *SQL* (*structured query language*). SQL is widely used because it works with a number of DBMSs (although some variations exist in syntax and allowed commands in different DBMSs) and it resembles English. You should be able to follow these two simple query examples here and you will learn more about SQL in the next chapter.

1. A query that uses the SQL SELECT command can return to the customers assigned to salesperson Garcia.

```
SELECT Cust_Code Cust_Name Cust_City

FROM CUSTOMERS

WHERE Salesperson = 'Garcia'
```

Cust_Code	Cust_Name	Cust_City
STANS	Stan's Cyclery	Hawthorne
WHEEL	Wheelaway Cycle Center	Campbell

You can see that there are two customers, STANS and WHEEL, who are assigned to salesperson Garcia.

2. You also can create more complex queries using the SELECT command. Consider the query shown here with its results:

```
SELECT SO_Number INVENTORY_ITEMS.Item_Number Sales_Price
Unit_Price

FROM SALES_LINES INVENTORY_ITEMS

WHERE Sales_Price <> Unit_Price AND INVENTORY_ITEMS.Item_Number
= SALES_LINES.Item_Number
```

SO_Number	Item_Number	Sales_Price	Unit_Price
1011	1001-1	$127.50	$150.00
1012	1001-1	$127.50	$150.00
1013	1001-1	$78.30	$150.00
1014	1003-1	$37.42	$60.93
1015	1003-1	$37.42	$60.93
1016	3965-1050	$33.00	$0.63

In this query, the SELECT command examines fields in both the SALES_LINES and INVENTORY_ITEMS tables and finds those items in the combined table that were sold at a price (Sales_Price) other than the price contained on the INVENTORY_ITEMS table (Unit_Price). The query result shows that there are six instances where this occurred.

In some cases, a user formulates a query and enters it to receive the query results immediately on the computer screen. In other cases, queries are placed into on-screen forms or reports that are generated by software within the DBMS. A third alternative is to include queries in the program code that uses the data in the DBMS. In the second and third cases, users might not be aware that a query was operating to assist them obtain the information. They simply open the form, print the report, or run the program.

Overcoming the Limitations of the Applications Approach

Earlier in this chapter, you learned about some of the limitations of the *applications approach to business event processing*. In this section you will learn how the database approach can overcome these limitations. You also will learn about other advantages of the database approach. Of course, the database approach has its own limitations. You will learn about those in this section also.

CONTROLS

- *Eliminating data redundancy.* With the database approach to business event processing, an item of data is stored only once. Applications that need data can access the data from the central database. For example, in Figure 5.1, part (a) (page 147), multiple versions are present of the inventory master data, while in part (b) of that figure only one exists. Further, Figure 5.2 (page 148) depicts the same data elements on more than one file, whereas Figure 5.3 (page 152) shows each data element only once. An organization using the applications approach to business event processing must incur the costs and risks of storing and maintaining these duplicate files and data elements.

- *Ease of maintenance.* Because each data element is stored only once, additions, deletions, or changes to the database are accomplished easily. Contrast this to the illustration in Figure 5.2 (page 148), where changes in a salesperson, territory, or customer combination would require changes in three different files.

- *Reduced storage costs.* By eliminating redundant data, storage space is reduced, resulting in associated cost savings. However, in most database installations, this savings is *more than offset* by the additional costs of DBMS software.

CONTROLS

- *Data integrity.* This advantage, like several others, results from eliminating data redundancy. As mentioned earlier, storing multiple versions of the same data element is bound to produce inconsistencies among the versions. For instance, the salesperson and sales territory data might differ among their many versions, not only because of clerical errors but because of timing differences in making *data maintenance* changes. Inconsistent data could also result from the timing differences that can occur during *business event processing* of the inventory master data by the sales and inventory applications. With only one version of each data element stored in the database, such inconsistencies are no longer a threat.

- *Data independence.* The database approach allows multiple application programs to use the data concurrently. The data can be accessed in several different ways (for example, through applications processing, online query, and report writing programs), and the access can be quickly changed by modifying the definition of the tables or views. With the traditional *applications approach to business event processing*, the programs would need revisions to provide access to more or less data.

CONTROLS

- *Privacy.* The security modules available in most DBMS software include powerful features to protect the database against unauthorized disclosure, alteration, or destruction. These modules implement the database controls shown in the AIS wheel at the beginning of this chapter. Control over data access can typically be exercised down to the data element level. Users can be granted access to data for reading or updating (add, revise, delete) data. Other ways to implement security include *data classification* (i.e., data objects are given classification levels and users are assigned clearance levels) and *data encryption* (discussed in Chapter 9).

Despite the many advantages of using a DBMS instead of an application approach, some organizations do not use a DBMS. A DBMS can be expensive to implement. In general, a DBMS requires more powerful, and thus more expensive, hardware. The DBMS itself costs money. Hiring people to maintain and operate the database can be more expensive than hiring application maintenance programmers. Also, drawbacks exist related to *operating* the DBMS. Operational issues can include the following:

- Although database sharing is an advantage, it carries with it a downside risk. If the DBMS fails, all of the organization's information processing halts.

- Because all applications depend on the DBMS, database recovery and *contingency planning* (discussed in Chapter 8) are more important than in the applications approach to data management.

- When more than one user attempts to access data at the *same* time, the database can face "contention" or "concurrency" problems. Procedures such as *record locking* can mitigate these problems, but these solutions are not foolproof. Further discussion of this topic is beyond the scope of this book.

- Territorial disputes can arise over who "owns" the data. For instance, disputes can arise regarding who is responsible for data maintenance (additions/deletions/changes) to customer data. The sales department might think it should own those data, but the credit department and the accountants managing accounts receivable might argue with that contention.

To cope with these and other problems, most companies that have adopted the database approach have found it necessary to create a database administrator function (see Technology Summary 5.2 on page 156).

DATABASE ESSENTIALS

The design and implementation of a DBMS can be a more complex process than creating specific applications with subordinate data. To understand how the database approach works, you need some background information in database essentials. You will learn about logical database structures and gain an understanding of some key database elements in this section. You also will be introduced to the process of designing and implementing a database. Chapter 6 includes a more detailed treatment of database design, implementation, and use.

Logical Database Models

Four types of logical DBMS models exist: hierarchical, network, relational, and object-oriented. As a *designer* or *user* of an AIS you will participate in the selection of the DBMS for your organization, and the choice from among these logical models will affect the speed and flexibility of the DBMS. In addition, as a user or auditor of business information systems, your effective use of a DBMS often depends on your understanding of these logical models.

The first DBMSs used a **hierarchical database model.** In this model, records are organized in a pyramid structure. The records at or near the top of the structure contain records below them. This structure works well for simple situations. For example, a bank that wants to record information about its customers and their accounts could use a hierarchical DBMS. The top-level records would hold information about customers. The next level down would include records with information about accounts. A customer might have a savings account, a checking account, and a loan account. All of a customer's

Technology Summary 5.2

Role of the Database Administrator

Discussions of the role and functions of the *database administrator (DBA)* occupy entire chapters in database texts. Therefore, the discussion here is only a survey of the topic. DBAs perform both administrative and technical functions; however, most experts agree that a DBA who has good people skills and is highly user-oriented is a better choice than a narrowly focused technical person.

The specific elements in a DBA's role can vary widely from organization to organization. Among the duties that a DBA might be expected to perform are the following (presented in no particular order of importance):

- *Database designer and maintainer.* The DBA is responsible for establishing and maintaining data definitions and authorizing views of the database for specific classes of users. Any new table and any new field in an existing table must be approved by the DBA.
- *Policy and procedure setter.* As part of installing and operating a DBMS, the DBA should play a key role in developing database policies and procedures. For instance, data ownership such as who can do what to which data should be clearly articulated in writing.
- *Security officer.* Typically, the DBA determines user-authorization privileges and monitors access to the database. From a control standpoint, the DBA's role as security officer has both benefits and drawbacks. Centralizing control in the DBA offers the advantage of not having control spread throughout the organization. However, the considerable power and responsibility that then resides in this single individual can create

security risks. Organizations that do not have a separate security officer should implement *compensatory controls.* For example, the increased involvement of the *internal audit* function in overseeing the DBA's activities can be one solution.
- *Consultant to users and programmers on use of DBMS.* In this role, the DBA offers a considerable amount of technical expertise. But often this function requires good interpersonal skills to sell the database approach to potential users and top-level management.
- *DBMS operations supervisor.* The DBA is responsible for specifying and implementing backup and recovery procedures. The DBA also oversees troubleshooting activities handled by the information technology staff in response to problems reported by users. The DBA also coordinates troubleshooting and solutions obtained from the DBMS software vendor.
- *DBMS performance evaluator.* The DBA should closely monitor the DBMS's efficiency and effectiveness. In many cases, the DBA is asked by management to justify database technology in cost/benefit terms.
- *Resource arbitrator.* Once users become accustomed to a database system approach, many companies find that users develop new ways to use the DBMS that can place increasing demands on system resources. It generally falls to the DBA to manage the resolution of multiple and sometimes conflicting demands for use of system resources.

accounts would be below that customer record in the hierarchy. The next level down would include records that stored information about increases and decreases in each account.

In a hierarchical DBMS, records that are included in a record one level above them are called **child records** and the records that include them (and reside one level above) are called **parent records**. Each parent record can have many child records, but each child record can have only one parent record. In the bank example, the customer records would be the parent records of the child account records, which in turn would be the parent records of the child records that stored information about account increases and decreases.

Hierarchical DBMSs work well for simple data structures; however, they fall apart quickly when the data becomes more complex. For example, the hierarchical bank example DBMS described previously could not handle joint accounts unless the joint owners were considered a single entity. To handle more complex data structures, database researchers created a different database model. In the **network database model**, a child record can have more than one parent record. This was a significant improvement over the early hierarchical designs. Network DBMSs were adopted by a number of organizations that had been frustrated by the limitations of hierarchical DBMSs. The wholesale move to network DBMSs was interrupted, however, by the development of a vastly more flexible model, the relational database.

Relational Database Model

In a **relational database model**, data are logically organized in two-dimensional tables. Each individual fact or type of information is stored in its own table. The relational model was developed using a branch of mathematics called *set theory*. In set theory, a two-dimensional collection of information is called a *relation* (thus the name "relational"). However, today most people call these collections of information "tables." A relational DBMS allows users to query the tables to obtain information from one or more tables in a very flexible way. The tables in Figure 5.3 (page 152) are relational tables.

The relational structure is attractive from a user's standpoint because end users often think of the data they need as a table. This mental picture translates well to the logical data model of a relational DBMS. The ability of a relational DBMS to handle complex queries also is important. Although the relational model is considered to be a dramatic improvement over the network and relational models, it does have two disadvantages. First, a relational DBMS requires much more computer memory and processing time than the earlier models. Increases in computer processing capabilities that are now available at very low costs have reduced the impact of this first disadvantage. The second disadvantage is that the relational model, as originally conceived, allows only text and numerical information to be stored in the database. It did not allow the inclusion of complex object types in the database such as graphics, audio, video, or geographic information. The desire to include these complex objects in databases led to the development of object-oriented databases.

Object-Oriented Database Model

In an **object-oriented database model**, both simple and complex objects can be stored. Earlier data models were designed to store text-based data (which includes numbers). In *object-oriented* data models, other types of data can be stored. For example, video clips or pictures can be stored in an object-oriented database. Object-oriented databases include **abstract data types** that allow users to define data to be stored in the database. This overcomes the limitations of relational databases. Relational databases limit the types of data that can be stored in table columns. Instead of tables, an object-oriented DBMS stores data in objects.

An object can store attributes (similar to the attributes stored in table columns in a relational database) and instructions for actions that can be performed on the object or its attributes. These instructions are called *encapsulated methods* ("encapsulated" because they are included as part of the object). Objects can be placed in a hierarchy so that other objects lower in the hierarchy (subclass objects) can obtain (inherit) attributes from objects higher in the hierarchy (superclass objects). Figure 5.4 shows three objects in an object-oriented DBMS. The superclass object EMPLOYEE provides the same set of attributes to both subclasses—MANAGER and ADMIN_STAFF. In other words, every MANAGER would have a Name, Address, and Employee_No (as would every ADMIN_STAFF). Objects are drawn using a rectangle with rounded corners, which is divided into three parts: the object name, the attributes, and any encapsulated methods.

Figure 5.4 Object-Oriented Database Model

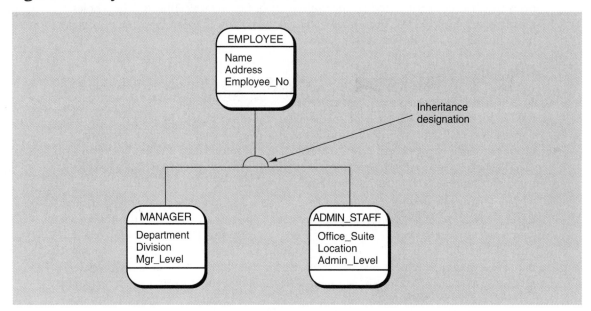

Although many researchers have argued that object-oriented DBMSs are superior to relational DBMSs, most organizations still use relational DBMSs. The main advantage of an object-oriented model is the storage of complex data types. In recent years, relational DBMSs have added the ability to store complex data types. These databases are sometimes called **object-relational databases**. Although developers continue to refine object-oriented DBMSs, most companies seem to be satisfied with relational or object-relational DBMSs at this time. The next section describes some of the important elements of relational databases.

Elements of Relational Databases

Although many different vendors offer DBMS software products, all of DBMSs have the same essential elements. In this section you will learn about these elements and some important concepts that underlie database design and implementation.

The elements that make up all DBMSs include **tables**, which provide a place to store the data; **queries**, which are tools that allow users and programmers to access the data stored in various tables; **forms**, which are on-screen presentations of data in tables and collected by queries from one or more tables; and **reports,** which provide printed lists and summaries of data stored in tables or collected by queries from one or more tables.

The most important step in creating a useful database is designing the tables properly. Each database table only stores data about one specific thing. It might be a person, such as a customer, an object, such as inventory, or an event, such as a sale. You are probably familiar with spreadsheet software. In spreadsheet software, the main element of the user interface is a worksheet. The worksheet has rows and columns.

A database table is like a worksheet in that it has rows and columns, but it is unlike a worksheet in that a database table has very strict rules about what can be put in those rows and columns. In a database table, a specific row contains all information about a particular instance of the type of thing stored in the table. For example, the first row in the CUSTOMERS table (see Figure 5.3 on page 152) stores all of the information about the customer Bikes Et Cetera. No other row can contain information about that customer. Database table columns each store one specific attribute of the type of things stored in the table. For example, the column labeled "Cust_Name" in the CUSTOMERS table in Figure 5.3 stores all of the customer names. No customer name can ever appear in any other column.

A spreadsheet cell (the intersection of a row and a column) can hold text, numbers, a formula, a graphic, a command button, a chart, or any of a number of different types of data. A cell in a database table can only hold the type of data allowed in its column and must contain the value of that specific attribute for the instance of the thing recorded in its row. For example, the first row of the SALES_LINES table (Figure 5.3, page 152) contains a number, 137.50, in the column titled "Sales_Price." This column contains the sales price of each item on each sales order. The values in this column must be numbers, and the numbers must each have two decimal places. The number in the first row is the sales price of the five Item Number 1000-1 products that were sold on sales order number 1010. This fact is stored in this row and column. It does not appear anywhere else in the database.

Each row in a database must be unique; that is, no other row can exist in the table that stores identical information. Each row must include a unique identifier that serves as an address for the row. This unique identifier is called the table's **primary key** and its value is often stored in the first column of the table. In Figure 5.3 (page 152), you can see that the primary key of the CUSTOMERS table is the first column of the table, labeled "Cust_Code." Some tables use two or more columns in combination to provide a primary key for each row. This type of key is called a **composite primary key**. The SALES_LINES table in Figure 5.3 has a composite primary key formed by combining the first two columns in that table. Note that each of the first two columns individually contains non-unique values in some rows, but when the two columns are combined, the resulting values across both columns are unique for all rows in the table.

The primary key fields in tables must be unique identifiers and that can present problems for database designers who are not very careful in creating the values to be used in these fields. For example, a designer who wants to create a primary key for an employee table might be tempted to use employees' last names as the value. As soon as the business hires more than one person with the same last name, the primary key becomes unworkable. Because the requirement that primary key fields contain unique values is so important, most database designers create an artificial value for each row in each table. They do this following procedures for classifying and coding that are described in Technology Summary 5.3 (pages 160–161).

Technology Summary 5.3

Classifying and Coding

Classifying and coding data are important elements of any database design. **Classifying** is the process of grouping or categorizing data according to common attributes. Your college or university probably has numerous occasions to classify you (and your peers who have the same characteristics) according to class (freshman, sophomore, etc.), housing (resident versus commuter), financial aid status, major, class enrollment (e.g., all students enrolled in section 001 of AC 340), and so forth.

To classify students into meaningful categories, schools do not create computer records that include values such as "junior," "resident," "work study assigned to department X," or "20-meal plan." To be efficient, they use a short-hand substitute for these long labels. The creation of these substitute values, or codes, is called **coding**. Many different coding schemes exist; the following list outlines the most common and useful examples. The accompanying figure illustrates five common coding types.

- *Sequential Coding.* **Sequential coding** (also known as **serial coding**) assigns numbers to objects in chronological sequence. This coding scheme provides limited flexibility. Additions can be made only at the end of the sequence; deletions result in unused numbers unless the numbers are recycled; and the codes tell nothing about the objects' attributes.
- *Block Coding.* In **block coding**, groups of numbers are dedicated to particular characteristics of the objects being identified. This provides some improvement over sequential coding. For example, in the universal product codes (UPCs) that supermarkets and other retailers use, the first block of five digits represents the manufacturer and the second block of five digits designates the product. However, within each block no significance is given to any of the digits. For example, Kellogg's has a manufacturer's code of 38000,

whereas Ralston Purina's code is 17800. Cracklin' Oat Bran™ (Kellogg's) has a 04510 product identifier, which appears to have no relationship to Ralston's Wheat Chex™ code, 15011. Within each block of digits, numbers are usually assigned sequentially (see the employee example in the accompanying figure), which means that block coding has the same limitations related to additions and deletions as sequential coding.

- *Significant Digit Coding.* **Significant digit coding** assigns meanings to specific digits. The accompanying figure shows how this method can be used for inventory items. Parts of the inventory item number describe the product group, the product type (part, subassembly, or end-item), the warehouse in which the part is stored, and a unique number that identifies the specific item. Significant digit codes are much better than the first two coding types.
- *Hierarchical Coding.* Like significant digit codes, hierarchical codes also attach specific meaning to particular character positions. **Hierarchical coding** orders items in descending order, where each successive rank order is a subset of the rank above it. Reading from left to right in a hierarchical code, each digit is a subcategory of the digit to its immediate left. The five-digit postal ZIP Code illustrated in the accompanying figure shows the hierarchical elements in this type of coding.
- *Mnemonic Coding.* Computers good at handling numeric data, and all of the previous coding schemes use numbers. Most humans, however, have trouble learning and remembering strings of numbers. In **mnemonic coding**, some or all of the code is made of letters. The word *mnemonic* comes from the Greek *mnemonikos, to remember*, and means "assisting or related to memory." The

accompanying figure shows a mnemonic code used for college courses.

- *Other Coding Schemes.* There are other coding schemes that can be useful in creating primary key fields in databases. A **self-checking digit code** includes an extra digit that can be used to check the accuracy of the code. The extra digit is computed by applying a mathematical formula to the primary code. For example, a bank account number of 1234-0784 might have an extra digit of 9 (it might appear on the account as 1234-0784-9). The number 9 is calculated from the other numbers using a formula. In this case, the formula is the sum of the last four digits (0 + 7 + 8 + 4 = 19) minus the sum of the first four digits (e.g., 1 + 2 + 3 + 4 = 10). If a data entry clerk enters the first eight digits incorrectly, the check digit will likely be different. The formulae used in practice are much more complex, but they work much the same as in this example.

Coding Type	Everyday Example(s)	Example Based on Employee ID Codes	
A. Sequential (serial)	• Student ID numbers • Ticket taken to identify your turn to be waited on at the supermarket deli counter	001 = first employee hired 002 = second employee hired ⋮ etc.	
B. Block	Universal product code (UPC): ⓐ 73805 80248 Manufacturer code Product identifier	001-100 fabricating department employees 101-200 assembly department employees ⋮ etc.	Within department blocks, codes are usually assigned to individual employees on a sequential basis.
C. Significant digit	Inventory item: 16 2 17 4389 Product group — Warehouse Part, subassembly or end-item — Unique item identifier	2 0 4 623 Work center — Pay rate code — Unique employee identifier Exempt or nonexempt	
D. Hierarchical	Postal ZIP Codes: 0 18 90 Section of country — Region within section — Locality (e.g., town) within region	01 3 9 623 Company division — Plant within division — Department within plant — Unique employee identifier	
E. Mnemonic	College course numbering: AC 340 = Accounting Information Systems EN 101 = English Composition	F M C 623 Female Married Caucasian — Unique employee identifier	

NOTE:

ⓐ The universal product code (UPC) is *physically* implemented through bar codes attached to the product or its container. Therefore ⟶

0 3

73805 80248

DBMSs have many built-in tools for creating tables and enforcing the strict rules on the columns and rows. Once the tables have been properly designed, the DBMS helps to enforce the design by using these tools. First, however, the tables need to be designed in accordance with the relational model. This design task is the subject of the next two sections.

Normalization in Relational Databases

Two approaches are used in designing a relational database: bottom-up and top-down. You will learn about top-down design in the next section. In the bottom-up design approach, the designer identifies the attributes that are of interest and organizes those attributes into tables. Referring back to Figure 5.3 (page 152), you can see that the attributes of sales events might include such things as customer name, customer city, salesperson, sales territory, credit limit, inventory item name, unit cost, unit price, sales order number, and so on.

The structure of the tables must comply with several rules that are based on set theory, the branch of mathematics on which relational database models are based. These rules are called **normal forms** and include specifications that must be met by relational database tables. Following the normal forms yields tables that prevent errors (also called **anomalies**) that otherwise might occur when adding, changing, or deleting data stored in the database.

Applying the normal forms to collections of data transforms tables that are not in normal form into tables that comply with the rules. The resulting tables are said to be "in normal form." There are six levels of normal form, but business systems usually work well if they comply with the first three. A table that is in first normal form (1NF) is better than a table that is not in 1NF; a table in second normal form (2NF) is better than a table in 1NF; and a table in third normal form (3NF) is better than a table in 2NF. The goal of normalization is to produce a database model that contains relations that are in 3NF. The normal forms are inclusive, which means that each higher normal form includes all lower normal forms. That is, a table in 3NF is in 1NF and in 2NF. Two concepts are essential to an understanding of normal forms: functional dependence and primary keys.

Functional Dependence and Primary Keys

An attribute (a column in a table) is **functionally dependent** on a second attribute (or a collection of other attributes), if a value for the first attribute determines a single value for the second attribute at any time. If functional dependence exists, one would say that "the first attribute determines the second attribute."

Consider a table that contains information about purchases in two columns, one for purchase order number (PO_Num) and another for purchase order date (PO_Date). A value in PO_Date does not determine the value in PO_Num because a particular date could have several purchase orders (and thus, several distinct values for PO_Num) associated with it. In this case, PO_Num is not functionally dependent on PO_Date. However, PO_Date is functionally dependent on PO_Num because the value in PO_Num will always be associated with a single value for PO_Date, the value will always be the date on which that purchase order was issued.

The second concept that is essential to understanding normalization is that of the primary key. Although you know from its definition earlier in this chapter that a primary key contains a value that uniquely identifies a specific row in a table, the use of this concept in normalization requires that you learn a more formal specific definition. A candidate attribute (a column or collection of columns) in a table is that table's primary key if:

1. All attributes in the table are functionally dependent on the candidate attribute.
2. No collection of other columns in the table, taken together, has the first property.

First Normal Form (1NF)

An **unnormalized table** is a table that contains repeating *attributes* (or *fields*) within each *row* (or *record*). We call these repeated attributes "repeating groups." Figure 5.5 is an unnormalized table because it contains repeating groups. Each sales order occupies one row, but then Item_Number, Item_Name, Qty_Ordered, Cust_Code and Cust_Name are repeated as many times as necessary.

Figure 5.5 Unnormalized Relation

SALES_ORDERS

SO_Number	Item_Number	Item_Name	Qty_Ordered	Cust_Code	Cust_Name
1010	2010-0050	Formed Handlebar	2	WHEEL	Wheelaway Cycle Center
	1000-1	20 in. Bicycle	5	WHEEL	Wheelaway Cycle Center
1011	1002-1	24 in. Bicycle	5	ETC	Bikes Et Cetera
	1001-1	26 in. Bicycle	10	ETC	Bikes Et Cetera
1012	1003-1	20 in. Bicycle	5	WHEEL	Wheelaway Cycle Center
	1001-1	26 in. Bicycle	10	WHEEL	Wheelaway Cycle Center
1013	1001-1	26 in. Bicycle	50	IBS	Inter. Bicycle Sales
1014	1003-1	20 in. Bicycle	25	ETC	Bikes Et Cetera
1015	1003-1	20 in. Bicycle	25	WHEEL	Wheelaway Cycle Center
1016	3961-1041	Tire Tube, 26 in.	5	ETC	Bikes Et Cetera
	3965-1050	Spoke Reflector	50	ETC	Bikes Et Cetera
	1003-1	20 in. Bicycle	5	ETC	Bikes Et Cetera
	1000-1	20 in. Bicycle	4	ETC	Bikes Et Cetera

A table is in **first normal form (1NF)** if it does not contain repeating groups. Transforming this table into 1NF requires the removal of the repeating groups. Figure 5.6 (page 164) shows the table SALES_ORDERS in 1NF. Instead of one row with repeating groups, each sales order is represented in the number of rows required. For example, sales order 1010 now has two rows, rather than the one row it had in Figure 5.5. The *primary key* for the new table is a combination of SO_Number and Item_Number. Recall that a primary key that is formed by the combination of two or more columns is called a *composite primary key*. The simpler table structure shown in Figure 5.6 solves a big problem. If a table has repeating groups, the designer must decide in advance how many repeats to allow. The risk is always that the designer will not allocate enough columns. With tables in 1NF, the designer does not need to speculate because the table expands vertically to accommodate any number of items.

Second Normal Form (2NF)

Although the table shown in Figure 5.6 is in 1NF, it still has problems. The table includes the following *functional dependencies*:

1. Item_Number functionally determines Item_Name. Therefore, item names, such as "26 in. Bicycle," are repeated several times. This data redundancy should be eliminated.

2. Cust_Code functionally determines Cust_Name.

3. The combination of SO_Number and Item_Number together functionally determine Item_Name, Qty_Ordered, Cust_Code, and Cust_Name.

Figure 5.6 Relation in First Normal Form (1NF)

Shaded_Attribute(s) = Primary Key

SALES_ORDERS

SO_Number	Item_Number	Item_Name	Qty_Ordered	Cust_Code	Cust_Name
1010	2010-0050	Formed Handlebar	2	WHEEL	Wheelaway Cycle Center
1010	1000-1	20 in. Bicycle	5	WHEEL	Wheelaway Cycle Center
1011	1002-1	24 in. Bicycle	5	ETC	Bikes Et Cetera
1011	1001-1	26 in. Bicycle	10	ETC	Bikes Et Cetera
1012	1003-1	20 in. Bicycle	5	WHEEL	Wheelaway Cycle Center
1012	1001-1	26 in. Bicycle	10	WHEEL	Wheelaway Cycle Center
1013	1001-1	26 in. Bicycle	50	IBS	Inter. Bicycle Sales
1014	1003-1	20 in. Bicycle	25	ETC	Bikes Et Cetera
1015	1003-1	20 in. Bicycle	25	WHEEL	Wheelaway Cycle Center
1016	3961-1041	Tire Tube, 26 in.	5	ETC	Bikes Et Cetera
1016	3965-1050	Spoke Reflector	50	ETC	Bikes Et Cetera
1016	1003-1	20 in. Bicycle	5	ETC	Bikes Et Cetera
1016	1000-1	20 in. Bicycle	4	ETC	Bikes Et Cetera

These dependencies cause several problems, called **update anomalies**:

1. *Update.* A change to the name of any item requires not one change but several. Each row in which any item, such as the 26 in. Bicycle, appears must be changed if the description is updated.

2. *Inconsistent data.* Nothing is preventing an item from having several different names in different rows of the table.

3. *Additions.* If a user tries to add a new inventory item to the database, a problem arises. Since the primary key to the table is the item number *and* the sales order number, a user cannot add a new inventory item to the database unless it has a sales order. This is an impossible requirement for a business, which would want to have information about inventory items stored in its database before accepting orders to sell those inventory items.

4. *Deletions.* Deleting an inventory item from the database (by deleting its row) could cause the table to lose the information it has stored about all sales orders that contained that item.

These problems arise because we have an attribute, Item_Name that is dependent on a portion of the primary key, Item_Number, *not* on the entire key. Database designers call this problem a **partial dependency**.

A table is in **second normal form (2NF)** if it is in first normal form and has no partial dependencies; that is, no non-key attribute is dependent on only a portion of the primary key. An attribute is a **non-key attribute** if it is not part of the primary key. For instance, in Figure 5.5 (page 163), Item_Name, Quantity_Ordered, Cust_Code, and Cust_Name are non-key attributes.

A designer would perform two steps to get this 1NF table into 2NF. First, create a new table for each subset of the table that is partially dependent on a part of the composite primary key (that is, SO_Number and Item_Number). In this case, that procedure would yield two new tables, one with SO_Number as its primary key (a

SALES_ORDERS table) and another with Item_Number as its primary key (an IN-VENTORY_ITEMS table). Second, place each of the non-key attributes that are dependent on a part of the composite primary key into the table that now has a primary key that is the field on which the non-key attribute is partially dependent. For example, the Item_Name field is partially dependent on the Item_Number field portion of the composite primary key, so it would be moved into the new INVENTORY_ITEMS table. This transformation yields the three tables shown in Figure 5.7.

Figure 5.7 Relations in Second Normal Form (2NF)

With this set of three tables, the *update anomaly* problems mentioned earlier are resolved. Users can add inventory items without having a sales order by adding them to the table INVENTORY_ITEMS. Since item names are stored only once, the potential for inconsistencies no longer exists, and updates to names will require only one change. Finally, users can delete inventory items from the database and not lose any sales order information.

Third Normal Form (3NF)

Before proceeding to third normal form, we need one more definition. A **transitive dependency** exists in a table when a non-key attribute is functionally dependent on another non-key attribute (of course, the second non-key attribute will be dependent on the primary key). If you examine the table SALES_ORDERS in Figure 5.7, you will notice that the values in Cust_Name are functionally dependent on Cust_Code, which is a non-key attribute. Thus, a transitive dependency exists in this table.

Some of the customer names—Wheelaway Cycle Center, for example—are repeated several times. This transitive dependency causes these *update anomalies*:

1. *Update.* A change to the name of any customer could require not one change but several. The user would have to change each row in which any customer appears. For example, changing Wheelaway's name would require changing three rows in the SALES_ORDERS table.

2. *Inconsistent data.* Nothing in this design prevents users from entering several different names for a single customer.

3. *Additions.* A new customer cannot be added to the database unless the customer already has a sales order. Good internal control dictates that an authorized customer should exist *before* a sales order can be created for that customer.

4. *Deletions.* If a user deletes a sales order from the database, the name of a customer might be erased from the database.

These problems arise because the transitive dependency exists in the table SALES_ORDERS. To summarize, a table is in **third normal form (3NF)** if it is in second normal form and if it has no transitive dependencies.

Figure 5.8 contains the 3NF tables that are the final result of the normalization process. The tables in Figure 5.8 are free of the anomalies outlined earlier. Users can add customers without sales orders. Since customer names are stored only once, each customer will have only one name and updates to names will require only one change. Finally, users can delete customers from the database without regard to the sales order information.

Using Entity-Relationship Models

Although it is possible to create a workable database design using a bottom-up approach as previously described, most database professionals prefer to use a top-down approach, described in this section, as a first step in creating a new database. Although the bottom-up approach is useful for checking the results obtained with a top-down approach, and the bottom-up approach is easier to learn and understand, the top-down approaches usually result in a better database design.

A **data model** depicts user requirements for data stored in a database. There are a number of approaches to data modeling, any of which can be used to implement top-down database design. The most popular data modeling approach is **entity-relationship modeling**, in which the designer identifies the important things (called **entities**) about which information will be stored[2] and then identifies how the things are related to each other (called **relationships**). Then the designer draws a diagram of the relational model. Because this diagram includes entities and relationships, it is called an **entity-relationship model**. You will often see "entity-relationship" abbreviated as "E-R." The **E-R diagram** (also called an **entity-relationship diagram**) reflects the system's key entities and the relationships among those entities. The E-R diagram represents the data model. Database designers use standard symbols when creating E-R diagrams; however, several sets of standard symbols do exist. This book uses one of the more popular sets of symbols, but you should keep in mind that you might see E-R diagrams in other books or in your practice of accounting that differ from the diagrams used here. Figure 5.9 (page 168) shows an E-R diagram in the form that we will be using in this book.

---

[2] Notice that this definition of entity—including events as it does—is broader than that introduced in Chapter 1.

Figure 5.8 Relations in Third Normal Form (3NF)

Shaded_Attribute(s)	= Primary Key

SALES_ORDERS

SO_Number	Cust_Code
1010	WHEEL
1011	ETC
1012	WHEEL
1013	IBS
1014	ETC
1015	WHEEL
1016	ETC

CUSTOMERS

Cust_Code	Cust_Name
ETC	Bikes Et Cetera
IBS	Inter. Bicycle Sales
RODEBYKE	Rodebyke Bic. & Mopeds
STANS	Stan's Cyclery
WHEEL	Wheelaway Cycle Center

INVENTORY_ITEMS

Item_Number	Item_Name
1000-1	20 in. Bicycle
1001-1	26 in. Bicycle
1002-1	24 in. Bicycle
1003-1	20 in. Bicycle
1280-054	Kickstand
2010-0050	Formed Handlebar
3050-2197	Pedal
3961-1010	Tire, 26 in.
3961-1041	Tire Tube, 26 in.
3965-1050	Spoke Reflector
3970-1011	Wheel, 26 in.

SALES_ORDER *line item* **INVENTORY**

SO_Number	Item_Number	Qty_Ordered
1010	2010-0050	2
1010	1000-1	5
1011	1002-1	5
1011	1001-1	10
1012	1003-1	5
1012	1001-1	10
1013	1001-1	50
1014	1003-1	25
1015	1003-1	25
1016	3961-1041	5
1016	3965-1050	50
1016	1003-1	5
1016	1000-1	4

Most E-R diagrams use rectangles, connecting lines, and diamonds. The rectangles represent entities and the connecting lines represent relationships. The diamonds are used to show the characteristics of relationships. In the E-R diagram shown in Figure 5.9, the entities include ORDERS, INVENTORY, CUSTOMERS, and SALES. The connecting lines show the five relationships in the data model. These relationships are between ORDERS and INVENTORY, ORDERS and CUSTOMERS, ORDERS and SALES, INVENTORY and SALES, and CUSTOMERS and SALES. The diamonds on the connecting lines provide some information about the relationships between the entities. For example, the relationship between ORDERS and CUSTOMERS occurs because orders are received from customers. Another database designer might have described this relationship as "place" because CUSTOMERS place ORDERS. Either description would be an acceptable way to describe this particular data model.

The first step in E-R modeling is to determine users' requirements for the database. This process is often incorporated into a process called *systems analysis* and is typically conducted by a person called a *systems analyst*. To discover user requirements, the systems analyst conducts interviews and observations and reviews existing system documentation. To document the existing system and the user's requirements for the new database, the analyst prepares narratives and diagrams, one of which is the E-R diagram.

Figure 5.9 Entity-Relationship (E-R) Diagram

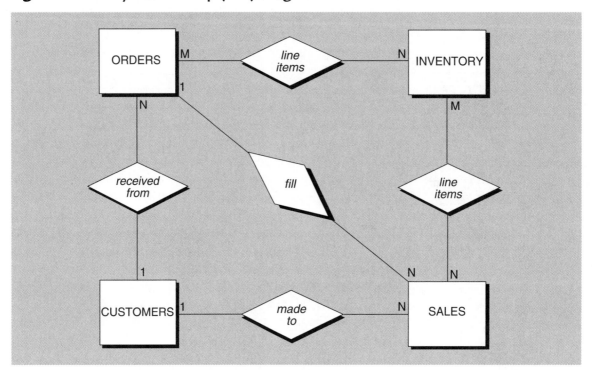

Part of the information collected by the analyst is the structure of the data being used in the activities of the organization. This information leads the analyst through three steps. First, the analyst identifies the entities. Second, the analyst identifies the relationships between the entities and learns more about the characteristics of those relationships. Finally, the analyst uses the information about the entities and relationships (which is summarized in the E-R diagram) to create database tables and define connections among those tables.

Identify Entities

The analyst first examines existing system documentation and talks with users to learn which entities are important to the business processes about which the database will store information. Any "thing" that is an important element in the business process can be modeled as an entity. If only one instance of a thing occurs in the process, it is not modeled as an entity. Entities become tables and if there is only one instance of a thing, you do not need a table to store information about it. For example if a small business has one sales manager, it does not need a table to store information about its sales managers. A larger company with several sales managers would probably want to use a table because it has multiple instances of the thing "sales manager."

Accounting researchers have identified categories of entities that commonly occur in systems that track accounting information. These categories include resources, events, agents, and locations. **Resources** are assets (tangible or intangible) that the company owns. Resources include things such as inventory, equipment, and cash. **Events** are occurrences related to resources that are of interest to the business. Events include orders, sales, and purchases. Agents are people or organizations that participate in events. Agents can be part of the company or they can be external to the company. Agents include customers, employees, and vendors. **Locations** are places or physical locations at which events occur, resources are stored, or agents participate in events. Many accounting systems researchers argue that a location owned by the company is a resource, but experts are not in complete agreement on that point. Locations can include countries, cities, stores, warehouses, and more precise categories such as bin or pallet.

Although many accountants find these categories to be useful organizing devices for thinking about entities, others simply identify entities without using these categories. The entity categories do not lead to any different treatment in the data modeling process. For example, an agent entity is modeled in an E-R diagram in the same way an event entity is.

Identify the Relationships That Connect the Entities

Next, the analyst identifies the relationships between and among the entities. The *relationships* are shown in the E-R diagram as connecting lines with diamonds that describe the nature of the relationship. Figure 5.9 shows an E-R diagram of a simple sales and order entry database. In this figure you can see that relationships can exist between:

- two events, such as SALES *fill* ORDERS.
- an agent and an event, such as ORDERS are *received from* CUSTOMERS or SALES are *made to* CUSTOMERS.
- a resource and an event, such as ORDERS have *line items* INVENTORY or INVENTORY line items SALE.

Characteristics of Relationships

The diamond on the left side of the diagram in Figure 5.9 includes one characteristic of the relationship between ORDERS and CUSTOMERS. It shows that an order is received from a customer. The formal notation for this relationship characteristic is "ORDERS are *received from* CUSTOMERS."

A person reading the diagram could be confused by the diagram and want to interpret its meaning as "CUSTOMERS are *received from* ORDERS." However, most users who are familiar with the business processes being modeled can usually interpret the diagram correctly because they know the context of the relationship.

In addition to the description of the relationship that appears in the diamond, each relationship has a characteristic, called a **cardinality** that shows the degree to which each entity participates in the relationship. A full discussion of cardinalities is quite complex and not really necessary for an understanding of E-R modeling. However, you should know that the discussion here is limited in scope and that you might see different notations used in practice to describe relationship cardinalities.

The **maximum cardinality** is a measure of the highest level of participation that one entity can have in another entity. In the cardinality notation used in this book, a maximum cardinality can have a value of "one" or "many." A value of one is shown as the digit "1" and a value of many is shown as the letter "N" or the letter "M." For example, the letter "N" beneath the ORDERS rectangle in Figure 5.9 means that each customer may have many (more than one) orders and the "1" above the CUSTOMERS rectangle means that each order is from only one customer. In reading this E-R diagram, one would say "the relationship between customers and orders is one-to-many." One could also say "the relationship between orders and customers is many-to-one."

In a relational database, a relationship between the entities will be one of three types (common notation is shown in parentheses): one-to-many (1:N), many-to-many (M:N), or one-to-one (1:1). A many-to-one (N:1) relationship is the same as a one-to-many relationship, but stated in reverse.

In Figure 5.9 (page 168), you can see that each inventory item can have many orders, and each order can have many inventory items. This relationship has a many-to-many (M:N) cardinality. The relationship between INVENTORY and SALES is also many-to-many (there can be many inventory items on a sale and each sale can have many inventory items).

The third cardinality, one-to-one, means that an instance of an entity is related to one specific instance of another entity. This cardinality is easier to visualize using tables. Recall that each entity in the E-R model will become a table in the database. If two entities (tables) have a one-to-one relationship, each row in the first table will be related to one (and only one) row in the second table. An analyst that identifies a one-to-one relationship will, in most cases, simply combine the two tables into one.

The E-R diagram in Figure 5.9 reflects only part of an organization's business processes. An organization would require more data than just the customers, orders, inventory, and sales shown in this diagram. It would require data related to purchases, payments, payroll, and so on. Before going on to the next step, the analyst would confirm the accuracy of the E-R diagram with the people in the organization who will use the database.

Create Tables and Relationships

Having completed a data model that captures users' requirements, the analyst continues the data modeling process transforming the data model into a *logical* design for the database. This logical design takes the user requirements and converts them into a usable database. This logical design of a database includes a definition of each table in the database and how each table is related to other tables in the database.

Figure 5.10 is the logical design for our database. It is the data model in Figure 5.9, implemented in a relational database. The analyst can create this logical model from the E-R diagram by following these five steps:

1. Create a relational table for each entity. In Figure 5.10 CUSTOMERS, INVENTORY, ORDERS, and SALES are the entity tables.

2. Determine a *primary key* for each of the entity tables. The primary key must uniquely identify each row within the table and it must contain a value in each row. A customer code or number (Cust_Code), stock number (Item_Number), and order number (SO_Number) are commonly used to identify customers, items of inventory, and orders. The SALES table uses the date (YYMMDD) followed by a three-digit sequentially assigned serial number (the *unique* portion of the Shipment_Number) to represent each shipment record (row).

3. Determine the *attributes* for each of the entities. An attribute is sometimes called a *field* and is represented in a database table as a column. The accepted custom among relational database designers is to put the primary key attribute in the first column of the table. User requirements determine the other attributes. The other columns shown in these entity tables contain typical attributes, but you will see different attributes included in databases used by different organizations.

4. Implement the relationships among the entities. This is accomplished by assuring that the primary key in one table also exists as an attribute in every table (entity)

Figure 5.10 Relational Database

Shaded_Attribute(s) = Primary Key

CUSTOMERS

Cust_Code	Cust_Name	Cust_City	Credit_Limit	Sales_YTD
ETC	Bikes Et Cetera	Elgin	10000.00	9561.55
IBS	Inter. Bicycle Sales	New York	5000.00	4191.18
RODEBYKE	Rodebyke Bic. & Mopeds	San Jose	2000.00	1142.50
STANS	Stan's Cyclery	Hawthorne	10000.00	8330.00
WHEEL	Wheelaway Cycle Center	Campbell	10000.00	6854.00

INVENTORY

Item_Number	Item_Name	Qty_On_Hand	Unit_Cost	Unit_Price
1000-1	20 in. Bicycle	247	55.00	137.50
1001-1	26 in. Bicycle	103	60.00	150.00
1002-1	24 in. Bicycle	484	60.00	150.00
1003-1	20 in. Bicycle	4	24.37	60.93
1280-054	Kickstand	72	6.50	16.25
2010-0050	Formed Handlebar	90	4.47	11.25
3050-2197	Pedal	23	0.75	1.88
3961-1010	Tire, 26 in.	42	1.45	3.13
3961-1041	Tire Tube, 26 in.	19	1.25	3.13
3965-1050	Spoke Reflector	232	0.29	0.63
3970-1011	Wheel, 26 in.	211	10.50	25.00

ORDERS

SO_Number	Cust_Code	Cust_Order_Number	SO_Date
1010	WHEEL	453	061205
1011	ETC	347	061205
1012	WHEEL	56-6	061205
1013	IBS	3422	061205
1014	ETC	778	061205
1015	WHEEL	5673	061206
1016	ETC	3345	061206

SALES

Shipment_Number	Invoice_Number	SO_Number	Cust_Code
021207028	35	1011	ETC
021207042	36	1012	WHEEL

ORDERS *line items* **INVENTORY**

SO_Number	Item_Number	Qty_Ordered	Sales_Price
1010	1000-1	5	137.50
1010	2010-0050	2	11.25
1011	1001-1	10	127.50
1011	1002-1	5	150.00
1012	1003-1	5	60.93
1012	1001-1	10	127.50
1013	1001-1	50	78.30
1014	1003-1	25	37.42
1015	1003-1	25	37.42
1016	1003-1	5	60.93
1016	3965-1050	50	33.00
1016	3961-1041	5	3.13
1016	1000-1	4	137.50

SALES *line items* **INVENTORY**

Shipment_Number	Item_Number	Qty_Shipped
021207028	1001-1	8
021207028	1002-1	4
021207042	1001-1	5

for which there is a relationship specified in the *entity-relationship diagram*. Implementing the many-to-many relationships requires the creation of tables, called **relationship tables** or **junction tables**. This is necessary because relational DBMSs do not have the ability to model a many-to-many relationship directly. Each many-to-many relationship must be modeled as a pair of one-to-many relationships. For example, the SALES and INVENTORY relationship (M:N) is modeled as two (1:N) relationships. One of these relationships is between SALES and the relationship table titled "SALES *line items* INVENTORY" and the other is between INVENTORY and "SALES *line items* INVENTORY." Relationship tables always have composite primary keys that are a combination of the primary keys of the entity tables that participate in the M:N relationship.

5. Determine the *attributes*, if any, for each of the relationship tables. Some relationship tables only need the columns that make up their composite primary keys. Other relationship tables provide a way to store interesting information that depends on the combination of the attributes contained in their composite primary keys. The two relationship tables shown in Figure 5.10 each have additional attributes. For example, the "SALES *line items* INVENTORY" table includes the attribute Qty_Shipped. This attribute stores the quantity of each item on a particular sale. This value is determined jointly by the Shipment_Number and the Item_Number, the two attributes that make up the table's composite primary key.

Select and Implement the Database Management System (DBMS)

Because the database itself may be quite complex, the programs that manage it are also complex and can be expensive to develop. For this reason, most companies do not design their own *DBMS*; instead, they purchase such systems.

Commercially developed DBMSs are available for all sizes of computers, from supercomputers to personal computers. Popular DBMS packages include Access, DB2, IMS, MySQL, Oracle, Paradox, SQL Server, Sybase, and R:BASE. The price and power of the DBMS decline as the computer on which the software will operate gets smaller. In addition to cost and speed, selection considerations include functionality (such as query languages supported, report writing tools, form building tools) and compatibility with existing hardware and software.

Once a DBMS has been chosen, it must be implemented. The supplement *Acquiring, Developing, and Implementing Accounting Information Systems* that accompanies this text describes the steps required to implement any system. These steps include such things as installing the DBMS, testing the new database design with a sample of data, completing documentation, training users, and converting to using the new DBMS. Coding of the logical model into the DBMS—roughly equivalent to writing the programs for an application—is the main activity undertaken during implementation of a DBMS.

AIDING MANAGEMENT DECISION MAKERS WITH INTELLIGENT SYSTEMS

Using relational databases can help organizations track accounting information better, but a major benefit of having information stored in a database is that it is easier to access the information in new and creative ways. This type of information access can help managers make better decisions. Each day hundreds of thousands of decisions are made in business organizations. In this section you will learn about the information tools that can help decision makers: *decision support systems*, *executive information systems*, *group support systems*, *expert systems*, and *intelligent agents*.

As you learned earlier in this book, many decisions—particularly important decisions made by high-level management—are predominantly unstructured. Four levels of expertise can be applied to these decision situations:

- Managers can make the decision without assistance, using their expertise.

- The decision maker can be assisted by problem-solving aids such as manuals and checklists. For example, an information systems auditor will use an *internal control questionnaire* to evaluate controls to ensure a comprehensive review.

- The checklists and manuals might be automated. An automated internal control questionnaire can incorporate thousands of factors, relationships, and rules of thumb. This automated expertise can assist the auditor in arriving at a conclusion regarding the effectiveness of the controls.

- The system itself can replace the decision maker, as when an *expert system* monitors the activity in a production line and adjusts the machinery as required.

Decision Support Systems, Executive Information Systems, and Group Support Systems

A number of automated tools exist that can assist or replace the decision maker. Technology Summary 5.4 (pages 174–175) describes *decision support systems (DSS)* and *executive information systems (EIS)*, both of which assist the manager by combining current and historical facts, numerical data, and statistics—from both inside and outside the organization—and by converting these data into information useful in making the decision.

Here is a comparison that shows the differences between a DSS and an EIS. A manager could use a spreadsheet—a typical component of a DSS—to calculate variances and to compare them to variances from a previous period. This information might help the manager measure current performance against budget. With the DSS, the decision maker prepares a presentation in a format that is suitable for *him or her* for *this* decision at *this* point in time. In contrast, an EIS would have its presentation formats programmed in advance. An executive using an EIS turns on his or her computer each morning and views a screen that contains icons for EIS applications that are available. An executive who wants to examine sales trends would click the "sales trends" icon. The EIS might ask some questions, such as the period of time and the geographical area to be used in the analysis, but the EIS would follow its programmed instructions to retrieve data and present the output, most likely in the form of graphs depicting sales trends. This sales trend information might alert the executive to some problem, that is, the *intelligence* step in a decision. To determine what to do, the executive might successively request more detailed information, a process known as "drill down."

DSS and EIS are similar in that neither tells the decision maker what to do; both simply provide views for interpreting the information. The knowledge and experience required to analyze the information, to make the judgments, and to take the actions required reside with the decision maker.

DSS and EIS help managers, who typically work alone, to make decisions. **Group support systems (GSS)**, also called **group decision support systems (GDSS)**, are computer-based systems that support collaborative intellectual work such as idea generation, elaboration, analysis, synthesis, information sharing, and decision making. GSS use technology to solve the time and place dimension problems associated with group work. That is, a GSS creates a "virtual meeting" for a group. While "attending" this meeting, members of the group work toward completion of their task and achievement of the group's objective(s).

Technology Summary 5.4

Decision Support Systems and Executive Information Systems

Decision support systems (DSS) are information systems that assist managers with unstructured decisions by retrieving and analyzing data for purposes of identifying and generating useful information. A DSS possesses interactive capabilities, aids in answering ad hoc queries, and provides data and modeling facilities (generally through the use of spreadsheet models and/or statistical analysis programs) to support non-

recurring, relatively unstructured decision making. The main components of a DSS appear in the accompanying figure. Notice that the data made available to the decision maker include both internal data from the enterprise database, and data obtained from outside the organization, such as Dow Jones financial information.

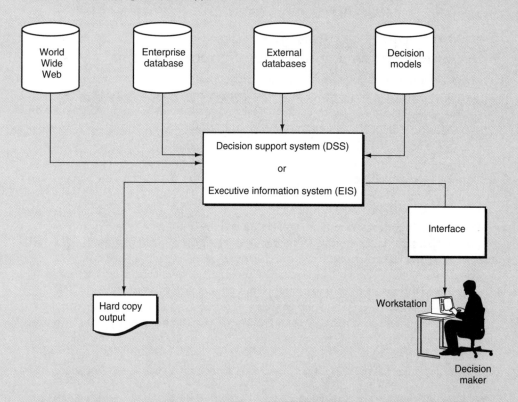

A DSS can provide the required relevant data and can model, simulate, and perform "what-if" analysis. The DSS is superior to normal computer programs because a DSS can work on loosely defined tasks, in areas of high uncertainty, and in situations where user requirements and data are in a constant state of change.

Over the years, the term "DSS" has become synonymous with financial modeling and ad hoc querying. To support managers at the top echelon of the organization, **executive informa-**

tion systems (EIS) have been developed (these also are called **executive support systems** or **ESS**). These systems, which can be considered a subset of DSS, combine information from the organization and the environment, organize and analyze the information, and present the information to the manager in a form that assists in decision making.

Most EISs have graphical user interfaces (GUIs). The typical EIS presents output using text, graphics, and color; has multiple presentation formats; and can be tailored and customized for each executive. The complexity of these systems has greatly increased in recent years as they have expanded to include the support of crisis management and as sources of information for dealing with media questioning during such crises. This expansion in complexity has been dovetailed with the development of data warehouses and can be used to search for data needed to answer questions during unexpected crises.

Although EIS originally were developed to support strategic-level managers and to relieve those managers of the burden of learning how to use a DSS, current EIS and ESS are virtually indistinguishable from DSS. Rather than concentrating on the name (DSS, EIS, or ESS) or the system's nature (GUI, color, preprogrammed), it is probably more useful to distinguish these systems by their *users* and their *purpose*. For example, if a system is used exclusively by upper management, it is an executive system.

Groupware, the software identified with GSS, focuses on such functions as e-mail, group scheduling, and document sharing. Technology Application 5.1 (page 176) describes PricewaterhouseCoopers' use of distributed database technology to facilitate audit team work.

Expert Systems

Many decision-making situations can benefit from an even higher level of support than that provided by the DSS, EIS, or GSS. Managers can use **expert systems (ES)** in these situations. Expert systems may be appropriate in situations that have the following characteristics:

- Decisions are extremely complex.
- Consistency of decision making is desirable.
- The decision maker wants to minimize time spent making the decision while *maximizing* the quality of the decision.
- Expert decision makers exist that are familiar with the knowledge context of the decision and their knowledge can be captured efficiently and modeled via computer software effectively.

Technology Application 5.2 (page 177) presents examples of expert systems used to assist in decision making. Companies sometimes use experts systems as a part of a downsizing strategy. In downsizing, much of an organization's collective knowledge and experience can be lost because employees with the most seniority and the highest pay are often the first to go. These employees often are exactly the people who have accumulated vast amounts of knowledge about the business and expertise in making decisions using that knowledge. The increasing complexity of the business organization and its operations along with the trend toward decentralization also prompt companies to implement expert systems. Expert systems can be used to:

- Capture and retain the expertise of the retiring employees.
- Distribute the expertise to the remaining employees.
- Distribute the expertise to the employees who cannot obtain timely access to the expert.
- Train new employees.
- Guide human experts by suggesting trends, asking questions, highlighting exceptions, and generally serving as an "electronic colleague."

Technology Application 5.1

Using Distributed Database Systems to Automate the Audit at PricewaterhouseCoopers

At the heart of PricewaterhouseCoopers Team-Mate software is a relational database that permits sorting and filtering of information by individual audit team members. The system captures, shares, and organizes audit-related information for the firm's auditors. In addition to the underlying database, TeamMate includes software modules developed at PricewaterhouseCoopers (PwC) along with spreadsheet and word processing programs. TeamMate runs on laptop computers used by PwC audit staff members.

At the start of the audit engagement, team members are given access rights to an intranet server that contains a master copy of the audit workpapers. These files include the audit programs—a listing of the work to be performed during the audit engagement. As auditors complete portions of the audit program, they update the shared set of audit workpapers, documenting the audit work performed, the conclusions reached, and any issues discovered. Once the workpapers are updated, the system automatically records electronic information related to when and by whom the workpapers were updated. Through the intranet server—*regardless of their location anywhere in the world*—all audit team members have virtually instant access to the updated versions of the audit workpapers. These updated versions reflect changes made to the workpapers by *all members of the audit engagement team*. Audit partners and managers—again, regardless of their location—can review workpapers and monitor the progress of the audit. PwC reports that TeamMate has enhanced the *efficiency* and *effectiveness* of its audit engagements. Additionally, PwC believes that TeamMate dramatically improves technical proficiency and accelerates ca-

reer development of new staff. Key features of TeamMate include:

1. TeamMate links elements of the workpapers together. For example, audit program steps are linked to the documentation of the work performed, and the work performed is linked together, regardless of its form—spreadsheet, word processing documents, etc. The linking provides for complete, consistent, and accessible audit documentation.

2. The status of the audit program (in progress, completed, and reviewed) is centrally reported to facilitate control by audit partners and managers. Additionally, the audit workpapers can be locked by the partners and managers to prohibit alteration after they have been reviewed.

3. TeamMate records and classifies open issues (problems, recommended financial statement adjustments, potential consulting services). These are centrally maintained and reported to permit timely resolution.

4. PwC's generic audit programs are stored on its intranet server. These programs are tailored for each audit engagement. Then, in each successive year, the previous audit files are automatically brought forward, updated, and used for the current year's audit.

5. Client files and documents also can be downloaded or scanned to the auditor's laptop computer for analysis and inclusion in the audit workpapers.

6. Paper documents and working papers are reduced or eliminated.

Source: "TeamMate98," PricewaterhouseCoopers, http://www.pwc.com, June 1999.

The benefits derived—increased productivity, improved decision making, competitive advantage, and so on—from an expert system must exceed the costs of development and maintenance of the system. A company also must be able to identify and extract the ex-

Technology Application 5.2

Uses of Expert Systems for Decision Making

Case 1

A product developed by Decision Support Systems, *The Expert Business Impact Analysis System*, provides an appraisal of business risks and recommendations for strategies to cope with said risks. The focus is on global risks that can threaten a company's operations. Once a key risk is identified, managers can use what-if analysis to identify the best defensive strategy.

Case 2

Contingency planning (which is discussed in greater detail in Chapter 8) is the process an organization goes through to ensure that it can get its information systems and operations up and running after experiencing a failure or disaster. Strohl Systems provides a package that aids in the assessment of potential risks and alternative strategies for preventing business interruptions. The software also aids the decision maker in putting together a contingency plan for recovering from outages, failures, and disasters that cannot be adequately controlled via prevention strategies.

Case 3

Business Foundations Software's *Internal Operations Risk Analysis* is a system that assesses internal control risks. This expert system uses 180 interview questions to identify and assess control strengths and weaknesses in an organization's business operations. The software provides an overall rating of controls strength that can be broken down by operational area. PricewaterhouseCoopers offers a similar system named *Controls.*

Source: Joel Siegel and Anique Qureshi, "The CPA and the Computer: Risk Analysis and Management Software and the CPA," *CPA Journal On-line,* http://www.nysscpa.org/cpajournal/1997/1297/dept/D651297.htm, December 1997.

pertise required and to enter that expertise into the expert system's knowledge base. Therefore, companies must carefully choose the areas in which they use expert systems.

Neural networks (NN) are computer hardware and software systems that mimic the human brain's ability to recognize patterns or predict outcomes using less than complete information. For example, NN are used to recognize faces, voices, and handwritten characters. NN also are used to sort good apples from bad, to detect fraudulent users of credit cards, and to manage investment funds.

Given a volume of data, an expert system makes a decision by using the knowledge it has acquired from outside experts. Neural networks, on the other hand, derive their knowledge from the data. For example, an expert system designed to predict bankruptcy would have a knowledge base that included the rules that experts have used to predict bankruptcy. A rule might be: "If the current ratio is less than X and interest has not been paid on long-term debt, then bankruptcy is likely." A neural network, on the other hand, would be given data on firms that have gone bankrupt and firms that have not (using an expert to decide which data are relevant). The neural network sifts through the data and decides how to determine whether a firm will go bankrupt. The neural network develops its own knowledge base. This knowledge base includes an understanding of the patterns underlying the data and the logic necessary to reconstruct the patterns to solve future problems. Technology Application 5.3 (page 178) offers some examples of neural networks used in business today. The ability of NN to discover patterns in large quantities of data makes them useful in decision making, performing well in areas that are difficult for ES, DSS, or EIS.

Technology Application 5.3

Uses of Neural Networks

These examples of neural networks (NN) can give you an understanding of how they operate and how useful they can be:

- At Signet Bank, neural networks read and automatically process student loan applications and canceled checks.
- A neural network helps manage the Fidelity Disciplined Equity Fund, a fund that has consistently beat the Standard & Poor's 500 Stock Index.
- Neuroscope is a neural network diagnostic tool that provides early warning of failure in industrial machinery.
- Foster Ousley Conley uses a neural network-based system for residential real estate appraisal. The system performs better than humans because it can review data from hundreds of houses and analyze the data in many different ways.

The following are accounting and auditing applications of neural networks:

- At Mellon Bank's Visa and MasterCard operations, neural networks outperform expert systems—and the experts themselves—in detecting credit card fraud. Since the neural network can learn by experience, it can find incidences of fraud *not anticipated by an expert*.
- Neural networks can be used to forecast a client's earnings. By comparing this forecast to actual results, the auditor can make a judgment as to the reasonableness of the actual results. The forecasted earnings also can indicate to the auditor if the client is likely to continue as a going concern.
- A cost accountant/consultant can use a neural network to determine optimal resource allocation and production schedules. The manipulation of the hundreds of variables and constraints has traditionally been undertaken using operations research models.
- The IRS in Taiwan is using a neural network to determine the likelihood of tax evasion and the necessity of further investigation.

Neural networks have become so common that they are emerging as the tool of choice for fraud detection and order checking. Future applications will likely move increasingly toward more intelligent versions that will require even less user intervention.

Sources: "An Interview with Industry: Marge Sherauld, Vice President, Ward Systems Group, Inc.," *AI/ES Update* 6(2) (1997): 2; Gene Bylinsky, "Computers that Learn by Doing," *Fortune* (September 6, 1993): 96–102; Kenneth O. Cogger, "A Primer on Neural Networks," *AI/ES Update* 6(2) (1997): 3–6; Harlan L. Etheridge and Richard C. Brooks, "Neural Networks: A New Technology," *The CPA Journal* (March 1994): 36–39, 52–55; Rebecca Chung-Fern Wu, "Integrating Neurocomputing and Auditing Expertise," *Managerial Auditing Journal* 9(3) (1994): 20–26.

Intelligent Agents

The greatest growth in intelligent systems currently underway is the development and application of *intelligent agents*. An **intelligent agent** is a software component integrated into a *decision support system* or other software tool (such as word processing, spreadsheet, or database packages). An intelligent agent might provide automated assistance or advice on the use of the software in to which it is embedded, identify factors that should be considered when using a system for decision making, or present a list of common responses made by other users. Most *intelligent agents* are designed to learn from the actions of the system's user and to respond based on the user's inputs or usage patterns. Technology Application 5.4 discusses the use of *intelligent agents* in the TurboTax tax compliance software package.

Technology Application 5.4

Use of Intelligent Agents in TurboTax

One of the most promising areas for the use of *intelligent agents* is helping novice decision makers use specialized software packages. One example of such use occurs in the tax return preparation software package, TurboTax. TurboTax uses *intelligent agents* to achieve three objectives: (1) support completing the entry of personal tax information, (2) use the available information to identify additional possible tax deductions, and (3) identify items that might trigger an audit of the return.

Support for Information Entry: Two agents are used to support the information entry process. The first agent monitors the information entered into the individual's tax return to control which questions are asked of the user. This prevents the software from asking questions that are not relevant to the individual's particular return. The second agent displays "frequently asked questions" on the margin along with explanations and answers as the user answers questions and enters information. This saves the user time by anticipating the questions the user might have while entering information.

Missing Tax Deductions: The agent for tax deductions monitors the individual's return and watches for patterns in the return that suggest legitimate tax deductions that the user might have missed. These patterns are based on historical information about tax returns and the relationships that TurboTax researchers identified among taxpayer activities. When the user is finished entering information, the system prompts the user for potential missing deductions.

Audit Flags: When the user is finished entering the information into the tax return and has a completed return, the audit flag agent looks for patterns in the information that might trigger an audit by the IRS. The user can review the information flagged before completing the return.

Source: *User's Guide TurboTax: Tax Year 1998* (Tucson, AZ: Intuit, Inc., 1998).

Here is a summary of what you have read in this section regarding systems that provide intelligence-based assistance to the management decision maker.

- To overcome the roadblocks to quality decision making, managers use decision support systems (DSS), executive information systems (EIS), group support systems (GSS), expert systems (ES), neural networks (NN) and intelligent agents.

- A DSS structures the available data to provide information about alternative courses of action without offering a solution. DSS work well with unstructured or semi-structured problems that have a quantifiable dimension.

- An EIS uses menus, graphics, and color to provide a friendly interface to the DSS for executives who want to minimize their interaction with the system.

- A GSS facilitates group interaction and group consensus-building.

- An ES applies expertise extracted from a human expert to provide specific recommendations on problems or decisions.

- Both a DSS and an ES can assist a user in problem solving, but in different ways. A DSS is a *passive tool*; it depends on the human user's knowledge and ability to provide the right data to the system's decision model. An ES is an *active* teacher or partner that can guide the user in deciding what data to enter and in providing hints about further actions that are indicated by the analysis to date.

- Neural networks supplement the expert system in areas where expertise has not yet been captured. By examining the data, the NN can identify and replicate the patterns that exist.

- Expert systems can automate portions of the decision-making activity. They can function independently and actually make the decision or they can assist the decision maker and recommend a course of action. The goal of ES is not to replace people. These systems make it possible for valuable expertise to be available in multiple locations.

- Intelligent agents can be embedded in software to help simplify or improve effective use of the software.

KNOWLEDGE MANAGEMENT

Susan O'Neill, deputy chief knowledge officer at PricewaterhouseCoopers, has stated that "Knowledge is what we're all about. All of our profitability and viability is about how good we are at leveraging the intellectual assets of our people and making that available to our clients." Indeed, a survey of 200 IT managers by *InformationWeek* shows that 94 percent of companies consider knowledge management strategic to their business or IT processes and that these companies are in the early stages of their knowledge-management efforts. Additional results reveal that, on average, companies are capturing only 45 percent of their intellectual capital.[3] A manager at Ernst & Young referred to knowledge management as the single biggest problem faced by the firm in trying to maintain the quality of service expected by its customers.[4]

Knowledge management is the process of capturing, storing, retrieving, and distributing the knowledge of the individuals in an organization for use by others in the organization to improve the quality and efficiency of decision making across the firm. The primary enabler of *knowledge management* efforts is information technology, in particular, database technology.

Effective *knowledge management* means that an organization must be able to connect the knowledge of one individual with other individuals in the firm that need the same knowledge. This "capture and distribute" need is well served by databases. Employees can access a database to contribute knowledge or extract knowledge from anywhere in the world. Databases also provide a mechanism for orderly storage and retrieval of the captured knowledge.

Storing Knowledge in Data Warehouses

At the heart of most knowledge management systems is a series of interconnected databases. Two contemporary concepts that are driving new database management systems implementations in organizations: *data warehousing* and *data mining*.

Data warehousing is the use of information systems facilities to focus on the collection, organization, integration, and long-term storage of entity-wide data. Its purpose is to provide users with easy access to large quantities of varied data from across the organization for the sole purpose of improving decision-making capabilities. A data warehouse

---

[3] Michael Schrage, "Senile Dementia for Artificial Intelligentsia?" *Computerworld* (May 9, 1994): 39.
[4] Constance Nagle, "Research Opportunities in Knowledge Management," *Mid-Year Meeting of the Auditing Section of the American Accounting Association* (January 14, 1999).

is created by copying data periodically from the transaction databases into a separate database where it is stored. Managers can gain important insights by analyzing this collected historical data with multidimensional analytic tools and exploratory techniques called **data mining**, which is the exploration, aggregation, and analysis of large quantities of varied data from across the organization to better understand an organization's business processes, trends within these processes, and potential opportunities to improve the effectiveness and efficiency of the organization. The "warehouses of data" analogy makes sense as the software to support data storage is akin to physical warehousing approaches used to store and retrieve inventory—when an item needs to be restocked on the store shelf, some system must exist whereby the item can be located in the warehouse and retrieved.

Data warehousing and *data mining* opportunities are enabled and enriched through the use of *event-driven* systems, which are focused on capturing data that provide comprehensive views of business events. However, neither effective *event-driven* systems nor *data warehouses* are possible without effective implementation of database management systems. Both objectives are dependent on the massive data integration and data independence made possible through database technology. At the same time, both objectives also may be limited in the future if well-designed database models that provide for future information needs are not effectively implemented. This starts with the information requirements analysis and successful attainment of an understanding of all users' potential data and information needs.

Intelligent Agents for Knowledge Retrieval

Intelligent agents (which you learned about earlier in this chapter) have greatly improved the usability and efficiency of knowledge management systems. Many organizations store documents such as memoranda and letters that explain problem resolutions that might be reusable with other customers and clients. Retrieving these documents when needed is a difficult task, but one with which intelligent agents can help.

Intelligent agents can learn about an individual's work tasks and search behavior to better understand the information the user is likely to be seeking. The intelligent agent can refine the search and filter out extraneous information that can be retrieved during a search. The intelligence in these agents can dramatically decrease the search time.

Although intelligent agents tend to be the dominant form of intelligent system used for *knowledge management*, other intelligent system components can be used in knowledge management systems. *Neural networks* can recognize patterns within stored information and can help pull together associated documents to recognize common threads between various documents and other stored information. *Expert systems* and *decision support systems* also are being used as integrated components in knowledge management systems.

Creating a Knowledge Culture

One major barrier to developing effective knowledge management systems is a behavior or culture issue. Knowledge enters the knowledge management system only if individuals within an organization develop the habit of entering information into the system. Employees resist doing this for two primary reasons: (1) the fear that their information is wrong and entering incorrect information can have repercussions for the employee entering it, and (2) the failure to remember to enter information into the system when a problem has been resolved.

The fear element can be difficult to overcome. Although many individuals feel quite expert in a given subject, those people can be apprehensive about presenting their ideas in person or in writing. Entering information into a knowledge management system presents a similar situation because many of an individual's peers will see the information. When a good job is done, however, many more people will recognize the good job that has been done. This is the message organizations need to convey to encourage individuals within their organization to participate.

The other problem is getting employees into the habit of entering information into the knowledge management system. Some organizations record employees' participation in the knowledge management system and make that participation a part of employees' annual personnel review. This practice provides an extrinsic reward that encourages knowledge sharing.

As organizations continue to struggle with the *knowledge management* issue, the one thing that is clear is that strategically organizations cannot afford to ignore the issues. *Knowledge management* is but one of many issues faced by organizations today as they attempt to implement information technologies that support their strategic mission. The challenge is in determining a logical plan for the development of intelligent technologies that provide maximum support for the strategic mission of the organization.

SUMMARY

In this chapter you learned how organizations use databases to store information about business events such as sales, purchases, cash receipts, and cash disbursements. You learned how data from these events are recorded and processed in database systems.

You learned about the types of databases and the basic elements of database design that organizations use when they create databases for their accounting information, including normalization and entity-relationship data modeling. You learned that larger organizations store information in data warehouses and that managers can gain important insights by analyzing the information in data warehouses. You learned that many companies combine their data resources with decision support systems, executive information systems, group decision systems, and other advanced technology-based systems to improve decision making and operations.

REVIEW QUESTIONS

RQ 5-1 What are the key elements in the data hierarchy used in file management systems?

RQ 5-2 What are the differences between the type of data stored in master files and the type of data stored in business event files in a file management system?

RQ 5-3 What is data redundancy? Explain why it is important in business information systems.

RQ 5-4 How can storing the same facts in different computer files potentially affect the integrity of data?

RQ 5-5 What is the relationship between database management systems and ERP systems in large companies?

RQ 5-6 How are the applications and the database approaches to business event processing the same? How are they different?

RQ 5-7 What are the main advantages and disadvantages of using a database approach when designing and implementing business information systems?

RQ 5-8 What are the main ways users can access information stored in a DBMS?

RQ 5-9 What are the most important limitations of the applications approach to business information system design?

RQ 5-10 What are the four main elements in a relational database?

RQ 5-11 What is a primary key? What is a composite primary key?

RQ 5-12 What is the purpose of database normalization in a relational database?

RQ 5-13 Explain the concept of functional dependence.

RQ 5-14 What is an entity in an entity-relationship model? How does it differ from the concept of "entity" used in creating data flow diagrams?

RQ 5-15 What is the cardinality of a relationship in a relational database?

RQ 5-16 Explain when a database designer might use a relationship table in constructing a relational database.

RQ 5-17 What functions does the database administrator perform?

RQ 5-18 What factors distinguish a DSS from an EIS?

RQ 5-19 Describe the basic differences between an ES and an NN.

RQ 5-20 Why have knowledge management systems become so important to businesses in recent years?

RQ 5-21 What role do intelligent agents play in the operation of a knowledge management system?

DISCUSSION QUESTIONS

DQ 5-1 Identify three specific anomalies that could arise when using a file management system for payroll processing that would be solved by using a database system instead.

DQ 5-2 What is data independence? Why is it important in a comparison of file management systems to database management systems?

DQ 5-3 What are the differences between a logical view and a physical view of a database? Which would be more important for accountants who are involved in the design of a database that will store business event information?

DQ 5-4 What problems are solved by transforming a set of relational tables from second normal form to third normal form?

DQ 5-5 "The database approach to data management is a good alternative to using enterprise systems such as ERP and CRM." Do you agree? Discuss fully.

DQ 5-6 Why have object-oriented databases not replaced relational databases in business information system applications?

DQ 5-7 Demonstrate your understanding of some of the coding schemes discussed in Technology Summary 5.3 (pages 160–161) by indicating which type of code is represented by each of the following. You should be prepared to explain and defend your answers.

a. The student ID codes used at your college

b. MICR codes used by the banking industry

c. The customer codes used in Figure 5.3 (page 152).

DQ 5-8 What are the comparative advantages of the various data *coding* types discussed in Technology Summary 5.3 (pages 160–161) when applied to each of the following? Discuss fully.

a. Employee ID numbers

b. Customer ID numbers

c. Vendor ID numbers

d. The general ledger chart of accounts

PROBLEMS

Notes regarding Problems 1 through 5

These problems should be completed with a database software package, such as Access. For Problems 1 through 3, you may use data that you (or your instructor) have *downloaded* from an accounting database. Problem 4 provides an alternative to Problems 1 through 3 by using the database structure and sample data from Figure 5.10 (page 171). This problem also may be completed using the software of your choosing.

P 5-1 Before starting this problem, you should consult the customer master data record layout in Figure 5.2 (page 148).

Using the database software indicated by your instructor:

a. Create the "structure" for the records in the customer data. Use Figure 5.2 as a general guide to the data elements to be included in the customer records. However, observe the following specific requirements:

(1) For the customer address, use four separate fields, one each for street address, city, state, and ZIP Code.

(2) Provide for two additional data elements that are not shown in Figure 5.2 (because they normally would be accessed from other files)—open sales orders and accounts receivable balance.

b. If the software package supports a function to design input screens, create the screen format to be used for entering customer data.

c. Create example customer records and enter them into the database. Use a variety of names, street addresses, states/ZIP Codes, open sales order amounts, accounts receivable balances, and credit limits. (The number of records will be indicated by your instructor.)

d. Obtain a printout of the database records.

P 5-2 *Note*: This problem is a continuation of Problem 1.

a. "Search" the database for all customers with a specific ZIP Code (choose a code that is common to at least two, but not to all, of your customers).

Obtain a printout of your search algorithm and a list of customers whose records met the search parameter.

b. "Sort" the database in *descending* order of credit limit amounts. Obtain a printout of your sort algorithm and a printout of the sorted list of customers.

c. Create a "Customer Status Report" (the report title). Observe the following specific requirements:

(1) Provide column headings, in left-to-right order, for customer name, credit limit, accounts receivable balance, and open orders.

(2) For each state, print subtotals of the accounts receivable balance and open orders columns.

P 5-3 *Note*: This problem is a continuation of Problem 1.

a. Write a "program" to enter customer order *amounts* into the database and to have the system either warn the user if the new order places the customer over his or her credit limit or advise the user if the credit limit is not exceeded.

b. Test the program developed in (a) by entering the amounts of customer order business event data (use a variety of order amounts and different customers, such that you test all possible combinations of variables involved in the credit-checking algorithm). (The number of order business event data will be indicated by your instructor.) Obtain hard copy evidence of the results of your testing.

P 5-4 Using the database structure and sample data in Figure 5.10 (page 171) as a starting point (rather than Figure 5.2, page 148), complete the requirements of Problems 1 through 3 (or whatever portions of those problems your instructor may indicate).

P 5-5 Use the database structure and sample data in Figure 5.10 (page 171) to:

a. Combine the tables to obtain a complete record of orders and shipments. Obtain a printout of the algorithm(s) used to combine the tables and a printout of the list of these records.

b. Write a query that selects the inventory items for which there is *no* order. Obtain printouts of the algorithm(s) you used and a list of the selected records.

c. Select those orders that have not yet been shipped (that is, open orders). Obtain printouts of the algorithm(s) you used and a list of the selected records.

d. Calculate the total value (price) of the inventory items that are on hand. Sort the items in descending order of value. Obtain printouts of the algorithm(s) you used and a list of the selected records.

P 5-6 A local accounting firm that is growing rapidly has asked for your help. The firm has four partners who are primarily responsible for developing new business. In addition to developing new business, the partners are very busy with their management tasks, so the partners need an easy way to record their new business development activities that does not take too much time or effort. The managing partner of the firm has asked you to develop a database that will help the four partners track their new business development efforts. After talking with the managing partner, you decide that the following information needs to be included in the database:

1. Identity of the partner who is developing the new business lead, including the partner's first name, middle initial, last name, and four-digit employee ID number

2. Identity of the client or potential client for which the work would be done, including the company name, the key contact persons at the company, and the company's address (street address, city, state, and ZIP Code)

3. Information about each new business lead, including the type of new business (the firm classifies its work into the following categories: Audit, accounting, tax compliance, tax research, litigation support, and other consulting) and an estimate of the revenue the firm could derive from the new business

4. Information about each contact made to develop each new business lead, including the date of the contact, how much time the partner spent on the contact (in hours), and a brief summary of important points discussed

Required:

Using the bottom-up approach described in the chapter, design a set of relational database tables that will include all needed information. Be sure that the tables are in third normal form. Your instructor might have you create the tables and their relationships in a DBMS such as Microsoft Access and enter a few rows of data into each table.

P 5-7 Review the E-R diagram in Figure 5.11 and:

a. List the resources, events, agents, and locations that are represented as entities in this diagram (*Note:* You might not find all four types of entities in this diagram).

b. Write a description for each of the six relationships in the diagram. In your description, include the cardinalities. For example, you might describe the relationship between CUSTOMERS and ORDERS as: "Orders are made by customers. A customer may make many (N) orders, but each order is from only one (1) customer."

P 5-8 This problem asks you to research the literature for applications of expert systems.

Develop a paper that outlines the use of expert systems in accounting and tax applications. Your paper should describe at least two expert systems and should evaluate the benefits and costs of the systems. If the systems you identify are proposed systems, you should estimate the costs and evaluate the anticipated benefits. The number of pages will be indicated by your instructor.

P 5-9 Transform the database structure that appears in Figure 5.12 (page 188) into third normal form (3NF).

P 5-10 This problem asks you to research the database integration features of an ERP software package and a CRM software package.

Figure 5.11 Entity-Relationship (E-R) Diagram for Problem 5-7

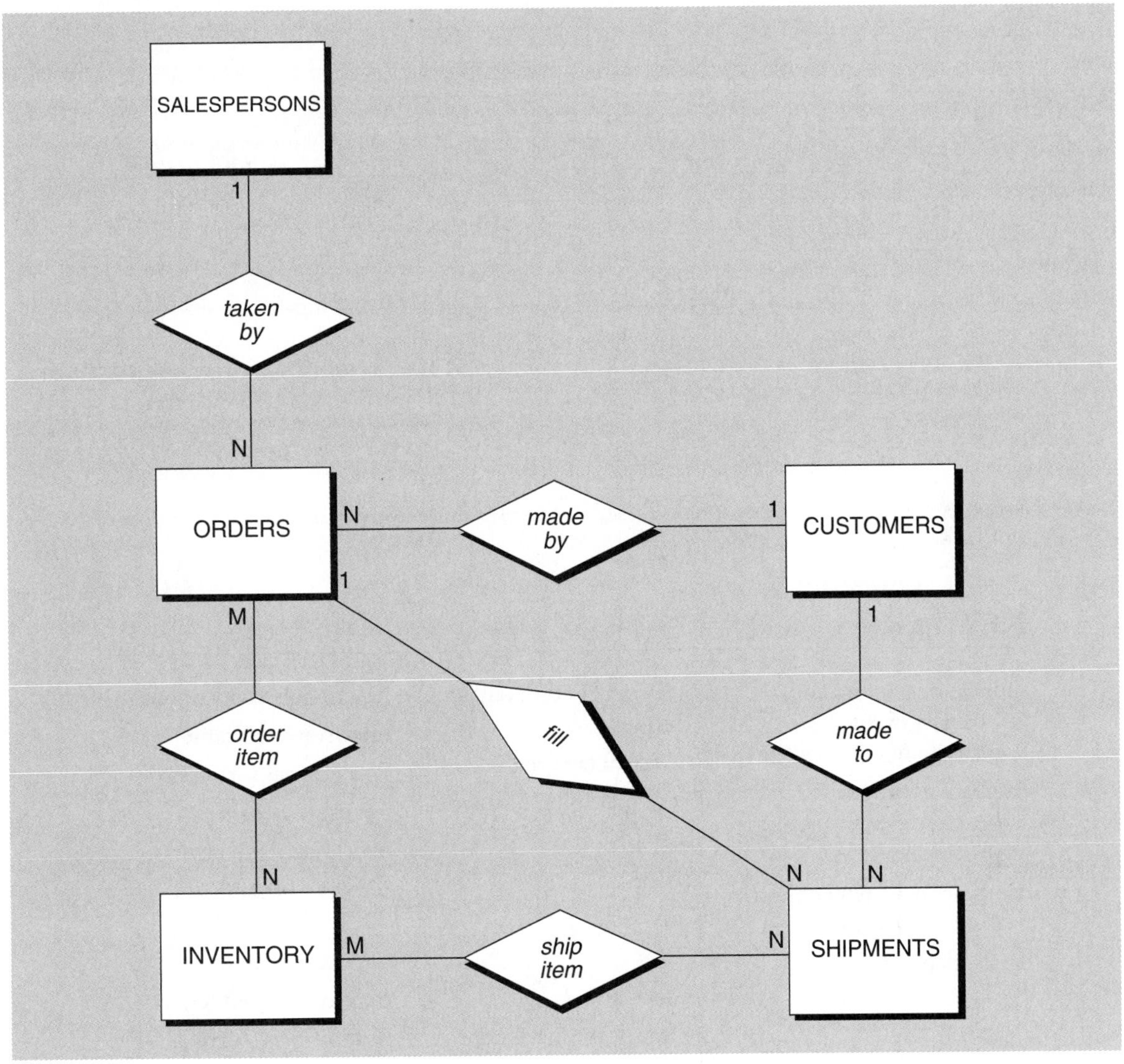

Using your school library or the Web, learn about the ERP products of SAP and the CRM products of Siebel. Select one specific product offered by each company and determine whether it includes its own database or must be used with an existing database. If the product requires an existing database, identify which DBMSs the product can use. Summarize your findings in a written report. The number of pages will be indicated by your instructor.

P 5-11 Technology Summary 5.3 (pages 160–161) uses examples of employee ID codes to illustrate five data coding types. Refer to those examples.

Create *customer* ID codes that illustrate each of the five coding schemes. Explain each of your examples.

Figure 5.12 Unnormalized Relation for Problem 5-9

| SOFTWARE | | | | | | | |
PACKID	TAGNUM	COMPID	INSTDATE	SOFTCOST	EMPNUM	EMPNAME	LOCATION
AC01	32808	M759	9/13/06	754.95	611	Dinh, Melissa	Accounting
DB32	32808	M759	12/13/06	380.00	611	Dinh, Melissa	Accounting
	37691	B121	06/15/06	380.00	124	Alvarez, Ramon	Sales
DB33	57772	C007	05/27/06	412.77	567	Feinstein, Betty	Info Systems
WP08	37691	B121	06/15/06	227.50	124	Alvarez, Ramon	Sales
	57772	C007	05/27/06	170.24	567	Feinstein, Betty	Info Systems
WP09	59836	B221	10/30/06	35.00	124	Alvarez, Ramon	Home
	77740	M759	05/27/06	35.00	567	Feinstein, Betty	Home

KEY:

PACKID = Software package identification code

TAGNUM = Fixed asset inventory tag number

COMPID = Computer model

INSTDATE = Date software was installed on the computer

SOFTCOST = Cost of the particular package installed

EMPNUM = Employee identification code

EMPNAME = Employee name

LOCATION = Location of the computer

Source: Table and data adapted from Philip J. Pratt and Joseph J. Adamski, *Database Systems Management and Design*, 3rd ed. (Danvers, MA: Boyd & Fraser Publishing Company, 1994): 218.

KEY TERMS

applications approach to business event processing

database approach to business event processing

database management system (DBMS)

data independence

schema

subschema

query language

data manipulation language (DML)

logical database view

physical database storage

hierarchical database model

child records

parent records

network database model

relational database model

object-oriented database model

abstract data types

object-relational databases

tables

queries

forms

reports

primary key

composite primary key

classifying

coding

sequential coding

serial coding

block coding

significant digit coding

hierarchical coding

mnemonic coding

self-checking digit code

normal forms

anomalies

functionally dependent

unnormalized table

first normal form (1NF)

update anomalies

partial dependency

second normal form (2NF)

non-key attribute

transitive dependency

third normal form (3NF)

data model

entity-relationship modeling

entities

relationships

entity-relationship model

E-R diagram

entity-relationship diagram

resources

events

agents

locations

cardinality

maximum cardinality

relationship tables

junction tables

decision support systems
(DSS)

executive information
systems (EIS)

executive support systems
(ESS)

group support systems
(GSS)

group decision support
systems (GDSS)

groupware

expert systems (ES)

neural networks (NN)

intelligent agent

knowledge management

data warehousing

data mining

Relational Databases and SQL

From 1997 to 2000 employee theft in U.S. stores jumped 34 percent to roughly $12.85 billion, while shoplifting losses rose a comparatively modest 14 percent to around $10.15 billion. Further, while shoplifting cost U.S. store owners an average of $158.86 per incident in 1999, the typical theft total for an employee was over six times higher at $1,004.35.[1]

Famous Footwear was incurring far greater rates of loss in its Madison Street (Chicago) location than what these national numbers portray. Employees would pull ruses such as billing a friend for a $2 bottle of shoe polish instead of $50 for a pair of shoes to fake out monitoring cameras by creating the illusion of a properly completed sale. To fend off the skyrocketing costs of such thefts, Famous Footwear began using its database of sales event information along with data mining techniques to identify patterns of sales behavior (such as unusually large numbers of refunds or voids, repeated sales of inexpensive items, etc.) that would aid in identifying employees who were likely engaging in such fraudulent transactions. The Madison Street store's inventory losses were quickly cut by 50 percent; in one store the manager actually turned herself in, assuming that she would be caught by the new data tracking and monitoring program. In this chapter, we extend our discussion of integrated databases and the value of enterprise-wide database information.

Learning Objectives

- To understand the techniques used to model complex accounting phenomena in an entity-relationship diagram.

- To develop entity-relationship diagrams that model effective accounting database structures using the Resources, Events, Agents (REA) approach.

- To recognize the components of relational tables and the keys to effective relational database design.

- To understand the use of SQL commands to create relational tables during implementation of the model.

- To be able to manipulate relational tables to extract the necessary data during decision making.

---

[1] The information for this vignette was primarily drawn from C. Coleman, "Sticky Fingers—As Thievery by Insiders Overtakes Shoplifting, Retailers Crack Down," *The Wall Street Journal* (September 8, 2000): A1, A6.

In this chapter we describe the REA (Resources, Events, Agents) approach for developing models of accounting databases and using those models to build relational databases. We also describe SQL, a database query language used to construct and manipulate relational databases. At the conclusion of your study of this chapter you should understand how enterprise databases, including database controls, are constructed and used in modern organizations.

SYNOPSIS

In this chapter, you will learn to develop more complex entity-relationship diagrams, integrate the REA concepts with E-R diagrams, create and manipulate relational databases with the SQL query language, and integrate control procedures into the database design. These advanced database techniques provide the foundation for understanding how *ERP systems* are constructed and how they function in a business environment. These advanced database skills also will aid you in designing effective accounting information systems, finding the data you need to perform accounting tasks, and creating report forms that provide your data in an easy-to-use format.

INTRODUCTION

In earlier chapters, you learned about the importance of well-designed information systems and database management systems to the effective support of decision making in organizations. You learned how to create data models using both bottom-up and top-down approaches and learned about alternative types of database management systems.

In this chapter, our goal is to increase your knowledge of database management systems, data modeling, database management systems implementation, and query languages. We will begin with a more in-depth discussion of *entity-relationship (E-R) modeling* and the REA approach to designing data models for accounting systems. This discussion is followed by an exploration of the key components and concepts underlying relational database management systems and how to build a working set of relational tables from an *E-R model*. We will then examine the core commands in the SQL query language for purposes of creating and manipulating relational databases. Finally, we discuss security and ethics-related issues surrounding database management systems.

We have discussed the importance of data to organizations in the information age. At the same time we have noted a shift in the focus of organizations from using information for operational control toward the use of information in decision support applications. Information systems today must effectively collect, organize, and integrate the data necessary to support decision making. The successful accountant of tomorrow will be the one who can manage the creation of *data warehouses* and effectively perform *data mining* to gather information that will help managers make better decisions.

REA Modeling

In Chapter 5, you learned some basic E-R modeling concepts, including *entities* and *attributes*. In this section, you will gain a deeper understanding of how database designers use the REA model to identify *entities* and *attributes* for accounting applications. The development of the REA approach is discussed in Technology Summary 6.1.

Entities and Attributes

Chapter 5 and Technology Summary 6.1 explain that an *entity* in an accounting system can be classified as a resource, event, agent, or location[2] about which data are collected. You learned that resources could include merchandise inventory, equipment, and cash. Events might include orders, sales, and purchases. Agents can be people such as customers and employees; agents also can be organizations, such as corporate vendors. Locations are physical objects or spaces that (according to most REA experts) are not owned by the company. Basically, an *entity* is anything in which we are interested that exists independently. An **instance** of an *entity* is one specific thing of the type defined by the *entity*. For example, the *agent entity* EMPLOYEE in a small company with three employees might have *instances* of Marge Evans, Roberto Garcia, and Arte Singh. In a relational database, the *entity* is represented as a table and the three *instances* of the *entity* are represented as rows in that table.

To understand which *entity* we are capturing in our database and, likewise, to identify that unique *entity* when we retrieve the data, we need to describe the *entity* in detail. Data models describe entities by capturing their essential characteristics. The essential characteristics of an entity are its *attributes*. An **attribute** is an item of data that characterizes an *entity* or relationship. Figure 6.1 (page 194) displays an attribute hierarchy for the agent entity CLIENT. To fully describe a CLIENT we need to record several attributes such as Name, Address, Contact_Person, and Phone_Number. Sometimes, *attributes* are a combination of parts that have unique meanings of their own. As you can see in Figure 6.1, the attribute Address can include several independent subattributes such as Street_Address, City, State, and ZIP_Code. Attributes that consist of multiple subattributes are referred to as **composite attributes**. The degree to which a database designer breaks down attributes is a matter of judgment. For example, the at-

---

[2] REA remained the name for this model even after the location entity was added.

Technology Summary 6.1

The REA Model

In 1982, accounting researcher William Mc-Carthy published a paper[a] that outlined the REA approach, which was a new way of thinking about accounting information. At that time, computerized accounting systems were designed to perform the same tasks that accountants performed in manual accounting systems. For example, the computer running a sales system would be programmed to maintain one file that stored sales records and another file that stored information about payments received. Periodically, the computer would run both files and update a third file that included the accounts receivable records.

The designers of these old accounting systems modeled the things that accountants did in manual systems instead of modeling the business events themselves. In other words, the computerized accounting systems were models of the existing accountant's model of business events (double-entry bookkeeping) instead of being modeled after the business events themselves.

McCarthy became interested in the E-R modeling techniques you learned about in Chapter 5. E-R modeling was still relatively new and was still a theoretical curiosity; computers powerful enough to implement relational databases for large companies did not exist in the late 1970s. McCarthy first wrote about the potential of E-R modeling for accounting applications in 1979, hopeful that the technology would eventually become available.[b] He was attracted by the E-R model's ability to capture the meaning (or **semantics**) of business events more efficiently and effectively than the double-entry bookkeeping model could. Instead of modeling the accounting artifacts of journals and ledgers, the E-R model-based systems could focus on the elements of transactions and other business events. McCarthy classified business information into three categories: resources, events, and agents. These categories formed the basis for the REA model.

The REA model opened the door to a new world of accounting system design. Other accounting researchers worked with McCarthy to refine and improve the REA model.[c] As computers become more powerful and relational DBMS software became easier to use, the REA model was used increasingly to design accounting systems that could be integrated with other enterprise data. These integrated, enterprise-wide databases are used today to control and plan every aspect of a company's business processes.

[a] William E. McCarthy, "The REA Accounting Model: A Generalized Framework for Accounting Systems in a Shared Data Environment," *The Accounting Review* 57(3) (July 1982): 554–578.
[b] William E. McCarthy, "An Entity-Relationship View of Accounting Models," *The Accounting Review* 54(4) (October 1979): 667–686.
[c] Recent publications that discuss and extend the REA model include: Guido Geerts and William E. McCarthy, "An Ontological Analysis of the Economic Primitives of the Extended-REA Enterprise Information Architecture," *International Journal of Accounting Information Systems* 3(1) (March 2002): 1–15; Cheryl Dunn and Severin Grabski, "An Investigation of Localization as an Element of Cognitive Fit in Accounting Model Representations," *Decision Sciences* 32(1) (Winter 2001): 55–98; Cheryl Dunn and William E. McCarthy, "The REA Accounting Model: Intellectual Heritage and Prospects for Progress," *Journal of Information Systems* 11(1) (Spring 1997): 31–50; and William E. McCarthy, "The REA Modeling Approach to Teaching Accounting Information Systems," *Issues in Accounting Education* 18(4) (November 2003): 427–441.

tribute Street_Address could be broken down into further subattributes such as Street_Number, Street_Name, Street_Type (road, avenue, lane, and so on), and Street_Directional_Suffix (N, S, E, NE, and so on). Although an important goal of attribute identification is to break the attributes down into small components, attributes do not need to be broken into the smallest possible units in every case.

Note that an important assumption lies behind our specification of the attributes for the *agent entity* CLIENT. We have assumed that a common set of attributes exists for

Figure 6.1 Attribute Hierarchy for the Entity CLIENT

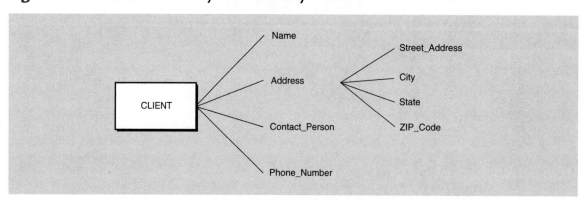

each *instance* of CLIENT.[3] That is, every client has a name, address, contact person, and phone number. To design an effective data model, you must learn to identify the complete set of entities and the common attributes that fully describe each entity. The REA approach helps the designers of accounting databases to identify a complete set of entities. It is important that the attributes allow the user of a database to uniquely identify each *entity* in the database.

To achieve the objective of uniquely identifying each *entity* to be stored in our database, it is necessary that one or more *attributes* be identified that will allow the user to access the *entity* that he or she is seeking. A **key attribute** is the *attribute* whose value is unique (i.e., different) for every *entity* that will ever appear in the database and is the most meaningful way of identifying each *entity*. This *key attribute* becomes the *primary key* (as discussed in Chapter 5). For our CLIENT agent entity, we might be tempted to use Name for the *key attribute*, but alphabetic-based *attributes* such as names are tricky because computers do not consistently distinguish between (or fail to distinguish between) uppercase and lowercase letters. Further, spellings and full names can be tricky in that one user might view the company name as "Arnold Consultants" while another user might use the full name, "Arnold Consultants, LLP." Similar problems can arise with company names such as "The Final Authority." A well-intentioned data entry clerk might enter that name as "Final Authority, The" or simply "Final Authority" after concluding that the article "The" is not an important part of the company name. Most designers would use a numeric-valued or a non-naming alphabetic *attribute* using one of the coding approaches you learned about in Chapter 5. For instance, an internally generated client number could be assigned to each *instance* in the CLIENT table. A numeric form using a *sequential coding* scheme might assign a number such as "12345." A non-naming alphabetic form using *block coding* to categorize companies by the first letter of a company's name might assign an alphanumeric such as "A1234" for the client number.

Figure 6.2, part (a), shows one common set of symbols that are used to represent *entities* and *attributes* in E-R diagrams. In Figure 6.2, part (b), the rectangle is used to represent the CLIENT agent entity. To map the *attributes* of an entity, we add ovals con-

---

[3] Technically, CLIENT would be an "entity type" in that it describes a collective group of *entities* (e.g., different clients). However, most database developers use the term *entity* rather than "entity type," as it is understood that all *entities* of interest will fall into some category of similar-type *entities*. We will use this common terminology throughout the remainder of our discussion.

Figure 6.2 Symbols Used in E-R and REA Diagrams

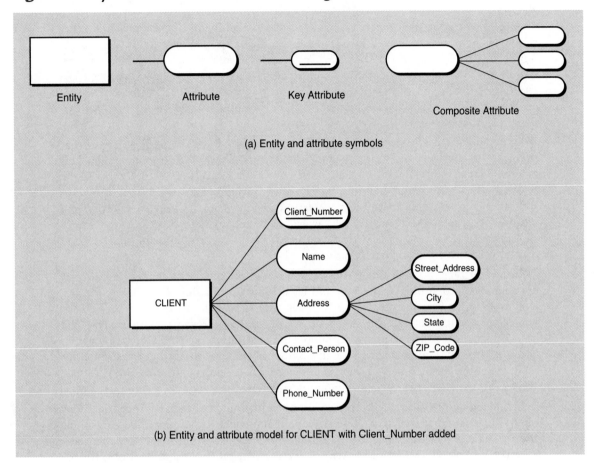

(a) Entity and attribute symbols

(b) Entity and attribute model for CLIENT with Client_Number added

nected to the entity (as shown in part a) for each attribute. Notice in part (b) that we have added an oval for each of the attributes shown in Figure 6.1. For the composite attribute Address, we use the same oval connectors for each of the subattributes of the main *attribute*. Note that we have added a new *attribute* to the set of attributes shown in Figure 6.1—Client_Number. This *attribute* is the CLIENT entity's *key attribute*. The underline beneath the attribute name documents its selection as the *key attribute*.

Relationships

In Chapter 5 we defined *relationships* as associations between *entities*. As you have learned, a database includes multiple *entities*. However, to make the data stored in *entities* available to users who might want to reconstruct descriptions of various business events, the *entities* must be logically linked to represent the *relationships* that exist between them. The ease with which a user can extract related data from a database is heavily dependent on the quality of the database's *logical design*—that is, effective identification of the *relationships* between different *entities*. These *relationships* map and define the way in which data can be extracted from the database in the future. The mapping of the *relationships* between *entities* (i.e., development of the E-R diagram) provides a roadmap for getting from one piece of data in the database to another related piece of data—much as a road map in an atlas might show you how to drive from one city to another.

A three-step strategy is generally most effective in identifying all the *relationships* that should be included in a model. First, identify users' existing and desired information requirements to determine whether *relationships* in the data model can fulfill those requirements. Second, evaluate each of the *entities* in pairs to determine whether one *entity* in the pair provides a better description of an *attribute* contained in the other entity in the pair. Third, evaluate each *entity* to determine if there would be any need for two occurrences of the same *entity* type to be linked.

In designing a database it is important that you learn about the business events that occur in the company and that you understand users' information requirements. This helps you identify all the ways in which different *entities* are related to each other in the company. This information will give you an idea of which *relationships* are required in the data model. The most common way to gather information about *relationships* in a particular company is to conduct interviews of the company's employees. All employees (not just managers) who work with the business process you are modeling can be good sources of information about *relationships*.

In this chapter, we will use as an illustrative example the client billing process that many public accounting, consulting, and legal firms use. In this client billing system, employees in the firm keep track of how much time they spend working on each client. Each employee fills out a weekly time sheet to record the time spent on each client. The hours spent on each client are then multiplied by the employee's billable rate for each hour worked. The cumulative fees for all employees' work are used to generate a bill for each client. The business process here is the capture of all information necessary to track employees' work hours and client billing information.

Examine Figure 6.3 briefly before we go on. The figure includes information about three *entities* and their *attributes*. Using the REA approach, we have identified one event and two agents that participate in the business process of billing for professional services. The WORK_COMPLETED *entity* is an *event*. The CLIENT and EMPLOYEE *entities* are *agents*. No *resources* or *locations* are tracked in this data model for the client billing business process.

Desirable linkages between *entities* will often be fairly easy to recognize when the *relationship* defines an *attribute*. If our billing system requires that we know for which client an employee has worked, the *entity* representing work completed needs to include a client number. This client number would link the WORK_COMPLETED entity to the CLIENT entity that provides us with a full description of the *attribute* denoted by client number in WORK_COMPLETED. As you can see in Figure 6.3, part (a), CLIENT is an entity and not an attribute of WORK_COMPLETED. However, CLIENT does improve the description of an attribute for the work completed—the client for whom the work was performed. This descriptive value suggests that a relationship exists between the CLIENT *entity* and the *entity* capturing the completed work as shown in Figure 6.3, part (a). Hence, we often can identify the need for defining *relationships* (such as Works_For) by examining the prescribed *entities* as pairs (in this case, we examined the pair CLIENT and WORK_COMPLETED) to identify logical linkages that would improve the description of an *entity's attributes*.

Another type of relationship is displayed in Figure 6.3, part (b). The *relationship* Supervises is called a *recursive relationship*. A **recursive relationship** is a *relationship* between two different *instances* of an *entity*. For example, most organizations have *rela-*

Figure 6.3 Relationship Types in the REA Model of the Client Billing Business Process

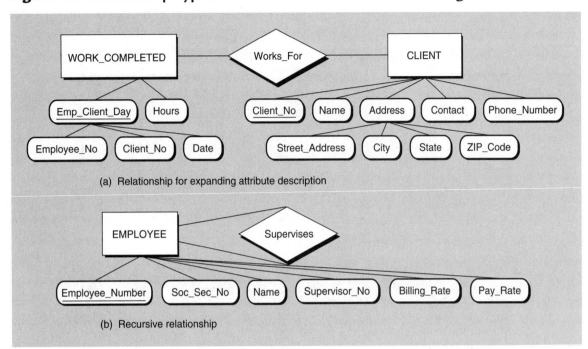

(a) Relationship for expanding attribute description

(b) Recursive relationship

tionships among employees in which one employee supervises other employees. This *relationship* is often important in business processes and in decision-making contexts. Thus, this *relationship* should be represented in our database. Figure 6.3, part (b) shows how a *recursive relationship* is displayed in an REA data model diagram. One tempting alternative is to represent supervisors and their supervised employees as separate *entities* in the model. Unfortunately, this separate *entity* approach yields data redundancies when the supervisor is supervised by a third employee. Thus, it is easier and more logically correct to use a recursive relationship to the *entity*, EMPLOYEE. In this recursive relationship, a link is created between the employee who is being supervised and another employee who is the supervisor. As shown in Figure 6.3, part (b), the diamond represents the recursive relationship, Supervises, just as it would be used to show any relationship (such as the Works_For relationship in part (a).

Model Constraints

In this section we explore the various types of *relationships* that can occur and discuss the constraints used to specify such *relationships*. In Chapter 5 we briefly explored three different relationship types: 1:N (read one-to-many), M:N (read many-to-many), and 1:1 (read one-to-one). You learned in Chapter 5 that the degree of these three relationship types is called *cardinality*.

Figure 6.4, part (a) (page 198) is an REA diagram that shows the maximum cardinalities for the Works relationship between the agent entity EMPLOYEE and the event entity WORK_COMPLETED in the client billing business process. The "1" above the left line of the relationship indicates that one employee performs each completed work entry. The "N" above the right line indicates that many work entries can be performed by an employee.

Figure 6.4 Relationship Constraints in the Client Billing Business Process

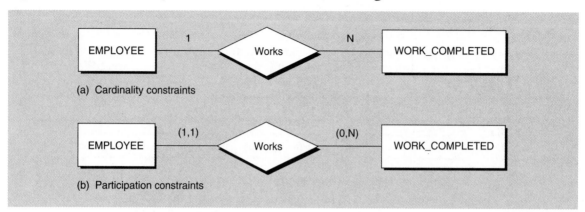

To determine the cardinality of a relationship, ask yourself the question, "How many items (records) in this entity could be related to any one item (record) in the other entity—one or many?" The answer determines that half of the *cardinality* ratio, and then the same question is asked in the reverse direction of the *relationship* to determine the other half of the *cardinality* ratio. In our example, we take the *relationship* in Figure 6.4, part (a), and ask the question, "How many work completed entries can an employee have?" The answer is many (based on the *attributes* specified for WORK_COMPLETED in Figure 6.3, part (a), which indicates that a given occurrence in the WORK_COMPLETED *entity* relates to one employee's time spent on a given client in a single time period. The question is then reversed and we ask, "How many employees can provide a specific work completed entry?" The maximum number will be one. Hence, the cardinality of the *relationship* is specified as one-to-many and indicated on the diagram with the "1" and "N" notation. Most DBMSs include a feature that enforces maximum constraints. In other words, the DBMS will ensure that data are never entered that connect more than one employee to a single work completed entry.

Cardinality is the most common constraint specified in *E-R diagrams*. The other meaningful constraint that may be specified is *participation*. The **participation constraint** specifies the degree of minimum participation of one entity in the *relationship* with the other entity. In Figure 6.4, part (b), the *participation constraints* appear in the diagram. In the Works *relationship*, not every employee will have completed a billable work activity. Some employees are new and are not yet billable, others might have non-client service responsibilities, such as training or new business development. The "many" *cardinality* that appears in part (a) of the diagram only specifies the maximum participation in the relationship, not the minimum. The minimum *participation* in the relationship can be zero or one. The notation (0,N) on the line on the right in part (b) reflects the range of zero to many occurrences of work being completed on client projects, where the numbers reflect (minimum, maximum). The notation (1,1) on the line on the left side in part (b), illustrates that for any given occurrence of work completed for a client, the maximum of one employee providing the specific service still holds. In this case, the minimum also will be one because an employee must perform a particular occurrence of the completed work. The (1,1) *relationship* reflects that there is a required *participation* of one, and only one, employee.

Although the *participation constraint* does provide more information, it is still used less frequently than the *cardinality constraint*. In this book, we will present the diagrams using the maximum *cardinality* and will omit the participation (or minimum) constraints. You should know that both types of constraints and notation are used because, as a member of the development team, as an auditor, or as a user, you will need to communicate using the methods selected by the organization with which you are working.

REA Data Models and E-R Diagrams

You now have all of the basic knowledge you need to develop effective REA models and their representations in *E-R diagrams*. You should be ready to start developing an integrated database model. Each of the data model segments included in Figures 6.1 through 6.4 (page 194, 195, 197, and 198) are parts of REA data models.

You might remember from earlier in this book that a fundamental requirement for moving toward an *event-driven* model is the complete integration of data related to an organization's business events. Although the development of a full comprehensive integrated data model for an entire organization is a major undertaking, you can use your data modeling skills to explore the integration of two business processes: client billing and human resources.

The objective in the development of an REA model is to integrate the data in a way that allows managers and other users access to the information they need to perform effectively. Figure 6.5 (page 200) presents the integrated REA data model for the billing and human resources business processes. Follow along with the REA diagram as we discuss the data relationships in the following scenario.

In a service organization such as a public accounting or consultancy firm, the billing of clients requires that the firm track the person-hours spent by each employee who is providing service. To execute the client billing process effectively, the database must capture data about all employees who provided client services. The database must record each employee's work to a specific client. Each employee can have a different billing rate for his or her time. To meet the needs of the billing process, the database must aggregate each employee's time worked, each employee's billing rate, and sufficient information about the client to deliver the billing statement. Three entities are involved in the billing process: the agent EMPLOYEE, the agent CLIENT, and the event WORK_COMPLETED. Note in Figure 6.5 that the three *entities* for the billing process are linked together on the right half of the diagram. The linkages allow us to pull together information related to the employees' hours worked on a specific client, their billing rates, and the contact address for sending the billing statement.

Service businesses also are interested in tracking employee work activities as part of the human resources process. The human resources process includes payroll activities, employee education and development, and other activities. To complete the payroll process, information is needed regarding work hours completed, pay rate, vacation time, sick days, and training time. Using the REA approach, we can identify two additional *entities*, the events RELEASE_TIME, and TRAINING_COMPLETED that are added to the model that also includes the previously identified agent entity EMPLOYEE and event entity WORK_COMPLETED. These four entities enable the database to aggregate the information it needs to determine the employee's pay rate, hours worked, hours spent in training, and hours of sick and vacation time used.

The human resources department needs information about employee education and development so it can monitor training activities and ensure that the employee is

Figure 6.5 An Integrated REA Model for the Client Billing and Human Resources Processes

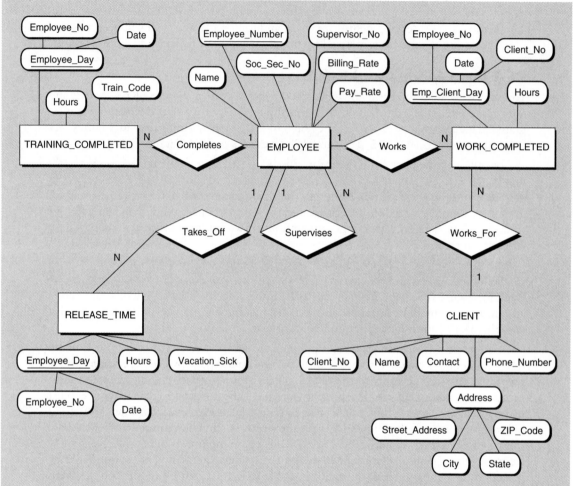

receiving enough continuing education to comply with state license requirements and the firm's policies. Human resources also will monitor the percentage of billable hours the employee has accumulated as a measure of job performance. To accomplish these activities, human resources must be able to link data about completed work activities and training programs to specific employees. This information can be drawn from the agent entity EMPLOYEE, the event entity TRAINING_COMPLETED, and the event entity WORK_COMPLETED. Human resources can use this information to accumulate a given employee's training record and calculate that employee's percentage of hours worked that were billable hours.

ENTERPRISE SYSTEMS   It is important to recognize that Figure 6.5 shows only a small part of the overall enterprise model that integrates all information across an the entire organization. The REA model effectively integrates the data required for the firm's business processes. As other business processes are examined, modeled, and integrated, the REA data model will continue to expand through an explosion of *entities* and *relationships*. Many organizations have moved toward integration of all data across the organization. These integrated enterprise models are the foundations for implementing *enterprise systems*, which you learned about in Chapter 2.

In the following sections, we describe how to implement the REA data model in a relational database system. Subsequently, we examine the use of SQL to create and manipulate the database.

RELATIONAL DATABASES

We briefly demonstrated the use of the *relational databases* in Chapter 5. In this section, we expand our examination of *relational databases* and explore a few of the more technical issues. Despite a push toward *object-oriented databases*, *relational database*-driven legacy systems exist in most large organizations, and the cost to switch them over is prohibitive. Many of these legacy systems (that is, systems that have existed in an organization over a period of time and were developed using an organization's previous computer hardware and software platforms) have been functioning reliably for decades. As an alternative to making costly changes to *object-oriented databases*, *relational database* vendors are providing modified versions of their software that support objects within the relational structure. It is likely that relational-based DBMSs will remain dominant in the near future.

Our exploration of *relational databases* is divided into two segments. First, we take a look at the basic concepts that underlie *relational databases*. Then we explore the task of mapping REA data models into *relational database* tables and *relationships*.

Relational Database Concepts

Relational databases often are perceived by users as a collection of tables. This is a reasonable perception because the logical view of the data are a tabular type format referred to as a *relation*. A **relation** is a collection of data representing multiple occurrences of a resource, event, or agent. These relations correspond to the entities in the E-R model and the REA model.

Figure 6.6 displays an example *relation* along with labels for each of the components (or *attributes*) of a *relation*. Consistent with a tabular representation, a *relation* consists of rows and columns. Rows are sometimes referred to as *tuples* and columns are referred

Figure 6.6 Example of a Relation (EMPLOYEE) and Its Parts

EMPLOYEE	Employee_Number	Soc_Sec_No	Name	Supervisor_No	Billing_Rate	Pay_Rate
	B432	305-45-9592	Carl Elks	A632	57.00	2,500
	A491	350-97-9030	Janet Robins	A632	57.00	2,500
	A632	125-87-8090	Greg Kinman	B122	100.00	4,500
	B011	178-78-0406	Christy Bazie	A632	57.00	2,600
	B122	123-78-0907	Elaine Kopp	Null	150.00	7,000
	A356	127-92-3453	John Mast	A632	57.00	2,600

Relation

Tuples

Attributes

to as *attributes*. A **tuple** is a set of data that describes a single *instance* of the *entity* represented by a *relation* (for example, one employee is an instance of the EMPLOYEE *relation*). *Attributes*, as in an *E-R model*, represent an item of *data* that characterizes an object, event, or agent. Attributes are often called *fields*.

In viewing the *relation* in Figure 6.6, note that the data contained in the table do not appear to be in any particular order. In a *relational database model* no ordering is given to the *tuples* contained within a *relation*. This is different from the traditional file structures and the database models that existed before the relational model that you learned about in Chapter 5. In those systems, sequence or keyed location could be critical. The ordering of the *tuples* in a relational database is unimportant because the *tuples* are recalled by the database by matching an *attribute's* value with some prescribed value, or through a query in which the ordering could be established on any attribute (for example, a query could sort on the Pay_Rate or Billing_Rate attribute).

To identify a *tuple* uniquely, it is critical that each *tuple* be distinct from all other *tuples*. This means that each *tuple* in a *relation* must be identified uniquely by a single *attribute* or some combination of multiple *attributes*. In each table, a *primary key* is specified to identify each *tuple* in the *relation*. Notice in Figure 6.6 that Employee_Number is the *primary key* and that it is unique for every *tuple*. Other attributes in the *relation* could serve as a *key attribute*. In a *relation* these additional *attributes* are secondary keys and are often called **candidate keys**. Any *attribute* that is specified as a *key attribute* must have a unique value that exists for each tuple. A missing value is called a **null** and key *attributes* are required to be **non-null** in every *tuple* in the relation. Notice that Soc_Sec_No would also be unique and could possibly be used as a *candidate key*, but constraints would have to be implemented that require every *tuple* to have a value because an employee might not have a Social Security number, especially if the firm has operations outside the United States.

CONTROLS   Additionally, constraints should be implemented to ensure that the *referential integrity* of the database is maintained. **Referential integrity** specifies that for every *attribute* value in one *relation* that has been specified to allow reference to another *relation*, the *tuple* being referenced must remain intact. For example, consider the *relation* EMPLOYEE in Figure 6.6. You might recall that EMPLOYEE was involved in a *recursive relation* in Figure 6.3, part (b) on page 197. In that *recursive relation*, Supervisor_No is used to reference the Employee_Number of the supervising employee. If the *tuple* for Greg Kinman were deleted from the database, four other employees would no longer have a valid Supervisor_No (because the Supervisor_No would be referencing a *tuple* that no longer exists). Thus, a *referential integrity constraint* would require the user to reassign the four employees to a new supervisor before the *tuple* for Greg Kinman could be deleted. Most DBMS software products have built-in mechanisms for enforcing *referential integrity*. For example, the Microsoft Access DBMS software provides a check box for that purpose when a designer is creating a relationship as shown in Figure 6.7.

Mapping an REA Model to a Relational DBMS

So far in this chapter, we have discussed the development of *REA models* and the foundations for implementing good *relational database models*. It is now time to put these two concepts together. This process is referred to as mapping an *REA model* onto a *logical database model*—in this case the *relational data model*.

In Chapter 5 we outlined a simple five-step process for creating tables and relationships based on an *E-R diagram*. We will now expand the five-step process to develop a

Figure 6.7 Enforcing Referential Integrity on a
Relationship in the Microsoft Access DBMS

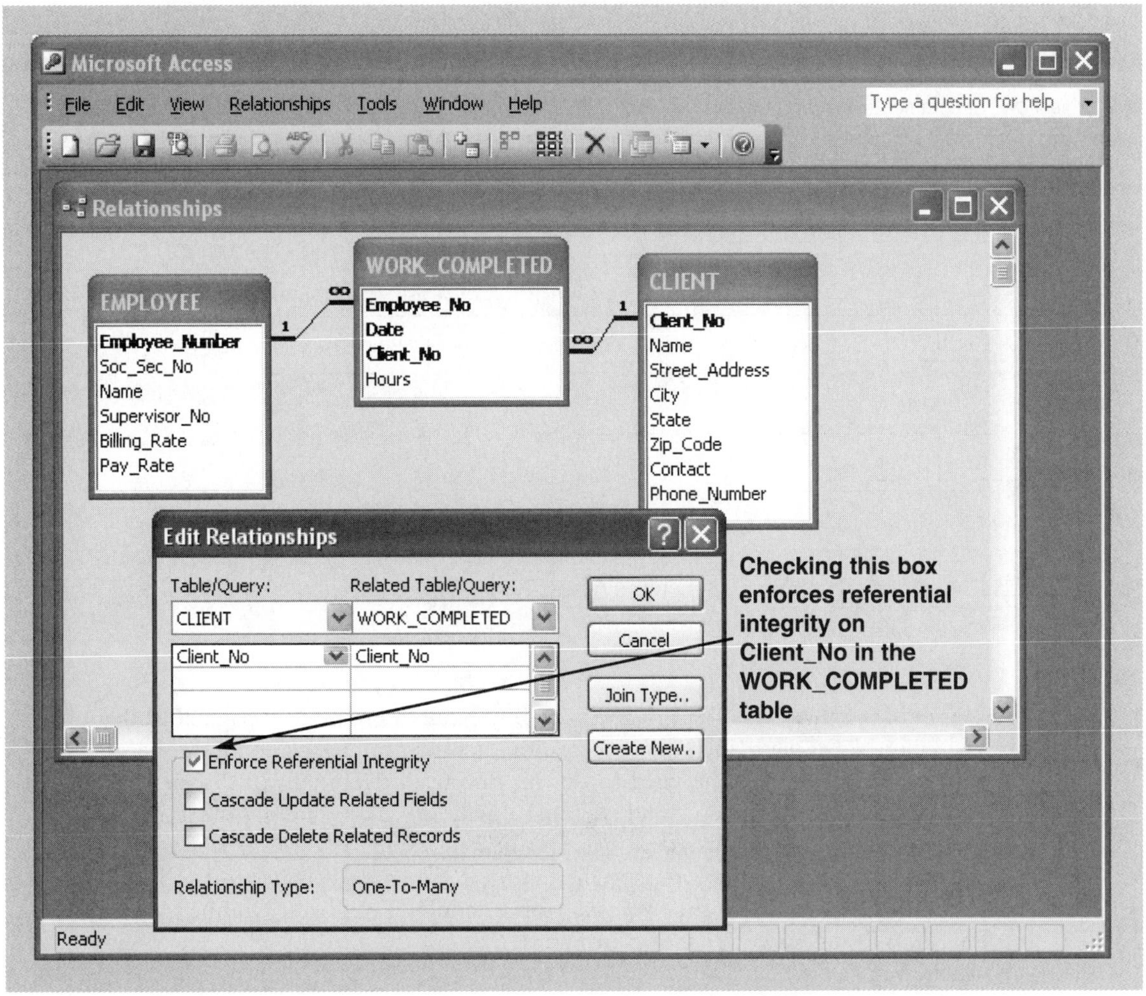

Source: Relationships Window, Microsoft Access 2003.

well-constrained *relational database* implementation. To aid in the comparability with our original discussion, we will reintroduce each of the five steps in the context of the discussion on this expanded mapping methodology. Follow along as we map the REA diagram in Figure 6.5 (page 200) to the relational database schema in Figure 6.8.

1. *Create a separate relational table for each entity.* This is a logical starting point whenever mapping an *REA model* onto a *relational database model.* As a starting point in this process, it is generally useful to first specify the database *schema* before proceeding to expansion of the *relations* to account for specific *tuples.* Notice that each of the entities in Figure 6.5 (page 200) has become a relation in Figure 6.8. To complete the schema, however, steps 2 and 3 also must be completed.

2. *Determine the primary key for each of the relations. The primary key must uniquely identify any row within the table.*

**Figure 6.8 Schema for the Client Billing and Human
Resources Portion of the Database**

CLIENT

Client_No	Name	Street_Address	City	State	ZIP_Code	Contact	Phone_Number

WORK_COMPLETED

Employee_No	Date	Client_No	Hours

EMPLOYEE

Employee_Number	Soc_Sec_No	Name	Supervisor_No	Billing_Rate	Pay_Rate

TRAINING_COMPLETED

Employee_No	Date	Hours	Train_Code

RELEASE_TIME

Employee_No	Date	Hours	Vacation_Sick

3. *Determine the attributes for each of the entities.* Note in Figure 6.5 (page 200) that a complete *REA model* includes specification of all attributes, including the *key attribute*. This eliminates the need to do this during development of the *relations*. Rather, the focus is on step 2 and is simply a matter of determining how to implement the prescribed *key attribute* within a *relation*. With a single *attribute* specified as the *key*, the *key attribute* specified in the *REA model* is matched to the corresponding *attribute* in the *relation* (for example, Employee_Number in the EMPLOYEE agent entity shown in Figure 6.5 and the EMPLOYEE agent relation in Figure 6.8).

To create a *composite primary key*, you simply break the key down into its component *subattributes*. For instance, in the implementation of the WORK_COMPLETED event *relation*, Employee_No, Date, and Client_No are three distinct *attributes* in the *relation*, but also combine to form the *composite primary key*. The completed *schema* is presented in Figure 6.8. Note the direct mapping between the *entities* and *attributes* in the *REA model* and the *relations* and *attributes*, respectively, in the *relational schema*.

4. *Implement the relationships among the entities by ensuring that the primary key in one table also exists as an attribute in every table for which there is a relationship specified in the REA diagram.* With the availability of the full *REA model*, the mapping of the *relationships* in the model to the *relationships* in the *relational schema* is straightforward. References to the *key attributes* of one *entity* are captured by including a corresponding *attribute* in the other *entity* that participates in the *relationship*. All of the relationships in this example are 1:N relationships, which sim-

plifies the process. Let's consider how the different degrees of *relationships* (i.e., *cardinality constraints*) can affect the mapping of relationships to the *schema*.

a. One-to-many (1:N or N:1) relationships are implemented by including the primary key of the table on the one side of the relationship as an attribute in the table on the many side of the relationship. This is the situation we have for all the relationships in Figure 6.5 (page 200). The linking between these relations in the schema are drawn in Figure 6.9. Note that Client_No in CLIENT and Employee_Number in EMPLOYEE provide the links to WORK_COMPLETED. Similarly, Employee_Number in EMPLOYEE provides links to TRAINING_COMPLETED and RELEASE_TIME. The recursive relationship with EMPLOYEE uses Supervisor_No to identify the correct EMPLOYEE as the supervisor.

Figure 6.9 Referential Constraints for the Relational Schema

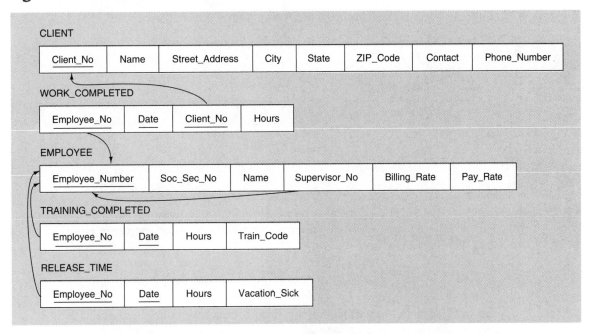

b. One-to-one (1:1) relationships are even easier. You can follow the same steps used for 1:N relationships, but you can start with either table. For example, if at present one entry in WORK_COMPLETED is sufficient to finish any client project, then a 1:1 relationship exists between WORK_COMPLETED and CLIENT. In this situation we could still select the Client_No in CLIENT to establish the primary key (see Figure 6.9). Starting with CLIENT has an advantage; if a client engagement in the future might require more than entry in WORK_COMPLETED to finish or more than one employee to complete, using Client_No in the CLIENT table would still work (that is, it would form the *many* dimension shown for the relationship Works_For in Figure 6.5, page 200).

c. Many-to-many (M:N) relationships are implemented by creating a new relation whose primary key is a composite of the primary keys of the relations to be linked. In our model we do not have any M:N relationships, but if we had not needed to record the Date and Hours in the WORK_COMPLETED entity, that entity would not have existed. Still, we would need a relationship between the EMPLOYEE and CLIENT entities, which would then be an M:N relationship. This creates problems because tables that have been normalized (as discussed in Chapter 5) cannot store multiple client numbers in a single EMPLOYEE tuple. Similarly, a single CLIENT tuple cannot store multiple employee numbers. In that situation, we would need to develop a relation to link the EMPLOYEE and CLIENT relations (see Figure 6.10). This new relation would have a composite key consisting of Employee_Number from EMPLOYEE and Client_No from CLIENT—similar to the composite key in the existing relation, WORK_COMPLETED (see Figure 6.8 on page 204).

Figure 6.10 Linking Two Relations in a Many-to-Many Relationship

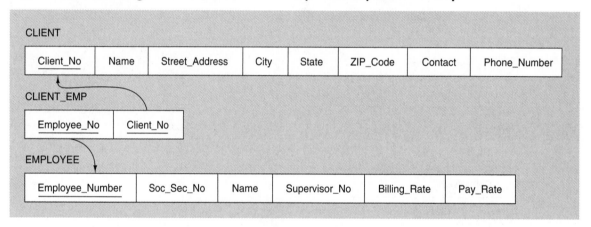

Beyond concerns over meeting the constraint requirements for *primary keys*, we also must ensure adherence to the *referential integrity constraints*. We identify the *referential integrity constraints* by locating the corresponding *attribute* in each *relation* that is linked via a *relationship*. We then determine which of the *relations* contain the *tuple* that if the reference attribute were deleted or changed would jeopardize the *integrity* of the database. In Figure 6.9 (page 205) the *referential integrity constraints* are represented by the arrow, with the destination of the arrow being the *attribute* that must be controlled to achieve *referential integrity*. In other words, changing the attribute to which the arrow points could cause an *attribute* not to have a matching value in the attribute at the source of the arrow. To achieve *referential integrity*, constraints should be established that assure Employee_Number is not altered or deleted for any EMPLOYEE until the referencing *attribute* values for the Employee_No *attributes* in WORK_COMPLETED, TRAINING_COMPLETED, and RELEASE_TIME have first been corrected. A similar constraint should be placed on Client_No in CLIENT until Client_No has been corrected in WORK_COMPLETED.

5. *Determine the attributes, if any, for each of the relationship tables.* Again, in the extended version of the *REA model*, the *attributes* map directly to the *relations*. The implementation of the *schema* is shown in Figure 6.11.

Figure 6.11 Implementation of the Relational Schema

EMPLOYEE	Employee_Number	Soc_Sec_No	Name	Supervisor_No	Billing_Rate	Pay_Rate
	B432	305-45-9592	Carl Elks	A632	57.00	2,500
	A491	350-97-9030	Janet Robins	A632	57.00	2,500
	A632	125-87-8090	Greg Kinman	B122	100.00	4,500
	B011	178-78-0406	Christy Bazie	A632	57.00	2,600
	B122	123-78-0907	Elaine Kopp	Null	150.00	7,000
	A356	127-92-3453	John Mast	A632	57.00	2,600

TRAINING_COMPLETED	Employee_No	Date	Hour	Train_Code
	A356	070823	8	32
	B011	070823	8	32
	B432	070823	8	32
	A491	070823	8	32
	A356	070824	8	32
	B011	070824	8	32
	B432	070824	8	32
	A491	070824	8	32
	A356	070825	8	32
	B011	070825	8	32
	B432	070825	8	32
	A491	070825	8	32

RELEASE_TIME	Employee_No	Date	Hour	Vacation_Sick
	B011	070826	8	V
	B011	070827	8	V

CLIENT	Client_No	Name	Street_Address	City	State	ZIP_Code	Contact	Phone_Number
	A12345	Arnold, LLP	11 Nayatt Dr.	Barrington	RI	02806	V. Arnold	401-792-8341
	F11555	Fleet Services	10 Mission Rd.	Providence	RI	02835	R. Grass	401-774-9843
	H12456	Hasbro, Inc.	4516 Burton Pike	Providence	RI	02844	T. Bayers	401-837-2132

WORK_COMPLETED	Employee_No	Client_No	Date	Hours
	B122	F11555	070823	8
	A632	F11555	070823	8
	B122	F11555	070824	8
	A632	F11555	070824	8
	B122	F11555	070825	8
	A632	F11555	070825	8
	B122	H12456	070826	8
	A632	H12456	070826	8
	A356	F11555	070826	8
	B432	H12456	070826	8
	A491	H12456	070826	8
	B122	F11555	070827	8
	A632	H12456	070827	8
	A356	F11555	070827	8
	B432	H12456	070827	8
	A491	H12456	070827	8

SQL: A Relational Database Query Language

In this section of the chapter, you will learn how SQL query language can be used to create a database, store data in the new database, and manipulate the data stored in the database.

SQL[4] is a powerful database language that can be used to define database systems, query the database for information, generate reports from the database, and access databases from within programs using embedded SQL commands. It has become the *de facto* standard database language—evidenced by continual efforts by industry to provide standardization guidelines for vendors and the number of variations of the language that exist in databases from supercomputers to personal computers. It has become so critical to many business organizations that increasingly software is being developed that provides intelligent interfaces that help the user generate queries more quickly. Figure 6.12 displays an example of a Query-By-Example (QBE) interface used in PeopleSoft's J.D. Edwards ERP software. Using an interface such as this, a user enters a description of the output he or she desires (e.g., Amount Open is greater than Zero) and the system generates an SQL query. However, these query utilities can be risky to use because they do not always generate the SQL query intended and it is imperative that the user thoroughly understands the queries to ensure the intended data is properly extracted from the database.

SQL is increasingly becoming a survival tool among accounting and business professionals. Once you complete your study of the material presented here, you should have the basic skills necessary to develop your own databases and retrieve data from many different databases. Our discussion of SQL will begin with the commands necessary to create databases. From there we will explore the basic querying commands that will allow us to update the database, retrieve data, and generate reports.

Constructing Relational Databases

SQL was first introduced as a query language named Structured English Query Language (SEQUEL). Much like this early name suggests, the language is an attempt to use somewhat normal English language as its commands. As such, SQL uses terms such as table, row, and column to describe *relations* during creation and manipulation of *relational databases*. Similarly, most commands use easily recognizable names.

Our first command of interest in creating the database structure is the CREATE command. As the name suggests, we will use it to create the *relations* that form the database structure. Browse the queries in Figure 6.13 (page 210) before reading the following discussion.

Use Figure 6.13 to follow the steps for creating a database structure with SQL as discussed next. To create a *relation* we must:

1. Assign the relation a name (which we have already done for our *relations* in defining the *schema* in Figure 6.8, page 204).

2. Assign each attribute a name. Again, in the schema demonstrated in Figure 6.8 we have already given our attributes names.

---

[4] SQL is pronounced two different ways because of an interesting fact in the language's history. The original implementation of the language many years ago was named "SEQUEL," but another company was already selling a product with that name and asserted its trademark rights to the name. So, the query language's name was changed to "SQL." As a result, older database designers usually pronounce the name "sequel." Younger designers are more likely to pronounce the name "ess-cue-el."

Figure 6.12 Executing a Query by Example in PeopleSoft's J.D. Edwards ERP Software

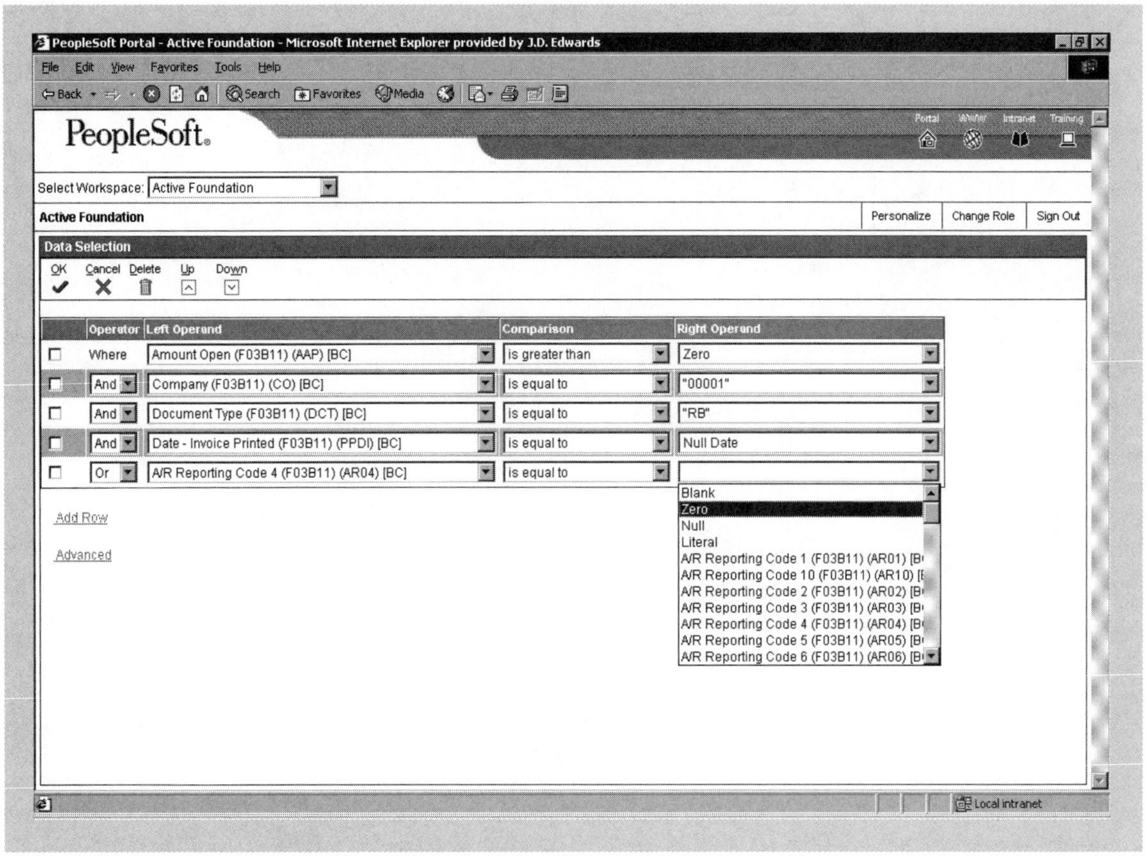

3. Specify the data type for each attribute. Data type descriptions generally include some combination of alphanumeric (e.g., with letters and/or symbols) or numeric values. Alphanumeric types include CHAR (for fixed-length strings) and VARCHAR (for varying length alphanumeric strings). Numeric data types include INTEGER, FLOAT (which has a floating decimal point), and DECIMAL (where the number of digits both left and right of the decimal point are fixed and defined).

4. Specify constraints, when appropriate, on the attributes. Most notably, we need to make sure that the primary key values are not left empty (i.e., null); otherwise there will be no key value by which to identify and pull the *tuple's* record from the database. We may wish to require that other attributes be assigned some value rather than having the option of being null. In each of these cases we can assign a value of "NOT NULL" as the constraint.

CONTROLS

The previous conventions are applied in Figure 6.13 to generate the *relations* specified in our earlier defined *schema* in Figure 6.8 (page 204). Carefully study how the various conventions have been applied. For instance, note in the EMPLOYEE *relation* that we have assigned a fixed-length character value (11 characters) for the *attribute* Soc_Sec_No. This accommodates the use of the hyphens in the number. In many cases,

Figure 6.13 SQL Commands for Creating Database Relations

```
CREATE TABLE EMPLOYEE          (Employee_Number   Char(4)          NOT NULL,
                                Soc_Sec_No         Char(11)         NOT NULL,
                                Name               VarChar(25)      NOT NULL,
                                Supervisor_No      Char(11),
                                Billing_Rate       Decimal(5,2),
                                Pay_Rate           Decimal(7,2);

CREATE TABLE TRAINING_COMPLETED (Employee_No       Char(11)         NOT NULL,
                                Date               Integer          NOT NULL,
                                Hour               Integer,
                                Train_Code         Integer);

CREATE TABLE RELEASE_TIME       (Employee_No       Char(11)         NOT NULL,
                                Date               Integer          NOT NULL,
                                Hour               Integer,
                                Vacation_Sick      Char(1));

CREATE TABLE CLIENT            (Client_No          Char(6)          NOT NULL,
                                Name               VarChar(25),
                                Street_Address     VarChar(30),
                                City               VarChar(15),
                                State              Char(2),
                                ZIP_Code           Integer,
                                Contact            VarChar(25)      NOT NULL,
                                Phone_Number       VarChar(12));

CREATE TABLE WORK_COMPLETED    (Employee_No        Char(11)         NOT NULL,
                                Client_No          Char(6)          NOT NULL,
                                Date               Integer          NOT NULL);

ALTER TABLE WORK_COMPLETED      (Hours             Integer);
```

a company might choose to omit the hyphens and even reflect the Social Security number as a numeric. Also, note that despite our longest employee name currently being 13 characters, we have allowed a variable length alphanumeric field of 25 characters to accommodate longer names that may be entered in the future. Similarly, additional size has been built into the specifications for Billing_Rate and Pay_Rate to accommodate future inflationary effects on the two rates.

At the bottom of Figure 6.13, note that we demonstrate a new command—ALTER. ALTER is SQL's way of recognizing that we may not always get the permanent design of a *relation* right the first time. In this way, additional *attributes* can be added to a *relation* at some future point in time. In our case, we accidentally left off the last *attribute* for WORK_COMPLETED when issuing the CREATE command and came back to add the missing attribute. Note that adding an attribute is fairly easy.

Before going on to updating the data, we should explain how to delete a table as well. If you have a *relation* you decide you no longer need, or that needs to be completely recreated from scratch rather than altering, you can drop a *relation* very quickly. The DROP command is as follows:

```
DROP TABLE [table name]
```

For instance, if we wanted to drop the WORK_COMPLETED table, we would enter the command:

```
DROP TABLE WORK_COMPLETED
```

Updating the Database

Data can be changed in the database in three ways. Our first concern is the loading of data into the structure we just created with the CREATE command. This is accomplished using the INSERT command to add new *tuples* to a *relation*. In the future, a user might wish to DELETE or UPDATE the data stored within relations, and we will review these commands in this section as well.

The INSERT command is used to add a single *tuple* to an existing *relation*. Hence, when you create a relational database using SQL you must first use the CREATE command to generate the structure of the relation and then use the INSERT command to enter the current data into the structure. The INSERT command in its simplest form only requires the user to specify the SQL table and the values to be inserted for each *attribute* if a value is provided for every *attribute*. This simple form of the INSERT command is demonstrated in Figure 6.14 by the command to enter the first tuple into the EMPLOYEE table—that is, the values for Carl Elks. This form of the command also is demonstrated in Figure 6.14 for entering the first record of the remaining tables.

Figure 6.14 SQL Commands to Add Data to the Database

```
INSERT INTO     EMPLOYEE
VALUES          ('B432','305-45-9592','Carl Elks','125-87-8090',57,2500)

INSERT INTO     EMPLOYEE
VALUES          ('A491','350-97-9030','Janet Robins','125-87-5090',57,2500)

INSERT INTO     EMPLOYEE
VALUES          ('A632','125-87-8090','Greg Kinman','123-78-0907',100,4500)

INSERT INTO     EMPLOYEE
VALUES          ('B011','178-78-0406','Christy Bazie','125-87-8090',57,2600)

INSERT INTO     EMPLOYEE (Employee_Number, Soc_Sec_No, Name, Billing_Rate, Pay_Rate
VALUES          ('B122','123-78-0907','Elaine Kopp',150,7000)

INSERT INTO     EMPLOYEE
VALUES          ('A356','127-92-3453','John Mast','125-87-8090',57,2600)

INSERT INTO     TRAINING_COMPLETED
VALUES          ('A356',990823,8,32)
        :               :    :    :
        :               :    :    :

INSERT INTO     RELEASE_TIME
VALUES          ('B011',990826,8,'V')
        :               :    :    :
        :               :    :    :

INSERT INTO     CLIENT
VALUES          ('A12345','Arnold,LLP','11 Nayatt Dr.','Barrington','RI',02806,
                'V. Arnold','401-792-8341')
        :               :    :    :
        :               :    :    :

INSERT INTO     WORK_COMPLETED
VALUES          ('B122','F11555',990823,8)
        :               :    :    :
        :               :    :    :
```

If values are not entered for all attributes for a given tuple, then the INSERT command must be specified more clearly. Namely, when the table is specified in the INSERT command, the attributes for which values are being provided must be specified. If we study Figure 6.14 again, we will notice that when we enter the fifth EMPLOYEE tuple we specify the attributes to receive values because Elaine Kopp, as the top-level manager, has no supervisor specified—that is, Supervisor_No is NULL.

CONTROLS   Before leaving the INSERT command, we should note that we can omit values for selected attributes of a tuple if, and only if, a database constraint has not been set to "NOT NULL" when creating the table. For instance, if we look back to Figure 6.13 (page 210) where we issued the CREATE commands, we will notice that a value must be entered for Employee_No in every instance of EMPLOYEE. Hence, if we had a new employee who did not have a Social Security number, we would need to assign that employee a temporary number before we could INSERT him or her into the database.

The DELETE command is, of course, the flip side of the INSERT command and is the method by which we delete a tuple from a relation. The DELETE command requires specification of the table name and inclusion of a WHERE condition, which is used to identify the unique tuple(s) for deletion. For instance, if the EMPLOYEE named Elaine Kopp decided to leave the firm, we could enter the following command to delete her from the EMPLOYEE table:

```
DELETE FROM   EMPLOYEE
WHERE         Employee_Number ='B122'
```

CONTROLS   Notice that we use the *primary key* (Employee_No) to identify the tuple for deletion. The use of the DELETE command demonstrates one of the weaknesses in most forms of SQL—the database will not enforce *referential integrity constraints*. If we delete Elaine Kopp from the database, we now have a number of other relations with instances of attributes referring to what would now be a deleted record (e.g., all relations would have referential integrity problems other than CLIENT, including the recursive relationship on EMPLOYEE). Most implementations of SQL will require the user to manage *referential integrity* rather than providing the means for implementing constraints through the database. Most DBMSs available today that include SQL also include mechanisms within the DBMS itself (and not within the SQL function) for establishing and enforcing referential integrity. We depicted one example of such a mechanism in in Figure 6.7 (page 203), which showed the procedure for enforcing referential integrity in Microsoft Access 2003.

The last command of interest in this segment is UPDATE. The UPDATE command is used when we want to change one or more attribute values for one or more tuples in a table. To accomplish a change of an attribute value, the UPDATE command must be able to identify the table with the value to be updated, the new values to be placed in the database, and the conditions for identifying the correct tuple for UPDATE. To make the change, we identify the tuple using the "WHERE" condition we just learned for deletion, and we change the existing values by using a "SET" command to set the new values for the database.

For example purposes, let's assume that our firm has decided to give Elaine Kopp a raise so that she will stay as an employee. We need to place her new Pay_Rate of $7,500 in her record in the database. To accomplish this, we execute the following UPDATE command:

```
UPDATE   EMPLOYEE
SET      Pay_Rate=7500
WHERE    Employee_Number ='B122'
```

Execution of the SQL command first finds the matching Employee_Number, deletes the existing attribute value (i.e., 7000), and enters the new value of 7500 into the Pay_Rate for the matching employee.

Basic Querying Commands

Queries of the database are driven by SELECT commands that allow us to develop elaborate conditions for narrowing our data search to a very narrow view. In their simplest form, SELECT commands retrieve the values for a list of attributes from the tuples of a single relation. In their most complex form, SELECT commands allow us to join data across multiple tables to link specific pieces of information that are of interest. In the following discussion, we outline the foundations from which such complex queries can be generated.

The SELECT statement consists of three parts: (1) a list of attributes that we wish to SELECT from the database, (2) a list of tables where these attributes can be found, and (3) a WHERE clause that sets the conditions under which attribute values are to be retrieved. For instance, if we wanted to retrieve a list of all employees with a pay rate over $3,000, we would issue the following SELECT command:

```
SELECT    Name
FROM      EMPLOYEE
WHERE     Pay_Rate>3000
```

SQL would first locate the table named EMPLOYEE, then search all the tuples to identify any with a Pay_Rate greater than 3000. From the identified tuples, the SELECT attributes are extracted and the values returned to the screen. Hence, the results of this query based on the values shown in Figure 6.11 (page 207) would be:

```
Greg Kinman
Elaine Kopp
```

Often, a user will want to aggregate data from more than one table. If we go back to our original reasons for designing this database, one goal was to facilitate the billing process. To process client billing, we need a combination of data from the EMPLOYEE, WORK_COMPLETED, and CLIENT relations. From the EMPLOYEE relation we need information on Billing_Rate for each record of WORK_COMPLETED. From the CLIENT relation we need data for Name, Street_Address, City, State, ZIP_Code, and Contact to send the bill to the correct client. From the WORK_COMPLETED relation we will match the previously noted information with the records of employees' completed work to provide line item detail on the date and hours of work completed. The SELECT command to aggregate the data for the billing for Hasbro, Inc., could be as follows:

```
SELECT    CLIENT.Name, Street_Address, City,
          State, ZIP_Code, Contact, Date, Hours,
          Billing_Rate
FROM      EMPLOYEE, CLIENT, WORK_COMPLETED
WHERE     Employee_Number=Employee_No AND
          CLIENT.Client_No='H12456' AND
          WORK_COMPLETED.Client_No='H12456'
```

Note the new conventions we have added in this query. First, in the SELECT attribute list, we used "CLIENT.Name" to identify the client name. The reason we attached the table name onto the front of the attribute name is because the attribute Name is ambiguous—that is, SQL would not be able to tell if we wanted the Name attribute from the EMPLOYEE or the CLIENT relation. We did the same thing in the WHERE clause for Client_No. In fact, the rule is that any time we reference an attribute in a SELECT statement and the attribute name appears in more than one relation in the table list specified on the FROM list, we must use the table name extension as a prefix to the attribute name.

The other convention is the use of the "AND" in the WHERE clause. We use connectors such as AND to link multiple conditions that must all be met when selecting tuples from one or more tables. The most common other connector is the OR connector, which allows for a tuple to be selected if either condition in the WHERE clause is true.

One final note on querying is consideration of the output that comes from the previous query. As shown in Figure 6.15, this query would attach the client name and address to every line of output generated when a row of WORK_COMPLETED is identified. Hence, for the seven lines of completed work that are returned in the query, there is a repetitive return of the client name and address each time. In this case, where the name, address, and contact person will be the same for every query response, it would make more sense to split the query into two parts. First, we would identify the client billing address information. Then, in a second query, we would pull out the multiple lines of billing information for completed work. This two-query approach and the related output are demonstrated in Figure 6.16.

Figure 6.15 Generation of Client Billing Information (Single Query Approach)

Name	Street_Address	City	State	ZIP_Code	Contact	Date	Hours	Billing_Rate
Hasbro, Inc.	4516 Burton Pike	Providence	RI	02844	T. Bayers	070826	8	150.00
Hasbro, Inc.	4516 Burton Pike	Providence	RI	02844	T. Bayers	070826	8	100.00
Hasbro, Inc.	4516 Burton Pike	Providence	RI	02844	T. Bayers	070826	8	57.00
Hasbro, Inc.	4516 Burton Pike	Providence	RI	02844	T. Bayers	070826	8	57.00
Hasbro, Inc.	4516 Burton Pike	Providence	RI	02844	T. Bayers	070827	8	100.00
Hasbro, Inc.	4516 Burton Pike	Providence	RI	02844	T. Bayers	070827	8	57.00
Hasbro, Inc.	4516 Burton Pike	Providence	RI	02844	T. Bayers	070827	8	57.00

Generating Standard Reports

To this point we have focused our discussion on designing a logical *relational database model* that efficiently stores the data in our database. This allows the user to easily manipulate the base level tables to generate information on an *ad hoc* (as needed) basis. This is the most effective way to provide data availability to users of the database when their information needs change on an ongoing basis.

However, many decisions are not *ad hoc*, but are made on an ongoing basis as part of regular business operations. For instance, the billing information we previously discussed will need to be performed on a regular basis. It would be much easier if the information required for the second part of the query in Figure 6.16 was already aggregated in a single source table within the database—but only if the data were not replicated, causing a redundancy. (Recall from Chapter 5 our discussion of the negative effects of data redundancy and our arguments for using database management systems as a solution to the problem.)

Figure 6.16 Generation of Client Billing Information (Double Query Approach)

```
SELECT      Name, Street_Address, City, State, ZIP_Code, Contact
FROM        CLIENT
WHERE       Client_No='H12456'
```

Output

Name	Street_Address	City	State	ZIP_Code	Contact
Hasbro, Inc.	4516 Burton Pike	Providence	RI	02844	T. Bayers

```
SELECT      Date, Hours, Billing_Rate
FROM        EMPLOYEE, WORK_COMPLETED
WHERE       Employee_Number=Employee_No AND Client_No='H12456'
```

Output

Date	Hours	Billing_Rate
070826	8	150.00
070826	8	100.00
070826	8	57.00
070826	8	57.00
070827	8	100.00
070827	8	57.00
070827	8	57.00

In a *relational database model* we can do just that. We can actually create *views* of the data that look like additional tables, but are just alternative ways to view the data that already exists in the database. The data are not copied to a second physical location in the database. Instead, a *view* creates the appearance of a different set of tables for the user in the format the user wants to see. We graphically present this concept in Figure 6.17.

Figure 6.17 Schema for the Client Billing and Human Resources Portion of the Database

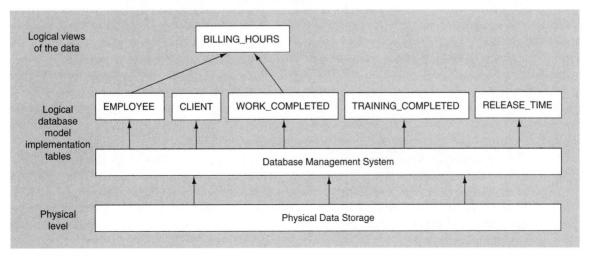

Note that the data at the lowest level (i.e., the physical level) are stored in a manner that users need not understand. The DBMS handles all the communication between the relational tables that are used to implement the database model and the physical storage of the data. Once the database model has been implemented into relational tables, we can then create as many *views* as we wish, based on some combination of attributes extracted from these base *relations*. These views do not replicate the data; they only provide alternative ways to examine the data.

To create a *view* of the data contained in the database tables, we simply tell SQL to do just that. We CREATE VIEW by using a SELECT statement, just as we did when querying the database, but in this case, we will be storing the results in a permanent view. Permanent views can be deleted using the DROP VIEW statement. In Figure 6.18 we issue the CREATE VIEW command to create the view BILLING_HOURS. Note after the query in Figure 6.18 the data that would be shown in the view based on the data from Figure 6.11 (page 207).

Figure 6.18 Creating a View of the Client Billing Detail with SQL

SQL commands

```
CREATE VIEW     BILLING_HOURS
AS SELECT       Employee_No, Client_No, Date, Hours, Billing_Rate
FROM            EMPLOYEE, WORK_COMPLETED
WHERE           Employee_No=Employee_Number
```

(Note: Employee_No would not have to be included except that it is needed to form a composite key for the view, BILLING_HOURS.)

Data in the view BILLING_HOURS:

BILLING_HOURS	Employee_No	Client_No	Date	Hours	Billing_Rate
	B122	F11555	070823	8	150
	A632	F11555	070823	8	100
	B122	F11555	070824	8	150
	A632	F11555	070824	8	100
	B122	F11555	070825	8	150
	A632	F11555	070825	8	100
	B122	H12456	070826	8	150
	A632	H12456	070826	8	100
	A356	F11555	070826	8	57
	B432	H12456	070826	8	57
	A491	H12456	070826	8	57
	B122	F11555	070827	8	150
	A632	H12456	070827	8	100
	A356	F11555	070827	8	57
	B432	H12456	070827	8	57
	B491	H12456	070827	8	57

Once a *view* has been created, the view can be used in other SQL queries the same as any of the tables that were created. Notice in Figure 6.18 that we have created a view that represents all employees' hours spent working for clients, matched with the employee billing rates. We can now issue a query directly to this view to aggregate billing information for a specific client (see Figure 6.19), instead of having to use the more

Figure 6.19 Query to Extract Client Billing Data for Hasbro, Inc.

```
SELECT      Date, Hours, Billing_Rate
FROM        BILLING_HOURS
WHERE       Client_No='H12456'
```

Output

Date	Hours	Billing_Rate
070826	8	150.00
070826	8	100.00
070826	8	57.00
070826	8	57.00
070827	8	100.00
070827	8	57.00
070827	8	57.00

complex query in Figure 6.16 (page 215). The result is exactly the same for the new query in Figure 6.19 as what we received from the second query in Figure 6.16.

Views can be used to generate standard reports or to provide all the data necessary to create such reports. This simplifies the process for users of the database and reduces the risk of the user producing incorrect queries. In other cases, an experienced user may decide to create views on a temporary basis for work on a given project and, once the project is completed, drop the view. Once the database design is complete, tables generally remain constant in a database except for maintenance and additions prompted by changes in business processes. Views, on the other hand, are much more likely to come and go in the database.

SUMMARY

As the information needs and wants of users continue to escalate, database integration has clearly become the norm rather than the exception. The focus is no longer on finding places in the business where implementing databases is useful. Instead, the focus has shifted to finding ways to integrate as much of the organization's data as possible into a single logical database. This shift in focus offers new opportunities and challenges for accountants as they strive to continue as the primary information providers in organizations.

With these opportunities and challenges come huge responsibilities. The very lifeblood of an organization today often resides in a database that contains all the organization's information. If the database is destroyed and cannot be recovered, the organization might not survive in today's business environment. Likewise, if competitors or other unauthorized persons gain access to the data, the organization's ability to compete can be jeopardized.

Safeguarding data while providing information to users who need it is not a simple task. In Chapters 8 and 9, our discussion will shift to the issues surrounding data reliability, access, and security. You will learn about procedures that organizations implement to ensure the reliability of information that is updated or added to the database. You will also learn about safeguarding the data and maintaining backups of data so that if something should happen to the database, it can be recovered in a timely manner to allow the organization to carry on its operations. These are truly challenging but exciting times for accountants who are prepared to operate in an information systems environment.

REVIEW QUESTIONS

RQ 6-1   a.   What is an entity?

b.   What is an attribute?

c.   What is a relationship?

d.   What is a key attribute?

e.   What is a composite primary key?

RQ 6-2   What coding techniques can be used to create good primary key attributes?

RQ 6-3   Why is it important that you identify all the important relationships when developing an REA model?

RQ 6-4   Identify and briefly define the four types of entities that can be modeled in the REA approach for accounting databases?

RQ 6-5   What is the most important distinction between a resource and a location in the REA approach?

RQ 6-6   What are the characteristics of recursive relationships that distinguish them from other types of relationships?

RQ 6-7   Describe a situation in which one entity has minimum participation in its relationship with another entity.

RQ 6-8   How can an REA model help an organization improve the level of data integration it achieves across multiple business processes?

RQ 6-9   a.   What is a relation?

b.   What is a tuple?

c.   What is an attribute in a relational data model?

d.   What is referential integrity?

RQ 6-10   How is referential integrity implemented in most relational DBMSs?

RQ 6-11   What is the difference in implementation of a one-to-many and a one-to-one relationship in a relational database model?

RQ 6-12   a.   What SQL command can be used to build a relation?

b.   What SQL command do we use to enter data in a relation?

c.   What SQL command do we use to query information from a relation?

d.   What SQL command do we use to build a standard report view in a relational database?

DISCUSSION QUESTIONS

DQ 6-1   Examine Figure 6.20, which contains the REA model for Davis Industrial Supply (DIS). The model is partially completed; it includes all entities and relationships, but it does not include cardinalities or descriptions of the relationships (which would appear in diamonds on the connecting lines between entities). DIS sells replacement parts for packaging machinery to companies in several states. DIS accepts orders over the telephone, via fax, and by mail. When an order arrives, one of the salespersons enters it as a sales order. The sales order includes the customer's name and a list of the inventory items that the customer wishes to purchase. This inventory list includes the quantity of each inventory item and the price at which DIS is currently selling the item. When the order is ready to ship, DIS completes an invoice and records the sale. Sometimes, inventory items that a customer has ordered are not in stock. In those cases, DIS will ship partial orders. Customers are expected to pay their invoices within 30 days. Most customers do pay on time; however, some customers make partial payments over two or more months. List each entity in the REA model and identify it as a resource, event, agent, or location. Redraw the REA model to include the diamonds for each relationship and include an appropriate description in each diamond.

Figure 6.20 Partially Completed REA Model of the Davis Industrial Supply Sales Business Process

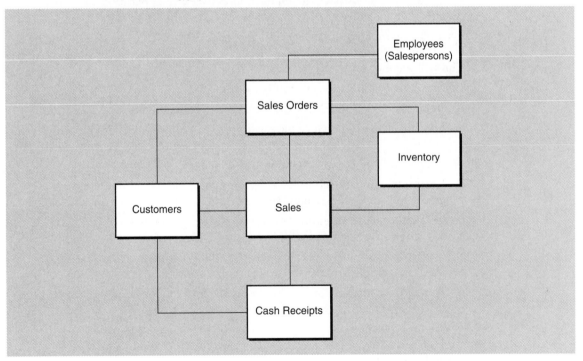

DQ 6-2 Examine the REA model for Davis Industrial Supply that appears in Figure 6.20. Determine the maximum cardinalities for each of the eight relationships indicated in the model. State any assumptions you needed to make and be prepared to defend the rationale for your selection.

DQ 6-3 Examine the REA model for Davis Industrial Supply that appears in Figure 6.20. For each of the six entities in the model, list the attributes that a database designer should include in each table. Identify primary key attributes with (PK) and composite primary key attributes with (CPK). State any assumptions you needed to make and be prepared to defend the rationale for the attributes you have chosen.

DQ 6-4 What SQL command(s) would you use to generate a standard report for human resources from the relational database represented in Figure 6.11 (page 207)? Assuming human resources will be interested in tracking work, vacation, and sick time for all employees, be sure to consider all of these factors in designing your report format.

DQ 6-5 What SQL command(s) would you use to extract data from the report view in Discussion Question 6-4 for Janet Robins?

PROBLEMS

Note: These problems should be completed with a database software package such as Access. For Problems 6-1 through 6-3, you may use data that you (or your instructor) have downloaded from an accounting database. Problem 6-4 demonstrates the interaction between an application software system and the database.

P 6-1 Using the information from Figures 6.11 (page 207), 6.13 (page 210), and 6.14 (page 211), create the database in the software package of your choice. This will require three steps:

a. Implement the relations from Figure 6.11.

b. Insert the data from Figure 6.11 into the relational tables.

c. Print the data from each of the relations to test for successful implementation.

P 6-2 *Note:* This problem is a continuation of Problem 6-1.

a. Create the standard report view for displaying the billing hours as suggested in Figure 6.18 (page 216).

b. Create the standard report view for displaying the human resources information as recommended in Discussion Question 6-4.

c. Extract from the billing hours view the billing information for Hasbro, Inc., and print the results.

d. Extract from the human resources view the information related to Janet Robins and print the results.

P 6-3 *Note:* This problem is a continuation of Problem 6-1, but requires access to the Internet, a site for posting the database on the Web, and an understanding of Internet access.

a. Take the database developed in Problem 6-1 and place it on the Internet (or your instructor may provide the same).

b. Access the database from your local computer using the appropriate address for the database. (Your software must be capable of using Internet addresses for locating the data.)

c. Use a series of queries similar to that in Figure 6.16 (page 215) to pull down the billing information for Fleet Services.

P 6-4 *Note:* This problem is a continuation of Problem 6-1, but requires use of a spreadsheet package that is capable of reading data from your database package (for example, Excel can import data from an Access database).

    a. Using your spreadsheet package, construct SQL queries (or use the software's menu generation for queries) to import the billing information for Fleet Services.

    b. Develop a report format for using the information from your queries to generate a nice-looking report in your spreadsheet package.

    c. Document the queries used in your spreadsheet package to access the data and explain what each step of the queries does.

P 6-5 Using the REA model in Figure 6.20 and your answers to Discussion Questions 6-1, 6-2, and 6-3, create a database for DIS in the software package of your choice. This will require that you:

    a. Create tables for each of the relations you identified in Discussion Question 6-1 that include the attributes you identified in Review Question 6-3.

    b. Insert a few tuples of sample data that you devise.

    c. Print the data from each of the relations to test for successful implementation.

KEY TERMS

semantics	recursive relationship	null
instance	participation constraint	non-null
attribute	relation	referential integrity
composite attributes	tuple	
key attribute	candidate keys	

Enterprise
Risk Management

Part Three

Controlling Information Systems: Introduction to Internal Control

The 21st century started with a bang! News of business scandals and corruptions blazed across worldwide media at the speed of light. CPA firms, investors, lenders, managers and innocent bystanders were deeply affected by the discovery, nature, and extent of corporate malfeasance. The direct injuries sustained by corporate stakeholders were staggering and the collateral damage inflicted on the public was frightening. Reports of corporate shenanigans dominated newspaper headlines:

- Enron Corporation: Upper managers used special purpose entities to hide billions of dollars in corporate liability. Once the house of cards fell and these entities collapsed, Enron was broke and millions of people lost billions of dollars.

- Arthur Andersen, LLP: The CPA firm, responsible for auditing Enron, experienced loss of credibility, trust, and integrity, and was viewed by the public as greedy and negligent. The firm imploded and thousands of employees were harmed, as was the whole accounting profession.

- WorldCom, Incorporated: Managers transferred billions of dollars in expenses to capital accounts, which violated generally accepted accounting principles. WorldCom's stock price plummeted and millions of investors lost huge sums of money. WorldCom filed for bankruptcy protection and struggled to reemerge as MCI.

- Adelphia Communications: Upper managers inflated the company's financial performance through misleading accounting practices. They also tapped the company's coffers for personal benefit without disclosure to the public or board of directors. Thousands of stakeholders were severely harmed.

- Tyco International: Three former executives are accused of looting the company of hundreds of millions of dollars. The public lost money and faith in the company.

- Quest Communications: Managers of Quest's Global Business Unit improperly inflated company revenues in order to meet earnings and revenue expectations. The company's stock nosedived and investors lost incredible sums of money.

Learning Objectives

- To learn the purpose of achieving an adequate level of control in business organizations.

- To understand that organizational and IT management employs control systems as part of organizational and IT governance initiatives.

- To appreciate the relationship between business ethics and sound internal control.

- To grasp the concepts of fraud, computer fraud, and computer abuse.

- To examine operations process and information process control goals.

- To describe the major categories of control plans.

As you can see by looking at the AIS Wheel icon, this chapter will introduce the concept of internal control, which includes pervasive, process, and database controls. You will learn about the vital importance that controls play in today's organizations, particularly in light of recent accounting scandals and frauds. No time in recent history has the issue of accounting information system controls been more publicly prominent and socially sensitive.

These are but a few of the more notable business and audit failures uncovered in the early part of the 21st century. How did these situations occur and what would have prevented them? We shall learn in this chapter that these companies created a *control environment* that permitted, and perhaps encouraged, employees to perpetrate these frauds. We will learn about systems of *internal control* that are designed to prevent such frauds from occurring and provide a means to detect when they have occurred.

SYNOPSIS

Can an organization's business processes operate without controls? Perhaps—but the odds against it are staggering! In the absence of controls, how would an organization attain its objectives? In this chapter, as well as Chapters 8 and 9, we attempt to make the case that controlling business processes is critically important to business organizations. These chapters should provide you with a solid foundation for the later study of the controls for specific business processes, which are covered in Chapters 10 through 15.

CONTROLS

We place a controls icon at the head of this synopsis to emphasize that the content of this chapter is entirely about controls. In this chapter we consider the importance of controls in organizations that are tightly integrated internally, such as with *enterprise systems*, or have multiple connections to its environment, such as e-Business architectures. Managers of these organizations must be confident that each component of the organization performs as expected, otherwise chaos will prevail and business partnerships will fail. In particular, organizations engaged in e-Business must have internal control processes in

ENTERPRISE SYSTEMS

E-BUSINESS

place to reduce the possibilities of fraud and other disruptive events, and to ensure compliance with applicable laws and regulations. For example, when engaged in Internet-based commerce, the organization may need to ensure the security of its own database, as well as the security of communication networks it operates in conjunction with trading partners; also, e-Business firms might have to comply with relevant privacy-related laws and regulations. We begin by discussing the need for control in organizations.

WHY DO WE NEED CONTROL?

The concept of *control* is likely not new to you. You may have read about control in a number of other courses. In business courses you would have learned that one of the three primary functions performed by managers (together with *planning* and *decision making*) is *controlling* business activities. Also, you may have learned in a biology course how the human body is controlled, or in an organizational behavior course how work-related activities of employees are controlled. Recall from Chapter 1 that organizations are composed of three major components: the management process, the operations process, and the information process. These chapters (Chapters 7–9) concentrate on controlling the *business processes* (i.e., the combined management, operations, and information processes) of an organization.

Management is responsible for exercising control over the organization's business processes. The major reasons for exercising such control are (1) to provide reasonable assurance that the goals of each business process are being achieved; (2) to mitigate the risk that the enterprise will be exposed to some type of harm, danger, or loss (including loss caused by *fraud* or other intentional and unintentional acts); and (3) to provide reasonable assurance that the company is in compliance with applicable legal and regulatory obligations.

Corporate Governance

Picture yourself as a passenger on an airplane coming in for a landing at a busy airport like Chicago's O'Hare or New York's JFK. Over the intercom system, you hear the captain announce, in a somewhat agitated tone, "Ladies and gentlemen, we have been informed by the tower that all air traffic controllers have just walked off the job. In addition, we have simultaneously experienced a sudden, unexplained, malfunction in our on-board radar and navigation instrumentation. Please remain in your seats, keep your seat belts fastened, and stay calm as we attempt to land the plane in this nasty weather."

Without the aid of control mechanisms that ordinarily exist, could our process (i.e., the aircraft) accomplish its *objective* of landing safely? While we can argue that process objectives might be achieved in the absence of these control mechanisms, the primary reason for control is to help *ensure* that process goals are achieved. For example, an element of control not mentioned in our example is the pilot. A skilled and experienced pilot *may* be able to land the plane safely. But, the air traffic controllers, radar, and other processes significantly reduce the risks involved by helping the pilot to identify and deal with the hazards, such as buildings, terrain, weather, and other aircraft—factors that make a safe landing so difficult.

To underscore the importance of the relationship of control and objectives, the Committee of Sponsoring Organizations (COSO) of the Treadway Commission (National Commission on Fraudulent Financial Reporting) stated in its framework for internal control that "to effect control, there need to be predetermined objectives. *Without ob-*

jectives, control has no meaning (emphasis added)." Further, the COSO report goes on to say that control "involves influencing someone and/or something—such as an entity's personnel, a business unit, or an entire enterprise—with the purpose of moving toward the objectives."[1]

Rather than express the purpose of control in positive terms (i.e., the good to be achieved), we can state its purpose in terms of the bad to be avoided. For instance, in our airplane illustration, is there a *risk* that the plane will crash and that lives will be lost? Obviously the possibility exists! Therefore, we conclude that a second reason for controlling processes is to *reduce the risk* that unwanted outcomes will occur. We define **risk** as the possibility that an event or action will cause an organization to fail to meet its objectives (or goals). Organizations must identify and assess the risk, literally the probability, that untoward events or actions will occur and then reduce the possibility that those events or actions will occur by designing and implementing systems of control.

Having made the case that the principal reason for controlling processes is to help achieve process objectives—or alternatively, to mitigate risk to the process—let's translate those two thoughts to the business environment by asking ourselves:

- What are the enterprise goals that internal control is designed to help achieve?
- What are the typical business risks or unwanted outcomes that the organization should try to avoid?

We devote a later section of the chapter to answering the first of these questions. At this point, let's briefly examine the second question. The set of nine *common business exposures* presented in Exhibit 7.1 (page 228) are examples of undesirable actions or events that an organization wants to avoid. These exposures might cause an organization to fail to meet its objectives or their realization might represent a breakdown in a company's control system. For example, a flood might cause an organization to have its *business interrupted* or have its *resources destroyed*. In many ways, however, these exposures occur when we fail to meet objectives. For example, by experiencing the exposure *statutory sanctions,* an organization fails to achieve a goal to comply with applicable laws, regulations, and contractual obligations.

Here is another important observation about Exhibit 7.1. As you read these definitions, be careful to distinguish causes and effects. Exposures do not *cause* adverse actions or events; rather, they may *result* from any of these actions or events. It may be poor judgment on management's part to fail to implement a certain control, but this failure does *not* constitute the exposure itself. Rather, a control weakness, such as *erroneous recordkeeping*, may subsequently *cause* an erroneous management decision to be made.

Internal control has recently become more important because of the emphasis placed by shareholders on *corporate governance* and the demands this places on boards of directors and executives to implement and demonstrate control over operations. Executives, in turn, must implement and demonstrate governance of IT operations. In both cases—corporate and IT governance—frameworks for control, such as those introduced here and expanded upon throughout this text, will be key elements in this governance process.

Sarbanes-Oxley Act

As a result of Enron, WorldCom, Tyco, Arthur Andersen, and the other business scandals noted in the introduction to this chapter, the federal government was forced to interject

---

[1] *Internal Control—Integrated Framework—Framework Volume* (New York: The Committee of Sponsoring Organizations of the Treadway Commission, 1992): 101.

Exhibit 7.1 Common Business Exposures

1. *Erroneous recordkeeping* is the recording of events contrary to established accounting policies. This exposure is often *caused* by the incomplete or inaccurate processing of an event.

2. *Unacceptable accounting* is the establishment or implementation of accounting policies that are not generally accepted or are inappropriate to the circumstances. This exposure is often *caused* by an improper interpretation or a willful disregard of GAAP or some other set of accounting regulations.

3. *Business interruption* may include anything from a temporary suspension of operations to a permanent termination of the enterprise. This exposure may be *caused* by a number of factors, including irreparable damage to an organization's database.

4. *Erroneous management decisions* are objectionable in themselves but may also lead to other exposures. This exposure is often *caused* by managers using misleading information or failing to acquire necessary information relative to a particular decision.

5. *Fraud and embezzlement* may be perpetrated at different levels (against management or by management). This exposure may be *caused* by direct misappropriation of funds or by deliberate communication of misinformation to management or investors.

6. *Statutory sanctions* are any of the various penalties that may be brought by judicial or regulatory authorities that have jurisdiction over an organization's operations. This exposure may be *caused* by a number of factors, including violation of the Foreign Corrupt Practices Act (FCPA), discussed in the next section of the chapter.

7. *Excessive costs* may include incurring unnecessary expenses involved in operating a business. This exposure may be *caused* by failing to require that all expenditures over a certain dollar amount be approved.

8. *Loss or destruction of resources* is *unintentional* loss of physical resources (cash, inventory, etc.) and the loss of information (inventory master data, accounts receivable master data, etc.). This exposure is often *caused* by a lack of adequate safeguards over an organization's resources.

9. *Competitive disadvantage* relates to any inability of an organization to remain abreast of the demands of the marketplace or to respond effectively to competitive challenges. This exposure may be *caused* by a number of factors, including the use of an outdated computer system that fails to respond to customer needs as effectively as do systems used by competitors.

Source: Adapted from William C. Mair, Donald R. Wood, and Keagle W. Davis, *Computer Control & Audit* (Altamonte Springs, FL: The Institute of Internal Auditors, 1982): 11–12.

its will into corporate governance affairs. Why? Because these business entities apparently failed to enact and enforce proper internal controls throughout their organizations, and as a result, some employees boldly violated ethical codes, business rules, regulatory requirements, and/or statutory mandates, which resulted in massive frauds. Investors and lenders lost huge sums of money, and public trust in corporate managers, public accounting firms, and federal regulators has been severely, perhaps irreparably, harmed. The federal government's duty is to protect its citizens from such abuses; accordingly, one of the measures taken by Congress was to pass the Sarbanes-Oxley Act (SOA) of 2002.

This section is aimed at placing the SOA into the context of corporate governance. If this is your first exposure to the act, it will undoubtedly be discussed in-depth in your financial accounting and auditing courses. However, it is worth including here because it highlights the critical role played by accountants and auditors in corporate governance; as well, it serves as a vivid reminder that it takes decades to build public trust and minutes to lose this sacred bond! The basic elements of the SOA are outlined in Exhibit 7.2.

Among other reforms, the SOA created a new accounting oversight board, strengthened auditor independence rules, increased accountability of company officers and directors, mandated upper management to take responsibility for the company's internal control structure, enhanced the quality of financial reporting, and put teeth into white-

Exhibit 7.2 Outline of the Sarbanes-Oxley Act of 2002[a]

The Sarbanes-Oxley Act (SOA) affects corporate managers, independent auditors, and other players who are integral to capital formation in the United States. This omnibus regulation will forever alter the face of corporate reporting and auditing. SOA titles and key sections are outlined herein.

1. *Title I—Public Company Accounting Oversight Board:* Section 101 establishes an independent board to oversee public company audits. Section 107 authorizes oversight and enforcement of the board to the Securities and Exchange Commission (SEC).

2. *Title II—Auditor Independence:* Section 201 prohibits a CPA firm that audits a public company to engage in certain non-audit services with the same client. Most relevant to accounting information systems is the prohibition of financial information systems design and implementation services to audit clients. Section 203 requires audit partner rotation in their fifth, sixth, or seventh year, depending on the partner's role in the audit.

3. *Title III—Corporate Responsibility:* Section 302 requires a company's chief executive officer (CEO) and chief financial officer (CFO) to certify quarterly and annual reports. They are certifying the following: they reviewed the reports; the reports are not materially untruthful or misleading; the financial statements fairly reflect in all material respects the financial position of the company; and they are responsible for designing, establishing, maintaining, and monitoring corporate disclosures, controls, and procedures. Section 303 makes it unlawful for corporate officers or directors to fraudulently influence, coerce, manipulate, or mislead any independent auditors who are engaged in auditing the firm's financial statements.

4. *Title IV—Enhanced Financial Disclosures:* Section 404 requires each annual report filed with the SEC to include an internal control report. The report shall: state the responsibility of management for establishing and maintaining an adequate internal control structure and procedures for financial reporting and assess, as of the end of the company's fiscal year, the effectiveness of the internal control structure and procedures of the company for financial reporting. The company's independent auditors must attest to and report on the assessments made by company management.

5. *Title V—Analysts Conflicts of Interests:* Requires financial analysts to properly disclose in research reports any conflicts of interest they might hold with the companies they recommend.

6. *Title VI—Commission Resources and Authority:* Authorizes the SEC to censure or deny any person the privilege of appearing or practicing before the SEC if that person is deemed to: be unqualified, have acted in an unethical manner, or have aided and abetted a violation of federal securities laws.

7. *Title VII—Studies and Reports:* Authorizes the General Accounting Office (GAO) to study the consolidation of public accounting firms since 1989 and offer solutions to any recognized problems.

8. *Title VIII—Corporate and Criminal Fraud Accountability:* Section 802 makes it a felony to knowingly destroy, alter, or create records and/or documents with the intent to impede, obstruct, or influence an ongoing or contemplated federal investigation. Section 806 offers legal protection to whistle-blowers who provide evidence of fraud.

9. *Title IX—White-Collar Crime Penalty Enhancements:* Section 906 sets forth criminal penalties applicable to CEOs and CFOs of up to $5 million and up to 20 years in prison if they certify and file false and/or misleading financial statements with the SEC.

10. *Title X—Corporate Tax Returns:* Section 1001 conveys a "sense of the Senate" that the corporate federal income tax returns are signed by the CEO.

11. *Title XI—Corporate Fraud and Accountability:* Section 1102 provides for fines and imprisonment of up to 20 years to individuals who corruptly alter, destroy, mutilate, or conceal documents with the intent to impair the document's integrity or availability for use in an official proceeding, or to otherwise obstruct, influence, or impede any official proceeding. Section 1105 authorizes the SEC to prohibit anyone from serving as an officer or director if the person has committed securities fraud.

[a] 107 P.L. 204, § 1, 116 Stat. 745, July 30, 2002.

collar crime penalties. Of particular note to students of accounting information systems, section 201 of the act prohibits audit firms from providing a wide array of non-audit services to audit clients; in particular, the act prohibits consulting engagements involving the design and implementation of financial information systems. Does this suggest that CPA firms will no longer offer systems-related consulting engagements? No—it means that CPA firm A cannot offer such services to audit client X, but CPA B can provide these services to client X. Thus, in all likelihood, non-audit engagements of this nature will swap around among CPA firms—not disappear altogether.

Two other striking mandates in the act are reflected in section 302, which specifies that CEOs and CFOs must certify quarterly and annual financial statements, and section 404, which mandates the annual filing of an internal control report to the SEC. The bottom-line observation regarding the SOA is the following: Corporate governance is neither a joke, nor management babble, nor an esoteric academic topic—it is real, palpable, and important, with serious consequences. Case in point: Recall what happened to the largest CPA firm in the world, Arthur Andersen? It will take years or perhaps decades for the accounting profession to regain the public's trust—this is a challenging matter indeed!

Fraud and Its Relationship to Control

In this section, we discuss fraud, computer fraud, and computer abuse. As noted earlier, there have been some highly publicized instances of management and employee fraud, some of which involved computer fraud and computer abuse. This topic has received so much media attention that we cover it in this separate section. Fraud is a deliberate act or untruth intended to obtain unfair or unlawful gain. Management's legal responsibility to prevent fraud and other irregularities is implied by laws such as the Foreign Corrupt Practices Act,[2] which states "a fundamental aspect of management's stewardship responsibility is to provide shareholders with reasonable assurance that the business is adequately controlled." Notice that section 1102 of the Sarbanes-Oxley Act specifically addresses corporate fraud. Instances of fraud undermine management's ability to convince various authorities that it is upholding its stewardship responsibility.

The accounting profession too has been proactive in dealing with corporate fraud, as it has launched an anti-fraud program. One of the manifestations of this initiative is Statement on Auditing Standards (SAS) Number 99, entitled Consideration of Fraud in a Financial Statement Audit. SAS 99 has the same title as its predecessor, SAS 82, but the new standard is much more encompassing than the old. For instance, SAS 99 emphasizes brainstorming fraud risks, increasing professional skepticism, using unpredictable audit test patterns, and detecting management override of internal controls.

Why are Congress, the accounting profession, the financial community, and others so impassioned about the subject of fraud? This is largely because of some highly publicized business failures in recent years that caught people completely by surprise, when the financial statements of these businesses showed that they were prospering. When these firms, such as Enron, went "belly-up," it was discovered that the seeming prosperity was an illusion concocted by "cooking the books" (i.e., creating false and misleading financial statements).

E-BUSINESS   Let's examine some fraud-related exposures that management must address when the organization is engaged in e-Business. First, an organization that receives payment via credit card, where the credit card is not present during the transaction (e.g., sales via Web site or telephone), absorbs the loss if a transaction is fraudulent. To prevent these exposures (i.e., *fraud, excessive cost*) the organization may install controls, such as anti-

---

[2] See Foreign Corrupt Practices Act (FCPA) of 1977 (P.L. 95-213).

fraud software. Also, some banks will drop merchants who have unacceptably high fraud rates. This would cause an organization to go out of business (i.e., *business interruption*).

Aside from some widely reported cases, is fraud really that prevalent in business? In March 1999, the Committee of Sponsoring Organizations of the Treadway Commission (COSO) reported on a study of fraudulent financial reporting. Technology Excerpt 7.1 includes the highlights of the report. In 2002, Ernst and Young, LLP conducted its eighth, biannual global fraud survey to find answers to these and other questions. The results of the latest survey are reported in Technology Excerpt 7.2 (page 232).

We can see from these reports that fraud is indeed a worldwide problem. Notice that **E-BUSINESS** both the COSO and Ernst & Young reports indicate that management was involved in the majority of frauds. The COSO findings suggest that internal pressure to improve financial performance may lead to fraudulent behavior. The Ernst & Young results show that the risk of external fraud increases when companies engage in e-Business. The implication is clear: A system of internal control, including an ongoing *process* of review, can reduce the incidents of fraud.

Implications of Computer Fraud and Abuse

Now let's turn our attention to computer fraud and abuse. The proliferation of computers in business organizations has created expanded opportunities for criminal infiltration. Computers have been used to commit a wide variety of crimes, including fraud, larceny, and embezzlement. Referring to Technology Excerpt 7.2, results of the Ernst and Young study indicate that one of managers' most worrisome concerns is the perpetration of fraud using computers. In general, computer-related crimes have been referred to as *computer fraud*, *computer abuse*, or *computer crime*.

Technology   Excerpt   7.1

COSO Report on Fraudulent Financial Reporting

The research team studied over 200 cases of fraudulent financial reporting that occurred between 1987 and 1997. Some of the key insights include:

- The companies where the frauds had been committed were small (size ranging below $100 million in assets) and were not listed on the New York or American Stock Exchanges.
- Some of the companies were at or near positions of net loss. Pressures to show better financial performance may have provided the incentive for the fraudulent activities.

- The companies' CEOs were involved in 72 percent of the cases and the CFOs in 43 percent of the cases.
- Typical techniques involved overstating revenues by recording revenues early or fictitiously, and overstating assets by overstating value and recording assets that did not exist.
- Consequences of the frauds often included bankruptcy, significant changes in ownership, delisting by national exchanges, as well as financial penalties (for the companies and the accused executives).

Source: *Fraudulent Financial Reporting: 1987–1997 An Analysis of U.S. Public Companies* (New York: The Committee of Sponsoring Organizations of the Treadway Commission, 1999): 2–4.

Technology Excerpt 7.2

Ernst & Young Fraud Survey

In 2002 Ernst & Young conducted its eighth, biannual fraud survey. Questionnaires were sent to key executives of major organizations in Africa, Australia, Europe, and the Americas. Among its key findings were:

- Around 85 percent of frauds were committed by company insiders.
- About 55 percent of fraud perpetrators were managers.
- Over one-half of the surveyed firms experienced significant frauds in the last year.
- Organizations engaged in e-Business were more vulnerable to the risk of external fraud.
- Fraud is not confined to any particular region of the globe; however, more frauds were perpetrated in less-developed regions than more-developed regions.
- Approximately 20 percent of frauds are known to the public, about 40 percent of frauds are kept confidential, and the remaining 40 percent of frauds have yet to be discovered.

- The expectation gap persists with regard to the auditors' roles in uncovering fraud during a financial statement audit, as 64 percent of respondents felt that auditors should be responsible for detecting fraud.
- Sound internal controls are the best way to prevent and detect fraud.
- The number one fraud worry on the minds of executives is asset misappropriation.
- The second most disconcerting fraud concern of executives is computer crime; most notably, electronic funds transfers, data abuses, confidentiality, and illegal software.
- For the first time in the 16 years during which the surveys have been administered, most organizations have formal fraud prevention policies, such as codes of corporate governance and employee conduct.
- The most useful fraud protection mechanisms are internal controls, management reviews, and internal audits.

Source: Ernst & Young LLP, *Fraud: The Unmanaged Risk*, 2002.

The majority of computer crimes consists of two basic types:

- The computer is used as the *tool* of the criminal to accomplish the illegal act. For instance, the perpetrator could illegally access one or more banking systems to make unauthorized transfers to a foreign bank account, and then go to the other country to enjoy the ill-gotten gain.

- The computer or the information stored in it is the *target* of the criminal. Recent, widely publicized instances of *computer viruses* fall into this category.

E-BUSINESS   Technology Summary 7.1 describes some of the better-known malicious coding techniques used to commit computer fraud or to damage computer resources. Be aware of two things: Insiders commit the majority of computer crimes, and the methods listed are by no means exhaustive. For instance, two abuses not shown in Technology Summary 7.1 that typically are perpetrated by someone outside the organization are *computer hacking* and *computer viruses*. Refer to Technology Summary 7.2 for a brief presentation of computer viruses. Computer hacking is discussed in Chapter 8. Both of these computer crimes, viruses and hacking, are major concerns to organizations engaged in e-Business because they affect the actual and perceived reliability and integrity of their electronic infrastructure.

Technology Summary 7.1

Malicious Code Technologies

Salami. Unauthorized instructions are inserted into a program to systematically steal very small amounts. For example, a program is written to calculate daily interest on savings accounts. A dishonest programmer includes an instruction that if the amount of interest to be credited to the account is other than an even penny (for example, $2.7345) the excess over the even amount (.0045) is to be credited to account number 673492, which just happens to be his own. While each credit to his account is minute, the total can accumulate very rapidly.

Trap Door (back door). During the development of a program, the programmer may insert a special code or password that enables him to bypass the security features of the program in order to simplify his work. These are meant to be removed when the programmer's work is done, but sometimes they aren't. Someone who knows the code or password can still get into the program.

Logic Bomb. Similar to the trap door, unauthorized code is inserted into a program at a time when a programmer has legitimate access to the program. When activated, the code causes a disaster, such as shutting the system down or destroying data. The technique is usually tied to

a specific future date or event, in which case it is a time bomb. For example, if the programmer's name no longer appears on the payroll records of the company, the bomb is activated, and the disaster occurs.

Trojan Horse. Like a logic bomb, a Trojan horse is a module of unauthorized instructions covertly placed in a program; a Trojan horse, unlike the logic bomb, lets the program execute its intended function while also performing an unauthorized act. Some Trojan horses are distributed by e-mail to steal passwords. This was an element of the ILOVEYOU virus of May 2000.

Worm. This program replicates itself on disks, in memory, and across networks. It uses computing resources to the point of denying access to these resources to others, thus effectively shutting down the system. They also may delete files and can be spread via e-mail. Many recent viruses have included these worm features.

Zombie. A program that secretly takes over another Internet-attached computer, then uses that computer to launch attacks that can't be traced to the zombie's creator. Zombies are elements of the denial-of-service attacks discussed in Chapter 8.

Sources: Esther C. Roditti, *Computer Contracts* (New York: Matthew Bender & Co., Inc., 1998); Steve Alexander, "Viruses, Worms, Trojan Horses and Zombies," *Computerworld* (May 1, 2000): 74.

Before leaving this section, let's make a few other points. First, systems have been manipulated in a number of different ways in perpetrating computer crimes. Manipulation of event-related data (i.e., the adding, altering, or deleting of events) represents one frequently employed method of committing computer fraud.

Second, regardless of the method used in committing computer crime, we must not overlook the real issue. Computer crime represents an interesting example of a process failure. It characterizes a poorly controlled process. Process failure can usually be corrected by a conscientious application of appropriate control plans. For example, inadequately controlled processes have allowed bank tellers to perpetrate major frauds. If access to the affected computer programs and data had been restricted, these tellers would not be able to manipulate data to perpetrate their frauds.

Finally, as seductive as the topic of computer fraud and abuse is for students, you should not leave this section with the mistaken impression that controls are important

Technology Summary 7.2

Computer Viruses

A **computer virus** is a program that can attach itself to other programs (including macros within word processing documents), thereby "infecting" those programs and macros. Computer viruses may also be inserted into the boot sectors[a] of PCs. Viruses are activated when you run an infected program, open an infected document, or boot the computer from an infected disk. Computer viruses alter their "host" programs, destroy data, or render computer resources (e.g., disk drives, central processor, networks) unavailable for use. Unlike other malicious programs such as logic bombs and Trojan horses, viruses differ in that they can *reproduce themselves* in a manner analogous to biological viruses.

Some viruses are fairly innocent—they might merely produce a message such as "GOTCHA" or play "The Blue Danube" through the computer's speakers. Other viruses can be more harmful. Some viruses will delete programs and files; some will even format your hard drive, thus wiping away all stored data! Viruses also can overload local area networks with "messages," making it impossible to send or receive e-mail or to connect to external sources, such as the Internet. Finally, some companies have experienced "denial of service attacks," where hackers continuously deluge Web servers with high volumes of messages (called mass mailers); as a result, the servers are so busy handling the onslaught of messages that legitimate customers are prohibited from gaining access and conducting business with the companies.

Viruses can enter an organization through PCs, electronic bulletin boards, software that is shared through the exchange of storage media and files attached to e-mail messages. Such exchanges allow viruses to quickly become an epidemic, much like a biological virus. The real fear that can cause information systems managers to lose sleep, of course, is that the virus will then spread to the organization's networks (and networked computing resources) and destroy the organization's most sensitive data or result in denial of service to customers.

How extensive is the virus problem? In its 2002 "Computer Virus Prevalence Survey,"[b] TrueSecure Corporation (formerly known as The National Computer Security Association) reported 105 monthly virus infection encounters per 1,000 PCs in 2002, up from 80 in 1999, 90 in 2000, and 103 in 2001. The vast majority of respondents believe that the virus problem is now much worse than in prior years. Eight of the top ten viruses in 2002 were classified as Internet worms. Some of the more notable, major outbreak viruses have been Melissa (1999), Loveletter (2000), Code Red (2001), Nimda (2001), Yaha (2002), Klez (2002), and Slammer (2003). Regarding the sources of viruses, 85 percent of infections in 2002 arose from e-mail attachments and 11 percent came from Internet downloads. First generation (1985–1994) viruses were primarily aimed at boot sectors; second generation (1995–1999) viruses mostly attached themselves to application macros; third generation (1999–2001) viruses mainly focused on mass mailings; fourth generation (2001–present) viruses are simultaneously aimed at multiple vulnerability points in operating systems, applications, and networks; and future viruses (fifth generation) are likely to affect broadband, wireless, PDAs, and cell phone communication systems. It is taking longer than every before to recover from virus attacks. The average number of days to recover was 20 in 2001 and 23 in 2002. The hard costs of each attack were $81,000 in 2002, up from $69,000 in 2001. These numbers do not include the most pervasive and perhaps expensive cost of a virus attack—loss of productivity.

How does one protect from a viral infection? If you are going to share files and disks with others, use virus protection software to scan all files and disks before the disks are used or the files are opened. This is especially true of files received as e-mail attachments. Back up your files regularly. Use an up-to-date virus program to scan your hard disk regularly. E-mail servers also can be set to block attachments written in Visual Basic script.

---

[a] The boot sector is the area of a hard or floppy disk containing the program kernel that loads the operating system.
[b] TruSecure® Corporation, ICSA Labs 8th Annual Computer Virus Prevalence Survey, 2003.

simply because they can protect against "rip-offs." It has been estimated that losses due to accidental, non-malicious acts far exceed those caused by willful, intentional misdeeds. Therefore, you should recognize that the computer must be protected by a system of controls capable not only of preventing crimes but also of minimizing simple, innocent errors and omissions.

DEFINING INTERNAL CONTROL

In the preceding sections, we discussed the importance of an organization achieving an adequate level of internal control. But what do we mean by *internal control*? Up to now we have only alluded to this term's meaning. In the next two sections we describe first the definitions of internal control found in the authoritative literature and then offer our own working definition.

The COSO Definition of Internal Control

The definition of internal control contained in the COSO report, mentioned earlier in the chapter, has become widely accepted and is the basis for definitions of control adopted for other international control frameworks:[3]

> Internal control is a process—effected by an entity's board of directors, management, and other personnel—designed to provide reasonable assurance regarding the achievement of objectives in the following categories:
>
> - Effectiveness and efficiency of operations
> - Reliability of financial reporting
> - Compliance with applicable laws and regulations[4]

In 1995, Statement on Auditing Standards No. 78 (SAS No. 78), "Consideration of the Internal Control in a Financial Statement Audit: An Amendment to Statement on Auditing Standards No. 55," adopted the COSO definition of internal control. The COSO report and SAS No. 78 went on to say that internal control comprises five interrelated components:

- *Control environment* sets the tone of an organization, influencing the control consciousness of its people. It is the foundation for all other components of internal control, providing discipline and structure.

- *Risk assessment* is the entity's identification and analysis of relevant risks to achievement of its objectives, forming a basis for determining how the risks should be managed.

---

[3] The influence of the COSO definition of internal control is apparent in the definitions adopted by the following: (a) the *Cadbury Report* published as *The Financial Aspects of Corporate Governance* (London: The Committee on the Financial Aspects of Corporate Governance, December 1, 1992); (b) *Preface to Guidance Issued by the Criteria of Control Board* (Toronto, Ontario, Canada: The Canadian Institute of Chartered Accountants, 1995); and (c) *Control Objectives for Information and Related Technology—Executive Summary* (Rolling Meadows, IL: The Information Systems Audit & Control Foundation, 2000).

[4] *Internal Control—Integrated Framework—Framework Volume* (New York: The Committee of Sponsoring Organizations of the Treadway Commission, 1992): 9, 12, and 14. Our working definition of control, presented in the next section, classifies control *goals* into two broad groups—those for the *operations process* and those for the *information process*. Our two groupings roughly parallel the first two COSO categories. In our control framework and control matrices in later chapters, we include COSO's third category—compliance with applicable laws, regulations, and contractual agreements—as one of the control goals of the *operations process.*

- *Control activities* are the policies and procedures that help ensure that management directives are carried out.

- *Information and communication* are the identification, capture, and exchange of information in a form and time frame that enables people to carry out their responsibilities.

- *Monitoring* is a process that assesses the quality of internal control performance over time.

On June 5, 2003, the Securities and Exchange Commission (SEC) issued the final rules related to implementation of the Sarbanes-Oxley Act, "Management's Reports on Internal Control Over Financial Reporting and Certification of Disclosure in Exchange Act Periodic Reports."[5] In the section addressing implementation of SOA section 404, the SEC used the COSO description of internal control. It went on to say that management must base its evaluation of the effectiveness of its internal control system on a framework such as COSO.

Earlier in this chapter, we discussed an important element of the COSO report—it proposed that the purpose of control is to accomplish objectives. Now that we have COSO's definition of internal control before us, we want to emphasize an additional idea that we get from COSO, and that is that internal control is a *process*. A **process** is a series of actions or operations leading to a particular and usually desirable result. Results could be effective internal control as proposed by COSO, or a specified output for a particular market or customer. The idea of process is important to our understanding of internal control and business processes in modern organizations, and in our discussions of *business process reengineering* in Chapter 2 of the supplement that accompanies this text.

A complementary perspective on internal control is found in Statement on Auditing Standards (SAS) 94, entitled "The Effect on Information Technology on the Auditor's Consideration of Internal Control in a Financial Statement Audit." This standard guides auditors in understanding the impact of IT on internal control and assessing IT-related control risks. Further, SAS 94 highlights how IT can be used to strengthen internal control, while at the same time emphasizing how IT can actually weaken some controls. Armed with this background perspective, let's now proceed to a working definition of internal control that will be used throughout the remainder of the text.

Our Working Definition of Internal Control

The common ground on which we have developed our working definition of internal control includes the following points of general agreement:

- As mentioned in the first section of this chapter, a system of internal control is not an end in itself. Rather, it is a *means to an end*—the end of attaining process objectives (or avoiding certain undesirable effects or exposures).

- Internal control itself is a *system*. Therefore, like any system it must (1) have clearly defined goals and (2) consist of interrelated components that act in concert to achieve those goals. We could also say that internal control, being a series of actions or operations leading to a desirable result (i.e., achievement of objectives), is a *process*.

- Establishing a viable internal control system is *management's responsibility*. In fact, ultimate ownership of the system should rest with the chief executive officer (CEO). Only if the primary responsibility for the system resides at the top can control effectively permeate the entire organization.

---

[5] SEC Release No. 33-8238, June 5, 2003.

- The strength of any internal control system is largely a function of the people who operate it. In other words, no matter how sound the control *processes* may be, they will fail unless the personnel who apply them are competent and honest. Because internal control is so people-dependent, we explore the ethical dimensions of control more fully in the next section.

- Partly because it depends on people to operate it and partly because it comes only at some cost to the organization, internal control cannot be expected to provide *absolute*, 100% assurance that the organization will reach its objectives. Rather, the operative phrase is that it should provide *reasonable assurance* to that effect.

- Internal control is not free; it has a cost associated with it. For that reason, it should result from management's thoughtful risk analysis and evaluation of cost/benefits. Later in this section we will say more about assessing the cost-effectiveness of control plans. For now, suffice it to say that controls should be "built in versus bolted on." That is, to be cost-effective, controls should not be superimposed on the existing organizational structure. Rather, they should be purposefully designed and integrated with existing operational activities. As the COSO report expressed it:

    > The internal control system is intertwined with the entity's operating activities and exists for fundamental business reasons. Internal control is most effective when controls are built into the entity's infrastructure and are part of the essence of the enterprise. "Built-in" controls support quality and empowerment initiatives, avoid unnecessary costs, and enable quick response to changing conditions.[6]

By blending the best of the thoughts expressed previously, we offer the following composite definition of control, which will be used to guide our study of the topic throughout the remainder of the text:

Internal control is defined in the Preface and Chapter 1 as a system of integrated elements—people, structure, processes, and procedures—acting in concert to provide reasonable assurance that an organization achieves its *business process* goals. The design and operation of the internal control system is the responsibility of top management and therefore should:

- Reflect management's careful assessment of risks.
- Be based on management's evaluation of costs versus benefits.
- Be built on management's strong sense of business ethics and personal integrity.

Figure 7.1 (page 238) depicts a general model for control that should help summarize our discussion of internal control.

1. Start at the lower right corner of the figure with "Establish desired state of process." This is where the organization establishes the *objectives* that it desires to achieve and toward which the control system is directed. For example, the organization may define one objective as "comply with applicable laws and regulations."

2. Next go to the top left of the figure: "Observe actual state of process" and "Document actual state of process." To perform these actions we can use the tools described in Chapter 4 (i.e., narrative, flowchart, etc.).

---

[6] *Internal Control—Integrated Framework—Executive Summary Volume* (New York: The Committee of Sponsoring Organizations of the Treadway Commission, 1992): 3.

Figure 7.1 A General Control Model

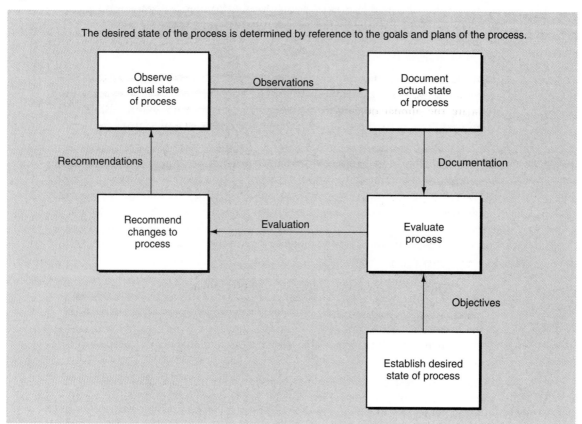

The desired state of the process is determined by reference to the goals and plans of the process.

Observe actual state of process → Observations → Document actual state of process

Recommendations

Documentation

Recommend changes to process ← Evaluation ← Evaluate process

Objectives

Establish desired state of process

Source: Adapted from "Report of the Committee on Accounting and Information Systems," *Committee Reports Supplement to Volume XLVI of the Accounting Review* (Sarasota, FL: American Accounting Association, 1971): 319.

3. The next step is: "Evaluate process." Notice that there are two inputs: the documentation and the process's objectives. Essentially, this reflects a comparison (variance analysis) of plan (or budget) to actual results. An evaluation of a control system is typically undertaken using a *control matrix* (Chapter 9)—a tool we can use to compare the performance of the process to the process's objectives.

4. The final step, if necessary, is to "Recommend changes to the process." Such recommendations must be made very carefully, as there are many cost-benefit factors to consider, as next illustrated.

Because control is an ongoing process, there are periodic iterations of the steps just outlined. For example, as we discussed with regard to fraud, there will be periodic reviews to determine the effectiveness of fraud prevention programs.

How do we determine that there may be sufficient *risk* that our objectives will not be achieved? That is, how do we decide what recommendations we will have when we evaluate a system of internal control? A dilemma exists regarding the costs and benefits of controls. An organization strives to have enough control to ensure that its goals are achieved. At the same time, the organization does not want to pay more for the controls than can be derived from their implementation. For example, suppose an organization installs a sophisticated fire-prevention and fire-detection system. This control should reduce the possibility of a fire destroying an organization's physical assets. But if the fire prevention system costs more than the assets being protected, the system obviously is not worthwhile from a financial perspective.

Many risk assessment models are used to determine whether a control should be implemented. As a practical matter, it is difficult to determine the amount to spend on a particular control or set of controls because an organization cannot afford to *prevent* all losses. One method that *can* be used is conceptually quite simple:

1. Estimate the annual dollar loss that would occur should a costly event, say a destructive fire, take place. For argument sake, say that the estimated loss is –$1,000,000.

2. Estimate the annual probability that the event will occur. Suppose the estimate is 5 percent.

3. Multiply item 1 by item 2 to get an initial *expected gross risk* (loss) of –$50,000 (–$1,000,000 × 0.05), which is the maximum amount or upper limit that should be paid for controls and the related risk reduction offered by such controls, in a given year. Next, we illustrate a recommendation plan using one *corrective* control, a fire insurance policy, and one *preventive* control, a sprinkler system.

4. Assume that the company would pay $1,000 annually (*cost of control*) for a $20,000 fire insurance policy (*reduced risk exposure due to control*). The estimated monetary damage remains at $1 million and *expected* gross risk (loss) remains at –$50,000, because there is still a 5 percent chance that a fire could occur. But, the company's *residual expected risk* exposure is now –$31,000 [–$50,000 + ($20,000 – $1,000)]. Our *expected* loss is reduced by the amount of the insurance policy (less the cost of the policy).

5. Next, you recommend that the company install a sprinkler system with a 5-year annualized cost (net present value) of $10,000 each year to install and maintain (*cost of control*). At this point you might be tempted to say that the company's *residual expected risk* just increased to –$41,000 (–$31,000 – $10,000), but wait! The sprinkler system lowered the likelihood of a damaging fire from 5 to 2 percent. In conjunction with this lower probability, the insurance company agreed to increase its coverage to $30,000 while holding the annual premium constant at $1,000.

6. Thus, the *residual expected risk* exposure is –$1,000, calculated as follows: Expected gross risk (–$20,000 or –$1,000,000 × 0.02) plus the insurance policy ($30,000) equals a gain of $10,000, but we must subtract the insurance premium ($1,000) and the sprinkler system ($10,000), leaving the residual expected risk at –$1,000.

Hence, *residual expected risk* is a function of *initial expected gross risk*, *reduced risk exposure due to controls*, and *cost of controls*. After all is said and done, however, a large dose of management judgment is required to determine a *reasonable* level of control.

Before discussing two key elements of our system of internal control, which we call *control goals* and *control plans*, let's pause to examine the very underpinnings of the system—namely, its ethical foundation.

Ethical Considerations and the Control Environment

COSO places integrity and ethical values at the heart of what it calls the *control environment*. In arguing the importance of integrity and ethics, COSO makes the case that the best-designed control systems are subject to failure caused by human error, faulty judgment, circumvention through collusion, and management override of the system. COSO goes on to state that:

> Ethical behavior and management integrity are products of the "corporate culture." Corporate culture includes ethical and behavioral standards, how they are communicated, and how they are reinforced in practice. Official policies specify what management wants to happen. Corporate culture determines what actually happens, and which rules are obeyed, bent, or ignored.[7]

There is some evidence to suggest that companies that have formal ethics policies might even lower their internal control costs. In a survey of 1,000 members of the Institute of Management Accountants' cost management group, 53 percent of those polled believed a strong, comprehensive ethics policy reduced the overall cost of internal control.[8] Cases in point: the business and audit failures noted at the beginning of this chapter arose primarily because upper management did not establish and/or reinforce ethical corporate cultures across their organizations, and in some cases, managers willfully violated any semblance of ethical behavior.

Management is responsible for internal control and can respond to this requirement legalistically or by creating a control environment. That is, management can follow the "letter of the law" (its form), or it can respond *substantively* to the need for control (its spirit). The **control environment** reflects the organization's (primarily the board of directors' and management's) general awareness of and commitment to the importance of control throughout the organization. In other words, by setting the example and by addressing the need for control in a positive manner at the top of the organization, management can make an organization *control conscious.*

For instance, reward systems might consider ethical, legal, and social performance, as well as the "bottom line."[9] Imagine the temptation to circumvent the control system or to "bend the rules" that could result from a reward system that pressures employees to meet unrealistic performance targets—such as happened at Enron Corporation—or that places upper and lower limits on employee bonus plans. Strategies should be developed so as not to create conflicts between business performance and legal requirements. Finally, management should consistently find it unacceptable for personnel to circumvent the organization's system of controls and, as importantly, the organization *should impose stiff sanctions for such unacceptable behavior.* These actions are included in what some call the "tone at the top" of the organization.

Aside from the companies mentioned in the introduction to this chapter, there are numerous examples of frauds and other illegal acts perpetrated by upper management. For example, at Sensormatic Electronics Corp. executives told underlings, including the IT manager, to doctor the books to create the appearance of more favorable financial results. In another case, the CEO and CFO at Bio Clinic falsified revenue and directed the IT manager to reprogram the accounting software to hide the falsified records.[10] An organization's board of directors, audit committee, and internal and external auditors must always be alert to the possibility that the "tone at the top" has become as distorted as these cases indicate.

---

[7] *Internal Control—Integrated Framework—Framework Volume* (New York: The Committee of Sponsoring Organizations of the Treadway Commission, 1992): 20.

[8] "Ethical Policies Help Reduce Internal Control Costs," *Journal of Accountancy* (April 1994): 14.

[9] COSO even goes as far as to suggest that responsibility for internal control should be an explicit or implicit part of everyone's job description.

[10] Kim Nash, "IT Staffers Charged in Accounting Frauds: SEC Cracks Down, Says IT Managers Should be Able to Catch Scams," *Computerworld* (December 13, 1999): 20.

One tangible way an increasing number of companies have articulated the ethical behavior expected of employees is to develop corporate *codes of conduct* that are periodically acknowledged (i.e., signed) by employees. The codes often address such matters as illegal or improper payments, conflicts of interest, insider trading, computer ethics including personal use of office e-mail systems and Internet connections, and software piracy.

BUSINESS PROCESS CONTROL GOALS AND CONTROL PLANS

Our working definition of *internal control* encompasses in a broad sense both selecting the ends to be attained (control goals) and specifying the means to ensure that the goals are attained (control plans). Control also extends to the processes of periodically reviewing a process to ensure that the goals of the process are being achieved, and to taking remedial action (if necessary) to correct any deficiencies in the system (i.e., what the COSO report calls "monitoring"). Control is concerned with discovering courses of action that contribute to the general welfare of the business enterprise (however defined) and with ensuring that the implementation of these actions produces the desired effects.

Because we believe that the driving force underlying control is to assist management in achieving its goals and objectives, we will discuss control goals before proceeding to control plans. To focus our discussion throughout the rest of the chapter, we will apply concepts to the Causeway Company's cash receipts process depicted in Figure 7.2 (page 242). The associated narrative is included in Exhibit 7.3 (page 243). Before proceeding, please acquaint yourself with the figure and exhibit.

Control goals are business process objectives that an internal control system is designed to achieve. Table 7.1 (page 244) provides an overview of the *generic* control goals of *operations processes* and of *information processes*. In the following paragraphs, we discuss each goal, and ask you to follow Table 7.1 and Figure 7.2 in the process.

Control Goals of Operations Processes

The first control goal, *ensure effectiveness of operations,* strives to ensure that a given operational process (e.g., Causeway's cash receipts process) is fulfilling the purpose for which it was intended. Notice that we must itemize the specific *operations process goals* to be achieved. These goals are created by humans, therefore subjective, and no uniform set of process goals exists. In each of the business process chapters, we provide a representative listing of operations process goals.[11]

The next goal, *ensure efficient employment of resources,* can be evaluated in only a relative sense. For example, let's assume that one of Causeway's effectiveness goals is to deposit all cash on the day received. To determine efficiency, we would need to know the cost of the people and computer equipment required to accomplish this goal. If the cost is more than the benefits obtained (e.g., security of the cash, interest earned), the system might be considered *inefficient*. Likewise, if the Causeway process costs more to operate than a process in a similar organization, we might also judge the system to be *inefficient*.

---

[11] As mentioned earlier in the chapter, we also include *compliance with applicable laws, regulations, and contractual agreements* (i.e., COSO's third category of entity objectives) as one of the goals of each operations process to which such laws, regulations, or agreements might be appropriate. For instance, compliance with the Robinson/Patman Act is shown as a legitimate goal of the order entry/sales system process in Chapter 10.

Figure 7.2 Causeway Company Systems Flowchart

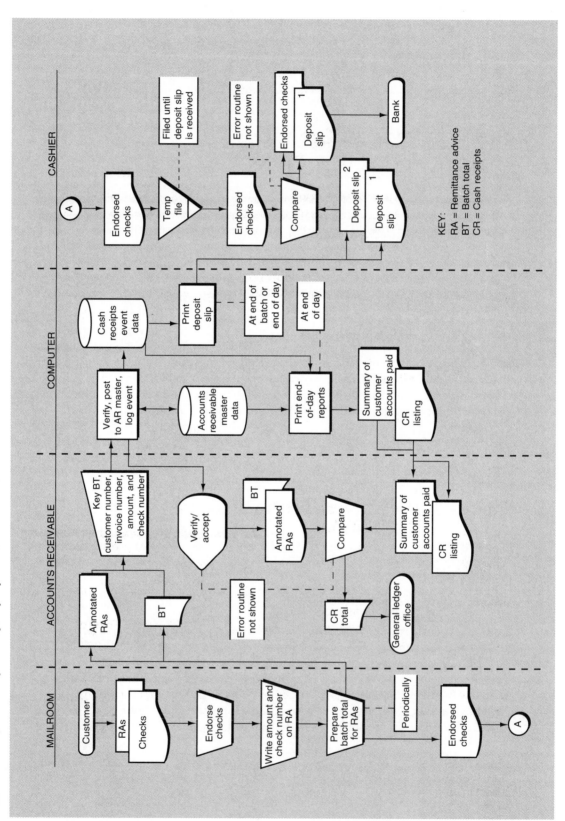

Exhibit 7.3 Causeway Company System Narrative

Causeway Company uses the following procedures to process the cash received from credit sales. Customers send checks and remittance advices to Causeway. The mailroom clerk at Causeway endorses the checks and writes the amount paid and the check number on the remittance advice. Periodically, the mailroom clerk prepares a batch total of the remittance advices and sends the batch of remittance advices to accounts receivable, along with a copy of the batch total. At the same time, the clerk sends the corresponding batch of checks to the cashier.

In accounts receivable, a clerk enters the batch into the computer by keying the batch total, the customer number, the invoice number, the amount paid, and the check number. After verifying that the invoice is open and that the correct amount is being paid, the computer updates the accounts receivable master data. If there are any discrepancies, the clerk is notified.

At the end of each batch (or at the end of the day), the computer prints a deposit slip in duplicate on the printer in the cashier's office. The cashier compares the deposit slip to the corresponding batch of checks and then takes the deposit to the bank.

As they are entered, the check number and the amount paid for each receipt are logged on a disk. This event data is used to create a cash receipts listing at the end of each day. A summary of customer accounts paid that day is also printed at this time. The accounts receivable clerk compares these reports to the remittance advices and batch totals and sends the total of the cash receipts to the general ledger office.

Let's now discuss the last operations process control goal in Table 7.1, *ensure security of resources*. As noted in the table, organizational resources take many forms, both physical and non-physical. Since the advent and proliferation of computer systems, information has become an increasingly important resource. For example, the information about Causeway's customers (as reflected in the accounts receivable data) represents an important resource for this company. Causeway must protect all of its resources, both tangible and intangible.

Control Goals of Information Processes

A glance at Table 7.1 reveals that the first three control goals related to information processes deal with entering event-related data into a system. Recall from Chapter 1 that data input includes *capturing* data (for example, completing a source document such as a sales order or, in Causeway's case, writing the check number and amount on the remittance advice). Also, data input includes, if necessary, *converting* the data to *machine-readable form* (for example, for Causeway, keying the remittance advices to add events to the cash receipts event data).[12] Therefore, *event data* are the targets of the *input* control goals shown in Table 7.1.

To illustrate the importance of achieving the first goal, *ensure input validity*, assume that Causeway's accounts receivable clerk processes a batch of 50 cash receipts or remittance advices (RAs). Further assume that 2 of the 50 RAs represent fictitious cash receipts (for example, a mailroom employee fabricates the phony remittance advices for relatives who are Causeway customers). What is the effect of processing the 50 RAs, including the 2 fictitious remittances? First, the cash receipts event data and the accounts receivable master data each have been corrupted by the addition of two bogus RAs. Second, if not

---

[12] As presented, the Causeway system is an automated equivalent of a manual system, such as the one depicted in Figure 3.1 (page 74). When inputs are keyed into a computer directly without the use of source documents (i.e., *online transaction entry [OLTE]* such as that depicted in Figure 3.2, page 76), the capture and conversion steps are combined. For instance, order entry clerks might key a customer telephone order without first transcribing it onto an order form.

Table 7.1 Control Goals

Control goal	Definitions	Discussion
Control goals of operations processes		
Ensure *effectiveness of operations* by achieving the following *operations process goals*: (itemize the specific goals for the process being analyzed)	**Effectiveness:** A measure of success in meeting one or more *operations process goals*, which reflect the criteria used to judge the effectiveness of various business processes.	If one of Causeway's operations process goals is to deposit cash receipts on the day received, the operations process is effective if cash receipts are deposited each day when received.
Ensure *efficient employment of resources*	**Efficiency:** A measure of the productivity of the resources applied to achieve a set of goals.	What is the cost of the people, computers, and other resources needed to deposit all cash on the day received?
Ensure *security of resources* (specify the applicable operations process and information process resources)	**Security of resources:** Protecting an organization's resources from loss, destruction, disclosure, copying, sale, or other misuse.	Are the physical (e.g., cash) and non-physical (e.g., information) resources available when required? Are they put to unauthorized use?
Control goals of information processes		
Ensure *input validity* (IV)	**Input validity:** A control goal that requires that input data be appropriately approved and represent actual economic events and objects.	Are all of the cash receipts (RAs) to be input into the Causeway process supported by actual customer payments?
Ensure *input completeness* (IC)	**Input completeness:** A control that requires that all valid events or objects be captured and entered into a system.	Are all valid customer payments captured on a remittance advice (RA) and entered into the Causeway process?
Ensure *input accuracy* (IA)	**Input accuracy:** A control goal that requires that events be correctly captured and entered into a system.	Is the correct payment amount and customer number transcribed onto the RA? Is the correct payment amount and customer number keyed into the Causeway computer? Is the customer number missing from the RA?
Ensure *update completeness*	**Update completeness:** A control goal that requires that all events entered into a computer are reflected in their respective master data.	Are all input cash receipts recorded in the Causeway accounts receivable master data?
Ensure *update accuracy*	**Update accuracy:** A control goal that requires that data entered into a computer are reflected correctly in their respective master data.	Are all input cash receipts correctly recorded in the Causeway accounts receivable master data?

detected and corrected, the pollution of these data will result in unreliable financial statements—overstated cash and understated accounts receivable—and other erroneous system outputs (e.g., cash receipts listings, customer monthly statements).

To discuss the second information process goal, *ensure input completeness,* let's return to the previous Causeway example and suppose that, while the 48 *valid* RAs are being key-entered (we'll ignore the 2 fictitious receipts in this example), the accounts receivable clerk decides to get a cup of coffee. As the clerk walks past the batch of 48 RAs, 10 are blown to the floor and are not entered into the system. What is the effect of processing 38 RAs, rather than the original 48? First, the cash receipts event data will be incomplete; that is, it will fail to reflect the true number of remittance events. Second, the incompleteness of the data will cause the resulting financial statements and other reports to be inaccurate (i.e., understated cash balance and overstated accounts receivable). In this example, the omission was unintentional. Fraudulent, intentional misstatements of the accounting data can be accomplished by omitting some events.

The goal of *input completeness* is concerned with the actual number of events or objects to be processed. Particular questions relative to this goal include the following:

- Is *every* event or object captured (for example, are source documents prepared for every valid event or object)?

- Is every captured event or object *entered into the computer* (or manually recorded in the books of original entry)? This was the breakdown in the Causeway example of 10 RAs getting blown to the floor and overlooked.

When dealing with input completeness, we are concerned with the documents or records representing an event or object, not the *correctness* or *accuracy* of the document or record. Accuracy issues are addressed by the third information process goal. Rather, when talking about input completeness, the act of capturing and entering all legitimate events and objects represents our only concern. Input completeness simply means that *all* of the events or objects that should be processed (i.e., the valid events and objects) are processed.

The third goal, *ensure input accuracy,* relates to the various data items that usually constitute a record of an event, such as a source document. To achieve this goal, we must minimize discrepancies between data items entered into a system and the economic events or objects they represent. Mathematical mistakes and inaccurate transcription of data from one document or medium to another may cause accuracy errors. Again, let's return to the Causeway example. Suppose that one of the *valid* RAs is from Acme Company, customer 159, in the amount of $125. The accounts receivable clerk mistakenly enters the customer number as 195, resulting in Ajax Inc.'s account (rather than Acme's) being credited with the $125. Missing data fields on a source document or computer screen represent another type of accuracy error. For Causeway, the absence of a customer number on a remittance advice would result in "unapplied" cash receipts (that is, receipts that can't be credited to a particular customer). We consider this type of system malfunction to be an accuracy error rather than a completeness error, because the mere presence of the source document suggests that the transaction itself has been captured and that the input data are, by our definition, therefore complete.

Two critical questions must be asked concerning the goal of input accuracy:

1. Is the initial capturing of data correct (for example, are data recorded accurately on source documents)?

2. Is the entering of data correct (for example, are data transcribed or recorded in the books of original entry or accurately converted from source documents into machine-readable form)? Again, in the Causeway example of keying an incorrect customer number, the flaws in the system lay here.

To achieve the goal of input accuracy, we must capture and enter into a system all important data elements. Thus, all important data elements must be identified for each economic event or object that we wish to include in a system's database. In general, you should find the following guidelines helpful in identifying important data elements:

- All financial data elements are usually important, such as numbers that enter into a calculation. For a Causeway cash receipt, the correctness of the gross invoice amount, discount taken, and net amount collected are crucial to "balancing" each RA.

- The accuracy of reference numbers, such as those for inventory product groups, customer numbers, and general ledger coding, is important. Among other reasons, accurate reference numbers are crucial to the proper *classification* of items in the financial statements.

- The accuracy of dates is very important, so that we can determine that events are recorded in the proper time period. For instance, if cash received by Causeway on December 29th was recorded as received on December 28th, would you as an auditor be concerned? Possibly, but not nearly as concerned as you would be if cash received on January 2nd was recorded as received on December 31st (assuming that Causeway's year-end is December 31st). Notice that this accuracy error causes cash receipts to be invalid in December (the cash was not received in December) and incomplete in January (a cash receipt that occurred in January has not been recorded in January).

Now let's examine the last two information process control goals shown in Table 7.1 (page 244). These goals deal with updating *master data*. As we learned in Chapter 1, master data update is an information processing activity whose function is to incorporate new data into existing master data. We also learned that there are two types of updates that can be made to master data: information processing and data maintenance. You also should remember from Chapter 1 that master data updates resulting from information processing are analogous to the *posting* step in a manual bookkeeping cycle. In this textbook, we emphasize information processing; therefore, our analysis of the internal controls related to data updates is restricted to data updates from information processing.

In a manual-based system, the goals of *ensure update completeness* and *ensure update accuracy* relate to updating various ledgers (for example, the accounts receivable subsidiary ledger) for data items entered into the books of original entry (e.g., the sales and cash receipts journals). In Causeway's process, the goal of *ensure update completeness* relates to crediting customer balances in the accounts receivable master data for *all* cash collections recorded in the cash receipts transaction data. The goal of *ensure update accuracy* relates to correctly crediting (e.g., correct customer, correct amount) customer balances in the accounts receivable master data.

Once valid data have been *completely* and *accurately* entered into a computer (i.e., added to transaction data such as Causeway's cash receipts transaction data), the data usually go through a series of processing steps. Several things can go wrong with the data once they have been entered into a computer for processing. Accordingly, the goals of update completeness and accuracy are aimed at minimizing processing errors.

In general, an awareness of the following types of processing errors should assist you in achieving the goals of update completeness and update accuracy:

- *Programming errors.* For example, logical or technical errors may exist in the program software. (For instance, instead of crediting Causeway's customers for cash collections, the cash receipts were *added* to accounts receivable balances.)

- *Operational errors.* For example, today's cash receipts data may be processed against an out-of-date (yesterday's) accounts receivable master data. Or we may fail to execute some intermediate steps in a process. This may happen if input data is used for more than one application and we fail to use the inputs for all of the intended processes. (Note that this should not be a problem with *enterprise systems* where one input automatically impacts all relevant applications.) Finally, some applications, such as in banking, process "memo" updates during the day to immediately reflect activity, such as cash withdrawals. But, the "real" updates take place overnight in a batch process. If we fail to properly execute the overnight process, the updates may be incomplete or inaccurate.

ENTERPRISE SYSTEMS

These two examples present illustrations of how things can go wrong while updating master data, even when the data are valid, complete, and accurate at the input stage. Controls that ensure *input* accuracy and completeness do not necessarily ensure *update* accuracy and completeness. We should note, however, that if the events or transactions are processed using an *online real-time processing* system such as the one depicted in Figure 3.3 (page 78), the input and update will occur nearly simultaneously. This will minimize the possibility that the update will be incomplete or inaccurate.

Note that we do *not* have a separate goal for *update validity* as we do for update completeness and update accuracy. The reason is that there is no inherent risk of having an invalid update to master data unless an invalid input data has been introduced into the system. Therefore, by controlling *input* validity, we automatically facilitate update validity.

Control Plans

Control plans reflect information processing policies and procedures that assist in accomplishing control goals. Control plans can be classified in a number of different ways that help us to understand them. Figure 7.3 (page 248) shows one such classification scheme—a control hierarchy that relates control plans to the *control environment*. The fact that the control environment appears at the top of the hierarchy illustrates that the control environment comprises a multitude of factors that can either reinforce or mitigate the effectiveness of the pervasive and application control plans.

The second level in the Figure 7.3 control hierarchy consists of pervasive control plans. **Pervasive control plans** relate to a multitude of goals and processes. Like the control environment, they provide a climate or set of surrounding conditions in which the various business processes operate. They are broad in scope and apply equally to all business processes, hence they *pervade* all systems. For example, preventing unauthorized access to the computer system would protect all of the specific AIS processes that run on the computer (such as order entry/sales, billing/accounts receivable/cash receipts, inventory, payroll, and so on). We discuss a major subset of these pervasive controls—IT processes (i.e., controls)—in Chapter 8.

Business process control plans relate to those controls particular to a specific process or subsystem, such as billing or cash receipts, or to a particular technology used to process the data. Business process control plans are the subject of the control framework introduced in Chapter 9.

Figure 7.3 A Control Hierarchy

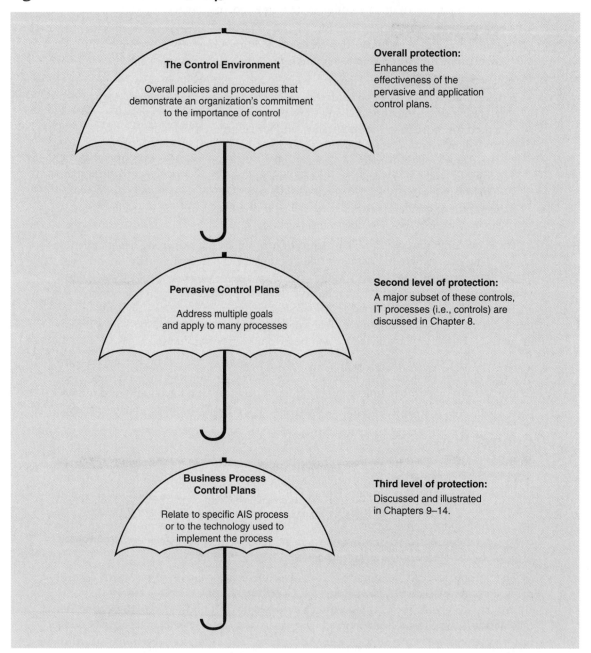

The Control Environment

Overall policies and procedures that demonstrate an organization's commitment to the importance of control

Overall protection:
Enhances the effectiveness of the pervasive and application control plans.

Pervasive Control Plans

Address multiple goals and apply to many processes

Second level of protection:
A major subset of these controls, IT processes (i.e., controls) are discussed in Chapter 8.

Business Process Control Plans

Relate to specific AIS process or to the technology used to implement the process

Third level of protection:
Discussed and illustrated in Chapters 9–14.

Another useful and common way to classify controls is in relation to the timing of their occurrence. **Preventive control plans** stop problems from occurring. **Detective control plans** discover that problems have occurred. **Corrective control plans** rectify problems that have occurred. Let's use the Causeway process again to illustrate. The programmed verification of customer number is an example of a *preventive* control; remittance advices with bad customer numbers should be rejected before they ever enter the computer system. At least two instances of *detective* controls are present in the Causeway process; they are shown by the manual processes (trapezoid symbols) labeled "Compare." The comparisons are done to ensure that no discrepancies exist between inputs (that is, remittance advices and batch totals) and outputs, either in the form of deposit slips or end-of-day reports. If discrepancies are *detected*, Causeway should have procedures for reprocessing the incorrect items. These procedures constitute *corrective* controls, which are not shown in Figure 7.2 (page 242).

Obviously, if we had our choice, we would implement preventive controls because, in the long run, it is less expensive and less disruptive to operations to prevent, rather than to detect and correct, problems. However, since no control can be made to be 100 percent effective, we need to implement a combination of preventive, detective, and corrective controls. Furthermore, it should go without saying that detective control plans often can help to prevent or deter fraudulent or careless acts. That is, if one knows that plans exist to detect or uncover fraud and carelessness, such knowledge can serve as one additional preventive measure.

SUMMARY

In the introduction and in the section on fraud, we gave some alarming examples of fraud and computer crime incidences. Future managers must confront this problem much more directly than have their predecessors, particularly in light of recent business and audit failures, which gave rise to the Sarbanes-Oxley Act. Also, as computer-based systems become more sophisticated, managers must continually question how such technological changes affect the system of internal controls. For example, some companies have already implemented paperless (totally electronic) information systems. Others employ electronic data interchange (EDI) technology, which we introduced in Chapter 3. The challenges to future managers are to keep pace with the development of these types of systems, and to ensure that changes in any process are complemented by enhancements in the company's system of internal controls.

Minimizing computer fraud and abuse is only one area of concern for today's managers. An organization's stakeholders—investors, customers, employees, taxpayers, government, etc.—have recently raised a number of *corporate (organizational) governance* issues to demonstrate their interest in and concern over how well organizations are being managed. For example, these stakeholders are asking how well the board of directors (BOD) governs its own performance and that of the organization's managers. And, how do the BOD and management implement *and demonstrate* that they have control over their operations? We submit that only through an effective system of internal control can these and other matters be adequately addressed and suitably resolved.

REVIEW QUESTIONS

RQ 7-1 What are the three primary reasons that management exercises control over operations processes and the information processes? Explain.

RQ 7-2 What gave rise to the Sarbanes-Oxley Act of 2002?

RQ 7-3 What does the term *exposure* mean as used in this chapter? What are the names and meanings of nine common business exposures?

RQ 7-4 What are the relationships between fraud, in general, and internal control? between computer fraud, in particular, and internal control? Name and explain in your own words at least three ways that computer crimes/computer abuses have typically been committed.

RQ 7-5 What is a computer virus?

RQ 7-6 Describe the elements common to most current definitions of internal control.

RQ 7-7 Explain what is meant by the *control environment*. What elements might comprise the control environment?

RQ 7-8 Explain how business ethics relate to internal control.

RQ 7-9 a. What are the three generic control goals of operations processes and the five generic control goals of the related information process?

b. Explain the difference between the following pairs of control goals: (1) ensure effectiveness of operations processes and ensure efficient employment of resources; (2) ensure efficient employment of resources and ensure security of resources; (3) ensure input validity and ensure input accuracy; (4) ensure input completeness and ensure input accuracy; (5) ensure input completeness and ensure update completeness; and (6) ensure input accuracy and ensure update accuracy.

RQ 7-10 What is the difference between the control environment, a pervasive control plan, and an application control plan?

DISCUSSION QUESTIONS

DQ 7-1 Recently, the U.S. federal government and the American Institute of Certified Public Accountants (AICPA) have taken aggressive steps aimed at ensuring the quality of corporate governance. What are these changes, how might they change corporate governance procedures, and do you believe that these actions will really improve internal control of business organizations?

DQ 7-2 Nine common business exposures were presented in the chapter. These exposures are not mutually exclusive. One example in support of this assertion is that the exposure of erroneous management decisions could be caused by erroneous recordkeeping. Give five other examples of possible causal relationships *between* exposures.

DQ 7-3 Controls can be categorized as preventative, detective, and corrective. Assume that you are the controller for a large corporation. You are concerned about the controls related to the privacy of employee information, such as employees' social security numbers, salaries, benefits, medical histories, and so on. Name two preventative, two detective, and two corrective controls you would design to ensure the privacy of sensitive employee information of this nature.

DQ 7-4 "If it weren't for the potential of computer abuse, the emphasis on controlling computer systems would decline significantly in importance." Do you agree? Discuss fully.

DQ 7-5 Provide five examples of potential conflict between the control goals of ensuring effectiveness of operations and of ensuring efficient employment of resources.

DQ 7-6 Discuss how the *efficiency* and *effectiveness* of a mass-transit system in a large city can be measured.

DQ 7-7 "If *input data* are entered into the system completely and accurately, then the information process control goals of *ensuring update completeness* and *ensuring update accuracy* will be automatically achieved." Do you agree? Discuss fully.

PROBLEMS

P 7-1 Conduct research to determine management's responsibility for establishing and maintaining an adequate system of internal control. Create a written report, in a manner prescribed by your instructor, describing applicable statutory and professional guidance, the implications of internal control obligations, and how management should discharge its internal control responsibilities.

P 7-2 In list 1 are 12 terms from this chapter or from Chapter 1, and in list 2 are 10 definitions or explanations of terms.

Match the definitions with the terms by placing a *capital* letter from list 1 on the blank line to the left of its corresponding definition in list 2. You should have two letters left over from list 1.

List 1—Terms

A. Business process control plan

B. Control environment

C. Control goal

D. Exposure

E. Data maintenance

F. Master data update

G. Input accuracy

H. Input completeness

I. Input validity

J. Pervasive control plan

K. Preventive control plan

L. Operations process goal

List 2—Definitions

_____ 1. The process of modifying the master data reflects the results of new events.

_____ 2. A control designed to keep problems from occurring.

_____ 3. A control goal of the information process that is directed at ensuring that fictitious or bogus events are not recorded.

_____ 4. A goal of an operations process that signifies the very reason for which that process exists.

_____ 5. The highest level in the control *hierarchy*, a control category that evidences management's commitment to the importance of control in the organization.

_____ 6. The process of modifying a master data's *standing data*.

_____ 7. A type of control that is exercised within each business process as that process' events are processed.

_____ 8. The potential adverse consequence that could result from an organization's objectives not being met.

_____ 9. Objectives to be achieved by the internal control system.

_____ 10. A control that addresses a multitude of goals across many business processes.

P 7-3 Nine common business exposures were presented in Exhibit 7.1 (page 228). In our discussions, we told you that an exposure is an undesirable action or event that may cause an organization to fail to meet operations process and information process goals. The purpose of this problem is to have you associate the nine exposures with the *unmet* goal(s) to which they relate. Assume, for the purpose of this problem only, that there are only four control goals.

The goals of the operations process are:

A. Effectiveness

B. Efficiency

C. Security of resources

The goal of the information process is:

D. Integrity of information (i.e., validity, completeness, and accuracy)

List the numbers 1 through 9 on a solution sheet. Each number represents the business exposure from the list in Exhibit 7.1. Match each exposure to the unmet goal(s) to which it relates by inserting opposite each number one or more letters (A through D from the list of goals). Provide a brief explanation (no more than two to three sentences for each exposure) of the relationship(s) you have chosen. The format of your solution should appear as follows:

Exposure Number	Unmet Goals of Goals (A through D)	Explanation
1	_____	_____
	_____	_____
	_____	_____
2	_____	_____
	_____	_____
	_____	_____

Important: Do *not* consider any relationships between or among exposures. Assume that the exposures are mutually exclusive, even though in practice they would not be.

P 7-4 Following is a list of eight generic control goals from the chapter, followed by eight descriptions of either process failures (i.e., control goals not met) or instances of successful control plans (i.e., plans that helped to achieve control goals).

List the numbers 1 through 8 on a solution sheet. Each number represents one of the described situations. Next to each number:

a. Place the *capital* letter of the control goal that *best* matches the situation described.

b. Provide a one- to two-sentence explanation of how the situation relates to the control goal you selected.

Hint: Some letters may be used more than once. Conversely, some letters may not apply at all.

Control Goals

A. Ensure effectiveness of the operations process

B. Ensure efficient employment of resources

C. Ensure security of resources

D. Ensure input validity

E. Ensure input completeness

F. Ensure input accuracy

G. Ensure update completeness

H. Ensure update accuracy

Situations

1. A company uses *prenumbered documents* (defined in a subsequent chapter) for recording its sales invoices to customers. When the invoices for a particular day were entered, the system noted that invoice #12345 appeared twice. The second entry (i.e., the duplicate) of this same number was rejected by the system because it was unsupported by a shipment.

2. In entering the invoices mentioned in situation 1, the data for salesperson number and sales terms were missing from invoice #12349 and therefore were not keyed into the computer.

3. Instead of preparing deposit slips by hand, Causeway Company has them generated by the computer. The company does so in order to speed up the deposit of cash.

4. In the Causeway Company cash receipts process, one of the earliest processes is to endorse each customer's check with the legend, "for deposit only to Causeway Company."

5. XYZ Co. prepares customer sales orders on a multipart form, one copy of which is sent to its billing department where it is placed in a temporary file pending shipping notification. Each morning, a billing clerk reviews the file of open sales orders and investigates with the shipping department any missing shipping notices for orders entered 48 hours or more earlier.

6. Referring to situation 5, once a shipping notice is received in the billing department, the first step in preparing the invoice to the customer is to compare the unit prices shown on the sales order with a standard price list kept in the billing department.

7. Alamo, Inc., posts its sales invoice event data against its accounts receivable master data each night. Before posting the new sales, the computer

program first checks the old master data to make sure that it is the version from the preceding day.

8. MiniScribe Corporation recorded as sales shipments of disk drives to their warehouse. These disks drives had not been ordered by anyone and were still the property of MiniScribe.

P 7-5 In the following first list are 10 examples of the items described in the second list.

Match the two lists by placing the *capital* letter from the first list on the blank line preceding the description to which it best relates. You should have two letters left over from list 1.

List 1—Examples

A. Management philosophy and operating style

B. Accounts receivable subsidiary ledger in a manual system

C. Customer name and address

D. The process of increasing customer balances for sales made

E. Cash receipts journal in a manual system

F. Fire extinguishers

G. Deleting an inactive customer's record from the accounts receivable master data

H. Ensure input validity

I. Ensure security of resources

J. Computer virus

List 2—Descriptions

_____ 1. *Event data* in a computer system.

_____ 2. A control goal of the *information process.*

_____ 3. An element included in the *control environment.*

_____ 4. An element of *standing data.*

_____ 5. A control goal of an *operations process.*

_____ 6. An instance of *data maintenance.*

_____ 7. *Master data* in a computerized system.

_____ 8. An illustration of a *master data update.*

P 7-6 The CFO of Synergein Corporation is very uncomfortable with its current risk exposure related to the possibility of business disruptions. Specifically, Synergein is heavily involved in e-Business and its internal information systems are tightly interlinked with its key customers' systems. The CFO has estimated that every hour of system downtime will cost the company about $10,000 in sales. The CFO and CIO (chief information officer) have further estimated that if the system were to fail, the average downtime would be 1 hour per incident. They have anticipated that Synergein will likely experience 50 downtime incidents in a given year due to internal computer system problems and another 50 incidents per year due to external problems; specifically, system failures with the Internet service provider (ISP). Currently, Synergein pays an annualized cost of $150,000 for redundant computer and communication systems, and $100,000 for Internet service provider (ISP) support just to keep the total expected number of incidents to 100 per year.

Required:

a. Given the information provided thus far, how much ($) is the company's current *residual expected risk*?

b. A further preventative control would be to purchase and maintain more redundant computers and communication lines where possible, at an annualized cost of $100,000, which would reduce the expected number of downtime incidents to 15 per year due to internal computer system problems. What would be the dollar amount of Synergien's current *residual expected risk* at this point?

c. An external threat still prevails, that is, the ISP could cause the business interruption. Hence, another preventative control would be to increase the annual service fee the company pays to its ISP to a higher level of guaranteed service, based on the following schedule:

Guaranteed Maximum Number of Downtime Incidents per Year:	Annual Cost of Service Support
50	$100,000 (current contract)
40	$150,000
30	$200,000
20	$300,000
10	$425,000
0	$550,000

Would you purchase a higher level of service from the ISP? If so, what level of service would you purchase? Please defend your answer both quantitatively and qualitatively.

P 7-7 Investigate the internal controls in one of the following (ask your instructor which): a local business, your home, your school, your place of employment. Report (in a manner prescribed by your instructor) on the controls that you found and the goals that they were designed to achieve.

KEY TERMS

risk	effectiveness	update accuracy
fraud	efficiency	control plans
computer virus	security of resources	pervasive control plans
process	input validity	business process control plans
internal control	input completeness	
control environment	input accuracy	preventive control plans
control goals	update completeness	detective control plans
		corrective control plans

Controlling Information Systems: IT Processes

As the computer security officer at DPI Merchant Services (DPI) ambled into work one cold morning in February 2003, he warmed up his computer while continuing to drink his daily cup of java. When he and his computer woke up, something seemed eerily wrong. He noticed some strange entries in his security log. After digging around for a few moments, he ran across some database transactions that were executed from an unknown source. After performing more detailed analyses, he was panic stricken— someone had gained access to the company's most sensitive information—personal credit card numbers! He quickly grabbed the phone, spilling his coffee into the keyboard, and immediately called his boss, the president of DPI, saying "Sir, we have a problem."[1]

DPI serves as an intermediary transaction processor between credit card companies and merchants. Through companies like DPI, sellers of goods and services can accept credit card payments from customers. Credit card companies such as Visa, MasterCard, Discover, and American Express use third-party intermediaries to manage credit card transactions between merchants and the financial institutions that issue the cards. Rather than breaking into a single credit card company's computer system to steal account numbers, this hacker found a more vulnerable spot where millions of credit card accounts from multiple credit card companies are stored. On that fateful morning in early February, a hacker had gained access to an estimated 8 million credit card accounts.

MasterCard revealed that 2.2 million of its cards were involved, Visa claimed that 3.4 million cards were affected and industry experts conjectured that around 2.4 million additional credit card accounts from Discover and American Express were likely compromised. A DPI spokesperson stated that "information targeted by the system intruder did not include any personal information that could relate a card number to an individual. . . . (P)ersonal information including account holder name, address, telephone number and Social Security number were not obtained through the attempted intrusion." Visa and MasterCard representatives reported no fraudulent use of the credit card accounts. As a precaution, Citizens Bank closed out 8,800 MasterCard accounts that had been accessed. A federal official who was

Learning Objectives

- To learn the major IT resources.
- To appreciate the problems involved in providing adequate control over IT resources.
- To study the major IT control processes and practices organizations use to manage the IT resources.
- To understand how IT and personnel control plans can help an organization achieve its strategic vision for IT.
- To overview the major steps in acquiring and implementing new IT resources.
- To examine business continuity and security controls that help ensure continuous, reliable IT service.
- To value the integral part played by the monitoring function in ensuring the overall effectiveness of a system of internal controls.

---

[1] The facts and circumstances surrounding how the hacker attack was discovered at DPI are fictionalized.

In this chapter, we continue our investigation of internal accounting controls, as indicated by the shaded areas on the AIS Wheel icon. Herein, you will learn how to control information technology resources and processes, which form the underpinning of accounting information systems. Importantly, you will be exposed to a fundamental control concept that must be incorporated into every aspect of an organization; that is, managers need to segregate four key functions—authorizing events, executing events, recording events, and safeguarding resources.

working on the case suggested that this is a clear example of a hacker whose apparent motive was to gain access to a secure server just for shear pleasure.

SYNOPSIS

This chapter provides a comprehensive discussion of information technology (IT) control processes, which are a major subset of pervasive control plans introduced in Chapter 7. These IT control processes are designed to manage IT resources so that an organization has the information it needs to achieve its objectives.

CONTROLS

We begin by introducing a hypothetical computer system and the information services function (ISF) that operates that system. This system has multiple connections among the IT resources within and outside of the organization. Internal interconnectedness of this nature is typical of organizations employing *enterprise systems*. The external interfaces are typical of organizations engaged in *e-Business*. The use of IT resources for enterprise systems and e-Business magnifies the importance of protecting such resources from various risk exposures. The interlinking of IT resources makes it much more difficult to provide protection, as compared to similar IT resources used in isolation.

ENTERPRISE SYSTEMS

E-BUSINESS

We also will discuss four broad IT control process domains. These domains reflect groupings of control processes (i.e., management practices) that serve to reduce the possibility that an organization will be susceptible to the nine categories of business exposures introduced in Chapter 7. We also explain how these control processes are directed at attaining the information qualities introduced in Chapter 1.

INTRODUCTION

Each year the Computer Security Institute (CSI) conducts the "Computer Crime and Security Survey" with the participation of the San Francisco Federal Bureau of Investigation's Computer Intrusion Squad. The 2003 survey included respondents from U.S. corporations, financial institutions, medical centers, universities, and governmental agencies. When asked if they had detected computer security breaches within the last 12 months, 92 percent of the respondents said "yes" and over 70 percent reported *serious* computer security breaches, including theft of proprietary information, denial of service attacks, financial fraud, system penetration from outsiders, and sabotage of data or networks. Quantifiable estimates of financial losses exceeded $200 million; the greatest loss ($70 million) came from theft of proprietary information and the second most expensive crime ($65 million) arose from denial of service attacks. Financial fraud accounted for around $9 million. Survey results further show that computer crime threats come from both inside and outside the organization's electronic perimeters. While many unauthorized accesses are attempted by insiders, even more attacks arise from the outside (78 percent from Internet connections). The 2002 Ernst & Young (E&Y) Information Security Survey supports these findings. Respondents to the E&Y survey reported serious threats from outside the organization (e.g., hackers, computer terrorists) and from inside the organization (e.g., unauthorized users, authorized employees, former employees, contract workers). The E&Y survey also reported that only 53 percent of organizations had prepared formal business continuity plans. Both the CSI/FBI and E&Y surveys noted a dramatic increase in denial of service attacks over prior years.[2] Our conclusion from these reports is that an organization must protect its IT resources from very real external and internal threats. This chapter describes some of the typical management practices/IT processes used to address these threats.

In Chapter 7, we defined *pervasive control plans* as those that relate to a multitude of control goals and to many information system processes. Like the control environment, also introduced in Chapter 7, pervasive control plans influence the effectiveness of the *business process control plans.* For example, a pervasive control plan that restricts access to data and programs stored on a computer can reduce the possibility that computer-based data (e.g., payroll or accounts receivable) will be altered without proper authorization. Thus, the pervasive control, (restricting access to the computer) will have an impact on *any* business process control intended to ensure the reliability of *any* related data. Recall that an organization establishes a system of controls to provide reasonable assurance that organizational objectives will be achieved (or, alternatively, that business risks will be reduced or avoided). The system of controls consists of the control environment, pervasive control plans, and business process control plans. In this chapter, we concentrate on IT control processes—also known as management practices—that are a major subset of pervasive control plans.

---

[2] *Issues and Trends: 2003 CSI/FBI Computer Crime and Security Survey* (San Francisco: Computer Security Institute, 2003). As of June 2003, highlights of this report are available at http://www.gocsi.com. *Global Information Security Survey 2002* (Ernst & Young LLP). As of June 2003, this report was available at http://www.ey.com.

COBIT (Control Objectives for Information and Related Technology) was developed by the Information Systems Audit and Control Foundation to provide guidance—to managers, users, and auditors—on the best practices for the management of information technology. According to COBIT, IT resources must be managed by IT control processes to ensure that the organization has the information it needs to achieve its objectives.[3] Exhibit 8.1 defines the IT resources that must be managed and Chapter 1 describes the qualities that this information must exhibit in order for it to be of value to the organization.

Exhibit 8.1 IT Resources

Data: Objects in their widest sense (i.e., external and internal), structured and nonstructured, graphics, sound, etc.

Application systems: Application systems are understood to be the sum of manual and programmed procedures reflecting business processes.

Technology: Technology covers hardware, operating systems, database management systems, networking, multimedia, etc.

Facilities: Facilities are all resources used to house and support information systems.

People: People include staff skills; awareness; and productivity to plan, organize, acquire, deliver, support, and monitor information systems and services.

Source: Adapted from *COBIT: Control Objectives for Information and Related Technology—Framework*, 3rd ed. (Rolling Meadows, IL: The Information Systems Audit and Control Foundation, 2000): 14.

Because the COBIT framework is a major source for the control processes described in this chapter, we should include here the COBIT definition for control. COBIT defines control as:[4]

> The policies, procedures, practices, and organizational structures designed to provide reasonable assurance that business objectives will be achieved and that undesired events will be prevented or detected and corrected.

Let's compare this to the COSO definition of internal control presented in Chapter 7. Notice that both the COSO and the COBIT definitions refer to the achievement of objectives. Whereas COSO makes these objectives explicit, the COBIT objectives are the qualities of information introduced in Chapter 1. Finally, the COBIT definition adds the idea that controls should address "undesired events." This is similar to our theme in this chapter that the IT processes should prevent exposures from occurring.

A Hypothetical Computer System

The IT resources are typically configured with some or all of the elements shown in Figure 8.1 (page 261) which we will use to focus our discussions. This computer system consists of one or more mainframe computers (perhaps one is called a *server*) housed in a computer room within the organization's headquarters This computer is connected to several networked *client computers* (CCs) and PCs located within the

---

[3] *COBIT: Control Objectives for Information and Related Technology—Framework*, 3rd ed. (Rolling Meadows, IL: The Information Systems Audit and Control Foundation, 2000): 6.

[4] *COBIT: Control Objectives for Information and Related Technology—Framework*, 3rd ed. (Rolling Meadows, IL: The Information Systems Audit and Control Foundation, 2000): 12.

Figure 8.1 A Hypothetical Computer System

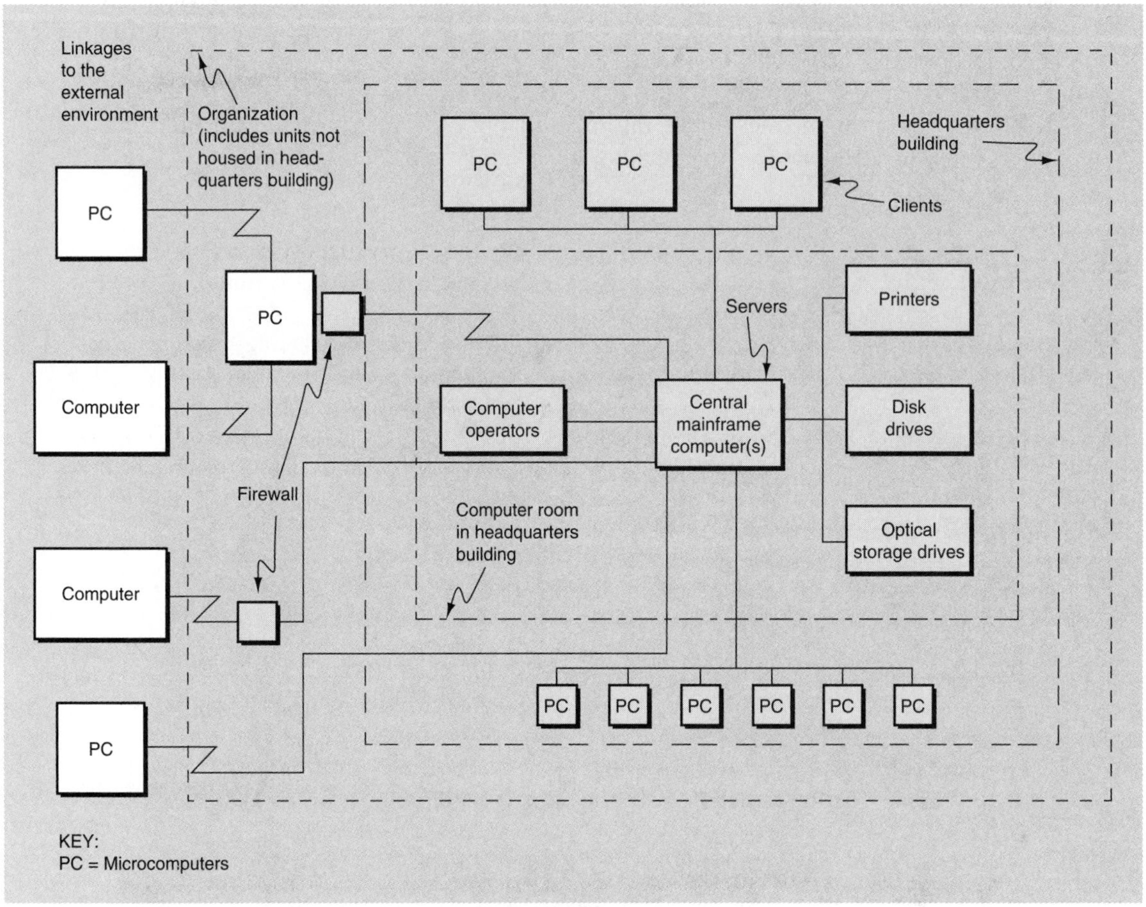

Linkages to the external environment

Organization (includes units not housed in head-quarters building)

Headquarters building

PC

PC · PC · PC

Clients

Servers

Printers

PC

Firewall

Computer operators

Central mainframe computer(s)

Disk drives

Computer room in headquarters building

Optical storage drives

Computer

PC

PC · PC · PC · PC · PC · PC

KEY:
PC = Microcomputers

building, perhaps through a *local area network (LAN)*, and to PCs and CCs located in the organization's other facilities, perhaps through a *wide area network (WAN)*. Finally, computer facilities operated by other organizations are connected, perhaps via the *Internet* and through a *firewall* (to be described later in the chapter), to the mainframe, servers, and PCs.

Controlling the operation of this configuration provides many challenges to the organization. To support organizational objectives and to provide an environment in which business process control plans can be effective, we must determine how we can protect the computer from misuse, whether intentional or inadvertent, from within and outside the organization. Furthermore, how do we protect the computer room, the headquarters building, and the rooms and buildings in which other connected facilities are located? In the event of a disaster, do we have plans in place for continuing our operations? What policies and procedures should be established (and documented) to provide for efficient, effective, and authorized use of the computer? What measures can we take to help ensure that the personnel who operate and use the computer are competent and honest? Answers to these and similar questions run to the heart of IT control processes.

The Information Systems Function

Before we begin the discussion of IT control processes, however, we need to take a look at the information systems function. This short digression will make your study of IT control processes more meaningful.

An organization's **information systems function (ISF)** is the department or function that develops and operates an organization's information system. The function (department) is composed of people, procedures, and equipment, and it is typically called the *information services department*, *IT department*, or *data processing department*.

Figure 8.2 reflects an organization chart of a typical **centralized information systems structure**. This type of structure places the information systems function under the line authority of the vice president of information systems (also known as the chief information officer or CIO). In practice, organizations have structured their information systems function in ways other than the centralized arrangement illustrated in Figure 8.2. These alternate structures include but are not limited to:

- *Decentralized* organization—assigns personnel to non-central (e.g., departments) organizational units.

- *Functional* organization—assigns personnel to skills-based units (e.g., programming, systems analysis). Used by both decentralized and centralized organizations.

Figure 8.2 Centralized Information Systems Organization

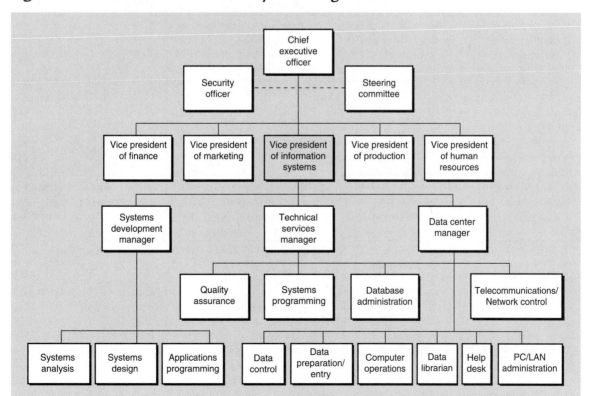

- *Matrix* organization—assembles work groups or teams, comprised of members from different functional areas, under the authority of a team leader.
- *Project* organization—establishes permanent systems development structures such as "Financial Systems Development."

Table 8.1 outlines the principal responsibilities, major duties, and key control concerns related to each information systems functional box depicted in Figure 8.2. We include key control concerns in Table 8.1 to raise your awareness of control issues related to particular functional activities and to the organization of the information system as a whole.[5]

Table 8.1 Summary of Information Systems Functions

Functional Title (See Fig. 8.2)	Principal Responsibilities	Major Duties	Key Control Concerns
Steering committee	Guide and advise the ISF.	Prioritize and select ISF projects and resources.	Corporate and ISF strategic objectives are misaligned.
Security officer	Ensure the security of all ISF resources.	Physical security (e.g., computer and telecommunications equipment) and logical security (enterprise data).	Disasters (e.g., hurricanes, tornadoes, terrorist attacks, power outages, fires, hackers, and crackers).
Vice president of information systems	Efficient, effective operation of information systems functions.	Plans resource acquisition and development; controls hardware and software operations.	IS function fails to support organization's mission.
Systems development manager	Delivers cost-effective, bug-free applications; advises systems development staff; implements systems development standards.	Supervises applications systems development; sets and monitors multiple project deadlines; sees that staff utilizes state-of-the-art development methods.	If systems development also operates the computer, they can develop and implement systems without management or user approval.
Systems analysis	Studies information-related problems and proposes solutions.	Analyzes existing system; writes new system specifications.	Combining analysis with programming or design precludes containment of analysis errors.
Systems design	Converts analyst's specifications into a design.	Devises program module specifications, report layouts, database design, implementation plans, test plans, and user procedures.	Combining design with analysis or programming precludes containment of design errors.

[5] See Chapter 2 of *Systems Auditability and Control Report, Module 1, Managing Computer Resources* (Altamonte Springs, FL: The Institute of Internal Auditors Research Foundation, 1991) for a discussion of the organization of the IS function.

Table 8.1 Summary of Information Systems Functions (*continued*)

Functional Title (See Fig. 8.2)	Principal Responsibilities	Major Duties	Key Control Concerns
Applications programming	Converts designer's specifications into applications programs.	Codes, tests, and debugs applications programs.	Combining programming with analysis or design precludes containment of programming errors.
Technical services manager	Manages miscellaneous specialized and technical functions.	Manages functional units such as networks, computer-aided design/computer-aided manufacturing (CAD/CAM), OCR, MICR, POS, DBA, systems programming, and program maintenance.	Access to this technology is a vulnerable point in the information system.
Quality assurance	Maintains quality management standards and systems. Ensures continuous improvement of systems development and data quality.	Conducts reviews to determine adherence to ISF standards and procedures and achievement of ISF objectives.	Developed systems fail to achieve objectives. Projects not completed on time and within budgets. Data fails to satisfy quality criteria.
Systems programming	Maintains systems software.	Modifies and adapts systems software, including operating systems and various utility routines.	Systems programmers can easily access applications programs and data.
Database administration (DBA)	Designs and controls the database.	Maintains database software; maintains data dictionary; monitors and controls access to database.	DBA is central point from which to control data *and* is a central point of vulnerability.
Telecommunications/Network control	Installs and supports organizational telecommunications and network hardware and software.	Acquires, installs, maintains, and secures telecommunications and network hardware and software.	Less than optimal performance of telecommunications and networks. Security breaches.
Data center manager	Plans, controls, and delivers data processing production activities.	Establishes and monitors computer operations policies and procedures; hires, schedules, and oversees personnel on multishift operations.	Development activities undertaken by operations can bypass normal controls.
Data control	Routes all work into and out of the data center; corrects errors; monitors all error correction.	Logs batches of data; checks input batches for authorization, completeness, and accuracy; checks output batches for completeness and accuracy; distributes output.	An independent data control function ensures completeness and accuracy of processing.

(continued)

Table 8.1 Summary of Information Systems Functions (*continued*)

Functional Title (See Fig. 8.2)	Principal Responsibilities	Major Duties	Key Control Concerns
Data preparation/entry	Prepares input for computer processing.	Keys data directly into computer; uses offline devices to record data on magnetic or optical disks.	High risk of data conversion errors, which have pervasive impact.
Computer operations	Provides efficient and effective operation of the computer equipment.	Mounts tapes, disks, and CDs; loads printer paper; responds to computer console messages; and monitors equipment operation.	An operator allowed to program the computer can make unauthorized software changes.
Data librarian	Maintains custody of and controls access to programs, files, and documentation.	Issues programs, data, and documentation to authorized users; maintains record of data, program, and documentation usage.	Controlled access to data, programs, and documentation reduces unauthorized program changes and unauthorized computer operations.
Help desk	Assists users with systems problems.	Answers help line phone calls and e-mail and resolves user problems; obtains technical support and vendor assistance as required.	Problems not resolved in a timely manner. Problems that cannot be resolved at the help desk should be referred to the appropriate function and tracked until resolved.
PC/LAN administration	Helps user departments attain optimal use of LANs and PCs.	Assists departments to acquire, set up, and properly utilize LANs and PCs.	Acquired technology is consistent with organizational resource plans and technology infrastructure.

Take some time now to study Figure 8.2 (page 262) and Table 8.1. Be sure you have a good understanding of the principal responsibilities, major duties, and key control concerns of each functional title.[6]

The remainder of the chapter presents the four broad domains of IT control processes. Recall from Chapter 7 the nine common business exposures (see Exhibit 7.1, page 228). As we discuss the pervasive controls, we will present them as plans designed to reduce the likelihood that these nine exposures will occur. The discussion will be sprinkled with actual case examples of system breakdowns caused by both unintentional acts and intentional (malicious) acts. Also, we will occasionally allude to the control

---

[6] We should point out that Figure 8.2 (page 262) and Table 8.1 (pages 263–264) show job titles that have *typically* existed in the IS function. However, as new technologies emerge, we can expect new jobs to appear and others perhaps to disappear.

goals and information qualities that the IT control processes help an organization achieve. In this way, we hope you will see controls help to both *achieve* organizational objectives and *prevent* exposures.

Four Broad IT Control Process Domains

CoBiT groups IT control processes into four broad domains: (1) planning and organization, (2) acquisition and implementation, (3) delivery and support, and (4) monitoring. Figure 8.3 depicts the relationship of these four domains and lists the IT control processes within each domain, for a total of 10 processes. Notice that the monitoring domain provides feedback to the other three domains.

**Figure 8.3 Four Broad IT Control Process Domains
(from CoBiT) and Ten Important IT Control Processes**

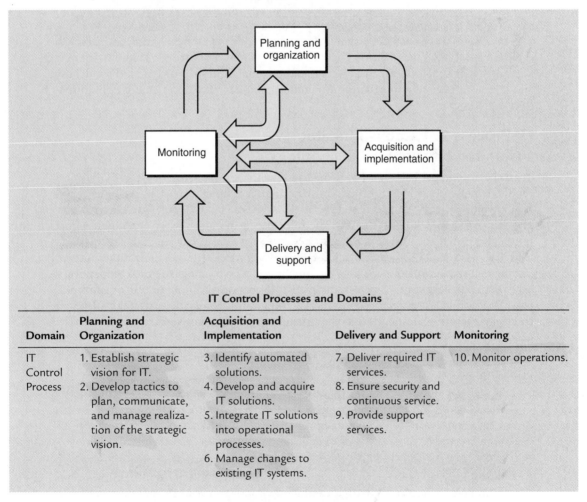

IT Control Processes and Domains

Domain	Planning and Organization	Acquisition and Implementation	Delivery and Support	Monitoring
IT Control Process	1. Establish strategic vision for IT. 2. Develop tactics to plan, communicate, and manage realization of the strategic vision.	3. Identify automated solutions. 4. Develop and acquire IT solutions. 5. Integrate IT solutions into operational processes. 6. Manage changes to existing IT systems.	7. Deliver required IT services. 8. Ensure security and continuous service. 9. Provide support services.	10. Monitor operations.

Before we move on to a discussion of the 10 IT control processes, let's discuss the concept of a control process. First, a "control process" could easily be, and often is, referred to as a "management practice." This latter terminology emphasizes management's responsibility for control in the organization and the practices or processes that will bring about achievement of an organization's objectives. Second, the prominence of "process" in this terminology reminds us of the COSO definition of control as "a process" and this text's definition of control as "a system." It is through a coordinated effort, across all IT resources and all organizational units, that the objectives of the organization are achieved.

PLANNING AND ORGANIZATION DOMAIN

Within the planning and organization domain are processes to develop the strategy and tactics for realizing an organization's information technology strategy. The overriding goal of these processes is to identify ways that IT can best contribute to the achievement of the organization's objectives. Once a strategic vision in this regard is set, management must communicate the vision to affected parties (within and outside the organization) and put in place the IT organization and technology infrastructure that enables that vision. Failure to implement these processes can lead to *competitive disadvantage, statutory sanctions, erroneous management decisions, fraud and embezzlement,* and *excessive costs* (see Exhibit 7.1, page 228). These exposures would result from a failure to identify and address external threats and internal and external IT requirements, and to identify and take advantage of opportunities for strategic implementation of emerging information technology.

IT Process 1: Establish Strategic Vision for Information Technology

To strike an optimal balance of information technology opportunities and IT business requirements, management of the information services function should adopt a process for developing a strategic plan for all of the organization's IT resources, and for converting that plan into short-term goals. The information systems strategic planning effort must ensure that the organization's strategic plan is supported and that information technology is used to the best advantage of the organization. An organization wants to be sure that the information systems function is prepared to anticipate the competition's actions and to take advantage of emerging information technology. An organization must establish links between organizational and information systems strategic planning to ensure that strategies plotted in the organizational plan receive the IT support they need.

Important strategic planning processes, and corresponding elements of strategic IT plans, include the following:

1. *A summary of the organizational strategic plan's goals and strategies, and how they are related to the information systems function.* This information is included to provide a framework for the strategic IT plan and to make sure that the plan is directed toward achievement of organizational objectives (see next item).

2. *IT goals and strategies, and a statement of how each will support organizational goals and strategies.* These strategies include a description of major information subsystems and applications. Mission-critical applications—those IS applications central to the successful competitive performance of the organization—must be separately identified and monitored.

E-BUSINESS   3. *An information architecture model encompassing the corporate data model and the associated information systems.* Plans for any new lines of business, such as e-Business, or changes in business processes, such as change over to an *enterprise system*, **ENTERPRISE** will require new data and relationships among the data. These data elements and **SYSTEMS** relationships must be incorporated into the organization's information architecture model.

4. *An inventory of current information systems capabilities.* The inventory should include hardware (computers and networks), software, personnel (quantities and skills), application systems, utilization rates, strengths, and weaknesses. This inventory should address both primary and backup facilities. A process must be in place to review IT capabilities to ensure that there is adequate technology to perform the IS function and to take advantage of emerging technology.

5. *Acquisition and development schedules for hardware, software, and application systems and for personnel and financial requirements.* These should be stated in detail for the following one or two years and should provide a basis for specific actions and for control.

6. *IT-related requirements to comply with industry, regulatory, legal, and contractual ob-* **E-BUSINESS** *ligations, including safety, privacy, transborder data flows, e-Business, and insurance contracts.* To avoid fines, sanctions, and loss of business, the organization must maintain procedures to ensure awareness and compliance with these obligations.

7. *IT risks and the risk action plan.* To ensure the achievement of IT objectives, in support of business objectives, and to respond to threats to the provision of IT services, management should establish a risk assessment framework, including risk identification, measurement, actions, and the formal acceptance and communication of the residual risk.

8. *Process for modifying the plan to accommodate changes to the organization's strategic plan and changes in information technology conditions.* The strategic IT plan should not be a static document. Rather, it should be kept up to date to accommodate changes in organizational objectives and to leverage opportunities to apply information technology for the strategic advantage of the organization.

IT Process 2: Develop Tactics to Plan, Communicate, and Manage Realization of the Strategic Vision

To ensure adequate funding for IT, controlled disbursement of financial resources, and effective and efficient utilization of IT resources, an organization must manage IT resources by using information services capital and operating budgets, by justifying IT expenditures, and by monitoring costs (in light of risks).

To ensure the overall effectiveness of the IS function, IS management must establish a direction and related policies addressing such aspects as positive control environment throughout the organization, code of conduct/ethics, quality, and security. Then, these policies must be communicated (internally and externally) to obtain commitment and compliance. IS management's direction and policies must be consistent with the *control environment* established by the organization's senior management.

To ensure that projects are completed on time and within budget and that projects are undertaken in order of importance, management must establish a project management framework to ensure that project selection is in line with plans and that a project management methodology is applied to each project undertaken.

Management should establish a quality assurance (QA) plan and implement related activities, including reviews, audits, and inspections, to ensure the attainment of IT customer requirements. A systems development life cycle methodology (SDLC) is an essential component of the QA plan.

To ensure that IT services are delivered in an efficient and effective manner, there must be adequate internal and external IT staff, administrative policies and procedures for all functions (with specific attention to organizational placement, roles and responsibilities, and segregation of duties), and an IT steering committee to determine prioritization of resource use. We divide these controls into two groups: *organizational control plans* and *personnel control plans.*

Organizational Control Plans

We will concentrate on two organizational control plans: segregation of duties and the information systems function.

Segregation of Duties Control Plan. Without proper segregation of duties, an organization might fail to achieve the control goals of *input accuracy* or *update accuracy*, leading to the exposures of *erroneous recordkeeping* and, if the incorrect records are used in a decision, *erroneous management decisions.* For example, assume that one person is responsible for recording all the data necessary to recognize a sales event. If that person were to make a mistake, then the stored data and output reports, such as the financial statements, would be misstated because no one else would have checked this person's work. This control plan also helps to ensure *security of resources* and prevent *embezzlement* and *loss of resources.* For example, the CEO and CFO of WorldCom, Inc., thwarted the system of internal controls by authorizing, executing, and recording false accounting transactions that resulted in bogus inflated revenues totaling around $11 billion. The board of directors, which is supposed to serve as a "watchdog" over upper management, was so passive that it failed to uncover the fraud that was taking place under its very nose.[7] The entire system of internal control and corporate governance apparently imploded at WorldCom.

Segregation of duties consists of separating the four basic functions of event processing. The functions are:

- *Function 1:* authorizing events
- *Function 2:* executing events
- *Function 3:* recording events
- *Function 4:* safeguarding resources resulting from consummating events

The concept underlying segregation of duties is simple enough: Through the design of an appropriate organizational structure, no single employee should be in a position both to perpetrate and conceal frauds, errors, or other kinds of system failures. A brief scenario should illustrate this point. John Singletary works in the general office of Small Company. He initiates a sales order and sends the picking ticket to the warehouse, resulting in inventory being shipped to his brother. When Sue Billings sends Singletary the customer invoice for the shipment, he records the sale as he would any sale. Sometime later, he writes his brother's account off as a bad debt. What is the result? Inventory was stolen and Singletary manipulated the information system to hide the theft. Had other employees been responsible for authorizing and recording the shipment or for the bad debt write-off, Singletary would have had a tougher time manipulating the system.

Table 8.2 illustrates segregation of duties in a manual system. Examine the top half of the table, which defines the four basic functions. The bottom half of the table extends

---

[7] Jim Hopkins, "Report: WorldCom Board Passive," *USA Today—Business* (June 10, 2003).

Table 8.2 Illustration of Segregation of Duties

Function 1	Function 2	Function 3	Function 4
			Safeguarding Resources Resulting from Consummating Events
Authorizing Events	**Executing Events**	**Recording Events**	
Activities · Approve phases of event processing.	· Physically move resources. · Complete source documents.	· Record events in books of original entry. · Post event summaries to the general ledger.	· Physically protect resources. · Maintain accountability of physical resources.
Example: Processing a credit sales event			

Activities · Approve customer credit.
· Approve picking inventory and sending inventory to shipping department.
· Approve shipping inventory to customer.
· Approve recording accounting entries.
	Physical Movement Resources
	· Pick inventory from bins.
	· Move inventory from warehouse to shipping department.
	· Ship inventory to customer.
	
	Complete Source Documents
	· Complete sales order.
	· Complete shipping document.
	· Complete invoice.
		Record Event Details
		DR AR—A/R Subsidiary Ledger
		CR Sales—Sales Journal
		DR Cost of Goods Sold—Inventory Ledger
		CR Inventory—Inventory Ledger
		
		Post Event
		GL Summaries
		DR AR
		   CR Sales
		DR Cost of Goods Sold
		   CR Inventory
			Physically Protect Resources
			· Safeguard inventory while in storage at warehouse, while in transit to shipping department, and while being prepared for shipment to customer.
			
			Maintain Accountability
			· Examine and count inventory periodically, and compare physical total to recorded total.

the coverage of segregation of duties by illustrating the processing of a credit sales event. The detail in the bottom half of the table is straightforward and should not require narrative interpretation.

Let's examine Table 8.2 as a means of better understanding the control notion underlying segregation of duties. Ideal segregation of duties requires that different units (departments) of an organization carry out each of the four phases of event processing. In this way, *collusion* would need to occur between one or more persons (departments) in order to exploit the system and conceal the abuse. Whenever collusion is necessary to commit a fraud, a greater likelihood exists that the perpetrators will be deterred by the risks associated with pursuing a colluding partner and that they will be caught. Thus, at a minimum, an organization must be large enough to support at least four independent units to implement segregation of duties *effectively*.

In practice, the customer service department might be responsible for accepting customer orders and completing sales orders. The credit department might be responsible for determining the existence of customers and approving their creditworthiness. The warehouse might be responsible for safeguarding inventory while it is being stored. The shipping department might be responsible for protecting inventory while it is awaiting shipment and for executing the shipment.

But how do we accomplish this in small organizations that have few employees? Perhaps we don't. At a minimum, we should strive to separate the critical duties. Also, in this kind of environment, we would place greater reliance on personnel control plans aimed at hiring honest employees and motivating those people to stay honest, coupled with close supervision by top management. These alternative control plans are commonly called *compensatory controls*.

E-BUSINESS   Controls to prevent *unauthorized* execution of events help prevent *unacceptable accounting* and *fraud* by ensuring that only *valid* events are recorded. Therefore, function 1, authorizing events, takes on particular significance in our segregation of duties model. Control plans for authorizing or approving events empower individuals or computers to initiate events and to approve actions taken subsequently in executing and recording events. Authorization control plans often take the form of policy statements, and are implemented by including necessary procedures and business process controls within the information system that will process the events. For example, through proper design of the sales order form, an organization can see that credit is granted by including a block on the document that requires the credit manager's signature. Or, a computer-based system can be designed to approve sales within some predetermined credit limits. In some e-Business trading partner arrangements, a retail store's computer is authorized to automatically send a stock replenishment order to a vendor when shelf inventory runs low. The vendor's computer automatically sends the goods to the retail store. In turn, the retail stores' computer automatically receives the goods and pays the vendor. In this example, computer-based rules authorized the purchase, sale, movement, and receipt of goods. These procedures receive management authorization when the system is approved during initial development, or when the system is changed.

Organizational Control Plans for the Information Systems Function. The information systems function (ISF) normally acts in a service capacity for other operating units in the organization. In this role, it should be limited to carrying out function 3 of Table 8.2 (page 269) recording events and posting event summaries. Approving and executing events along with safeguarding resources should be carried out by departments other than IS. This arrangement allows for the effective implementation of segregation of duties. Situations exist, however, where the functional divisions we mentioned can be violated. For instance, some ISFs do authorize and execute events; for example, the computer might be programmed to approve purchase, receipts, and payments, as previously mentioned. However, with this example, the authorization actually occurred when an authorized manger developed and implemented the computer-based rules. And, the safeguarding of assets (inventory received) was in the hands of the receiving function. Any changes to such rules must be restricted to authorized persons only who are not part of the ISF.

Within the ISF we segregate duties to control unauthorized use of and/or changes to the computer and its stored data and programs. Segregation of duties within the ISF can be accomplished in a number of ways. For example, in examining Figure 8.2 (page 262), we see that *systems development, technical services,* and *data center management* are segregated. A method of separating systems development and operations is to prevent programmers from operating the computer, thus reducing the possibilities of unauthorized data input or unauthorized modification of stored data and programs.

The data librarian also assists in separating key functions. For example, a librarian function grants access to stored data and programs to authorized personnel only. This separation reduces the risk of unauthorized computer operation or unauthorized programming by operators. Librarian controls, combined with restricting access to the database and making the *security officer* responsible for assigning *passwords*, are critical to separating key functions within the ISF and limiting access to computing resources.

In addition to assigning passwords, the **security officer** might perform a multitude of control-related activities such as monitoring employees' network access, granting security clearance for sensitive projects, and working with human resources to ensure that interview practices such as thorough background checks are conducted during the hiring process.

The senior management in many organizations has appointed a committee to oversee the ISF and its activities. The **information technology steering committee** coordinates the organizational and IT strategic planning processes and reviews and approves the strategic IT plan. The steering committee can provide significant help to the organization in establishing and meeting user information requirements and in ensuring the effective and efficient use of the organization's IT resources. The committee should consist of about seven executives from major functional areas of the organization, including the information systems executive; report to senior management; and meet regularly.

Figure 8.4 (page 272) provides a summary of the preceding discussion. Since this section deals with organizational control plans, the figure is presented in the form of two organization charts—one general and one specific to the information systems function—preceded by a summary of the key control issues presented in this section.

Personnel Control Plans

IT personnel resources must be managed so as to maximize their contributions to the IT processes. Specific attention must be paid to recruitment, promotion, personnel qualifications, training, backup, performance evaluation, job change, and termination. As we discussed earlier in the chapter, an organization that does not have a critical mass of honest, competent employees will find it virtually impossible to implement other control plans.

Personnel control plans help to protect an organization against certain types of exposures. For example, hiring incompetent employees could result in time and money being wasted on futile training programs. This exposes a company to *excessive cost*. Alternatively, offering employment to an individual unqualified to fill a position may preclude efficient, effective operations or, if the person cannot follow instructions, may lead to inaccurate information processing. Obviously, hiring an employee with a prior record of dishonesty exposes the organization to a greater possibility of *fraud and embezzlement*.

Figure 8.5 (page 273) summarizes a number of personnel control plans aimed at mitigating the effects of these types of exposures. As you study each plan, think of the exposures that the plan can prevent or the control goal that could be achieved by implementing the plan.

Selection and Hiring Control Plans. Candidates applying for positions should be carefully screened, selected, and hired. The requirement for a technical background and

Figure 8.4 Summary of Organizational Control Plans

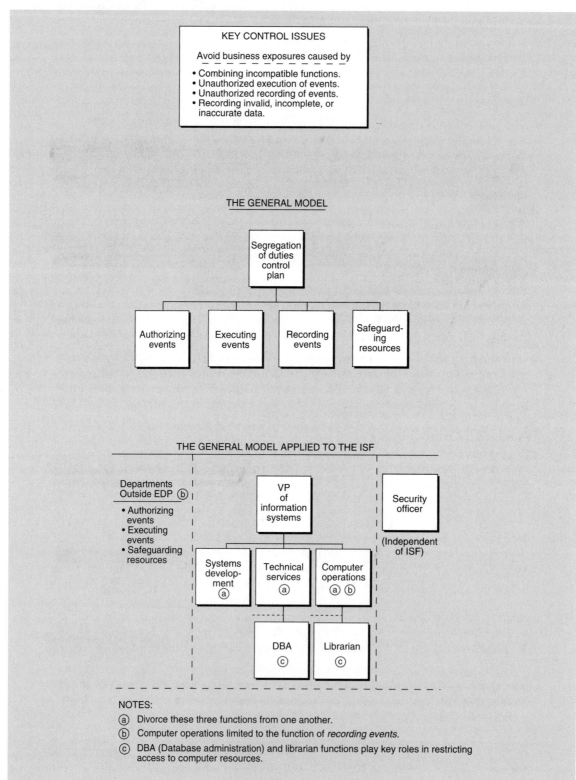

NOTES:

ⓐ Divorce these three functions from one another.

ⓑ Computer operations limited to the function of *recording events*.

ⓒ DBA (Database administration) and librarian functions play key roles in restricting access to computer resources.

Figure 8.5 Summary of Personnel Control Plans

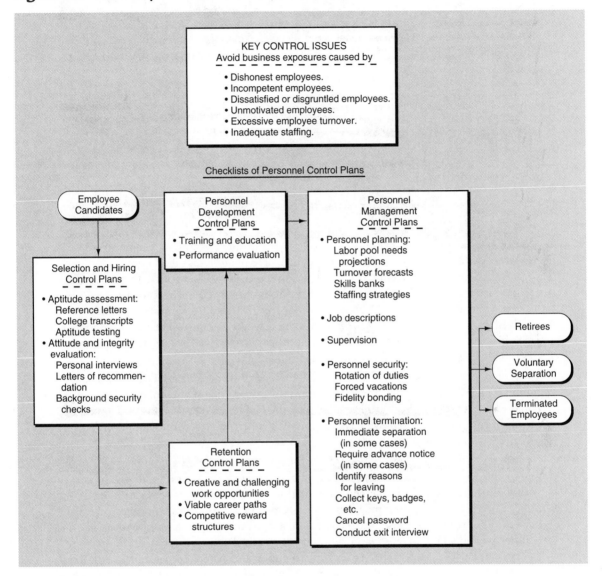

the shortage of qualified applicants make the selection and hiring of systems personnel particularly important.

Retention Control Plans. Retaining qualified personnel can be even more difficult than hiring them. Again, the problem is especially critical when dealing with systems personnel. Companies should make every effort to provide creative and challenging work opportunities and, when possible, to offer open channels to management-level positions.

Personnel Development Control Plans. Training must be regular, not haphazard. Deficiencies noted in an employee's background should be rectified through proper training or education. Training must be preeminent in an employee's work schedule. In general, performance reviews are performed for at least four reasons. First, a review determines whether an employee is satisfying the requirements of a position as indicated by a job description. Second, it assesses an employee's strengths and weaknesses. Third, it assists management in determining whether to make salary adjustments and whether to promote an employee. Finally, it identifies opportunities for training and for personal growth.

Personnel Management Control Plans. *Personnel planning control plans* project future managerial and technical skills of the staff, anticipate turnover, and develop a strategy for filling necessary positions. *Job description control plans* lay out the responsibilities for each position on an organization chart and identify the resources to be used in performing those responsibilities. *Supervision control plans* involve the processes of approving, monitoring, and observing the work of others.

Personnel security control plans prevent the organization's own personnel from committing acts of computer abuse, fraud, or theft of assets. **Rotation of duties** is a policy of requiring an employee to alternate jobs periodically. **Forced vacations** is a policy of requiring an employee to take leave from the job and substituting another employee in his or her place. The control notion underlying these plans is that if an employee is perpetrating some kind of irregularity, that irregularity will be *detected* by the substitute. Furthermore, if these plans are in place, they should act as a deterrent to the irregularity ever occurring in the first place (i.e., preventive). Beyond the control considerations involved, these two plans also help mitigate the disruption that might be caused when an employee leaves the organization. Since another person(s) is familiar with the job duties of each position, no single employee is irreplaceable.

What if personnel security control plans fail to prevent employee dishonesty? By bonding their key employees, many organizations insure against the financial losses that could result. A **fidelity bond** indemnifies a company in case it suffers losses from defalcations committed by its employees. Employees who have access to cash and other negotiable assets are usually bonded.

Termination control plans define the set of procedures a company follows when an employee voluntarily or involuntarily leaves an organization. Although all departments within a company should implement termination policies, rigorous application of these policies is particularly important in the ISF. Disgruntled employees working in the ISF have the opportunity to cause much damage in a short time. For example, computer operations personnel could erase large amounts of stored data in a matter of minutes. For this reason, key employees who have access to important stored data and programs may be asked to leave the facility immediately, and in some cases company security personnel may escort them off the premises.

ACQUISITION AND IMPLEMENTATION DOMAIN

Processes within the acquisition and implementation domain are designed to identify, develop or acquire, and implement IT solutions, and integrate them into the business process. Once installed, procedures must also be in place to maintain and manage changes to existing systems. Failure to successfully execute these processes can lead to *all* of the nine common business exposures. For example, if we do not correctly determine the requirements for a new information system *and* see that those requirements are satisfied by the new system, the new system could cause us to violate accounting standards (*unacceptable accounting*) or perform calculations incorrectly (*erroneous recordkeeping* leading to *erroneous management decisions* or *statutory sanctions*). Or we may not complete the development on time (leading to *competitive disadvantage* if our competition implements such a system first) and within budget (causing *excessive cost*). Finally, should we fail to develop proper controls for the new system, we could experience *business interruption*, *fraud and embezzlement*, or *loss or destruction of resources*.

Our discussion of this domain is brief here because these processes are analyzed in depth in the systems analysis and design supplement to this text. The following discussion often refers to the *systems development life cycle* or *SDLC*. The term **systems development life cycle (SDLC)** is used in several ways. It can mean:

1. A formal set of activities, or a *process*, used to develop and implement a new or modified information system. (In the text supplement *Acquiring, Developing, and Implementing Accounting Information Systems*, we refer to this as a *systems development methodology*.)

2. The documentation that specifies the systems development process. (In the text supplement *Acquiring, Developing, and Implementing Accounting Information Systems*, we refer to this as the *systems development standards manual*.)

3. The progression of information systems through the systems development process, from birth, through implementation, to ongoing use. The "life cycle" idea comes from this last definition.

IT Process 3: Identify Automated Solutions

To ensure the selection of the best approach to satisfying users' IT requirements, an organization's *SDLC* must include procedures to define information requirements; formulate alternative courses of action; perform technological, economic, and operational feasibility studies; and assess risks. These solutions should be consistent with the strategic information technology plan, and the technology infrastructure and information architecture contained therein. At the completion of this process, an organization must decide what approach will be taken to satisfy users' requirements, and whether it will develop the IT solution in-house or will contract with third parties for all or part of the development.

IT Process 4: Develop and Acquire IT Solutions

Once IT solutions have been identified and approval to proceed has been received, development and/or appropriate acquisition of the application (i.e., business process) software, infrastructure, and procedures may begin. Note: We use the term *business process* to describe conceptually the related flow of economic events under consideration. When discussing the actual computer software that is used to facilitate the execution of a given business process, we use the term *application software*. A given business process may utilize more than one application. For instance, a sales process might have one application for customer relationships, one for sales orders, and another for sales payments. In all likelihood, these applications would be linked to one another; nevertheless, they might actually represent three distinct applications. Thus, application software reflects instantiations or artifacts of a higher-level concept known as the *business process*.

Develop and Acquire Application Software

To ensure that applications will satisfy users' IT requirements, an organization's *SDLC* should include procedures to create design specifications for each new, or significantly modified, application and to verify those specifications against the user requirements. The specifications should be developed with systems users and approved by management and user departments. Design specifications include those for inputs, outputs, processes, programs, and stored data.

Acquire Technology Infrastructure

The *SDLC* should include procedures to ensure that platforms (hardware and systems software) support the new or modified application. Further, an assessment should be made of the impact of new hardware and software on the performance of the overall system. Finally, procedures should be in place to ensure that hardware and systems software are installed, maintained, and changed so as to continue to support business processes.

Develop Service Level Requirements and Application Documentation

ENTERPRISE SYSTEMS

E-BUSINESS

To ensure the ongoing, effective use of IT, the organization's *SDLC* should provide for the preparation and maintenance of service level requirements and application documentation. *Service level requirements* include such items as availability, reliability, performance, capacity for growth, levels of user support, disaster recovery, security, minimal system functionality, and service charges. These requirements become benchmarks for the ongoing operation of the system. As IT organizations become larger and more complex, especially those that must implement and operate *enterprise systems*, these service level requirements become important methods for communicating the expectations of the business units for IT services. Further, if the organization is engaged in *e-Business* these service levels become benchmarks for service on a Web site or with business partners engaged in electronic commerce.

The *SDLC* should include processes to ensure that comprehensive documentation is developed for each application to enable the effective use, operation, and maintenance of the application. *Application documentation* typically includes the following:

1. *Systems documentation* provides an overall description of the application, including the system's purpose; an overview of system procedures; and sample source documents, outputs, and reports.

2. *Program documentation* provides a description of an application program and usually includes the program's purpose; program flowcharts; source code listings; descriptions of inputs, data, and outputs; program test data and test results; and a history of program changes and approvals of such changes.

3. *Operations run manuals* give detailed instructions to *computer operators* and to *data control* about a particular application. These manuals typically specify input source, form, and when received; output form and distribution; and computer operation instructions, including setup, required data, restart procedures, and error messages.

4. *User manuals* describe user procedures for an application. These instructions, which assist users in preparing inputs and using outputs, include a description of the application, procedures for completing source documents, instructions on how to input data to the computer, descriptions of manual files and computerized data, instructions on how to perform manual and automated processing, explanations of controls (including how to detect and correct errors), and procedures for distributing and utilizing normal outputs.

5. *Training materials* help users learn their jobs and perform consistently in those jobs.

IT Process 5: Integrate IT Solutions into Operational Processes

To ensure that a new or significantly revised system is suitable, the organization's *SDLC* should provide for a planned, tested, controlled, and approved conversion to the new system. After installation, the SDLC should call for a review to determine that the new system has met users' needs in a cost-effective manner. When organizations implement *enterprise systems*, the successful integration of new information systems modules into existing information and operations processes becomes more difficult and more important. The challenges are the result of the interdependence of the business processes and the complexity of these processes and their connections. Any failure in a new system can have catastrophic results.

ENTERPRISE SYSTEMS

IT Process 6: Manage Changes to Existing IT Systems

To ensure processing integrity between versions of systems and to ensure consistency of results from period to period, changes to the IT infrastructure (hardware, systems software, and applications) must be managed via change request, impact assessment, documentation, authorization, release and distribution policies, and procedures.

Program change controls provide assurance that all modifications to programs are authorized, and ensure that the changes are completed, tested, and properly implemented. Changes in documentation should mirror the changes made to the related programs. Figure 8.6 depicts the stages through which programs should progress to ensure that only authorized and tested programs are placed in production. Notice that separate organizational entities (see Figure 8.2, page 262) are responsible for each stage in the change process. These controls take on an even higher level of significance with *enterprise systems*. Should unauthorized or untested changes be made to such systems, the results could be disastrous. For example, assume that a change is made to the inventory module of an ERP system without testing to see the impact that change will have on the sales module used to enter customer orders. Because these two modules work together,

ENTERPRISE SYSTEMS

Figure 8.6 Illustration of Program Change Controls

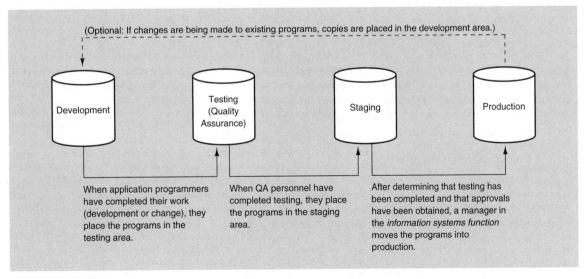

and orders from customers for inventory cannot be processed without the inventory module, changes to either module must be carefully planned and executed.

DELIVERY AND SUPPORT DOMAIN

The delivery and support domain includes processes to deliver required IT services; ensure security and continuity of services; set up support services, including training; and ensure integrity of application data. Failure to implement these processes can lead to *erroneous recordkeeping*, *erroneous management decisions*, and *statutory sanctions* resulting from a failure to maintain the *integrity* of the application programs and data. Failure of these processes also can result in computing resources being lost or destroyed or becoming unavailable for use, leading to *business interruption*, *statutory sanctions*, *excessive costs*, *loss or destruction of resources*, and *competitive disadvantage*. Finally, unauthorized use of the computing resources can lead to *fraud and embezzlement*, *excessive costs*, and *loss and destruction of resources*.

IT Process 7: Deliver Required IT Services

This process includes activities related to the delivery of the IT services that were planned by the IT processes in the planning and organization domain, and developed and implemented by the IT processes in the acquisition and implementation domain. Table 8.3 describes some of the key service-delivery activities.

IT Process 8: Ensure Security and Continuous Service

In addition to managing ongoing IT operations, the IS function must see that IT services continue to be provided at the levels expected by the users. To do so, they must provide a secure operating environment for IT and plan for increases in required capacity and losses of usable resources. To ensure that sufficient capacity of IT resources remain available for optimal use to satisfy organizational requirements, management should establish a process to monitor the capacity and performance of all IT resources. Capacity of all IT resources must be determined and managed, and resource modifications (increases or decreases) must be properly planned. To ensure that IT assets are not lost or altered, or used without authorization, management should establish a process to account for all IT components, including applications, technology, and facilities, and to prevent unauthorized alterations of assets or use of unauthorized assets. To ensure that barriers to efficient and effective use of the IT resource are prevented or eliminated and that the IT resource remains available, processes should be in place to identify, track, and resolve in a timely manner problems and incidents that occur. Three important aspects of the IT processes designed to address these issues are discussed in the following sections: ensuring continuous service, restricting access to computing resources, and ensuring physical security.

Ensure Continuous Service

To ensure that sufficient IT resources continue to be available for use in the event of a service disruption, management should establish a process, coordinated with the overall business continuity strategy, which includes business continuity or contingency planning as well as disaster recovery planning for all IT resources and related business resources, both internal and external. These control plans are directed at potential calamitous losses of resources or disruptions of business processes, for both the organization and its business partners, which could imperil the organization's very survival. Catastrophes like Hurricanes Andrew, Floyd, and George; earthquakes in Los Angeles and San Francisco;

Table 8.3 Delivering Required Services

Activity	Discussion
Define service levels	To ensure that internal and third-party IT services are effectively delivered, service level requirements must be defined. Service levels are the organizational requirements for the minimum levels of the quantity and quality of IT services.
Manage third-party services	To ensure that IT services delivered by third parties continue to satisfy organizational requirements, processes must be in place to identify, manage, and monitor nonentity IT resources.
Manage IT operations	To ensure that important IT functions are performed regularly and in an orderly fashion, the information services function should establish and document standard procedures for IT operations.
Manage data	To ensure that data remain *complete*, *accurate*, and *valid*, management should establish a combination of business process and general controls. *Business process controls* relate directly to the data as it is being processed. *General controls* ensure data integrity once the data has been processed and include *production backup* and *recovery control plans* that address short-term disruptions to IT operations. Production backup and recovery starts with making a copy (i.e., a *backup*) of the database, programs, and documentation. The copies are then used for day-to-day operations, and the originals are stored in a safe place. Should any of the working copies be damaged or completely destroyed, the originals are retrieved (i.e., the *recovery*) from safekeeping.
Identify and allocate costs	To ensure that IT resources are delivered in a cost-effective manner and that they are used wisely, information services management should identify the costs of providing IT services and should allocate those costs to the users of those services.

terrorist attacks on the World Trade Center and the Pentagon; the massive dockworker strike that left hundreds of ships afloat up and down the California coast with no place to unload their goods; flooding caused by the Chicago River; and the Con Edison fire that crippled Wall Street for several days have struck fear in the hearts of many executives that their firms might be brought to their knees by natural or man-made disasters. The processes covered in this section have been referred to in a variety of ways, including but not limited to **disaster recovery planning**, **contingency planning**, **business interruption planning**, and **business continuity planning**.

A number of business continuity planning models are available. The following are the six stages reflected in a business continuity management life cycle model developed by the Business Continuity Institute.[8] Think about a wagon wheel, with a center hub and five spokes. The first five stages form the spokes of the wheel and the last stage serves as the hub that glues the entire business continuity life cycle together.

1. *Understand your business:* Conduct a business impact analysis and perform a risk assessment and control study.

[8] "Business Continuity Management: Good Practice Guidelines," Dr. David J. Smith ed., sponsored by the Business Continuity Institute. They are available, as of June 2003, on the BCI Web site at http://www.thebci.org.

2. *Create business continuity strategies:* Design continuity and recovery strategies for the entire organization and all business processes.

3. *Develop and implement a business continuity management response:* Formalize a response plan; consider outsourcing some recovery functions to external parties if necessary; determine how to define and handle crises and incidents; create emergency response teams and related communication networks; and decide how to handle public relations and the media.

4. *Build and embed a business continuity management culture in the organization:* Engage in ongoing programs of education, awareness, and training.

5. *Maintain and audit the business continuity plan:* Rehearse the plan with affected parties, test the technology and other business continuity systems, and continually maintain and update the plans. Remember, business continuity planning reflects an ongoing process.

6. *Establish a formal business continuity management program* [the hub of the wheel previously described]: Gain the approval and proactive participation of the board of directors; define roles, accountability, responsibility, and authority; determine necessary levels of finances and resources; develop metrics, scorecards, and/or benchmarks for evaluating the effectiveness and efficiency of the program.

E-BUSINESS   Before we go further, let us alert you to the fact that contingency planning extends beyond the mere backup and recovery of stored computer data, programs, and documentation. The planning involves procedures for backing up the physical computer facilities; computer; and other equipment (such as communications equipment, which is a vital resource in the event of a catastrophe), supplies, and personnel. Furthermore, it reaches beyond the IS function to providing backup for these same resources residing in operational business units of the organization. Finally, the plan may extend beyond the organization for key resources provided by third parties. You also might note that the current thinking is that we should plan contingencies for important *processes* rather than individual *resources.* Thus we would develop a contingency plan for our Internet presence, rather than for our Web servers, networks, and other related resources that enable that presence.

E-BUSINESS   Numerous disaster backup and recovery strategies are available that may be included in an organization's contingency plan. Some industries require instant recovery and must incur the cost of maintaining two or more sites. One such option is to run two processing sites, a primary site and a **mirror site** that maintains copies of the primary site's programs and data. During normal processing activities master data is updated at both the primary and mirror sites. Located miles away from the primary site, the mirror site can take over in seconds if the primary site goes down. Mirror sites are very popular with airline and *e-Business* organizations because they need to keep their systems and Internet commerce sites online at all times. **Server clustering** also can be used to disperse the processing load among servers so that if one server fails, another can take over. These clustered servers are essentially mirror sites for each other. Due to lowered cost of servers and supporting software, server clustering is now cost-effective for all businesses—large and small.[9]

E-BUSINESS   Here is one example of the importance of these contingency processes to *e-Business.* In June 1999 the Web site for eBay, Inc., the online auctioneer, was un-

---

[9] Joe Brockmeier, "Will Server Clusters Swarm the Mainstream?" Linuxtoday, http://www.linuxtoday.com/, March 28, 2003 (story available as of June 2003).

available for 22 hours. This *business interruption* caused eBay to forego $3 to $5 million in fees (i.e., *loss of resources*) and some erosion of customer loyalty (i.e., *competitive disadvantage*). This failure spurred eBay to accelerate its plans for a better *backup* system.[10]

A less expensive alternative to mirror sites or server clustering is **electronic vaulting**, also known as **shadowing** or **replication**, a process that automatically transmits *event-related data* or actual *master data changes* (i.e., the results of processing the event data) on a continuous basis to an off-site electronic vault. Unlike the mirror site, the remote site does not contain the programs or processing capability required to take over processing for the primary site.

For most companies, maintaining duplicate equipment is cost prohibitive. Therefore, a good control strategy is to make arrangements with hardware vendors, service centers, or others for the standby use of compatible computer equipment. These arrangements are generally of two types—*hot sites* or *cold sites*.

A **hot site** is a fully equipped data center, often housed in bunker-like facilities, that can accommodate many businesses and that is made available to client companies for a monthly subscriber fee. Less costly, but obviously less responsive, is a **cold site**. It is a facility usually comprising air-conditioned space with a raised floor, telephone connections, and computer ports into which a subscriber can move equipment. The disaster recovery contractor or the manufacturer provides the necessary equipment. For example, IBM has a mobile recovery center on a converted 18-wheel truck fitted with 32 workstations, along with telephone lines and PCs, which can tap into LANs using wireless technology.[11] Obviously, it is necessary to have a contract for the delivery of the replacement equipment to ensure that it will be available when needed. As described in Technology Application 8.1, a company that contracts for either a hot site or a cold site should expect some delay in getting operations up and running after a disaster strikes since, at a minimum, it must relocate operations to that site.

Ensuring continuous service in a mainframe environment has become fairly straight-forward. We know that we need to back up important stored data, programs, and documentation; move those backups to recovery sites; and begin processing at that site. However, ISF environments are seldom just mainframe-oriented. As depicted in Figure 8.1 (page 261), client-server applications and other distributed applications and connections may exist. For example, a company doing business on the Internet would need to include that application in their continuity plan. However, few companies have an Internet business recovery plan in place. **E-BUSINESS**

Client-server applications also present problems because dozens or even hundreds of sites may exist, each with their own type of hardware and software. It is problematic to identify all those sites and to provide all the resources needed to bring them back to operational status after a disaster.

In the spring of 2000, several organizations, including Yahoo!, eBay, CNN.com, and Amazon.com, experienced a serious threat to their ability to ensure continuous service to their customers. The culprit was a relatively new phenomenon, the *distributed denial of service attack*. Technology Summary 8.1 describes these attacks and the processes that might be put in place to detect and correct them to ensure that organizations achieve **E-BUSINESS**

[10] George Anders, "eBay To Refund Millions in Listings Fees as Outage Halts Bids for About 22 Hours," *The Wall Street Journal* (June 4, 1999): B8.
[11] "IBM Hitting the Road with Recovery Truck," *PC Week* (July 21, 1997): 88.

Technology Application 8.1

Disaster Recovery Stories

Case 1—Verizon Communications Inc.

While many companies in New York City were prepared for small, contained, and localized IT disruptions, very few were ready for the widespread damage inflicted by terrorists on September 11, 2001. On that fateful day, the nation's economic well being hung in balance as the telecommunication infrastructure that powered the New York Stock Exchange, the mayor's command center, city hall, a city police plaza, and a federal plaza was virtually destroyed. One of the telecommunication giants, Verizon Communications Inc.—a major service provider in the NYC area—was critically wounded. President George W. Bush insisted that telecommunications service to the New York Stock Exchange be restored within days. While Verizon did not have a specific business continuity plan for such a catastrophe, the company had formed effective disaster recovery plans and teams that went into immediate action. One of Verizon's facilities, located at 140 West Street, was virtually destroyed. This facility housed four million data circuits and 300,000 dial tone lines. Meanwhile, at the Pentagon, Verizon sustained considerable damage to a switching network that serviced around 25,000 Pentagon phones. Indeed, Verizon had its plate full and the race was on to beat the clock. Because the company had planned for disasters, although not nearly as cataclysmic as these, the existing recovery plans and teams were flexible and adaptable enough to reconfigure, regroup and respond as events unfolded. Verizon restored telecommunications just hours before the re-opening of the New York Stock Exchange—only four days after the terrorist attack. The rest of the damaged telecommunications in NYC and at the Pentagon was restored within 90 days. This is an example of a disaster for which no specific plan existed; but, the existence of an ongoing business continuity management strategy greatly aided in the final recovery.

Source: D. Lenckus, "Verizon Quickly Restored Service After Terrorist Attacks," *Business Insurance* (April 7, 2003).

Case 2—Federal Employees Credit Union

On April 19, 1995, at 9:03 in the morning, the bombing of the Alfred P. Murrah Federal Building in Oklahoma City directly and indirectly traumatized thousands of people. In the wake of this tragedy, the Federal Employees Credit Union was completely destroyed. But, due to exceptional contingency planning, the credit union was back in operation 48 hours and 30 minutes later! Among the many features of the disaster recovery plan, all of the credit union's computer records were stored off-site in a concrete reinforced vault, 12 blocks away from the bomb site. The Rock Island Group, a company specializing in disaster recovery operations, owned and operated the vault. The credit union's data backup plan cost the credit union a mere $245 per month. Also, the credit union's standard operating procedure manual was stored off -site, as were supplies such as blank checks and computer forms. Many of the credit union's 15,800 members were faced with the sudden and sad task of planning for funerals of loved ones who lost their lives in the blast. The quick re-opening of the credit union was a stunning technological feat, but more importantly, it revealed the humanity of designing an effective business continuity plan.

Source: "Coping With Disaster—Federal Employees Credit Union," *Management Review* 85 (5) (1996): 3.

the level of service that they plan. The attacks that occurred in February 2000, caused *business interruptions* and *loss of resources*. The Yankee Group estimated that the overall cost of these attacks was $1.2 billion. For example, the Yahoo! site was unavailable for

---

Technology Summary 8.1

Denial of Service Attacks

In a **denial of service attack** a Web site is overwhelmed by an intentional onslaught of thousands of simultaneous messages, making it impossible for the attacked site to engage in its normal activities. A **distributed denial of service attack** uses many computers (called "zombies") that unwittingly cooperate in a *denial of service attack* by sending messages to the target Web sites. Unfortunately, the distributed version is more effective because the number of computers responding multiplies the number of attack messages. And, because each computer has its own IP address, it is more difficult to detect that an attack is taking place than it would be if all the messages were coming from one address. Denial of service attacks can be categorized into four levels, with progressively more severe consequences: (1) inundating the server with bogus requests; (2) consuming CPU cycles, memory, and other resources; (3) disabling Web traffic by misconfiguring routers; and (4) sending mail-bombs to individuals, lists, or domains.

Currently, no easy *preventive* controls exist. To *detect* a denial of service attack, Web sites may employ *filters* to sense the multiple messages and block traffic from the sites sending them, and *switches* to move their legitimate traffic to servers and Internet service providers (ISPs) that are not under attack (i.e., *corrective*). However, attackers can hide their identity by creating false IP addresses for *each* message, making many filtering defenses slow to respond or virtually ineffective. An organization might also carry insurance to reimburse it for any losses suffered from an attack (i.e., *corrective*).

---

three hours, costing Yahoo! $500,000. Amazon's site was down for an hour and they may have lost $240,000.[12]

Restrict Access to Computing Resources

As noted at the beginning of this chapter, respondents to the surveys conducted by the CSI/FBI and by E&Y reported substantial levels of unauthorized access to computing resources. To ensure that organizational information is not subjected to unauthorized use, disclosure, modification, damage, or loss, management should implement logical and physical access controls to ensure that access to computing resources—systems, data, and programs—is restricted to authorized users for authorized uses by implementing two types of plans:

1. Control plans that restrict physical access to computer facilities.

2. Control plans that restrict logical access to stored programs, data, and documentation.

Figure 8.7 (page 284) shows the levels (or layers) of protection included in each of these categories. Use Figure 8.7 as a road map to the discussion that follows. As you study this section consider how much more important these controls become when the organization engages in *e-Business* and has electronic connections to customers and business partners.   **E-BUSINESS**

Control Plans for Restricting Physical Access to Computer Facilities. Naturally, only authorized personnel should be allowed access to the computer facility. As shown

---

[12] Ann Harrison and Kathleen Ohlson, "Surviving Costly Web Strikes," *Computerworld* (February 21, 2000): 6.

Figure 8.7 Restricting Access to Computing Resources—Layers of Protection

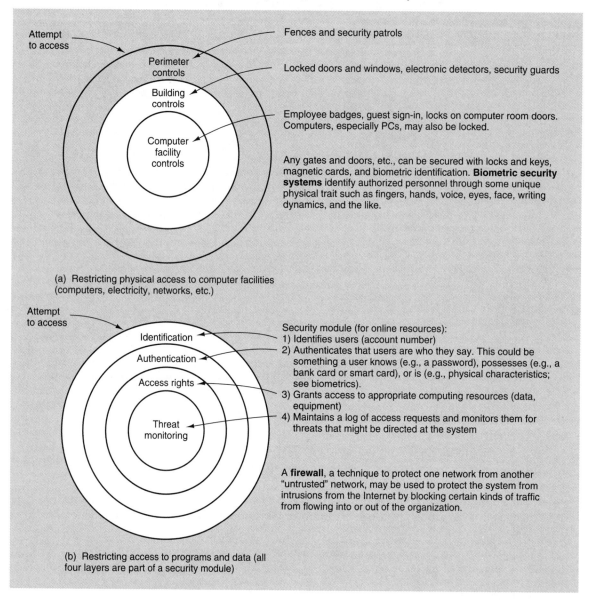

(a) Restricting physical access to computer facilities (computers, electricity, networks, etc.)

(b) Restricting access to programs and data (all four layers are part of a security module)

in Figure 8.7, control plans for restricting physical access to computer facilities encompass three layers of controls.

One important type of control is *biometric identification*, something that until recently you might have seen only in science fiction movies. Although not foolproof, the technology has improved dramatically in recent years, leading to the widening use of such systems in practice. The most common biometric devices are those that read finger- or thumbprints. In fact, biometric identification is used to secure physical access to many different types of facilities. For example, London City Airport, in response to the 9/11 terrorist attacks, is one of the first in Europe to use fingerprint identification to control access to its secure areas for 1,600 employees.[13] While controls for restricting physical access to computer facilities seem straightforward and are generally accepted as good practice, they are not always effectively implemented. Some of the security lapses uncovered by security consulting firms include:[14]

- Metal detectors at a front entrance that can be bypassed by taking a series of elevators and hallways to an unguarded door.

- Unlocked doors to computer rooms and utility rooms housing electrical connections and network wiring.

- Sensitive files, containing modem telephone numbers, passwords, confidential information, etc., lying out on desks in unsecured areas.

- Unrestricted access to devices that are printing confidential information.

Control Plans for Restricting Logical Access to Stored Programs, Data, and Documentation. Control plans for restricting logical access to stored programs, data, and documentation entail a number of techniques aimed at controlling *online* and *offline* systems. In an online environment, access control software called the **security module** will (1) ensure that only authorized users gain access to a system through a process of *identification* and *authentication*, (2) associate with authorized users the computing resources they are permitted to access and the action privileges they have with respect to those resources (*access rights*), and (3) report violation attempts. These steps are depicted in part (b) of Figure 8.7.

Biometric identification, mentioned earlier, is not only used to secure physical computing resources, but also logical resources. Fingerprint readers are available for use with PCs and laptops, and can cost as little as $50. Computer vendors are moving into this technology. For instance, IBM has integrated fingerprint security technology, from a company called AuthenTec, into IBM laptops.[15] This technology allows users to employ a fingerprint authenticator card by Targus to achieve touch-and-go laptop security. In addition, AuthenTec and Microsoft announced an agreement to integrate native biometric software into the Microsoft operating system, thereby resulting in the first biometrically enabled operating system on the market.[16]

The *threat monitoring* portion of the security module may employ intrusion detection software to monitor and "learn" how users typically behave on the system. The typical behavior is accumulated in *user profiles*. Subsequently, when usage patterns differ from the normal profile, the exceptional activity is flagged and reported. Intrusion detection systems can be used to detect attacks from outside the organization, such as *denial of service attacks*, or from inside the organization, as when authorized users attempt to undertake *un*authorized actions.

The primary plans for restricting access in an offline environment involve the use of *segregation of duties*, restriction of access to computer facilities, *program change controls*, and library controls. The first three plans have been defined and discussed in previous

---

[13] "Airport Rolls Out Biometric Security," CNN, http://www.cnn.com/2003/WORLD/europe/05/27/biz.trav.biometric.airport/index.html, May 27, 2003 (story available as of June 2003).
[14] Robert L. Scheier, "Lock the Damned Door!" *Computerworld* (February 10, 1997): 66–68.
[15] Tim McDonald, "IBM Buys Biometric Laptop Security," Newsfactor, http://newsfactor.com, April 1, 2002 (story available as of June 2003).
[16] "AuthenTec and Microsoft Collaborate on Biometric Authentication," Authentec, http://www.authentec.com/news/, April 23, 2003 (story available as of June 2003).

sections. Figure 8.8 depicts how some **library controls** restrict access to data, programs, and documentation. Library controls are provided by a *librarian function*, a combination of people, procedures, and computer software that serves two major purposes. First, library controls limit the use of stored data, programs, and documentation to authenticated users with authorized requests. Second, they maintain the storage media (e.g., disks, tapes).

Figure 8.8 Library Controls

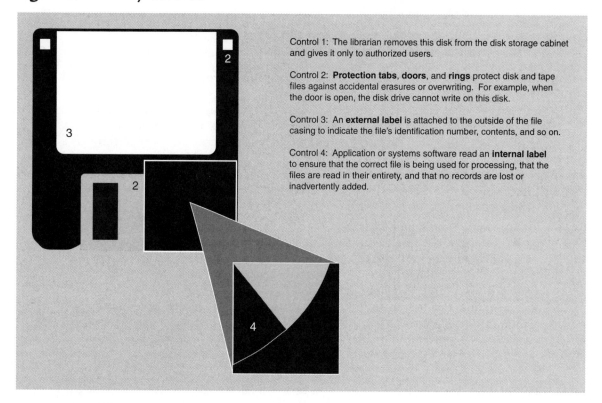

Control 1: The librarian removes this disk from the disk storage cabinet and gives it only to authorized users.

Control 2: **Protection tabs**, **doors**, and **rings** protect disk and tape files against accidental erasures or overwriting. For example, when the door is open, the disk drive cannot write on this disk.

Control 3: An **external label** is attached to the outside of the file casing to indicate the file's identification number, contents, and so on.

Control 4: Application or systems software read an **internal label** to ensure that the correct file is being used for processing, that the files are read in their entirety, and that no records are lost or inadvertently added.

In online environments, librarian software is used to restrict access to online programs, data, and documentation. For example, the software will keep track of the many versions of event and master data and ensure that the latest versions of such data are used. The software can also permit appropriate access to development, testing, staging, and production versions of programs (see Figure 8.6, page 277).

Before we leave this section, let's explore a topic that always receives much media attention, *computer hacking*. We discuss this topic in Technology Summary 8.2. Recently, a new type of hacker has been reported. "Hacktivists" are computer hackers with a political agenda. They vandalize government Web sites, such as the Federal Bureau of Investigation and the U.S. Army.[17] Interestingly, some security companies are hiring young, technology-savvy teenagers to try to break into clients' computer systems to find weaknesses. These bands of "white hat" hackers are let loose in an "information secu-

---

[17] Jon G.-Auerbach and William M. Bulkeley, "Web in Modern Age Is Arena for Activism, Terrorism, Even War," *The Wall Street Journal* (February 10, 2000): B1.

Technology   Summary   8.2

Computer Hackers and Crackers

In simple terms, **computer hacking and cracking** reflect the intentional penetration of an organization's computer system, accomplished by bypassing the system's access security controls. You can think of these acts as illegal breaking and entering. Usually, but not always, a person outside the organization does the hacking or cracking. A hacker is someone who gets a kick out of knowing the "ins and outs" of a computer system. Generally, hackers do not hold malicious intentions to destroy or steal; rather, they feel clever, powerful, and proud of their hacking successes. They enjoy building sought-after reputations among the underground world of hackers. On the other hand, while crackers employ many of the same penetration techniques as hackers, they do so with sinister motives that are bent on crime, theft, and destruction. However, as benign as hackers like to think they are, their illegal attempts to gain access into the computers and networks of others can result in serious damage and unwanted personal consequences. One renowned case of a so-called benign-motive type of hacking occurred in 1988 when a Cornell University graduate student infiltrated the Internet and planted a virus that he thought would not be destructive. However, it proved to be extremely so. It crashed some 6,000 computers on that network; as a result, the student gained more notoriety by becoming the first person charged with violating the Federal Computer Fraud and Abuse Act.

Hackers/crackers take a variety of steps to get the information they need to bypass security modules and firewalls—some ploys are ingenious, others mundane. Some of them merely "schmooze" unsuspecting employees to learn passwords.[a] This technique might work as follows:

> The hacker/cracker will call the "target" and claim that it appears that the "target" is trying to break into a key system— say accounting. The "target" will deny it vehemently, and when the panicked "target" thinks he or she is in real trouble, the hacker will ask, "Well, then, what user name are you using now?" The "target" will give his or her user name. Then, the hacker/cracker finishes it off with, "Well, then you are using the wrong password with that account. Are you using the new password?" The "target" will respond, "What new password?" Then the hacker/cracker will say, "Oh great! Now this is really messed up! What password are you using?" The "target" then gives up his or her password.[b]

Others employ "dumpster diving," searching through rubbish for system information such as passwords.[c] Some use "sniffer" programs that travel over telephone lines gathering passwords. Still others simply try to log on to a system by using commonly used passwords. Some of these techniques are now being used by businesses engaged in counter-hacking/cracking, known also as penetration testing. Clients hire these companies, including at least one Big Four accounting firm, to test the clients' computer systems for security weaknesses by attempting to legally hack their way into those systems.

[a] One security expert reports that a third of the computer crime cases that he has investigated involved an individual who had been talked out of a critical password. "Cyber Crime," *Business Week* (February 21, 2000): 42.
[b] "Securing the Network: Data Security Essentials," *Getting Results* (March 1997): 5.
[c] A case in point concerned a New York telephone company that sent a promotional letter to calling card customers, with PIN numbers printed on the letter. Dumpster divers scrambled for the discarded letters.

rity sandbox" to determine vulnerable spots in computers and networks: "Fortified by pizza and soda, they [study] a computer systems weaknesses, looking for ways to break in and steal information."[18]

[18] "Enlisting the Young as White Hat Hackers," *The New York Times* (May 29, 2003).

Ensure Physical Security

To protect the IT facilities against man-made and natural hazards, the organization must install and regularly review suitable environmental and physical controls. These plans reduce losses caused by a variety of physical, mechanical, and environmental events. Fire and water damages represent major threats to most businesses, as do power outages and lax data backup procedures. Table 8.4 summarizes some of the more common controls directed at these environmental hazards.

Table 8.4 Environmental Controls

Environmental Hazard	Controls
Fire	Smoke detectors, fire alarms, fire extinguishers, fire-resistant construction materials, insurance
Water damage	Waterproof ceilings, walls, and floors; adequate drainage; water and moisture detection alarms; insurance
Dust, coffee, tea, soft drinks	Regular cleaning of rooms and equipment, dust-collecting rugs at entrances, separate dust-generating activities from computer, good housekeeping
Energy increase, decrease, loss	Voltage regulators, backup batteries and generators

The advanced state of today's hardware technology results in a high degree of equipment reliability; unless the system is quite old, hardware malfunctions are rare. Even if a malfunction occurs, it is usually detected and corrected automatically. In addition to relying on the controls contained within the computer hardware, organizations should perform regular **preventive maintenance** (periodic cleaning, testing, and adjusting of computer equipment) to ensure its continued efficient and correct operation.

IT Process 9: Provide Support Services

To ensure that users make effective use of IT, management should identify the training needs of all personnel, internal and external, who make use of the organization's information services, and should see that timely training sessions are conducted. To effectively utilize IT resources, users often require advice about how to properly utilize IT resources, and may require assistance to overcome problems encountered in using those resources. This assistance is generally delivered via a "help desk" function.

MONITORING DOMAIN

Within the monitoring domain is a process to assess IT services for quality and to ensure compliance with control requirements. Monitoring may be performed as a self-assessment activity within an organizational unit such as the ISF, by an entity's internal/IT audit group, or by an external organization such as a public accounting firm. Failure to implement an adequate monitoring function can lead to *all* nine of the exposures described in Exhibit 7.1 (page 228) because without the feedback provided by this process, the system of internal control is not complete.

IT Process 10: Monitor Operations

To ensure the achievement of IT process objectives, management should establish a system for defining performance indicators (service levels), gathering data about all processes, and generating performance reports. Management should review these reports to measure progress toward identified goals. To increase confidence that IT objectives are being achieved and that controls are in place, and to benefit from advice regarding best practices for IT, independent audits should be conducted on a regular basis.

As previously mentioned in Chapter 1, the American Institute of Certified Public **E-BUSINESS** Accountants and Canadian Institute of Chartered Accountants have developed a set of professional assurance and advisory services based on a common set of Trust Service principles, which are outlined in Table 8.5. These principles apply to WebTrust and SysTrust engagements, among others. The WebTrust (version 3.0) family of services offers best practices and *e-Business* solutions related to business-to-consumer and business-to-business electronic commerce. Some of the services within the family include WebTrust Confidentiality, WebTrust Online Privacy, and WebTrust Consumer Protection. SysTrust (version 2.0) is an assurance service designed to test and monitor the reliability of an entity's information system and databases, including ERP systems. As you can see, the accounting profession is very involved with not only the monitoring domain (see Figure 8.3 on page 265), but also the planning and organization, acquisition and implementation, and delivery and support domains outlined in the COBIT framework.[19]

Table 8.5 Trust Services Principles

Principle	Description
Security	Determines whether the system is protected against unauthorized access (both physical and logical).
Availability	Determines whether the system is available for operation and use as committed or agreed.
Processing Integrity	Determines whether processing is complete, accurate, timely, and authorized.
Online Privacy	Determines whether private information obtained as a result of electronic commerce is collected, used, disclosed, and retained as committed or agreed.
Confidentiality	Determines whether business information designated as confidential is protected as committed or agreed.

Source: "Suitable Trust Services Criteria and Illustrations for Security, Availability, Processing Integrity, Online Privacy, and Confidentiality (Including WebTrust® and SysTrust®)," http://www.aicpa.org. Copyright © 2003 by American Institute of Certified Public Accountants, Inc. and Canadian Institute of Chartered Accountants. Used with permission.

---

[19] These services are introduced in Chapter 1.

SUMMARY

In this chapter, we discussed the problems inherent in controlling the activities of the information systems function. We suggested some controls that can help reduce IT exposures and take advantage of opportunities for strategic implementation of emerging information technology. To put these IT processes/control plans into perspective once again, return to the hierarchy shown in Figure 7.3 (page 248). Note that pervasive control plans, including the IT processes discussed in this chapter, provide a second umbrella of protection, in addition to the control environment, over all AIS business processes. In Chapter 9, we will begin to examine the third level in the hierarchy, business process control plans, by looking at those controls associated with the technology used to implement a business process. Then, in Chapters 10 through 15, we continue the coverage of application control plans by examining those related to each specific AIS subsystem.

REVIEW QUESTIONS

RQ 8-1 What is the difference between a business process control plan, a pervasive control plan, and an IT control process?

RQ 8-2 Name and describe the five IT resources.

RQ 8-3 How does the COBIT framework define control?

RQ 8-4 What are the principal responsibilities, major duties, and key control concerns of *each* functional position pictured in Figure 8.2 on page 262 (i.e., the organization chart of a centralized information systems department)?

RQ 8-5 What are the four IT control process domains?

RQ 8-6 a. What is the purpose of the strategic IT plan?

b. What are the major elements of the strategic IT plan?

RQ 8-7 a. What are two organizational control-related exposures and their possible causes?

b. Segregation of duties consists of separating what four basic functions? Briefly define each function.

RQ 8-8 Name some compensating controls that can be used to reduce exposures when it is not possible to properly segregate duties in a small organization.

RQ 8-9 What functions within the *Information Services Function* should be segregated.

RQ 8-10 What is the function of the security officer?

RQ 8-11 What is the function of the IT steering committee?

RQ 8-12 What are two personnel control-related exposures and their possible causes?

RQ 8-13 What are the personnel control plans? Define the plans.

RQ 8-14 What exposures might be associated with the acquisition and implementation domain? What are their possible causes?

RQ 8-15 Name and describe the four IT control processes in the acquisition and implementation domain.

RQ 8-16 What types of documentation constitute a well-documented application? Describe each type.

RQ 8-17 What are the four stages through which a program should move as it is being developed? Who should have responsibility for each of those phases?

RQ 8-18 What exposures might be associated with the delivery and support domain? What are their possible causes?

RQ 8-19 What steps are commonly included in a contingency planning methodology?

RQ 8-20 Describe a *mirror site, server clustering*, and *electronic vaulting*.

RQ 8-21 What is the difference between a *hot site* and a *cold site*?

RQ 8-22 Describe a *denial of service attack*. What controls are recommended to detect or correct such an attack?

RQ 8-23 a. What are the control plans for restricting physical access to computer facilities? What three layers of control do these plans represent? Explain each layer.

b. Explain what is meant by the term *biometrics*.

RQ 8-24 a. What are the control plans for restricting logical access to stored programs, data, and documentation? Which of these plans apply to an online environment, and which plans apply to an offline environment?

b. How does a security module work?

RQ 8-25 Define *computer hacking* and *cracking* and explain how they undermine resource security.

RQ 8-26 a. What kinds of damage are included in the category of environmental hazards?

b. What control plans are designed to *prevent* such hazards from occurring?

c. What control plans are designed to *limit losses* resulting from such hazards or to recover from such hazards?

RQ 8-27 a. Why should an organization conduct monitoring activities?

b. Who might conduct monitoring activities?

DISCUSSION QUESTIONS

DQ 8-1 What, if anything, is wrong with the following control hierarchy? Discuss fully.

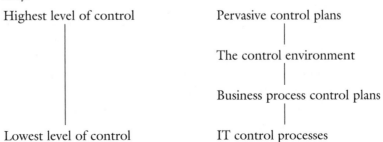

Highest level of control	Pervasive control plans
	The control environment
	Business process control plans
Lowest level of control	IT control processes

DQ 8-2 Compare and contrast the COBIT definition of control in this chapter (page 259) with the COSO and this textbook's definition of control in Chapter 7 (page 235).

DQ 8-3 "The information systems function of *systems programmer* presents particular threats to the organization—much more so than does that of *applications programmer*." Do you agree? Discuss fully.

DQ 8-4 "The information systems function of *database administrator* is really a 'two-edged sword.' It presents the organization with both control problems and opportunities to tighten control." Explain fully.

DQ 8-5 "In small companies with few employees, it is virtually impossible to implement the *segregation of duties* control plan." Do you agree? Discuss fully.

DQ 8-6 "No matter how sophisticated a system of internal control is, its success ultimately requires that you place your trust in certain key personnel." Do you agree? Discuss fully.

DQ 8-7 Debate the following point. "*Business continuity planning* is really an IT issue."

DQ 8-8 "Contracting for a standby *hot site* is too cost-prohibitive except in the rarest of circumstances. Therefore, the vast majority of companies should think in terms of providing for a *cold site* at most." Discuss fully.

DQ 8-9 What exposures might a *denial of service attack* cause? Also, what information criteria might an organization fail to attain as a result of such an attack? For each, describe a possible control.

DQ 8-10 "Using both external and internal file labels is an unnecessary duplication." Do you agree? Discuss fully.

DQ 8-11 "The monitor operations activity in IT process 10 must be performed by an independent function such as a CPA." Do you agree? Discuss fully.

DQ 8-12 Your boss was heard to say, "If we implemented every control plan discussed in this chapter, we'd never get any work done around here." Do you agree? Discuss fully.

PROBLEMS

P 8-1 Three lists follow. The first is a list of 10 situations that have control implications, the second is a list of 12 control plans from this chapter, and the third is the list of 9 common business exposures.

Control Situations

1. During a violent electrical storm, an employee was keying data at one of the computers in the order entry department. After about an hour of data entry, lightning caused a company-wide power failure. When power was restored, the employee had to rekey all the data from scratch.

2. The users' manual for the accounts payable department did not contain detailed instructions for completing the input form for approved vouchers. All the vouchers added to the accounts payable master data for the last month lacked the field for "due date." As a result, several vouchers were paid late and the company lost cash discounts on several other vendor payments.

3. Your instructor made arrangements for your AIS class to take a guided tour of the computer center at a large metropolitan bank. The father of one of your classmates had recently been fired as a teller at that bank. That classmate kept his visitor's badge and gave it to his father, who used it to access the computer center the next day. The father then erased stored programs and data.

4. The customer service representatives at We-Sell-Everything, a catalog sales company, have been complaining that the computer system response time is very slow. They find themselves apologizing to customers who are waiting on the phone for their order to be completed.

5. At Culpepper Company, most transaction processing is automated. When an inventory item reaches its reorder point, the computer automatically prints a purchase order for the economic order quantity (EOQ). Purchase orders of $500 or more require the signature of the purchasing manager; those under $500 are mailed to vendors without being signed. An applications programmer, who was in collusion with the vendor who supplied part 1234, altered the computer program and the inventory master data for that part. He reduced the EOQ and made certain program alterations, such that every time part 1234 reached its reorder point, two purchase orders were produced, each of which was under the $500 threshold.

6. The résumé of an applicant for the job of controller at OYnot Mills showed that the candidate had graduated, some 10 years earlier, magna cum laude from Large State University (LSU) with a major in accounting. LSU's accounting program was well respected, and OYnot had hired several of its graduates over the years. In his second month on the job, the new controller became tongue-tied when the vice president of finance asked him a technical question about earnings per share reporting. When later it was discovered that the controller's degree from LSU was in mechanical engineering, he was dismissed.

7. June Plugger, the company cashier, was known throughout the company as a workaholic. After three years on the job, June suddenly suffered a gall-bladder attack and was incapacitated for several weeks. While she was ill, the treasurer temporarily assumed the cashier's duties and discovered that June had misappropriated several thousand dollars since she was hired.

8. A hacker accessed the Web site at Deuteronomy, Inc., and changed some of the graphics. Being confused by these changes, some customers took their business elsewhere.

9. During a normal workday, Sydney entered Acme Company's offices and was able to find and remove some computer printouts containing user IDs and other sensitive information. He later used that information to gain access to Acme's computer system.

10. John, an employee at Smith & Company, successfully accessed the order entry system at Smith and entered some orders for goods to be shipped to his cousin.

Control Plans

A. Personnel termination control plans

B. Biometric security systems

C. Personnel selection and hiring control plans

D. Rotation of duties and forced vacations

E. Program change controls

F. Backup and recovery controls

G. Service level agreements

H. Firewall

I. Protection tabs, doors, and rings

J. Security guards

K. Application documentation

L. Security module

Common Business Exposures

1. Erroneous recordkeeping

2. Unacceptable accounting

3. Business interruption

4. Erroneous management decisions

5. Fraud and embezzlement

6. Statutory sanctions

7. Excessive costs

8. Loss or destruction of resources

9. Competitive disadvantage

Match the 10 situations from the first list with the items in the two remaining lists by completing a table similar to the following, and completing columns 2, "Control Plan," and 3, "Exposures." In column 2 insert *one* letter to identify the control plan that would *best* prevent the system failure from occurring. Because there are 12 plans in the second list, you should have 2 letters left over. In column 3, insert *one or more numbers* to indicate exposures that would result from each system failure.

Control situation	Control plan	Exposures
1	___	___
2	___	___
3	___	___

P 8-2 Listed here are several control plans discussed in the chapter. On the blank line to the left of each control plan, insert a P (preventive), D (detective), or C (corrective) to classify that control most accurately. If you think that more than one code could apply to a particular plan, insert all appropriate codes and briefly explain your answer:

Code   Control Plan

_____ 1. Internal and external file labels

_____ 2. Program change controls

_____ 3. Fire and water alarms

_____ 4. Adequate fire and water insurance

_____ 5. Install batteries to provide backup for temporary loss in power

_____ 6. Backup and recovery procedures

_____ 7. Service level agreements

_____ 8. IT steering committee

_____ 9. Security officer

_____ 10. Operations run manuals

_____ 11. Rotation of duties and forced vacations

_____ 12. Fidelity bonding

_____ 13. Adequate personnel supervision

_____ 14. Standardized personnel termination procedures

_____ 15. Segregation of duties

_____ 16. IT strategic plan

_____ 17. Disaster recovery planning

_____ 18. Restrict entry to the computer facility through the use of security guards, locks, badges, and identification cards

_____ 19. Computer security module

_____ 20. Computer library controls

P 8-3 Examine the last column in Table 8.1 (pages 263–264) for the following personnel only: vice president of information systems, systems development manager, systems analysis, quality assurance, and systems programming.

For each of the five functions, list *one* control plan from this chapter that would address the control concern described in the last column of Table 8.1 for that function. Explain how the plan might address the concern mentioned. Do not use the same plan twice; use five different plans.

P 8-4 Three lists follow. The first is a list of 10 situations that have control implications, the second is a list of 12 control plans from this chapter, and the third is the list of 9 common business exposures.

Situations

1. A computer programmer was fired for gross incompetence. During the 2-week notice period, the programmer destroyed the documentation for all programs that he had developed since being hired.

2. A fire destroyed part of the computer room and the adjacent library of computer disks. It took several months to reconstruct the data from manual source documents and other hard copy records.

3. A competitor flooded the Oak Company Web server with false messages (i.e., a denial of service attack). The Web server, unable to handle all of this traffic, shut down for several hours until the messages could be cleared.

4. A junior high school computer hacker created a program to generate random telephone numbers and passwords. Through a modem in his microcomputer, he used the random number program to "crack" the computer system of a major international corporation.

5. A computer room operator experienced an abnormal ending (i.e., an "abend," in computer parlance) during the nightly run of updates to the inventory master data. In a state of panic, he woke his supervisor from a sound sleep at 3:00 A.M. to get help in getting the job restarted.

6. During the nightly computer run to update bank customers' accounts for deposits and withdrawals for that day, an electrical storm caused a temporary power failure. The run had to be reprocessed from the beginning, resulting in certain other computer jobs not being completed on schedule.

7. A group of anti-nuclear demonstrators broke into a public utility's computer center overnight and destroyed computer equipment worth several thousand dollars.

8. The computer users at the Less-Than-Quick Company do not know how to use the computer very well.

9. A disgruntled applications programmer planted a logic bomb in the computer program that produced weekly payroll checks. The bomb was triggered to "go off" if the programmer were ever terminated. When the programmer was fired for continued absenteeism, the next weekly payroll run destroyed all the company's payroll master data.

10. The computer systems at Coughlin, Inc., were destroyed in a recent fire. It took Coughlin several days to get its IT functions operating again.

Control Plans

A. Off-site storage of backup computer programs and data

B. User training

C. Personnel termination procedures

D. Security guards

E. Program change controls

F. Operations run manuals

G. Firewall

H. Batteries and backup generations

I. Help desk

J. Identification badges and visitor's log

K. Hot site

L. Security modules

Common Business Exposures

1. Erroneous recordkeeping

2. Unacceptable accounting

3. Business interruption

4. Erroneous management decisions

5. Fraud and embezzlement

6. Statutory sanctions

7. Excessive costs

8. Loss or destruction of resources

9. Competitive disadvantage

Match the 10 situations from the first list with the items in the two other lists by making a table like that shown for Problem 1. In column 2, insert *one* letter to identify the control plan that would *best* prevent the system failure from occurring. Because there are 12 plans in the second list, you should have two letters left over. In column 3, insert *one or more numbers* from the third list to indicate exposures that would result from each system failure.

P 8-5 Assume that accounts payable are processed on a computer and that the options in the accounts payable system module are as follows:

1. Maintain vendor master data (i.e., add, change, or delete vendors in the vendor master data).
2. Record vendor invoices.
3. Record vendor credit memos.
4. Select vendor invoices for payment.
5. Print checks and record payments.
6. Print accounts payable reports.

Further assume that personnel in the accounts payable department include the department manager and two clerks, R. Romeo and J. Juliet.

By placing a "Y" for yes or an "N" for no in the following table, show which users, if any, should (or should not) have access to each of the six accounts payable options. Make and state whatever assumptions you think are necessary. In one or two paragraphs explain how your matrix design would optimize the segregation of duties control plan.

Option	Manager	Romeo	Juliet
1	___	___	___
2	___	___	___
3	___	___	___
4	___	___	___
5	___	___	___
6	___	___	___

P 8-6 Triune Corporation performs the following functions:

1. Receive checks and remittance advices from customers.
2. Approve vendor invoices for payment and prepare checks.
3. Approve credit memoranda for customer sales returns.
4. Record collections on account from customers.
5. Record customer sales returns.
6. Make daily deposits of cash receipts.
7. Sign payment checks and mail them to vendors.
8. Record cash payments to vendors.
9. Record purchase returns and allowances.
10. Reconcile bank account each month.

Triune has 3 employees, Winken, Blinken, and Nod, any of whom is capable of performing any of the 10 functions.

Explain how you would divide the 10 functions among the 3 employees to optimize the segregation of duties control plan discussed in the chapter. Consider only control aspects when allocating the duties. In other words, ignore factors such as the workload of each employee, except that any one employee should be assigned a minimum of two functions. Your solution should also include a one-paragraph explanation of how your design accomplishes the control goals that segregation of duties is supposed to achieve.

P 8-7   Research the Internet, newspapers, magazines, and journals to find recent incidences of outages of one or more Web sites. Develop a report (format and length to be determined by your instructor) describing how long the site(s) were not available and how it was they came to be out of service. Describe in your report controls that would have *prevented*, *detected*, or *corrected* the outages.

P 8-8   Research the Internet, newspapers, magazines, and journals to find recent incidences of *denial of service attacks* on one or more Web sites. Develop a report (format and length to be determined by your instructor) describing how long the site(s) were not available and how it was they came to be out of service. Describe in your report controls that would have *prevented*, *detected*, or *corrected* the attacks and resulting outages.

P 8-9   The American Institute of Certified Public Accountants (AICPA) has adopted a framework called Trust Service Principles.

a.   Look up this framework on the Internet and explain each of the principles.

b.   What types of assurance services are already based on the Trust Service Principles?

c.   Create two additional assurance services, not already in place or under consideration by the AICPA, which can use Trust Services Principles. For each additional service you recommend, please explain which principles would apply, how, and why.

KEY TERMS

information systems function (ISF)

centralized information systems structure

segregation of duties

security officer

information technology steering committee

rotation of duties

forced vacations

fidelity bond

systems development life cycle (SDLC)

program change controls

disaster recovery planning

contingency planning

business interruption planning

business continuity planning

mirror site

server clustering

electronic vaulting

shadowing

replication

hot site

cold site

denial of service attack

distributed denial of service attack

library controls

computer hacking and cracking

preventive maintenance

chapter

9

- To understand the steps in the control framework.

- To know how to prepare a control matrix.

- To comprehend the generic business process control plans introduced in this chapter.

- To be able to describe how the business process controls accomplish control goals.

- To appreciate the importance of controls to organizations with enterprise systems.

- To appreciate the importance of controls to organizations engaging in e-Business.

Controlling Information Systems: Business Process Controls

It was 3:55 P.M. EST, just before the 4:00 P.M. closing of the New York Stock Exchange. A clerk on the trading floor of Salomon Brothers, Inc., misread a program-trading order. Instead of entering the order correctly to sell $11 million of this particular stock, the clerk typed "11 million" into the box on his computer screen that asked for the number of shares to be sold. Like most such firms, Salomon has direct computer links to the New York Stock Exchange (NYSE) that allow it to process security trades with lightning speed. When a second clerk failed to double-check the order as required by company policy, most of the trade as entered— amounting to $500 million, not $11 million—was sent to the NYSE's computer system. Although the firm's computer system did catch the error shortly after it was made and kept at least part of the trade from being executed, it was not before the error sent the stock market tumbling and caused near chaos at the Big Board. This internal control failure, and many like it, will be discussed in this chapter along with methods to ensure that errors like this cannot occur.

In this chapter, we spotlight one layer of controls—process controls—as indicated by the AIS Wheel. First, you will learn how to assess the nature and extent of process control goals by decomposing them into operation process goals and information process goals. Further, operations process goals are subdivided into effectiveness, efficiency, and security goals; and information process goals are split into input and update goals. For each category of control goals, you will recommend effective control plans. When control goals and plans are combined, you will understand how to develop the control matrix, which will serve as the basis for evaluating process controls in later chapters.

SYNOPSIS

CONTROLS   This chapter presents a conceptual framework for the analysis of controls in business systems. We apply the control framework by describing business process controls that may be found in any information system. These controls will help us to *prevent* (or *detect* or *correct*) problems such as the one that occurred at Salomon Brothers.

ENTERPRISE SYSTEMS   Many of the controls described in this chapter provide assurance about the quality of the data entry process. Such controls take on increased importance with *enterprise systems* because they *prevent* erroneous data from entering the system and negatively impacting the many tightly connected processes that follow initial entry of the data. For example, we want to have good controls over the entry of customer orders so that we correctly perform and record data about the customer order; shipment; inventory balance; customer's invoice; general ledger entries for sales, accounts receivable, inventory, and costs of goods sold; and inventory replenishment process.

E-BUSINESS   Good data entry controls also are important for those engaging in *e-Business*. For example, if we are to receive customer orders electronically, our systems must have sufficient controls within them so that they accept only authorized, accurate order data. If we don't have these controls, we may make inaccurate shipments or shipments to those who have no intention of paying for the goods being shipped.

INTRODUCTION

Having covered the control environment in Chapter 7 and IT control processes in Chapter 8, we are now ready to move to the third level of control plans appearing in the hierarchy shown in Figure 7.3 (page 248)—business process control plans. We start by defining the components of a control framework and introduce the tools used to implement it. Then, we apply the control framework to a few generic business processes. These generic processes include controls that may be found in any information system. In Chapters 10 through 16 we will examine controls that might be found in particular business processes (e.g., order entry/sales, billing, accounts receivable, and so forth).

THE CONTROL FRAMEWORK

In this section we introduce a control framework that is specific to the control requirements of the operations process and the information process.[1] We again use the Causeway Company cash receipts system that you first saw in Chapter 4. This time we use it to illustrate the control framework.

The control framework provides you with a structure for analyzing the internal controls of business organizations. However, structure alone is of little practical value to you. To make the framework functional, you need to become familiar with and comfortable in using the tools for implementing the framework. Chapter 4 introduced you to one of the key tools—the systems flowchart. Now we introduce a related important tool—the control matrix.

The Control Matrix

The **control matrix** is a tool designed to assist you in analyzing a systems flowchart and related narrative. It establishes the criteria to be used in evaluating the controls in a particular business process.

Figure 9.1 (pages 302–303) presents a "bare-bones" outline of the control matrix, and Figure 9.2 (page 304) is the "annotated" flowchart produced as a foundation for completing the matrix. We explain how to annotate a flowchart later in this section. *We cannot overemphasize that our intent in Figure 9.1 is **not** to have you learn about the control goals and control plans for a cash receipts process. Those are covered in Chapter 11. Rather, we are giving you an overview of the control matrix elements and how they relate to each other, and walking you through the steps in preparing the matrix.* Please follow along in the figure as we describe how to prepare the control matrix.

Steps in Preparing the Control Matrix

I. *Specifying control goals* represents the first step in building a control matrix. The goals are listed across the top row of the matrix; they should be familiar to you from discussions in Chapter 7. Indeed, in Figure 9.1, we have merely tailored the generic goals shown in Table 7.1 (page 244) to Causeway's cash receipts system. The tailoring involves:

  1. *Identifying operations process goals:* In determining which operations process goals are appropriate for the business process under review, you may find it

---

[1] For simplicity, our control framework does not analyze the control requirements of the third business process component, the management process.

Figure 9.1 Sample Control Matrix

Recommended Control Plans (b)	Control Goals of the (Cash Receipts) Business Process								
	Control Goals of the Operations Process (a)				Control Goals of the Information Process (a)				
	Ensure effectiveness of operations		Ensure efficient employment of resources (people, computers)	Ensure security of resources (cash, accounts receivable master data)	For remittance advice inputs (i.e., cash receipts), ensure:			For accounts receivable master data, ensure:	
	A	B			IV	IC	IA	UC	UA
Present Controls									
P-1: Immediately endorse incoming checks				P-1 (c)					
P-2: Write amount and check number on remittance advices (RAs)					P-2		P-2		
P-3 through P-9									
Missing Controls									
M-1: Immediately separate checks and remittance advices (RAs)	M-1	M-1		M-1					
M-2: Assess resource efficiency			M-2						
M-3 through M-n									

Four key elements of the control matrix:
(a) Control goals
(b) Recommended control plans
(c) Cell entries
(d) Legend (below)

Legend (d)

Effectiveness goals:
A = To accelerate cash flow by promptly depositing cash receipts.
B = To ensure compliance with compensating balance agreements with the depository bank.

IV = Input validity
IC = Input completeness
IA = Input accuracy
UC = Update completeness
UA = Update accuracy

(continued)

helpful to first ask yourself, "What are the purposes of the business process, which resources are utilized in executing the process, are the resources used efficiently, how secure are the resources, and what are the undesirable risks to which the operations are exposed?" For example, in deciding on Causeway's operations process goal of accelerating cash flow by promptly depositing cash receipts, we may first have speculated that there was a possibility the mailroom could delay the processing of incoming remittance advices, the cashier could

Figure 9.1 Sample Control Matrix (*continued*)

Recommended control plans:
P-1:   Immediately endorse incoming checks.
       Security of resources: A restrictive check endorsement ("deposit only to the account of Causeway Company") ensures security of the cash resource by preventing the check from being misappropriated.
P-2:   Write amount and check number on remittance advices (RAs).
       Input validity: Ensures that the cash receipts are supported by actual customer payments.
       Input accuracy: Ensures that the correct payment amount is entered into the Causeway computer.
P-3 through P-*n*: Describe . . .
M-1:   Immediately separate checks and remittance advices (RAs).
       Effectiveness goals A and B: Immediately separating the checks from the RAs allows the checks to be deposited without being delayed by processing of the RAs, thereby, accelerating cash flows (*Effectiveness goal A*) and improving cash balances (*Effectiveness goal B*).
       Security of resources: If the checks and RAs are processed separately, the person handling the checks (i.e., the negotiable instruments comprising the cash asset) is a different person (or process) than the one who records the checks from information on the RA. By separating these functions, we improve security of the cash asset because there is less opportunity for misappropriation of the checks to be covered up while recording the RA.
M-2:   Assess resource efficiency.
       Efficiency of resources: Periodically (at least once each year), management should assess the extent to which the current cash receipts process efficiently utilizes people and computers. As well, management should consider whether technological advances have progressed to the point where this business process could be further automated, thus increasing *input accuracy* and improving resource utilization.
M-3 through M-*n*: Describe . . .

hold endorsed checks for a time before taking them to the bank, and so forth. Operations process goals can be subdivided into effectiveness, efficiency, and security (see Table 7.1), as follows:

a. *Effectiveness goals*

   i.   The purpose of *effectiveness* control goals of the operations process is to ensure the successful accomplishment of the goals set forth for the business process under consideration.

   ii. For Causeway's cash receipts process we include only two examples here: Goal A—to accelerate cash flow by promptly depositing cash receipts. Goal B—to ensure compliance with compensating balance agreements with the depository bank.[2] Other possible goals of a cash receipts would be shown as goals C, D, and so forth, and described at the bottom of the matrix (in the matrix *legend*).

   iii. With respect to other business processes, such as production, we might be concerned with effectiveness goals related to the following: Goal A—to maintain customer satisfaction by finishing production orders on time. Goal B—to increase market share by ensuring the highest quality of finished goods.

---

[2] Remember that one of the goals of any business process may be in compliance with applicable laws, regulations, and *contractual agreements*. Depending on the particular system being analyzed, we tailor the matrix to identify the specific law, regulation, or agreement with which we desire to achieve compliance. In Causeway's case, we assume that its loan agreements with its bank require that it maintain certain minimum cash balances, known as compensating balances, on deposit.

Figure 9.2 Causeway Company Annotated Systems Flowchart

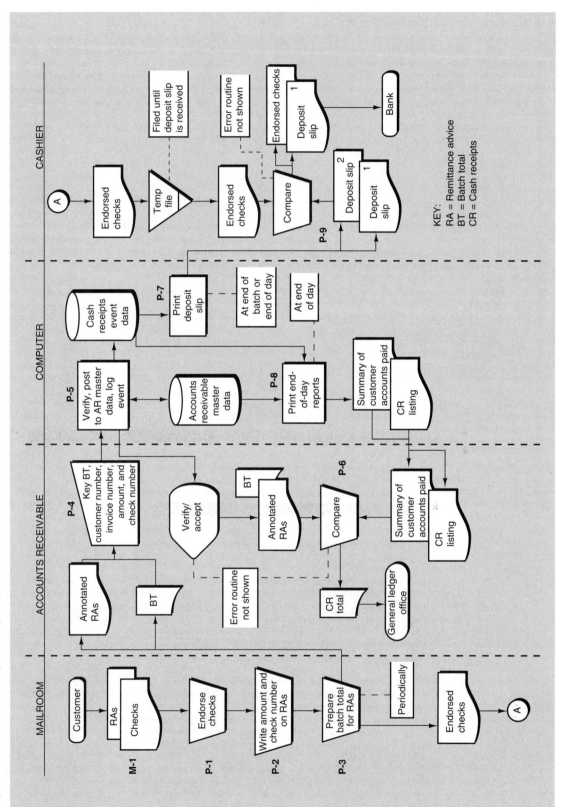

b. *Efficiency goals*

i. The purpose of *efficiency* control goals of the operations process is to ensure that all resources used throughout the business process are being employed in the most productive manner.

ii. In parentheses, notice that we have listed two resources of the cash receipts process for which efficiency is applicable—people and computers. In fact, people and computers would always be considered in the efficiency assessments related to accounting information systems.

iii. In other business processes, such as receiving goods and supplies, we might also be concerned with the productive use of equipment such as trucks, forklifts, and hand-held scanners.

c. *Security goals*

i. The purpose of *security* control goals of the operations process is to ensure that entity resources are protected from loss, destruction, disclosure, copying, sale, or other misuse.

ii. In parentheses, we have included two resources of the cash receipts process over which security must be ensured—cash and information (accounts receivable master data). With any business process, we are concerned with information that is added, changed, or deleted as a result of executing the process, as well as assets that are brought into or taken out of the organization as a result of the process, such as cash, inventory, and fixed assets.

iii. With regard to other business processes, such as shipping, we might include customer master data and shipping data. Note: The security over hard assets used to execute business processes, such as computer equipment, trucks, trailers, and loading docks, is handled through pervasive controls (discussed in Chapter 7).

2. *Identifying information process goals:* When deciding what information process goals are appropriate for the business process under evaluation, you may find it helpful to first ask yourself, "What information will be affected during the input and update processes, and what are the undesirable risks to which the information is exposed?" For instance, with respect to Causeway's information process goals, we recognized that remittance advices, reflecting cash receipts, will be entered into the system. We also understood that the receipts are coming from sales that took place on credit, so they would be used to update the customer's accounts receivable data. You should reason through the information process and examine the process on the systems flowchart (see Figure 9.2). The following discussion takes a deeper look into input and update goals of the information process:

a. *Input goals*

i. The purpose of *input* goals of the information process is to ensure input validity (IV), input completeness (IC), and input accuracy (IA) with respect to all business process data entering the system.

ii. With the cash receipts process, we are concerned with input validity, accuracy, and completeness over cash receipts (here, they are in the form of remittance advices). Notice that we specifically name the input data of concern in parentheses.

iii. With respect to other business processes, such as hiring employees, we would be concerned with other inputs, such as employee, payroll, and benefit plan data.

b. *Update goals*

i. The purpose of *update* control goals of the information process is to ensure the update completeness (UC) and update accuracy (UA) of the business process input data. Update goals must consider all related information that will be affected in some manner by the input data, such as master file data and ledger data.

ii. With regard to the cash receipts information process, we recognize that the accounts receivable data will be updated by cash receipts (cash received reflects the *debit* and customer account reflects the *credit*). Notice that we list *accounts receivable master data* in the control matrix.

iii. Other business processes, such as cash payments, would involve different update concerns, such as vendor, payroll, or accounts payable master data.

II. *Recommending control plans* for the business process under evaluation is the second step in the construction of a control matrix. Notice that the first step, specifying control goals, recognizes undesirable risk exposures. This step focuses on the nature and extent of control plans that should be in place to minimize such risks to an acceptable level of residual risk. In the final analysis, the comfort level that management and auditors reach with respect to residual risk is a matter of professional judgment.

For a given business process, each operations and information process goal should be addressed by one or more control plans. For instance, as with Causeway, one or more control plans should cover the effectiveness goals (A and B), the efficiency goal, the security goal, and each of the information process goals (IV, IC, IA, UC, and UA). The following advice will help you to structure your thinking with regard to control plans.

1. *Annotating "Present" Control Plans:* Start on the upper left-hand column of the systems flowchart and spot the first manual keying symbol, manual process symbol, or computer process symbol (refer back to Figure 4.6 on page 114 for flowcharting symbols used in a systems flowchart). For ease of description, hereafter we will refer to these as *process-related* symbols. Then, follow the sequential logic of the systems flowchart and identify all of the process-related symbols. Each process-related symbol reflects an internal control plan which is already *present*. It is important to recognize that while a control plan may be present, it may not be working as effectively as it should; thus, you might recommend ways to strengthen or augment existing control plans (this concept will be discussed in the following section #3).

a. Reviewing the Causeway systems flowchart (Figure 9.2), you will find that the first process-related symbol is entitled "Endorse checks." Because this process appears on the flowchart, this control plan already exists, meaning, it is *present* as opposed to *missing*. Accordingly, place a P- beside the process, indicating that is it present, and a *1* beside the P- reflecting the first present control plan on the flowchart. As a result, you should have *annotated* the systems flowchart with a P-1.

b. Continue reviewing the systems flowchart by following its sequential logic, annotating the flowchart with P-2, P-3, and so on until you have accounted for all *present* control plans. Notice on Figure 9-2, that eight control plans (P-1–P-8) are already present at Causeway.

2. *Evaluating "Present" Control Plans:* Write number (P-1, P-2, P-3 through P-*n*) and name of each control plan in the left-hand column of the control matrix. Then, starting with P-1, look across the row and determine which control goals the plan addresses and place a P-1 in each *cell* of the matrix for which P-1 is applicable. It is possible that a given control plan can attend to more than one control goal. Continue this procedure for each of the *present* control plans. Simultaneously, in the legend of the matrix, describe *how* the control plan addresses each noted control goal. Students usually have the most difficulty in providing these explanations. Yet, we believe this element is the most important part of the matrix because the purpose of the matrix is to relate plans to goals. Unless you can explain the association between plans and goals, there's a good possibility you may have guessed at the cell entry. Sometimes you'll guess right, but it's just as likely you'll guess wrong. Don't play the guessing game! Be prepared to defend your cell entries.

   a. To illustrate, we list two representative control plans (P-1 and P-2) for the cash receipts process at Causeway in the left column of Figure 9.1. Each of these plans (and others) will be further explained in Chapter 11. The other six *present* plans listed in Figure 9.1 are identified merely as plans P-3 through P-8.

   b. P-1 (Endorse checks) ensures the security of the cash equivalent (checks) by stamping the checks with a restrictive endorsement, which can prevent the check from being misappropriated by an employee.

   c. P-2 (Write amount and check number on the remittance advices [RAs]) ensures input validity (IV) and input accuracy (IA). IV is ensured because the cash receipt (as reflected by the remittance advice) to be input into the system is supported by an actual customer payment. IA is ensured because the event (cash receipt) is correctly captured and entered into the system.

3. *Identifying and Evaluating "Missing" Control Plans:* The next step in recommending control plans is to determine if additional controls are needed to address missing control goal areas, *strengthen present control plans*, or both.

   a. *Examining the controls matrix:* The first place to start is to look at the control matrix and see if there are any control goals (operations or information) for which no present control plan is addressing. If so, you need to do the following:

      i. In the left-hand column of the matrix, number the first missing control plan as M-1 and label or title the plan.

      ii. Across the matrix row, place M-1 in each cell for which the missing control is designed.

      iii. In the legend of the matrix, explain how the missing control will address each noted control goal.

      iv. On the systems flowchart, annotate M-1 where the control should be inserted.

      v. If there are still control goals for which no control plan has addressed, develop another plan (M-2) and repeat the four previous steps (i through iv). Continue this procedure until each control goal on the matrix is addressed by at least one control plan.

vi. *Exception to the rule:* For many business processes, the systems flowchart will not necessarily include a control plan for ensuring the efficient employment of resources. Nevertheless, management should periodically make an efficiency assessment. If the insertion of M-X (reflecting a control goal to ensure efficiency) does not logically fit into the systems flowchart, annotate M-X on the bottom, left-hand side of the systems flowchart, as shown on Figure 9-2 (M-2).

vii. With regard to Causeway, we have noted two missing control plans (M-1 and M-2), although more might exist. Recall that the purpose of this chapter is to offer guidelines for creating a controls matrix, not to completely analyze Causeway's cash receipts system. We noted in M-1 that Causeway should immediately separate checks and remittance advices, for this control plan can help to mitigate risks related to both effectiveness control goals, as well as to ensure the security of resources. The other noted missing control plan (M-2) deals with assessing and perhaps improving the efficient utilization of resources.

b. *Evaluating the systems flowchart:* Even though all of the control goals on the matrix are now addressed by one or more control plans, it is worthwhile to closely scrutinize the systems flowchart one more time. Such analysis can reveal areas where further controls are needed. Just because all of the control goals on the matrix now have one or more associated control plans, it may be necessary to add more control plans or strengthen existing plans to further reduce residual risk to an acceptable level in certain areas. It takes training and experience to spot risks and weaknesses of this nature. In Chapters 10 through 16 you will learn more about how to make such critical internal control assessments.

When your assessment leads you to the identification (and correction) of control weaknesses, as reflected in missing control plans or recommendations for strengthening present control plans, you are essentially recommending remedial changes to the system (if necessary) to correct deficiencies in the system.

In addition to telling you about the control strengths and weaknesses of a particular system, a completed matrix and annotated systems flowchart also facilitates your evaluation from the perspectives of *control effectiveness* (are all the control goals achieved?), *control efficiency* (do individual control plans address multiple goals?), and *control redundancy* (are too many goals directed at the same goal?).

Exhibit 9.1 summarizes the steps we have just undertaken in preparing the illustrative control matrix in Figure 9.1 (pages 302–303). Combined with the preceding discussion and illustration, the steps should be self-explanatory. You should take time now to study each of the steps and to make sure that you have a reasonable understanding of them.

SAMPLE CONTROL PLANS FOR DATA INPUT

In the preceding section we described the framework used to analyze business process controls. The framework consists of two main elements: specifying controls goals and recommending control plans. In the following sections we describe three methods for processing input data: (1) without access to master data, (2) with access to master data,

Exhibit 9.1 Steps in Preparing a Control Matrix

Step I *Specifying control goals:* Review the systems flowchart and related narrative description to become familiar with the system under examination. Identify the business process (e.g., cash receipts); the key relevant resources (e.g., cash, accounts receivable master data); the input (e.g., the remittance advice); storage, if any, for the input data (e.g., cash receipts event data); and the master data being updated (e.g., accounts receivable master data). With regard to the business process under consideration:

1. Identify operations process goals

   a. Effectiveness goals (there may be more than one)

   b. Efficiency goals (related plans may not logically fit on the systems flowchart)

   c. Security goals (consider all affected data and tangible assets)

2. Identify information process goals

   a. Input goals (input validity, completeness, and accuracy)

   b. Update goals (update completeness, and accuracy)

Step II *Recommending control plans:* List a set of recommended control plans that is appropriate for the process being analyzed. The list should include both plans related to the operations process (e.g., the cash receipts process) and those related to the information processing methods (e.g., data entry controls, batch controls). In Figure 9.1, we presented only two illustrative *present* plans for Causeway's system and two *missing* plans.

1. Annotate *present* controls on the systems flowchart by placing P-1, P-2 through P-*n* beside all manual keying, manual process and computer process symbols. Start on the upper left-hand column of the flowchart and follow the sequential processing logic of the flowchart.

2. Evaluate the *present* control plans by placing the number and name of the plan on the controls matrix, and explaining the nature and extent of the control plan on the matrix legend.

3. Identify and evaluate missing control plans (M-1, M-2 through M-*n*).

   a. Examine the control matrix and see if there are any control goals for which no control plan exists. If so, develop a control plan designed to minimize associated risks (control goals). Explain the nature and extent of the missing plan in the legend of the matrix. Repeat this procedure until all control goals on the matrix are addressed by one or more control plans.

   b. Analyze the systems flowchart for further risk exposures for which you would recommend adding additional controls or strengthening existing controls. Note any further additions or refinements on the controls matrix using the same procedures described for present or missing controls plans.

and (3) batch input. For each of these methods we describe the processing logic, present a systems flowchart, and describe and analyze the controls with a control matrix and control explanations.

Perhaps the most error-prone and inefficient steps in an operations or information process are the steps during which data is entered into a system. While much has been done to improve the accuracy and efficiency of the data entry process, problems still remain, especially when humans enter data into a system. Thus we begin our discussion of process controls by describing those controls that improve the data entry process.

As you study these controls keep in mind the following improvements that have been made to address the errors and inefficiencies of the data entry process.

- The data entry process may be automated. Documents may be scanned with bar codes or OCR for data entry. This automation reduces or eliminates manual keying.

E-BUSINESS
- Business events, such as purchases, may be initiated in one (buying) organization and transmitted to another (selling) organization via the Internet or electronic data interchange (EDI). In this case, the receiving (selling) organization need not enter the data at all.

ENTERPRISE SYSTEMS
- The multiple steps in a business process may be tightly integrated, such as in an enterprise system. In these cases the number of data entry steps is greatly reduced. For example, there may be no need to enter a shipment (sale) into the billing system because the billing system has been integrated with the shipping system.

CONTROL PLANS FOR DATA ENTRY WITHOUT MASTER DATA

System Description and Flowchart

Figure 9.3 shows an annotated systems flowchart for a hypothetical system that we will use to describe our first set of controls. The processing starts in the first column of Figure 9.3 with the clerk manually keying the input data. Normally the data entry program presents the clerk with a preformatted input screen and then prompts the user to enter certain data into fields on that screen (e.g., *customer code, item numbers,* and so on).

Recall in the last section of this chapter, you were instructed to look for process-related symbols (including manual keying) to identify the presence of controls. Begin by looking at the upper left-hand column of the flowchart and look for the first process-related symbol. Then, follow the sequential processing logic back and forth across and down the columns following the sequential flow of work activities.

Note that the first process-related symbol appears as "key document" in the first column (data entry clerk 1). As will be discussed soon, when evaluating controls related to manual keying of input documents, you should look for well-designed documents (P-1), written approvals signifying the validity of the underlying event (P-2), preformatted screens that complement the input document (P-3), and online prompting (P-4). The next process-related symbol (edit input) appears in the second column (data entry devices). The editing (P-5) is done through various *programmed edit checks,* which are discussed later in this section. Having edited the input, the computer displays a message to the user indicating that the input either is acceptable or contains errors. If errors exist, procedures should exist for resolving any discrepancies (P-6). Once any corrections are made, the user keys a code or clicks the mouse button to instruct the system to accept the input (P-7). That action triggers the computer to simultaneously:

- *Record* the input in machine-readable form—the event data table on the disk (P-8).
- *Inform* the user that the input data has been accepted (P-9).

The user waits to be notified to ensure that the input was accepted for processing.

In some instances, to verify that the event data were keyed correctly, the documents could be forwarded to a second clerk who would key the data again (M-1). This procedure is called *key verification,* which is typically applied only to important fields on low-volume inputs.

Our flowchart stops at this point *without* depicting the update of any master data. Certainly our system could continue with an update process. We have not shown it here so that we can concentrate on the *input* controls.

Figure 9.3 Systems Flowchart: Data Entry Without Master Data Available

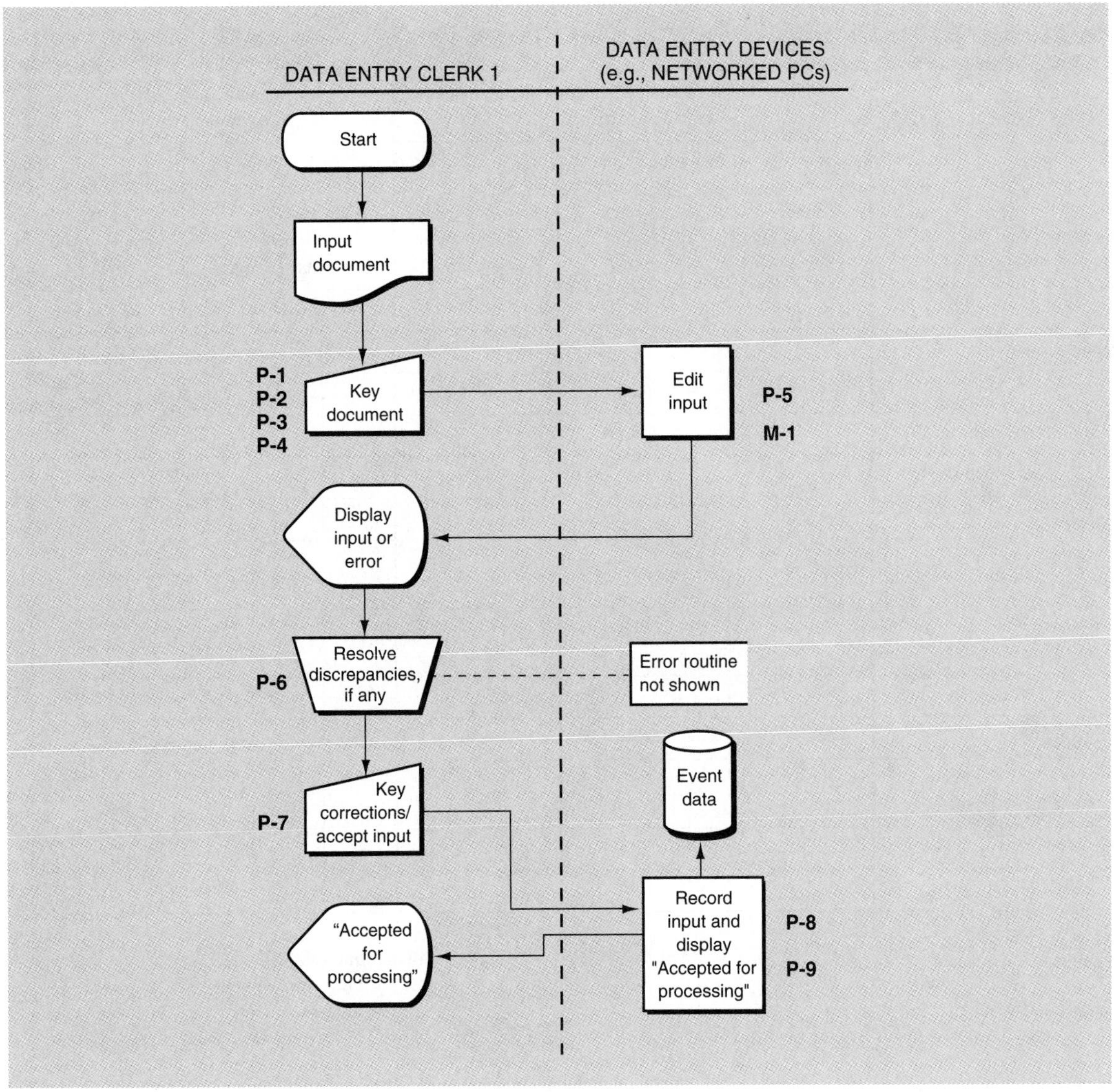

Applying the Control Framework

In this section, we apply the control framework to the generic system just described. Figure 9.4 (page 312) presents a sample control matrix for the systems flowchart shown in Figure 9.3. Through the symbols P-1 through P-9 we have annotated the flowchart to show where specific control plans are already implemented. We also have one control plan that we *assume* is missing (code M-1) because the narrative did not mention it specifically. The UC and UA columns in the matrix have been shaded to emphasize that they do not apply to this analysis because there is no update of any master data in Figure 9.3. Recall in the last section that you were instructed to make sure that at least one *present* or *missing* control plan covered each of the operations and information process control goals. Naturally, one has to use common sense in the application of this rule.

Figure 9.4 Control Matrix for Data Entry Without Master Data

Recommended Control Plans	Control Goals of the (blank) Business Process								
	Control Goals of the Operations Process			Control Goals of the Information Process					
	Ensure effectiveness of operations	Ensure efficient employment of resources (people, computers)	Ensure security of resources (event data)	For the (blank) inputs, ensure:			For the (blank) master data, ensure:		
	A			IV	IC	IA	UC	UA	
Present Controls									
P-1: Document design	P-1	P-1	P-1			P-1			
P-2: Written approvals				P-2					
P-3: Preformatted screens	P-3	P-3				P-3			
P-4: Online prompting	P-4	P-4				P-4			
P-5: Programmed edit checks	P-5	P-5				P-5			
P-6: Procedures for rejected inputs					P-6				
P-7: Key corrections						P-7			
P-8: Record input	P-8	P-8							
P-9: Interactive feedback checks					P-9				
Missing Controls									
M-1: Key verification						M-1			

Legend:

Effectiveness goals:
A = To ensure timely input of (blank) event data.

Recommended control plans:
See Exhibit 9.2 (page 316) for a complete explanation of control plans and cell entries.

IV = Input validity
IC = Input completeness
IA = Input accuracy
UC = Update completeness
UA = Update accuracy

That is, when depicting only an input process, no updating takes place; thus, update control goals do not apply to this particular business process (data input).

In Figure 9.4 under the operations process section, we have shown only one system goal for illustrative purposes—although there may be more than one effectiveness goal. We identify the goal as goal A: To ensure *timely* input of (blank) event data (whatever those data happen to be). In the business process chapters (Chapters 10 through 14) we will show you how to tailor the goals to the business process discussed in those chapters.

The recommended control plans are listed in the first column in Figure 9.4. Notice that the control goals (effectiveness, efficiency, and security) and input goals (validity, completeness, and accuracy) are covered by one or more recommended control plans. Please keep in mind that the systems flowchart (Figure 9-3) and related control matrix (Figure 9-4) are shown here for illustrative purposes only; thus, they may be incomplete in some respects. To help you in future assessments of this nature, we next present a list of control issues that are representative of those commonly associated with controlling the data entry process, all of which were applied to our example.

The purpose of this presentation is to give you a sense of the multitude of control plans available for controlling data input systems.[3] Once again, we remind you that the plans are *not* unique to a specific process such as order entry/sales, billings, cash receipts, and so forth. Rather, they apply to *any* data entry process. Therefore, when the technology of a system is appropriate, these controls should be incorporated into the list of recommended control plans:

P-1: **Document design** is a control plan in which a source document is designed in such a way as to make it easier to prepare the document initially and later to input data from the document. In our example, we assume that the organization has properly designed this document to facilitate the data preparation and data entry processes. Another control aspect of using input documents is that the data entry clerk does not have access to the underlying resource reflected on the document (e.g., cash, inventory or fixed asset), therefore facilitating the security of such resources by segregating recording events from safeguarding resources (as discussed in Chapter 8).

P-2: **Written approvals** take the form of a signature or initials on a document to indicate that that person has authorized the event. This control ensures that the data input arises from a valid business event, thus, it definitely needs to be included as an input control. Once again referring to Chapter 8, this control segregates authorizing events from recording events.

P-3: **Preformatted screens** control the entry of data by defining the acceptable *format* of each data field. For example, the screen might force users to key exactly nine alphabetic characters in one field and exactly five numerals in another field. To facilitate the data entry process the cursor may *automatically move* to the next field on the screen. The program may require that certain fields be completed, thus preventing the user from omitting any *mandatory* data sets. Finally, the system may *automatically populate* certain fields with data, such as the current date and default shipping methods, sales tax rates, and other terms of a business event. This reduces the number of keystrokes required, making data entry quicker and more efficient. Also, with fewer keystrokes and by utilizing the default data, fewer keying mistakes are expected; thus, data entry is more accurate. To ensure that the system has not provided inappropriate defaults, the clerk must compare the data provided by the system with that of the input.

P-4: **Online prompting** requests user input or asks questions that the user must answer. For example, after entering all the input data for a particular customer sales order, you might be presented with three options: (A)ccept the completed screen, (E)dit the completed screen, or (R)eject the completed screen. By forcing you to

---

[3] Many of the controls in this section are adapted from material contained in *Handbook of IT Auditing 2001 Edition* (Chapters D2, D3, and D4 primarily) (Boston:Warren, Gorham & Lamont, 2000). Copyright © 2000 by PricewaterhouseCoopers L.L.P.

stop and accept the order, online prompting is, in a sense, advising you to check your data entries before moving on. In addition, many systems provide *context-sensitive help* whereby the user is automatically provided with, or can ask for, descriptions of the data to be entered into each input field.

P-5:   **Programmed edit checks** are automatically performed by data entry programs upon entry of the input data. Erroneous data may be highlighted on the terminal screen to allow the operator to take corrective action immediately. Programmed edits can highlight actual or potential input errors, and allow them to be corrected quickly and efficiently. The most common types of programmed edit checks are the following:

a. **Reasonableness checks**, also known as **limit checks**, test whether the contents (e.g., values) of the data entered fall within predetermined limits. The limits may describe a standard range (e.g., customer numbers must be between 0001 and 5000, months must be 01 to 12) or maximum values (e.g., no normal hours worked greater than 40 and no overtime hours greater than 20). The presence of a reasonableness check may have prevented the mishap at Salomon Brothers described in the opening vignette.

b. **Document/record hash totals** reflect a summarization of any numeric data field within the input document or record, such as item numbers or quantities on a customer order. The totaling of these numbers typically serves no purpose other than as a control. Calculated before and then again after entry of the document or record, this total can be used to determine that the applicable fields were entered accurately and completely.

c. **Mathematical accuracy checks** compare calculations performed manually to those performed by the computer to determine if a document has been entered correctly. For this check the user might enter the individual items (e.g., quantity purchased, unit cost, tax, shipping cost) on a document, such as an invoice, and the total for that document. Then the computer adds the individual items and compares that total to the one input by the user. If they don't agree, something has likely been entered erroneously. Alternatively, the user can review the computer calculations and compare them to totals prepared before input.

d. **Check digit verification** involves the inclusion of an extra digit—a check digit—in the identification number of entities such as customers and vendors. More than likely you have a check digit as part of the ID on your ATM card. The check digit is calculated originally by applying a formula to an identification number; the check digit then is appended to the identification number. For instance, the digit 6 might be appended to the customer code 123 so that the entire ID becomes 1236. In this highly oversimplified example, the digit 6 was derived by adding together the digits 1, 2, and 3. Whenever the identification number is entered later by a data entry person, the computer program applies the mathematical formula to verify the check digit. In our illustration, if the ID were input as 1246, the entry would be rejected because the digits 1, 2, and 4 do not add up to 6. We know you are already saying to yourself, "But what about a transposition like 1326?" This would not be rejected; we told you that our example was highly oversimplified. In practice, check digits are assigned by using much more sophisticated formulas than simple cross-addition; those formulas are designed to detect a variety of input errors, including transpositions.

P-6: **Procedures for rejected inputs** are designed to ensure that erroneous data—not accepted for processing—are corrected and resubmitted for processing. To make sure that the corrected input does not still contain errors, the corrected input data should undergo all routines through which the input was processed originally. A "suspense file" of rejected inputs is often retained (manually or by the computer) to ensure timely clearing of rejected items. To reduce the clutter in the simple flowcharts in this text, we often depict such routines with the annotation "Error routine not shown."

P-7: **Keying corrections** into the computer is how the clerk completes the procedures for rejected inputs, thus ensuring that the input is accurate.

P-8: **Interactive feedback checks** are controls in which the data entry program informs the user that the input has been accepted and recorded or rejected for processing. The program may flash a message on the screen telling a user that the input has been *accepted* or *rejected* for processing.

P-9: **Record input** takes place automatically. This process stores the accurate, valid input data onto digital media for subsequent updating procedures (not shown) in a timely manner with minimal use of resources.

M-1: **Key verification** takes place when documents are keyed by one individual and rekeyed by a second individual. The data entry software compares the second keystroking to the first keystroking. If there are differences, it is assumed that one person misread or miskeyed the data. Someone, perhaps a supervisor or the second clerk, would determine which keying was correct, the first or the second, and make corrections as appropriate.

Now that you are armed with an understanding of the basic fundamentals of these control plans, look at Exhibit 9.2 (page 316) and decide if you agree with (and understand) the relationship between each plan and the goal(s) that it addresses. Remember, your ability to explain the relationships among plans and goals is more important than wrote memorization.

CONTROL PLANS FOR DATA ENTRY WITH MASTER DATA

Having just discussed input controls for data entry without master data, we will now discuss input controls that may be applied when we do have access to master data during the input process. The availability of such data can greatly enhance the control and efficiencies that can be gained in the data entry process. For example, let's say that we are entering orders from our customers. If we have available to us data entry programs such as those depicted in Figure 9.3 (page 311), we can check to see if the customer number is in the range of valid numbers (i.e., a *limit check*) or has been entered without error (e.g., *check digit verification*). But these edits determine only that the customer number *might* be correct or incorrect. If we have available the actual customer master data, we can use the customer number to call up the stored customer master data and determine if the customer number has been entered correctly, if the customer exists, the customer's correct address, and so forth. Follow with us in the next section as we describe the *additional* controls available to us when master data is available during data entry.

Exhibit 9.2 Explanation of Cell Entries for Control Matrix in Figure 9.4

P-1: *Document design.*

Effectiveness goal A, Efficient employment of resources: A well-designed document can be completed more quickly (Effectiveness Goal A) and can be prepared with less effort (Efficiency).

Security of resources: The input clerk only has access to the input document, not the resources reflected on the document, such as cash, inventory, fixed assets, and so on.

Input accuracy: We tend to fill in a well-designed document completely and legibly. And, if a document is legible, data entry errors will occur less frequently.

P-2: *Written approvals.*

Input validity: By checking to see that approvals are present on all input documents, we reduce the possibility that invalid (unauthorized) event data will be input.

P-3: *Preformatted screens.*

Effectiveness goal A, Efficient employment of resources: By structuring the data entry process, automatically populating fields, and preventing errors, preformatted screens simplify data input and save time (Effectiveness goal A) allowing a user to input more data over a period of time (Efficiency).

Input accuracy: As each data field is completed on a preformatted screen, the cursor moves to the next field on the screen, thus preventing the user from omitting any required data set. The data for fields that are automatically populated need not be manually entered, thus reducing input errors. Incorrectly formatted fields are rejected.

P-4: *Online prompting.*

Effectiveness goal A, Efficient employment of resources: By asking questions and providing online guidance, this plan ensures a quicker data entry process (Effectiveness goal A) and allows the user to input more data over a period of time (Efficiency).

Input accuracy: The online guidance should reduce input errors.

P-5: *Programmed edit checks.*

Effectiveness goal A, Efficient employment of resources: Event data can be processed on a timelier basis (Effectiveness goal A) and at a lower cost if errors are detected and prevented from entering the system in the first place (Efficiency).

Input accuracy: The edits identify erroneous or suspect data and reduce input errors.

P-6: *Procedures for rejected inputs.*

Input completeness: The rejection procedures (i.e., "Error routine not shown" annotations) are designed to ensure that erroneous data not accepted for processing are corrected and resubmitted for processing.

P-7: *Key corrections.*

Input accuracy: This step completes the rejection procedures (i.e., "Error routine not shown" annotations) by ensure that the corrections are submitted for processing.

P-8: *Record input.*

Effectiveness goal A, Efficient employment of resources: Automatic recording of input event data is fast and reliable.

P-9: *Interactive feedback checks.*

Input completeness: By advising the user that input has been accepted, interactive feedback checks help ensure input completeness.

M-1: *Key verification.*

Input accuracy: By having one data entry person key the data and a second person rekey that same data, we should detect the majority of keying errors.

System Description and Flowchart

Figure 9.5 depicts another hypothetical system. As with Figure 9.3 (page 311) we have made some assumptions in its creation. First, we have event data entering the system from a *remote* location to reinforce the fact that communications with the data entry system may be from sites that are geographically dispersed from the computer center. For instance, a field salesperson might enter customer orders from each customer's office using a laptop computer equipped with a *modem* or *wireless* telecommunication device. Secondly, we show that the events are keyed into the system without using a source doc-

Figure 9.5 Systems Flowchart: Data Entry With Master Data Available

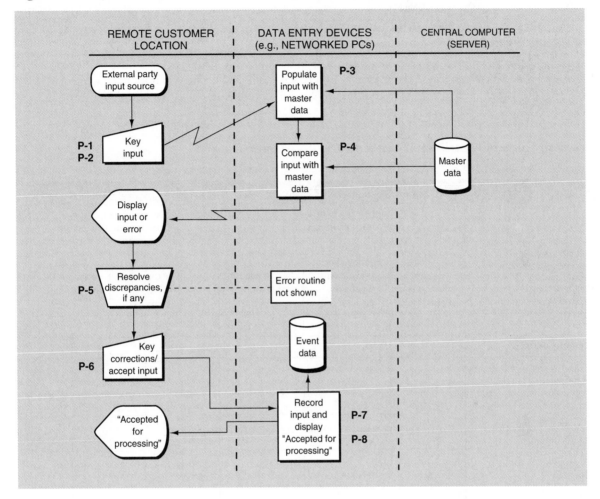

ument. Naturally, source documents might be used such as they were in Figure 9.3. Hence, the salesperson enters data close to the originating source (P-1) and uses an authentication mechanism (i.e., digital signature) (P-2) to authorize the input.

Note that at this point, the system populates (P-3) and compares (P-4) the input by reference to master data—unlike Figure 9.3. Normally, if the user enters *valid data* such as a valid customer code, the system would automatically retrieve certain standing *master data* such as the customer name and address. After processing the input, the user compares the input with the master data to determine whether the input either is acceptable or contains errors (P-5). Once corrections are made, the user keys a code or clicks the mouse button to instruct the system to accept the input (P-6). As in Figure 9.3 (page 311), that action triggers the computer to simultaneously record the input (P-7) and inform the user that the input data has been accepted (P-8). The user waits to be notified to ensure that the input was accepted for further processing.

As with Figure 9.3, our flowchart stops at this point *without* depicting the update of any master data so that we can concentrate on the input controls.

Applying the Control Framework

In this section, we apply the control framework to the generic system previously described. Figure 9.6 presents a completed control matrix for the systems flowchart shown in Figure 9.5.

We have formatted this matrix in a manner and with assumptions similar to those made when we created the matrix in Figure 9.4 (page 312). The recommended control plans listed in the first column in Figure 9.6 are representative of those commonly asso-

Figure 9.6 Control Matrix for Data Entry With Master Data

Recommended Control Plans	Control Goals of the (blank) Business Process								
	Control Goals of the Operations Process			Control Goals of the Information Process					
	Ensure effectiveness of operations	Ensure efficient employment of resources (people, computers)	Ensure security of resources (event data)	For the (blank) inputs, ensure:			For the (blank) master data, ensure:	
	A			IV	IC	IA	UC	UA
Present Controls									
P-1: Enter data close to the originating source	P-1	P-1			P-1	P-1		
P-2: Digital signatures			P-2	P-2		P2		
P-3: Populate input with master data	P-3	P-3		P-3		P-3		
P-4: Compare input with master data	P-4	P-4		P-4		P-4		
P-5: Procedures for rejected inputs					P-5			
P-6: Key corrections						P-6		
P-7: Record input	P-7	P-7						
P-8: Interactive feedback checks					P-8			
Missing Controls									
None noted									

Legend:

Effectiveness goals:
A = To ensure timely input of (blank) event data.

Recommended control plans:
See Exhibit 9.3 (page 319) for a complete explanation of control plans and cell entries.

IV = Input validity
IC = Input completeness
IA = Input accuracy
UC = Update completeness
UA = Update accuracy

ciated with controlling the data entry process when master data is available. Most if not all of the control plans described with Figures 9.3 and 9.4 (pages 311 and 312) may also be applicable, but for simplicity we will not repeat them here.

In this section, we first describe in general terms how several of the control plans work.[4] Then, in Exhibit 9.3, we explain each of the cell entries in the control matrix. As you study the control plans, be sure to see where they are located on the systems flowchart.

Exhibit 9.3 Explanation of Cell Entries for Control Matrix in Figure 9.6

P-1: *Enter data close to the originating source.*

Effectiveness goal A, Efficient employment of resources: This strategy places users in a position to process events immediately (i.e., no time taken to send to a data entry location). Being familiar with the input may allow the user to input the events more quickly. The direct entry of input data by operations personnel eliminates the cost associated with the handling of the event data by additional entities.

Input completeness: Because the inputs are captured at the source, they are less likely to be lost as they are transported to the data entry location.

Input accuracy: Because operations personnel are familiar with the type of event being entered, they are less likely to make input errors and can more readily correct these errors if they occur.

P-2: *Digital signatures.*

Security of resources, Input validity: Digital signatures authenticate that the sender of the message has authority to send it and thus prevents the unauthorized diversion of resources. This also determines that the message itself is genuine.

Input accuracy: Detects messages that have been altered in transit, thus preventing input of inaccurate data.

P-3: *Populate input with master data.*

Effectiveness goal A, Efficient employment of resources: Automatic population of inputs from master data results in fewer keystrokes, which should improve the speed and productivity of the data entry personnel.

Input validity: The code entered by the user calls up data from existing records (e.g., a customer record, a sales order record) and those data establish authorization for the transaction. For

example, without a customer record, the sales order cannot be entered.

Input accuracy: Fewer keystrokes and the use of data called up from existing records reduce the possibility of input errors.

P-4: *Compare input data with master data.*

Effectiveness goal A, Efficient employment of resources: Events can be processed on a timelier basis and at a lower cost if errors are detected and prevented from entering the system in the first place.

Input validity: The edits identify erroneous or suspect data and reduce the possibility of the input of invalid events.

Input accuracy: The edits identify erroneous or suspect data and reduce input errors.

P-5: *Procedures for rejected inputs.*

Input completeness: The rejection procedures (i.e., "Error routine not shown" annotations) are designed to ensure that erroneous data not accepted for processing are corrected and resubmitted for processing.

P-6: *Key corrections.*

Input accuracy: This step completes the rejection procedures (i.e., "Error routine not shown" annotations) by ensure that the corrections are submitted for processing.

P-7: *Record input.*

Effectiveness goal A, Efficient employment of resources: Automatic recording of input event data is fast and reliable.

P-8: *Interactive feedback checks.*

Input completeness: By advising the user that input has been accepted, interactive feedback checks help ensure input completeness.

---

[4] Many of the controls in this section are adapted from material contained in *Handbook of IT Auditing 2001 Edition* (Chapters D2, D3, and D4 primarily) (Boston: Warren, Gorham & Lamont, 2000). Copyright © 2000 by PricewaterhouseCoopers L.L.P.

P-1:   *Enter data close to the originating source.* This is a strategy for the capture and entry of event-related data close to the place (and probably time) that an event occurs. *Online transaction entry (OLTE), online real-time processing (OLRT),* and *online transaction processing (OLTP)* are all examples of this processing strategy. When this strategy is employed, databases are more current and subsequent events can occur in a *timelier* manner. Because data are not transported to a data entry location, there is less risk that inputs will be lost (*input completeness*). Also, the input can be more accurate because the data entry person may be in a position to recognize and immediately correct input errors (*input accuracy*). Finally, some *efficiencies* can be gained by reducing the number of entities handling the event data.

E-BUSINESS   P-2:   *Digital signatures.* Whenever data are entered from remote locations via telecommunications channels, the risk is present that the communication may have been sent by an unauthorized system user or may have been intercepted/modified in transit. To guard against such risks, many organizations employ *digital signatures* to *authenticate* the user's identity and to verify the integrity of the message being transmitted. **Digital signature** is a technology that validates the identity of the sender and the integrity of an electronic message. To appreciate how digital signatures work, you first must understand the basic mechanics of *data encryption* and *public-key cryptography*, topics discussed in Appendix 9A (pages 330–335).

P-3:   *Populate input with master data.* At this point in the data entry routine, the program automatically populates inputs with master data. Numeric, alphabetic, and other designators are usually assigned to entities such as customers, vendors, and employees. When we **populate inputs with master data**, the system user merely enters an entity's identification code and the system then retrieves certain data about that entity from existing master data. For example, in our earlier example of entering a customer order, the user might be prompted to enter the customer ID (code). Then, by accessing the customer master data, the system automatically provides data such as the customer's name and address, the salesperson's name, and the sales terms. This reduces the number of keystrokes required, making data entry quicker and more efficient. With fewer keystrokes and by utilizing the existing data, fewer keying mistakes are expected.

P-4:   *Compare input with master data.* A data entry program can be designed to compare the input data to data that has been previously recorded. When we **compare input data with master data**, we can determine the accuracy and validity of the input data. Here are just two types of comparisons that can be made:

a.   *Input/master data dependency checks.* These edits test whether the contents of two or more data elements or fields on an event description bear the correct logical relationship. For example, input sales events can be tested to determine whether the salesperson works in the customer's territory. If these two items don't match, there is some evidence that the customer number or the salesperson identification was input erroneously.

b.   *Input/master data validity and accuracy checks.* These edits test whether master data supports the validity and accuracy of the input. For example, this edit might prevent the input of a shipment when no record of a corresponding customer order exists. If no match is made, we may have input some data incorrectly, or the shipment might simply be invalid. We might also compare elements *within* the input and master data. For example, we can compare the quantities to be shipped to the quantities ordered. Quantities that do not match *may* have been picked from the shelf or entered into the computer incorrectly.

P-5: *Procedures for rejected inputs.* These procedures are designed to ensure that erroneous data—not accepted for processing—are corrected and resubmitted for processing.

P-6: *Key corrections.* The clerk completes the procedures for rejected inputs by keying the corrections into the computer thus ensuring that the input is accurate.

P-7: *Record input.* Once all necessary corrections are made, the user accepts the input. This action triggers the computer to simultaneously *record* the input in the transaction file and *inform* the user that the input data has been accepted.

P-8: *Interactive feedback checks.* These interactive programmed features inform the user that the input has been accepted and recorded or rejected for processing.

Explanation of Control Matrix Cell Entries

Let's now turn our attention to Exhibit 9.3 (page 319). Do you agree with (and understand) the relationship between each plan and the goal(s) that it addresses? As mentioned earlier, your ability to *explain* the relationships between plans and goals is more important than your memorization of the cell entries themselves.

CONTROL PLANS FOR DATA ENTRY WITH BATCHES

In this section, we introduce you to a hypothetical system wherein we use the example of a shipping and billing process to illustrate certain points. The distinguishing control-related feature in this system is that it processes event data in batches. Once again we describe the system, walk you through its systems flowchart, list and explain the control plans associated with batch-oriented systems, and incorporate those plans into a control matrix for the system.

System Description and Flowchart

Figure 9.7 (page 322) shows the systems flowchart for our hypothetical batch processing system. Follow along in the flowchart as we describe the system and discuss some of the assumptions we used in its creation.

Processing begins in the first column of the flowchart with picking tickets that have been received in the shipping department from the warehouse (P-1). Let's assume that accompanying these picking tickets are goods that are about to be shipped to customers. Upon receipt of the picking tickets, a shipping department employee assembles them into groups or batches (P-2). Let's assume that the employee batches the documents in groups of 25 and calculates batch totals (the nature of the totals that could be taken is discussed in the next section).

The batch of documents is then scanned onto a magnetic disk (P-3). As the batch is recorded onto this disk, the data entry program calculates one or more totals for the batch and displays those batch totals to the shipping clerk. The clerk determines if the displayed totals agree with the ones previously calculated (P-4). If they don't, an error-correcting routine (not shown) is performed. This process is repeated throughout the day as picking tickets are received in the shipping department.

Periodically, the shipment data is sent to the computer for processing by the shipment programs (P-5). This program records the inputs on the sales journal (sales event data)

Figure 9.7 Systems Flowchart: Data Entry With Batches

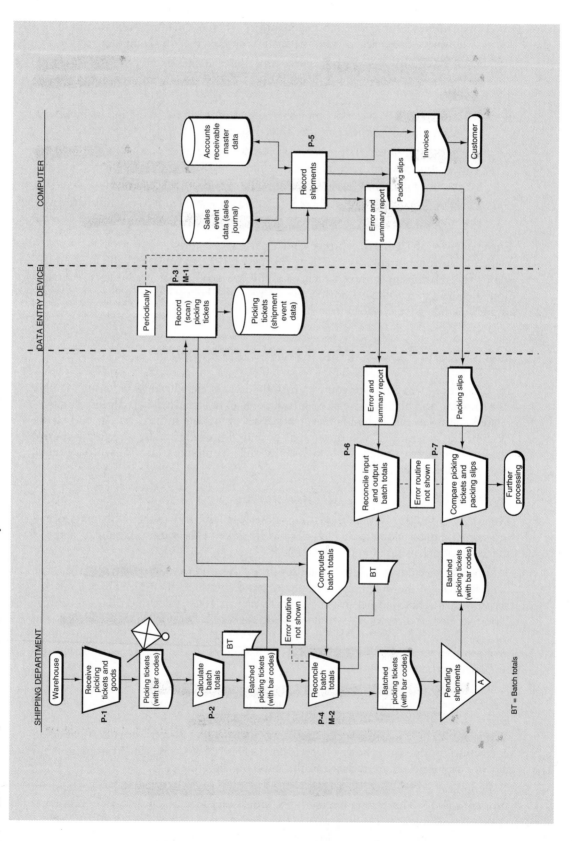

and updates the accounts receivable master data to reflect a new open receivable. Invoices are printed and sent to the customer. Packing slips are printed and sent to the shipping department where they are matched with the picking ticket before the goods are sent to the customer. "Further processing" includes packing and shipping the goods.

One of the system outputs is usually an **exception and summary report**. This report reflects the events—either in detail, summary, or both—that were accepted or rejected by the system. Even though the keyed input was edited and validated, some data still could be rejected at the update stage of processing. In our system a clerk in shipping compares the totals on this report to the input batch totals (P-6). Finally, picking tickets and packing slips are compared to ensure that they agree and that no picking tickets remain unshipped for an unduly long period of time (P-7).

Applying the Control Framework

In this section, we apply the control framework to the generic batch processing system previously described. Figure 9.8 (page 324) presents a completed control matrix for the systems flowchart shown in Figure 9.7, which has been annotated to show the location of recommended control plans that exist in the system (codes P-1, P-2, . . . P-7). We also have some control plans that we *assume* are missing (codes M-1 and M-2) because the narrative system description did not mention them specifically. In Figures 9.4 and 9.6 (pages 312 and 318, respectively) we could not complete certain parts of the top of the control matrix. However, for this example we know the nature of the input (i.e., picking tickets), the resources that are to be protected (i.e., the inventory and the accounts receivable master data), and the data that is to be updated (i.e., the AR master data). Therefore, we have completed these elements in Figure 9.8.

In this section, we discuss each of the recommended control plans listed in the first column of the matrix.[5] First we describe how the plans work; then, we explain the cell entries appearing in the control matrix. Be sure to trace each plan to the flowchart location where it is implemented (or could be implemented in the case of a missing plan).

Before we start, let's explain what we mean by *batch controls*. **Batch control plans** regulate information processing by calculating control totals at various points in a processing run and subsequently comparing these totals. When the various batch totals fail to agree, evidence exists that an event description(s) may have been lost (completeness exposure), added (validity exposure), or changed (accuracy exposure). Once established, batch totals can be reconciled manually or the computer can reconcile them. In general, for batch control plans to be effective, they should ensure that:

- *All* documents are batched; in other words, the batch totals should be established close to the time that the source documents are created or are received from external entities.
- *All* batches are submitted for processing; batch transmittals and batch logs are useful in protecting against the loss of entire batches.
- *All* batches are accepted by the computer; the user should be instrumental in performing this checking.
- *All* differences disclosed by reconciliations are investigated and corrected on a timely basis.

---

[5] Many of the controls in this section are adapted from material contained in *Handbook of IT Auditing 2001 Edition* (Chapters D2, D3, and D4 primarily) (Boston: Warren, Gorham & Lamont, 2000). Copyright © 2000 by PricewaterhouseCoopers L.L.P.

Figure 9.8 Control Matrix for Data Entry With Batches

Recommended Control Plans	Control Goals of the (blank) Business Process							
	Control Goals of the Operations Process			Control Goals of the Information Process			
	Ensure effectiveness of operations	Ensure efficient employment of resources (people, computers)	Ensure security of resources (inventory, AR master data)	For the picking ticket inputs, ensure:			For the AR master data, ensure:	
	A			IV	IC	IA	UC	UA
Present Controls								
P-1: Receive turnaround documents	P-1	P-1		P-1		P-1		
P-2: Calculate batch totals				P-2	P2			
P-3: Record picking tickets	P-3	P-3		P-3				
P-4: Manually reconcile batch totals				P-4	P-4	P-4		
P-5: Record shipments	P-5	P-5		P-5		P-5		P-5
P-6: Reconcile input and output batch totals			P-6	P-6	P-6	P-6	P-6	P-6
P-7: Compare picking tickets and packing slips (one-for-one checking)	P-7		P-7	P-7	P-7	P-7	P-7	P-7
Missing Controls								
M-1: Automated sequence checks				M-1	M-1			
M-2: Computer agreement of batch totals	M-2	M-2		M-2	M-2	M-2		

Legend:

Effectiveness goals:
A = To ensure timely input and processing of (blank) event data.

Recommended control plans:
See Exhibit 9.4 (pages 329–330) for a complete explanation of control plans and cell entries.

IV = Input validity
IC = Input completeness
IA = Input accuracy
UC = Update completeness
UA = Update accuracy

Batch control procedures must start by grouping event data and then calculating a control total(s) for the group. For example, Figure 9.7 (page 322) shows the shipping department employee preparing batch totals for the picking tickets documents to be scanned.

Several different types of batch control totals can be calculated, as discussed in the following paragraphs. You will note in the following discussion that certain types of batch totals are better than others in addressing the information process control goals of input validity, input completeness, and input accuracy.

Document/record counts are simple counts of the number of documents entered (e.g., 25 documents in a batch). This procedure represents the minimum level required to control *input completeness*. It is not sufficient if more than one event description can appear on a document. For example, consider the event "sale of goods" where each document reflects a sale. If each document can include one or more line items (say, one television set and three chairs are listed as a single sale), then a document/record count would not reflect multiple sale items. Also, because one document could be intentionally replaced with another, this control is not effective for ensuring input *validity* and says nothing about input *accuracy*.

Item or line counts are counts of the number of items or lines of data entered, such as a count of the number of invoices being paid by all the customer remittances. By reducing the possibility that line items or entire documents could be added to the batch or not be input, this control improves input *validity, completeness,* and *accuracy*. Remember, a missing event record is a *completeness* error and a data set missing from an event record is an *accuracy* error.

Dollar totals are a summation of the dollar value of items in the batch, such as the total dollar value of all remittance advices in a batch. By reducing the possibility that entire documents could be added to or lost from the batch or that dollar amounts were incorrectly input, this control improves input *validity, completeness,* and *accuracy.*

Hash totals are a summation of any numeric data existing for all documents in the batch, such as a total of customer numbers or invoice numbers in the case of remittance advices. Unlike dollar totals, hash totals normally serve no purpose other than control. Hash totals can be a powerful batch control because they can determine if inputs have been altered, added, or deleted. These *batch* hash totals operate for a batch in a manner similar to the operation of *document/record hash totals* for individual inputs.

Now we proceed with an explanation of the controls plans in Figures 9.7 (page 322) and 9.8 by following the logical order of processing.

P-1: *Receive turnaround documents.* **Turnaround documents** are used to capture and input a *subsequent* event. Picking tickets, inventory count cards, remittance advice stubs attached to customer invoices, and payroll time cards are all examples of turnaround documents. For example, we have seen picking tickets that are printed by the computer, used to pick the goods, and sent to shipping where the bar code on the picking ticket is scanned to trigger the recording of the shipment.

P-2: *Calculate batch totals.* Calculation of batch totals ensures that the data input arises from legitimate events (*input validity*) and that all events in the batch are captured (*input completeness*). However, batch totals in isolation do not necessarily ensure input accuracy—that takes place in the reconciliation, which is discussed in P-4.

P-3: *Record picking tickets.* The picking tickets are automatically recorded (scanned) into the computer using a bar code. This process stores the accurate, valid input data onto digital media for subsequent updating procedures in a timely manner with minimal use of resources. In addition, the automatic calculation of the batch totals will ensure an efficient and effective subsequent reconciliation of the inputs.

We notice at this point that a sequence check is not applied to the input documents. Read on about a type of control that could have been applied at this point.

M-1: *Automated sequence checks.* Whenever documents are numbered sequentially—either assigned a number when the document is prepared or prepared using *pre-numbered documents*—a **sequence check** can be automatically applied to those documents. One of two kinds of sequence checks may be used—either a batch sequence check or cumulative sequence check.

In a **batch sequence check**, the event data within a batch are checked as follows:

a. The range of serial numbers constituting the batch is entered.

b. Each individual, serially pre-numbered event data is entered.

c. The computer program sorts the event data into numerical order; checks the documents against the sequence number range; and reports missing, duplicate, and out-of-range event data.

Batch sequence checks work best when we can control the input process and the serial numbers of the input data, such as payroll checks. For example, this control would not work for entering customer orders that had a variety of numbers assigned by many customers.

A slight variation on the batch sequence check is the cumulative sequence check. The **cumulative sequence check** provides input control in those situations in which the serial numbers are assigned within the organization (e.g., sales order numbers issued by the sales order department) but later are not entered in perfect serial number sequence (i.e., picking tickets might contain broken sets of numbers). In this case, the matching of individual event data (picking ticket) numbers is made to a file that contains *all* document numbers (all sales order numbers). *Periodically*, reports of missing numbers are produced for manual follow-up.

Reconciling a checkbook is another example of a situation in which numbers (the check numbers) are issued in sequence. When we receive a bank statement, the batch may not contain a complete sequence of checks. Our check register assists us in performing a cumulative sequence check to make sure that all checks are eventually cleared.

P-4: *Manually reconcile batch totals.* The **manual reconciliation of batch totals** control plan operates in the following manner:

a. First, one or more of the batch totals are established manually (i.e., in the shipping department in Figure 9.7, page 322).

b. As individual event descriptions are entered (or scanned), the data entry program accumulates independent batch totals.

c. The computer produces reports (or displays) at the end of either the input process or update process, or both. The report (or display) includes the relevant control totals that must be manually reconciled to the totals established prior to the particular process.

d. The person who reconciles the batch total (see the shipping department employee in Figure 9.7) must determine why the totals do not agree and make corrections as necessary to ensure the integrity of the input data.

We notice at this point that the clerk must perform a manual reconciliation of the batch totals. Read on about a more efficient means for performing that reconciliation.

M-2: *Computer agreement of batch totals.* This control plan does not exist in Figure 9.7 and therefore is shown as a missing plan. Note in Figure 9.7 where we have placed the M-2 annotation. The **computer agreement of batch totals** plan is pictured in Figure 9.9 and works in the following manner:

a. First, one or more of the batch totals are established manually (i.e., in the user department in Figure 9.9).

Figure 9.9 Computer Agreement of Batch Totals Control Plan

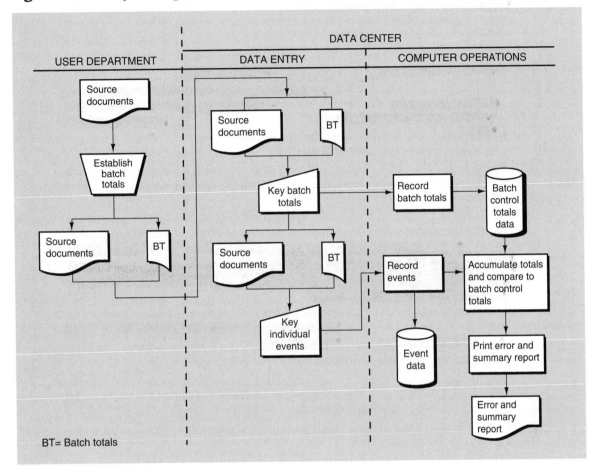

BT= Batch totals

b. Then, the manually prepared total is entered into the computer and is written to the computer batch control totals data.

c. As individual event descriptions are entered, a computer program accumulates independent batch totals and compares these totals to the ones prepared manually and entered at the start of the processing.

d. The computer prepares a report, which usually contains details of each batch, together with an indication of whether the totals agreed or disagreed. Batches that do not balance are normally rejected, and discrepancies are manually investigated. Such an analysis would be included in a report similar to the "Error and summary report" in Figures 9.7 (page 322) and 9.9.

P-5: *Record shipments.* Picking ticket data and accounts receivable master data are used to record shipments, which in turn updates the sales transaction data. As we have noted before, such automatic recording stores the accurate, valid input data onto digital media in a timely manner with minimal use of resources.

P-6: *Reconcile input and output batch totals (agreement of run-to-run totals).* This is a variation of the agreement of batch totals controls. With **agreement of run-to-run totals**, totals prepared before a computer process has begun are compared, manually or by the computer, to totals prepared at the completion of the computer process. These post-process controls are often found on an *error and summary report.* When totals agree, we have evidence that the input *and* the update took place correctly. This control is especially useful when there are several intermediate steps between the beginning and the end of the process and we want to be assured of the integrity of each process.

P-7: *Compare picking tickets (from a tickler file) and packing slips (one-for-one checking).* This has two purposes: one is to ensure that all picking tickets are linked to an associated packing slip, and the other is to ensure that all items on related picking tickets and packing slips match. Both of these objectives are facilitated by a **tickler file**, which is reviewed on a regular basis for the purpose of taking action to clear items from that file. While Figure 9.7 (page 322) shows a file of picking tickets items that should be shipped ("Pending Shipments" file), tickler files also may be digitized computer records reflecting events that need to be completed, such as open sales orders, open purchase orders, and so forth. Should tickler file documents remain in the file for an extended period of time, the person or computer monitoring the file would determine the nature and extent of the delay. In our example, once packing slips are received, the picking tickets are compared to their associated packing slips using a procedure called **one-for-one checking**, which involves a detailed comparison of the individual elements of two or more data sources to determine that they agree. This control is often used to compare a source document to an output produced later in a process. Differences may indicate errors in input or update. This procedure provides us detail as to *what* is incorrect within a batch. Being very expensive to perform, one-for-one checking should be reserved for low-volume, high-value events.

Having examined what each of the recommended control plans means and how each operates, we can now look at how the plans meet the control goals. Exhibit 9.4 explains the relationship between each control plan and each control goal that it helps to achieve. As you study Exhibit 9.4, we again urge you to concentrate your energies on understanding these relationships.

SUMMARY

In this chapter, we began our study of business process control plans, the third level in the control hierarchy shown in Figure 7.3 on page 248. Our study of business process control plans will continue in Chapters 10–14, where we will apply the control framework and explore those controls that are unique to each business process.

Before we leave, let's address one more aspect of business process controls. Many of these controls attempt to detect data that *may* be in error. For example, a reasonableness test may reject a price change that is beyond a normal limit. But it may be that the price change has been authorized and correctly entered. As another example, perhaps a customer order is rejected because it does not pass the credit check, but it might be that it is in the best interest of the company to permit the sale. In these cases, we need to be able to *override* the control and permit the event to process. If our control system is to remain effective, these overrides must be used sparingly and securely (e.g., requiring a *password* or key and signature to effect the override). Finally, a record of all overrides should be periodically reviewed to determine that the override authority is not being abused.

Exhibit 9.4 Explanation of Cell Entries for Control Matrix in Figure 9.8

P-1: *Receive turnaround documents.*

Effectiveness goal A, Efficient employment of resources: By reducing the amount of data that must be input to record the shipment we improve the speed and productivity of the data entry personnel.

Input validity: The turnaround documents were printed in a different functional area. Therefore, the shipping department employee who calculates the batch totals must presume that the picking tickets are valid. This also serves to separate event authorization (as reflected by the picking ticket) from execution (as represented by the packing slips).

Input accuracy: Using a pre-recorded bar code to trigger the event reduces the possibility of input errors.

P-2: *Calculate batch totals.*

Input validity, Input completeness: Batch totals arise from legitimate source documents (*input validity*). Batch totals ensure that all of the batched data is recorded (*input completeness*). As suggested earlier, the nature and extent of batch totals can vary: they can account for only the number of events, the number of items or lines of data, dollar amounts, and/or hash totals. As such, batch totals themselves ensure the validity and completeness of the counts and amounts they represent. However, they do not necessarily ensure input accuracy—that takes place in the reconciliation, which is discussed in control plan P-4.

P-3: *Record picking tickets.*

Effectiveness goal A, Efficient employment of resources: Using the bar code on the picking ticket to scan items and quantities is fast and resource-conserving.

Input validity: Since the picking ticket is a turn-around document, the picking and shipping of goods must be valid, as the picking ticket was generated from a customer order (unless some sort of unintentional or intentional error produced the ticket in the first place).

P-4: *Manually reconcile batch totals.*

Input validity, Input completeness, Input accuracy: Agreement of the batch totals at this point ensures that only valid source documents comprising the original batch have been input (*input validity*), that all source documents were input (*input completeness*), and that data elements appearing on the source documents have been input correctly (*input accuracy*).

P-5: *Record shipments.*

Effectiveness goal A, Efficiency employment of resources: Shipments result from sales orders and picking tickets and the recording is automated (*efficiency of resources*), hence, timely (*Effectiveness goal A*).

Input validity, Input Accuracy, Update Accuracy: By automatically recording shipments from picking tickets and sales orders (from valid customers), we ensure that the shipment is legitimate (*input validity*) and precise (*input accuracy*). In addition, we ensure that the shipment is updated correctly to the appropriate record in the AR master data (*update accuracy*). But, we do not know if the input or update was complete.

P-6: *Reconcile input and output batch totals (agreement of run-to-run totals).*

Security of resources, Input validity: By determining that updates to the accounts receivable master data reflect goods picked and about to be shipped, we reduce the possibility of recording an invalid sales event and shipping to customers who did not order, and will not pay for, the goods.

Input completeness, Input accuracy, Update completeness, Update accuracy: By comparing totals prepared before the input to those produced after the update, we ensure that all events were input (*input completeness*), all events were input correctly (*input accuracy*), all events were updated to the master data (*update completeness*), and all events were updated correctly to the master data (*update accuracy*).

P-7: *Compare picking tickets (from tickler file) and packing slips (one-for-one checking).*

Effectiveness goal A: A file of picking tickets is retained in shipping awaiting packing slips. If the packing slips are received in a timely manner, and the corresponding picking ticket removed from the "Pending shipments" file, we can ensure that goods will be shipped in a timely manner and that the picking tickets were indeed input and the master data updated. If picking slips do not receive packing slips within a rea-

(continued)

Exhibit 9.4 Explanation of Cell Entries for Control Matrix in Figure 9.8 (*continued*)

sonable period of time, then an inquiry procedure is initiated to determine the nature and extent of the delay.

Security of resources, Input validity: By matching details on the picking tickets with the data on the packing slips produced by the computer, we reduce the possibility that an invalid sales event has been recorded and that we will not ship goods to customers who did not order, and will not pay for, the goods.

Input completeness, Input accuracy, Update completeness, Update accuracy: By matching details on the picking tickets (i.e., the inputs) with the details on the packing slips produced by the computer, we ensure that all events were input (*input completeness*), all events were input correctly (*input accuracy*), all events were updated to the master data (*update completeness*), and all events were updated correctly to the master data (*update accuracy*).

M-1: *Automated sequence checks.*

Input validity, Input completeness: By comparing an expected sequence of documents to those actu-

ally input, computerized sequence checks can detect a second occurrence of a particular document number, which would suggest that the second event is invalid, and can detect missing document numbers, suggesting that not all events had been input.

M-2: *Computer agreement of batch totals.*

Effectiveness goal A, Efficient employment of resources: Had the computer been used to reconcile the control totals, the processing of the events would have been completed more quickly and with less human effort.

Input validity, Input completeness, Input accuracy: Regarding these control goals, the effect of this control is the same as P-4. Agreement of the batch totals at this point would have ensured that only valid source documents comprising the original batch had been input, that all source documents were input, and that data elements appearing on the source documents had been input correctly.

APPENDIX 9A

Data Encryption and Public-Key Cryptography

E-BUSINESS **Data encryption** is a process that employs mathematical algorithms and encryption keys to encode data (i.e., change it from plain text to a coded text form) so that it is unintelligible to the human eye and therefore useless to those who should not have access to it. Encryption is used (or should be used) in situations where the data are of such a sensitive nature that we want to preserve the data's privacy and confidentiality. For example, people are asking for and obtaining security of their Internet transmissions through cryptography. Technology Application 9.1 (at the end of this Appendix on pages 334–335) describes three methods for conducting secure electronic commerce on the Internet using data encryption and public-key cryptography.

One of the earliest and most elementary uses of encryption dates back to the first century B.C. During the Gallic Wars, Julius Caesar encoded his messages by shifting the alphabet three letters forward so that an A became a D, an X became an A, and so on. For instance, if the message is NED IS A NERD—called *plaintext* in cryptography lingo—the *ciphertext* would appear as QHG LV D QHUG. The *Caesar cipher*—an example of a simple one-for-one letter substitution system—in effect used a *key* of 3 and an encrypting *algorithm* of addition. We still see examples of this type of encryption in the cryptograms or cryptoquotes that are published in the puzzle pages of our daily newspapers.

With the use of more complex *algorithms* and encryption *keys*, coding a message can be made much more powerful than in the preceding example. Figure 9.10 contains an illustration of how the message NED IS A NERD could be made more difficult to decode. Keep in mind, however, that the figure also is a very basic, rudimentary example intended to convey the bare-bones mechanics of how encryption works. In practice, algorithms and keys are much more sophisticated, so much so that good encryption schemes are virtually impossible to break.

Figure 9.10 Example of Data Encryption

Encrypt (i.e., encode a message):										
1. Plaintext message	N	E	D	I	S	A	N	E	R	D
2. (Letter of the alphabet)	(14	5	4	9	19	1	14	5	18	4)
3. Encryption algorithm	+	-	+	-	+	-	+	-	+	-
4. Key	3	1	7	6	3	4	8	6	7	9
5. (Letter of the alphabet)	(17	4	11	3	22	23	22	25	25	21)
6. Ciphertext	Q	D	K	C	V	W	V	Y	Y	U
Decrypt (i.e., decode a message):										
7. Ciphertext (from line 6)	Q	D	K	C	V	W	V	Y	Y	U
8. (Letter of the alphabet)	(17	4	11	3	22	23	22	25	25	21)
9. Decryption algorithm	-	+	-	+	-	+	-	+	-	+
10. Key (same as line 4)	3	1	7	6	3	4	8	6	7	9
11. (Letter of the alphabet)	(14	5	4	9	19	1	14	5	18	4)
12. Decoded message	N	E	D	I	S	A	N	E	R	D

Please note the following about Figure 9.10:

- Each letter of the alphabet is assigned a number—A=1 through Z=26—to designate its position in the alphabet.
- If symbols as well as letters appeared in the character set, they would be designated by the numbers 27, 28, etc.
- The key can be any string of random numbers, one number for each character in the message. In conventional, single-key encryption, the *same* key (see lines 4 and 10) is used both to encrypt and decrypt the message.
- The mathematical formula (i.e., algorithm) on line 3 is used to apply the key (line 4) to the plaintext message. In this simplistic example, we use an algorithm that alternates the basic math functions of plus and minus (i.e., plus for the first character, minus for the second, plus for the third, and so forth).
- The decryption algorithm on line 9 is the reverse of that on line 3 (i.e., each plus on line 3 is a minus on line 9 and vice versa).
- Unlike the simple puzzle-page cryptogram in our first example, a particular plaintext character—such as the N in *NED* and in *NERD*—does not translate on a one-

for-one basis into a single ciphertext character. For instance, the first N on line 1 becomes a Q on line 6, whereas the second N becomes a V.

As shown in Figure 9.10, the crux of conventional encryption procedures is the *single key* used both by the sender to encrypt the message and by the receiver to decrypt it. A major drawback to such systems is that the key itself has to be transmitted by secure channels. If the key is not kept secret, the security of the entire system is compromised. *Public-key cryptography* helps to solve this problem by employing a *pair* of matched keys for each system user, one private (i.e., known only to the party who possesses it) and one public. The public key corresponds to but is not the same as the user's private key. As its name implies, the public key is assumed to be public knowledge and even could be published in a directory, in much the same way as a person's telephone number.

Figure 9.11 illustrates how public-key cryptography is used both to *encrypt* messages (part (a) of the figure) and to *authenticate* a message by appending a digital signature to it (part (b) of the figure). Please note that although we show both parts (a) and (b) being executed, in practice the parts are separable. That is, a message could be encrypted as shown in part (a) without having a *digital signature* added to it. Digital signatures enhance security by ensuring that the "signature" cannot be forged (i.e., that the message comes from an authorized source) and that the message has not been changed in any way in transmission.

We believe that the figure tells the story. Therefore, we discuss it only briefly. First note that Sally Sender and Ray Receiver each have a *pair* of keys. In part (a), Ray's *public* key is used to encrypt *all* messages sent to him. Privacy of the messages is ensured because only Ray's *private* key can decrypt the messages. The messages *cannot* be decoded using Ray's public key. Furthermore, the private decryption key never has to be transmitted; it is always in Ray's exclusive possession.

In part (b), Sally first uses a hashing function to translate the plaintext message into a binary number. Any message *other* than NED IS A NERD would not "hash" into the number 11010010. By then using her *private* key to encrypt the binary number, Sally, in effect, has digitally "signed" the message. On the right side of part (b), Ray Receiver employs Sally's *public* key to decrypt her "signature." Because no public key except Sally's will work, Ray knows that the message comes from her. Note that *anyone* could use Sally's public key to decode her signature, but that is not important. The object is not to keep the signature secret or private, but rather to *authenticate* that it was Sally, and *only* she, who "signed" the message.

To ensure the *integrity of the message* (received in part (a) of the figure), Ray

- runs the decrypted message, NED IS A NERD, through a hashing function—the same hashing function used by Sally—and
- compares the decoded digital signature (11010010) with the hashed output of the message *received* (11010010). If the two numbers don't agree, Ray knows that the message is not the same as the one Sally sent. For example, assume that Ted Tamperer was able to intercept Sally's encrypted message in part (a) and change it so that when Ray decoded it, he read NED IS A NICE GUY. This message would *not* hash into the number 11010010; therefore, it would not match the decrypted digital signature from Sally.

E-BUSINESS   Some experts predict that digital signatures will soon pave the way for a truly cashless society, which has been talked about for years. The digital signatures will be used to create electronic cash, checks, and other forms of payment that can be used in electronic commerce (see Technology Application 9.1 for examples). Others foresee digital signa-

Figure 9.11 Illustration of Public-Key Cryptography and Digital Signatures

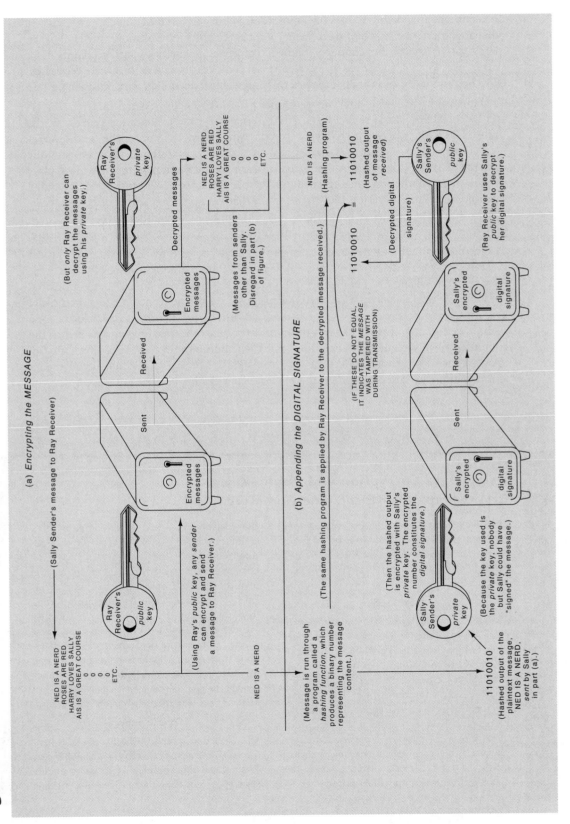

tures replacing handwritten ones on a multitude of business and legal documents, such as purchase orders, checks, court documents, and tax returns. The Millennium Digital Commerce Act of 2002 makes contracts "signed" by electronic methods legally valid in all 50 states. This law was designed to accelerate the rate of growth of business-to-business (B2B) *e-Business* by allowing companies to immediately execute documents online.

Digital signatures also offer an additional benefit to e-Business transactions. Buyers and sellers of goods and services over the Internet can only feel comfortable about the business transaction if one party is sure that the other party will not renege on the agreement. One way for a party to back off from an agreement is to repudiate or disclaim the agreement. If the other party cannot prove that a legally binding agreement took place in the first place, the reneging party might be successful. To ward off this threat, digital signatures are used to ensure *non-repudiation*; that is, digital signatures offer the necessary proof that a legal "meeting of the minds" took place, as neither party can successfully dispute or repudiate the existence and authenticity of a document and/or signature.

One final thought—for public-key cryptography to be effective the *private* keys must be kept *private*. To do that we can employ a variety of techniques, some of which were introduced in Chapter 8. For example, the private key might be kept within a protected computer or device such as a *cryptographic box*. Access to the device, and to the private key, must then be protected with *passwords* or other *authentication* procedures. One such procedure involves the use of a thumbprint reader or retinal imager attached to the computer. With such devices, users must put their thumb onto the reader or eye into an imager before the private key can be used to "sign" a message. The thumbprint reader and retinal imager are examples of the *biometric* devices introduced in Chapter 8.

Technology Application 9.1

Using Data Encryption and Public-Key Cryptography for Electronic Commerce

Data encryption and public-key cryptography are being used to secure business transactions on the Internet. Following are three examples. While all three are currently in use, only SSL is widely used.

Case 1: SSL

The secure sockets layer (SSL) handshake protocol was developed by Netscape Communications Company and uses public-key cryptography to secure communications on the Internet. With SSL, a secure session is established during which messages transmitted between two parties are protected via encryption. For example, before a consumer transmits a credit card number to a merchant, the merchant's server establishes a secure session. The merchant receives the message, decrypts it, extracts the credit card number, and submits a charge to the consumer's credit card company (i.e., credit card issuing bank) to clear the transaction using traditional means. With SSL, the consumer is protected from interception and unauthorized use of the purchase and credit card information while on the Internet (i.e., from the consumer's Web browser to the merchant's Web server). Normally, the merchant cannot authenticate the transmission to determine from whom the message originated, and the consumer has only moderate assurance that he or she has sent his or her credit card number to a legitimate merchant.

Case 2: eCheck

The electronic check (eCheck) is a payment mechanism developed by the Financial Services Technology Consortium (FSTC). Using public-key cryptography and digital signatures, trading partners and their banks can transmit secure messages and payment information. eCheck certificates would be issued by banks certifying that the holder of the certificate has an account at that bank. Payments would be processed automatically through the existing bank systems. Payments would be checks drawn on bank accounts. A feature beyond SSL is that the eCheck protocol defines message formats, such as purchase orders, acknowledgments, and invoices, which can be processed automatically by trading parties. The basic technology developed for eCheck is being used by Xign Corp. for the Internet-based purchasing/payment system it hosts for buying and selling organizations. Also, the U. S. Department of the Treasury is piloting an Internet Payment Platform, supported by Xign Corp.

Case 3: Smart Cards

In an increasingly online environment, where critical corporate information and business transactions are exchanged over open networks, privacy and security are essential. A possible solution to ensuring such privacy and security is a smart card, which is a small electronic device about the size of a credit card that includes embedded memory and sometimes integrated circuits. Smart cards utilize the public key infrastructure (PKI) technology to provide everything from digital cash, signatures, authentication, authorization, and security on a single card platform. Because PKI technology is built into smart cards, should you lose your card, no one else can use it without your private key. Smart cards are presently used in a wide array of transactions, such as telephone, banking, and healthcare—both on and off the Internet. While the popularity of smart cards is growing rapidly in the United States, they are already used extensively in Europe and Japan. Some reasons to use smart cards—they are more reliable, can store more information, and are more tamper-resistant than magnetic stripe cards; smart cards can be disposed or reused; they can be programmed to perform single or multiple functions; and, smart cards are compatible with portable electronic devices and personal computers. In fact, when President Bill Clinton signed the Millennium Digital Commerce Act of 2002, he did not use the traditional quill pen, rather, he used a smart card that contained his digital signature!

Sources: For information about SSL, go to http://developer.netscape.com/docs/manuals/security/sslin.For information about e-Check, go to http://www.echeck.org. For information about Xign Corp., go to http://www.xign.com. For information about Internet Payment Platform, go to http://www.ipp.gov.

REVIEW QUESTIONS

RQ 9-1 Explain the difference between the category of business process control plans covered in this chapter and the business process controls to be covered in Chapters 10 through 16.

RQ 9-2 Describe the relationship between the *control matrix* and the *systems flowchart*.

RQ 9-3 What are the steps involved in preparing a control matrix?

RQ 9-4 a. How would the control matrix be useful in evaluating control *effectiveness*, control *efficiency*, and control *redundancy*? Include in your answer a definition of these three terms.

b. How could the control matrix be used to recommend changes in the system in order to improve control of that system?

RQ 9-5 How does each control plan listed Exhibit 9.2 work?

RQ 9-6 What are two common *programmed edit checks*? Describe each check.

RQ 9-7 How does each control plan listed in the control matrix in Figure 9.6 work?

RQ 9-8 In examining the systems flowchart in Figure 9.7, how would you discern from the symbols used (or perhaps the lack of certain other symbols) whether the system (a) employs online data entry; (b) uses data communications technology; (c) processes events individually, rather than in groups of similar events; and (d) updates master data continuously?

RQ 9-9 How does each control plan listed in the control matrix in Figure 9.8 work?

RQ 9-10 Name and explain three different types of batch totals that could be calculated in a batch processing system.

RQ 9-11 Referring to Appendix 9A, distinguish among data encryption, public-key cryptography, and digital signatures.

DISCUSSION QUESTIONS

DQ 9-1 Discuss why the control matrix is custom-tailored for each business process.

DQ 9-2 Explain why input controls are so important. Discuss fully.

DQ 9-3 In evaluating business process controls, some auditors differentiate between the point in the system at which the control is "established" and the *later* point at which *that* control is "exercised." Speculate about the meaning of the terms *establish a control* and *exercise a control* by discussing those terms in the context of:

 a. Batch total procedures.

 b. Turnaround documents.

 c. Tickler files.

DQ 9-4 "The mere fact that event data appear on a pre-numbered document is no proof of the validity of the event. Someone intent on defrauding a system, by introducing a fictitious event, probably would be clever enough to get access to the pre-numbered documents or would replicate those documents so as to make the event appear genuine."

 a. Do you agree with this comment? Why or why not?

 b. Without prejudice to your answer to part (a), assume that the comment is true. Present (and explain) a "statement of relationship" between the control plan of using pre-numbered documents and the information system control goal of event "validity."

DQ 9-5 Describe situations in your daily activities, working or not, where you have experienced or employed controls discussed in this chapter.

DQ 9-6 When we record our exams into the spreadsheet used for our gradebook, we employ the following procedures:

 a. For each exam, manually add up the grade and record on the front page.

 b. Manually calculate the average grade for all of the exams.

 c. Input the score for each part of each exam into the spreadsheet.

 d. Compare the exam total on the front page of the exam to the total prepared by the computer.

 e. After all the exams have been entered, compare the average grade calculated by the computer with that calculated manually.

Describe how this process employs controls discussed in this chapter.

DQ 9-7 Referring to Appendix 9A, "Protecting the private key is a critical element in public-key cryptography." Discuss fully.

DQ 9-8 On October 2, 2002, a clerk at Bear Stearns had erroneously entered an order to sell nearly $4 billion worth of securities. The trader had sent an order to sell $4 million worth. Only $622 million of the orders were executed, the remainder of the orders were canceled prior to execution. Reports stated that it was a human error, not a computer error and that it was the fault of the clerk, not the trader. What is your opinion of these reports? What controls could have *prevented* this error?

PROBLEMS

P 9-1 You worked with the Causeway Company cash receipts system in Chapter 4. The narrative of that system and its systems flowchart are reproduced in Exhibit 9.5 and Figure 9.12 (page 338), respectively.

Using Exhibit 9.5 and Figure 9.12, do the following:

a. Prepare a control matrix, including explanations of how each recommended control plan helps to accomplish—or would accomplish in the case of missing plans—each related control goal. Your choice of recommended control plans should come from Exhibits 9.2, 9.3, or 9.4 as appropriate. Be sure to tailor the matrix columns to conform to the specifics of the Causeway system. In doing so, assume the following two operations process goals only:

- To deposit cash receipts on the same day received.
- To assure that customer balances in the accounts receivable master data reflect account activity on a timely basis.

b. Annotate the systems flowchart in Figure 9.12 to show the location of each control plan listed in the control matrix.

Exhibit 9.5 Causeway Company System Narrative to Accompany Problem 9-1

Causeway Company uses the following procedures to process the cash received from credit sales. Customers send checks and remittance advices to Causeway. The mailroom clerk at Causeway endorses the checks and writes the amount paid and the check number on the remittance advice. Periodically, the mailroom clerk prepares a batch total of the remittance advices and sends the batch of remittance advices to accounts receivable, along with a copy of the batch total. At the same time, the clerk sends the corresponding batch of checks to the cashier.

In accounts receivable, a clerk enters the batch into the computer by keying the batch total, the customer number, the invoice number, the amount paid, and the check number. After verifying that the invoice is open and that the correct amount is being paid, the computer updates the accounts receivable master data. If there are any discrepancies, the clerk is notified.

At the end of each batch (or at the end of the day), the computer prints a deposit slip in duplicate on the printer in the cashier's office. The cashier compares the deposit slip to the corresponding batch of checks and then takes the deposit to the bank.

As they are entered, the check number and the amount paid for each receipt are logged on a disk. This event data is used to create a cash receipts listing at the end of each day. A summary of customer accounts paid that day is also printed at this time. The accounts receivable clerk compares these reports to the remittance advices and batch totals and sends the total of the cash receipts to the general ledger office.

Figure 9.12 Causeway Company Systems Flowchart to Accompany Problem 9-1

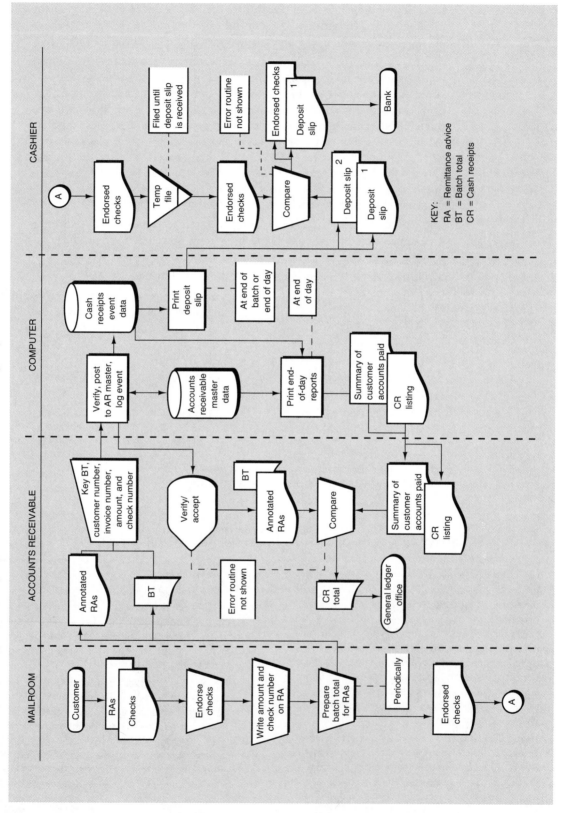

P 9-2 The following narrative describes the processing of customer mail orders at Technotronic Company:

Technotronic Company is a small manufacturing operation engaged in the selling of digital identification chips that can be implanted into household pets, such as cats and dogs. Customer mail orders are received in the sales order department, where sales order clerks open the orders and review them for accuracy. The clerks enter each order into the computer, where they are edited by comparing them to customer master data (stored on a disk). The computer displays the edited order on the clerk's computer. The clerk reviews and accepts the order. The order is then added to the sales event data (stored on a disk) and updates the sales order master data (also stored on a disk). As the order is recorded, it is printed on a printer in the warehouse (the picking ticket). A copy of the sales order is also printed in the sales order department and is sent to the customer (a customer acknowledgment).

(Complete only those requirements specified by your instructor.)

a. Prepare a table of entities and activities.

b. Draw a context diagram.

c. Draw a physical data flow diagram (DFD).

d. Indicate on the table of entities and activities prepared for part a, the groupings, bubble numbers, and titles to be used in preparing a level 0 logical DFD.

e. Draw a level 0 logical DFD.

f. Draw a systems flowchart.

g. Prepare a control matrix, including explanations of how each recommended existing control plan helps to accomplish—or would accomplish in the case of missing plans—each related control goal. Your choice of recommended control plans should come from Exhibits 9.2, 9.3, or 9.4 as appropriate. Be sure to tailor the matrix columns to conform to the specifics of the Technotronic Company system. In doing so, assume the following two operations process goals only:

  • To provide timely acknowledgment of customer orders.

  • To provide timely shipment of goods to customers.

h. Annotate the systems flowchart prepared in requirement (f) to show the location of each control plan listed in the control matrix.

P 9-3 The following is a list of 14 control plans from this chapter:

Control Plans

A. Populate inputs with master data

B. Batch sequence check

C. Interactive feedback checks

D. Programmed edit checks

E. Manual agreement of batch totals

F. Online prompting

G. Cumulative sequence check

H. Written approvals

I. Key verification

J. Document design

K. Procedures for resolving discrepancies

L. Compare input data with master data

M. Turnaround documents

N. Digital signatures

Listed following are 10 system failures that have control implications. On your solution sheet, list the numbers 1 through 10. Next to each number, insert the *capital* letter from the previous list for the best control plan to *prevent* the system failure from occurring. (If you can't find a control that will prevent the failure, choose a *detective* plan or, as a last resort, a *corrective* control plan.) A letter should be used only once, with four letters left over.

System Failures

1. Occasionally, the order entry system at Dorsam Inc. fails to record a customer order. After failing to receive an acknowledgment, the customer will call to inquire. Inevitably, the sales clerk will find the customer's order filed with other customer orders that had been entered into the computer. In each case, all indications are that the order had been entered.

2. At Syncheck Inc., data entry clerks receive a variety of documents from many departments throughout the company. In some cases, unauthorized inputs are keyed and entered into the computer.

3. The tellers at Bucks Bank have been having difficulty reconciling their cash drawers. All customer events are entered online at a teller terminal. At the end of the shift, the computer prints a list of the events that have occurred during the shift. The tellers must then review the list to determine that their drawers contain checks, cash, and other documents to support each entry on the list.

4. Data entry clerks at Visitron Company use networked PCs to enter data into the computer. Recently, a number of errors have been found in key numeric fields. The supervisor would like to implement a control to reduce the transcription errors being made by the clerks.

5. At Helm Inc., clerks in the accounting offices of Helm's three divisions prepare pre-numbered general ledger voucher documents. Once prepared, the vouchers are given to each office's data entry clerk, who keys them into an online terminal. The computer records whatever general ledger adjustment was indicated by the voucher. The controller has found that several vouchers were never recorded, and some vouchers were recorded twice.

6. Purchase orders are prepared online by purchasing clerks. Recently, the purchasing manager discovered that many purchase orders are being sent to the wrong vendor, for the wrong items, and for quantities far greater than would normally be requested.

7. Refer to the vignette at the beginning of the chapter. It describes a botched securities trade caused by a clerk mistakenly entering the dollar amount of a trade into the box on the computer screen reserved for the number of shares to be sold, and then transmitting the incorrect trade to the stock exchange's computer.

8. At Baltimore Company, clerks in the cash applications area of the accounts receivable office open mail containing checks from customers.

They prepare a remittance advice (RA) containing the customer number, invoice numbers, amount owed, amount paid, and check number. Once prepared, the RAs are sent to a clerk who keys them into an on-line computer terminal. The accounts receivable manager has been complaining that the RA entry process is slow and error-prone.

9. Stoughton Company enters shipping notices in batches. Upon entry, the computer performs certain edits to eliminate those notices that have errors. As a result, many actual shipments never get recorded.

10. A computer hacker gained access to the computer system of Big Bucks Bank and entered an event to transfer funds to his bank account in Switzerland.

P 9-4 The following is a list of 12 controls from Chapter 9:

Controls

A. Limit checks

B. Tickler files

C. Public-key cryptography

D. Written approvals

E. Batch sequence check

F. Document/record counts

G. One-for-one checking

H. Hash totals (for a batch)

I. Turnaround documents

J. Procedures for resolving discrepancies

K. Digital signatures

L. Interactive feedback checks

Listed below are 10 definitions or descriptions. List the numbers 1 through 10 on your solution sheet. Next to each number, insert the *capital* letter from the previous list for the term that *best* matches the definition. A letter should be used only once, with two letters left over.

Definitions or Descriptions

1. A business process control plan that implements the *pervasive* control (see Chapter 8) of general or specific authorization.

2. Ensures that transmitted messages can be read only by authorized receivers.

3. A control plan that cannot be implemented unless source documents are pre-numbered.

4. In systems where accountable documents are not used, this control plan helps assure input completeness by informing the data entry person that events have been accepted by the computer system.

5. Used to detect changes in batches of events to ensure the validity, completeness, and accuracy of the batch.

6. Used to determine that a message has not been altered and has actually been sent by the person claiming to have sent the message.

7. Data related to open sales orders is periodically reviewed to ensure the timely shipment of goods.

8. Sales orders are compared to packing slips and the goods to determine that what was ordered is what is about to be shipped.

9. A system output becomes an input source in a *subsequent* event.

10. A type of programmed edit that is synonymous with a reasonableness test.

P 9-5 Big Al's Drive-In is a very popular restaurant located in Brunswick, Maine. Customers come from all over to savor Big Al's seafood delicates. There is no inside seating area, rather, customers eat their food in their cars. Here is how the business works: A customer drives into a parking spot and orders a meal from a touch-screen pad. For instance, a customer will press a button labeled "Scallop Dinner," the computer then asks "How Many" and the customer presses the "1" key to indicate that he or she wants only one dinner. The same process is used for each menu item selected. When the customer finishes ordering, he or she presses a button labeled "Done Ordering." The order shows up on a computer screen inside the restaurant where cooks prepare the meal. When the order is ready, an attendant brings the tray of food and drinks to the car and places it near the driver's window. Once the customer is finished eating (after, perhaps, ordering more food, drinks, and dessert!), they request a bill on the touch pad and the bill prints out on a small printer located below the touch pad. The customer can either pay the bill on-site with a credit card (the reader is located near the touch pad) or the attendant can collect cash payments. Once paid, the printer leaves a receipt with the customer.

Big Al has been having problems lately and is asking you for advice. First, some customers are simply driving off without paying. Also, Big Al suspects that some attendants are letting their friends eat free. Another problem is that when a customer presses "Done Ordering" but later orders a second round of food, the computer system treats this as two orders—each which must be paid separately. Customers are not at all happy with this situation—particularly when they order many times. Finally, Big Al has been experiencing a growing problem with "order changes." For example, say that a customer orders a lobster roll from the touch pad. When the order arrives, the customer swears that he did not order a lobster roll; rather, he ordered a cheeseburger. Currently, the attendant takes back the lobster roll and the cook prepares a cheeseburger instead. The lobster roll disappears (mysteriously). This repudiation problem is getting worse.

Required:

a. Draw a systems flowchart. Make reasonable assumptions where necessary.

b. Prepare a control matrix, including explanations of how each recommended control plan helps to accomplish—or would accomplish in the case of missing plans—each related control goal. Your choice of recommended control plans should come from Exhibits 9.2, 9.3, or 9.4 as appropriate. Be sure to tailor the matrix columns to conform to the specifics of Big Al's Drive-In. In doing so, assume the following operations process goal:

   • To provide timely service to customers.

c. Annotate the systems flowchart prepared in requirement (a) to show the location of each control plan listed in the control matrix.

d. Discuss the nature of the repudiation problem described by Big Al, and explain fully how your recommended control plan would help to assure non-repudiation.

P 9-6 Figure 9.13 is a systems flowchart for the first few steps in an order entry process. Some, but not all, of the controls have been annotated on the flowchart. Figure 9.14 (page 344) is a partially completed control matrix for the system in Figure 9.13. Some controls are not on the matrix at all. For some controls not all of the cells have been completed. Exhibit 9.6 (page 345) is a partially completed set of explanations of the cell entries in Figure 9.14.

Figure 9.13 Flowchart to Accompany Problem 9-6

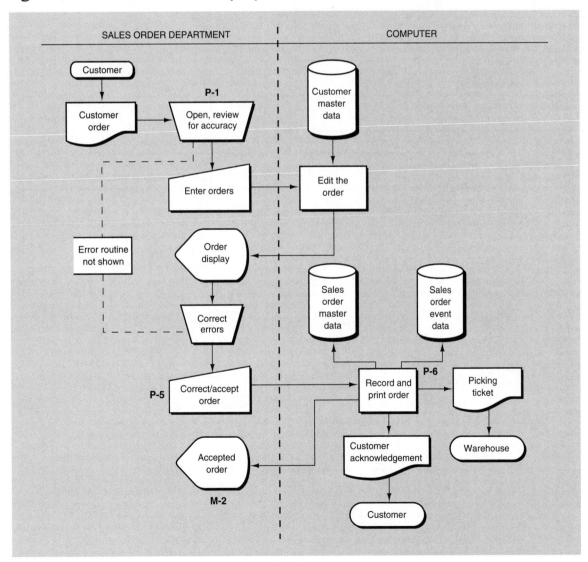

Figure 9.14 Control Matrix for Figure 9.13 to Accompany Problem 9-6

Recommended Control Plans	Control Goals of the Order Entry Business Process								
	Control Goals of the Operations Process			Control Goals of the Information Process				
	Ensure effectiveness of operations		Ensure efficient employment of resources (people, computers)	Ensure security of resources (inventory, customer data)	For the sales order inputs, ensure:			For the sales order master data, ensure:	
	A	B			IV	IC	IA	UC	UA
Present Controls									
P-1: Review document for accuracy									
P-4: Procedures for rejected input									
P-5: Key corrections							P-5		
P-6: Record input	P-6	P-6	P-6						
P-7: Interactive feedback checks									
Missing Controls									
M-2: Manual reconciliation of batch totals				M-2	M-2	M-2	M-2	M-2	M-2

Legend:

Effectiveness goals:
A = Provide timely acknowledgement of customer orders.
B = Provide timely shipment of goods to customers.

IV = Input validity
IC = Input completeness
IA = Input accuracy
UC = Update completeness
UA = Update accuracy

See Exhibit 9.6 (page 345) for a complete explanation of control plans and cell entries.

Required:

a. Annotate the flowchart to indicate additional present and missing controls. (Some controls that are on the matrix are not annotated on the flowchart. Others are missing from both the flowchart and the matrix.)

b. Complete the control matrix by adding new controls (ones you added to the flowchart, or ones that were on the flowchart but not on the matrix) and by adding cell entries to controls that are already on the matrix.

c. Complete the control explanations to reflect changes that you made to the flowchart and matrix.

Exhibit 9.6 Explanation of Cell Entries for Control Matrix
in Figure 9.14 to Accompany Problem 9-6

P-1: *Review document for accuracy.*

P-2: *Pre-formatted screens.*

Effectiveness goals A and B, Efficient employment of resources: By structuring the data entry process, automatically populating fields, and by preventing errors, pre-formatted screens simplify data input and save time (*Effectiveness goals A and B*) allowing a user to input more data over a period of time (*Efficiency*).

Input accuracy: As each data field is completed on a pre-formatted screen, the cursor moves to the next field on the screen, thus preventing the user from omitting any required data set. The data for fields that are automatically populated need not be manually entered, thus reducing input errors. Incorrectly formatted fields are rejected.

P-4: *Procedures for rejected inputs.*

P-5: *Key corrections.*

P-6: *Record input.*

Effectiveness goal A, Efficient employment of resources: Automatic recording of input event data is fast and reliable.

P-7: *Interactive feedback checks.*

M-2: *Manually reconcile batch totals.*

Security of resources: Agreement of the batch totals at this point would ensure that only valid source documents have been input and that invalid picking tickets have not been sent to the warehouse leading to inappropriate shipments of inventory.

Input validity, Input completeness, Input accuracy: Agreement of the batch totals at this point would ensure that only valid source documents comprising the original batch have been input (*input validity*), that all source documents were input (*input completeness*), and that data elements appearing on the source documents have been input correctly (*input accuracy*).

Update completeness, Update accuracy: Reconciliation of batch totals from before input to those after update would ensure complete and accurate update of master data.

KEY TERMS

control matrix

document design

written approvals

preformatted screens

online prompting

programmed edit checks

reasonableness checks

limit checks

document/record hash totals

mathematical accuracy checks

check digit verification

procedures for rejected inputs

interactive feedback checks

record input

key verification

digital signature

populate inputs with master data

compare input data with master data

exception and summary report

batch control plans

document/record counts

item or line counts

dollar totals

hash totals

turnaround documents

sequence check

batch sequence check

cumulative sequence check

manual reconciliation of batch totals

computer agreement of batch totals

agreement of run-to-run totals

tickler file

one-for-one checking

data encryption

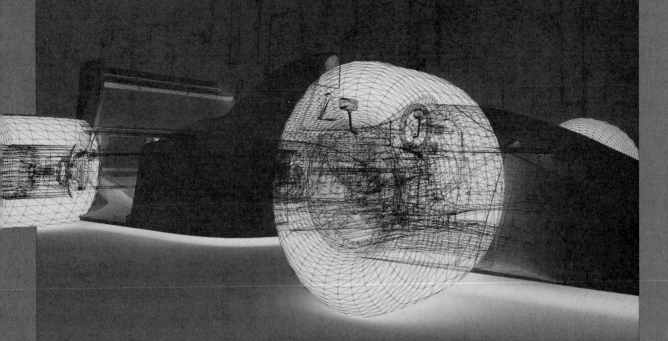

Business Processes

Part Four

The Order Entry/ Sales (OE/S) Process

chapter

10

Boise Office Solutions sells office products, furniture, technology, and services to businesses. It was one of the first companies in the industry to take orders over the Web and by late 1999, it was still a major player in the B2B marketplace. However, the industry was rapidly changing. Superstores such as Staples and industry consolidation had made office products a commodity. Margins and service differences between competitors were diminishing. Boise believed that it needed to give its customers a good reason to choose Boise. Consequently, it embarked on a multiyear, $25 million project to understand its customers better than anyone else and personalize customer service. This, it thought, would allow the company to differentiate itself from its competitors, and charge a premium for its products and services.

In the course of the project Boise discovered, for example, that some of its customers interacted with them 400,000 times per year! And, as the company developed a customer touchpoint map detailing how its customers contact Boise, it learned that customers were using many contact routes. Common methods included calling a sales representative, calling a customer service representative, accepting a delivery from one of its drivers, and ordering products online or via fax.

Once its customer profiles had been identified, Boise reengineered its customer sales and service processes and consolidated separate business units. Customers were given a 10-digit personal identification number that they used for any interaction with Boise. This allowed Boise to offer a personalized service to every customer.

The project led to savings of $3.5 million annually while at the same time increasing customer retention. Overall gross margins increased, the least profitable (yet very large) customer was eliminated, and Boise won a price increase from Boeing, one of their least-profitable customers.[1]

Learning Objectives

- To understand the relationship between the OE/S process and its business environment.

- To appreciate the potential of the OE/S process to assist management decision making.

- To become familiar with technologies commonly used in contemporary implementations for the OE/S process.

- To demonstrate how the integration provided by enterprise systems and electronic commerce add-ons can improve effectiveness and efficiency of the OE/S process.

- To achieve a reasonable level of understanding of the OE/S process' logical and physical characteristics.

- To know the OE/S operations process and information process control goals and to recognize the significance of some business process control plans commonly used to control those processes.

[1] Alice Dragoon, "This Changes Everything," *Darwin Magazine*, http://www.darwinmag.com, March 2002; Christopher Milliken, "A CRM Success Story," *CIO Magazine*, http://www.cio.com, November 1, 2002.

In this chapter, we spotlight one business process, the order entry/sales (OE/S) process. We will describe the various users of the OE/S process, each having their own view of the enterprise system and enterprise database. In addition, we will analyze the process controls related to the OE/S process.

SYNOPSIS

In business process analysis and design, we must carefully consider the business process as a whole—including all the interrelated parts that work toward the common purpose of meeting business process requirements. We follow this model in examining each of the business processes that enable organizations to successfully achieve their organizational goals. Accordingly, Chapters 10 through 15 will explore topics from the following possibilities:

- Process definition and functions.
- Organizational setting of the process.
- E-Business technology used to implement the process.   **E-BUSINESS**
- Enterprise system integration of related process activities.
- Decision making supported by the information system.   **ENTERPRISE SYSTEMS**
- Logical process features.
- Logical database design.
- Physical process features.
- Control analysis applied to the process (including an examination of process goals).   **CONTROLS**

INTRODUCTION

The order entry/sales (OE/S) process includes the first four steps in the order-to-cash process in Figure 2.7 (page 60), pre-sales activities, sales order processing, picking and packing the goods, and shipping. The last two steps in Figure 2.7, billing and processing the customer payment, are described in Chapter 11, the billing/accounts receivable/cash receipts process.

Examination of the OE/S process is an important part of your study of AIS. As noted in Chapter 1, we want you to understand both the *operations process* and *information process* functions of each business process. The operational aspects of the OE/S process are critical to the success—in fact the very survival—of businesses today and in the future. Indeed, many organizations, such as Boise Office Solutions, focus the bulk of their strategic information systems investment on supporting OE/S process effectiveness. Customers want to be able to place their orders quickly and easily. They want immediate pricing and material availability information. They expect convenient and timely access to information about their order from order initiation, through product delivery, and until after the bill has been paid! This is why later sections of the chapter discuss the vital topics of *decision making*, satisfying customer needs, employing technology to gain competitive advantage, and other issues that transcend the mere processing of accounting entries.

PROCESS DEFINITION AND FUNCTIONS

The **order entry/sales (OE/S) process** reflects an interacting structure of people, equipment, methods, and controls that is designed to achieve certain goals. The primary function of the OE/S process is to create information flows that support the following:

1. Repetitive work routines of the sales order department, the credit department, and the shipping department.[2]

2. Decision needs of those who manage various sales and marketing functions.

Let's take a few minutes to examine each of these functions. First, the OE/S process supports the repetitive work routines of the sales order, credit, and shipping departments by capturing and recording sales-related data. For example, a sales order form (whether paper or electronic) often supports the repetitive work routines of the sales order department by capturing vital customer and order data, by facilitating the process of granting credit to customers, and by helping to ensure the timely shipment of goods to customers. To further illustrate this point, we can consider that a copy of a sales order may serve as a communications medium to inform workers in the warehouse that certain goods need to be picked and transported to the shipping department. Additional discussions and illustrations of this function will be provided throughout the chapter.

Second, the OE/S process supports the decision needs of various sales and marketing managers. Obviously, in addition to these managers, any number of people within a given organization may benefit from information generated by the OE/S process. Later chapter sections discuss the relationship between the OE/S process and managerial decision making and provide some examples of related information that might facilitate decision making.

---

[2] To focus our discussion, we have assumed that these departments are the primary ones related to the OE/S process. For a given organization, however, the departments associated with the OE/S process may differ.

ORGANIZATIONAL SETTING

In this section, we take both a horizontal and vertical view of how the OE/S process fits into the organizational setting of a company. The horizontal perspective will enhance your appreciation of how the OE/S process relates to the repetitive work routines of the sales order, credit, and shipping departments. Conversely, the vertical perspective will sharpen your understanding of how the OE/S process relates to managerial decision making within the marketing function.

A Horizontal Perspective

Figure 10.1 (page 352) and Table 10.1 (page 353) present a horizontal view of the relationship between the OE/S process and its organizational environment. The figure shows the various information flows generated or captured through the OE/S process. The information flows are superimposed onto the organizational structures that house the departments. The figure also illustrates the multiple entities with which the OE/S process interacts (customers, carriers, other business processes, and so forth).

As you examine this figure and the number of interacting organizational units, consider again the discussion of *value chain* in Chapter 2. The ultimate goal of the activities depicted in Figure 10.1 is to create value for the customer. Organizations often assign an owner to this process (often called the order fulfillment process) to coordinate the activities to ensure that customer value expectations are met. The order fulfillment process owner must balance the goals of making goods available in a timely manner with the goal of maximizing profit. To do so, the process owner must ensure, for example, that just enough inventory is carried to meet expected demand; that customer orders are relayed accurately and promptly; and that customers receive the right goods in the right condition, on time, and at the expected price.

Figure 10.1 reveals nine information flows that function as vital communications links among the various operations departments. The information flows also connect those departments with the entities residing in the relevant environment of the OE/S process.

For example, the first information flow apprises representatives in the sales order department of a customer request for goods. This information flow might take the physical form of a telephone call, an entry on a Web site, or a faxed or mailed *customer order*. In turn, flow 5 informs workers in the shipping department of a pending sale; this communication facilitates the operational planning and related activities associated with the shipping function. This information flow might take the form of a copy of a *sales order* or it might be an electronic image appearing on a computer workstation located in the shipping department. Take some time now to review the remaining information flows.

A Vertical Perspective

To understand the relationship between the OE/S process and managerial decision making, you need to become familiar with the key players involved in the marketing function. Figure 10.2 (page 353) presents these players in the form of an organization chart. Take some time now to study the chart.

As the figure illustrates, sales-related data are captured in the sales order department and then flow vertically (in a summarized format) to managers housed within the marketing organizational structure. Much of this information was traditionally based on sales-related events and was captured through the use of a sales order form or through

Figure 10.1 A Horizontal Perspective of the OE/S Process

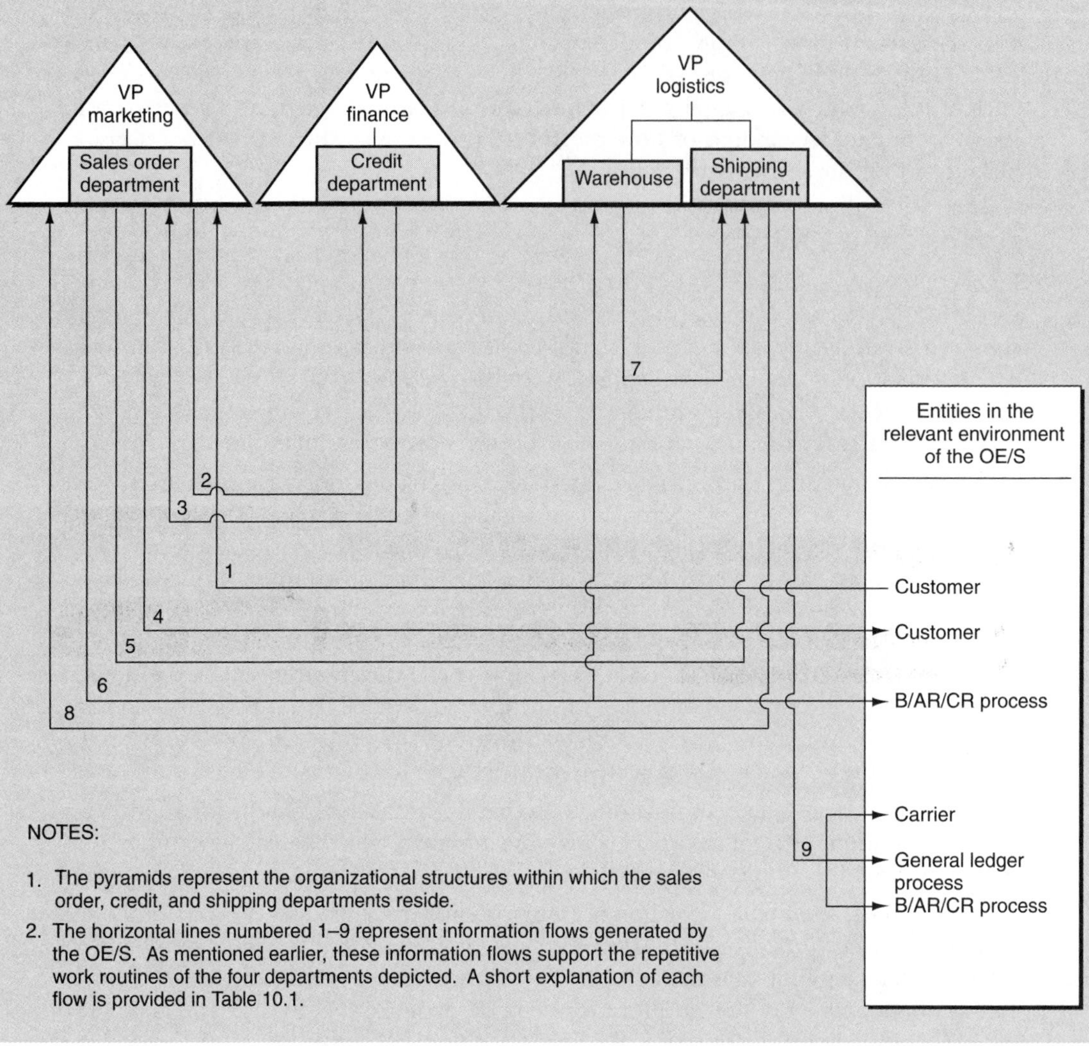

NOTES:

1. The pyramids represent the organizational structures within which the sales order, credit, and shipping departments reside.

2. The horizontal lines numbered 1–9 represent information flows generated by the OE/S. As mentioned earlier, these information flows support the repetitive work routines of the four departments depicted. A short explanation of each flow is provided in Table 10.1.

entry of data directly into a database. However, as organizations become increasingly focused on customers, the information needs for decision making are less accounting entry-oriented and more focused on customer characteristics, needs, and preferences as described for Boise Office Solutions. The next section provides an overview of the relationship between management decision making and the OE/S process, and how information technology facilitates the demands of decision makers.

MANAGING THE OE/S PROCESS: SATISFYING CUSTOMER NEEDS

In recent years, the print media has been glutted with articles stressing that the most critical success factor for businesses entering the new millennium is their ability to know

Table 10.1 Description of Horizontal Information Flows

Flow No.	Description
1	Customer places order.
2	Sales order department requests credit approval from credit department.
3	Credit department informs sales order department of disposition of credit request.
4	Sales order department acknowledges order to the customer.
5	Sales order department notifies shipping department of sales order.
6	Sales order department notifies warehouse and B/AR/CR process of shipment.
7	Warehouse sends completed picking ticket to shipping.
8	Shipping department informs sales order department of shipment.
9	Shipping department informs carrier, B/AR/CR process, and general ledger process of shipment.

Figure 10.2 A Vertical Perspective of the OE/S Process

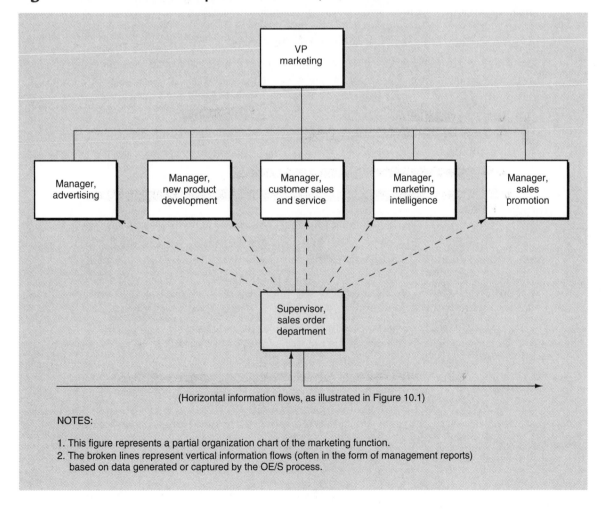

(Horizontal information flows, as illustrated in Figure 10.1)

NOTES:

1. This figure represents a partial organization chart of the marketing function.
2. The broken lines represent vertical information flows (often in the form of management reports) based on data generated or captured by the OE/S process.

their customers better and, armed with such knowledge, to serve their customers better than their competition. With companies facing increasing global competition, a new emphasis on satisfying customer needs has emerged. To effectively compete, firms must improve the quality of their service to customers. Firms are recognizing that their most important asset—one that is not capitalized on the balance sheet—is a happy customer. A satisfied customer tends to remain a customer, and it is less costly to retain existing customers than to attract new ones. Certainly, efforts to form closer partnerships with customers would top the priority list of several of the marketing managers shown in Figure 10.2.

ENTERPRISE SYSTEMS

What does this situation mean for the OE/S process? Most importantly, it has expanded the type and amount of data collected by the OE/S process regarding a firm's customer population. To respond to the increasing information demand, many organizations have developed a separate marketing information system to assist decision making in the marketing function. These are often tightly coupled with the information systems supporting the OE/S process. For companies using *enterprise systems, customer relationship management (CRM) systems* often share the same underlying database (a topic we will explore in greater detail shortly). The focus of these new systems is generally on replacing mass marketing or segmented marketing strategies with approaches that use new and more powerful computing resources to zero in on increasingly smaller portions of the customer population, with the ultimate aim being to concentrate on the smallest component of that population—the individual consumer.

Decision Making and Kinds of Decisions

Now let's look at one brief example of the decisions that marketing managers must confront. Put yourself in the position of the advertising manager shown in Figure 10.2 (page 353). A few representative questions for which you might need answers are

- Where is sales volume (quantity and dollars) concentrated?
- Who are the specific major customers (by sales and by profitability), both present and potential?
- What opportunities exist to sell after-sales services?
- What types of advertising and promotions have the greatest influence on customers?

Could the information system help you to obtain the answers? Certainly, at least to the extent that it has captured and stored historical data related to sales events and hopefully through additional customer information stores. To answer the first question, you might find a sales report by region helpful. A sales report by customer could provide *some* answers to the second question. An organization's own sales database should provide answers to the third question.

Where might you find answers to questions like the fourth one? It depends. If you want to know which advertising and promotions have had an impact on your own customers, you would need to gather that data as sales take place. Otherwise, you would need to use census reports, market research questionnaires, and trade journals. Also, research houses garner vast amounts of information from public records—drivers' licenses, automobile registrations, tax rolls, mortgage registrations, and the like—and sell that information to other companies. In certain industries, the mechanisms to collect data regarding customers, their buying habits, and other demographics have become quite sophisticated. Recent advances in database management systems and the underlying technologies are leading to a focus on the use of *data warehousing* and *data mining* techniques (as discussed in Chapter 5) to support marketing analysis. Let us take a closer look at some of the key technologies supporting these efforts.

Using Data Mining to Support Marketing

Data warehousing applications in organizations are usually viewed as being focused on either operational or analytical applications. Operational applications focus on providing decision makers with the information they need to monitor and control their organization. Analytical applications, which include *data mining*, are intended to allow the use of sophisticated statistical and other analytical software to help an organization's members develop insights about customers, processes, and markets.[3] Two analytical applications are discussed in Technology Application 10.1.

ENTERPRISE SYSTEMS

Data warehousing can be a massive effort for a company. For instance, Home Depot Inc. has planned a 60-terabyte Web-accessible data warehouse that will cost tens of millions of dollars to implement.[4] For many companies, such integration of corporate-wide data is a taxing process that requires several years of development. This complexity is raised as companies increasingly focus on using the data warehousing tools in contemporary ERP systems to merge the data captured through ERP processing with other types of data desired in a data warehouse. Thus, many companies that desire the

ENTERPRISE SYSTEMS

Technology Application 10.1

Applications of Data Mining

Case 1

National Australia Bank recently implemented data mining tools from the SAS Institute to aid in the area of predictive marketing. The tools are used to extract and analyze data in the bank's Oracle database. Specific applications focus on assessing how competitors' initiatives are impacting the bank's bottom line. The data mining tools are used to generate market analysis models from disaggregated historical data recorded in event-level form. The addition of data mining tools is one more step in a strategic set of initiatives focusing on the development of a comprehensive data warehouse. National Australia Bank considers the data warehousing initiatives to be crucial to maintaining an edge in the increasingly competitive financial services marketplace.

Case 2

digiMine Inc. installs software on customer databases, collects data, encrypts it, and transfers it to its data center. There it cleans the data, installs it in a secure data warehouse, and uses a set of proprietary algorithms to analyze the data. digiMine reports will tell its customers what works and doesn't work on its Web sites and can forecast future customer moves. The reports also can tell how many visitors are repeat users or are new, and how much time users spend on the site. They also can report what activities a particular customer segment is using on the site.

Sources: Iain Ferguson, "Data Mining Lifts Competitive Edge," *Computerworld* (February 6, 1998): 18; Nicole Harris, "Data-Mining Company Helps Business Analyze Customers," *The Wall Street Journal* (August 9, 2001): B10.

---

[3] Shaku Atre, "Defining Your Warehouse Goals," *Computerworld* (January 30, 1998): 35.

[4] Marc L. Songini, "Home Depot's Next IT Project: Data Warehouse," *Computerworld* (October 7, 2002): 1, 16.

availability of detailed marketing data will resort to *data marts*, which are subsets of an overall warehouse and are customized for a specific department. **Data marts** are designed to provide detailed data for a specific set of users while avoiding the costly development and extensive time delays that come from the development of a comprehensive *data warehouse*.

E-BUSINESS   Once the marketing department is armed with this massive array of data from which customer buying habits, characteristics, and addresses can be analyzed and linked, extensive study can be undertaken. Researchers armed with *neural networks* (as discussed in Chapter 5), comprehensive statistical analysis packages, and graphical presentation software can rapidly begin to develop insights about relationships within the marketing information. Finally, Technology Application 10.2 describes how companies can obtain assistance, over the Internet, from vendors providing data warehousing and data mining services.

Technology Application 10.2

Web-based Smart Pricing

How does your local department store decide when to reduce the price of swimsuits? Does the answer to that question differ in various parts of a country and the world? The answer to the first question is often not clear and the answer to the second is certainly! Sometimes companies make pricing decisions by looking at the cost of an item (and then applying some multiplier or margin requirement) or by using their gut feeling or experience. This often leads to under- and overpricing, lost sales, and lost profit. But, help is on the way from a variety of vendors who are using *data warehousing, data mining, data marts*, and some Web-based tools to take the guess work out of pricing.

These tools analyze data about orders, promotions, product revenues, and inventory balances to dynamically suggest optimal prices. For example, prices can be reduced for swimsuits sold in the northeast United States in August, when historical data indicates that sales decline, and held at full price in the southern United States throughout the year.

Prices for these tools start at $3 million for licensing fees, services, and training. Typically, these tools consist of modules that may be connected to data warehouse and legacy systems to analyze historical sales volume (POS for retail sales), pricing, promotions, and product mix. Combining this with price history of competitors, these tools provide a picture of price sensitivity on each item sold (each SKU), factoring in seasonality and sales locations. Some modules can analyze customer responses to price changes, promotion, etc. Others can provide support for testing of pricing and promotions.

Hewlett-Packard has used these tools to decide when to discount the price of an aging line of servers as they introduce a replacement for that line. General Electric uses 300 factors to respond to 55,000 annual pricing requests to reduce the quote process from 30 days to 6 hours. DHL used Web software to test prices in 43 worldwide markets. With more competitive pricing DHL increased cold-caller revenue by over 13 percent by turning 25 percent (versus 17 percent) of callers into customers. Oh, and the retailers? JCPenney Co. increased quarterly revenue on markdowns by $15 to $20 million. Dillard's Inc. saw a 5 to 6 percent increase in gross margins. And, The Casual Male increased the gross margin on discounts by 25 percent.

Sources: Faith Keenan, "The Price Is Really Right," *BusinessWeek* (March 31, 2003): 18; http://www.demandtec.com, July 2003; http://www.profitlogic.com, July 2003; http://www.zilliant.com, July 2003.

Mastering Global E-Business

E-Business systems can be used to penetrate global markets by allowing trading partners **E-BUSINESS** and customers to easily process international orders without a physical presence. E-Business systems are broken into two categories: buy-side and sell-side.[5]

Buy-side systems use the Internet to automate and manage corporate vendors and purchases. The predominant technology in this area is *electronic data interchange (EDI)*. A variety of software solutions are available that can take a company's business information transmitted over the Internet and convert it into EDI format. Likewise, when EDI information is transmitted to the company, the software translates the EDI format into an Internet transmission form that provides compatible business information for the organization's internal systems. Examples of other buy-side e-commerce software applications are supply chain management (allows an organization to manage the entire purchase-to-pay business cycle with worldwide trading partners), e-procurement (automates corporate purchasing), and e-sourcing (sets up auctions among various vendors for products and services).

Sell-side systems are designed to allow a company to market, sell, deliver, and service goods and services to customers throughout the world via the Internet. Sell-side applications can handle both B2B and B2C business transactions. For instance, sell-side applications can process many customer-related functions, such as browsing, sales, payments, support, and analytics. One facet of sell-side systems is known as *customer relationship management (CRM)* applications, as discussed later in this chapter. Other examples of sell-side applications include marketing management (used to manage campaigns and promotions), catalog management (allows a company to keep its catalog up-to-date), e-payment (designed to handle global credit authorizations and currency transactions), and order management (administers order information).

Technology Summary 10.1 (page 358) describes Web Services, a technology used to **ENTERPRISE** automate buy-side and sell-side enterprise applications. By combining *enterprise systems* **SYSTEMS** with buy-side and sell-side applications, an organization can seamlessly conduct e-business across the globe. We will discuss some of the systems described in this section in later chapters.

Customer Relationship Management (CRM) Systems

In Chapter 2 we introduced you to *customer relationship management (CRM)* software, **ENTERPRISE** along with related *customer self-service software*, and *sales force automation (SFA) soft-* **SYSTEMS** *ware*. Recall that CRM software is designed to manage all the data related to customers, such as marketing, field service, and contact management data. CRM has become the **CONTROLS** focus of ERP vendors who realize the need to tap into this growing market and to integrate CRM data with the other data already residing within the ERP system's database.

The concept behind CRM is that better customer service means happier customers and yields greater sales—particularly repeat sales. Part of the service concept is field-service support and contact management. Contact management facilitates the recording and storing of information related to each contact a salesperson has with a client and the context of the conversation or meeting. Additionally, each time the client makes contact regarding queries or service help, this information also is recorded (field service records). The result is that a salesperson can review all the historical information

---

[5] F. Biscotti and R. Fulton, "Infrastructure and Applications Worldwide Software Market Definitions," *Gartner Dataquest* (June 2002).

Technology Summary 10.1

Web Services

Web Services is a process and set of protocols for directly connecting enterprise systems over the Internet. Earlier Web protocols that we now take for granted, such as HTTP (HyperText Transfer Protocol), FTP (File Transfer Protocol), and SMTP (Simple Mail Transfer Protocol), enabled early communication across the Web. Web Services goes one step further and enables communication between computer systems (e.g., enterprise system-to-enterprise system, software-to-software, computer application-to-computer application) without human intervention. Web Services is, then, a replacement for *EDI*. But, it is much more in that it is a protocol for interoperation of systems, not just communication between systems.

Web Services relies on three key underlying technologies. **Universal Description, Discovery, and Integration (UDDI)** is a protocol for registering a business in an Internet directory so that companies can find one another and carry out business over the Web. **Web Services De-** scription Language (WSDL) is an XML-based format for describing how one software system can connect and utilize the services of another software system over the Internet. **Simple Object Access Protocol (SOAP)** is an XML-based protocol for encoding Web Service messages. So, UDDI tells where you are and what you do, WSDL describes how two services (systems) can be connected, and SOAP describes a common language for two services to talk to each other.

XML (eXtensible Markup Language) is a generalized system for the customized tagging of data to enable the definition, transmission, and interpretation of data exchanged by systems over the Internet. As noted previously, WSDL and SOAP are applications of XML for Web Services. In Chapter 16, we describe another extension of XML, XBRL, a language for reporting business information, such as financial statements, over the Web.

Source: Frank P. Coyle, "Web Services, Simply Put," *Computerworld* (May 19, 2003): 38–39.

---

before calling on a customer and be better prepared to provide that customer with targeted products and services. These systems also support the recording of information about the customer contact such as spouse's name, children, hobbies, etc., that help facilitate the salesperson in making quality contact with the customer.

ENTERPRISE SYSTEMS   At the same time, the software supports the organizing and retrieving of information on historical sales activities and promotions planning. This facilitates the matching of sales promotions with customers' buying trends. This is a particularly crucial area for integration with any existing ERP system because much of the information necessary to support sales analyses comes from data captured during the recording of sales event data in the ERP system. The buzzword for this CRM application is "segmentation," the grouping of customers into categories based on key characteristics. These categories might represent customers likely to respond to a marketing campaign, high-end customers who should receive "high-touch" customer service, and low-end customers who should be directed to self-service options.

A third area that is prevalent in CRMs is support for customer service—particularly for phone operators handling customer support call-in centers. For many organizations, phone operators who have not had previous contact with the customer handle the bulk of customer service activities. The CRM quickly provides the phone operator with information on the customer's history and usually links the operator with a database of solutions for various problems about which a customer may be inquiring. These solutions may simply be warranty or contract information, or at a more complex level, solutions to operations or maintenance problems on machinery or equipment. All this information can be efficiently stored for quick retrieval by the system's user. Technology Application 10.3 describes the CRM software chosen to support the newly reengineered customer sales and service processes at Boise Office Solutions described at the beginning of this chapter.

LOGICAL DESCRIPTION OF THE OE/S PROCESS

Using data flow diagrams, this section provides a logical view of a typical OE/S process. Although the narrative highlights certain key points that you should discern from the diagrams, your study of Chapter 4 should have equipped you to glean much knowledge simply from a careful study of the diagrams themselves. We conclude the section with a description of the data created or used by the OE/S process.[6]

Logical Data Flow Diagrams

Our first view of the process is a general one. Figure 10.3 (page 360) portrays the OE/S process in the form of a *context diagram* and delineates the domain of our study. In

---

Technology Application 10.3

CRM at Boise Office Solutions

As noted at the beginning of this chapter, Boise Office Solutions sells office products, furniture, technology, and services to businesses. To address the increasingly competitive situation in its industry, Boise embarked on a project with the goal to provide its customers "with greater economic value." Once its needs had been identified and its customer sales and service processes reengineered, Boise implemented a customer relationship management (CRM) system. Boise chose a best-of-breed approach to acquiring CRM software. It chose, for example, separate vendors for the core CRM module, customer interaction, and marketing campaign management. The implementation included loading and cleansing 2.2 million customer records from multiple databases into the CRM software.

The CRM project led to savings of $3.5 million annually and an increase of customer retention. Gross margins were increased, the least-profitable (yet very large) customer was eliminated, and Boise won a price increase from Boeing, one of their least-profitable customers. How did it achieve this success, when up to 70 percent of CRM implementations fail? The company adopted a customer-centric culture and saw this project as a way to improve customer service, rather than as a technology solution. Its customer-centric focus included creating a single customer database that captured data from every customer touch point and by keeping track of customer likes and dislikes and responding to those preferences with customer service and tailored product offerings.

Sources: Alice Dragoon, "This Changes Everything," *Darwin Magazine*, http://www.darwinmag.com, March 2002; Christopher Milliken, "A CRM Success Story," *CIO Magazine*, http://www.cio.com, November 1, 2002.

---

[6] As we have indicated in earlier chapters, whenever we show data being stored in separate data stores, you should recognize that such data stores represent a process's view of data that in reality may reside in an *enterprise database*.

Figure 10.3 The OE/S Process—Context Diagram

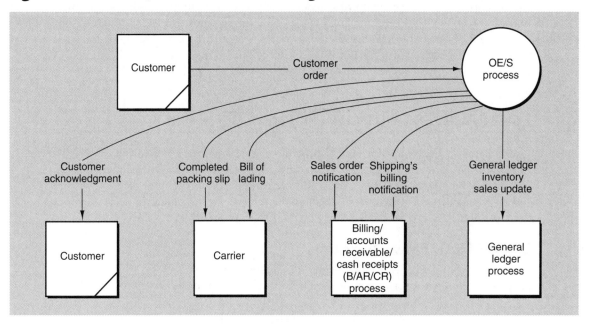

examining Figure 10.3, you should observe one input entering the process and six outputs emerging. Also notice the entities in the relevant environment with which the OE/S process interacts. Some of these entities reside outside the organization (Customer and Carrier), whereas one is internal to the organization but external to the OE/S process (the Billing/Accounts Receivable/Cash Receipts [B/AR/CR] process).[7]

Notice that this process begins after the "Pre-sales activities" depicted in Figure 2.7 (page 60). Those activities would include such things as salespersons contacting customers and recording information about that contact in the *CRM system*, customer inquiries regarding price and availability of goods, customer formal request for a quote (RFQ), and responses to those with a quotation. The customer order entering our process indicates that a customer has decided to place an order.

Figure 10.4 presents a *level 0 diagram* of the OE/S process. In examining the figure, observe that the inputs and outputs are identical to those presented in Figure 10.3. Recall that this *balancing* of inputs and outputs is an important convention to observe when constructing a set of data flow diagrams. The single bubble in Figure 10.3 has been divided into three bubbles in Figure 10.4, one for each of the three major processes performed by the OE/S process.[8] Additional data flows connecting the newly partitioned bubbles appear, as do the data stores used to store various sets of data. Take some time now to study the data flows, processes, and data stores shown in Figure 10.4.[9]

Each of the three processes shown in Figure 10.4 will now be decomposed (that is, "exploded") into lower-level diagrams. Figure 10.5 (page 362) decomposes bubble 1.0

---

[7] The slash on the lower right corner of the Customer entity square indicates that there is another occurrence of this entity on the diagram.

[8] To focus our discussion, we have assumed that the OE/S process performs three major processes. A given process, however, may perform more or fewer processes than we have chosen to illustrate here.

[9] The line enclosing the right side of the Sales order master data indicates that there is another occurrence of that data store on the diagram.

Figure 10.4 The OE/S Process—Level 0 Diagram

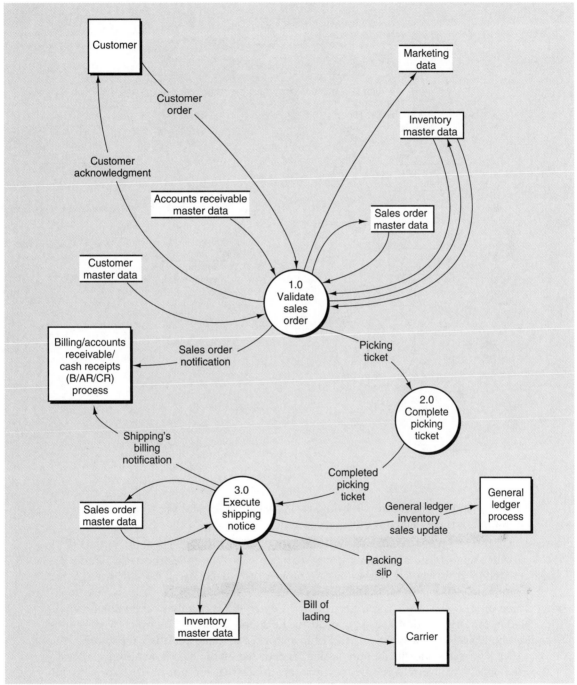

of Figure 10.4. Notice, first, that the inputs and outputs in this figure do not match those for bubble 1.0 in Figure 10.4. We see here the convention, first mentioned in Chapter 4, of showing *reject stubs* only below level 0 DFDs. Therefore, the three flows

Figure 10.5 The OE/S Process—Diagram 1

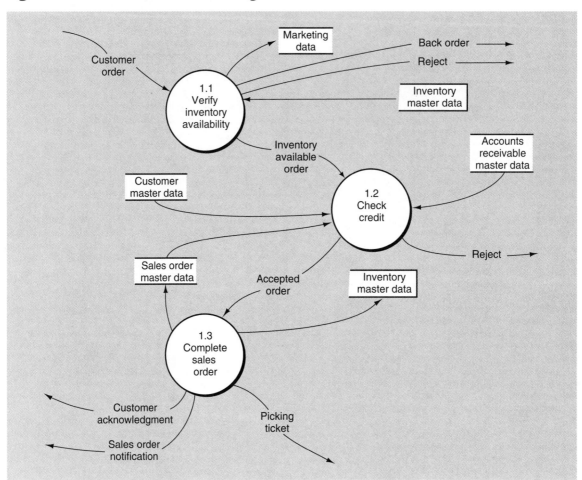

seen here and not in Figure 10.4 (i.e., two "Reject" stubs and the flow "Back order") do not make these diagrams out of balance.

ENTERPRISE
SYSTEMS

Customer order is the *trigger* that initiates process 1.1.[10] How does the OE/S process then validate a customer order? First, process 1.1 verifies the availability of requested inventory by consulting the inventory master data. Recall from Chapter 2 that determining inventory availability—"available to promise (ATP)"—can be a complicated process that would be facilitated by an *enterprise system* that can look worldwide within the organization and up and down the supply chain to determine when goods can be delivered. If a sufficient level of inventory is on hand to satisfy the request, the order is forwarded for further processing, as depicted by the data flow "Inventory available order." Conversely, if a customer orders goods that are not in stock, process 1.1 runs a special back order routine. This routine determines the inventory requirement necessary to satisfy the order and then sends the back order request to the purchasing department. This activity is depicted by the "Back order" data flow, which in reality is a specific type of *exception routine* (i.e., a specific type of reject stub). Once the goods are

---

[10] We use the term *trigger* to refer to any data flow or event that causes a process to begin.

received, the order is routinely processed. If the customer refuses to accept a back order, then the sales event is terminated and the order is rejected, as shown by the "Reject" data flow. Information from the order (e.g., sale region, customer demographics, and order characteristics that reflect buying habits) that has potential value to marketing would be recorded in the marketing data store.

After assuring inventory availability, process 1.2 establishes the customer's existence and then approves credit. With an *enterprise system* one record should exist for each customer, wherever he or she is located and from whatever parts of the organization he or she makes purchases. This allows an organization to readily determine the amount of credit available to that customer worldwide. Without this central database a customer could incur multiple receivable balances that in total exceed an amount the selling organization considers desirable.

ENTERPRISE SYSTEMS

How does the process complete the sales order? First, process 1.3 receives an accepted order from process 1.2. It then completes the order by adding price information, which is ascertained from the inventory master data. As noted earlier, this could be a complicated calculation based on who and where the customer is and if the item is to be discounted. Then, process 1.3 performs the following activities simultaneously:[11]

- Updates the inventory master data to allocate the quantity ordered to the sales order.
- Updates the sales order master data to indicate that a completed sales order has been created.
- Disseminates the sales order.

The physical means used to disseminate the order may vary from using a multipart sales order form to using electronic images appearing on various computer screens (illustrated in Figure 10.6 on page 364) or as a record in a computer data store. Notice in Figure 10.6 the quantity and nature of information that is available in a sales order record. For example see the ship-to party and the delivering plant. Data on the shipping tab will suggest the route that should be taken between the plant and customer. The item quantity, item number, and description as well as the net value of the order are shown (the individual selling price is not shown in this view). Finally, we also can see that the terms of payment are also on this screen.

ENTERPRISE SYSTEMS

Regardless of the physical form used, we generally expect the dissemination to include the following data flows:

- A **picking ticket** authorizes the warehouse to "pick" the goods from the shelf and send them to shipping. The picking ticket identifies the goods to be picked and usually indicates the warehouse location.
- A **customer acknowledgment** is sent to the customer to notify him or her of the order's acceptance and the expected shipment date.
- A sales order notification is sent to the billing department to notify them of a pending shipment (this could take many forms including a message received on a computer screen or a report of pending shipments).

Figure 10.7 (page 364), a lower-level view of bubble 2.0 of Figure 10.4 (page 361), describes activities that normally take place in a warehouse. Warehouse personnel receive a picking ticket, locate the goods, take the goods off the shelf (i.e., "pick" the goods), and match the goods with the picking ticket.

---

[11] We say *simultaneously* when there is no reason, inherent in the logical process being performed, to preclude simultaneous activities.

Figure 10.6 SAP Sales Order Inquiry Screen

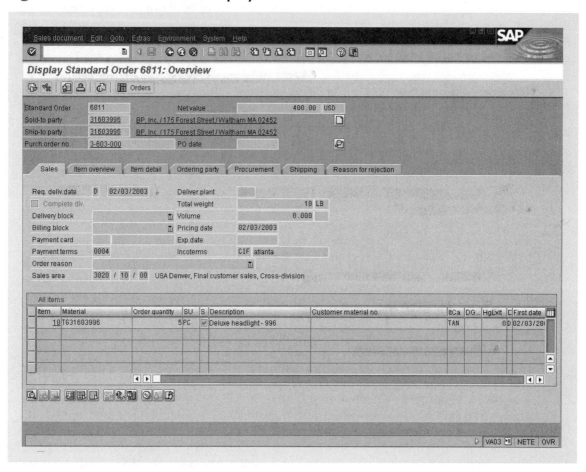

Source: Reprinted with permission from SAP.

Figure 10.7 The OE/S Process—Diagram 2

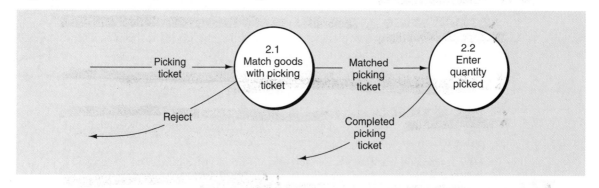

The reject stub coming from bubble 2.1 indicates at least two situations that might occur at this point. First, the goods pulled from the shelf might not be those indicated on the picking ticket (i.e., goods have been placed in the wrong warehouse location).

Second, sufficient goods may not exist to satisfy the quantity requested. The second situation may arise when goods have been misplaced or when the actual physical balance does not agree with the perpetual inventory balance indicated in the inventory data. These predicaments must be resolved and a back order routine may be initiated to order the missing goods for the customer.

In process 2.2, warehouse personnel write the quantities "picked" on the picking ticket (thus "completing" the ticket) and forward the picking ticket (along with the goods) to the shipping department.

Figure 10.8, a lower-level view of bubble 3.0 in Figure 10.4 (page 361), describes activities that normally take place in a shipping department. The figure tells us that process 3.1 receives two data flows; namely, the completed picking ticket from process 2.2 of Figure 10.7 and data retrieved from the sales order master data table. The shipping clerk would match the quantity of the goods, the quantity on the picking ticket, and the quantity stored in the sales order data store (i.e., the quantity ordered in Figure 10.7). If the details agree, the matched sales order is forwarded to process 3.2. If the details of the data flows do not agree, process 3.1 rejects the order and initiates procedures for resolving any discrepancies.

Figure 10.8 The OE/S Process—Diagram 3

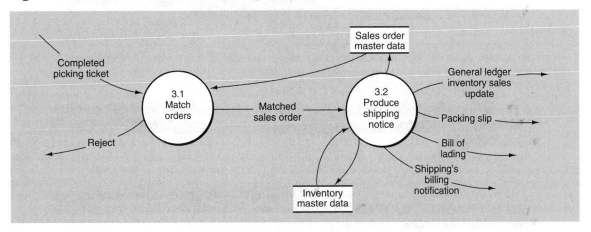

When process 3.2 receives a matched sales order from process 3.1, it produces and disseminates notices of the shipment and updates the sales order and inventory master data tables. The sales order master data is updated to reflect that the goods have been picked, packed, and shipped. The inventory master data is updated to change the quantity allocated for the sales order to an actual shipment, thus reducing the quantity of inventory on hand. We generally expect the dissemination of notices will include the following data flows:

- Shipping's billing notification (to notify billing to begin the billing process).

- **Bill of lading,** a contract between the shipper and the carrier in which the carrier agrees to transport the goods to the shipper's customer. The carrier's signature on the bill of lading, and/or the customer's signature on some other form of receipt, substantiates the shipment.

- A **packing slip** is attached to the outside of a package and identifies the customer and the contents of the package.
- General ledger inventory sales update to notify the general ledger process that inventory has been sold and the cost of goods sold has increased.

Logical Data Descriptions

Figure 10.4 (page 361) shows that the OE/S process employs the following five data stores:

- Marketing data
- Customer master data
- Inventory master data
- Accounts receivable master data
- Sales order master data

With the exception of the inventory and accounts receivable master data, the other three data stores are "owned" by the OE/S system, meaning that the OE/S system has the responsibility for performing *data maintenance* and *master data updates* on these data stores. This section discusses the purpose and contents of each of these three data stores.

Earlier, we noted that the *marketing data* is the repository of a variety of sales-oriented data, some of which result from recording sales events (i.e., processed sales orders) and some of which originate from activities that do not culminate in completed sales, such as pre-sales activities. Typically, these data include items discussed in an earlier section, such as economic forecasts, census reports, responses to market research questionnaires, customer buying habits, customer demographics, and the like. Collection and maintenance of these data are activities of the *CRM system*.

Customer master data includes data that identify the particular characteristics of each customer, such as name, address, telephone number, and so forth. It also stores various credit data. Although customer data may be altered directly, proper control techniques require that all such master data changes (i.e., *data maintenance*) be documented and approved, and that a report of all data changes be printed periodically.

As shown in the data flow diagrams, records in the **sales order master data** are created on completion of a sales order. Then, once the goods have been shipped, the sales order record is updated. See Figure 10.6 (page 364) for examples of the kinds of data stored. Depending on how the OE/S process is designed and how many updates take place during the process, the sales order master data may include the time and date of the picking, packing, and shipment of the goods and who completed each step.

Logical Database Design

In Chapter 5, we compared data as it would be stored in a file(s) with that same data when stored in a database, with emphasis on the relational database model (see in particular Figures 5.2 and 5.3 on pages 148 and 152, respectively). In this section, we will depict the relational tables for the data we have just mentioned in the discussion of the customer master data and the sales order master data.

To do so, we are well advised to first redraw the E-R diagram appearing in Figure 5.9 on page 168. Figure 10.9 is our new E-R diagram. It differs from Figure 5.9 in that the SALES event in Chapter 5 now has been divided into three events comprising the sale—namely, picking goods (STOCK PICK event in Figure 10.9), shipping goods (SHIPMENTS event), and billing the customer for the shipment (SALES INVOICES event).

Figure 10.9 Entity-Relationship (E-R) Diagram for the OE/S Process

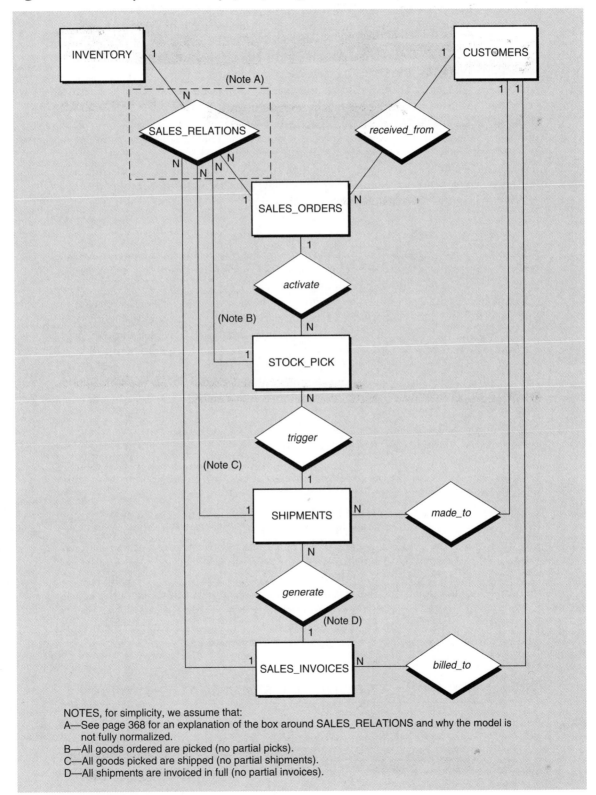

NOTES, for simplicity, we assume that:
A—See page 368 for an explanation of the box around SALES_RELATIONS and why the model is
   not fully normalized.
B—All goods ordered are picked (no partial picks).
C—All goods picked are shipped (no partial shipments).
D—All shipments are invoiced in full (no partial invoices).

Before proceeding, take some time to study Figure 10.9 and compare it to Figure 5.9. From Figure 10.9, we have developed the relational tables appearing in Figure 10.10.

Before going on we should note three things about these figures. First, you should observe that the SALES_RELATIONS relationship and table gradually accumulate a record of the events as they progress from a customer's order through to sending an invoice to the customer. The box around this relationship indicates that we will have a relation in our database for this relationship while the other relationships will not have a corresponding relation. Second, if you look carefully, you will see that some of the relationships, and attributes in the relations, really aren't needed. For example, we actually don't need the *activate* relationship, nor do we need the related sales order number in the STOCK_PICK relation; we can get that from SALES_RELATIONS. You see, this model is not fully normalized yet. We include the "extra" relationships and redundant attributes to help you see the logical sequence of events. Third, the notes on Figure 10.9 indicate that this is a simplified model. Certainly realistic models must deal with partial picking, shipping, and invoicing.

Compare the CUSTOMERS relation in Figure 10.10 with the discussion of the customer master data and observe that the data elements (attributes) are *essentially* the same. Note that the relation allows for both a customer address and "ship to" address, each being subdivided into four attributes—street address, city, state, and ZIP Code—to facilitate database inquiries using any of these attributes. Now compare the SALES_ORDERS and SALES_RELATIONS relations to the sales order in Figure 10.6 (page 364) and the discussion of the sales order master data. Here we see some marked differences. The two sales order tables contain far fewer data elements than the sales order display itself because many of the elements needed to complete the display are available from other relations. Recall that a major advantage of a database approach to data management is the elimination of redundant data items. Therefore, using the Cust_No from SALES_ORDERS, we can obtain the customer's name, address, ship-to name, ship-to address, and credit terms from the CUSTOMERS relation. Likewise, using Item_No from SALES_RELATIONS, we can obtain from the INVENTORY relation the description of the goods and unit selling price. Finally, using the primary key from SALES_RELATIONS (i.e., the *combination* of SO_No/Item_No), we can determine the quantity picked/shipped.

We believe that the remainder of Figure 10.10 needs no particular comment, except to note once again that many relations contain relatively few attributes because most of the data needed to complete a picking ticket or shipping notice reside in other relations. For example, an actual picking ticket often takes the physical form of a duplicate copy of the sales order document. The primary item that differentiates the two documents is the warehouse location, which must appear on the picking ticket to facilitate the actual picking of the goods. Once the goods are picked, the picking ticket *document* can be *completed* by adding the quantity picked, date picked, and identification of the person who picked the items, attributes that appear in the two relations.

ADVANCES IN ELECTRONIC COMMUNICATION

E-BUSINESS   Before describing a "typical" physical implementation of an OE/S process, two key technologies should be mentioned that enable modern sales order processes. Without a doubt, the key enabler of the transition from primarily *periodic mode* systems to primarily *immediate mode* systems required for the OE/S process has been electronic

Figure 10.10 Selected Relational Tables (*Partial*) for the OE/S Process

Shaded_Attribute(s) = Primary Key

CUSTOMERS

Cust_No	Cust_Name	Cust_Street	Cust_City	Cust_State	Cust_ZIP	Ship_to_Name	Ship_to_Street	Ship_to_City	Ship_to_State	Ship_to_ZIP	Credit_Limit	Last_Revised	Credit_Terms
1234	Acme Co.	175 Fifth St	Beaufort	SC	29902	Same	Same	Same	Same	Same	5000	20060101	2/10,n/30
1235	Robbins, Inc	220 North Rd	Columbia	SC	29801	Aline Fabric	2 Main St	Greenwood	SC	29845	10000	20070915	n/60
1236	Jazzy Corp.	45 Ocean Dr	Hilton Hd	SC	29910	Same	Same	Same	Same	Same	0	20070610	COD

SALES_ORDERS

SO_No	SO_Date	Cust_No	Cust_PO_No	Cust_PO_Date	Ship_Via	FOB_Terms
5677	20071216	1235	41523	20071212	UPS	Ship Pt
5678	20071216	1276	A1190	20071214	Best way	Ship Pt
5679	20071216	1236	9422	20071216	Fed Ex	Destin

STOCK_PICK

Pick_No	Pick_Date	Picked_By	SO_No	Ship_No
9436	20071215	Butch	5676	94101
9437	20071215	Rachel	5677	94102
9438	20071216	Ace	5678	94103

INVENTORY

Item_No	Item_Name	Price	Location	Qty_on_Hand	Reorder_Pt
936	Machine Plates	39.50	Macomb	1,500	950
1001	Gaskets	9.50	Macomb	10,002	3,500
1010	Crank Shafts	115.00	Tampa	952	500
1025	Manifolds	45.00	Tampa	402	400

SHIPMENTS

Ship_No	Ship_Date	Shipped_By	Cust_No	Invoice_No
94101	20071215	Jason	1293	964
94102	20071216	Carol	1235	965
94103	20071216	Jason	1249	966

SALES_INVOICES

Invoice_No	Invoice_Date	Invoice_Total	Cust_No
964	20071216	549.00	1293
965	20071216	9575.00	1235
966	20071217	1580.00	1249

SALES_RELATIONS

SO_No	Item_No	Qty_Ordered	Pick_No	Qty_Picked	Ship_No	Qty_Shipped	Invoice_No	Qty_Invoiced	Amt_Invoiced
5676	1074	60	9436	60	94101	60	964	60	549.00
5677	1001	100	9437	100	94102	100	965	100	950.00
5677	1010	75	9437	75	94102	75	965	75	8625.00
5678	936	40	9438	40	94103	40	966	40	1580.00

communications technology. The most important advancements have largely been in the area of image-based technologies. These technological advances are discussed in this section.

Contemporary electronic communications-based systems that facilitate the processing, storage, and management of image-based data require the use of different types of related technologies that facilitate the effective capturing of data to support business information processing through the use of imaging technology.

Automated Data Entry

CONTROLS   While a variety of methods exist for electronic data capturing, the interest here is in image-based technologies used to electronically capture data. Increasingly, optical-based technologies are being used to eliminate the need to key data (a major source of data entry error) and to eliminate voluminous files of paper documents by maintaining electronic copies.

E-BUSINESS   The most common technology is probably that of bar coding. **Bar code readers** are devices that use light reflection to read differences in bar code patterns in order to identify a labeled item. While the most common place for bar code readers is in grocery and department stores, bar coding systems also are used extensively by warehouses for inventory tracking. Similarly, delivery and courier companies frequently use such coding systems to track inventory items and packages during shipping transfers (if you have received a delivery from Federal Express or United Parcel Services recently, you may have noticed the bar codes on the package that were used to track its delivery to you).

In many cases, bar coding schemes are not feasible. For instance, when customers mail payments, converting payment amounts into bar codes is not necessary. On the other hand, utility and credit card companies frequently ask customers to handwrite the amount of the payment on the remittance slip. In such cases, **optical character recognition** is used—similar to the way *bar code readers* work—for pattern recognition of handwritten or printed characters. While such systems have more difficulty than *bar code readers* in consistently reading data (due mainly to inconsistencies in writing characters), *optical character recognition* fulfills a need where bar coding is not feasible. Note, however, that both *bar code readers* and *optical character recognition* are technologies designed to eliminate the need for individuals to key data and the accompanying potential risk of error.

The third major optical input technology is the *scanner*. **Scanners** are input devices that capture printed images or documents and convert them into electronic digital signals (i.e., into binary representations of the printed image or document) that can be stored on computer media. *Scanners* are key to the increased use of electronic digital imaging to drive business processes and facilitate management decision making.

Digital Image Processing

E-BUSINESS   **Digital image processing systems** are computer-based systems for capture, storage, retrieval, and presentation of images of real or simulated objects. In a typical business application, the images are usually documents. Once the domain of large mainframe computers only, these systems are now frequently implemented on personal computer platforms. The following briefly describes the major steps in a typical digital image processing system.

In the *input* stage, *scanners* are generally used to capture images or documents. In this case, pieces of data from the source documents are keyed (i.e., data that could not be read directly by the *OCR* incorporated into the scanner) while the entire document is scanned separately to allow future review of the original document image.

A clerk uses a PC or workstation to retrieve the image of a source document. For example, the clerk inputs the customer number to obtain a list of related source document images, such as customer orders, for that customer. One of the documents—the one with the sought-after information—is then selected for display. In addition to screen output, images also may be printed.

After a document has been input, additional processing may take place. For example, additional data related to the document might be added, or someone might act on data contained in, or associated with, the document. Retrieval and processing capabilities may be incorporated into existing applications. In this way the images become an integral part of the information system. Recall that in Chapter 5 we discussed the move toward object-oriented databases that are capable of handling object data—such as images—and that we noted the move toward enabling object storage within relational databases. A major part of the demand for object-capable databases is the management of a vast array of document images. Linkages of these images into an *enterprise system* can make accessibility much greater and easier as the information can readily be distributed throughout the organization to where it is needed.

ENTERPRISE SYSTEMS

PHYSICAL DESCRIPTION OF THE OE/S PROCESS

We have assumed a particular physical model to illustrate the OE/S process. As you examine the process' physical features, you should notice a close resemblance between them and the logical design of the OE/S process, as presented in Figures 10.3, 10.4, 10.5, 10.7 and 10.8 (pages 360, 361, 362, 364, and 365). You also should see that this system demonstrates the use of an *enterprise system* and several features of the technology discussed earlier in this chapter.

ENTERPRISE SYSTEMS

The OE/S Process

Figure 10.11 (page 372) presents a systems flowchart of the model. Take some time now to examine the flowchart. We start with customer calls received in the customer service center. Customer service representatives may perform a number of services for a customer including:[12]

- Checking the availability of inventory.
- Determining the status of open orders.
- Initiating sales.
- Confirming orders.

Let's assume that the customer sales representative (CSR) invokes the option to enter a sales order and sees a screen much like the one in Figure 10.6 (page 364). First, the system prompts the CSR to enter the *customer number*. If the CSR enters a customer number for which the system has no record, the system rejects the order, and the recording of the event is terminated.

Assuming the CSR enters a valid customer number, the system automatically retrieves certain *standing data*, such as customer name(s), address(es), and credit terms, from the

---

[12] Note that salespeople may not have access to all the menu options. For example, they may not have access to certain *data maintenance* functions or reporting options.

Figure 10.11 OE/S Process Flowchart

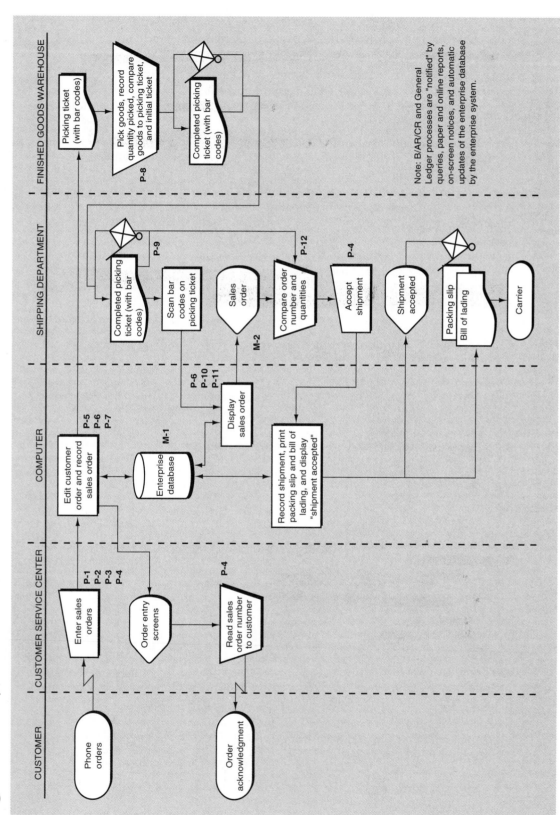

customer master data. Next, the CSR enters the other data in the sales order, guided by the cursor moving to each new position in the *preformatted screen*.

When the CSR enters data for each item ordered, starting with the part number, the system automatically displays the description and price. Finally, the CSR enters the quantity ordered. If the total amount of the current order, any open orders, and the outstanding receivable balance exceeds the customer's credit limit, the operator is warned of this fact, the order is suspended, and credit rejection procedures are initiated. If the total amount falls within the customer's credit range, the processing continues. Should the balance shown on the inventory data be less than the quantity ordered, back order procedures are initiated.

Once the customer service representative has finished entering the order data, the computer updates the sales order and inventory master data, and gives the CSR a sales order number that is then relayed to the customer. Simultaneously, a picking ticket, containing a bar code of the sales order number, is printed in the warehouse.

As each item is picked, warehouse personnel insert the picked quantities on the picking ticket. When all the goods have been picked, they compare the goods to the picking ticket, initial the ticket, and then move the goods and the completed picking ticket to the shipping department.

Shipping personnel scan the bar code on the picking ticket to bring the sales order up on their computer screen. After they confirm that this is the correct order and that the quantities are correct, they select the option to record the shipment. This action causes the computer to update the sales order, inventory, and general ledger master data to reflect the shipment and to print a packing slip and bill of lading (a shipping label for the common carrier). The goods are packed, with the packing slip inside, the shipping label (bill of lading) is attached to the box, and the box is given to the carrier for delivery. The completed picking ticket is discarded.

Error routines would be initiated if the customer record did not exist, the customer's credit limit was not sufficient, the goods were not available in the correct quantity, or the goods to be shipped did not match the picking ticket and the sales order.

Management Reporting

In an online system that incorporates an inquiry processing capability, the need for regular preparation of printed management reports is reduced or eliminated. Instead, each manager can use a PC to access a database and retrieve relevant management information. For example, a sales manager could access the marketing database at any time and assess the performance of particular salespeople.

Alternatively, sales reports in many desired formats can be obtained, on demand. For example, some of the report options could include sales analyses by part number, product group, customer, or salesperson as well as open order status, sorted and accumulated in a variety of ways. Notice, for example, in Figure 10.6 (page 364) that the sales area is part of the sales order master data. A manager could run a report analyzing the relative performance of sales areas. Figure 10.12 (page 374) illustrates part of one such report. This report can be previewed on screen as shown and can then be printed, if desired. This report shows sales by customer (sold-to party), including incoming orders, by dollar and quantity, and the amounts for open orders, those that have not yet been shipped. Monitoring these open orders to ensure prompt shipment is a form of *tickler file*.

ENTERPRISE SYSTEMS

Figure 10.12 Sample SAP Sales Analysis Report

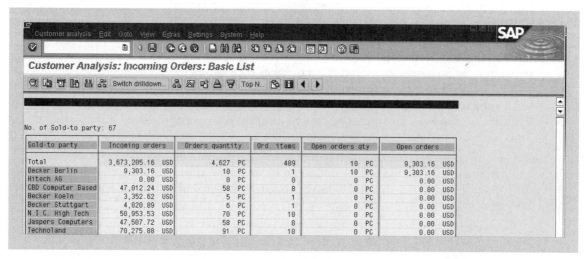

Source: Reprinted with permission from SAP.

APPLICATION OF THE CONTROL FRAMEWORK

CONTROLS The methodology for studying application controls was presented in Chapter 9. You might want to review that material before proceeding. In this section, we apply the control framework to the OE/S process. Figure 10.13 (pages 376–377) presents a completed control matrix for the systems flowchart presented in Figure 10.11 (page 372). The flowchart is annotated to show the location of the various application control plans.

Control Goals

The control goals listed across the top of the matrix are no different from the generic goals presented in Chapter 7, except that they have been *tailored* to the specifics of the OE/S process.

Two categories of control goals are presented in the matrix. The *operations process control goals* are:

- *Effectiveness of operations.* A through D in Figure 10.13 identify four representative effectiveness goals for the OE/S process. These goals relate to the reason(s) for which the process exists. In the case of the OE/S process, notice that for the most part these goals address the issue of satisfying customers, a topic discussed earlier in the chapter.

- *Efficient employment of resources.* As noted in Chapter 9, people and computers are the resources found in most business processes.

- *Resource security.* Note that in this column we have named two specific resources that are of concern to the OE/S process. Control plans should be in place to prevent theft or unauthorized sale of merchandise inventory. Equally important are plans designed to preclude unauthorized access to or copying, changing, selling, or destruction of the customer master data.

The *information process control goals* comprise the other category. These goals are divided into two sections—one section for sales order inputs and a second section for shipping notice inputs. To focus our discussion, we have not included other system inputs (i.e., customer inquiries, credit applications, credit-limit changes, and management inquiries). The information system control goals are:

- *Input validity (IV)*. A *valid* sales order is one from an existing customer—one contained in the customer master data—whose current order falls within authorized credit limits. To be added to the customer master data, a customer should pass an initial credit investigation. By adding the customer to the customer master data, management has provided *authorization* to do business with that customer. *Valid* shipping notice events are those that are supported by both an approved sales order and an *actual* shipment of goods.

- *Input completeness (IC) and input accuracy (IA)* of sales orders or shipping notices.

- *Update completeness (UC) and update accuracy (UA) of the sales order and inventory master data*.[13] We have seen earlier in the chapter that the sales order master data is updated twice—once when a new sales order is created, and later to reflect the shipment of that order. The single inventory master data update occurs at the same time the new sales order is created.[14]

Recommended Control Plans

Exhibit 10.1 (pages 378–380) contains a discussion of each recommended control plan listed in the control matrix, including an explanation of how each plan meets the related control goals. As you study the control plans, be sure to see where they are located on the systems flowchart. Also, see whether you agree with (and understand) the relationship between each plan and the goal(s) that it addresses. Remember that your ability to *explain* the relationships between plans and goals is more important than your memorization of the cell entries themselves.

Recall that application control plans include both those that are characteristic of a particular AIS process and those that relate to the technology used to implement the application. For simplicity, we have assumed that most of the plans exist in our system (i.e., is a "P" plan), regardless of whether it was specifically mentioned in the narrative or not. One of the control plans described in Chapter 9—namely, *digital signatures*—is not used in this particular system because the customer sales representatives (CSRs) communicate directly with the computer.

Many of the plans listed in Exhibit 10.1 were discussed in Chapter 9, including an explanation of how each plan helps to attain specific control goals. That discussion will not need repeating here except to point out, as necessary, how and where the plan is implemented in the OE/S process pictured in Figure 10.11 (page 372). If you cannot explain in your own words the relationship between the plans and goals, you should review the explanations in Chapter 9.

---

[13] Again, to focus our discussion, we have limited our coverage of system updates to just the sales order and inventory master data.

[14] In many OE/S processes the inventory data is updated at the time that the sales order is created to show that the inventory has been allocated to a particular order. Then, at the time of the shipment the inventory is updated again to reduce the balance on hand.

Figure 10.13 Control Matrix for the OE/S Business Process

Recommended Control Plans	Control Goals of the OE/S Business Process															
	Control Goals of the Operations Process						Control Goals of the Information Process									
	Ensure effectiveness of operations				Ensure efficient employment of resources (people, computers)	Ensure security of resources (inventory, customer data)	For sales order inputs (i.e., customer orders), ensure:			For sales order and inventory master data, ensure:		For shipping notice inputs (i.e., shipment data), ensure:			For sales order master data, ensure:	
	A	*B*	*C*	*D*			*IV*	*IC*	*IA*	*UC*	*UA*	*IV*	*IC*	*IA*	*UC*	*UA*
Present Controls																
P-1: Enter customer order close to where the order is received	P-1	P-1		P-1	P-1			P-1	P-1	P-1	P-1					
P-2: Preformatted screens	P-2	P-2		P-2	P-2				P-2		P-2					
P-3: Online prompting	P-3	P-3		P-3	P-3				P-3		P-3					
P-4: Interactive feedback check								P-4		P-4			P-4		P-4	
P-5: Customer credit check			P-5			P-5	P-5									
P-6: Populate inputs with master data	P-6	P-6		P-6		P-6	P-6		P-6		P-6	P-6		P-6		P-6
P-7: Programmed edit checks	P-7	P-7		P-7	P-7				P-7		P-7					
P-8: One-for-one checking of picking tickets with the goods				P-8	P-8	P-8						P-8		P-8		
P-9: Receive and input turnaround document (picking ticket)				P-9	P-9							P-9		P-9		

Figure 10.13   Control Matrix for the OE/S Business Process (*continued*)

	Control Goals of the OE/S Business Process																		
	Control Goals of the Operations Process					Control Goals of the Information Process													
Recommended Control Plans	Ensure effectiveness of operations			Ensure efficient employment of resources (people, computers)	Ensure security of resources (inventory, customer data)	For sales order inputs (i.e., customer orders), ensure:			For sales order and inventory master data, ensure:			For shipping notice inputs (i.e., shipment data), ensure:				For sales order master data, ensure:		
	A	B	C	D			IV	IC	IA	IV	IC	UC	UA	IV	IC	IA	UC	UA
Present Controls																			
P-10: Independent shipping authorization					P-10						P-10								
P-11: Compare input with master data				P-11	P-11						P-11			P-11	P-11	P-11		
P-12: One-for-one checking of goods, picking ticket, sales order					P-12										P-12	P-12		P-12
Missing Controls																			
M-1: Independent customer master data maintenance		M-1			M-1		M-1											
M-2: Review open sales orders (tickler file)				M-2												M-2	M-2	

Legend:

Effectiveness goals:
A = Provide timely response to customer inquiries.
B = Provide timely acknowledgment of customer orders.
C = Provide assurance of customer's creditworthiness.
D = Provide timely shipment of goods to customers.

IV = Input validity
IC = Input completeness
IA = Input accuracy
UC = Update completeness
UA = Update accuracy

See Exhibit 10.1 (pages 378–380) for a complete explanation of control plans and cell entries.

Exhibit 10.1 Explanation of Cell Entries for Control Matrix in Figure 10.13

P-1: *Enter customer order close to where the order is received.*

Effectiveness goals A, B, and D, Efficient employment of resources: Use of this strategy places customer service representatives (CSRs) in a position to process customer orders immediately and to respond quickly to customer inquiries. Being familiar with the orders allows the CSRs to input the orders more quickly. Finally, the direct entry by the CSRs eliminates the costs associated with the handling of orders by additional entities.

Sales order input completeness, Master data update completeness: By having the CSRs enter the sales data rather than forwarding to a data entry function, the risk of orders getting lost should be reduced. The master data is updated concurrent with data input.

Sales order input accuracy, Master data update accuracy: Because CSRs are familiar with the type of data being entered and can correct any input errors "on the spot," input accuracy should be improved. The master data is updated concurrent with data input.

P-2: *Preformatted screens.*

Effectiveness goals A, B, and D, Efficient employment of resources: This simplifies the data entry process, allowing the CSR to enter orders more quickly and allowing more orders to be input over a period of time.

Sales order input accuracy, Master data update accuracy: Preformatted screens may prevent the CSR from omitting data, populate certain fields, and reject incorrectly formatted fields thus reducing input errors. The master data is updated concurrent with data input.

P-3: *Online prompting.*

Effectiveness goals A, B, and D, Efficient employment of resources: Prompting helps the CSR understand very quickly which data should be entered, making the data input process quicker and more efficient.

Sales order input accuracy, Master data update accuracy: By forcing the CSR to stop and "accept" the order, online prompting is, in a sense, advising you to check your data entries before moving on. The master data is updated concurrent with data input.

P-4: *Interactive feedback checks.*

Sales order and shipping notice input completeness, Master data update completeness: The system tells the CSR and the shipping clerk that the order and the shipment have been *accepted.* The master data is updated concurrent with data input.

P-5: *Customer credit check.*

Effectiveness goal C: The credit check is performed by ascertaining that the amount of the customer order (plus the amount of any open orders and the amount of any outstanding balance) falls within the credit limit established by the credit department. If the request falls outside the limit, then the control terminates the sale.

Security of resources: Termination of orders exceeding credit limits ensures that the organization protects its resources by dealing only with customers who have demonstrated an ability to satisfy their liabilities.

Sales input validity: Valid sales orders include those that fall within authorized credit limits.

P-6: *Populate inputs with master data.*

Effectiveness goals A, B, and D, Efficient employment of resources: Because the inputs (customer order and shipping notice) are populated with data from customer, inventory, and sales order master data, the CSR and the shipping clerks use fewer keystrokes for each input, enter data more quickly, and provide more timely responses to customer inquiries, acknowledgment of customer orders, and shipment of goods to customers.

Sales input validity: If the CSR *correctly* enters a customer code and the system does not populate the input with customer master data, we presume that there is no matching customer master data and no authorized customer. This prevents the entry of invalid orders.

Shipping notice input validity: When the shipping clerk scans the picking ticket, the system should populate the input with sales order master data. If not, we presume that there is no matching sales order master data and no *authorized* order. This prevents the entry of invalid shipments.

Sales order input accuracy, Master data update accuracy: The automatic retrieval of customer infor-

Exhibit 10.1 Explanation of Cell Entries for Control Matrix in Figure 10.13 (*continued*)

mation when the customer code has been entered helps ensure the accuracy of the input data because the CSR keys less data and makes use of the customer and inventory master data that were previously entered and reviewed for accuracy. This automatically facilitates the accuracy of master data updates that are performed concurrent with data input.

Shipping notice input accuracy, Sales order master data update accuracy: When the picking ticket bar codes are scanned, the input data related to the shipment are automatically captured, reducing the risk of erroneous input. The sales order master data is updated concurrent with input.

P-7: *Programmed edit checks.*

Effectiveness goals A, B and D: By editing and correcting data as it is input, rather than later, we can process orders in a more timely manner.

Efficient employment of resources: Programmed edits provide quick, low-cost editing of event data.

Sales order input accuracy, Master data update accuracy: Various spots in the narrative talk about the system rejecting erroneous data input. The master data is updated concurrent with data input.

P-8: *One-for-one checking of picking tickets with the goods.*

Effectiveness goal D, Efficient employment of resources: By comparing the goods to the picking ticket (and correcting any picking errors) in the warehouse, rather than later in shipping, we can process shipments in a more timely manner and more efficiently (the warehouse clerk is in a better position to correct picking errors than is the shipping clerk).

Security of resources: By correcting picking errors we ensure that only goods that were ordered leave the warehouse.

Shipping notice input validity and accuracy: The shipping clerk sends only the quantity of goods that were on the picking ticket, thus ensuring that the goods entered are shipments that will be valid and accurate.

P-9: *Receive and input turnaround document (picking ticket).*

Effectiveness goal D, Efficient employment of resources: By reducing the amount of data that must be

input to record the shipment, we improve the speed and productivity of the shipping personnel.

Shipping notice input validity: The turnaround documents were printed in the warehouse. Thus, the shipping clerks are precluded from entering unauthorized shipments.

Shipping notice input accuracy: Using the prerecorded bar code to trigger the event reduces the possibility of input errors.

P-10: *Independent shipping authorization.*

Security of resources: To provide security over merchandise inventory, the plan requires that the system provide the shipping department with an independent authorization (i.e., an open sales order in the enterprise database) to ship inventory to a customer. In addition, the plan calls for the system to provide an independent authorization (i.e., a *picking ticket*) to the warehouse to pick goods and send them to the shipping department.

Shipping notice input validity: The shipping department will not record a shipment unless they have received independent authorization to do so. This independent authorization comes in the form of *picking tickets* and the *open sales order* executed by independent functions.

P-11: *Compare input with master data.*

Effectiveness goal D, Efficient employment of resources: Shipments may be processed more quickly and at a lower cost if errors are detected and prevented from entering the system.

Security of resources, Shipping notice input validity: If there is no open order in the sales order master data or if the shipment quantities exceed the open quantities, the input shipment may not be authorized.

Shipping notice input accuracy: By comparing the input shipping notice to the sales order master data, erroneous or suspect input data may be identified.

P-12: *One-for-one checking of goods, picking ticket, sales order.*

Security of resources: By comparing data on the *sales order* with the data on the *picking ticket* and then comparing these data sets to the actual goods being shipped, this plan ascertains that inventory shipments have been authorized.

(*continued*)

Exhibit 10.1 Explanation of Cell Entries for Control Matrix in Figure 10.13 (*continued*)

The master data is updated as the input is accepted.

Shipping notice input validity, Master data update accuracy: By comparing the goods to the *sales order*, we ensure that shipping notice inputs are represented by an actual shipment of goods.

Shipping notice input accuracy: By comparing such items as item numbers, quantities, and customer identification, we can ensure that the input of shipping events is accurate.

M-1: *Independent customer master data maintenance.*

Effectiveness goal C: Only personnel in the credit department, a function that is separate from the sales department, should add new customers to the customer master data.

Security of resources: By precluding sales being made to customers who may not be creditworthy, the organization helps to ensure the security of its resources.

Input validity: Valid sales orders include those that are made to customers for whom management has provided prior *authorization*. This is accomplished here by having the records entered by the credit department.

M-2: *Review open sales orders (tickler file).*

Effectiveness goal D: A tickler file of open sales orders maintained in the enterprise database allows the shipping department to investigate any orders that are open for an unreasonable period of time. Therefore, the plan would provide assurance that goods are shipped to customers on a timely basis.

Shipping notice input completeness, Master data update completeness: If action is taken to expedite shipments for *all* open sales orders, the plan also would address the goal of input and update completeness of shipping notices (we are reviewing master data for incomplete shipments).

SUMMARY

The OE/S process is critical to revenue generation for the organization and as such is often a priority process for new technology integration. We have demonstrated one such system in this chapter. You should be aware that different organizations will have very differing levels of technology integration into their business processes. As these levels of technology change, the business processes also are altered accordingly. As the business process evolves, so also must the specific internal control procedures necessary to maintain the security and integrity of the process. Keep this in mind as you explore alternative levels of technology. Think about how the control systems change and how the controls in the OE/S process would similarly change given similar technology-drivers for the business process.

E-BUSINESS   In this chapter, we presented a technologically advanced order entry system. What's in the future? Well, consider an Internet storefront. Buyers can use their PCs to browse through electronic catalogs and compare prices and product specifications, and can make purchases at any hour. Consider that the only recently tapped market of B2B e-commerce is many times larger than predicted. As of May 2003, the value of B2B e-commerce in 2003 was $2.4 trillion and the value of B2C e-commerce was $96 billion.[15]

CONTROLS   Also, *expert systems* (described in Chapter 5) are used increasingly in practical business applications, including OE/S systems. For example, the American Express Company has developed an expert system called Authorizer's Assistant that helps the credit authorization staff to approve customer charges. The Authorizer's Assistant searches through 13 databases and makes recommendations to the person who makes the authorization de-

---

[15] "The E-Biz Surprise," *BusinessWeek* (May 12, 2003): 61.

cision. Authorizer's Assistant raises the user's productivity by 20 percent and reduces losses from overextension of credit. In addition to the cost savings, this expert system application allows American Express to differentiate itself from its competition by offering individualized credit limits.

REVIEW QUESTIONS

RQ 10-1 Describe the major functions performed by the OE/S process.

RQ 10-2 Each of the following questions concerns Figure 10.1 and Table 10.1 (pages 352 and 353):

    a. Which entities, shown as external to the OE/S process, also are outside the "boundary" of the total organization? Which are not?

    b. The B/AR/CR process is notified of the sale in flow 6 and the shipment in flow 9. Which of the two flows is the "trigger" for invoicing the customer?

RQ 10-3 What "key players" would you expect to find in the marketing function's organization chart?

RQ 10-4 Discuss the advantages and disadvantages of using *data marts* versus *data warehouses* to support marketing decision makers.

RQ 10-5 Discuss how customer relationship management (CRM) systems aid a customer service representative (CSR) in providing service to customers.

RQ 10-6 The following questions concern the logical description of the OE/S process:

    a. What are the three major processes? Describe the subsidiary processes of each major process.

    b. What three exception routines may occur when a customer order is processed?

RQ 10-7 How is each lower-level DFD (Figures 10.5, 10.7, and 10.8 (pages 362, 364, and 365) "balanced" with the level 0 diagram in Figure 10.4 (page 361)?

RQ 10-8 The following questions concern the logical database design of the OE/S process:

    a. What data stores does the OE/S process "own"? Describe each data store.

    b. What data stores are owned by *other* AIS processes that provide data to the OE/S process? What data does the OE/S process obtain from these stores?

RQ 10-9 a. Explain how bar code readers work.

    b. Explain how optical character recognition works and how it differs from bar code technology.

    c. Explain how scanners are used to capture data.

RQ 10-10 How is digital image processing used to support the keying in of data?

RQ 10-11 In examining the systems flowchart in Figure 10.11 (page 372), how would you discern from the symbols used (or perhaps the lack of certain other symbols) that the system (a) employs online data entry; (b) uses data communications technology; (c) processes event occurrences individually, rather than in groups of similar events; and (d) updates data records continuously?

RQ 10-12 How does each control plan listed in the control matrix in Figure 10.13 (pages 376–377) work?

RQ 10-13 Each of the following questions concerns the control matrix for the OE/S process (Figure 10.13, pages 376–377) and its related annotated systems flowchart (Figure 10.11, page 372):

    a. What four effectiveness goals does the matrix show?

    b. In this process, what particular resources do we wish to secure?

    c. What are the two kinds of data inputs in this system?

    d. What constitutes a valid sales order? a valid shipping notice?

    e. For what master data(s) do we want to ensure UC and UA?

RQ 10-14 What do the terms *picking ticket, packing slip, bill of lading, tickler file*, and *one-for-one checking* mean?

DISCUSSION QUESTIONS

DQ 10-1 Among the three functional entities shown in Figure 10.1 (page 352), what goal conflicts could exist, and how might this affect results of the OE/S process?

DQ 10-2 The chapter presented a brief example of how the OE/S process might or might not support the decision-making needs of the advertising manager. For each of the other functional positions shown in the organization chart of Figure 10.2 (page 353), speculate about the kinds of information needed to support decision making and indicate whether the typical OE/S process would provide that information. Be specific.

DQ 10-3 Explain how and where operations process goals would be shown in the goal columns of a control matrix prepared for the OE/S process. At a minimum, include in your discussion the following topics from Chapter 7:

    a. Differentiation between operations process control goals and information process control goals.

    b. Distinction between effectiveness and efficiency, and between effectiveness and security of resources.

DQ 10-4 "A control plan that helps to attain operational effectiveness by 'providing assurance of creditworthiness of customers' also helps to achieve the information process control goal of sales order input validity." Do you agree? Discuss fully.

DQ 10-5 Examine the systems flowchart in Figure 10.11 (page 372). Discuss how this process implements the concept of segregation of duties, discussed in Chapter 8. Be specific as to which entity (or entities) performs each of the four processing functions mentioned in Chapter 8 (assuming that all four functions are illustrated by the process).

DQ 10-6 What goals for the OE/S process (both operations process and information process goals) would be more difficult to achieve with an enterprise system?

DQ 10-7 Describe how *data mining* and a CRM *system* might be used by any of the managers depicted in Figure 10.1 (page 352), a horizontal perspective of the OE/S process, or in Figure 10.2 (page 353), a vertical perspective of the OE/S process.

DQ 10-8 An *enterprise system* supports a business process by:

    a. Facilitating the functioning of the business process.

    b. Providing records that business events have occurred.

    c. Storing data for decision making.

Describe how the enterprise system depicted in Figure 10.11 (page 372) provides support in these three areas.

PROBLEMS

Note: The first problems in this and several other application chapters ask you to perform activities that are based on processes of specific companies. The narrative descriptions of those processes (the cases) precede each chapter's problems. If your instructor assigns problems related to these cases, he or she will indicate which of them to study.

CASE STUDIES

CASE A: Speedy Grocers, Inc.

Speedy Grocers is an online grocery service that provides home delivery of groceries purchased via the Internet. Speedy operates in the greater Tulsa area and provides delivery to pre-certified customers. In order to be certified, the customer must have a user account with an established credit or charge line and rent a refrigerated unit to store delivered goods at their residence should they not be home at the time of delivery.

To enter an order the customer must log on to the Speedy Web site with a username and password. Using the customer database, the system confirms that the customer has a refrigerator unit in place and that the customer is in good standing. Once approved, the customer can browse and add products from the product list that is generated from the inventory database to the shopping cart. When finished, the customer can proceed to the checkout screen, where unwanted products can be removed. When the customer is satisfied with his/her selections, the customer will authorize the billing amount to be charged to his/her account. When the order is submitted, items are allocated in the inventory database and a new order is recorded in the order database.

In the warehouse, a clerk downloads an outstanding order from the order database to a handheld computer. The downloaded order provides an electronic picking ticket for use in assembling the customer's order. The order is assembled, placed in a box, recorded via the handheld computer as completed by item, which simultaneously updates the inventory database, a bar code is printed on the handheld computer and affixed to the outside of the box, and placed on a conveyor belt to delivery services.

In delivery services, the delivery person uses another handheld computer device to read the barcode and access the sales order information from the order database. The items in the box for delivery are rechecked per the order and loaded for delivery to the customer. Keying in the confirmation of the order contents by the delivery person triggers the printing of delivery directions and receipt. Upon delivering the groceries and receipt to the customer, the delivery person once again reads the barcode with the handheld device, and presses the button for confirmation of delivery. The completion of the delivery is automatically recorded in the order database. The system at this time also updates the customer's master data for billing purposes.

CASE B: Supplies R' Us Company

The Supplies R' Us Company is a wholesale distributor of office supplies, such as diskettes, stationary, file cabinets, and related items. Customers receive an updated catalog annually and place orders over the phone.

When a customer calls in with an order, a clerk would first ask for the customer ID and name. The clerk would then key in the customer info and retrieve the customer record from the customer database. The clerk would compare the name to the data on the screen to ensure that the customer is legitimate and has an acceptable credit record. If everything checks out, the clerk enters the customer's order. Once the order is entered, the computer compares the amount of the order to the available credit to ensure that the purchase does not exceed the credit amount limit.

This results in the creation of an entry in the sales order event data store and an allocation of inventory. At the end of the day, the data is processed against the customer data and the inventory data and the sales order is recorded in the sales order master data store. At the same time a customer acknowledgment is printed in the mailroom and is mailed to the customer. Also a picking ticket is printed in the warehouse and used to assemble the customer's order.

The completed order (goods and attached picking ticket) is forwarded to the shipping department. The shipping clerk keys the sales order number into the computer and the order is displayed on the screen. The shipping clerk keys in the items and quantities being shipped and, after the computer displays the shipment data, accepts the input. Once the shipment is accepted, the computer updates the sales order and inventory master data and creates a record for billing (in the billing due list data store). The computer also prints a packing slip and bill of lading on a printer in the shipping department. These shipping documents and the goods are given to the carrier for shipment to the customer.

P 10-1 For the company assigned by your instructor, complete the following requirements:

a. Prepare a table of entities and activities.

b. Draw a context diagram.

c. Draw a physical data flow diagram (DFD).

    d. Prepare an annotated table of entities and activities. Indicate on this table the groupings, bubble numbers, and bubble titles to be used in preparing a level 0 logical DFD.

    e. Draw a level 0 logical DFD.

P 10-2 For the company assigned by your instructor, complete the following requirements:

    a. Draw a systems flowchart.

    b. Prepare a control matrix, including explanations of how each recommended existing control plan helps to accomplish—or would accomplish in the case of missing plans—each related control goal. Your choice of recommended control plans should come from Exhibit 10.1 (pages 378–380) plus any additional technology-related control plans from Chapter 9 that are germane to your company's process.

    c. Annotate the flowchart prepared in part a to indicate the points where the control plans are being applied (codes P-1 . . . P-*n*) or the points where they could be applied but are not (codes M-1 . . . M-*n*).

P 10-3 Using the following table as a guide, describe for each function from Figure 10.1 (page 352):

    a. A risk (an event or action that will cause the organization to fail to meet it goals/objectives)

    b. A control/process or use of technology that will address the risk.

	Function	**Risks**	**Controls and technology**
Manager	Marketing		
	Finance		
Operations process	Sales (see Sales Order Department)		
	Logistics		

P 10-4 The following capsule cases present short narratives of processes used by three actual companies whose names have been changed for the purpose of this problem. You will use the cases to practice the mechanics of drawing data flow diagrams.

CAPSULE CASE 1: Bambino's Pizzeria

For its chain of fast food outlets, Bambino's Pizzeria recently installed a microcomputer-based system to speed its pizza deliveries. In each of its stores, Bambino's has PCs connected to incoming phone lines. When a customer calls in an order to have pizza delivered, an employee answers and asks for the customer's phone number, which is entered on the PC. If the order is for a repeat customer, the system matches the number with the customer database and displays the customer record on the screen. (Customer records contain a variety of information, including whether the customer's dog bites.) For first-time customers, the employee keys the caller's phone number, name, and address to create a record in the customer database.

    The order-taker then keys the customer's pizza order. The system prints a three-part order on a printer located in the kitchen. The original is used by the cook to prepare the order. When the order is ready, the cook marks the other two copies completed and gives them to the delivery driver to serve as delivery receipts for the driver and customer, respectively. At the same time that the order is printed, the order-taker's computer displays a city locator grid, which is used to help dispatch the drivers. From a copy of the display, a dispatch slip showing the customer's street and connecting roads is printed for the driver. The final system output generated at this time is a record of the order, which is the source for the event data written to the PC's hard drive. The data will be used later to tally sales, calculate the driver's pay, and generate other reports. (*Note:* For this problem, assume that these activities are beyond the order-taking system's context.)

CAPSULE CASE 2: Royal Casino

Waiters and waitresses at the Royal Casino's main dining room in Las Vegas use handheld, radio-frequency data terminals to take diners' orders and relay the orders to the kitchen. The data entry terminals weigh just a few ounces and open like a wallet to reveal function keys and a two-line LCD screen. The terminals are connected by radio signal to the dining room's PC-based computer system. As diners place their orders, the terminal prompts the waiter through the order. For instance, if the customer asks for a sirloin steak, the terminal asks the waiter to choose a function key corresponding to the desired degree of doneness (i.e., rare, medium rare, and so forth).

When the customer has completed ordering, the waiter hits a function key to indicate that fact. The PC system prints or displays the incoming order for cooks in the kitchen. When the dining party has finished its meal, the waiter indicates this fact by pressing the appropriate function key on the handheld terminal. The PC system communicates, over conventional wiring, with a point-of-sale (POS) computer at the cash register station, which prints out a guest check (which is given to the customer). At this time, the system also records the sales event data on the host PC's hard drive.

CAPSULE CASE 3: Pix for Pay

Background Information

Pix for Pay (PFP) is a company that offers pay-television movies and other cable television programming to subscribers for a fee. This case involves those subscribers who receive PFP's TV signal through a satellite dish. To restrict delivery of PFP broadcasts to paying subscribers only, the company scrambles its signal. A subscriber must have a descrambler box attached to the receiving dish and must pay a monthly subscription fee in order to receive a clear picture. Each descrambler box has its own unique ID number, so it will respond only to "on" signals meant for it. The descrambler boxes were designed by Spacecom, Inc., located in Los Angeles, California.

The Order Entry Process

When a customer places an order for pay-TV service with a PFP-affiliated cable TV company, the cable company telephones that order to PFP's telemarketing center in Cincinnati. There, a customer service representative enters the order, together with the customer's descrambler ID number, via a terminal that is connected through a leased telephone line to PFP's mainframe in New York City. The mainframe creates a customer order on the customer cable orders data and sends the descrambler code to a computer at Spacecom in Los Angeles, which then sends an encrypted activation message to PFP's uplink center in Buffalo, New York. The uplink center beams the activation message to a space satellite, and the message is echoed down to earth to the customer's satellite dish. The customer's descrambler box deciphers the encrypted message, which allows the customer to start receiving PFP's programming. From the time the customer places the order, the entire process takes less than a minute.

For the capsule case assigned by your instructor, complete the following requirements:

a. Prepare a table of entities and activities.

b. Draw a context diagram.

c. Draw a physical data flow diagram (DFD).

d. Prepare an annotated table of entities and activities. Indicate on this table the groupings, bubble numbers, and bubble titles to be used in preparing a level 0 logical DFD.

e. Draw a level 0 logical DFD.

P 10-5 The following is a list of 12 control plans from this chapter or from Chapters 8 and 9.

Control Plans

A. Enter customer order close to where customer order is prepared

B. Customer credit check

C. Independent shipping authorization

D. Populate inputs with master data

E. One-for-one checking of the goods, picking ticket, and sales order

F. Preformatted screens

G. Interactive feedback check

H. Reasonableness check

I. Backup procedures (for data)

J. Program change controls

K. Librarian controls

L. Personnel termination controls

The following are 10 system failures that have control implications. List the numbers 1 through 10 on your solution sheet. Next to each number, insert *one* letter from the preceding list, identifying the control plan that would *best* prevent the system failure from occurring. Also, give a brief (one- to two-sentence) explanation of your choice.

A letter should be used only once, with four letters left over.

System Failures

1. A clerk logged on to the online order entry system by entering the date of June 39, 20XX, instead of the correct date of June 29, 20XX. As a result, all sales orders entered that day were dated incorrectly.

2. Customer sales representatives at Wiscasset Company enter customer orders received in the mail. A recent audit of the order entry process

determined that the clerks were making many errors in entering data such as the customer's name and address.

3. A former employee of the order entry department gained access to the department after hours and logged on to the system at one of the PCs. He entered an order for a legitimate customer but instructed the system to ship the goods to his home address. Consequently, several thousand dollars worth of inventory was shipped to him. When the misappropriation was discovered, he had long since left the company and had changed addresses.

4. Century Inc.'s field salespeople record customer orders on prenumbered order forms and then forward the forms to central headquarters in Milwaukee for processing. Fred Friendly, one of Century's top salespeople, had a very good week; he mailed 40 customer orders to headquarters on Friday afternoon. Unfortunately, they were misplaced in the mail and did not reach Milwaukee until two weeks later. Needless to say, those 40 customers were more than a little displeased at the delay in their orders being filled.

5. Ajax Corporation recently converted to an online order entry system. Clerks key in order data at one of several PCs. In the first week of operations, every sales order produced by the computer was missing the data for the "ship-to" address.

6. At XYZ Co. the finished goods warehouse delivers goods to the shipping department, accompanied by the picking ticket. Then the shipping department prepares a three-part shipping notice, one copy of which serves as the packing slip. A recent audit discovered that a dishonest warehouse employee had been forging picking ticket documents, allowing her to have goods shipped to an accomplice.

7. The job of a systems programmer included doing maintenance programming for the order entry application. He altered the programs so that the credit-checking routine was bypassed for one of the customers, a company owned by his uncle. The uncle obtained several thousand dollars of merchandise before his firm went bankrupt.

8. To encourage new business, Carefree Industries adopted a policy of shipping up to $1,000 of orders to new customers during the period in which the customer's credit was being investigated. A recently terminated order entry manager at Carefree, aware of the policy, placed several bogus telephone orders, disguised each time as a first-time customer. She absconded with over $10,000 of merchandise that was shipped to her.

9. Clerks in the shipping department at Storrs, Inc., scan picking tickets to bring up the appropriate open sales order and then scan another bar code on the picking ticket to trigger the recording of the shipment. They then put the box on the conveyor to the loading dock. They have discovered that some shipments are not being recorded by the system.

10. Customers of Fribble Company have complained that the goods received are not accurate. Sometimes they receive the wrong goods and sometimes the wrong quantity.

P 10-6 The following is a list of 12 control plans from this chapter or from Chapters 8 and 9.

Control Plans

A. Customer credit check

B. Review open sales orders

C. Reconcile batch totals

D. Populate inputs with master data

E. Online prompting

F. Preformatted screens

G. Programmed edit checks

H. Protection tabs, doors, rings

I. Internal labels

J. Operates run manual

K. Segregation of duties

L. Open sales order data

The following are 10 statements describing either the achievement of a control goal (i.e., a system success) or a system deficiency. List the numbers 1 through 10 on your solution sheet. Next to each number, insert *one* letter from the preceding list, identifying the *best* control plan to achieve the desired goal or to address the system deficiency described.

A letter should be used only once, with two letters left over.

Control Goals or System Deficiencies

1. Should have precluded the erasure of the customer master data tape, which was inadvertently mounted as an output tape by an inexperienced computer operator.

2. Helps to ensure the effectiveness goal of timely shipment of goods to customers.

3. Results in the efficient employment of resources; when the order entry clerk keys the customer number, the computer program supplies the customer name, billing address, and other standing data about the customer.

4. Meets both the effectiveness goal that sales are made only to creditworthy customers and the information systems control goal of sales order input validity.

5. Helps to achieve the information systems control goal of input accuracy by ensuring that dates are entered as MM/DD/YY.

6. Helps to achieve the information systems control goal of input accuracy by providing interactive dialogue with the data entry person.

7. Results in the efficient employment of resources by providing detailed instructions to computer operations personnel for running production jobs.

8. Addresses the information system control goals of both input accuracy and input completeness.

9. Could have prevented the clerk from entering 10 boxes of an item when a customer ordered 10 each of an item.

10. Can be compared to the goods and the picking ticket to prevent unauthorized shipments.

P 10-7 For Figure 10.4 (page 361):

- Indicate the sequence of activities by putting numbers next to the data flows. For example, the Customer order in the upper left of the diagram would be number "1." Restart the numbers for each bubble. Assign the same number to simultaneous data flows. For example, several different data flows coming out of bubble 3.0 should get the same number.

- For each process bubble, indicate, by placing a "T" on the flow, the flow that triggers the processing activities.

- Label each flow into and out of the data stores and to and from the other processes. These labels should describe the purpose of the flow.

- Annotate each data store to indicate the data's major elements.

- Include on the diagram one-sentence descriptions of each process bubble's activities.

P 10-8 Use the data flow diagrams in Figures 10.4, 10.5, 10.7, and 10.8 (pages 361, 362, 364, and 365) to solve this problem.

Prepare a four-column table that summarizes the OE/S processes, inputs, and outputs. In the first column, list the three processes shown in the level 0 diagram (Figure 10.4). In the second column, list the subsidiary functions shown in the three lower-level diagrams (Figures 10.5, 10.7, and 10.8). For *each* subsidiary process listed in column 2, list the data flow names or the data stores that are inputs to that process (column 3) or outputs of that process (column 4). (See note.) The following table has been started for you to indicate the format for your solution.

Note: To simplify the solution, do *not* show any reject stubs in column 4.

Solution Format

Summary of the OE/S system's processes, subsidiary functions, inputs, outputs, and data stores

Process	Subsidiary Functions	Inputs	Outputs
1.0 Validate sales order	1.1 Verify inventory availability	Customer order Inventory master data	Marketing data Inventory available—order
	1.2 Check credit	. . . Continue solution . . .	. . . Continue solution . . .

KEY TERMS

order entry/sales (OE/S) process

data marts

Web Services

Universal Description, Discovery, and Integration (UDDI)

Web Services Description Language (WSDL)

Simple Object Access Protocol (SOAP)

XML (eXtensible Markup
    Language)
picking ticket
customer acknowledgment
bill of lading

packing slip
customer master data
sales order master data
bar code readers

optical character
    recognition
scanners
digital image processing
    systems

chapter 11

The Billing/Accounts Receivable/Cash Receipts (B/AR/CR) Process

Stacey Cox is the vice president and chief financial officer (CFO) at CableSystems, Inc., an independent provider of cable television and high-speed Internet services.[1] Stacey has developed a new way to bill customers and receive payments. This is how Stacey, in her own words, described the proposed system to Chuck Wild, the president and CEO of CableSystems, and other VPs.

> For some time now we have known that we need to reduce the number of days between the date customers are billed each month and the date the customers' payments become available to CableSystems. This is what I propose.
>
> Each month we will place customer bills on our Web site and send an e-mail telling each customer that his or her bill is there. This is called *electronic bill presentment*.
>
> Customers will log onto our Web site, view the bill, and execute payment. This is called *electronic bill payment*.
>
> Because customers will receive their bills more quickly and make their payments in a timelier manner, the cash flow for CableSystems will improve and we will have additional funds available to invest in new technology and programming.

Dora Wolman, the VP of marketing, liked the idea of customers coming to the Web site each month. Cablesystems could place advertising on the site to encourage customers to buy additional goods and services.

Bill Shuman, the VP and chief information officer (CIO), added that the Web site also could be designed to provide customer information and services. For example, customers could review their bills and send e-mails to customer service if they wanted to dispute any portion of it. Dora particularly liked Bill's idea because she has been trying to reduce the billing-related calls to the customer service center.

By the end of the meeting the group decided that the development of an Electronic Bill Presentment and Payment system was going to create great advantages for CableSystems, Inc. Chuck thanked Stacey for her presentation and gave the go-ahead for the project.

[1] The story of CableSystems, Inc., and the cast of characters are disguised and adapted from a number of sources describing Electronic Bill Presentment and Payment (EBPP) services at real-world companies.

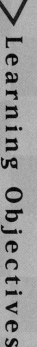

Learning Objectives

- To understand the relationship between the B/AR/CR process and its environment.
- To understand the relationship between the B/AR/CR process and management problem solving at various levels in the organization.
- To become familiar with some of the technology used in implementing the B/AR/CR process.
- To achieve a reasonable level of understanding of the logical and physical characteristics of the process.
- To gain a foundation level of understanding as to how enterprise systems impact the processing of information in the B/AR/CR process.
- To know some typical operations process and information process control goals.
- To recognize some plans commonly used to control the B/AR/CR process.

In this chapter we spotlight one business process, the billing/accounts receivable/cash receipts (B/AR/CR) process. We will describe the various users of the (B/AR/CR) process, each having their own view of the enterprise system and enterprise database. In addition, we will analyze the process controls related to the (B/AR/CR) process.

SYNOPSIS

This chapter covers the billing/accounts receivable/cash receipts (B/AR/CR) process. A close relationship exists between this process and the order entry/sales (OE/S) process you studied in Chapter 10. In fact, many firms do not distinguish the two processes as clearly as we do in this book. In combination, the OE/S and B/AR/CR processes comprise the order-to-cash process depicted in Figure 2.7 on page 60.

ENTERPRISE SYSTEMS

This chapter first defines the B/AR/CR process and describes its functions. In addition to the recording of the relevant business events, we emphasize the importance of this process in meeting customer needs and show how companies have used the B/AR/CR process to gain competitive advantage. This includes exploration of the technologies used to leverage the process and to compete in an increasingly *enterprise systems* and *e-business* driven environment. Based on this business environment, we explore the imprint of the B/AR/CR process on the organization, again taking both a horizontal and vertical perspective. We follow this with discussion of both the logical and physical process implementation. As in Chapter 10, *control* issues are dispersed throughout the chapter and are summarized by application of the control framework of Chapter 9.

ENTERPRISE SYSTEMS

E-BUSINESS

CONTROLS

INTRODUCTION

The OE/S process performs the critical tasks of (1) processing customer orders and (2) shipping goods to customers. The B/AR/CR process completes the order-to-cash process by accomplishing three separate yet related activities: (1) billing customers, (2) managing customer accounts, and (3) securing payment for goods sold or services rendered.

The **billing/accounts receivable/cash receipts (B/AR/CR) process** is an interacting structure of people, equipment, methods, and controls designed to create information flows and records that accomplish the following:

1. Support the repetitive work routines of the credit department, the cashier, and the accounts receivable department.[2]

2. Support the problem-solving processes of financial managers.

3. Assist in the preparation of internal and external reports.

First, the B/AR/CR process supports the repetitive work routines of the departments listed by capturing, recording, and communicating data resulting from the tasks of billing customers, managing customer accounts, and collecting amounts due from customers. Next, the B/AR/CR process supports the problem-solving processes involved in managing the controller and treasury functions. For example, the credit manager, reporting to the treasurer, might use an accounts receivable aging report in making decisions about extending further credit to customers, dunning customers for payment, or writing off worthless accounts. Finally, the B/AR/CR process assists in the preparation of internal and external reports, including GAAP-based financial statements.

The B/AR/CR process occupies a position of critical importance to an organization. For example, an organization needs a rapid billing process, followed by close monitoring of receivables, and a quick cash collections process to convert sales into working resources (e.g., cash) in a timely manner. Keeping receivables at a minimum should be a major objective of a B/AR/CR process. While we tend to associate the B/AR/CR process with mundane recordkeeping activities, the process also can be used to improve customer relations and competitive advantage. We discuss more about the strategic importance of the B/AR/CR process later in this chapter. First, let's take a look at the organizational aspects of the B/AR/CR process.

ORGANIZATIONAL SETTING

Figure 11.1 and Table 11.1 (page 396) present a horizontal view of the relationship between the B/AR/CR process and its organizational environment. Like their counterparts in Chapter 10, they show typical information flows handled by the B/AR/CR process. The flows provide an important communications medium among and between departments and entities in their relevant environment. The objective here is to have you identify the major information flows of the B/AR/CR process. Please take some time now to review the information flows of Figure 11.1.

CONTROLS   Next, we introduce the key players shown within the *finance* entity of Figure 11.1 (i.e., those boxes appearing in the right-most triangle of that figure). As illustrated by the figure, the major organizational subdivision within the finance area is between the treasury and controller functions. Most organizations divorce the operational responsibility over the security and management of funds (treasury) from the recording of events (controller). The pervasive control plans (see Chapter 8) of *segregation of duties* and *physical security of resources* guide us toward this decision and assist us in implementing the division between the treasury and the controller functions.

Within the treasury function, the activities having the greatest effect on the B/AR/CR process relate to the credit function (credit manager) and the custodial function (cashier).

---

[2] To focus our discussion, we have assumed that these departments are the primary ones related to the B/AR/CR process. For a given organization, however, the departments associated with the B/AR/CR process may differ.

Figure 11.1 A Horizontal View of the B/AR/CR Process

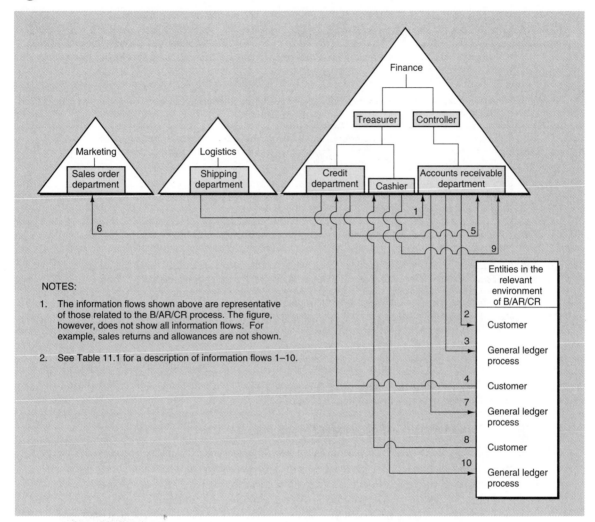

NOTES:

1. The information flows shown above are representative of those related to the B/AR/CR process. The figure, however, does not show all information flows. For example, sales returns and allowances are not shown.

2. See Table 11.1 for a description of information flows 1–10.

First, note that the credit manager is housed within the finance area rather than within marketing. This separation of the credit and the sales functions is not atypical. It is often defended on the grounds that if the credit function were part of marketing, credit might be extended to high-risk customers simply to achieve an optimistic sales target.

It is important also to separate the credit function (event authorization) from the *recordkeeping* functions of the controller's area. Within the controller's area, the major activities involved with the B/AR/CR process are those of the accounts receivable department. This functional area is primarily involved in recordkeeping activities.

MANAGING THE B/AR/CR PROCESS: LEVERAGING CASH RESOURCES

It seems a simple concept—to increase returns on the same amount of sales you must reduce your costs. The B/AR/CR process provides several opportunities to cut costs

Table 11.1 Description of Horizontal Information Flows

Flow No.	Description
1	Shipping department informs the accounts receivable department (billing section) of shipment.
2	Accounts receivable department (billing) sends invoice to customer.
3	Accounts receivable department (billing) informs general ledger process that invoice was sent to customer.
4	Customer, by defaulting on amount due, informs credit department of nonpayment.
5	Credit department recommends write-off of the receivable and informs accounts receivable department.
6	Credit department, by changing credit limits, informs sales order department to terminate credit sales to customer.
7	Accounts receivable department informs general ledger process of write-off.
8	Customer makes payment on account.
9	Cashier informs accounts receivable department (cash applications section) of payment.
10	Cashier informs general ledger process of payment.

through emerging technologies and improved management processes. We discuss three frequently used methods in this section: (1) customer self-service systems, (2) digital image processing systems, and (3) cash receipts management.

CRM: Customer Self-Service Systems

Chapter 10 described *customer relationship management (CRM)* systems (introduced in Chapter 2) and how they can be used to improve customer management and service during the OE/S process. We extend that discussion here by looking at another common feature of CRM systems: *customer self-service systems*. Recall from Chapter 2 that a customer self-service system is a CRM system extension that allows a customer to complete an inquiry or perform a task within an organization's business process without the aid of the organization's employees.

Banks were probably the first industry to widely implement such systems with the introduction of ATMs. ATMs allow a customer to withdraw cash, make deposits, transfer funds between accounts, and so forth without a teller. Another example is the so-called "pay-at-the-pump" systems for purchasing gasoline. In many cases, a human worker is not even required on-site; a set of gasoline pumps are provided on location and purchases are made with a credit card, a debit card, or a "fob," such as the "Speedpass" wand issued by the Mobil Oil Company.

E-BUSINESS *Customer self-service systems* are currently prevalent in many sectors, primarily through the use of automated telephone systems where the customer selects options and enters account information via the number keys on the telephone. A more recent trend that has received positive public feedback is the move to Internet systems that provide access to customer information. While these systems tend to take the same time to use as telephone-based systems, studies show that consumers enjoy Internet-based systems more than the much-maligned phone-based systems. Internet-based systems also bring greater capability to systems. For instance, most of the courier companies (i.e., FedEx, UPS, etc.) now allow users to connect through the Internet and identify where their package for delivery is currently located and if delivered who signed for the receipt of the package.

A major extension to these systems is the interconnection of customer self-service systems with *enterprise systems*. In some cases, customers can check their orders as they progress through the manufacturing process or even check inventory availability before placing orders. Some of the more advanced systems also allow customers to check production planning for future manufacturing to determine if goods will be available when they are needed.

Why are companies so interested in customer self-service systems and willing to allow access to information in their internal systems? Quite simply, the payback on such systems is huge when consideration is given to the reduced number of people that are needed to staff customer call centers. Reduction of staffing needs for call centers is particularly beneficial because of the high turnover such centers incur due to the high boredom factor associated with the job.

ENTERPRISE SYSTEMS

Digital Image Processing Systems

Many of the capabilities of digital image processing systems were explored in Chapter 10. Here, we take a brief look at the use of digital image processing systems in the B/AR/CR process. Because of the quantity of paper documents that typically flow through the B/AR/CR process, the ability to quickly scan, store, add information to, and retrieve documents on an as-needed basis can significantly reduce both labor costs for filing and the physical storage space and structures necessary for storing paper-based files.

Here is how it typically works. Given the abundance of digital image documents that rapidly stack up in a large payment processing center, these documents need to be organized and filed (much like their paper counterparts). Thus, electronic folders are created to store and organize related documents. The folders are retrievable via their electronic tabs. As a result, the image processes logically parallel the same processes used in traditional paper systems, without the headache of storing the mounds of paper and delivering requested documents by hand across the building or even across the world. The digital image processing system can make an electronic image instantly available anywhere in the world where a connection to the system can be established. Likewise, if a customer contacts a customer service representative, the representative can quickly retrieve the digital images of customer-related documents by computer and provide the customer a timely response—avoiding wasted time retrieving paper documents and returning calls to the customer. We will take another look at the use of digital image processing during the controls discussion later in this chapter.

Cash Receipts Management

The advent of electronic banking has made treasurers acutely aware of the critical importance of sound *cash management* to improving earnings performance. The name of the cash management game is to free up funds so that they either can be invested to earn interest or used to reduce debt, thus saving interest charges. Of course, before cash can be invested or used for debt reduction, it first must be received and deposited. Therefore, a central theme of this chapter is that of managing cash receipts. The overall management objective is to shorten, as much as possible, the time from the beginning of the selling process to the ultimate collection of funds.

In the billing function, the goal is to get invoices to customers as quickly as possible; with the hope of reducing the time it then takes to obtain customer payments. Having the B/AR/CR process produce invoices *automatically* helps ensure that invoices are sent to customers shortly after the goods have been shipped.

Another major concern of the treasurer is that of potential delays in collecting/depositing customer cash receipts and having those receipts clear the banking system. **Float**, when applied to cash receipts, is the time between the customer tendering payment and the availability of good funds. **Good funds** are funds on deposit and available for use. Float is a real cost to a firm and may be measured by the firm's marginal borrowing rate, assuming some type of borrowing occurs to finance the float period.

The following procedures are designed to reduce or eliminate the float associated with cash receipts:

- When checks are used for the settlement of accounts, *magnetic ink character recognition (MICR)* expedites the processing of those checks through the banking channels. High-speed electronic equipment is able to read the MICR code and sort checks at speeds approaching 100,000 checks per hour.
- A **charge card**—also known as a **credit card**—is a method of payment whereby a third party, for a fee, removes from the collector the risk of noncollection of the account receivable. The retailer submits the charges to the credit card company for reimbursement. The credit card company bills the consumer.
- A **debit card** is a form of payment authorizing the collector to transfer funds electronically from the payer's to the collector's balance. Some retailers find the notion of direct debit attractive because it represents the elimination of float.

Technology Summary 11.1 discusses four other solutions, perhaps less familiar to you, that organizations have used to shorten float, improve Internet business practices, or achieve other economies. Technology Summary 11.2 (page 400) describes the *electronic bill presentment and payment (EBPP)* systems introduced at the start of the chapter in the CableSystems story.

The Fraud Connection

In Chapters 7 and 8, we saw some cases of "cooking the books" by inflating revenues and accounts receivable. A recent example involved Take-Two Interactive Software, Inc., which sells the hit game "Grand Theft Auto." In 2001 Take-Two restated earnings of $15.4 million of sales that had been recorded over seven previous quarters. This restatement followed an SEC investigation of accounting practices in the videogame industry. The SEC found that companies in the industry engaged in accounting practices that led to inflated earnings and revenue. In the case of Take-Two, they had recorded as sales shipments to distributors that were returned in subsequent quarters. Other videogame companies were found to have booked revenues on shipments of products that were held in a warehouse until the buyer was ready to take delivery. In some cases these accounting treatments are questionable, in some cases they are found to be fraudulent.[3]

CONTROLS   Moving to the realm of intentional malfeasance, we find an abundance of illustrations of wrongdoing entailing the theft of cash—not surprising, since this is the most liquid

[3] Don Clark and Deborah Solomon, "Leading the News: SEC Focuses on Videogame Industry; Three Software Firms Say They Are Cooperating in Accounting Investigation," *The Wall Street Journal* (July 21, 2003): A3.

Technology Summary 11.1

Solutions for the Float Problem

One of the earliest initiatives in the realm of **electronic funds transfer (EFT)** is the **automated clearing house (ACH)**. If you have ever had your paycheck deposited directly to your checking account, you have been a party to an ACH transaction. Over 40,000 companies use the ACH, most of them for direct deposit. In addition, the government is a big user of the ACH. For instance, each month millions of senior citizens have their Social Security checks deposited electronically through the ACH banking network. Conceptually, the essence of the ACH system is not dissimilar to that of the debit card. Through a prearranged agreement between the trading parties, the collector's bank account is credited and the payer's account is debited for the amount of the payment. This might happen at specified recurring intervals as in the case of direct deposit, or it might be initiated by the payer—a so-called customer-initiated payment (CIP)—via a touch-tone or operator-assisted phone call or through a personal computer.

Another solution is the use of a lockbox for processing customer payments. A **lockbox** is a postal address, maintained by the firm's bank, which is used solely for the purpose of collecting checks. A firm will generally select a variety of banks with lockboxes across the country so that customer mail arrives quickly at the lockbox. The bank constantly processes the lockbox receipts, providing a quick update to the firm's bank balance. To provide the collecting company with the information to update customer accounts, the lockbox bank traditionally sends the company the remittance advices (RAs), photocopies of the checks, and a listing of the remittances, prepared by scanning the MICR-encoded RAs. Many banks now offer an **electronic lockbox** service, by which the lockbox bank scans the payer's remittance advice details into its computer system and then transfers the remittance advice data electronically to the collector's accounts receivable computer system. Obviously, the electronic lockbox allows the company to post cash receipts more rapidly, at reduced cost, and with more accuracy.

The other two technologies of interest here relate to emerging payment methods for Internet commerce. A major problem for Internet commerce concerns payment by the individual customer. Many individuals are hesitant to transmit personal credit card information across the Web, and others do not have sufficient credit card funds available to use. An alternative is to use either *electronic check* or *electronic cash*. An **electronic check** closely resembles a paper check with the inclusion of the customer's name, the seller's name, the customer's financial institution, the check amount, and a *digital signature*. Public-key cryptography is used to protect the customer's account from illicit activity. Electronic cash has been slower to catch on, as banks are only beginning to support the cash form, and accessibility to customers for use is still limited. With **electronic cash**, a financial institution issues an individual cash that is placed into an electronic wallet. The cash is issued in an electronic form much the way it would be in paper form. The individual spends out of the electronic wallet by transferring the electronic cash as payment. However, unlike using a check, the individual making the cash transfer is generally not traceable.

---

of a company's assets. Without recounting those cases here, we would merely point out that in all too many of them improper *segregation of duties* (see Chapter 8) occurred between the functions of handling cash (*custody of resources*) and *recording* cash transactions. Where inadequate segregation of duties exists, a common scheme for misappropriating cash involves "lapping" of customer accounts. Simply put, a lapping fraud might work as follows:

- Wanda Wayward is the bookkeeper for Honest Harry's House of Horticulture (4Hs). She also handles cash for the company.

Technology Summary 1 1 . 2

Electronic Bill Presentment and Payment (EBPP) Systems

Electronic bill presentment and payment (EBPP) systems are Internet-based systems for sending bills/invoices to customers and receiving the customer payment electronically. Two major types of EPBB systems exist. One is the "biller direct" method whereby a company posts its bills/invoices to its own Web site (or to a Web site hosted for them by a third party) and sends an e-mail notification to its customers telling them that their bill has been posted. The customers log on to the Web site, access their account, and decide what and how much to pay.[a] The details of the payment, such as customer name, customer number, bank account number, and amount to be paid, are captured at the Web site and sent to the third-party payment processor. The processor sends back a verification that allows the billing company to reduce the receivable (by posting an expected payment to the accounts receivable master data) and to notify the customer that the payment has been accepted.

At the end of each day the third-party processor consolidates all payments made that day (by the billers that are their customers) and prepares an ACH file containing all of the electronic fund transfers to be made to clear the day's payments.[b] The file is submitted through the ACH network into the banking system. Each bank receives the transfers relevant to its cus-

tomers, makes the appropriate transfers, and prepares a file to be sent to each customer every evening. The files contain a list of the customer payments (customer name, number, items paid, and amount). When the payment file is received from the bank, the billing companies change their accounts receivable data to reflect that an expected payment has been received. A record of the payment also is recorded in the cash receipts event data and the general ledger data.

The second EBPP method is the "consolidation/aggregation" method whereby the bills are not posted to the billing company's Web site (or to one hosted for them) but are posted to a Web site, such as CheckFree (see http://www.checkfree.com), that posts the bills from a number of companies. This method allows a customer to go to one site to pay bills received from many companies. For example, if you were to pay your bills with the biller direct method you would need to log on to the Web sites for your credit card companies, your cable company, your electric company, etc. But, with the consolidation method you would log on to one site to pay all of your bills. Once the bill payer logs on and decides what and how much to pay, the payment proceeds as it would under the direct biller method.

---

[a] Payment options include credit card, debit card, or bank account transfer.
[b] Some payments to the biller may be made using a paper check or with a credit or debit card.

- Wanda pockets cash received on account from customer A. She neither deposits the cash to 4Hs' bank account nor records it as received from A.
- So that customer A will not complain that the cash payment was never credited, Wanda deposits cash that is later received from customer B but credits A's account for the payment.
- So that customer B will not complain, Wanda deposits cash that is later received from customer C but credits B's account for the payment. And on it goes.

Some lapping scams have become so large and unmanageable for the perpetrator to keep covered up that there simply weren't enough hours available in the working day for the dishonest employee to manipulate the accounting records. The embezzler had to take the records, such as aged trial balances, home at night and doctor them there.

LOGICAL PROCESS DESCRIPTION

The principal activities of the B/AR/CR process are to bill customers, collect and deposit cash received from those customers, record the invoices and cash collections in customer subsidiary ledgers, and inform the general ledger process to make entries for sales and cash receipts. In addition to the billing (B) and cash receipts (CR) functions, the B/AR/CR process *manages customer accounts* (AR). Activities normally included in this process are sales returns and allowances and bad debts as well as sending periodic statements to customers. This chapter also shows and explains the key *event data* and *master data* used by the process.

Logical Data Flow Diagrams

As you learned in Chapter 4 and saw applied in Chapter 10, our first view of the process is a general one, shown in the form of a *context diagram*. For the B/AR/CR process, that view appears in Figure 11.2. Take some time to examine that figure and to note the external entities with which this process interacts and the data flows running to and from those entities.

Figure 11.2 The B/AR/CR Process—Context Diagram

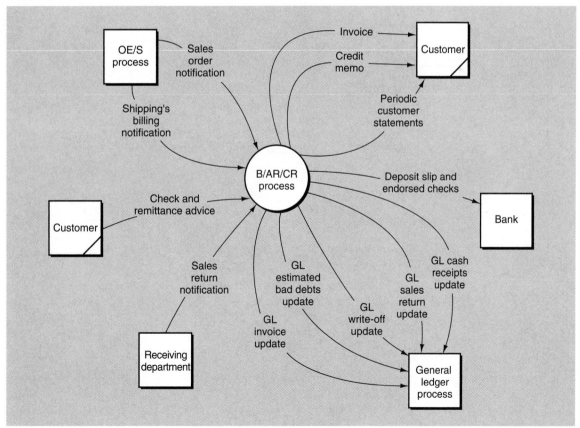

Now let's explode Figure 11.2 into the level 0 diagram reflected in Figure 11.3. In this expanded view of the process, we see that the single bubble in Figure 11.2 has become three process bubbles. We also see the event and master data for this process. At this point, review Figure 11.3 and compare it to Figure 11.2 to confirm that the two figures are "in balance" with each other.

Figure 11.3 B/AR/CR Process—Level 0 Diagram

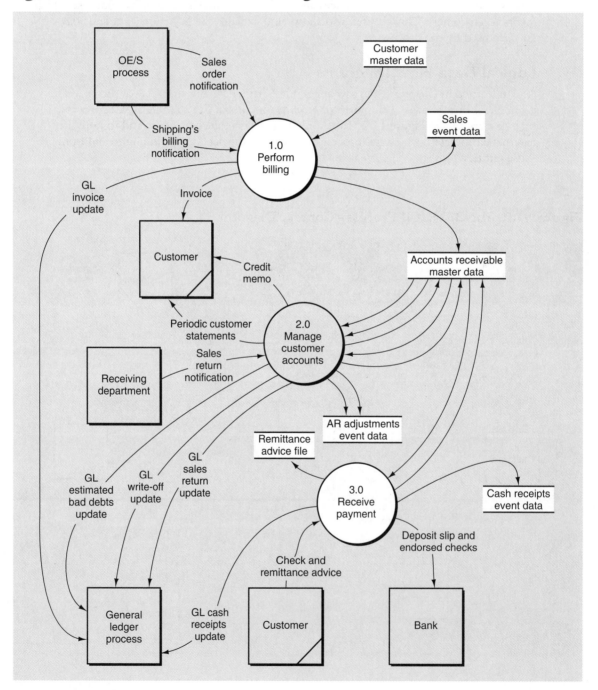

We will now decompose each of the three processes shown in the level 0 diagram into their lower-level diagrams. Figure 11.4 decomposes bubble 1.0 of Figure 11.3.

Figure 11.4 B/AR/CR Process—Diagram 1

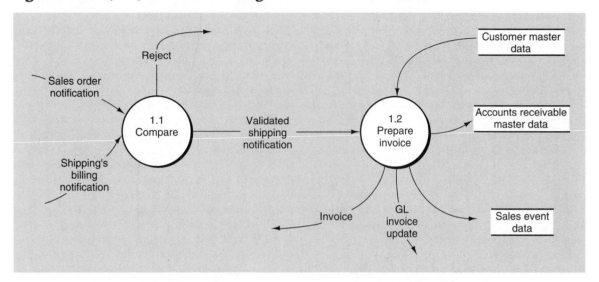

Most of Figure 11.4 should be self-explanatory. Therefore, we will comment only briefly on it. As you saw in Chapter 10, when the OE/S process produces a *sales order*, it notifies the B/AR/CR process to that effect.[4] When *triggered* by the data flow "Shipping's billing notification," process 1.1 validates the sale by comparing the details on the sales order notification to those shown on shipping's billing notification. Essentially, this is a comparison of the order (what was supposed to be shipped) with the shipment (what was shipped). If discrepancies are noted, the request is rejected, as shown by the reject stub coming from bubble 1.1. Rejected requests later would be processed through a separate *exception routine*.

If the data flows match, process 1.1 sends a validated shipping notification to process 1.2. Process 1.2 then performs the following actions simultaneously:

- Obtains from the customer master data certain standing data needed to produce the invoice.
- Creates the invoice and sends it to the customer.
- Updates the accounts receivable master data.
- Adds an invoice to the sales event data.
- Notifies the general ledger process that a sale has occurred (GL invoice update).

In the next section we define or explain *accounts receivable master data* and *sales event data*. Before proceeding, let's take a brief look at the information content of an invoice. Figure 11.5 (page 404) shows a sample invoice record for a customer.

The **invoice** is a business document used to notify the customer of an obligation to pay the seller for the merchandise (or service) ordered and shipped (or provided, if a

---

[4] Please recognize that, *physically*, this data flow could take the form of an open sales order (i.e., an order not yet shipped) in a *sales order master data store* or SALES_ORDERS relational table, both of which you saw in Chapter 10.

Figure 11.5 Sample SAP Invoice Data Screen

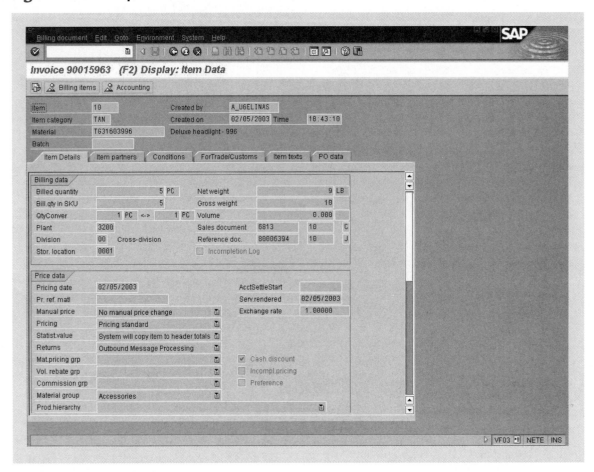

service). Notice that the top portion of the invoice screen identifies the invoice line item being displayed (Item 10, subsequent lines would be 20, 30, etc.), the material, and when the invoice was created and by whom. The tabs can be accessed to learn the sales order number, shipping plant, and quantity (Item Details tab), who ordered the goods and who should be billed (Item partners tab), pricing and terms information (Conditions tab), and details of the customer's order (PO data tab).

Now let's take a closer look at process 2.0 in Figure 11.3 (page 402). Figure 11.6 is the lower-level diagram of that process.

As mentioned earlier, managing customer accounts involves an array of activities that typically occur between customer billing and later cash collection. Three of those activities are reflected in Figure 11.6: (1) sending periodic statements of account to customers, (2) accounting for sales returns and allowances or other accounts receivable adjustments, and (3) accounting for bad debts. The tasks required to properly maintain customer accounts can be fairly resource-intensive for an organization, as discussed in Technology Application 11.1 (page 406).

Figure 11.6 B/AR/CR Process—Diagram 2

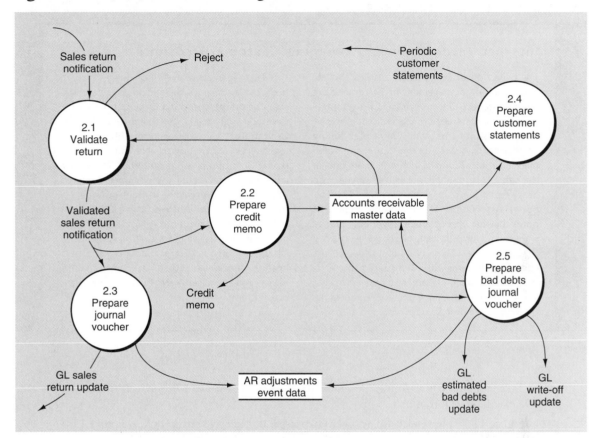

Let's examine briefly the processes that are diagrammed in Figure 11.6. In general, adjustments will always be necessary to account for sales returns, allowances for defective products or partial shipments, reversals of mispostings and other errors, estimates of uncollectible accounts, and bad debt write-offs. In Figure 11.6, processes 2.1 through 2.3 relate to sales returns adjustments. Process 2.5, "Prepare bad debts journal voucher," is triggered by a *temporal* event; namely, the periodic review of aging details obtained from the accounts receivable master data. One of two types of adjustments might result from this review:

- The recurring adjusting entry for *estimated* bad debts.
- The periodic write-off of "definitely worthless" customer accounts.

Note that, regardless of type, adjustments are recorded in the event data, updated to customer balances in the accounts receivable master data, and summarized and posted to the general ledger master data by the general ledger process.

Like process 2.5, bubble 2.4, "Prepare customer statements," also is triggered by a temporal event. In other words, it recurs at specified intervals, often on a monthly basis in practice. Details of unpaid invoices are extracted from the accounts receivable master data and are summarized in a statement of account that is mailed to customers. The statement both confirms with the customer the balance still owing and reminds the customer that payment is due. Therefore, it serves both operating and control purposes.

Source: Hurwitz Group, Inc., *The Future of Trade Receivables in Business* (March 2000).

Take some time now to track all these activities in Figure 11.6. Resolve any questions you may have before moving on.

Figure 11.7, a lower-level diagram of process 3.0, "Receive payment," in Figure 11.3 (page 402), completes our analysis of the events comprising the B/AR/CR process. In this diagram, we see our earlier activities culminate in the collection of cash from customers.

The check and remittance advice trigger the *receive payment* process. A **remittance advice (RA)** is a business document used by the payer to notify the payee of the items being paid. The RA can take various forms. For instance, it may be a copy of the invoice, a detachable RA delivered as part of a statement periodically sent to the customer (often a "stub" attached to the statement, a *turnaround document*), or a stub attached to the payer's check. In any case, B/AR/CR uses the RA to initiate the recording of a cash receipt.

Upon receipt of the check and remittance advice from a customer, process 3.1 first validates the remittance by comparing the check to the RA. Mismatches are rejected for later processing. If the check and RA agree, the validated remittance is sent to process 3.2, which endorses the check and separates it from the RA. Process 3.3 accumulates a number of endorsed checks, prepares and sends a bank deposit to the bank, records the collection with the *cash receipts events data*, and notifies the general ledger process of the amount of the cash deposited.

While process 3.3 is preparing the deposit, process 3.4 uses the RA to update the *accounts receivable master data* to reflect the customer's payment and then files the RA in the remittance advice file.

Figure 11.7 B/AR/CR Process—Diagram 3

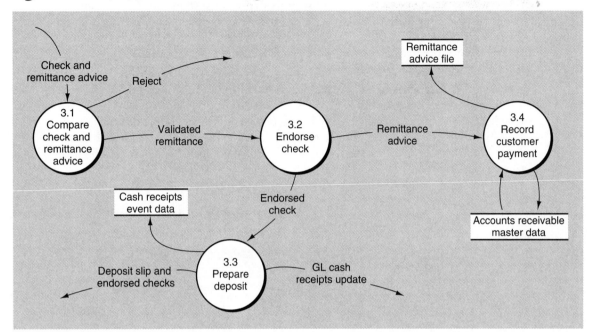

Logical Data Descriptions

Six data stores appear in Figure 11.3 (page 402), the level 0 diagram, four of which are related to event occurrences. Of the two *master data stores*, the *customer master* was defined in Chapter 10.

The **accounts receivable master data** is a repository of all unpaid invoices issued by an organization and awaiting final disposition. As the invoice is created, a record of the receivable is entered in the master data. Subsequently, the records are updated—i.e., the receivable balance is reduced—at the time that the customer makes the payment. As you learned in the previous section, the records also could be updated to reflect sales returns and allowances, bad debt write-offs, or other adjustments.

The accounts receivable master data provides information useful in minimizing outstanding customer balances and in prompting customers to pay in a timely manner. Two types of accounts receivable systems exist: (1) the *balance-only system*, and (2) the *open-item system*. Both are characterized by a different method of storing and reporting information, and both result in a different format for the periodic customer statements produced from the master data.

In a **balance-only system**, accounts receivable records consist of a customer's current balance due, past-due balance, and the finance charges and payments related to the account. Monthly statements display current charges, past-due charges, payments, finance charges, and the total balance due. Each month, unpaid current balances are rolled into the past-due balances. Electric and gas utility companies typically use balance-only systems. Usually, the only details supporting the amount of current charges are beginning and ending meter readings, total kilowatt-hours used for the period, and rate(s) per kwh.

In the balance-only system, customers usually pay from the periodic statement rather than paying individual invoices. In contrast, the **open-item system** is the more complex and is appropriate in situations where the customer typically makes payments for specific invoices when those invoices are due. The accounts receivable master data is organized such that each record consists of individual open invoices, against which all payments and other adjustments are applied.

On the periodic customer statement of account, a "lump sum" beginning balance is not shown. Rather, all invoices that are yet to be settled continue to be listed, along with payment details. Also, each open invoice is grouped by aging category and aged individually. Monthly, or at specified times, the customer accounts are aged and an aging schedule is printed. Figure 11.8 illustrates an aging report for an open-item system using SAP R/3.

Figure 11.8 Sample Accounts Receivable Aging Report in SAP

Customer	0 - 15	16 - 30	31 - 45	> 45
Elektromarkt Bamby	427,575.75	4,411,049.25	0.00	0.00
Lampen-Markt GmbH	606,743.45	1,039,404.50	0.00	0.00
Becker AG	14,030.00	0.00	571,527.00	0.00
N.I.C. High Tech	0.00	395,997.63	0.00	0.00
Christal Clear	0.00	458,892.55	0.00	0.00
C.A.S. Computer Applicatio	177,262.15	0.00	0.00	175,413.18
Speed & Partner	517,500.00	0.00	0.00	138,000.00
COMPU Tech. AG	0.00	227,154.87	0.00	0.00
Software Systeme GmbH	0.00	203,662.10	0.00	0.00
Carbor GmbH	716,013.00	0.00	0.00	0.00
SudaTech GmbH	0.00	417,715.65	0.00	0.00
Hitech AG	206,425.00	0.00	690.00	0.00
Motor Sports	0.00	101,731.14	0.00	0.00
HTG Komponente GmbH	0.00	425,276.90	0.00	0.00
Karsson High Tech Markt	0.00	133,010.15	0.00	0.00
CBD Computer Based Design	10,350.00	214,672.80	0.00	0.00
Amadeus Software Solutions	154,412.80	0.00	0.00	181,196.51
Motomarkt Stuttgart GmbH	0.00	80,500.00	0.00	0.00
Motomarkt Heidelberg GmbH	0.00	116,995.25	0.00	0.00
Autohaus Franzl GmbH	0.00	0.00	0.00	0.00
Computer Competence Center	9,257.50	0.00	0.00	0.00
Hallmann Anlagenbau GmbH	0.00	0.00	0.00	0.00
IDES France SA	0.00	0.00	0.00	0.00
Technik und Systeme GmbH	0.00	0.00	0.00	0.00
Total	2,839,569.65	8,226,062.79	572,217.00	494,609.69

Company code IDES AG — Country Total — Due in ... days — Key date: 12.02.1998 — Values in: UNI

Source: Reprinted with permission from SAP.

Now let's look at the event data maintained in the B/AR/CR process. First, the process records an entry for the sales data after it has validated the shipment and as it produces an invoice. The logical data definition for the **sales event data** would essentially comprise one or more invoice records. In a manual process, the sales data would be called a *sales journal*, with which you may be familiar from earlier accounting courses.

Recall that the **accounts receivable adjustments data** is created as sales returns, bad debt write-offs, estimated doubtful accounts, or similar adjustments and are processed as part of managing customer accounts. As in any event data, the records in this data store are typically keyed by date. The other essential data elements usually comprise journal voucher number, customer identification, adjustment type, account(s) and amount(s) to be debited, account(s) and amount(s) to be credited, and authorization indicator (i.e., approval code, signature, or the like).

The **cash receipts data,** created when customer payments are recorded, contains the details of each payment as reflected on the *remittance advice* accompanying a payment. Accordingly, each record in this data normally shows the date the payment is recorded, customer identification, invoice number(s) and gross invoice amount(s), cash discount(s) taken on each invoice, net invoice amount(s), check amount, and check number. Finally, as its name suggests, the *remittance advice file* stores copies of the remittance advices themselves.

Logical Database Design

We now look at how B/AR/CR data is structured, assuming a *database approach* to data management is employed. To keep the discussion simple, we will look at only two basic economic events as they relate to this process: sales invoicing and cash receipts. We also looked at sales invoicing in Chapter 10 because it is that event that is the bridge between the OE/S process and the B/AR/CR process. We will not cover adjustments resulting from sales returns, bad debt write-offs, and estimated doubtful accounts. Figure 11.9 (page 410) illustrates an E-R diagram of the invoicing and cash receipts events.

The shaded portion at the top of the diagram is repeated from Chapter 10 (Figure 10.9 on page 367). To the entities from Figure 10.9 we have added the CASH_RE-CEIPTS, DEPOSITS, BANKS, and EMPLOYEES entities. As it was in Figure 10.9, SALES_RELATIONS relationship accumulates a record of events as they progress. In this case we add the cash receipts event to this relationship. Recall from Figure 10.9 that this relationship already has accumulated a record of the SALES_ORDERS, STOCK_PICK, and SHIPMENTS, which we repeat here to emphasize that the invoice is generated after the goods are ordered, picked, and shipped. The box around this relationship indicates that we will have a relation in our database for this relationship while the other relationships will not have a corresponding relation.

As with Figure 10.9, the model in Figure 11.9 is not fully normalized yet. We include the "extra" relationships and redundant attributes to help you see the logical sequence of events. Also, the notes on Figure 11.9 indicate that this is a simplified model. Certainly realistic models must deal with partial picking, shipping, invoicing, and payments.

Finally, notice the interesting phenomenon in note E. There is *no separate accounts receivable* entity! Rather, accounts receivable balances (and/or deferred revenue balances) at any point in time are computed as the *difference* between the continuous events, SALES_INVOICES and CASH_RECEIPTS.[5]

Let's next translate the E-R diagram into relations (i.e., relational tables); Figure 11.10 (page 411) is designed to do that.

---

[5] William E. McCarthy—in his article, "The REA Accounting Model: A Generalized Framework for Accounting Systems in a Shared Environment," *The Accounting Review* (July 1982): 554–578—describes what is portrayed here as a process of producing information "snapshots" from records of continuing activities.

Figure 11.9 Entity-Relationship (E-R) Diagram (*Partial*) for the B/AR/CR Process

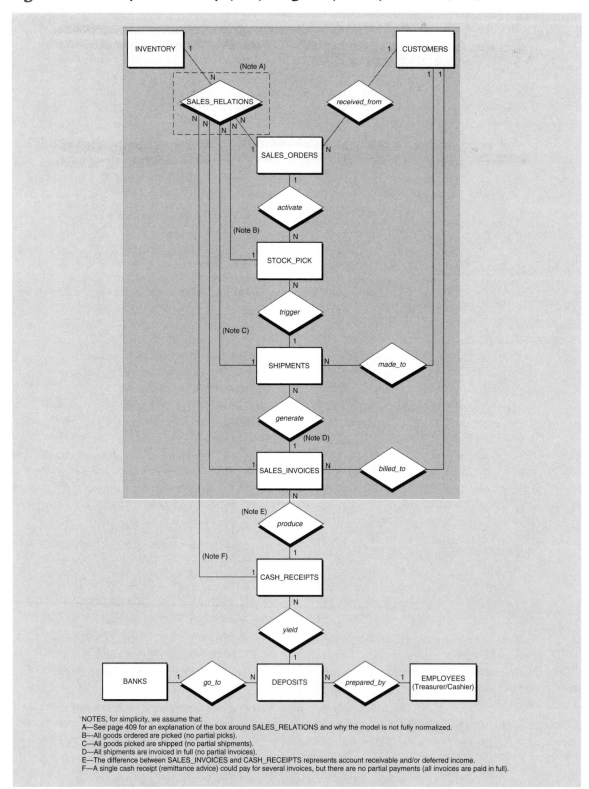

NOTES, for simplicity, we assume that:
A—See page 409 for an explanation of the box around SALES_RELATIONS and why the model is not fully normalized.
B—All goods ordered are picked (no partial picks).
C—All goods picked are shipped (no partial shipments).
D—All shipments are invoiced in full (no partial invoices).
E—The difference between SALES_INVOICES and CASH_RECEIPTS represents account receivable and/or deferred income.
F—A single cash receipt (remittance advice) could pay for several invoices, but there are no partial payments (all invoices are paid in full).

Figure 11.10 Selected Relational Table (*Partial*) for the B/AR/CR Process

Shaded_Attribute(s) = Primary Key

CUSTOMERS

Cust_No	Cust_Name	Cust_Street	Cust_City	Cust_State	Cust_ZIP	Ship_to_Name	Ship_to_Street	Ship_to_City	Ship_to_State	Ship_to_ZIP	Credit_Limit	Last_Revised	Credit_Terms
1234	Acme Co.	175 Fifth St	Beaufort	SC	29902	Same	Same	Same	Same	Same	5000	20060101	2/10,n/30
1235	Robbins, Inc	220 North Rd	Columbia	SC	29801	ALine Fabric	2 Main St	Greenwood	SC	29845	10000	20070915	n/60
1236	Jazzy Corp.	45 Ocean Dr	Hilton Hd	SC	29910	Same	Same	Same	Same	Same	0	20070610	COD

INVENTORY

Item_No	Item_Name	Price	Location	Qty_on_Hand	Reorder_Pt
936	Machine Plates	39.50	Macomb	1,500	950
1001	Gaskets	9.50	Macomb	10,002	3,500
1010	Crank Shafts	115.00	Tampa	952	500
1025	Manifolds	45.00	Tampa	402	400

SALES ORDERS

SO_No	SO_Date	Cust_No	Cust_PO_No	Cust_PO_Date	Ship_Via	FOB_Terms
5677	20071216	1235	41523	20071212	UPS	Ship Pt
5678	20071216	1276	A1190	20071214	Best way	Ship Pt
5679	20071216	1236	9422	20071216	Fed Ex	Destin

STOCK PICK

Pick_No	Pick_Date	Picked_By	SO_No	Ship_No
9436	20071215	Butch	5676	94101
9437	20071215	Rachel	5677	94102
9438	20071216	Ace	5678	94103

SHIPMENTS

Ship_No	Ship_Date	Shipped_By	Cust_No	Invoice_No
94101	20071215	Jason	1293	964
94102	20071216	Carol	1235	965
94103	20071216	Jason	1249	966

CASH RECEIPTS

Remit_No	Dep_No	Total_Rec	Remit_Date
9529	116-334	1962.35	20080110
9530	116-335	369.28	20070110

BANKS

Bank_No	Bank_Name
2239	Acme
2240	Benton

SALES_RELATIONS

SO_No	Item_No	Qty_Ordered	Pick_No	Qty_Picked	Ship_No	Qty_Shipped	Invoice_No	Qty_Invoiced	Remit_No	Amt_Invoiced
5676	1074	60	9436	60	94101	60	964	60	9529	549.00
5677	1001	100	9437	100	94102	100	965	100		950.00
5677	1010	75	9437	75	94102	75	965	75		8625.00
5678	936	40	9438	40	94103	40	966	40		1580.00

SALES INVOICES

Invoice_No	Invoice_Date	Invoice_Total	Cust_No	Remit_No
964	20071216	549.00	1293	9529
965	20071216	9575.00	1235	
966	20071217	1580.00	1249	

DEPOSITS

Deposit_No	Dep_Date	Deposit_Amt	Emp_No (Treasurer/Cashier)	Bank_No
116-334	20080112	1962.35	D762	2239
116-335	20080112	329.28	D762	2239

We repeat here from Figure 10.10 (page 369) the CUSTOMERS, INVENTORY, SALES_ORDERS, STOCK_PICK, SHIPMENTS, SALES_INVOICES, and SALES_RELATIONS relations to emphasize the connections (linkages) among relations and to remind you that before invoicing a customer, we first have accepted a customer's sales order, picked the goods, and shipped the goods to the customer.

To simplify the tables, we have assumed that each inventory line item picked and shipped is billed at a single unit sales price from the INVENTORY relation. Further, SALES_INVOICES ignores freight, sales taxes, or other items that might be billed to a customer. By using the SALES_INVOICES relation and extracting other data, as needed, from other relations, contemplate how you would prepare the invoice *document* to be sent to the customer.

The CASH_RECEIPTS and the attributes added to the end of the SALES_RELATIONS relation (i.e., Remit_No and Remit_Amt) substitute for the cash receipts data and remittance advice data discussed in the preceding section. For simplicity, we have ignored customer cash discounts in the relations shown. First, note that Cust_No in CASH_RECEIPTS allows us to associate cash receipts with particular customers for the purpose of monitoring customer accounts and assessing any needed bad debt adjustments. In addition, Invoice_No in SALES_RELATIONS can be used to apply collections against specific open invoices (as in an *open-item accounts receivable system*, for instance). Finally, the linkages among CASH_RECEIPTS, SALES_RELATIONS, SALES_INVOICES, and CUSTOMERS can be used to determine customer accounts receivable balances at any moment in time, as shown in the E-R diagram and explained previously.

Types of Billing Systems

In general, two kinds of billing systems exist. In a **post-billing system**, invoices are prepared after goods have been shipped and the sales order notification has been matched to shipping's billing notification. The data flow diagrams in this section and in Chapter 10 assumed a post-billing system.

In a **pre-billing system**, invoices are prepared immediately on acceptance of a customer order—that is, after inventory and credit checks have been accomplished. Pre-billing systems often occur in situations where there is little or no delay between receipt of the customer's order and its shipment. For instance, pre-billing systems are not uncommon in catalog sales operations such as that of L.L.Bean. In such systems, there is no separate sales order document as such; copies of the invoice serve as the picking ticket, packing slip, and other functions required by the OE/S process.[6] In other words, the customer is billed (and the inventory, accounts receivable, and general ledger master data are updated) at the time the customer order is entered. However, the customer copy of the invoice is not released until shipment has been made. For this type of system to operate efficiently, the inventory control system must be very reliable. If an order is accepted and an item then turns out to be unavailable, all accounting entries would have to be reversed.

PHYSICAL PROCESS DESCRIPTION OF THE BILLING FUNCTION

ENTERPRISE SYSTEMS

Figure 11.11 presents a physical process for billing. From Chapter 10, you should have a good understanding of the order entry and shipping functions leading up to billing.

---

[6] By eliminating one source document (the sales order) and a separate data transcription step (from shipping documents to the customer invoice), pre-billing helps to ensure certain control goals. For that reason, we include pre-billing procedures as a control plan for the billing process in a later chapter section.

Figure 11.11 Systems Flowchart of the Billing Function

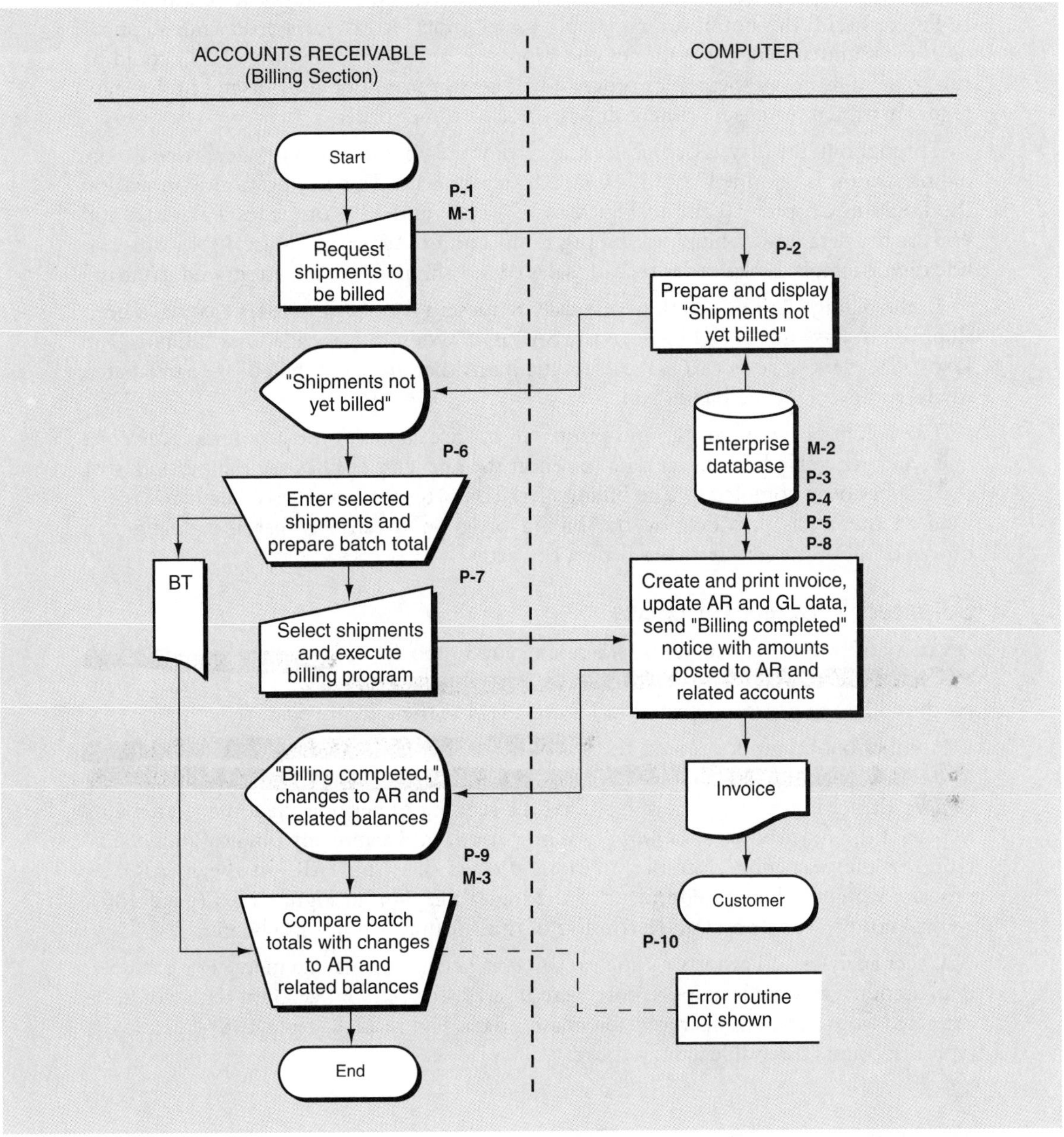

Take some time now to review the flowchart for general ideas. You should notice a close resemblance between this process's physical features and the logical design of the billing process as presented in Figures 11.2, 11.3, and 11.4. You should also see that this system demonstrates the use of an *enterprise system* and several features of the technology discussed earlier in this chapter.

The Billing Process

At the time the sales order was recorded in the order entry department, the billing section of the accounts receivable department was "notified" that a sales order had been created. This notification is shown on the DFDs in Chapter 10 and in Figures 11.2, 11.3, and 11.4 on pages 401, 402, and 403) as the data flow "Sales order notification." In Figure 11.11, this notification is simply a sales order record (sales orders not shipped) on the integrated database. Queries and reports (not shown in Figure 11.11) could be run to get a listing of these sales orders. Such listings would be most useful in the shipping department to ensure timely shipment of customer orders.

Throughout the day, as shipments are recorded in the shipping department, the billing section is "notified" by the shipping department. This notification is shown on the DFDs in Chapter 10 and in Figures 11.2, 11.3, and 11.4 on pages 401, 402, and 403) as the data flow "Shipping's billing notification." Again, in Figure 11.11, this notification is simply a sales order record (sales orders shipped) on the integrated database.

In the billing section, a clerk periodically requests a list of sales orders that have been shipped but have not been billed. In the SAP R/3 system this is called the "Billing Due List." The clerk reviews this list, selects the items that are to be billed, prepares batch totals, and executes the billing run.

The billing program creates and prints[7] an invoice, updates the accounts receivable, sales, and general ledger master data to reflect the sale, and notifies the billing clerk that the run has been completed. The billing clerk compares the previously calculated batch total to the totals provided by the billing program to ensure that the billing run processed all of the selected sales orders correctly.

Selected Process Outputs

A variety of outputs (documents, statements, and reports) are generated either during normal processing runs or during special report-generation runs. The key document produced by the process depicted in Figure 11.11 is the sales invoice.

Another important document, the *customer monthly statement,* is prepared at the end of each month from data appearing in each customer's accounts receivable master data record. Earlier in the chapter, we included the sending of periodic customer statements as part of the function of *managing customer accounts*. Because any physical implementation of the managing customer accounts process (i.e., the "AR" in the B/AR/CR process) would be highly redundant of the logical diagram in Figure 11.6 (page 405), we will not present a physical description of the AR function in this chapter.

Other analyses and reports can be prepared as needed by management. For example, if an accounts receivable aging report were desired, the relevant account data would be extracted from the accounts receivable master data. Figure 11.8 (page 408) illustrated a typical accounts receivable aging report.

APPLICATION OF THE CONTROL FRAMEWORK FOR THE BILLING FUNCTION

CONTROLS   In this section, the control framework is applied to the billing function. Figure 11.12 presents a completed *control matrix* for the systems flowchart depicted in Figure 11.11 (page 413). Figure 11.11 is annotated to show the location of the control plans keyed to the control matrix.

---

[7] The billing program could create an electronic invoice to be sent to the customer.

Figure 11.12 Control Matrix for the Billing Business Process

Recommended Control Plans	Control Goals of the Operations Process — Ensure effectiveness of operations (A)	(B)	(C)	Ensure efficient employment of resources (people, computers)	Ensure security of resources (accounts receivable master data)	For completed shipping notice inputs, ensure: IV	IC	IA	For the accounts receivable master data, ensure: UC	UA
Present Controls										
P-1: Review shipped not billed sales orders (tickler file)	P-1					P-1				
P-2: Edit the shipping notification for accuracy (e.g., programmed edits)								P-2		P-2
P-3: Independent billing authorization						P-3				
P-4: Check for authorized prices, terms, freight, and discounts						P-4		P-4		
P-5: Independent pricing data			P-5			P-5		P-5		
P-6: Calculate batch totals						P-6	P-6			
P-7: Interactive feedback						P-7		P-7		
P-8: Record input		P-8		P-8		P-8	P-8	P-8	P-8	
P-9: Reconcile input and output batch totals						P-9	P-9	P-9	P-9	P-9
P-10: Procedures for rejected inputs						P-10		P-10		
Missing Controls										
M-1: Employ a pre-billing system	M-1			M-1				M-1		
M-2: Confirm customer accounts regularly		M-2				M-2		M-2		M-2
M-3: Computer agreement of batch totals				M-3		M-3	M-3	M-3	M-3	M-3

Legend:
Possible effectiveness goals include:
A = Bill customers promptly upon evidence of shipment.
B = Provide for query and reporting functions that support accountability and meet specific problem-solving requirements (e.g., accounts receivable listings by invoice due date, aging reports).
C = Comply with the four pricing requirements of the Robinson-Patman Act.
See Exhibit 11.1 (pages 417–418) for a complete explanation of control plans and cell entries.

IV = Input validity
IC = Input completeness
IA = Input accuracy
UC = Update completeness
UA = Update accuracy

Control Goals

The control goals listed across the top of the matrix are derived from the framework presented in Chapter 9. We will comment briefly on a few of those goals.

Under effectiveness of operations, we have listed three representative *effectiveness* goals. Obviously, in actual billing processes, other goals are possible. In addition, as mentioned in Chapters 7 and 9, the control matrices in this text incorporate as one of the system goals, when applicable, the COSO report's goal of complying with laws, regulations, and contractual agreements. For this reason, we include goal C for the Billing business process—Comply with the fair pricing requirements of the Robinson-Patman Act of 1936. Briefly stated, the act makes it illegal in industrial and wholesale markets for a seller to charge different prices to two competing buyers under identical circumstances unless the seller can justify the pricing differential based on differences in its cost to manufacture, sell, and deliver the goods.

As mentioned in Chapter 9 and reinforced in Chapter 10, the resource security column should identify only the assets that are *directly* at risk. For that reason, cash is not listed because it is only indirectly affected by the validity of the billings. The resource that is of interest here is the accounts receivable master data. Controls should prevent unauthorized access, copying, changing, selling, or destruction of the accounts receivable master data.

To focus our discussion, we have limited our coverage of process inputs to just the shipping notice (i.e., the shipments not yet billed). Note, however, that other process inputs could be included in the matrix. From the point of view of the billing process, valid billings are those that are properly authorized and reflect actual credit sales; for example, a billing should be supported by a proper shipping notification and should be billed at authorized prices, terms, freight, and discounts.

Recommended Control Plans

Each of the recommended control plans listed in the first column of the control matrix is discussed in Exhibit 11.1 (pages 417–418). As usual, you will find that some of the recommended control plans are present in the process, whereas others are missing. As you study the control plans, be sure to notice where they are located on the systems flowchart.

PHYSICAL PROCESS DESCRIPTION OF THE CASH RECEIPTS FUNCTION

As discussed earlier, the procedures employed in collecting cash can vary widely. For example, some companies ask customers to mail checks along with remittance advices to the company, others ask customers to send payments to a designated bank lockbox, while in electronic commerce environments some form of electronic funds transfer is generally used. Figure 11.13 (page 419) depicts a process where customer payments are received by mail. The source documents include checks and remittance advices.

Each day, the process begins with mailroom clerks opening the mail. Immediately, the clerks endorse all checks. They assemble enclosed statements (remittance advices that come in the form of billing statement detachments from the customer invoice—i.e., *turnaround documents*) in batches and prepare batch totals for control purposes.

Exhibit 11.1 Explanation of Cell Entries for Control Matrix in Figure 11.12

P-1: *Review shipped not billed sales orders (tickler file).*

Effectiveness goal A, Completed shipping notice input completeness: By monitoring the sales orders that have been shipped but not yet billed, we can ensure that *all* shipping notices are billed in a *timely* manner.

P-2: *Edit the shipping notification for accuracy.*

Completed shipping notice input accuracy: We can greatly increase the accuracy of entering shipment data by utilizing the computer to edit the data input (i.e., *programmed edits*).

Accounts receivable master data update accuracy: Since the AR data is updated simultaneously with the editing of the inputs, these programmed edits ensure update accuracy.

P-3: *Independent billing authorization.*

Completed shipping notice input validity: Comparison of sales orders, entered at order entry, with shipping notifications entered by shipping, can reduce the possibility that shipping notifications are invalid by verifying that each shipment is supported by an approved sales order.

P-4: *Check for authorized prices, terms, freight, and discounts.*

Completed shipping notice input validity: The billing process in Figure 11.11 has an implicit, *independent* check for *authorized* prices, terms, discounts, and freight charges at the time that the invoices are prepared. Note that the operative word, "authorized," speaks to the control goal of input validity.

Completed shipping notice input accuracy: We see prices, terms, freight, and discounts being calculated during the billing process using an approved set of criteria, data, and table in the integrated database. At a minimum, we would expect to see access to the inventory master data for a price check for the items shipped. Criteria for the terms, discount, and freight *might* be located on the customer master data (or accounts receivable master data) or within the billing program.

P-5: *Independent pricing data.*

Effectiveness goal C: In this system, unit selling prices are obtained from the inventory master data. In this way, the inventory master data serves as an *independent* source of those prices. Therefore, determining the price to be charged

a customer is beyond the control of the salesperson and others involved in the selling function. This independent pricing of orders helps to ensure that the company does not engage in discriminatory pricing practices in violation of the Robinson-Patman Act.

Shipping notice input validity: Automatic pricing presumes that previously authorized prices are used in the billing process.

Shipping notice input accuracy: Automatic pricing ensures that a price will be entered and that it will be a correct price.

P-6: *Calculate batch totals.*

Shipping notice input validity and input completeness: Batch totals arise from legitimate source documents (*input validity*). Batch totals ensure that all of the batched data is recorded (*input completeness*). As suggested earlier, the nature and extent of batch totals can vary: they can account for only the number of transactions, the number of items or lines of data, dollar amounts, and/or hash totals. As such, batch totals themselves ensure the validity and completeness of the counts and amounts they represent. However, they do not necessarily ensure input accuracy—that takes place in the reconciliation, which is discussed in control plan P-9.

P-7: *Interactive feedback checks.*

Shipping notice input completeness: By advising the user that input has been accepted, interactive feedback checks help ensure input completeness.

Accounts receivable master data update accuracy: Since the feedback is provided after the AR data is updated, this feedback ensures update accuracy.

P-8: *Record input.*

Effectiveness goal A, and Efficient employment of resources, Shipping notice input completeness and accuracy, Accounts receivable master data update completeness and accuracy: Automatic recording of input event data is fast and reliable.

P-9: *Reconcile input and output batch totals.*

Completed shipping notice input validity, completeness, and accuracy: The billing clerk reconciles the input totals to the totals produced by the computer after the updates have occurred. If we assume that the batch total is either a dollar total or hash total, we are justified in making cell

(continued)

Exhibit 11.1 Explanation of Cell Entries for Control Matrix in Figure 11.12 (*continued*)

entries in all three columns: input *validity (IV)*, input *completeness (IC)*, and input *accuracy (IA)*. On the other hand, item or line counts help to ensure IC and IA (*not* IV), while document or record counts address the goal of IC only.

Accounts receivable master data update completeness and accuracy: Since the output totals are produced after the AR update, we show entries in the columns for update *completeness (UC)* and update *accuracy (UA)*. Again, if the batch totals comprised only document/record counts, we could not justify a cell entry in the UA column.

P-10: *Procedures for rejected inputs.*

Completed shipping notice input and accounts receivable master data update completeness: The cell entries in the IC and UC columns of the control matrix presume that corrective action will be taken to investigate all rejected items, remedy any errors, and resubmit the corrected input for reprocessing. We can include UC because the output totals are produced after the AR master data update.

M-1: *Employ a pre-billing system.*

Effectiveness goal A: If a pre-billing system were used, it would shorten the time needed to bill customers and thus help to ensure effectiveness goal A—to bill customers promptly upon evidence of shipment. Upon notification that the shipment had been made, billing the customer would involve simply releasing (mailing) the customer copy of the invoice.

Efficient employment of resources: By collapsing two processes—preparing the sales order and generating the customer invoice—into a single operation, a pre-billing system employs system resources more efficiently.

Completed shipping notice input accuracy: Collapsing sales order preparation and customer invoice generation into a single operation improves billing accuracy by eliminating a separate data entry step.

M-2: *Confirm customer accounts regularly.*

Effectiveness goal B: The customer statements, and summary reports produced with them, would provide the reporting and accountability functions suggested by goal B.

Completed shipping notice input validity, Completed shipping notice input accuracy: The customer can be utilized as a means of controlling the billing process. By sending regular customer statements, we use the customer to check that invoices were valid and accurate. Most organizations send statements, but that process is beyond the scope of that depicted in Figure 11.11 (page 413).

Accounts receivable master data update accuracy: Since statements would be produced from the accounts receivable master data, the customer also determines the accuracy of accounts receivable updates.

M-3: *Computer agreement of batch totals.*

Efficient employment of resources: Computer agreement of batch controls would improve efficiency through automation of the process.

Input and update control goals: This control does not appear in the flowchart nor is it mentioned in the physical process description narrative. Therefore we cannot make any of the P (present) entries made for control plan P-8.

The receipts data—batch total and remittance details from the customer billing statements—are then entered into the computer system via a scanning process and use of optical character recognition (OCR, as discussed in Chapter 10) technology in the mailroom. The computer edits the data as the data are entered and computes batch totals. Once the data are verified as correct, the details are written to the *cash receipts event data* in the integrated database. The batched statements are sent to the accounts receivable department for filing, and the checks are transferred to the cashier.

For most processes of the type illustrated in Figure 11.13, input requirements are minimal. As indicated, the editing process verifies the correctness of the entered data, including customer number and so forth. By accessing open invoice data that reside with

Figure 11.13 Systems Flowchart of the Cash Receipts Business Process

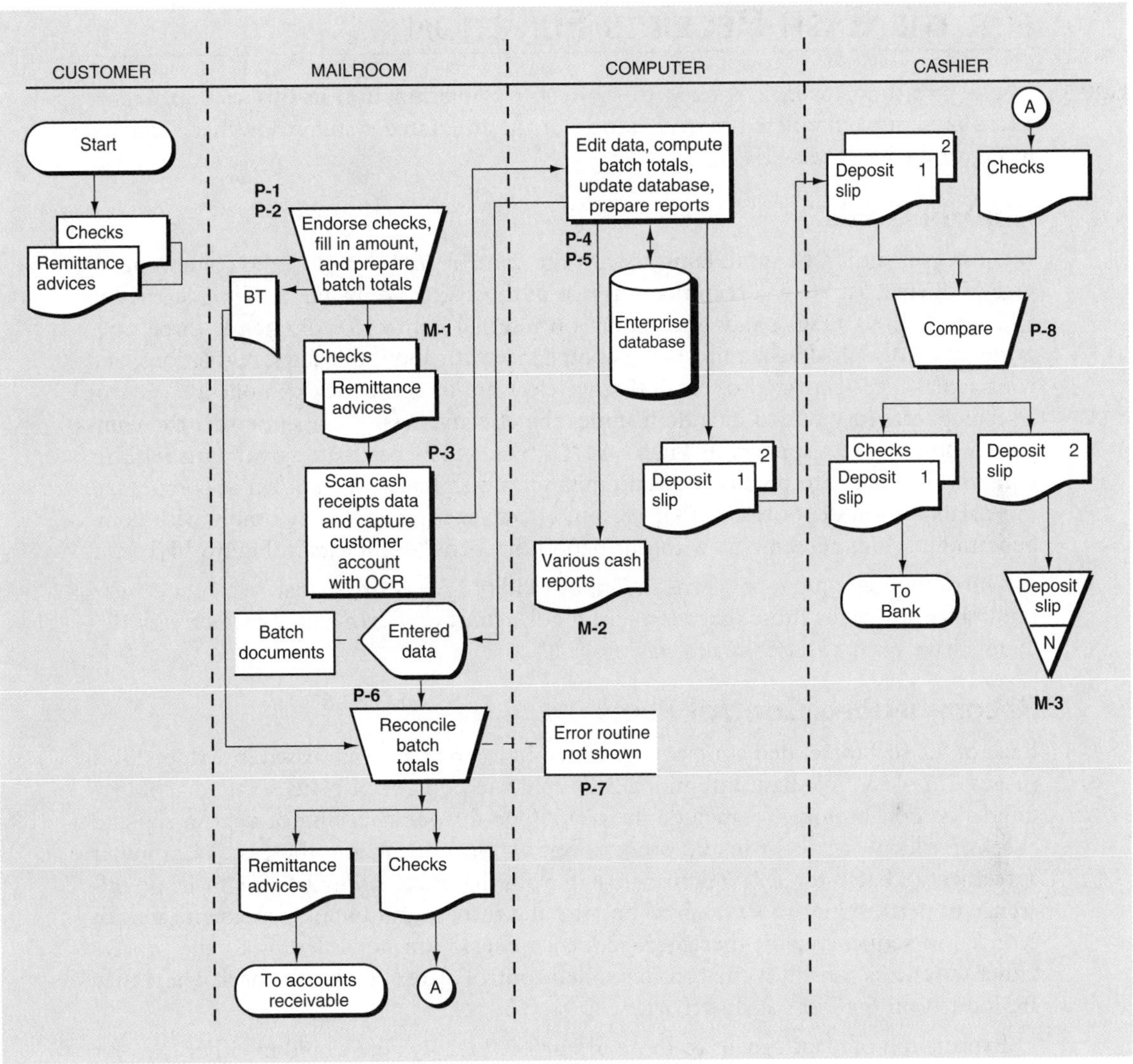

the accounts receivable master data in the integrated database, the process also verifies that any cash discounts taken by the customer are legitimate (i.e., they have been *authorized*). To check the dollar amount of each invoice remitted, the system calculates the balance due by adding the cash payment to the cash discount taken (if any); it then compares the computed balance-due total to the balance-due total scanned by the mailroom clerk.

Once the data have passed all the control checks, the accounts receivable, cash receipts, and general ledger data in the enterprise database are updated. Also, the computer generates various cash reports and prepares the deposit slip. The deposit slip is transferred to the cashier. The cashier compares the checks and the deposit slip; if they agree, all documents are sent to the bank.

APPLICATION OF THE CONTROL FRAMEWORK FOR THE CASH RECEIPTS FUNCTION

CONTROLS   The control framework is applied to the cash receipts function in this section. Figure 11.14 presents a completed *control matrix* for the annotated systems flowchart depicted in Figure 11.13 (page 419).

Control Goals

By now, you should be quite familiar with the control goals listed in the column headings of the matrix. We will comment on two of those goals only. First, as you learned in Chapter 7, the COSO study and report on internal control recommends three categories of control goals, the third being compliance with applicable laws, regulations, and contractual agreements. Also, recall that we elect not to show the "compliance" goal as a separate category but to include it under the effectiveness. We assume that the company whose process appears in Figure 11.13 (page 419) has loan agreements with its bank that require it to maintain certain minimum cash balances—known as compensating balances—on deposit. For that reason, effectiveness goal C—"Comply with compensating balance agreements with our depository bank"—appears in Figure 11.14.

Our second comment concerns the input validity (IV) control goal. We define *valid* remittance advices as those that represent funds *actually received* and for which cash discounts have been *authorized* and *approved*.

Recommended Control Plans

Each of the recommended control plans listed in the matrix is discussed in Exhibit 11.2 (pages 422–423). We have intentionally limited the number of plans so as to avoid redundancy. For instance, we include the plan "One-for-one checking of deposit slip and checks," which does exist in the process, but we do not include the plan "Computer agreement of batch totals," which is missing from the process. Further, we make no reference to performing *sequence checks* because the turnaround billing statements are not received in sequence and, therefore, sequence checks are not relevant to the process under review. As you study the recommended control plans, be sure to check where they are located on the systems flowchart.

Explanation of plans similar to those in Exhibit 11.2 was presented in either Chapter 9 or 10 or earlier in this chapter in Exhibit 11.1 (pages 417–418) for the billing function. Therefore, some explanations contain highlights only.

In addition to the control plans discussed in Exhibit 11.2, an organization should *reconcile subsidiary ledgers and control accounts regularly.* This control plan is discussed in Chapter 16. Also, you should note that the control plan of regularly confirming customer accounts, discussed earlier under the control plans for the billing process, serves to check the validity and accuracy of *both* customer billings and cash receipts.

SUMMARY

With the conclusion of this chapter, we complete the second business process in the order-to-cash process depicted in Figure 2.7 (page 60). In later chapters, we discuss the interaction of the OE/S and B/AR/CR processes with the other key business processes in an organization.

Figure 11.14 Control Matrix for the Cash Receipts Function

Recommended Control Plans	Control Goals of the Cash Receipts Business Process									
	Control Goals of the Operations Process					Control Goals of the Information Process				
	Ensure effectiveness of operations			Ensure efficient employment of resources (people, computers)	Ensure security of resources (cash, accounts receivable master data)	For remittance advice inputs (i.e., cash receipts), ensure:			For the accounts receivable master data, ensure:	
	A	*B*	*C*			*IV*	*IC*	*IA*	*UC*	*UA*
Present Controls										
P-1: Immediately endorse incoming checks					P-1					
P-2: Receive turnaround documents				P-2		P-2		P-2		
P-3: Enter cash receipts close to where cash is received				P-3				P-3		
P-4: Edit cash receipts for accuracy				P-4				P-4		
P-5: Compare input data with master data	P-5			P-5		P-5		P-5		P-5
P-6: Manual agreement of batch totals						P-6	P-6	P-6	P-6	P-6
P-7: Procedures for rejected inputs							P-7		P-7	
P-8: One-for-one checking of deposit slip and checks						P-8	P-8	P-8		
Missing Controls										
M-1: Immediately separate checks and remittance advices	M-1	M-1	M-1		M-1					
M-2: Reconcile bank account regularly						M-2		M-2		
M-3: Review deposit slip file	M-3		M-3		M-3					

Legend:

Possible effectiveness goals include:

A = Optimize cash flow by minimizing overdue accounts and reducing the investment in accounts receivable.

B = Provide for query and reporting functions that support accountability and meet specific problem-solving requirements (e.g., accounts receivable listings by invoice due date, cash on deposit by bank).

C = Comply with compensating balance agreements with our depository bank.

IV = Input validity
IC = Input completeness
IA = Input accuracy
UC = Update completeness
UA = Update accuracy

See Exhibit 11.2 (pages 422–423) for a complete explanation of control plans and cell entries.

Exhibit 11.2 Explanation of Cell Entries for Control Matrix in Figure 11.14

P-1: *Immediately endorse incoming checks.*

Security of resources: To protect the checks from being fraudulently appropriated, the checks should be restrictively endorsed as soon as possible following their receipt in the organization. *Lockboxes* provide even more protection for the cash by having cash receipts sent directly to a bank.

P-2: *Receive turnaround documents.*

Efficient employment of resources: The use of the billing statement as a turnaround document reduces the data entry that must be completed. Only the amount paid needs to be manually recorded by data entry personnel. Performance of this function early in the process—before the check and statement have been separated—facilitates a more efficient correction of errors.

Remittance advice input validity: By using the customer billing statement as the remittance advice, the turnaround document provides assurance on the validity of the cash receipt source. Since we assume that the clerk enters the actual amount of the payment, we also know that the input amount is valid (supported by an actual payment).

Remittance advice input accuracy: Scanning the computer-readable turnaround document reduces the risk of data entry errors, thereby improving accuracy.

P-3: *Enter cash receipts close to where cash is received.*

Efficient employment of resources: The direct entry of cash receipts data by mailroom personnel provides for a more efficient employment of resources because this arrangement eliminates the costs associated with the handling of the cash receipts data by additional entities.

Remittance advice input accuracy: Because mailroom personnel would have both the check and the paid billing statement (e.g., remittance advice), they would be in a position to correct many input errors "on the spot," thereby improving input accuracy.

P-4: *Edit cash receipts for accuracy.*

Efficient employment of resources: Programmed edits provide quick, low-cost editing of data.

Remittance advice input accuracy: By identifying erroneous or suspect data and preventing these data from entering the system, programmed edit checks help to ensure input accuracy.

P-5: *Compare input data with master data.*

Effectiveness goal A, Efficient employment of resources: Cash receipts data can be entered more quickly and at a lower cost if errors are detected and prevented from entering the system.

Remittance advice input validity: The matching process verifies that any cash discounts deducted by customers have been *authorized*.

Remittance advice input accuracy, Accounts receivable update accuracy: Comparison to the accounts receivable master data should reduce input errors. Updates to the accounts receivable data occur simultaneously with input.

P-6: *Manual agreement of batch totals.*

P-7: *Procedures for rejected inputs.*

(Plans P-6 and P-7 were discussed in Exhibit 11.1, pages 417–418. Refer to that discussion for an explanation of the cell entries in the cash receipts control matrix.)

P-8: *One-for-one checking of deposit slip and checks (tickler file).*

Remittance advice input validity: This plan helps to ensure input validity because each recorded receipt reflected on the deposit slip is represented by funds actually received (i.e., an actual customer check).

Remittance advice input completeness: The cashier should monitor the temporary file of checks to ensure that a deposit slip is received for *all* cash receipts. Since the deposit slip is prepared from the cash receipts data, this plan helps to ensure the completeness of cash receipts inputs.

Remittance advice input accuracy: Since the cashier compares the details of the deposit slip to the checks themselves, the accuracy of remittance advice inputs is ensured.

M-1: *Immediately separate checks and remittance advices.*

Effectiveness goals A, B, and C: The checks should be separated from the remittance advices and the checks deposited as quickly as possible. This helps to optimize cash flow and to ensure that the organization complies with compensating balance requirements of loan agreements with its bank.

If the remittance advices were immediately separated from the checks, the process of *recording* the remittance advices also could be accelerated in that the customer payment could

Exhibit 11.2 **Explanation of Cell Entries for Control Matrix in Figure 11.14 (*continued*)**

be recorded at the same time that the deposit is being prepared. Faster recording of the remittance advices (i.e., updating customer balances more quickly) would help to minimize overdue accounts and reduce the investment in accounts receivable. Furthermore, since the information available from the system would be more up to date, this plan also would address the providing of more meaningful query and reporting functions.

Security of resources: The faster the checks are deposited, the less chance that the cash can be diverted. At a minimum, cash should be deposited once a day.

M-2: *Reconcile bank account regularly.*

Remittance advice input validity, Remittance advice input accuracy: By regularly reconciling the bank account, the organization confirms the validity and accuracy of the recorded cash receipts. The bank statement and *validated* deposit slips will reflect actual cash deposits and the correct amount of those deposits. Ideally, a person

who is independent of those who handle and record cash receipts and disbursements should perform the reconciliation.

M-3: *Review deposit slip file (i.e., tickler file).*

Effectiveness goals A and C: Because the flowchart does not depict a process for periodically reviewing this file to determine if deposit slips are returned promptly from the bank, we mark this as a missing control. This file should be reviewed regularly to ensure that deposits are made promptly, to optimize cash flow, and to ensure that the organization complies with compensating balance requirements of loan agreements with its bank.

Security of resources: By maintaining a completed deposit slip file, the cashier provides an *audit trail* to support each deposit, thereby protecting deposits from misappropriation. The deposit slip should be filed prior to deposit and the *validated* deposit slip should be filed when it is returned from the bank.

This chapter presented a number of ways that technology can affect the operations of the B/AR/CR process. For example, technology was discussed as a means of solving certain problems regarding cash flow. What's in the future? We are rapidly moving toward a checkless society. Even cash is becoming less of an accepted medium for payment. Your challenge will be to keep abreast of the ways accountants are affected by the transition from checks and cash to electronic transfers of money.

REVIEW QUESTIONS

RQ 11-1 What is the billing/accounts receivable/cash receipts (B/AR/CR) process?

RQ 11-2 What primary functions does the B/AR/CR process perform? Explain each function.

RQ 11-3 How does the B/AR/CR process relate to its organizational setting?

RQ 11-4 Why are customer self-service systems generally helpful in cutting customer service costs?

RQ 11-5 What are the relative advantages of checks, charge cards, and debit cards from the collector's standpoint?

RQ 11-6 Describe several ways that companies have reduced the *float* connected with cash receipts.

RQ 11-7 What is a lockbox? Why is a lockbox used?

RQ 11-8 What is lapping?

RQ 11-9 What is a remittance advice (RA)?

RQ 11-10 What is the accounts receivable data store?

RQ 11-11 What are the major features of a balance-only and an open-item accounts receivable system?

RQ 11-12 What is the difference between a post-billing system and a pre-billing system?

RQ 11-13 What controls are associated with the billing business process? Explain each control.

RQ 11-14 What controls are associated with the cash receipts billing process? Explain each control.

Discussion Questions

DQ 11-1 Develop several examples of possible goal conflicts among the various managers and supervisors depicted in Figure 11.1 (page 395).

DQ 11-2 Based on the definition of *float* presented in the chapter, discuss several possibilities for improving the cash float for your company, assuming you are the cashier.

DQ 11-3 Using Figure 11.6 (page 405), speculate about the kinds of data that might be running along the data flow that comes from the accounts receivable master data to bubble 2.1. Be specific, and be prepared to defend your answer by discussing the use(s) to which *each* of those data elements could be put.

DQ 11-4 Discuss the information content of Figure 11.8 (page 408). How might this report be used by the credit manager or by the accounts receivable manager? If you were either of these managers, what other reports concerning accounts receivable might you find useful, and how would you use them? Be specific.

DQ 11-5 Consult the systems flowcharts of Figures 11.11 and 11.13 (pages 413 and 419). Discuss how each of these processes implements the concept of segregation of duties discussed in Chapter 8. For each of the two processes, be specific as to which entity (or entities) performs each of the four data processing functions mentioned in Chapter 8 (assuming that all four functions are illustrated by the process).

DQ 11-6 Discuss the relative advantages of lockbox systems, charge cards, and debit cards from the standpoint of *both* the party making the payment and the party receiving the payment.

DQ 11-7 a. Discuss the conditions under which each of the following billing systems would be most appropriate: (1) pre-billing system and (2) post-billing system.

b. Discuss the relative advantages of each of the billing systems mentioned in part a, from the standpoint of both the selling company and the customer.

Note: As mentioned in Chapter 10, the first couple of problems in the application chapters are based on the processes of specific companies. Therefore, the problem material starts with case narratives of those processes.

CASE STUDIES

CASE A: Trusty Insurance Co.

Background Information

Trusty Insurance Co. is a major property/casualty underwriter based in St. Louis. It uses over 5,000 independent insurance agents to market its products and collect the premiums. In the past, the agents typically have remitted the premiums to Trusty at a predetermined time each month by mailing the checks to a lockbox site or to a regional office of the insurance company. This method of cash collections has been slow, and accounting for the agents' payments has been fraught with problems. Therefore, Trusty sought the help of National One Bank (NOB) in developing a more automated collection process. NOB responded by developing an ACH-based "Customer-Initiated Payment Service (CIPS)" that allows the independent agents to pay Trusty with ACH debits initiated via a toll-free phone call, or PC. The next section describes how the CIPS process works; for simplicity, the description is limited to PC-initiated payments.

Operation of the CIPS Process

By 5:00 P.M. EST on the 15th of each month, an agent logs onto the NOB Web site and creates a Smartcheck for Trusty. The agent must fill out the Smartcheck with Trusty's four-digit company number, payment amount, and effective date of payment.

Once the agent submits the Smartcheck, the information is stored in a payment database that is formatted to ACH standards. On each effective payment date, NOB credits Trusty's account and sends the ACH payment data to the Federal Reserve Bank where it is used to debit the account for the agent's bank and to credit NOB's account.

The evening of the payment date, NOB also transmits electronically a data file of the settled payments to Trusty's data center in Delaware. The data center uses the payments data to update its agents' accounts receivable database and to post the payments to the general ledger. The following morning, the database is used to generate several accounting reports, which can be viewed online or printed, depending on the option chosen by the users (i.e., by managers who access the database from Trusty's St. Louis office).

CASE B: Bentley Department Stores, Inc. (I)

Bentley Department Stores, Inc., operates at 50 locations in California and Kansas. The company's headquarters are in Kansas City. The company accepts cash, national credit cards (VISA and MasterCard), and its own Bentley charge card (BCC). Procedures for cash receipts are standard at each location. BCC billing and the treasury function are located at headquarters.

Customers present their purchases at a central checkout location at each store. Point-of-sale (POS) terminals provide immediate updates to quantities on hand in the inventory master data, compile detailed data on sales, and accumulate "proof figures" used in cashing out the drawer at the end of each shift. Each store's terminals are tied to the central computer system in Kansas City for access to the inventory and sales data. The proof totals are stored on each POS terminal.

At the beginning of the shift, a clerk must log onto the terminal with a four-digit identifier. When the clerk logs on, the proof total is set to zero automatically. Throughout the shift, the clerk will process the several forms of sales, and proof totals are updated as each sale occurs. At the end of the shift, the clerk prints the proof totals, logs off, and takes the proof totals and the clerk's drawer to the cashier. The cashier reconciles the drawer to the totals, prepares a two-part "cash out report" for each clerk on the shift, and enters and updates the over and short summary data maintained for each clerk on the Kansas City computer.

Store deposits are made whenever the cash-on-hand balance reaches $25,000 and at the end of the day. For each deposit, the cashier makes out a deposit slip. A designated employee makes the trip to the local bank. The employee brings back a receipted deposit slip. Daily, the cashier transmits the credit card sales (including BCC sales) electronically using a credit card authorization device. A batch report is created by the authorization device when the transmission is complete. The BCC slips, batch report, a copy of the cash out report, and the day's deposit slips are sent to Kansas City at 5:00 P.M. by courier mail.

In the cash receipts section at Kansas City, a sales report is obtained from the computer at the end of each day. That report is reconciled to the cash out report and the deposit slips. BCC sales automatically updates the account receivable master data stored on the Kansas City computer.

CASE C: Bentley Department Stores, Inc. (II)

Before starting this case, review the facts in Case B. Assume that holders of the Bentley credit card have been billed and that the NCC Company has sent payments to Bentley's bank in Kansas City where they are deposited directly in Bentley's account.

Bentley cash receipts clerks can log on to the bank account to see the status of receipts from the national credit cards. A clerk in the cash receipts section reconciles the deposit amount and the batch report. All receipts from the company's proprietary cards (BCCs) are received in Bentley's office in Kansas City. The company uses a turnaround document, so it receives a check and a portion of the monthly charge card statement (on which the customer has filled in the amount remitted). The cash receipts clerk compares the check to the amount written on the document, and, in a space reserved, enters the amount received on the document so that it can be computer scanned.

Checks and turnaround documents are batched. The turnaround documents are sent to the IT department. The deposit slip is photocopied and the checks are deposited. Copies of the batch totals and the deposit slips are filed separately by date. A copy of the deposit slip is sent to the treasurer's office.

IT uses an optical scanner to process the turnaround documents. This run occurs each evening at 10:00 P.M. Customers' accounts are posted, and a cash receipts listing is produced and sent to cash receipts each morning, where it is checked against and filed with the related batch totals. A copy of the cash receipts listing is sent to the treasurer's office.

PROBLEMS

P 11-1 For the company assigned by your instructor,[8] complete the following requirements:

  a. Prepare a table of entities and activities.

  b. Draw a context diagram.

  c. Draw a physical data flow diagram (DFD).

  d. Prepare an annotated table of entities and activities. Indicate on this table the groupings, bubble numbers, and bubble titles to be used in preparing a level 0 logical DFD.

  e. Draw a level 0 logical DFD.

P 11-2 For the company assigned by your instructor, complete the following requirements:

  a. Draw a systems flowchart.

  b. Prepare a control matrix, including explanations of how each recommended existing control plan helps to accomplish—or would accomplish in the case of missing plans—each related control goal. Your choice of recommended control plans should come from Exhibit 11.1 and/or 11.2 (pages 417–418 and 422–423) plus any other control plans from Chapters 9 or 10 that are germane to your company's process.

  c. Annotate the flowchart prepared in part a to indicate the points where the control plans are being applied (codes P-1 . . . P-*n*) or the points where they could be applied but are not (codes M-1 . . . M-*n*).

P 11-3 Using the following two tables, describe for each function (see Figure 11.1, page 395):

  a. A risk (an event or action that will cause the organization to fail to meet it goals/objectives).

  b. A control/process or use of technology that will address the risk.

  c. Do the same for the accounting entries.

	Function	Risks	Controls and technology
Manager	Marketing		
	Finance		
Operations process	Billing		
	Collections		

Event	Entry	Risks	Controls and technology
Shipment	AR		
	Sales		
Cash receipt	Cash		
	AR		

---

[8] For problems P 11-1 and P 11-2 if the assigned case is an extension of an earlier case, limit your solution to the narrative contained in the assigned case.

P 11-4 The following capsule cases present short narratives of processes used by three actual organizations whose names have been changed for the purpose of this problem. You will use the cases to practice the mechanics of drawing data flow diagrams.

CAPSULE CASE 1: Cumberland County Registry of Motor Vehicles

The Registry of Motor Vehicles (RMV) in Cumberland County, Kansas, has recently simplified its license renewal process by automating the test-taking and fee-collection steps. RMV notifies drivers when their licenses are about to expire. Drivers who renew their licenses in person at the RMV work with an interactive terminal that looks and functions like an ATM machine. The process is described in the following paragraphs.

After keying his or her current driver's license number, the applicant is presented with a touch-screen display that pulls up test questions stored on a laser disc within the terminal. Short video clips of typical traffic situations are shown, and questions are asked about each clip. The applicant responds to the questions by selecting from options presented on the screen.

The terminal scores the test and "collects" the renewal fee. The user "pays" the fee by inserting his or her VISA or MasterCard into a designated slot on the terminal.

The terminal then prints a scored answer sheet, which the applicant takes to a registry clerk. The clerk completes the process by administering a vision test, taking a picture of the applicant, and issuing a license.

CAPSULE CASE 2: Down Under Airlines

Background Information

Down Under Airlines (DUA) processes over 400 million tickets a year. The process of issuing the tickets is highly automated; a record of each ticket sold is stored in DUA's mainframe database. But when passengers turn in tickets, gate agents stuff the flight coupons into envelopes and ship them to DUA's Denver headquarters. Because of discrepancies between the original records housed in the ticket database and actual ticket use as reflected by the flight coupons (see the following *Note*), DUA, like other airlines, has to match every coupon against every ticket in the database in order to accurately account for passenger revenues. With the volume of tickets involved, manual matching is a daunting task. Image processing to the rescue!

Note: For example, passengers might use a ticket from one airline to fly with another, or they might use only the A-B leg of an A-B-C flight, and so forth.

Description of the New Image Processing System

DUA's new system, designed by one of the Big Four public accounting firms, functions as follows (all data stores are disk files):

When a ticket is sold to a passenger by a travel agent or by one of DUA's own 30,000 ticket agents, the seller enters a record of the ticket into DUA's mainframe database, just as in the past. However, when flight coupons are received in Denver, they are now read by an image scanner that captures the images and stores them in an optical storage and retrieval library, called Big File.

The ticket number appearing on the flight coupon is also scanned by an optical character recognition (OCR) system. The ticket numbers—an index to the ticket images themselves—are stored in a relational database, which is used to track the location of each ticket image in Big File.

Operators use a network of workstations to begin the audit process. Special audit software matches each ticket image in Big File with ticket records in the mainframe database. If the image and record do not match (for instance, a three-leg ticket sold but only two legs used), the ticket number is included in the audit data. If the image and record do match, the ticket record is written to the passenger revenue data.

CAPSULE CASE 3: Rosebud Supermarkets

Background Information

Rosebud Supermarkets, Inc., operates a chain of grocery stores in Vermont. Rosebud is one of the supermarket chains that accepts credit cards and debit cards at the point of sale (POS). To offer this service to customers, Rosebud has placed a pinstripe terminal within reach of the customer at each checkout counter. The terminal, which is attached to the transport belt area that moves the groceries past the cashier, interfaces with the POS cash register. For customers who want to pay for their orders using a means *other* than cash, the system works as follows:

Partial Description of Rosebud's Checkout Process

(*Note:* Exception routines are among the features not described.)

When a customer presents his or her order at the checkout station, the cashier uses a POS scanner at the end of the belt area to ring the customer's order in the cash register and to produce a register tape for the customer. After the groceries have been scanned, the cashier obtains the POS register total for the groceries purchased. A screen display appears on the pinstripe terminal that shows the purchase total and asks the customer what type of payment option is desired. The customer selects from three options—credit card, direct debit (through local participating banks), or check authorization—by pressing a key opposite that option and then presses "enter."

In the case of credit, the customer runs the credit card through the terminal's magnetic stripe reader. The request for credit authorization is then transmitted to the appropriate credit card company. The credit card company sends back a credit authorization number for the purchased amount.

For the debit option, the customer runs a bank debit card through the card reader and then enters his or her PIN. As in the case of credit purchases, the data is transmitted to the appropriate bank. The bank responds by transmitting back an approval message.

For check authorization, Rosebud uses paper courtesy cards. This requires that the cashier enter the courtesy card number on a PIN pad attached to the terminal. The courtesy card number and grocery total are transmitted to Rosebud's internal check authorization system. The authorization system looks up the customer in its courtesy card data (on disk) and notifies the cashier whether the check should be accepted.

For the capsule case assigned by your instructor, complete the following requirements:

a. Prepare a table of entities and activities.

b. Draw a context diagram.

c. Draw a physical data flow diagram (DFD).

d. Prepare an annotated table of entities and activities. Indicate on this table the groupings, bubble numbers, and bubble titles to be used in preparing a level 0 logical DFD.

e. Draw a level 0 logical DFD.

P 11-5 (*Note:* You can do this problem only if you have access to a computer-based electronic spreadsheet, such as Excel, or to a database software package, such as Access.)

Problem Data

Gateway Industries is a retailer of bicycles and bicycle parts. It sells on credit terms of net 30 days. As of May 31, 20XX, its subsidiary ledger of customer balances reflects the following details:

Customer Name	Invoice Number	Due Date	Invoice Amount	Total Balance
Bikes Et	1965	2/15/20XX	$1,427.86	
Cetera	2016	3/23	721.40	
	2092	4/16	713.49	
	2163	5/14	853.02	
	2184	5/30	562.92	
	2202	6/13	734.47	
	2235	6/20	622.88	$5,636.04
International	1993	3/15	$ 333.24	
Bicycle	2010	3/20	564.49	
Sales	2112	4/24	400.69	
	2170	5/16	363.60	
	2182	5/29	1,255.91	$2,917.93
Rodebyke	2075	4/10	$ 634.84	
Bicycles	2133	4/28	370.97	
& Mopeds	2159	5/7	371.49	
	2174	5/22	498.75	
	2197	6/8	713.54	
	2222	6/18	451.11	
Finance Charge		6/30	10.06	$3,050.76
Stan's	1974	2/27	$ 575.00	
Cyclery	2000	3/18	536.82	
	2019	3/25	641.60	
	2108	4/22	629.94	
	2125	4/26	682.50	
	2164	5/14	292.36	
	2215	6/16	249.04	$3,607.26

Customer Name	Invoice Number	Due Date	Invoice Amount	Total Balance
Wheelaway	2117	4/25	$ 819.55	
Cycle	2140	5/4	745.54	
Center	2171	5/16	490.00	
	2178	5/25	587.80	
	2192	6/3	1,045.23	
	2219	6/17	475.87	
	2234	6/20	257.37	
	2250	6/29	700.03	$5,121.39

Using the computer electronic spreadsheet or database software indicated by your instructor, prepare an accounts receivable aging report as of May 31, 20XX. Observe the following specific requirements:

a. In addition to a report heading, the report should contain column headings for:

- Customer name
- Total balance
- Current balance
- Past-due balance, with supporting columns for 1 to 30 days, 31 to 60 days, 61 to 90 days, Over 90 days

b. Each individual open invoice and its due date should be entered into the computer software. However, those details should *not* appear in the report. Instead, for each customer, show the total outstanding balance and the total amount in each age category.

c. Print totals for each money column and verify that the totals of the aging columns cross-add to the grand total of all outstanding balances.

P 11-6 The following is a list of 13 control plans from this chapter or from Chapter 9.

Control Plans

A. Independent billing authorization

B. Review shipped not billed sales orders

C. Compare input data with master data and invoice

D. Programmed edits of shipping notification

E. Interactive feedback check

F. Computer agreement of batch totals

G. Cumulative sequence check

H. Document design

I. Pre-numbered documents

J. Procedures for rejected inputs

K. Receive and input turn-around documents

L. One-for-one checking of deposit slip and checks

M. Review deposit slip file

The following 10 statements describe either the achievement of a control goal (i.e., a system success) or a system deficiency (i.e., a system failure). List the numbers 1 through 10 on your solution sheet. Next to each item, insert *one* letter from the preceding list indicating the *best* control to achieve the desired goal or to address the system deficiency described. A letter should be used only once, with three letters left over.

Control Goals or System Deficiencies

1. Helps to ensure the validity of shipping notifications.
2. Provides a detective control to help ensure the accuracy of billing inputs.
3. Provides a preventive control to help ensure the accuracy of billing inputs.
4. By preventing duplicate document numbers from entering the system, helps to ensure input validity.
5. Helps to identify duplicate, missing, and out-of-range numbers by comparing input numbers to a previously stored number range.
6. Should have precluded a field salesperson from omitting the sales terms from the sales order, thereby causing the order to be rejected by the computer when it was entered by data entry personnel.
7. In a periodic/batch environment, helps to ensure the information system control goal of input completeness.
8. Helps to ensure that all shipments are billed in a timely manner.
9. Meets the operations system control goal of efficiency of resource use by reducing the number of data elements to be entered from source documents.
10. Provides an "audit trail" of deposits and helps to ensure that deposits are made in a timely manner.

P 11-7 The following is a list of 14 control plans from this chapter or from Chapters 9 and 10.

Control Plans

A. Review shipped but not billed sales orders

B. Confirm customer balances regularly

C. Enter shipping notice close to location where order is shipped

D. Check for authorized prices, terms, freight, and discounts

E. Hash totals (e.g., of customer ID numbers)

F. Computer agreement of batch totals

G. Manual agreement of batch totals

H. Batch sequence check

I. Key verification

J. Written approvals

K. Immediately endorse incoming checks

L. One-for-one checking of checks and remittance advices

M. Immediately separate checks and remittance advices

N. Reconcile bank account regularly

The following are 10 system failures that have control implications. List the numbers 1 through 10 on your solution sheet. Next to each number, insert *one* letter from the preceding list corresponding to the control plan that would *best* prevent the system failure from occurring. Also, give a brief (one- to two-sentence) explanation of your choice. A letter should be used only once, with four letters left over.

System Failures

1. Once goods are delivered to the common carrier, the shipping department at Goodtimes Video Corp. prepares a three-part shipping notice. Copy 2 of the notice is sent to billing to initiate the billing process. Many shipping notices have either been lost in transit or have been delayed in reaching the billing section.

2. A dishonest order entry clerk bypasses the credit-checking procedures every time a customer order is received from his brother-in-law's firm. The clerk releases sales order copies to the warehouse and to the shipping department without submitting the orders to the credit department.

3. Because the mailroom clerks at Laxx Company do not take batch totals of incoming customer checks, the cashier has misappropriated several thousand dollars over the years by depositing company checks to his personal bank account.

4. Potpourri Merchandising Mart uses periodic processing for entering sales invoice inputs and updating customer accounts. Although it uses certain batch total procedures, Potpourri has experienced a number of instances of recording sales invoices to incorrect customer accounts.

5. The billing department at Gerrymander Corp. employs batch processing and uses pre-numbered invoice documents. Nevertheless, a number of duplicate invoice numbers has been processed, resulting in numerous customer complaints.

6. Because Abraham Co. had been privately owned for years, it had never undergone an independent audit. When Abraham finally went public, the Securities and Exchange Commission required an audit of its financial statements. As part of its audit, the independent CPA firm found a large discrepancy between the accounts receivable general ledger balance and the underlying details of individual customer balances.

7. At Jonquil, Inc., billing sends shipping notices to the data entry group in data processing where they are keyed. During the last month, an inexperienced data entry clerk made several errors in keying the shipping notices. The errors were discovered by the internal auditors as part of their routine examination of the data processing department.

8. Sales at Defrod Corporation have declined considerably compared to those of the preceding year. In an effort to improve the financial statements, the vice president of finance obtained a supply of blank shipping notices on which she fabricated 100 fictitious shipments. She submitted the fictitious documents to data processing for billing.

9. The mailroom at Whipoorwill Co. forwards checks and remittance advices to the accounts receivable department. A clerk checks the

remittance advices against open invoices, as reflected on the accounts receivable subsidiary ledger data. It is not uncommon for the clerk to note discrepancies, in which case the customer is contacted in an effort to reconcile the differences. Once all the discrepancies have been investigated and cleared, the accounts receivable clerk releases the checks to the cashier for deposit.

10. Clerks in the billing department at Abacus Enterprises, Inc., prepare sales invoices from a copy of the packing slip received from the shipping department. Recently, the company has experienced a rash of customer complaints that the customers have been billed for freight charges, despite the fact that the freight terms were FOB destination.

P 11-8 Conduct research on electronic bill presentment and payment (EBPP) systems (see Technology Summary 11.2, page 400). Write a paper describing the advantages and disadvantages, to both the payer and payee, of the two methods for implementing these systems, the biller direct and the consolidation/aggregation methods.

P 11-9 a. Redraw the appropriate part of Figure 11.3 (page 402), assuming a lockbox system is used. Also, prepare a lower-level data flow diagram for the cash receipts function, using the same assumption.

b. Redraw the appropriate part of Figure 11.3 assuming that, in addition to cash collections from charge customers, the organization also has cash sales and receives cash from the sale of equity securities. Prepare a brief, one- to two-sentence defense for each of the changes made.

Do *not* draw an entirely new Figure 11.3 for either part a or part b. You might want to photocopy the figure from the chapter and then draw your additions and changes on the photocopy.

P 11-10 For Figure 11.3 (page 402):

a. Indicate the sequence of activities by putting numbers next to the data flows. For example, the "Sales order notification" in the upper left of the diagram would be number "1." Restart the numbers for each bubble. Assign the same number to simultaneous data flows. For example, "Invoice" and "GL invoice update" coming out of bubble 1.0 should get the same number.

b. For each process bubble, indicate, by placing a "T" on the flow, the flow that triggers the processing activities.

c. Label each flow into and out of the data stores and to and from the other processes. These labels should describe the purpose of the flow.

d. Annotate each data store to indicate the data's major elements.

e. Include on the diagram one-sentence descriptions of each process bubble's activities.

P 11-11 Use the data flow diagrams in Figures 11.3, 11.4, 11.6, and 11.7 (pages 402, 403, 405, and 407) to solve this problem.

Prepare a 4-column table that summarizes the B/AR/CR process's processes, inputs, and outputs. In the first column, list the three processes shown in the level 0 diagram (Figure 11.3). In the second column, list the subsidiary functions shown in the three lower-level diagrams (Figures 11.4,

11.6, and 11.7). For *each* subsidiary function listed in column 2, list the data flow names or the data stores that are inputs to that process (column 3) or outputs of that process (column 4). (See *Note.*) The following table has been started for you to indicate the format for your solution.

Note: To simplify the solution, do *not* show any reject stubs in column 4.

Solution Format

Summary of the B/AR/CR processes, subsidiary functions, inputs, outputs, and data stores

Process	Subsidiary Functions	Inputs	Outputs
1.0 Perform billing	1.1 Compare	Sales order notification Shipping's billing notification	Validated shipping notification
	1.2 Prepare invoice	Validated shipping notification Customer master data	. . . Continue solution . . .

KEY TERMS

billing/accounts receivable/cash receipts (B/AR/CR) process

float

good funds

charge card

credit card

debit card

electronic funds transfer (EFT)

automated clearing house (ACH)

lockbox

electronic lockbox

electronic check

electronic cash

electronic bill presentment and payment (EBPP)

invoice

remittance advice (RA)

accounts receivable master data

balance-only system

open-item system

sales event data

accounts receivable adjustments data

cash receipts data

post-billing system

pre-billing system

The Purchasing Process

This is a classic story. In the 1980s Wal-Mart and Procter & Gamble (P&G) built a software system that linked P&G to Wal-Mart's distribution centers. When a P&G product ran low in a Wal-Mart distribution center, the system sent a message to P&G. Then, P&G initiated a shipment to the Wal-Mart distribution center or perhaps to a Wal-Mart store. Enhancements to the system have allowed P&G to know when any P&G product is scanned at the checkout at any Wal-Mart store. Purchase orders, shipments, invoices, and payments are all automatic. As a result P&G knows when to make and ship products to Wal-Mart, without maintaining excessive inventory. Wal-Mart has less inventory on hand, lower costs (savings passed on from P&G), and higher product availability. P&G, Wal-Mart, and most importantly, Wal-Mart customers are happier with this system. In this chapter, we will explore the processes, systems, and controls that should be in place to ensure that the purchasing process operates efficiently (i.e., low cost) and effectively (i.e., high customer value). Particular attention will be paid to processes used to determine when and how much to purchase.

Learning Objectives

- To know the definition and basic functions of the purchasing process.
- To understand the relationship between the purchasing process and its environment.
- To know the purchasing function's place in an organization's supply chain.
- To achieve a reasonable level of understanding of the logical and physical characteristics of a typical purchasing process.
- To become familiar with some of the technology used to implement the purchasing process.
- To appreciate the implications of implementing a supply chain management system in a global business environment.
- To know some process goals and the plans used to control a typical purchasing process.

In this chapter, we spotlight one business process, the Purchasing Process. We will describe the various users of the purchasing process, each having their own view of the enterprise system and enterprise database. In addition, we will analyze the process controls related to the purchasing process.

SYNOPSIS

This chapter presents our third business process, the purchasing process. The purchasing process includes the first three steps, requirements determination, purchase order processing, and goods receipt, in the purchase-to-pay process (see Figure 2.10 on page 62). After we introduce the players involved in the purchasing process, we describe an organization's connections to its suppliers and customers (i.e., its supply chain) to set the stage for the complexities of the purchasing process. In addition, we call your attention to the sections on Physical Process Description and the Application of the Control Framework. These sections cover state-of-the-art material on current and evolving technology and provide reading that we hope you will find both interesting and informative.

INTRODUCTION

As previously noted, the purchasing process comprises the first three steps in the purchase-to-pay process (Figure 2.10, page 62). Let's take a closer look at the purchasing process.

PROCESS DEFINITION AND FUNCTIONS

The **purchasing process** is an interacting structure of people, equipment, methods, and controls that is designed to accomplish the following primary functions:

1. Handle the repetitive work routines of the purchasing department and the receiving department.[1]

---

[1] To focus our discussion, we have assumed that these two departments are the primary operating units related to the purchasing process. For a given organization, however, the departments associated with the process may differ.

2. Support the decision needs of those who manage the purchasing and receiving departments.

3. Assist in the preparation of internal and external reports.

First, the purchasing process handles the repetitive work routines of the purchasing and receiving departments by capturing and recording data related to the day-to-day operations of the departments. The recorded data then may be used to generate source documents (such as purchase orders and receiving reports) and to produce internal and external reports.

The purchasing process prepares a number of reports that personnel at various levels of management use. For example, the manager of the purchasing department might use an open purchase order report to ascertain which orders have yet to be filled.

Before leaving this section, we need to clarify two terms that we will be using throughout the chapter: *goods* and *services*. *Goods* are raw materials, merchandise, supplies, fixed assets, or intangible assets. *Services* cover work performed by outside vendors, including contractors, catering firms, towel services, consultants, auditors, and the like.

ORGANIZATIONAL SETTING

The purchasing process is closely linked to functions and processes within and outside the organization. Let's take a look at those links and the impact that they have on the operation of the purchasing process.

An Internal Perspective

Figure 12.1 and Table 12.1 present an internal view of the relationship between the purchasing process and its organizational environment. They show the various information flows generated or captured by the process. Take some time now to study the figure to acquaint yourself with the entities with which the process interacts. The data flows in Table 12.1 indicate the nature of these interactions.

The chief purchasing executive in an organization assumes various titles in different companies, such as manager of purchasing, director of purchasing, or purchasing agent. We use the term *purchasing manager*. The purchasing manager usually performs major buying activities as well as the required administrative duties of running a department. In many organizations, the actual buying is done by professional *buyers*. As we will see in Chapter 13, the purchasing and receiving departments will interact internally with:

- Departments within the organization making requests for the purchase of goods and services.
- The accounts payable department who must pay for the purchased goods.

The *receiving supervisor* is responsible for receiving incoming goods, signing the bill of lading presented by the carrier or the supplier in connection with the shipment, reporting the receipt of goods,[2] and making prompt transfer of goods to the appropriate warehouse or department.

---

[2] In this section and the section describing the logical purchasing process, we assume that the receiving supervisor also is responsible for indicating that services have been received. In practice, the receipt of services might well be reported by various operating departments instead.

Figure 12.1 An Internal Perspective of the Purchasing Process

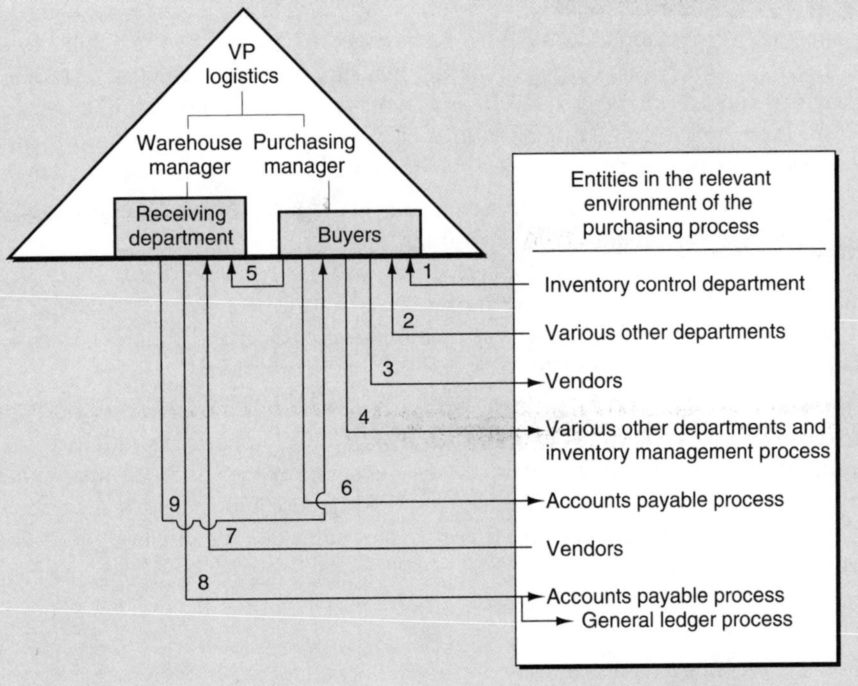

NOTES:

1. The information flows are representative of those related to the purchasing process. The figure, however, does not show all information flows. For example, purchase returns are not shown.

2. See Table 12.1 for a description of information flows 1–9.

Table 12.1 Description of Information Flows

Flow No.	Description
1	Purchase requisition sent from inventory control department to purchasing department
2	Purchase requisitions from various other departments sent to purchasing department
3	Purchase order sent to vendor
4	Purchase order notification sent to various other departments or to inventory management process
5	Purchase order notification sent to receiving department
6	Purchase order notification sent to accounts payable process
7	Goods and services received from vendor
8	Receiving notification sent to accounts payable and general ledger processes
9	Receiving notification sent to purchasing department

Goal Conflicts and Ambiguities in the Organization

The goals of individual managers may conflict with (i.e., are not in *congruence* with) overall organizational objectives. For instance, some of the managers and supervisors shown in the organization chart (Figure 12.1, page 439) might be "marching to different drummers." For example, the purchasing manager probably will want to buy in large quantities to take advantage of quantity discounts and to reduce ordering costs. Receiving, inspecting, and storing large quantities of inventory, however, will more than likely present problems for the receiving department supervisor and the warehouse manager.

In addition to goal conflicts between managers, ambiguity often exists in defining goals and success in meeting goals. For instance, one of the purchasing goals might be *to select a vendor who will provide the best quality at the lowest price by the promised delivery date.* But what does this goal mean precisely? Does it mean that a particular vendor must satisfy all three conditions of best quality, lowest price, and timely delivery? Realistically, one vendor probably will not satisfy all three conditions.

Prioritization of goals is often necessary in choosing the *best* solution given the various conflicts and constraints placed on the process. This implies that trade-offs must be made in prioritizing among the goals that conflict. For example, if a company operates in an industry that is extremely sensitive to satisfying customer needs, it may be willing to incur an excessive price to ensure that it is procuring the best quality goods and obtaining them when needed.

An External Perspective

ENTERPRISE SYSTEMS Figure 12.2 presents an external view of the relationship between the purchasing process and its environment. The connections between an organization, including the flow of

Figure 12.2 An External Perspective of the Purchasing Process: The Organization's Supply Chain (A Value System)

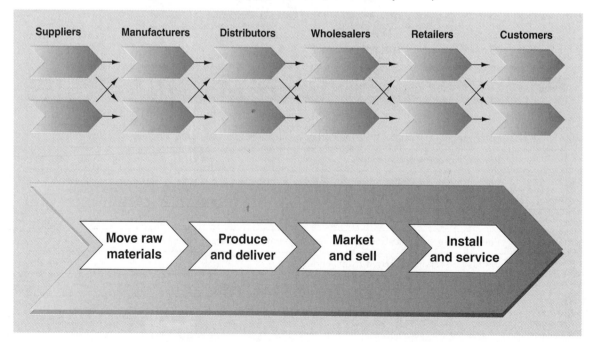

information, materials, and services, from suppliers of merchandise and raw materials **E-BUSINESS**
through to the organization's customers, are its **supply chain**. We depict the supply
chain as a value system (see Figure 2.2 on page 49) because each player in the supply
chain is performing a set of activities to transform inputs into outputs valued by its customers (i.e., a *value chain*). As discussed in Chapter 2, the value chain within an organization is facilitated by its *enterprise system*. And, you should notice that the links between the organizations in the supply chain are normally global, *e-Business* connections.

In our discussion here we will assume the role of the retailer in Figure 12.2 and not
consider the manufacturer. In Chapter 14 we will discuss the role of the manufacturing
process in the supply chain. For now, assume we are a retailer, such as Wal-Mart, Target, or Staples, and we need to manage the links in our supply chain so that we can get
the rights goods on our shelves, in the right amount, at the right time, at minimal cost
(i.e., *efficiency*), so as to create maximum value for our customers (i.e., *effectiveness*).
How we do that is discussed next.

Supply Chain Management

Supply chain management (SCM) is the combination of processes and procedures **E-BUSINESS**
used to ensure the delivery of goods and services to customers at the lowest cost while
providing the highest value to the customers. As previously noted, the goal of SCM is **ENTERPRISE**
to increase product availability while reducing inventory across the supply chain. To do **SYSTEMS**
this, supply chain partners must coordinate the flow of information and physical goods
among members of the supply chain. Technology Summary 12.1 describes a model for
SCM developed by the Supply-Chain Council and adopted by over 500 companies
worldwide.[3] How important is supply chain management? Technology Excerpt 12.1
(page 442) summarizes a few SCM metrics. Notice the relationship between supply
chains, enterprise systems, and B2B. Many of the external links noted in Figure 12.2 are
via the Internet and the internal links are via an organization's *enterprise system*.

Technology Summary 12.1

Supply-Chain Operations Reference-Model (SCOR)

The SCOR-model is a process reference tool that allows companies to benchmark their sup-ply chain processes and to identify how to make improvements in the processes and relation-ships that it has with partners, suppliers, and customers. The model defines five basic com-ponents for supply chain management:

1. *Plan.* Measure customer demand for a product or service and develop a course of action to source, produce, and de-liver the product or service.
2. *Source.* Select supply sources and pro-cure the goods and services to meet the planned or actual demand, receive product, and authorize payments to suppliers.
3. *Make.* Transform a product to a fin-ished state to meet planned or actual demand.
4. *Deliver.* This is the order fulfillment step. Receive customer orders, provide goods or service to customers, and in-voice customers.
5. *Return.* Perform post-delivery customer support and receive defective or excess products back from customers.

Source: *Supply-Chain Operations Reference-Model: SCOR Version 6.0*, Supply Chain Council, Inc., http://www.supply-chain.org, 2003.

---

[3] "Companies Worldwide Turn to Supply-Chain Council's SCOR-model for Efficient Supply Chain Manage-ment," *Supply-Chain Newsletter*, http://www.supply-chain.org, June 2003.

Technology Excerpt 12.1

Selected Supply Chain Management Metrics

- B2B exchanges will take off in 2003 thanks to better customer-supplier integration.
- Nearly 10 percent of direct goods and services are purchased online.
- U.S. firms will spend $35 billion over the next 5 years to improve their supply chain processes.

- Companies that put the most effort into online buying see the greatest savings.
- Internet purchases can reduce costs and time by 70 percent, saving the average mid-size firm $2 million annually.

Source: http://www.cio.com, July 30, 2003.

Supply chain management software helps an organization execute the steps in the supply chain. Software products are available to perform individual functions within each of the five steps in *SCM* (i.e., steps in Technology Summary 12.1) and products are available to perform complete steps or several of the steps. The products can be divided into two categories. The first, *supply chain planning* software accumulates data about orders from retail customers, sales from retail outlets, and data about manufacturing and delivery capability to assist in planning for each of the SCM steps. The most valuable, and problematic, of these products is demand planning software used to determine how much product is needed to satisfy customer demand.

ENTERPRISE SYSTEMS

E-BUSINESS

The second category of supply chain software, *supply chain execution* software, automates the *SCM* steps. *ERP* software is assigned to this category as it receives customer orders, routes orders to an appropriate warehouse, and executes the invoice for the sale. As previously noted, many of the connections between players in the supply chain are B2B automated interfaces. For example, the sourcing step may be implemented through an automatic order sent to a supplier via the Internet.

At the beginning of this chapter we briefly described the advantages that P&G and Wal-Mart achieved by managing their supply chain. In general, management of the supply chain leads to some or all of the following benefits:

- Lower costs to the customer
- Higher availability of product (for the customer, for production, etc.)
- Higher response to customer request for product customization and other specifications
- Reduced inventories along the supply chain
- Improved relationships between buyers and sellers
- Smooth workloads due to planned goods arrivals and departures, leading to reduced overtime costs
- Reduced item costs as a result of planned purchases through contracts and other arrangements
- Increased customer orders due to improved customer responsiveness
- Reduced product defects through specifying quality during planning and sharing defect information with suppliers during execution

Are all *SCM* initiatives successful? No. Here are some things that can go wrong and, in some cases, how to avoid those problems.

ENTERPRISE SYSTEMS

CONTROLS

E-BUSINESS

- Data is not collected or is not shared across functional boundaries. For example:
    - Up-to-date real-time sales data must be fed to the SCM demand forecasting system. An *enterprise system* and Internet (i.e., B2B) connections typically facilitate this process.
    - Supply chain performance is not fed back to the planning system. Again, an enterprise system can relay purchasing, receiving, transportation, and other logistics data.
    - Data such as customer, location, warranty, and service contracts, needed for post-customer support is not available. This data must be collected during sales processing and made available to the appropriate functions.
- Confused lines of responsibility and lack of trust can lead to lack of sharing of information between supply chain partners. These issues must be worked out in the SCM planning phase.
- Inaccurate data within the supply chain can negatively affect the entire chain. Implementation of the controls, such as those introduced in Chapters 8 and 9 and discussed throughout the business process chapters, should reduce this problem.
- Over-reliance on demand forecasting software can lead to inaccurate forecasts. Good demand forecasting requires an intelligent combination of software tools and human experience.
- Competing objectives can lead to unrealistic forecasts. For example, marketing may want a high target to ensure a successful product (i.e., promotion and production budgets will be based on the forecast). Sales, on the other hand, will be evaluated on its ability to meet sales quotas and wants a lower demand forecast. Deference to the modeling tools and to objective arbitration should reduce this conflict.

Several methods have been developed for managing the supply chain and implementing the SCOR-model described in Technology Summary 12.1 (page 441). Technology Summary 12.2 (pages 443–444) describes an evolution of those techniques and Technology Summary 12.3 (page 445) details the most recent, CPFR.

Technology Summary 12.2

Selected Methods for Information Sharing (Collaboration) in the Supply Chain

Collaboration Type	Features	Discussion
Continuous Replenishment (CRP) [also known as Vendor Managed Inventory (VMI) and Supplier Managed Inventory (SMI)]	A vendor (i.e., the seller/supplier) obtains, in real-time, a buyer's current sales, demand, and inventory data and replenishes the buyer's inventory. Stock management information such as reorder point is used to make the replenishment decision (i.e., quantity, timing).	CRP is an example of Quick Response (QR) and Efficient Consumer Response (ECR) umbrella concepts directed at improving and optimizing aspects of the supply chain. One key concept is to provide advance notice for situations with uncertain demand, such as promotions.

Collaboration Type	Features	Discussion
Continuous Replenishment (CRP) (*continued*)	Sales and demand data may be warehouse withdrawal, production control (for manufacturing), or retail point-of-sale (POS).	CRP was started in 1987 with P&G shipping Pampers to Wal-Mart.
	Data may be sent via EDI or accessed by vendor via a Web interface into the buyer's system (e.g., actual system or data extracts) or a hosted hub (e.g., SAP's Inventory Collaboration Hub).	Benefits: • Vendor has less uncertainty and can provide specified level of service with minimum cost (e.g., inventory, production, freight [expediting]) • Buyer has better balance of inventory cost and customer service (e.g., fewer stock-outs/higher fill rates)
	Replenishment is based on actual (pull) rather than plan because it recognizes changes such as changed production schedule, unplanned maintenance downtime, quality problems, failure to follow plan.	• Reduced production downtime (for buyer) • Lower costs are passed on to partner/customer
Co-Managed Inventory (a form of CRP)	The vendor replenishes standard merchandise while the buyer manages the replenishment of promotion merchandise.	In 1992 Wal-Mart added retailer-provided sales forecast to CRP. The buyer manages exceptions.
Collaborative Forecasting and Replenishment (CFAR) [was a precursor of CPFR]	Retailer and manufacturer forecast demand and schedule production jointly.	Starting in 1995/1996 Warner Lambert and Wal-Mart forecasted the demand for Listerine. Introduces sales forecast collaboration.
Collaborative Planning Forecasting and Replenishment (CPFR)	Collaborative processes across the supply chain using a set of processes and technology models.	An initiative of the Voluntary Interindustry Commerce Standards (VICS) Association, 1998.
	Trading partners share plans, forecasts, and other data over the Internet.	Adds planning (joint business plan [category and promotion planning]) to CFAR.
	During planning and execution, partners negotiate resolution to exception such as: • Dramatic change in plans • Plans do not match • Forecasts accuracy is out of tolerance • Overstock and understock conditions	Promotion process/messages never standardized.

How does the supply chain operate without using some of the techniques described in Technology Summary 12.2? Not well. Here are some things that can happen.

- An organization in the chain can relay a false demand signal. For example, a retailer could misread retail demand and so it doubles its normal order. Assume further that the wholesaler in response doubles its normal order (now four times the retail order) and so on up the chain to the manufacturer and its supplier. The multiplication of these orders up the supply chain can cause wild demand and supply fluctuations known as the *bullwhip effect*.

- Any member of the supply chain can increase its orders for reasons other than expected increase in demand. For example, a wholesaler might plan a promotion, or a retailer might order extra product one month to take advantage of a sales price, or a distributor could increase its order in anticipation of rationing, hoping to lower the reduction that it will receive from its supplier.

Supply chain management solutions can reduce the impact of the *bullwhip effect* and other negative effects of a dysfunctional supply chain by:

- Sharing information such as demand, forecasts, sales data, and planned promotions. This allows each member of the supply chain to plan its orders and production.

- Coordinate pricing, transportation, and product ownership.

- Obtain operational efficiencies by reducing ordering and carrying costs.

Technology Application 12.1 describes some successful supply chain collaborations.

Technology Summary 12.3

CPFR Process

Collaborative Planning

1. Develop front-end agreement (yearly). Establish a scorecard to track key supply chain metrics relative to success criteria.
2. Create joint business plan (quarterly). Identify planned promotions, inventory policy changes, store openings/closing, product changes.

Collaborative Sales Forecasting (weekly/daily). Share demand forecast. Identify and resolve exceptions.

3. Create sales forecast.
4. Identify sales forecast exceptions.
5. Collaborate on exception items.

Collaborative Order Forecasting (weekly/daily). Share replenishment plans. Identify and resolve exceptions.

6. Create order forecast.
7. Identify order forecast exceptions.
8. Collaborate on exception items.

Order Generation

9. Generate order. Generate orders based upon the consensus order forecast at an agreed time horizon.

Delivery Execution

Source: http://www.cpfr.org.

Supply Chain Collaboration Success Stories

Case 1

Diageo, manufacturer of Guinness, Johnnie Walker, and José Cuervo, will implement CPFR in 2003. It will combine weekly data from sales, on-hand inventory, and distributors' receipts with promotional information to generate detailed forecasts that will be sent automatically to 120 distributors. Diageo and its distributors then collaborate on the forecast that is loaded into a replenishment system to establish inventory levels and sales. Diageo expects to save $1.1 million in inventory costs and $600,000 in logistics cost, and increase sales by 1.1 percent or $3.3 million. Distributors also should cut inventory costs.

Case 2

A global auto manufacturer needed to reform its supply chain to lower inventories and be more responsive to dealer demands. The manufacturer made the following changes in its supply chain:

1. *Plan.* Dealers provide annual sales projections, by month and model via an online system.

2. *Forecast.* The manufacturer rolls the dealer plans into a wholesale plan and provides production plans to dealers.
3. *Order.* Dealers order vehicles and participate in online auctions for excess vehicles.
4. *Make.* The vehicles are manufactured.
5. *Deliver.* The vehicles are delivered in frequent shipments to reduce buffer stocks throughout the chain.

Improvements included a $900 million reduction in inventory, $13 million lower logistics costs, and dealer delivery reduced to 40 days from 100 days.

Case 3

Procter & Gamble (P&G) with almost $40 billion in revenues and 300 brands has set up an elaborate supply chain platform that includes in-house applications as well as CPFR. P&G uses Syncra Systems' CPFR offering, a Web-based collaboration platform, to link with retail partners to gauge demand and make needed adjustments to production and shipping. Through CPFR, P&G has reduced stock inventory by more than 10 percent.

Sources: Beth Bacheldor, "Diageo Overhauls Supply Chain," *InformationWeek.com* (April 8, 2003); "Automaker Case Study," http://www.coplenish.com/experience/casestudy.htm, August 1, 2002.

LOGICAL PROCESS DESCRIPTION

This section expands on the purchasing process. Once again, logical data flow diagrams are used to present the basic composition of a typical process. We also discuss the relationship between certain goals of the process and the process's logical design. The section includes brief discussions of the interfaces between the purchasing and inventory processes. We also describe and illustrate the process's major data stores.[4]

Discussion and Illustration

Figure 12.3 is the context diagram for our purchasing process. Notice that the process responds to requests for goods and services (i.e., purchase requisitions) received from the inventory process and from various departments and sends a purchase order to the

[4] As we have in several earlier chapters, we remind you once again that the data stores in the logical DFDs might well be the purchasing process's view of an *enterprise database.*

Figure 12.3 Purchasing Process—Context Diagram

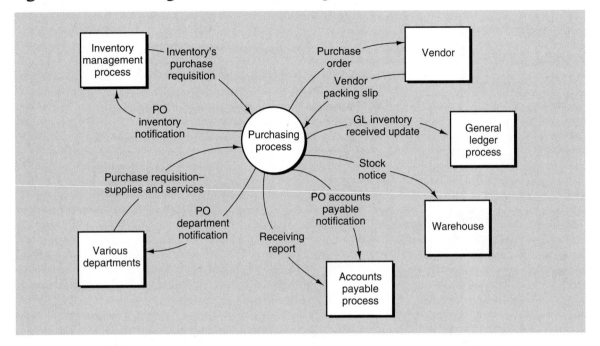

vendor and various notices to other departments and processes. Vendors respond by sending goods and services (i.e., vendor packing slip), which results in additional notices being sent out. As depicted, we do not see the vendor receiving inventory and sales data and responding with automatic shipments as they might if we were using some of the supply chain techniques depicted in Technology Summary 12.2 (pages 443–444).

Figure 12.4 (page 448) reflects the level 0 data flow diagram for our purchasing process. Take some time to study the figure. To focus our discussion, we have assumed that the purchasing process performs three major processes, represented by the three bubbles in the DFD. The next three sections describe each of those bubbles.

Determine Requirements

Note that purchase requisitions are initiated by entities that are outside the context of the purchasing process. The purchasing process begins with each department identifying its need for goods and services. These needs are depicted by one of two data flows entering bubble 1.0: *inventory's purchase requisition* or *purchase requisition—supplies and services.*

Figure 12.5 (page 449) is an example screen for an electronic **purchase requisition,** which is an internal request to acquire goods and services. Take some time to examine the figure, observing the various items included in the requisition such as the person placing the order, for which plant, the item, the quantity, and the unit cost. The requisition is usually approved by the requisitioning department supervisor.

Figure 12.6 (page 449) is a lower-level view of bubble 1.0 in Figure 12.4 (page 448). At first glance, the processes involved in determining an organization's requirements for goods and services may appear to be quite simple and straightforward. However, the earlier section about *supply chain management* should make it clear that the techniques and methods involved in determining *what* inventory to order, *when* to order it, and

ENTERPRISE SYSTEMS

Figure 12.4 Purchasing Process—Level 0 Diagram

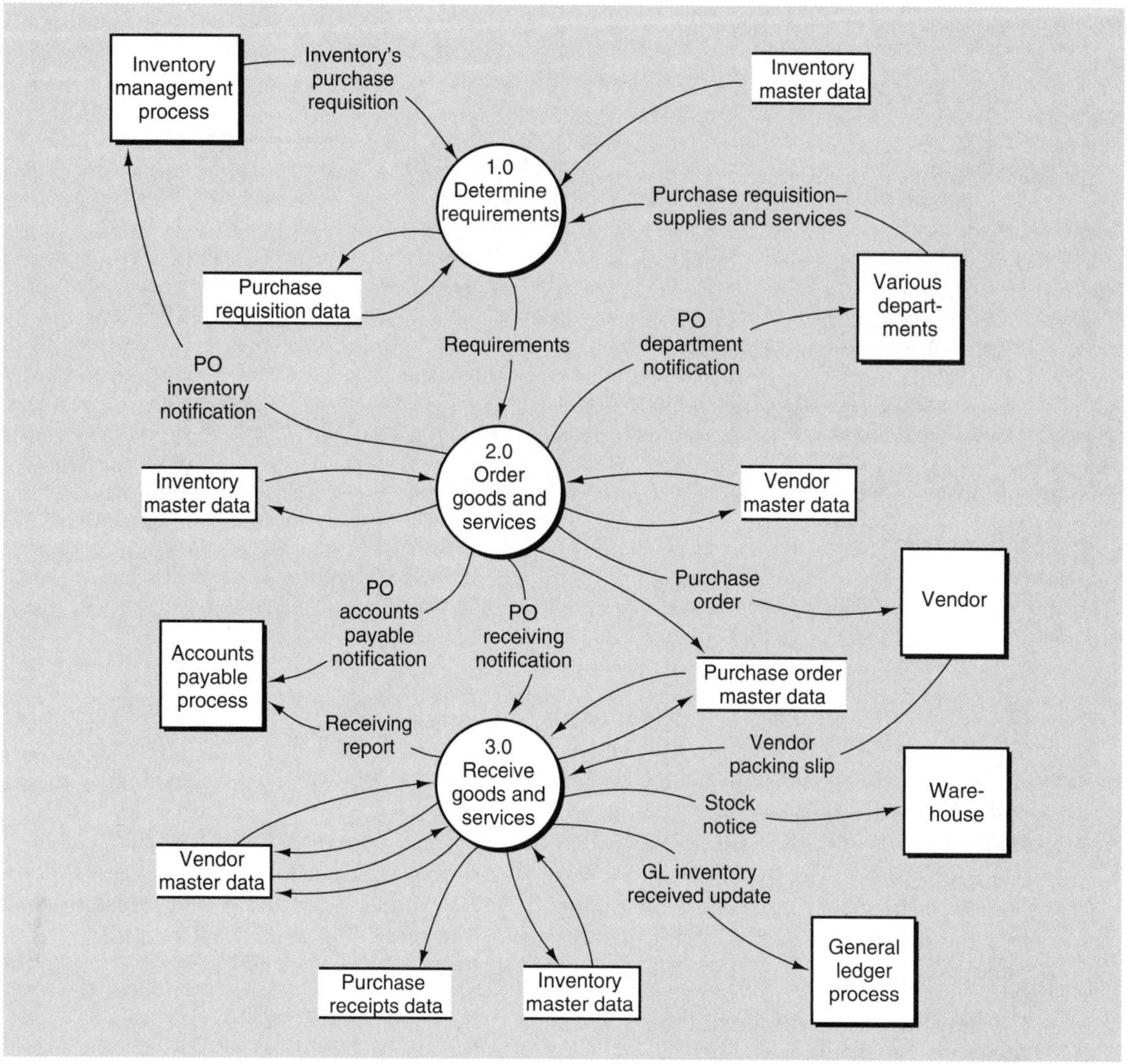

how much to order are considerably more intricate and complex than we might first imagine.

The processes associated with reordering inventory involve several important concepts and techniques, such as cyclical reordering, reorder point analysis, economic order quantity (EOQ) analysis, and ABC analysis. We discuss each of these methods briefly before going on.

- **Reorder point (ROP) analysis** recognizes that each item of inventory is unique with respect to the rate at which it is sold. Based on each inventory item's sales rate, a reorder point is determined. Thus, when the on-hand level for an item falls to its specified reorder point, the item is reordered. This might lead to the flow from the inventory master data into bubble 1.1 in Figure 12.6.

Figure 12.5 Sample Purchase Requisition Screen (J.D. Edwards)

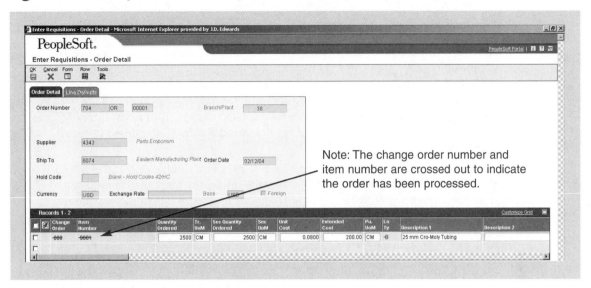

Figure 12.6 Purchasing Process—Diagram 1

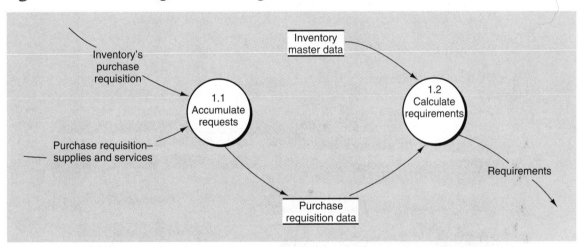

- **Economic order quantity (EOQ)** is a technique of analyzing all incremental costs associated with acquiring and carrying particular items of inventory. *Inventory carrying costs* are composed of five cost elements: (1) opportunity cost of investment funds, (2) insurance costs, (3) property taxes, (4) storage costs, and (5) cost of obsolescence and deterioration. The EOQ might be used in bubble 1.2 in Figure 12.6 to help determine how much inventory to order.

- **ABC analysis** is a technique for ranking items in a group based on the output of the items. ABC analysis can be used to categorize inventory items according to their importance. A given organization, for example, may have a situation where

15 percent of its inventory items accounts for 70 percent of its sales. Let's call this portion group A. Furthermore, an organization may find that an additional 10 percent of its inventory items accounts for an additional 20 percent of its sales. Let's call this portion group B. From this assessment, we can now deduce that the remaining 75 percent of the organization's inventory items constitutes only 10 percent of its sales. With this information, the supervisor of inventory control can decide which items of inventory are relatively more important to an organization and, consequently, require more attention and control. For instance, category C items might be ordered only when there is a specific request from a customer (i.e., no stock is kept on hand), whereas categories A and B might be ordered using *reorder point* analysis.

Now let's describe the process depicted in Figure 12.6. Bubble 1.1 receives and stores the requests received from inventory control (inventory's purchase requisition) and various departments (purchase requisition—goods and services). In this way an organization can consolidate requests, submit larger orders to vendors, and presumably receive concessions in price and payment terms for these larger purchases. Obviously, this benefit must be traded off with the costs associated with delaying a purchase and suffering the consequences of not having inventory available when needed.

At predetermined intervals, bubble 1.2 accesses the accumulated requests held in the purchase requisition data and combines that data with the inventory master data to determine what purchases need to be made. Requirements stored in the inventory master data might have been developed during *supply chain management* planning steps such as those described in Technology Summaries 12.1, 12.2, and 12.3 (pages 441, 443–444, and 445, respectively). For example, data about sales forecasts and scheduled promotions stored in the inventory master data might cause bubble 1.2 to adjust requested amounts.

Order Goods and Services

Figure 12.7, a lower-level view of bubble 2.0 in Figure 12.4 (page 448), provides a look at the logical functions involved in ordering goods and services. The first process involves vendor selection (bubble 2.1). A buyer generally consults the vendor master data to identify potential suppliers and then evaluates each prospective vendor.

Buyers often attempt to combine as many orders as possible with the same vendor by using *blanket orders* and/or *annual agreements*. If large expenditures for new or specially made parts are involved, the buyer may need to obtain *competitive bids* by sending a *request for quotation (RFQ)* to prospective vendors.

Vendor selection can have a significant impact on the success of an organization's inventory control and manufacturing functions. In Chapter 15 we describe manufacturing processes and just-in-time (JIT) inventory management. With JIT inventory management, parts arrive when needed, thus saving the interest costs associated with storing "excess" inventory and reducing the possibility of inventory becoming obsolete. To use JIT systems effectively, organizations must find and retain reliable vendors.

ENTERPRISE SYSTEMS

After the vendor has been selected, the buyer prepares a **purchase order**, which is a request for the purchase of goods or services from a vendor. Typically, a purchase order contains data regarding the needed quantities, expected unit prices, required delivery date, terms, and other conditions. Figure 12.8 (page 452) displays a requisition record with the necessary information to release the associated purchase order.

Process bubble 2.2 of Figure 12.7 depicts the process of preparing a purchase order. Process 2.2 first checks the inventory master data to obtain additional information with

Figure 12.7 Purchasing Process—Diagram 2

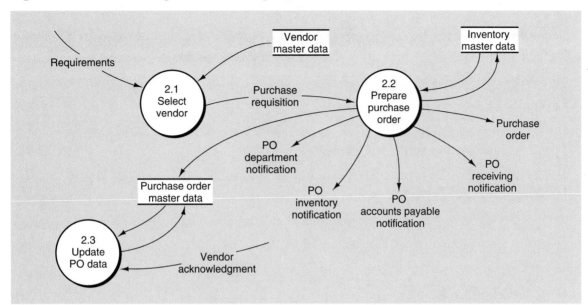

which to prepare the purchase order. The purchase order data flow out of process 2.2 is sent to the vendor. At the same time, the inventory master data is updated to reflect the goods on order. The purchase order information is distributed to several departments and processes as shown by the four other data flows out of process 2.2.

CONTROLS

The purchase order notifications could take a number of forms, including paper or electronic. It is not uncommon for the copy available for the receiving department to be a **blind copy**, meaning that certain data is blanked out (i.e., blinded). For instance, the quantities ordered might be blanked out so that the receiving personnel will not be influenced by this information when counting the goods. Price data may also be blinded because receiving personnel have no need to know that information.

Receive Goods and Services

CONTROLS

Figure 12.9 (page 453) is the lower-level diagram for process 3.0 in Figure 12.4 (page 448). In the case of inventory, the **vendor packing slip**, which accompanies the purchased inventory from the vendor and identifies the shipment, triggers the receiving process.[5] As indicated by bubble 3.1 of the figure, goods arriving at the receiving department are inspected and counted. This process helps to achieve a major process objective: *to ensure that the right goods in the correct amount are received in acceptable condition.* Nonconforming goods are denoted by the *reject* stub out of process 3.1. Notation of rejected goods is added to the vendor service record in the vendor master data.

Once the condition of the goods has been approved, process 3.2 completes the receiving report by noting the quantity received on the approved PO receiving notification. Once annotated with the quantity received, the PO receiving notification becomes a **receiving report,** which is the form used to record merchandise receipts. Process 3.3 compares the receiving report to the information stored in the purchase order master

---

[5] The vendor may push the shipment to the organization without a request, such as would happen in a *vendor managed inventory (VMI)* arrangement.

Figure 12.8 Sample Purchase Order Release Screen (J.D. Edwards)

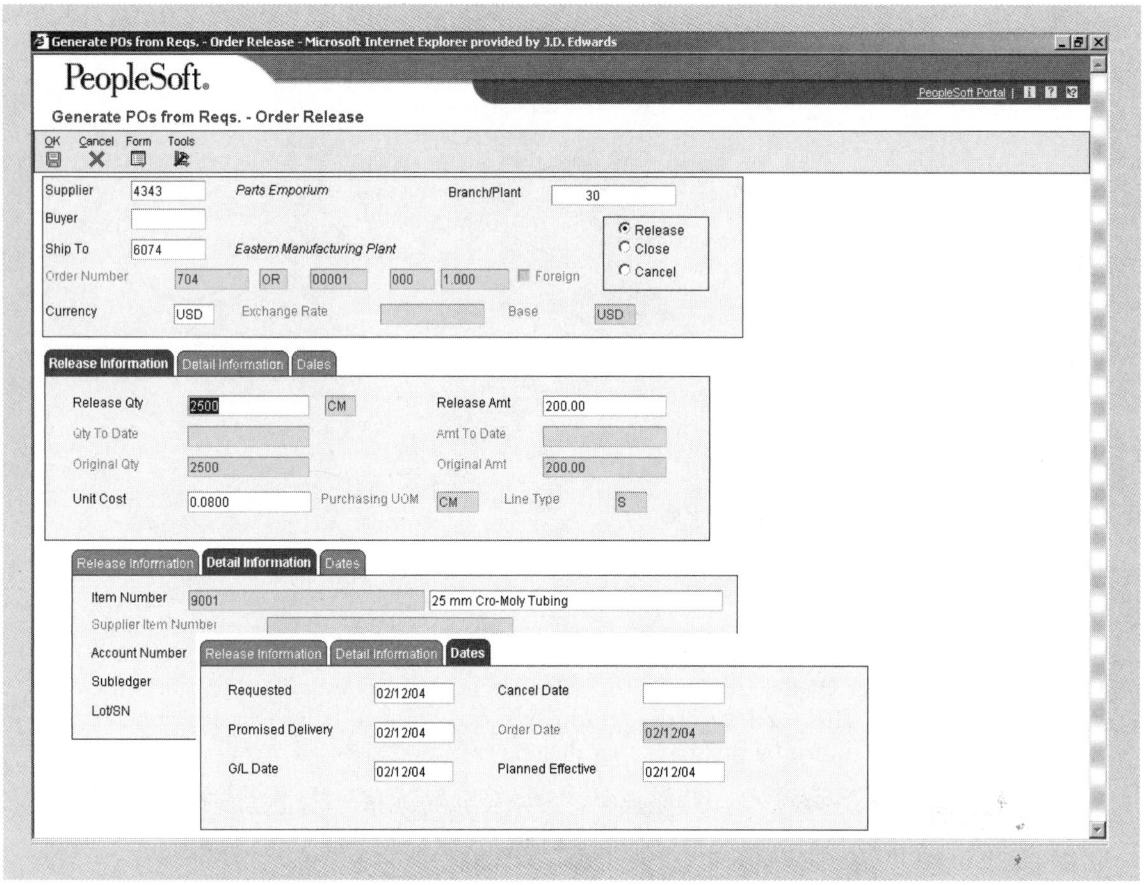

data—a process that often is automatically completed by the information system. Bubble 3.3 also reflects the following activities:

- Data about vendor compliance with the order terms (product quality, meeting promised delivery dates, etc.) is added to the vendor master data.
- Receiving report data may be accessed by the accounts payable process (i.e., the receiving report) and the warehouse (i.e., the stock notice). Data reflecting the receipt is stored as a copy of the receiving report document, if there is one, or as a computer data table (see the data store "Purchase receipts data").
- The inventory master data are updated to reflect the additional inventory on hand.
- The cost of the inventory received is relayed to the general ledger process (see the data flow "GL inventory received update").
- Finally, the purchase order master data are updated to reflect the receipt of the goods.

As in the case of the receipt of goods, services received also should be documented properly. Some organizations use an **acceptance report** to acknowledge formally the satis-

Figure 12.9 Purchasing Process—Diagram 3

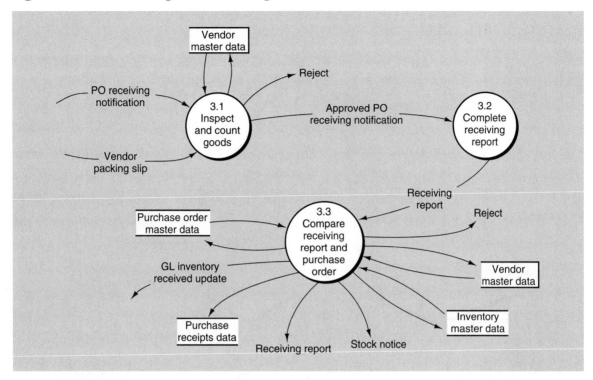

factory completion of a service contract. The acceptance report data supports the payment due to the vendor in the same way as the receiving report.[6]

Logical Data Descriptions

The purchasing process entails several different data stores. The **inventory master data** contains a record of each inventory item that is stocked in the warehouse or is regularly ordered from a vendor. These records are used to manage the inventory and to support the inventory balance in the general ledger. The **vendor master data** is usually accessed by purchasing personnel when selecting an appropriate vendor. In addition to storing identification data, the vendor data is used by management to evaluate vendor performance and to make various ordering decisions.

The **purchase requisitions master data** is a compilation of the *purchase requisitions*, requests for goods and services from authorized personal within an organization and for inventory replenishment from automated inventory replenishment systems, such as *supply chain management* processes. The **purchase order master data** is a compilation of open purchase orders and includes the status of each item on order. Finally, the **purchase receipts data** is an event data store with each record reflecting a receipt of goods and services.

---

[6] For simplicity in drawing the DFDs, we intend that the single data flow labeled *receiving report* represents either a receiving report (goods) or acceptance report (services).

Logical Database Design

The entity-relationship diagram applicable to the purchasing process is shown on Figure 12.10. The INVENTORY, VENDORS, PURCHASE_REQUISITIONS, PUR-CHASE_ORDERS and PURCHASE_RECEIPTS entities were described in the previous section. The EMPLOYEES entity contains specific information about each employee, including his/her authorization levels regarding generating purchase requisitions, preparing purchase orders, receiving goods, and so on. This entity will be discussed more fully in Chapter 14.

Figure 12.10 Entity-Relationship (E-R) Diagram (*Partial*) for the Purchasing Process

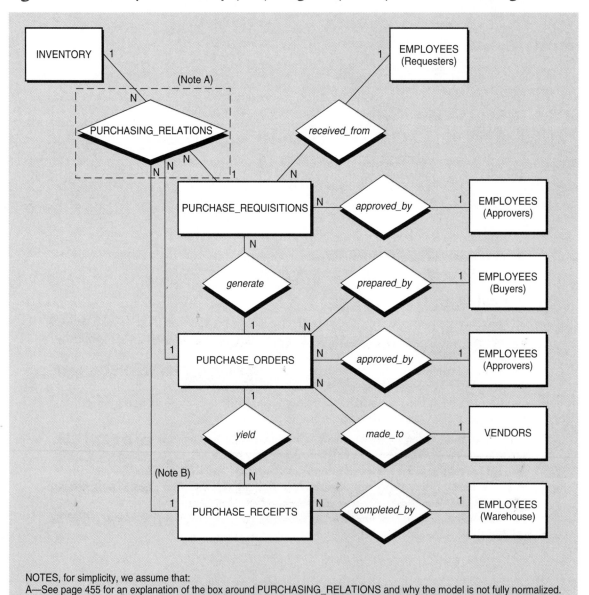

NOTES, for simplicity, we assume that:
A—See page 455 for an explanation of the box around PURCHASING_RELATIONS and why the model is not fully normalized.
B—There are no partial receipts of any line item on a PO.

The PURCHASING_RELATIONS relationship accumulates a record of purchasing-related events—PURCHASE_REQUISITIONS, PURCHASE_ORDERS, and PUR-CHASE_RECEIPTS—as they progress. The box around this relationship indicates that we will have a relation in our database for this relationship while the other relationships will not have a corresponding relation.

As with Figures 10.9 and 11.9 (pages 367 and 410, respectively), Figure 12.10 is not fully normalized yet. We include the "extra" relationships and redundant attributes to help you see the logical sequence of events. Also, note B on Figure 12.10 indicates that this is a simplified model. Certainly realistic models must deal with partial receipts.

The relational tables for the purchasing process are shown in Figure 12.11 (page 456). Notice that each table includes a primary key. In some tables, such as INVEN-TORY, a single primary key is included. One table, PURCHASE_RELATIONS, has a primary key from the PURCHASE_REQUISITIONS and INVENTORY tables to form a composite (multiple) key. Each relation (row) in this table records the details of each requested item from requisition (the first three columns) to purchase order (the fourth and fifth columns), to receipt (the last two columns).

TECHNOLOGY TRENDS AND DEVELOPMENTS

E-BUSINESS

You may also recall in Chapter 3 that we discussed the emergence of electronic market-places that create a more competitive purchasing market. A primary area of introduction of these marketplaces into the business processes of major business organizations is usually the purchasing process. Accordingly, we explore several examples of such market-places arising in certain industries as described in Technology Application 12.2 (page 457). Recall from Chapter 3, however, that many risks are involved in the move toward electronic marketplaces, and these may limit their success in the short term.

Another technology development that has had a significant effect on *supply chain management* and the purchasing process is radio-frequency identification (RFID) technology that is described in Technology Summary 12.4 (page 458). Technology Application 12.3 (page 459) describes some early RFID uses.

PHYSICAL PROCESS DESCRIPTION

E-BUSINESS

ENTERPRISE SYSTEMS

As the name implies, **paperless systems** *eliminate* documents and forms as the medium for conducting business. In a truly paperless system, printed reports disappear and are replaced with computer screen displays of requested information. With the increasing use of *Web services*, *RFID*, *EDI*, *electronic funds transfer (EFT)*, *digital image processing*, *electronic mail*, *workflow software*, *enterprise systems*, and similar technologies, is the "paperless office" at hand? We are certainly close in many contemporary environments. In fact, a growing number of organizations arguably operate the bulk of their business processes using *paperless systems*. The major roadblocks are more organizational and behavioral/psychological than technological in nature. Over time, these cultural barriers to the paperless office continue to disintegrate as a new generation of managers—who have grown up with the computer as a fact of their daily lives—emerges.

The physical model of the purchasing process presented in this section employs much of the technology mentioned previously. Although the process is not completely *paperless*, hard copy documents are held to a minimum.

Figure 12.11 Selected Relational Tables (*Partial*) for the Purchasing Process

Shaded_Attribute(s) | = Primary Key

INVENTORY

Item_No	Item_Name	Price	Location	Qty_on_Hand	Reorder_Pt
936	Machine Plates	39.50	Macomb	1,500	950
1001	Gaskets	9.50	Macomb	10,002	3,500
1010	Crank Shafts	115.00	Tampa	952	500
1025	Manifolds	45.00	Tampa	402	400

EMPLOYEES

Emp_No	Emp_First_Name	Emp_Last_Name	Soc_Sec_No	Emp_Dept
B432	Carl	Mast	125-87-8090	492-01
A491	Janet	Kopp	127-93-3453	639-04
A632	Greg	Bazie	350-97-9030	538-22
B011	Christy	Kinman	123-78-0097	298-12

VENDORS

Vend_No	Vend_Name	Vend_Street	Vend_City	Vend_State	Vend_ZIP	Vend_Tel	Vend_Contact	Credit_Terms	FOB_Terms
539	Ace Widget Co.	190 Shore Dr.	Charleston	SC	29915	803-995-3764	S. Emerson	2/10,n/30	Ship Pt
540	Babcock Supply Co.	22 Ribaut Rd.	Beaufort	SC	29902	803-552-4788	Frank Roy	n/60	Destin
541	Webster Steel Corp.	49 Abercorn St.	Savannah	GA	30901	912-433-1750	Wilbur Cox	2/10,n/30	Ship Pt

PURCHASE_REQUISITIONS

PR_No	PR_Date	Emp_No (PR_Requestor)[a]	Emp_No (PR_Approver)[b]	PO_No
53948	20071215	A491	E745	4346
53949	20071215	C457	A632	4350
53950	20071216	9999	540-32	4347
53951	20071216	F494	D548	4352

PURCHASE_ORDERS

PO_No	PO_Date	Vend_No	Ship_Via	Emp_No (Buyer)	Emp_No (PO_Approver)	PO_Status
4345	20071218	539	Best Way	F395	F349	Open
4346	20071220	541	FedEx	C932	F349	Sent
4347	20071222	562	UPS	E049	D932	Acknowledged

PURCHASE_RECEIPTS

Rec_No	Rec_Date	Emp_No (Receiving)	PO_No	Invoice_No
42944	20071216	B260	4322	7-945
42945	20071216	B260	4339	9542-4
42946	20071216	B260	4345	535

PURCHASE_RELATIONS

PR_No	Item_No	Qty_Requested	PO_No	Qty_Ordered	Rec_No	Qty_Received
53947	1005	200	4345	200	42946	200
53947	1006	50	4345	50	42946	50
53947	1015	25	4345	25	42946	25

[a] If automatic purchase requisition, then 9999; if employee, then employee number.
[b] If automatic purchase requisition, then contract number of trading partner; if employee, then employee number.

Technology   Application   1 2 . 2

Uses of Business-to-Business (B2B) Marketplaces for the Purchasing Process

Case 1

A trend in the B2B electronic marketplaces environment has been a move toward consolidation of the numerous marketplaces that popped up quickly in the early 2000s. One example of this is the merger between MyAircraft and AirNewco—two early entrants into the electronic marketplaces for supplying aviation-related supplies and materials. MyAircraft was a joint venture by supplier organizations such as United Technologies Corp., Honeywell International Inc., and Goodrich Corporation. On the other hand, AirNewco was a joint venture by buyer organizations, including eight major international airlines and the United Parcel Service of America, Inc. The result of the merger is a single major exchange that has both the interests of suppliers and buyers represented.

Case 2

In one of the earliest major marketplaces to arise, Covisint quickly gained the attention of the Federal Trade Commission (FTC) due to possible limitations on fair trade. Covisint is a joint venture of the Big Three U.S. automakers and, as a result, has the potential to radically change the pricing and partnering structures of the three automakers with the numerous automotive parts suppliers that previously serviced the automakers. The FTC ultimately gave its

blessings to the new electronic marketplace in September 2000, after apparently recognizing the enormous cost savings and efficiencies that would likely result from such a venture through the sharply reduced sales and distributions costs and through the streamlining of purchasing operations at the automakers.

Case 3

An alternative to the creation of a public electronic marketplace such as Covisint is the creation of a private network such as the approach used by Toyota Motor Sales, U.S.A., Inc. Toyota hopes to decrease its inventory levels by about $175 million (roughly 50 percent) by using a private electronic marketplace to rapidly replenish necessary automotive parts supplies from its established set of suppliers. It is anticipated that the reduction in inventory will save $30 million per year once the exchange is operating in full. Toyota is not the only company turning to private exchanges with their own supplier networks. While there are an estimated 600 planned or operating public electronic exchanges, about 30,000 such private exchanges are planned. These exchanges may link as few as a half-dozen suppliers in some cases, but are still anticipated to provide most of the benefits of larger public exchanges without many of the risks.

Sources: Todd R. Weiss, "Two Aviation Industry B2B Marketplaces Agree to Merge," *Computerworld Online* (October 26, 2000); John R. Wilke, "Green Light is Likely for Auto-Parts Site," *The Wall Street Journal* (September 11, 2000): A3; Steve Ulfelder, "Members Only Exchanges—Building a Private Business-to-Business Exchange Has its Benefits—and Challenges," *Computerworld Online* (October 23, 2000).

Discussion and Illustration

Figure 12.12 (pages 460–461) presents a systems flowchart of the purchasing process. At several points in the flowchart, you will see notations that *exception routines* are not flowcharted. They also are omitted from the discussion in the following paragraphs.

Requisition and Order Merchandise

As shown in the first column, the purchasing process begins when a cost center employee establishes a need. The *enterprise system* displays a screen similar to the one depicted in Figure 12.5 (page 449) and the requisitioner keys in a description of the items desired, as well as information about the cost center making the request.

ENTERPRISE SYSTEMS

Technology Summary 12.4

Radio-Frequency Identification Technology (RFID)

Radio-frequency identification (RFID) is a chip with an antenna that can send and receive data from an RFID reader. RFID chips can be attached to groups of items, such as pallets of groceries, or to individual items, such as shaving razors or pieces of clothing. RFID readers do not require that there be line-of-sight to a chip to be able to read the chip. A reader can obtain data from chips attached to items packed within boxes as the boxes pass near the reader.

RFID's most useful application to date is to track items through the supply chain. For example, a manufacturer, such as Gillette, would attach an RFID tag to each razor destined for Wal-Mart. RFID readers at the Gillette shipping dock would record the movement of the razors and send data to Gillette's *enterprise system* to record the shipment/sale. At Wal-Mart's warehouse an RFID reader would read the chips and record the receipt of the razors. Readers throughout the warehouse and retail stores can keep track of the location of the razors. When the razors are sold, RFID readers will read the data and record the sale of each razor, in a manner similar to that used for many years with *scanners*, UPC codes, and point of sale (POS) systems. In fact, an electronic product code

(EPC), has been developed for use with RFID technology, much like the UPC is used with bar codes.

Since RFID does not require line-of-sight between chip and reader, and the reading step is passive (e.g., the reader will locate every chip that passes by), this technology can help to reduce theft. At the same time, this feature has caused some privacy concerns because the chips are not necessarily turned off when the item is sold. Left activated, the chip can track the location of the person carrying the item.

Data on the chips can record the manufacturing date, color, and size of an item. Expiration dates, if any, can be stored and relayed to monitoring systems to move product into sales, price reduction, or disposal, as appropriate. At a cost of 30 cents each, it is presently more feasible to tag groups of items. The price is expected to soon reach 5 cents each and probably needs to reach 1 to 2 cents each before the technology can be widely adopted.

Advantages, then, of the RFID technology include increased data accuracy, reduced product theft, quicker retail checkout (or self-service checkout), reduced stockouts, more timely deliveries, and better customer service.

Sources: "Wal-Mart Put a Date on RFID Implementation: January 2005. Will Suppliers and the Technology be Ready?" *Information-Week* (June 16, 2003); Gerry Khermouch and Heather Green, "Bar Codes Better Watch Their Backs," *BusinessWeek* (July 14, 2003): 42.

CONTROLS The completed requisition is routed via the system to a cost center supervisor for approval. Depending on the amount and nature of the requisition, several approvals may be required. Approval is granted in the system by forwarding the requisition to the next person on the list; approval codes are attached to the record along the way and are displayed in the appropriate boxes on the requisition form. When all approvals have been obtained, the approved requisition is automatically sent to an audit file and routed to the purchasing department.

ENTERPRISE SYSTEMS Periodically, the *enterprise system* displays requirements—including requisitions from various departments, orders from inventory control, and requests based on forecast data—on the screen of the appropriate buyer. The system also displays a list of approved vendors who can provide the required items. The buyer selects a vendor and establishes the price and terms of the purchase. Final vendor selection and price determination may require contact with the potential vendor. When the vendor choice is settled, the buyer

Technology   Application   1 2 . 3

Uses of Radio-Frequency Identification (RFID) for the Purchasing Process

Case 1

In June 2003, Wal-Mart announced that 100 key suppliers must, by 2005, use RFID to track pallets of goods through the supply chain. Getting ready for this implementation, Wal-Mart has tracked individual items with Gillette; cases with Coca-Cola, Kraft, P&G, and Unilever; and pallets of paper towels.

Case 2

Associated Food Stores, Inc., has placed RFID chips on each of its trailers to obtain real-time data about the location and internal temperature of each trailer. The data from the chips is read every four minutes, fed to its supply chain management system via cables and the Internet, and used to track shipments and to ensure that goods are maintained at required temperatures. Associated expects to utilize its fleet of trailers more effectively to cut down on leasing and personnel costs and to reduce product spoilage by $100,000 each year.

Case 3

Many of you may be using RFID and not know it. RFID is the technology behind ExxonMobil's Speedpass used for gas purchases and E-ZPass used for paying highway tolls. In each case the consumer carries the RFID chip (in the Speedpass fob or in the windshield-mounted E-ZPass) that is read at the gas pump or at the toll booth. The individual (and car or truck) is then charged for the gas or toll.

Sources: "Wal-Mart Put a Date on RFID Implementation: January 2005. Will Suppliers and the Technology be Ready?" *Information-Week* (June 16, 2003); Marc L. Songini, "IT Plays Radio Tag," *Computerworld* (April 8, 2002): 46.

converts the requisition to a purchase order and adds any necessary details, such as vendor, price, and terms.

Next, the system routes the purchase order to the purchasing manager for approval. The manager approves and releases the purchase order. The system records the approval, updates the inventory master data to reflect the quantity on order, and confirms the order to the requisitioner. The purchasing process releases the PO to the EDI translator where it is converted to the appropriate EDI format. The translation software also *encrypts* the EDI message and appends a *digital signature* to it (procedures discussed in Chapter 9).

E-BUSINESS

CONTROLS

Receive Merchandise

On the second page of the flowchart, we see that receiving department personnel receive the merchandise sent by the vendor. They enter the purchase order number into the system and an *RFID* reader reads the item numbers and quantities from the RFID chips attached to each item in the shipment. The *enterprise system* compares the items and quantities received to those on the open purchase order master data.[7] If the shipment is correct, the system accepts the shipment, creates a record in the receiving report data, updates the status field in the purchase order data, records the receipt in the inventory master data, updates the general ledger to reflect the receipt, prints a stock notice, and displays the receiving report number. The receiving clerk attaches the stock

ENTERPRISE SYSTEMS

[7] The database controls prevent receiving personnel from accessing price data in the purchase order master data. In this way, the process implements the *blind copy* concept explained earlier.

Figure 12.12 Purchasing Process—Systems Flowchart

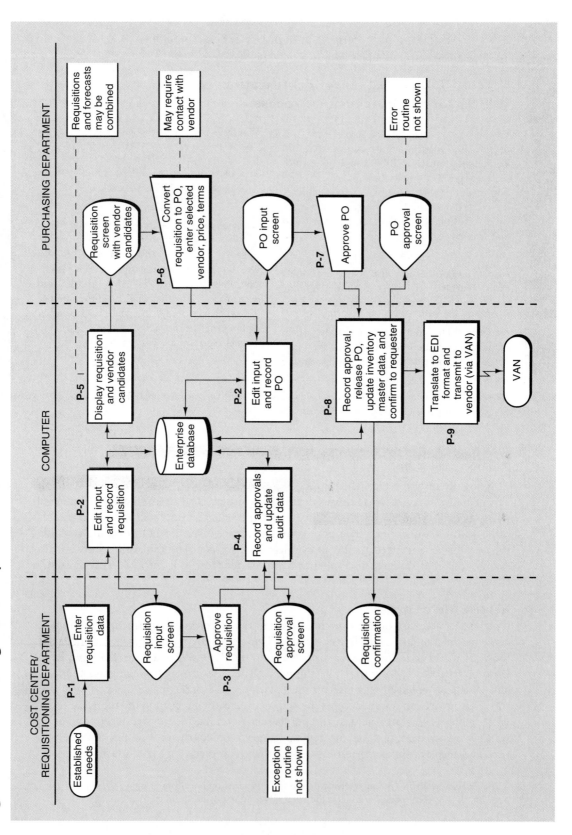

Figure 12.12 Purchasing Process—Systems Flowchart (*continued*)

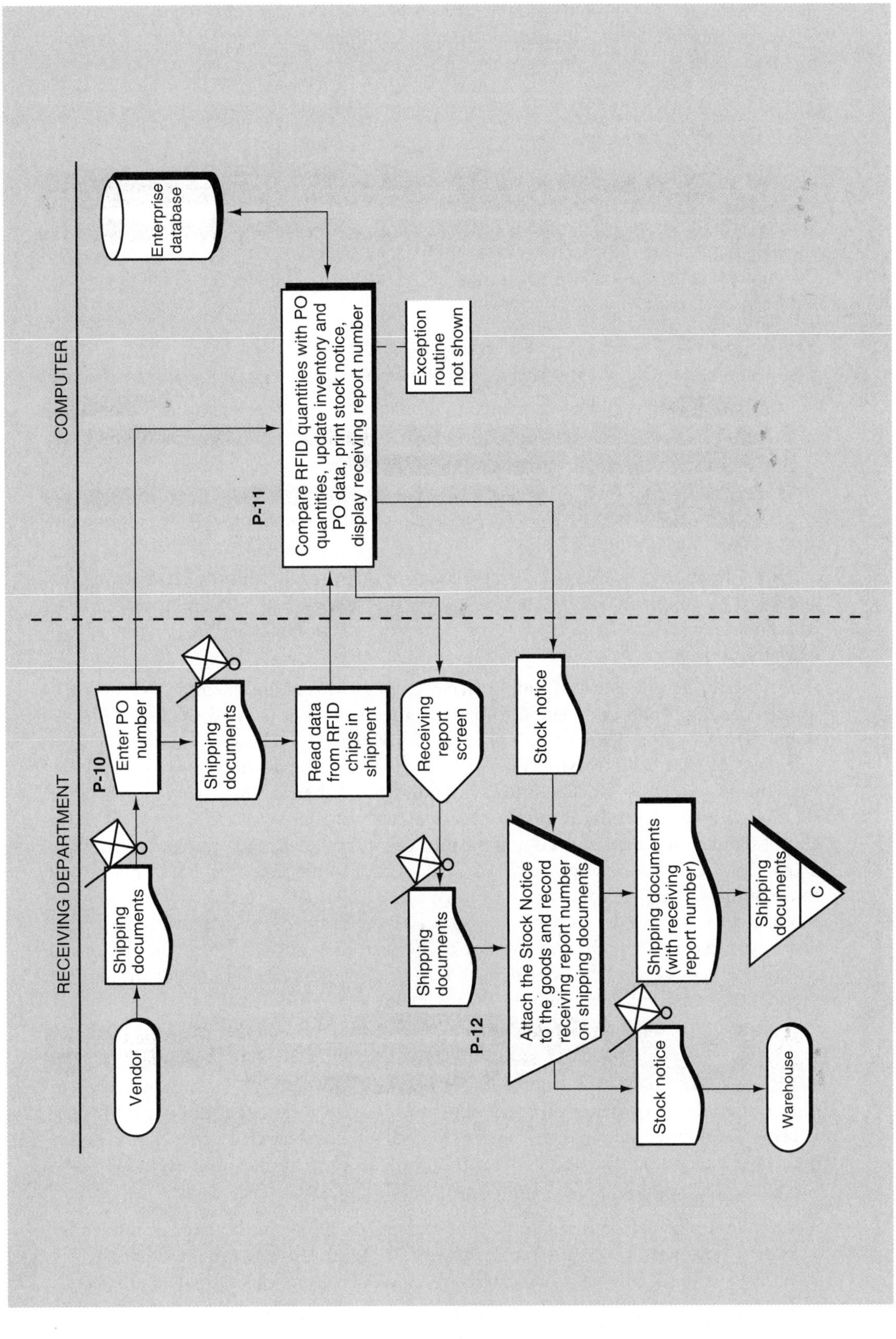

notice to the goods and sends them to the warehouse. The clerk also records the receiving report number on the shipping documents and files them in chronological sequence for *audit trail* purposes. Alternatively, an *image* of the shipping documents might be stored on the computer.

The Fraud Connection

Since the purchasing process is part of the *purchase-to-pay process* that culminates with the payment of cash—a firm's most liquid asset—it should not surprise you that this process is rife with potential for *exposing* an organization to fraud and embezzlement. Indeed, many of the most serious cases of process abuse have involved manipulation of the purchasing process. In this section, we present some of the ways in which the process has been manipulated.

Fraud and the Purchasing Function

The typical cases included in this category of process exploitation are instances in which:

- An employee (e.g., a buyer, purchasing manager, or other person) places purchase orders with a particular vendor(s) in exchange for a kickback, secret commission, or other form of inducement from the vendor(s).

- An employee has a *conflict of interest* between his responsibilities to his employer and his financial interest—direct or indirect—in a company with whom the employer does business.

As we mentioned in Chapter 7, these kinds of quasi-legal/ethical scenarios are often addressed by an organization as part of a *code of conduct,* which all employees are asked to acknowledge periodically by attesting that they have not engaged in activities that violate the code.

Cases of bribery, kickbacks, and the like present an interesting dilemma. It is accepted business practice for a salesperson to treat a buyer to lunch, to send the buyer promotional "gifts" (e.g., a sleeve of golf balls imprinted with the selling company's logo), or to extend other small favors in order to make sales. When do such actions stop being "acceptable" and cross the line into being improper, either in substance or appearance? We can't answer that ethical question here except to offer one case example that was clearly fraud. This case involved a company (customer) that made purchases from foreign suppliers. The company's president made it clear to the suppliers that if they wanted to do business with the company, they must agree to pay 2 percent of any business they transacted to the president's personal bank account. In turn, the suppliers inflated their invoices to the company by the amount of the secret commission they paid. To ensure that the higher cost would not be detected by anyone in the purchasing department, the president approved all such invoices for payment.

In purchasing activities, conflicts of interest often arise in situations where an employee with the authority to make (or approve) purchases for an organization has some kind of financial stake in a company that sells to the organization. For instance, the employee might be an owner or principal of the vendor-company, either directly or through a relative, and therefore stands to benefit by placing business with that vendor. This condition presents one of the knottier control problems confronting business today.

Here is a brief example of a *conflict of interest* fraud:

Over an 8-year period, Frick (a fictitious name), a director of buying for toys and related products at a major retailer (Wombat, Inc.), placed some $3 million of business with 12 companies operated by Frack. Although Frick signed annual conflict of interest statements, he did not disclose his significant ownership interest in those 12 companies. When other toy suppliers reported to one of Wombat's directors that they had trouble obtaining sales to Wombat, an investigation ensued. It was discovered that Frick had received over $500,000 in cash and benefits from the 12 companies.

APPLICATION OF THE CONTROL FRAMEWORK TO PURCHASING

In this section, we apply the control framework from Chapter 7 to the purchasing process. Figure 12.13 (pages 464–465) presents a completed *control matrix* for the annotated systems flowchart shown in Figure 12.12 (pages 460–461). After briefly discussing the control goals shown as column headings in the matrix, we then describe in Exhibit 12.1 (pages 466–467) each of the recommended control plans listed. As you study the control plans, be sure to see where they are located on the systems flowchart.

Control Goals

The following control goal categories are presented in the matrix. Those for the operations process are as follows:

- *Effectiveness of operations.* In addition to the two in the matrix, one each for the requisition/purchase order process and the goods receipt process, we include one for complying with the organization's code of conduct concerning conflicts of interest, accepting illegal or improper payments, and like matters. Recall from Chapter 7 that one of the three categories of control objectives recommended by the COSO report on internal control is compliance with applicable laws, regulations, and contractual agreements. For each process to which it applies, we have elected to include COSO's "compliance" objective under our operations goals. As you saw in Chapter 7 and earlier in this chapter in the "Fraud Connection" section, many organizations are addressing some of the thorny ethical issues that they face by adopting a corporate code of conduct, giving that code wide publicity throughout the organization, and having employees subscribe to that code by periodically attesting that they have abided by its provisions. In that sense, then, the code of conduct becomes a type of contractual agreement between the company and its employees.
- *Efficiency of the use of people and computers by the purchasing and receiving processes.*
- *Resource security.* Note that the resources include the cash asset and the information resources represented by the purchase order master data.

Those for the information process are as follows:

- *Input validity (IV) of input events.*[8]
- *Input completeness (IC) and input accuracy (IA).*

---

[8] In the matrix, please note that the inputs and master data vary for each of the processes. These variations can be summarized as follows:

Process	Nature of inputs	Updated master data
purchasing	purchase requisition	purchase order
receiving	vendor packing slip	purchase order

Figure 12.13 Control Matrix for the Purchasing Process

	Control Goals of the Purchasing Business Process														
	Control Goals of the Operations Process					Control Goals of the Information Process									
	Ensure effectiveness of operations			Ensure efficient employment of resources (people, computers)	Ensure security of resources (inventory, purchase order master data)	For purchase requisition inputs, ensure:			For purchase order master data, ensure:		For vendor packing slip inputs, ensure:			For purchase order master data, ensure:	
Recommended Control Plans	A	B	C			IV	IC	IA	UC	UA	IV	IC	IA	UC	UA
Present Controls															
P-1: Preformatted screens				P-1				P-1							
P-2: Programmed edit checks				P-2				P-2		P-2					
P-3: Written approvals						P-3									
P-4: Requisition audit data							P-4		P-4						
P-5: Authorized vendor data	P-5		P-5	P-5		P-5									
P-6: Compare vendors for favorable prices, terms, quality, and product availability	P-6														
P-7: Approve vendor selection	P-7		P-7			P-7									
P-8: Requisition confirmation to originating department							P-8		P-8						
P-9: Digital signatures						P-9	P-9	P-9		P-9					

Figure 12.13 Control Matrix for the Purchasing Process (*continued*)

Recommended Control Plans	Control Goals of the Operations Process					Control Goals of the Information Process									
	Ensure effectiveness of operations			Ensure efficient employment of resources (people, computers)	Ensure security of resources (inventory, purchase order master data)	For purchase requisition inputs, ensure:			For purchase order master data, ensure:		For vendor packing slip inputs, ensure:			For purchase order master data, ensure:	
	A	B	C			IV	IC	IA	UC	UA	IV	IC	IA	UC	UA
Present Controls															
P-10: Enter receipt data in the receiving department		P-10		P-10	P-10						P-10	P-10	P-10		P-10
P-11: Compare inputs with master data		P-11											P-11		P-11
P-12: Create audit trail for receipts		P-12			P-12								P-12		P-12
Missing Controls															
None noted															

Legend:

Effectiveness goals:
A = Select a vendor that will provide the best quality at the lowest price by the required delivery date.
B = Ensure that the right goods in the correct amount are received in acceptable condition.
C = Comply with corporate code of conduct.

See Exhibit 12.1 (pages 466–467) for a complete explanation of control plans and cell entries.

IV = Input validity
IC = Input completeness
IA = Input accuracy
UC = Update completeness
UA = Update accuracy

- *Update completeness (UC) and update accuracy (UA).*

Input validity for each input event type can be summarized as follows:

- *Purchase requisitions.* Those that have been properly approved and that utilize existing (real) and approved vendors.

- *Vendor packing slips.* Those that are supported by authorized purchase orders and that represent existing (real) receipts of goods and services.

Recommended Control Plans

Study the explanations of the cell entries appearing in the control matrix in Exhibit 12.1. As you know from your studies in prior chapters, understanding how the recommended control plans relate to specific control goals is the most important aspect of applying the control framework.

Exhibit 12.1 Explanation of Cell Entries for Control Matrix in Figure 12.13

P-1: *Preformatted screens.*

Efficient employment of resources: By structuring the data entry process, automatically populating fields, and preventing errors, preformatted screens simplify data input and save time allowing a user to input more data over a period of time.

Purchase requisition input accuracy: As each data field is completed on a preformatted screen, the cursor moves to the next field on the screen, thus preventing the user from omitting any required data set. The data for fields that are automatically populated need not be manually entered, thus reducing input errors. Incorrectly formatted fields are rejected.

P-2: *Programmed edit checks.*

Efficient employment of resources: Event data can be processed on a timelier basis and at a lower cost if errors are detected and prevented from entering the system in the first place.

Purchase requisition input accuracy: The edits identify erroneous or suspect data and reduce input errors.

Update accuracy: Edits performed when the purchase requisition is converted to a purchase order also ensure update accuracy since the purchase order is created at this time.

P-3: *Written approvals.*

Purchase requisition input validity: By obtaining approvals for all purchase requisitions, we reduce the possibility that invalid (unauthorized) requisitions will be input.

P-4: *Requisition audit data.*

Purchase requisition input completeness: After all necessary approvals have been obtained, a copy of the requisition is automatically added to the audit data. This control plan ensures that a complete record is maintained of *all* requisition activity.

P-5: *Authorized vendor data.*

Effectiveness goal A: Buyers in the purchasing department are presented with a list of vendor candidates that contains only those vendors with whom the company is authorized to do business. The screening of vendors that preceded their being added to the authorized data should help ensure *selection of a vendor who will provide the best quality at the lowest price by the promised delivery date.*

Effectiveness goal C: Screening of vendors helps to ensure that company employees do not have financial interests in a vendor that would jeopardize their ability to be impartial in selecting a vendor with whom to place an order.

Efficient employment of resources: People resources (buyers' time) are used efficiently because time is not wasted in searching for vendors that might not even supply the required goods or services.

Purchase requisition input validity: The *blanket* approval accorded to vendors who are placed on the authorized vendor data also helps ensure the validity of purchase orders issued.

Exhibit 12.1 Explanation of Cell Entries for Control Matrix in Figure 12.13 (*continued*)

P-6: *Compare vendors for favorable prices, terms, quality, and product availability.*

Effectiveness goal A: The comparison of vendors should help ensure *selection of a vendor who will provide the best quality at the lowest price by the promised delivery date.*

P-7: *Approve vendor selection.*

Effectiveness goal A: After the purchase order is checked against the requisition details, it is approved by the purchasing manager—by adding an approval code to the purchase order record. The manager's approval includes the vendor chosen by the buyer.

Effectiveness goal C: This control plan could flag situations in which certain vendors appear to be favored in the vendor-selection process.

Purchase requisition input validity: Approval by the purchasing manager helps to ensure validity of the purchase order.

P-8: *Requisition confirmation to originating department.*

Purchase requisition input completeness: Once the purchase order has been released by the purchasing manager, a confirmation of the requisition is sent to the requisitioner. Should the confirmation not be received in a timely manner the requester will follow up to see that the request is processed.

Update completeness: Confirmation is received after the purchase order data has been updated.

P-9: *Digital signatures.*

Security of resources, Purchase requisition input validity: Digital signatures will allow the vendor to determine that the sender of the message has authority to send it and thus prevents an unauthorized purchase and diversion of resources. This also determines that the message itself is genuine.

Purchase requisition input accuracy, Update accuracy: Detects messages that have been altered in transit, thus preventing the use of data by the vendor that is not reflected in the purchase requisition input and the purchase order master record.

P-10: *Enter receipt data in receiving department.*

Effectiveness goal B: Receiving personnel, with goods in hand and the PO data available, are in a good position to ensure that the correct goods are received.

Efficient employment of resources: The direct entry of input data by operations personnel eliminates the cost associated with the handling of the event data by additional entities.

Vendor packing slip input validity: Because the receipts are captured in the receiving department, they are more likely to reflect actual product receipts.

Vendor packing slip input completeness, Update completeness: Because the receipts are captured at the receiving department, they are less likely to be lost as they are transported to a data entry location. The master data is updated simultaneously with the input of the receipt data.

Vendor packing slip input accuracy, Update accuracy: Because receiving personnel are familiar with the data being entered, they are less likely to make input errors and can more readily correct these errors if they occur. The master data is updated simultaneously with the input of the receipt data.

P-11: *Compare inputs with master data.*

Effectiveness goal B, Vendor packing slip input validity: By comparing the open purchase order to the data on the RFID chips we can ensure that we have received the goods that were ordered.

Vendor packing slip input accuracy, Update accuracy: The comparison identifies erroneous or suspect data and reduces input errors. The master data is updated simultaneously with the input of the receipt data.

P-12: *Create audit trail for receipts.*

Effectiveness goal B, Security of resources, Vendor packing slip input validity: The audit trail may be examined to ensure that the correct goods have been received, recorded, and sent to the warehouse.

Vendor packing slip input accuracy, Update accuracy: The audit trail may be examined to ensure that the receipts were accurately recorded. The master data is updated simultaneously with the input of the receipt data.

Summary

This chapter has covered the purchasing process, which is the backbone of the *purchase-to-pay process* introduced in Chapter 2. Like the OE/S process in the *order-to-cash process*, the purchasing component of the purchase-to-pay process fills a central coordinating role as it supports the supplies and inventory components of an organization's operations.

The physical process implementation presented in this chapter evidences many attributes of the paperless office of the future. Are these visions of a paperless society that far-fetched? Hardly. The technology exists today, and many companies have availed themselves of some, if not all, of that technology.

Review Questions

RQ 12-1 How, in your own words, would you define the purchasing process?

RQ 12-2 What primary functions does the purchasing process perform?

RQ 12-3 How does the purchasing process relate to its environment inside and outside the organization?

RQ 12-4 What are the fundamental responsibilities of each position: receiving supervisor, purchasing manager, and buyer?

RQ 12-5 What major *logical* processes does the purchasing process perform?

RQ 12-6 Describe supply chain management.

RQ 12-7 Describe how Radio-frequency identification (RFID) works.

RQ 12-8 What are operations process (effectiveness) goals of the purchasing process? Provide an example illustrating each goal.

RQ 12-9 In designing vendor records to be incorporated into the vendor master data, what specific data elements would you include to help you select the best vendor? Be specific as to the nature of the data stored and how it will be used in the selection process.

RQ 12-10 Select three control plans presented in the chapter. How does each relate to the purchasing process presented in Figure 12.12 (pages 460–461)?

Discussion Questions

DQ 12-1 Refer to the operations process (effectiveness) goals shown in the control matrix (goals A and B in Figure 12.13, pages 464–465). For the two activities (purchasing and, receiving), describe an operations goal other than the one discussed in the chapter.

DQ 12-2 Explain why ambiguities and conflicts exist among operations process goals, and discuss potential ambiguities and conflicts relative to the effectiveness goals you described in DQ 12-1.

DQ 12-3 Discuss how, if at all, a "year-to-date purchases" field in the vendor record might be of use in selecting a vendor.

DQ 12-4 Without redrawing the figures, discuss how Figures 12.3, 12.4, 12.6, 12.7, and 12.9 (pages 447, 448, 449, 451, 453) would change as a result of purchasing a technical product that could not be inspected in the receiving department but had to undergo quality control testing before being accepted.

DQ 12-5 Figure 12.9 on page 453 (the DFD depicting the receipt of goods and services) shows an update to the vendor master data from bubble 3.1 and another update to that same data from bubble 3.3. Discuss the *difference(s)* between these two updates. Be specific as to the nature of the data being updated in each case. How would your answer to this question be affected by your assumption about whether the purchase order receiving notification entering bubble 3.1 was "blind" as to quantities? Explain.

DQ 12-6 In terms of effectiveness and efficiency of operations, as well as of meeting the generic information system control goals of validity, completeness, and accuracy, what are the arguments for and against each of the following?

    a. Sending a copy of the purchase order from the purchasing department to the receiving department.

    b. Having the "quantity ordered" field "blinded" on the receiving department copy of the purchase order.

DQ 12-7 "Auditors will never allow an organization to adopt a paperless system, so why do we waste our time bothering to study them?" Discuss fully.

DQ 12-8 Refer to Figure 12.12 on pages 460–461 (the systems flowchart for the purchasing process). After all necessary approvals have been added to the purchase requisition, the audit data are updated on the enterprise database. Speculate about the nature and purpose of the audit data. Who might access this data and for what purposes? Discuss fully. *Hint*: You might want to consider the purposes that such data could serve in a completely "paperless" system.

PROBLEMS

Note: As mentioned in Chapters 10 and 11, the first few problems in the business process chapters are based on the processes of specific companies. Therefore, the problem material starts with case narratives of those processes. (Note: These cases continue in Chapter 13.)

CASE STUDIES

CASE A: Speedy Grocers, Inc. (I)

Speedy Grocers is an online grocery service that provides home delivery of groceries purchased via the Internet. Speedy operates in the greater Tulsa area and provides delivery to pre-certified customers. Because of the perishable nature of many grocery products, the bulk of orders must be handled similarly to that used for just-in-time processes.

For each good there is a quantity on hand and a desired quantity on hand in the inventory database. When the quantity on hand falls below the desired quantity on hand, a screen will automatically pop up in the purchasing manager's computer, alerting the manager to reorder the goods. The manager can approve the reordering of goods simply by checking the acceptance box. When the acceptance box is checked, the purchase order and inventory databases are updated. In addition, the vendor is notified electronically through a transmission from the purchasing system. This transmission takes the form of an electronic purchase order.

When the goods are received from the vendor, a printout of the authorized purchase order is attached. The receiving department keys in the purchase order number to retrieve the electronic authorization from the purchasing database. Accepted goods are recorded as received in the purchasing and inventory databases and bar codes are automatically printed in the receiving department, to label the crates/boxes received. The goods are stored in the warehouse. Upon acceptance, accounts payable balances are updated.

CASE B: Healthy Medical Supplies (I)

Healthy Medical Supplies makes a variety of medical supplies such as test tubes, thermometers, and disposable surgical garments. Healthy employs the following procedures for purchasing and receiving.

Supplies are maintained on a real-time basis in an inventory database in an enterprise system. The inventory records include reorder points for all regularly used items. Each day, the supplies clerk reviews an online report listing those items that have reached their reorder point. The clerk creates a requisition by filling out a requisition form in the company's enterprise system. Each requisition form has a unique identifier and after creation, the purchasing and inventory databases are updated to reflect the purchase requisition. Production manager approval is required for items that cost over $100 and are not covered by a blanket order. The production manager can log onto the enterprise system anytime to look at open requisitions that require approval and to approve those requisitions by checking the acceptance box.

Some supplies that are used in large quantities come under "blanket" purchase orders. Blanket orders are based on agreements between Healthy and different vendors to buy a *minimum* amount of supplies over a specified period of time at a guaranteed price. Purchase requisitions against these orders do not require the production manager's approval, as long as the agreed minimum is not surpassed.

Each day, the purchasing department reviews approved requisitions, selects a vendor from the vendor database, and prepares a pre-numbered purchase order on the enterprise system. Once the purchase order is saved, the purchase and inventory databases are updated. The completed purchase order is then printed in the purchasing department and mailed to the vendor.

The receiving department counts the goods when they are received, compares the count to the packing slip, pulls up the purchase order in the enterprise system, and records the quantity received. The purchase order and inventory database are updated once the receiving record is saved.

P 12-1 For the company assigned by your instructor, complete the following requirements:

  a. Prepare a table of entities and activities.

  b. Draw a context diagram.

  c. Draw a *physical* data flow diagram (DFD).

  d. Prepare an annotated table of entities and activities. Indicate on this table the groupings, bubble numbers, and bubble titles to be used in preparing a level 0 logical DFD.

  e. Draw a level 0 *logical* DFD.

P 12-2 For the company assigned by your instructor, complete the following requirements:

  a. Draw a systems flowchart.

  b. Prepare a control matrix, including explanations of how each recommended existing control plan helps to accomplish—or would accomplish in the case of missing plans—each related control goal. Your choice of recommended control plans should come from this chapter plus any controls from Chapters 9 through 11 that are germane to your company's process.

  c. Annotate the flowchart prepared in part a to indicate the points where the control plans are being applied (codes P-1 . . . P-*n*) or the points where they could be applied but are not (codes M-1 . . . M-*n*).

P 12-3 The following describes a purchasing process at Mountain Bay Company, a manufacturer of skis, snowshoes, and other winter recreational gear. The description here is limited to the process for ordering and receiving parts for repairing and maintaining manufacturing equipment. Please read the narrative and answer the questions that follow.

  A small inventory of parts is located in the plant maintenance office. When that inventory needs to be replenished, the maintenance manager fills out a purchase requisition and brings it to the purchasing department. A similar process is used when parts are not available in inventory and are needed immediately to repair or service a machine.

  Once received in purchasing, the buyer responsible for plant maintenance purchase requisitions looks up any approved supplier in the corporate book of approved vendors. If an appropriate vendor is not found, the buyer looks in a card file of local suppliers. Once a vendor is chosen the buyer enters the requisition into the purchasing computer system and prints the purchase order.

  The purchasing manager at Mountain Bay must sign all purchase orders, about 75 each day. This is a tedious process. There is no review, just a signature. The PO is a two-part carbon and so each PO must be signed by hand. Several POs to the same vendor may be prepared each day. The purchasing manager gives the POs to a secretary who mails the original to the vendor and files the copy in a paper file by vendor number.

  When goods are received from the vendor, a receiving clerk calls up the purchase order on the computer screen, does a quick visual inspection and count, and labels the shipment "on hold." The clerk notifies the Quality Control (QC) department of the shipment. QC performs the required quality tests and, if appropriate, changes the "on hold" label to "released." At that point the goods are moved to the warehouse and the receipt is entered into the computer to clear the PO and update the inventory balance.

a. Comment on the efficiency and effectiveness of the purchasing process at Mountain Bay.

b. Draw a systems flowchart of a revised process that would solve the problems identified in part a.

P 12-4 The following capsule case presents a short narrative of a process used by an actual organization whose name has been changed for the purpose of this problem. You will use the case to practice the mechanics of drawing data flow diagrams.

CAPSULE CASE: Baby Bell Telephone Co.

Baby Bell Telephone Co. uses a purchasing process that utilizes EDI functionality. An abbreviated description of the process follows (the description covers only the purchase by field technicians of items to be delivered by suppliers directly to the technicians in the field).

The company's field technicians continually need to replace items such as small hand tools, wire, and power tools. (*Note*: Assume that an external entity called "Field Inventory System" triggers the process by identifying a "Field inventory replacement need.") They do so by using handheld computers to log into the system. Users have log-in IDs and passwords that allow them access only to information for which they have clearance. Once logged in, a technician enters the requested item's stock number. The system presents the user with a display showing the item's description, size, and so forth. Information on price, brand, or supplier is not provided to most users because it is information they don't need to know. To complete the order request, the user visually verifies the information shown in the display, keys the quantity ordered, and presses an "enter" key.

The system records the order in the purchase order master data. The order is routed through a wide area network to the workstation of an available clerk in the purchasing department. The clerk enters a code that requests the system to match the item's stock number with the supplier code in the inventory master data. The system then retrieves the supplier's *standing data* (e.g., name, address, whether an EDI vendor, and so forth) from the vendor master data and displays it on the workstation screen. The purchasing clerk next enters another code that either transmits the order electronically to the vendor through an EDI VAN or prints a hard copy purchase order document that is mailed to the vendor, in the case of a supplier that does not have EDI capability. In either case, the purchase order master data is updated to show that the PO has been issued. Hard copy purchase orders are put in envelopes and mailed.

P 12-5 Figure 12.1 (page 439) presents only the "normal" horizontal flows for the purchasing process. In other words, that figure intentionally ignores flows related to exception routines.

Using Figure 12.1 as the model, create a figure that shows all the horizontal data flows related to handling purchase returns to vendors. Observe the following specific requirements:

a. At the top of the figure, draw triangles to show the functional entities involved in processing purchase returns. Enter the titles of the specific managers that are involved, including any *new* managers not shown in Figure 12.1.

b. Near the right margin, draw a vertical line to demarcate the purchasing process from the "environment." As you draw the horizontal flows, insert any necessary external entities to the right of the vertical line.

c. Draw all of the horizontal flow lines (and their directions) needed to process purchase returns. Number each flow, starting with 1.

d. List the numbers 1 . . . *n* to correspond to each flow line added to the diagram in part c. Provide a brief description of each information flow number.

P 12-6 Draw a DFD to reflect the exception routine of handling purchase returns and allowances.

P 12-7 *Note*: If you were assigned DQ12-4, consult your solution to it. Modify the DFDs in Figures 12.3, 12.4, 12.6, 12.7, and 12.9 (pages 447, 448, 449, 451, and 453), as appropriate, to reflect the purchasing of a technical product that could not be inspected in the receiving department but had to undergo quality control testing before being accepted.

P 12-8 Modify the DFDs in Figures 12.3, 12.4, 12.6, 12.7, and 12.9, as appropriate, to reflect that the purchase from our vendor was "drop-shipped" to one of our customers instead of being shipped to us.

P 12-9 The following are five process failures that indicate weaknesses in control.

Process Failures

1. A purchasing agent ordered unneeded inventory items from a supplier company of which he is one of the officers.

2. The vendor shipped goods that were never ordered. The invoice for those goods was paid.

3. Goods were stolen by storeroom personnel. When the shortage was discovered, the storeroom personnel claimed that the goods had never been delivered to them from the receiving department.

4. An organization seems to regularly run out of inventory for some of its most popular items.

5. The materials going into production do not meet quality standards.

List the numbers 1 through 5 on your solution sheet. For each of the five process failures described, provide a two- to three-sentence description of the control plan that you believe would *best* address that deficiency. Obviously, there could be more than one plan that is germane to a particular situation. However, select *only one* plan for each of the five process failures and include in your description a justification of why you believe it is *best*. When in doubt, opt for the plan that is *preventive* in nature, as opposed to plans that are *detective* or *corrective*.

P 12-10 Using the following two tables as a guide, describe for each function (see Figure 12.1 on page 439):

a. A risk (an event or action that will cause the organization to fail to meet it goals/objectives)

b. A control/process or use of technology that will address the risk.

Do the same for the accounting entry.

	Function	Risks	Controls and technology
Manager	Logistics		
Operations process	Purchasing		
	Receiving		

Event	Entry	Risks	Controls and technology
Record receipt	**Inventory** ???		

P 12-11 Use the data flow diagrams in Figures 12.4, 12.6, 12.7, and 12.9 (pages 448, 449, 451, and 453), to solve this problem.

Prepare a four-column table that summarizes the purchasing processes, inputs, and outputs. In the first column, list the three processes shown in the level 0 diagram (Figure 12.4). In the second column, list the subsidiary functions shown in the three lower-level diagrams (Figures 12.6, 12.7, and 12.9). For each subsidiary process listed in column 2, list the data flow names or the data stores that are inputs to that process (column 3) or outputs of that process (column 4). (See *Note.*) The following table has been started for you to indicate the format for your solution.

Note: To simplify the solution, do not show any reject stubs in column 4.

Solution Format

**Summary of the Purchasing processes,
inputs, outputs, and data stores**

Process	Subsidiary Functions	Inputs	Outputs
1.0 Determine requirements	1.1 Accumulate requests	Inventory's purchase requisition Purchase requisition—supplies and services	Purchase requisition data
	1.2 Calculate requirements	Purchase requisition data Inventory master data	. . . Continue solution . . .

KEY TERMS

purchasing process

supply chain

supply chain management
(SCM)

supply chain management
software

purchase requisition

reorder point (ROP)
analysis

economic order quantity
(EOQ)

ABC analysis

purchase order

blind copy

vendor packing slip

receiving report

acceptance report

inventory master data

vendor master data

purchase requisitions
master data

purchase order master data

purchase receipts data

radio-frequency
identification (RFID)

paperless systems

The Accounts Payable/Cash Disbursements (AP/CD) Process

T-Mobile USA (formerly VoiceStream Wireless) is a nationwide wireless carrier providing voice, messaging, and high-speed wireless services to 11 million customers. As T-Mobile's business grew through acquisitions, it made more purchases and more payments to its vendors. As a result, it experienced an escalating volume of phone calls from vendors requesting payment status. To handle the increased volumes, it became imperative that T-Mobile automate its accounts payable/cash disbursement process. One solution considered by Susan Felix, the director of accounting at T-Mobile, was the electronic funds transfer (EFT) capability of its PeopleSoft ERP Accounts Payable system. But, while this solution would automate the payment process, T-Mobile accounts payables clerks would still need to perform inquiries into the accounts payable system to answer vendor questions. T-Mobile's choice was the outsourced ePayables solution hosted by Xign Corporation.

Now, T-Mobile vendors, such as Nokia, Samsung, and Motorola, submit their invoices electronically to T-Mobile through the Xign Payment Services Network (XPSN). The XPSN system routes the invoices to the appropriate people at T-Mobile for approval. When T-Mobile is ready to pay the invoice, it selects the invoice for payment and the XPSN system posts the payment to the T-Mobile systems and prepares an electronic payment. At any time during this process, T-Mobile and its vendors can query the XPSN system to determine the status of invoices and payments.

T-Mobile reports that the Xign solution has lowered operating costs (e.g., T-Mobile no longer needs to enter invoices), reduced vendor inquiries (vendors use the self-service features of the XPSN system), significantly cut the number of erroneous payments (e.g., the XPSN system facilitates the matching of vendors, purchases and receipts before a payment is authorized), and increased the level of security and ability to audit the payment process (the XPSN maintains an audit trail on the secure XPSN server). In addition, T-Mobile suppliers receive quicker payments (payments are electronic) and additional information because

Learning Objectives

- To know the definition and basic functions of the AP/CD process.
- To understand the relationship between the AP/CD process and its environment.
- To achieve a reasonable level of understanding of the logical and physical characteristics of a typical AP/CD process.
- To become familiar with various technologies used to implement the AP/CD process.
- To know core process goals and the plans used to control a typical AP/CD process.

In this chapter, we spotlight one business process, the accounts payable/cash disbursements (AP/CD) process and explore the processes, systems, and controls that should be in place to ensure that the accounts payable/cash disbursement process operates efficiently and effectively. Additionally, we will examine specific process control procedures that help ensure all accounts payable are paid in a timely fashion.

information such as payment status and detailed remittance information is always available on the XPSN server.[1]

SYNOPSIS

This chapter presents our fourth business process, the accounts payable/cash disbursements (AP/CD) process. The AP/CD process includes the last two steps, invoice verification and payment processing, in the purchase-to-pay process (see Figure 2.10 on page 62). After we introduce the players involved in the AP/CD process, we describe the logic and data typically employed in the process. In addition, we call your attention to the sections on Physical Process Description and the Application of the Control Framework. These sections cover state-of-the-art material on current and evolving technology and provide reading that we hope you will find both interesting and informative.

INTRODUCTION

As previously noted, the AP/CD process comprises the last two steps in the purchase-to-pay process (Figure 2.10, page 62). Let's take a closer look at the AP/CD process.

---

[1] "T-Mobile Success with ePayables," Xign, http://www.xign.com, August 7, 2003.

PROCESS DEFINITION AND FUNCTIONS

The **accounts payable/cash disbursements (AP/CD) process** is an interacting structure of people, equipment, methods, and controls that is designed to accomplish the following primary functions:

1. Handle the repetitive work routines of the accounts payable department and the cashier.[2]

2. Support the decision needs of those who manage the accounts payable department and cashier.

3. Assist in the preparation of internal and external reports.

First, the AP/CD process handles the repetitive work routines of the accounts payable department and cashier by capturing and recording data related to their day-to-day operations, such as recording vendor invoices and paying those invoices. The recorded data then may be used to generate source documents (such as disbursement vouchers and vendor payment) and to produce internal and external reports.

The AP/CD process prepares a number of reports that personnel at various levels of management use. For example, the cashier might use an accounts payable aging report to plan cash availability. The cash disbursements manager might use a cash requirements forecast to help decide which invoice(s) to pay next.

Finally, the AP/CD process assists in the preparation of external financial statements. The process supplies the general ledger with data concerning various events related to the procurement activities of an organization. This data includes data related to accounts payable, the related expenses incurred or assets acquired, and the cash that is disbursed.

ORGANIZATIONAL SETTING

The AP/CD process is closely linked to functions and processes within and outside the organization. Let's take a look at those links and the impact that they have on the operation of the AP/CD process.

A Horizontal Perspective

Figure 13.1 and Table 13.1 present a horizontal view of the relationship between the AP/CD process and its organizational environment. They show the various information flows generated or captured by the process. Take some time now to study the figure to acquaint yourself with the number of entities with which the process interacts. The data flows in Table 13.1 indicate the nature of these interactions.

A Vertical Perspective

Figure 13.2 (page 480) presents a representative organization chart for the purchasing process (Chapter 12) and the AP/CD process described in this chapter. We put them together here so that we can discuss the interactions of these processes and the players involved. In Chapter 12 we introduced the functions reporting to the VP of logistics. The new players here include the *accounts payable department* who is responsible for

---

[2] To focus our discussion, we have assumed that these two departments are the primary operating units related to the AP/CD process. For a given organization, however, the departments associated with the process may differ.

Figure 13.1 A Horizontal Perspective of the AP/CD Process

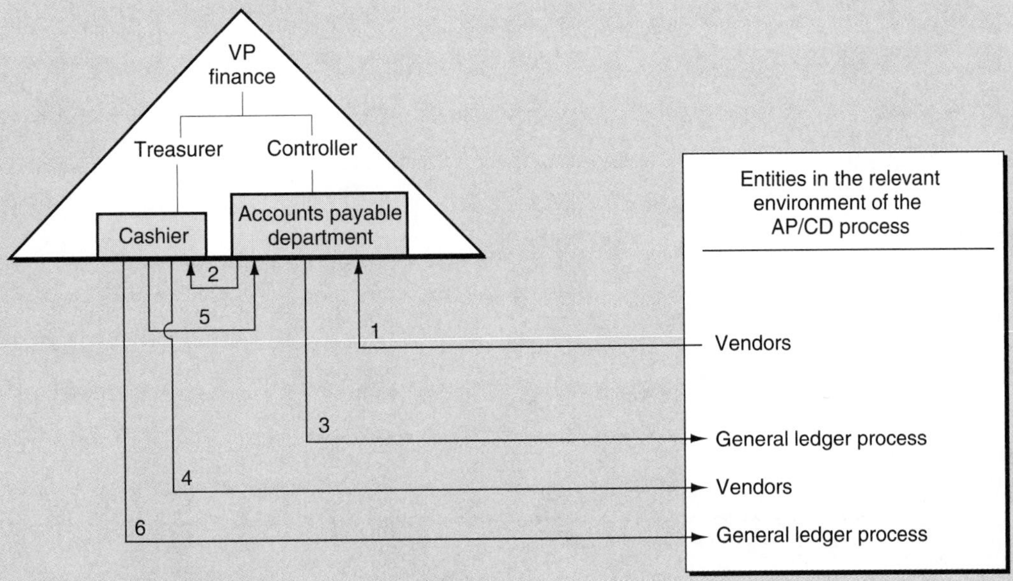

NOTES:

1. The information flows are representative of those related to the AP/CD process. The figure, however, does not show all information flows. For example, purchase returns are not shown.

2. See Table 13.1 for a description of information flows 1–6.

Table 13.1 Description of Information Flows

Flow No.	Description
1	Invoice received from vendor
2	Approved voucher sent to cashier
3	Accounts payable notification sent to general ledger process
4	Check sent to vendor by cashier
5	Paid voucher returned to the accounts payable department
6	Notification of the cash disbursement sent from the cashier to the general ledger process

processing invoices received from vendors, preparing payment vouchers for the subsequent disbursement of cash for goods or services received, and recording purchase and disbursement events. The *cashier* has custody of the organization's cash and makes the payments authorized by the accounts payable department.

Figure 13.2 A Vertical Perspective of the Purchasing and AP/CD Processes

(Horizontal information flows, as illustrated in Figures 12.1 and 13.1)

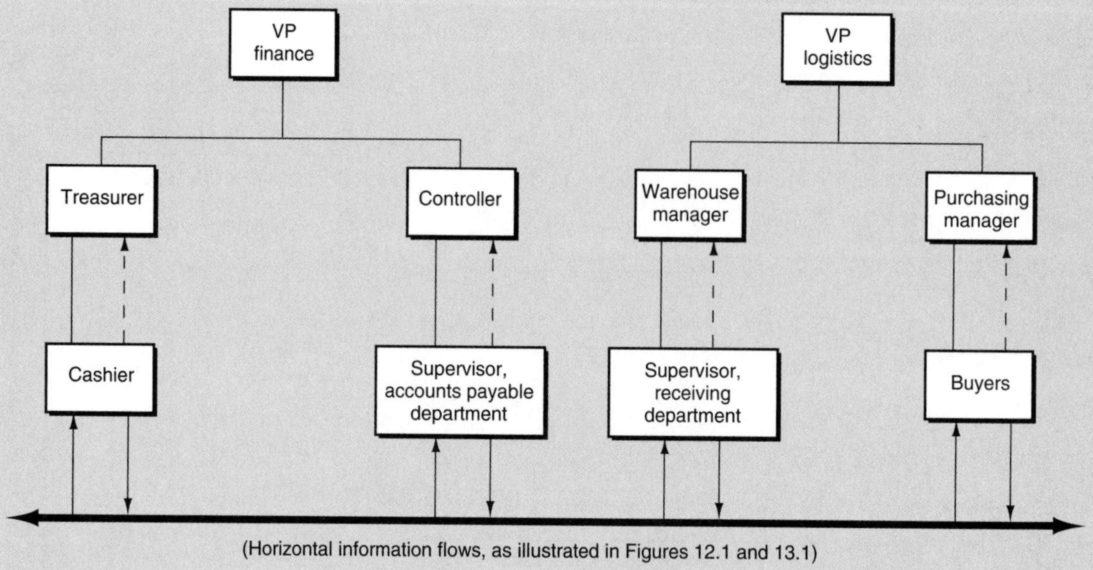

NOTES:

1. This figure represents a partial organization chart for the finance and logistics functions.

2. The broken lines represent vertical information flows (often in the form of management reports) based on data captured or generated by the purchasing and AP/CD processes.

The relationship between these groups, logistics and finance, are very similar to the relationships among the marketing, logistics, and finance functions described in Chapters 10 and 11. For example, we see processes such as order entry and shipping that begin a larger process—order-to-cash—working in conjunction with processes, such as billing and cash receipts, that complete the larger process. In Figure 13.2 we represent the functions that start the purchase-to-pay process, purchasing and receiving, and the functions that complete the process, accounts payable and the cashier.

In addition to cooperating in completing these larger processes, these functions, and the processes for which they are responsible, share data with which the processes operate on a day-to-day basis and make important management decisions. For example, the warehouse manager uses purchasing data to schedule personnel to handle incoming shipments and provide storage space for the goods to be received. The controller uses the purchasing and receiving data to validate incoming vendor invoices. The treasurer uses purchasing data to ensure that funds will be available to meet future obligations. Finally, data also is used "up stream" (i.e., left to right in Figure 13.2). For example, purchasing supervisors may use data about available funds to schedule purchases.

LOGICAL PROCESS DESCRIPTION

This section expands on the AP/CD process. Once again, logical data flow diagrams are used to present the basic composition of a typical process. We also discuss the relationship between certain goals of the process and the process's logical design. The section includes brief discussions of *exception routines* and processing noninvoiced disbursements. We also describe and illustrate the process's major data stores.[3]

Discussion and Illustration

Figure 13.3 reflects the level 0 data flow diagram for a typical AP/CD process. Take some time to study the figure. To focus our discussion, we have assumed that the AP/CD process performs two major processes, represented by the two bubbles in the DFD. The next two sections describe the processes within those two bubbles.

Figure 13.3 The AP/CD Process—Level 0 Diagram

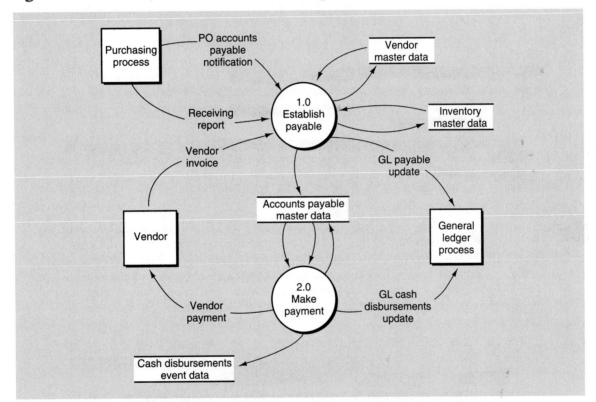

Establish Payable (Invoice Verification)

Figure 13.4 (page 482) presents a data flow diagram for establishing accounts payable. As shown by bubble 1.1, the first step in establishing the payable involves validating the vendor invoice. This process is triggered by receipt of the **vendor invoice**, a business document that notifies the purchaser of an obligation to pay the vendor for goods or services that were ordered by and shipped to the purchaser. Figure 11.5 (page 404) depicts a typical invoice screen. Process 1.1 comprises a number of steps. First, the vendor invoice is compared against purchase order data (PO accounts payable notification) to make sure that (1) the purchase has been authorized and (2) invoiced quantities, prices,

CONTROLS

---

[3] As we have in several earlier chapters, we remind you once again that the data stores in the logical DFDs might well be the AP/CD process's view of an *enterprise database*.

Figure 13.4 AP/CD Process—Diagram 1

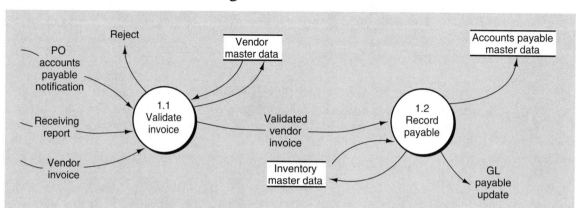

and terms conform to the purchase order agreement. Next, the invoice is matched against the receiving report data to determine that the goods or services actually have been received. Finally, the invoice is checked for accuracy of computed discounts, extensions, and total amount due.

If the data items do not agree, the invoice is rejected and follow-up procedures are initiated (see the reject stub emanating from bubble 1.1). If the data items agree, the invoice is approved, and the validated invoice is sent on to the next step to be used to record the payable. Note that the vendor master data is also updated at this point to reflect purchase history data.

ENTERPRISE SYSTEMS

Figure 13.5 depicts the purchase order and related data that can be displayed in the SAP R/3 system. At the top of this display is the purchase order data. We can drill down here to find the related purchase requisition. At the bottom of the screen you can see the purchase order history, including the goods receipt and the invoice. Before the invoice was accepted, a match was performed (i.e., invoice verification) to determine that the purchase order, goods receipt, and invoice matched (within tolerances chosen by the user).

Bubble 1.2 in Figure 13.4 depicts the process of recording the payable in the accounts payable master data. A payable is recognized and recorded by simultaneously:

- Creating a record in the accounts payable master data.
- Updating the inventory master data for the cost of the items received.
- Notifying the general ledger of the amount of the payable that was recorded (see the data flow "GL payable update").

Figure 13.4 assumes that a non-voucher process is used. Alternatively, a voucher process might be employed. A **disbursement voucher** is designed to reflect formal approval of the voucher for payment and to provide such added data as the account distribution and the amounts to be debited. Several invoices from a single vendor are often listed on one disbursement voucher so that fewer checks need to be written during the cash disbursement procedure. In the section on "Processing Noninvoiced Disbursements," we elaborate on the use of a voucher process.

CONTROLS

To help achieve an operations process (effectiveness) goal, *to optimize cash discounts,* the responsibility for ensuring savings through cash discounts includes (1) seeing that

Figure 13.5 Sample SAP Purchase Order Data Screen

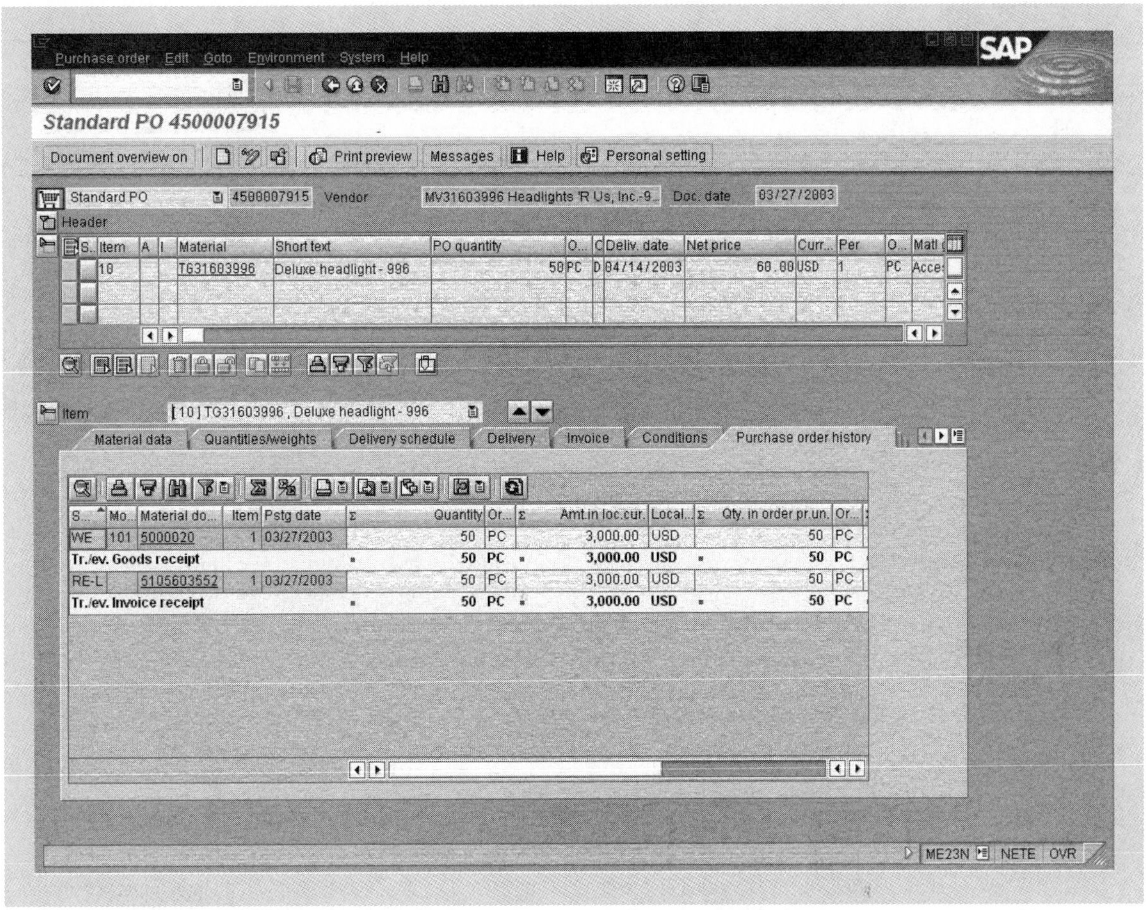

Source: Reprinted with permission from SAP.

proper cash discount terms are incorporated in the order; (2) securing invoices promptly from vendors; (3) processing invoices promptly and getting them to the disbursing office within the discount period; and (4) when unavoidable delays are encountered because of some fault of the seller, making sure that the discount privilege is not waived and that the vendor is notified to this effect.

Make Payment

Figure 13.6 (page 484) presents a data flow diagram of the cash disbursements process. We remind you as you study the figure that the payment process is *triggered* by payment due-date information residing on the accounts payable master data (i.e., a temporal event).

As you can see, the payment process begins with the preparation of a check (bubble 2.1) equal to the amount of the invoice, less any discount taken. The check is then recorded (bubble 2.2) by marking the invoice as paid and making an entry in the cash disbursements event data store. Finally, the recorded check is issued (bubble 2.3) and the general ledger process is notified of the payment.

Figure 13.6 AP/CD Process—Diagram 2

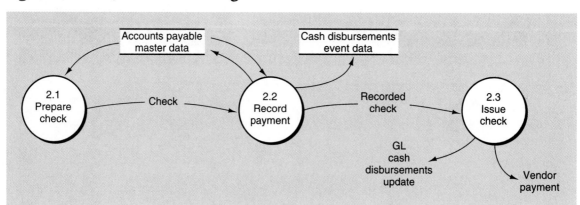

The payment schedule adopted will depend on the availability of any favorable discounts for prompt payment and on the organization's current cash position. Some companies will pay multiple invoices with one check to minimize the cost of processing invoices. Most cash managers will attempt to optimize cash balances to help achieve another operations process (effectiveness) goal: *to ensure that the amount of cash maintained in demand deposit accounts is sufficient (but not excessive) to satisfy expected cash disbursements.* To accomplish this goal, many banks offer their commercial customers a cash management service by which the bank transfers from the customer's money market or other investment account into its checking account the exact amount needed to cover the checks that clear each day.

Exception Routines

In the data flow diagrams, you saw a number of *reject* data flows; they occur for a number of reasons. **Purchase returns and allowances** frequently arise with respect to purchases. This *exception routine* usually begins at the point of inspecting and counting the goods (bubble 3.1 of Figure 12.9, page 453) or at the point of *validating* vendor invoices (bubble 1.1 of Figure 13.4, page 482).

To initiate an adjustment for returned goods or for a price allowance in the case of otherwise nonconforming goods, someone usually prepares a *debit memorandum* and transmits it to the vendor; the vendor commonly acknowledges it by returning a *credit memorandum.* The debit memo data also is transmitted to the accounts payable department. In the case of a return, data also is made accessible to the storeroom and shipping department. The merchandise to be returned then is released from the storeroom and sent to the shipping department. There the items to be returned are counted, recorded to the debit memorandum, and shipped. The shipping department's recording of the debit memo data also is made available to the accounts payable department.

Processing Noninvoiced Disbursements

Figures 13.4 (page 482) and 13.6 demonstrate only those events for which an invoice is received from the vendor for purchases of *goods* or *services.* But what about disbursements that are not typically supported by invoices, such as for payroll, payroll taxes, corporate income taxes, rent, security investments, repayment of debt obligations and interest, and the like? In this section, we examine how such noninvoiced disbursements are processed.

Figure 13.7 is a logical data flow diagram that shows the processing of noninvoiced payments under two different assumptions: (1) a true *voucher process* is used in which all expenditures must be vouchered—that is, formally approved for payment and recorded as a payable—before they can be paid, and (2) a non-voucher process is employed.

Figure 13.7 Processing Noninvoiced Disbursements

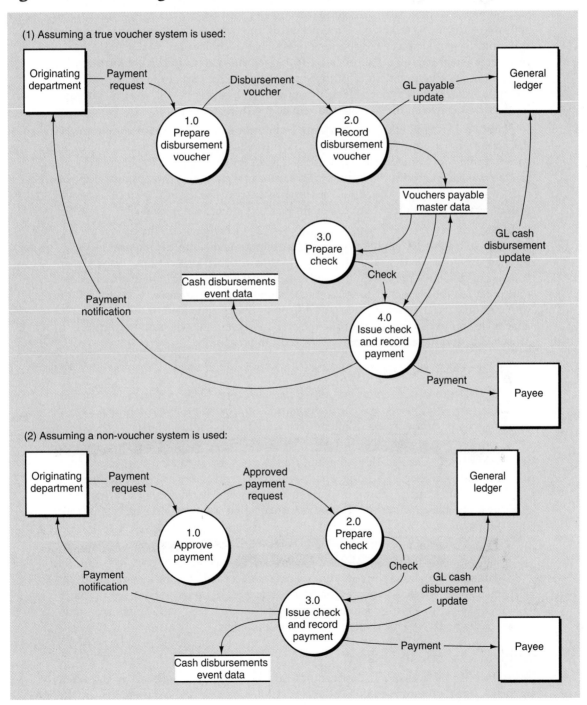

As you can see in Figure 13.7, the trigger for either process is a payment request from an originating department. The originator might be the treasurer in the case of payments for investment or financing activities, the controller's department in the case of tax payments, or even an accounts payable software module for recurring monthly payments such as rent. Upon receipt of the payment request, the processing in the voucher versus non-voucher process varies primarily in the formality of the payment approval process. In the voucher process shown in part (1) of the figure, all payments for whatever purpose and no matter how small—even petty cash reimbursements—are formally approved—that is, "vouchered"—in process 1.0. In process 1.0, the proper account distribution also is added to the disbursement voucher document. All vouchered items are then recorded as payables (see process 2.0) before they are paid. This means that from an accounting standpoint, the distribution of charges to asset, expense, or other accounts is reported to the general ledger by process 2.0; in process 4.0, the general ledger is notified to eliminate the payable and reduce the cash account.

Note also in part (1) that the data store is the *vouchers* payable master data instead of the *accounts* payable master data shown in the previous DFDs in this chapter. This difference is significant. For example, as mentioned in an earlier section, it implies that for *invoiced* payables, more than one vendor invoice may be combined into a single disbursement voucher. Therefore, you should be aware that records linked to the vouchers payable master data are for individual disbursement vouchers rather than individual invoices.

In the non-voucher process depicted in part (2) of Figure 13.7, the payment also is approved in bubble 1.0, and the account distribution is added to the request. However, the approval process is less formal than in the voucher process—no disbursement voucher document is prepared. Physically, the approved payment request that is passed to process 2.0 usually would comprise the same document that entered process 1.0 but with authorized signatures and account distribution now appended. In this process, the general ledger recording of the distribution of accounting charges is triggered by process 3.0, and the cash balance is decreased simultaneously.

Logical Data Descriptions

The AP/CD process entails several different data stores. The *inventory master data, vendor master data, purchase requisitions master data, purchase order master data*, and *purchase receipts data* were described in Chapter 12. Two additional data stores are:

- **Accounts payable master data**. This data store is a repository of all unpaid vendor invoices. The data design should consider how the data will be processed when the cash manager is deciding what payments to make. For example, the manager may want to merge vendor invoices so that the total amount due each vendor can be accumulated. Alternatively, the manager might want to select specific invoices for payment.

- **Cash disbursements data**. The purpose of this data is to show, in chronological sequence, the details of each cash payment made. Accordingly, each record in this data normally shows the date the payment is recorded, vendor identification, disbursement voucher number (if a voucher process is used), vendor invoice number(s) and gross invoice amount(s), cash discount(s) taken on each invoice, net invoice amount(s), check amount, and check number.

Logical Database Design

As in the prior three chapters, this section focuses on a *database approach* to data management. On the bottom portion of Figure 13.8, we portray the data model for the

Figure 13.8 Entity-Relationship (E-R) Diagram (*Partial*) for the AP/CD Process

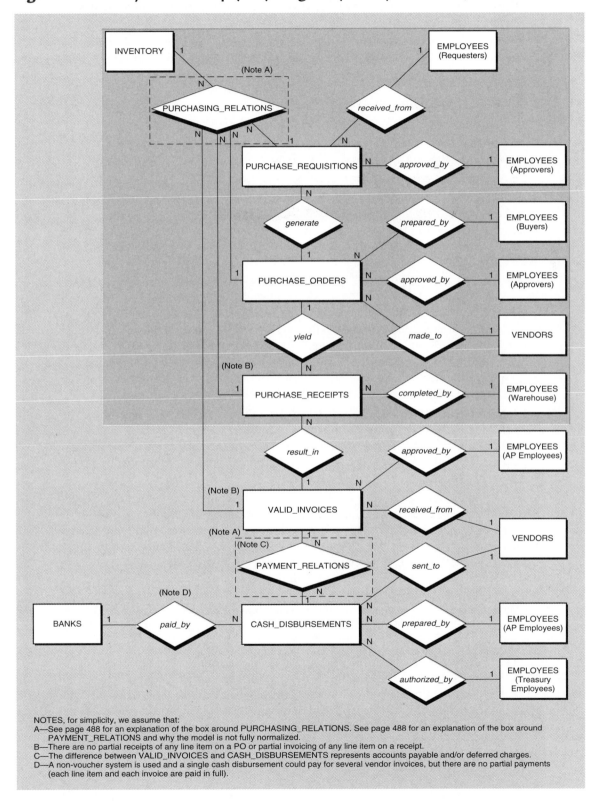

NOTES, for simplicity, we assume that:
A—See page 488 for an explanation of the box around PURCHASING_RELATIONS. See page 488 for an explanation of the box around PAYMENT_RELATIONS and why the model is not fully normalized.
B—There are no partial receipts of any line item on a PO or partial invoicing of any line item on a receipt.
C—The difference between VALID_INVOICES and CASH_DISBURSEMENTS represents accounts payable and/or deferred charges.
D—A non-voucher system is used and a single cash disbursement could pay for several vendor invoices, but there are no partial payments (each line item and each invoice are paid in full).

AP/CD process in an *entity-relationship (E-R) diagram.* We also show (shaded) the entities and relationships from Chapter 12, since these two chapters are interrelated from a database design perspective.

In examining the figure, you'll notice that the *events* of validating invoices and disbursing cash are depicted by two entity boxes (VALID_INVOICES and CASH_DISBURSEMENTS). The E-R diagram reflects how these events relate to prior events (PURCHASE_REQUISITIONS, PURCHASE_ORDERS and PURCHASE_RECEIPTS), agents (EMPLOYEES and VENDORS), and *resources* (INVENTORY and BANKS). To simplify the figure, we have:

- Assumed that all purchase orders are for merchandise inventory items (i.e., purchases of other goods and services are ignored).

- Assumed that a *non*-voucher process is employed.

As in its counterpart in Chapter 11 (see Figure 11.9 on page 410), Figure 13.8 shows that there is no need for a separate entity for accounts payable. Rather, accounts payable balances at any point in time—or their counterpart, deferred charges—are computed as the difference between the continuous events, VALID_INVOICES and CASH_DISBURSEMENTS.

Also carried over from Figure 12.10 (page 454) is the relationship PURCHASING_RELATIONS. As it was in Figure 12.10, this relationship accumulates a record of events as they progress. In this case we add the VALID_INVOICES event (i.e., receipt and recording of the vendor invoice) to this relationship. Recall from Figure 12.10 that this relationship already has accumulated a record of the PURCHASE_REQUISITIONS, PURCHASE_ORDERS, and PURCHASE_RECEIPTS. The box around this relationship indicates that we will have a relation in our database for this relationship while the other relationships will not have a corresponding relation.

As with Figures 10.9, 11.9, and 12.10 (pages 367, 410, and 454, respectively), the model in Figure 13.8 is not fully normalized yet. We include the "extra" relationships and redundant attributes to help you see the logical sequence of events. Also, the notes on Figure 13.8 indicate that this is a simplified model. Certainly realistic models must deal with partial receipts, invoices, and payments.

From Figure 13.8, we developed the relational tables shown in Figure 13.9 (pages 489–490). As with the E-R diagram, many of the relational tables are the same as shown in Chapter 12 (Figure 12.11, page 456), as these two chapters are tightly integrated from a database perspective. We repeat here from Figure 12.11 all but the last three relations shown in Figure 13.9 to emphasize the connections (linkages) among relations and to remind you that before making a cash disbursement, we have requisitioned the goods (or services), sent a purchase order to a vendor, received the goods, and received the vendor invoice. Also note that the relations in Figure 13.9 are not dissimilar to those shown in Figure 10.9 (page 367) (e.g., VENDORS is similar to CUSTOMERS, PURCHASE_ORDERS resembles SALES_ORDERS, and so forth).

Finally, we should note that the primary key of the relationship PAYMENT_RELATIONS is a composite key comprised of the invoice number (from VALID_INVOICES) and the cash disbursement number (from CASH_DISBURSEMENTS). This relationship matches the invoices with the disbursements and allows us to easily obtain the total amount of each disbursement. The box around this relationship indicates that we will have a relation in our database for this relationship while the other relationships will not have a corresponding relation.

Figure 13.9 Selected Relational Tables (*Partial*) for the AP/CD Process

Shaded_Attribute(s) = Primary Key

INVENTORY

Item_No	Item_Name	Price	Location	Qty_on_Hand	Reorder_Pt
936	Machine Plates	39.50	Macomb	1,500	950
1001	Gaskets	9.50	Macomb	10,002	3,500
1010	Crank Shafts	115.00	Tampa	952	500
1025	Manifolds	45.00	Tampa	402	400

EMPLOYEES

Emp_No	Emp_First_Name	Emp_Last_Name	Soc_Sec_No	Emp_Dept
B432	Carl	Mast	125-87-8090	492-01
A491	Janet	Kopp	127-93-3453	639-04
A632	Greg	Bazie	350-97-9030	538-22
B011	Christy	Kinman	123-78-0097	298-12

VENDORS

Vend_No	Vend_Name	Vend_Street	Vend_City	Vend_State	Vend_ZIP	Vend_Tel	Vend_Contact	Credit_Terms	FOB_Terms
539	Ace Widget Co.	190 Shore Dr.	Charleston	SC	29915	803-995-3764	S. Emerson	2/10,n/30	Ship Pt
540	Babcock Supply Co.	22 Ribaut Rd.	Beaufort	SC	29902	803-552-4788	Frank Roy	n/60	Destin
541	Webster Steel Corp.	49 Abercorn St.	Savannah	GA	30901	912-433-1750	Wilbur Cox	2/10,n/30	Ship Pt

PURCHASE_REQUISITIONS

PR_No	PR_Date	Emp_No (PR_Requestor)[a]	Emp_No (PR_Approver)[b]	PO_No
53948	20071215	A491	E745	4346
53949	20071215	C457	A632	4350
53950	20071216	9999	540-32	4347
53951	20071216	F494	D548	4352

PURCHASE_ORDERS

PO_No	PO_Date	Vend_No	Ship_Via	Emp_No (Buyer)	Emp_No (PO_Approver)	PO_Status
4345	20071218	539	Best Way	F395	F349	Open
4346	20071220	541	FedEx	C932	F349	Sent
4347	20071222	562	UPS	E049	D932	Acknowledged

PURCHASE_RECEIPTS

Rec_No	Rec_Date	Emp_No (Receiving)	PO_No	Invoice_No
42944	20071216	B260	4322	7-945
42945	20071216	B260	4339	9542-4
42946	20071216	B260	4345	535

(continued)

Figure 13.9 Selected Relational Tables (*Partial*) for the AP/CD Process (*continued*)

VALID_INVOICES

Invoice_No	Invoice_Date	Vend_No	Emp_No (AP)
4388	20071224	524	G232
92360	20071223	572	G232
535	20071224	539	D923

PURCHASE_RELATIONS

PR_No	Item_No	Qty_Requested	PO_No	Qty_Ordered	Rec_No	Qty_Received	Inv_No	Qty_Invoiced	Amt_Invoiced
53947	1005	200	4345	200	42946	200	535	200	1200.00
53947	1006	50	4345	50	42946	50	535	50	212.50
53947	1015	25	4345	25	42946	25	535	25	418.75

CASH_DISBURSEMENTS

CD_No	CD_Date	Emp_No (AP)	Emp_No (Treasury)	Amount	Vend_No	Bank
9561	20080102	H263	M0513	1782.10	524	2239
9562	20080102	H263	M513	432.50	572	2240
9563	20080102	H263	E219	1831.25	539	2239

BANKS

Bank_No	Bank_Name
2239	Acme
2240	Benton

PAYMENT_RELATIONS

Invoice_No	CD_No	Amount
4388	9561	1782.10
92360	9562	432.50
535	9563	1831.25

[a] If automatic purchase requisition, then 9999; if employee, then employee number.
[b] If automatic purchase requisition, then contract number of trading partner; if employee, then employee number.

TECHNOLOGY TRENDS AND DEVELOPMENTS

You will recall from Chapter 3 that we noted the rapid movement toward using electronic document interchange (EDI) to improve the transaction process between two organizations that are exchanging goods. In this chapter, we explore the use of EDI in terms of the impact on business processes and in particular the impact on performance and control of the AP/CD process.

E-BUSINESS

The AP/CD process is the primary candidate for EDI in major organizations (although they certainly may use this technology in the OE/S, B/AR/CR, and purchasing processes as well). As noted in Technology Application 13.1, several major companies have implemented EDI systems into the AP/CD process, resulting in significant cost savings. An increasing trend among some of these major companies is to require all vendors to use EDI in their transactions with the company. If the vendor does not implement EDI technologies, the major companies simply find a new supplier. This trend is indicative of the major cost savings companies have enjoyed with the use of EDI.

Technology Application 13.1

Uses of Electronic Data Interchange for the AP/CD Process

Case 1

Kaiser Permanente of Southern California is a pioneer in trying to cut medical costs, and one way to do so is through the accounts payable and cash disbursements process. The Southern California region alone processes more than 1 million invoices and 800,000 claims with over 500,000 payments. A small cut in the cost of processing each transaction can add up quickly. The solution was to move to EDI for its patient care providers—both inside and outside the managed care program. Kaiser implemented the ANSI X12 837 healthcare claims standard specifically designed for the detailed health care information required for claims processing. In cases where the provider only accepts a check, check processing has been outsourced at a savings of 35 to 40 percent, and for vendors who accept electronic funds transfers (EFT), the savings are even greater.

Case 2

John Hancock Mutual Life Insurance Co. spent $337 million in 1997 on supplies needed to run its business. Only 8 percent of these purchases went through the central purchasing department, though. The result was huge losses over the prices that could have been negotiated on bulk purchases. Armed with a new intranet system, Hancock Mutual now works to process 85 percent of those purchases through central processing while maintaining zero growth in staffing of the purchasing department. The key is to run all small-ticket items such as office supplies and business cards through central purchasing along with big-ticket items such as personal computers and contract labor. But it has to be easy for the workers using such systems. Thus the use of an intranet where employees simply point and click to select items from the Web page displaying available goods and services. Orders route through an automatic electronic approval process based on the individual's purchasing privileges and authorized purchases are transferred electronically to central purchasing. Another key to the system is that the intranet system is integrated into the enterprise system to make sure orders pass through back-end processing and to facilitate payment through the EDI system, which further minimizes transaction costs.

Sources: Sharon Watson, "Kaiser Taking Advantage of EDI to Process Claims Online," *Computerworld* (August 8, 1997); Carol Sliwa, "Purchasing Via Web to Save Big Bucks," *Computerworld* (July 20, 1998): 1, 14.

In the last few years, several alternatives to EDI have been deployed. These new technologies, based, for example, on XML or IP-based EDI (Internet EDI), have not replaced EDI. The services provided by the value-added networks (VANs) and the high degree of EDI standardization make EDI an attractive method for fully digital B2B collaboration among trading partners for years to come.[4]

E-BUSINESS

CONTROLS

As noted in the story at the start of this chapter, however, many organizations are using Web-based payment systems such as those offered by Xign Corporation. Technology Application 13.2 gives you a little more detail about how the Xign system works and the control techniques that it incorporates.

PHYSICAL PROCESS DESCRIPTION

E-BUSINESS

ENTERPRISE SYSTEMS

The physical model of the AP/CD process presented in this section employs an *enterprise system, electronic payments,* and *data communications* technology. As with the purchasing process, this process is not completely *paperless,* but hard copy documents are held to a minimum.

Discussion and Illustration

Figure 13.10 (page 494) presents a systems flowchart of the process. At several points in the flowchart, you will see notations that *exception routines* are not flowcharted. They also are omitted from the discussion in the following paragraphs.

Establish Accounts Payable

E-BUSINESS

Our organization's system picks up the vendor's invoice at the VAN and routes it to the EDI translator. The EDI translator converts the invoice to the appropriate format and records it in the incoming invoice data. Triggered by the receipt of a batch of EDI invoices, the accounts payable application accesses the purchase order and receiving report data and compares the items, quantities, prices, and terms on the invoice to comparable data from the PO and receiving report data. If the data correspond, a payable is created, and the general ledger is updated.

Make Payments

E-BUSINESS

Our organization utilizes EDI to make the payment. Banks that are members of the *National Automated Clearing House (ACH) Association* combine EDI and *electronic funds transfer (EFT)* standards to transmit electronic payments between companies and their trading partners.

As shown in Figure 13.10, the accounts payable master data is searched each day for approved vendor invoices due that day. The cash disbursements clerk selects invoices for payment and prepares batch totals. The totals include total accounts payable being paid, discounts taken, and total dollars disbursed. The cash disbursements application prepares the payment order and remittance advice, updates the accounts payable master data and the general ledger for the payment, displays the payment totals (i.e., AP, discounts, cash disbursed), and sends the data to the EDI translator. The translator converts the data to the appropriate format, encrypts the message, adds a digital signature, and sends the EDI payment order and remittance advice to the VAN, for pickup by the

---

[4] F. Kenney and B. Lheureux, "EDI: A New Look at an Established Technology," Gartner, Inc. publication AV-16-6758, May 22, 2002.

Technology Application 13.2

Using an Outsourced Epayables Solution for the AP/CD Process

Many companies, including Charles Schwab, Sprint, T-Mobile USA, Bristol-Myers Squibb Company, and Armstrong Holdings, Inc., use the ePayables solution hosted by Xign Corporation for their accounts payable/cash disbursements process. Companies using this system, the Xign Payment Services Network (XPSN), report operational savings of millions of dollars each year, in addition to savings that come from capturing early payment discounts.

The XPSN system operates as follows. The buying organization creates purchase orders as it normally would and sends them to a Xign "enterprise adapter" to be translated into the XPSN format. The POs are then sent over the Internet to the XPSN server. The selling organization (i.e., the vendor) logs on to the Xign server using a standard Web browser and reads and acts on its PO (it can only see POs intended for it). A selling organization can contract with Xign to have this PO data automatically imported into its order entry systems via electronic file uploads called *eFiles*. When it comes time to bill the buyer, the vendor sends an invoice to the vendor in one of three ways. First, it can log onto the XPSN server and convert the PO into an invoice. As the vendor converts (or "flips") a PO into an invoice, it makes changes as needed, such as adding charges not included on the PO. Second, it can use an eFile to directly link its billing system with the XPSN system. Finally, if no PO is created, it can use a Web template to create an invoice.

The XPSN system sends the invoice through the enterprise adapter to the buyer's accounts payable system. The invoice is routed, using the workflow capability of the buyer's enterprise system, to those who need to approve the invoice. The XPSN system applies buyer-specified rules to validate the invoice. Once approved, the invoice is posted to the buyer's accounts payable system. During this process the vendor can query the XPSN system to determine the status of the invoice.

The buyer acts on the invoice as it normally would and makes a payment through the XPSN system (i.e., through the enterprise adapter to the XPSN server). The complete history of the purchase is stored on the XPSN server to facilitate research required to authorize the payment. This data is also useful to vendors wishing to determine the status of payments due to them. This data includes an audit trail of all payments, including who authorized each payment. The XPSN system posts the remittance data on the XPSN server and processes a digitally signed electronic payment over a secure network through the banking system using the payment method (e.g., ACH, EFT) selected by the vendor. Detailed remittance information may be sent to the vendor in an eFile.

Savings from using the Xign ePayables solution come from reduced manual processing increased efficiency in routing and approval of vendor invoices, and reduction in vendor calls inquiring about the status of payments. The information on the XPSN server facilitates cash planning for disbursements and cash receipts. Early payment discounts are more easily obtained because data is more accurate (e.g., the PO flip leads to accurate invoices) and easier, quicker approval of payments.

Sources: Xign Corporation press releases, the Xign Web site (http://www.xign.com), and interviews with Xign officers and users of the Xign system.

---

bank. The dotted line between the batch totals and the display of the payment totals indicates that the disbursement clerk would manually reconcile the totals.

What happens next is not depicted on the flowchart. The bank debits the paying organization's account and then sends the payment order to an automated clearing house for processing. The automated clearing house sends the data to the vendor's bank, where it is automatically credited to the vendor's bank account. Finally, the vendor's

Figure 13.10 AP/CD Process—Systems Flowchart

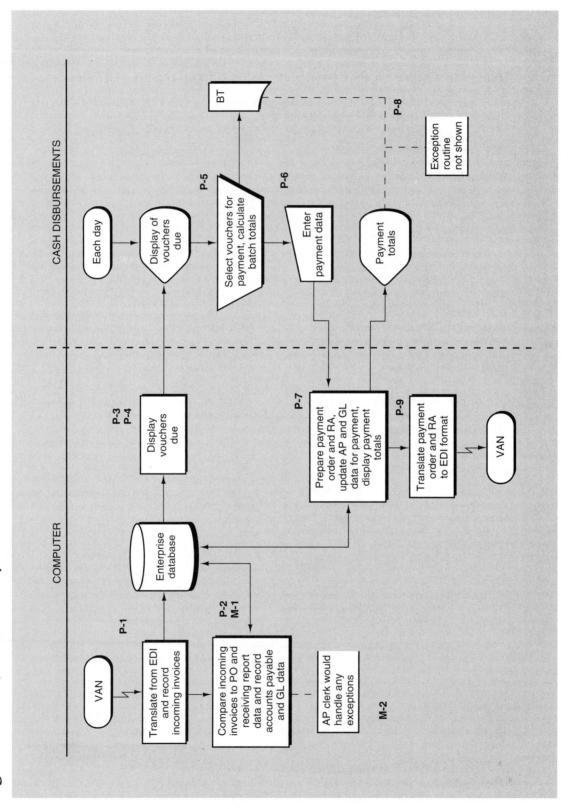

bank transmits the RA and payment data to the vendor. If the electronic remittance advice does not accompany the payment order through the banking system, it would be forwarded directly (via VAN) to the supplier.[5]

The Fraud Connection

As noted in Chapter 12, the AP/CD process is part of the *purchase-to-pay process* that culminates with the payment of cash and has a high potential for *exposing* an organization to fraud and embezzlement. In this section, we continue the Chapter 12 discussion of these abuses by presenting some of the ways the AP/CD process has been manipulated.

Fraud and the Accounts Payable Function

Abuses in this part of the AP/CD process usually entail creating phony vendors in the approved vendor data and/or submitting fictitious invoices. Some examples taken from actual incidents follow:

- Stanley opened a business account at his local bank in the name of SRJ Enterprises. He deposited $100 and told the bank that the company was located at the home address of his girlfriend, Phoebe, a disgruntled colleague from his employer's accounting department. Using his home computer, Stanley printed bogus invoices in the name of SRJ Enterprises. Phoebe created a vendor record for SRJ Enterprises on the company's computer and put the bogus invoice in a stack of much larger invoices for payment and approval. This scheme continued for a year and netted over $700,000 for Stanley and Phoebe. Stanley's wife became suspicious and called the organization's internal auditor who tracked down the fraud. As first time offenders Phoebe and Stanley only got probation. But both Phoebe and Stanley's wife left him![6]

- Veronica was an accounting clerk at a dental supply wholesaler responsible for processing invoices for payment. One vendor, a dental appliance manufacturer, printed its invoices in black ink on plain paper. Veronica would make a copy of the invoice and process them both for payment, one a few days after the other. When the vendor recognized the duplicate payment, it sent a refund check that was sent to Veronica! She simply deposited the check in her own bank account. The scheme was discovered by a colleague who saw Veronica pocket some checks and turned her in to the organization's internal auditor.[7]

Fraud and the Cash Disbursements Function

Frauds in this category are more direct and less subtle than in the purchasing and accounts payable functions. Usually, the theft of cash entails check forgery or fraudulent wire transfers. Before the advent of computers, fraud committed via bogus corporate checks first required that the thief steal a supply of blank checks. Now, however, those checks can be counterfeited using a laser scanner, a personal computer, and a color printer. For an investment of under $1,000, the counterfeiter can set up shop.

---

[5] You should be aware that using electronic funds transfer (EFT) to wire funds between banks and employing EDI to transmit remittance data from the payer's to the vendor's computer system do *not* necessarily go hand in hand. For instance, a company could utilize EFT to make payments but still rely on paper remittance advices to notify the vendor of the details of what is being paid.

[6] Joseph T. Wells, "Billing Schemes, Part 1: Shell Companies That Don't Deliver," *Journal of Accountancy* (July 2002): 76–79.

[7] Joseph T. Wells, "Billing Schemes, Part 3: Pay-and-Return Invoicing," *Journal of Accountancy* (September 2002): 96–98.

The risk from computer-generated forgeries has escalated significantly in the past few years. Cheap color ink jet printers can now generate such perfect replicas that even counterfeiting of currency has become a desktop computer operation. It is a primary reason for the U.S. Treasury's redesign of its currency, starting with the $20 bill.

What about checks that are legitimate, made out correctly, and sent to your vendor? Will they be routed to your vendor and result in absolution of your payable? Not always. When the check gets to your vendor an unscrupulous clerk can simply deposit the check to his or her account or use it to pay their credit card bill, or whatever. How do you prevent that? How about digitally signed electronic payments? These are either sent to the bank directly and cannot be diverted by the clerk or if sent directly to the vendor cannot be altered with alerting the bank to the clerk's fraudulent change when the clerk attempts to deposit the altered check.

Exposure to Loss and Destruction of Resources

In Chapter 7, we cautioned you that although the subject of fraud and embezzlement is seductively interesting, resource losses due to unintentional mistakes and inadvertent errors are as costly as—or more costly than—those caused by intentional acts of malfeasance. One major source of loss is the overpayment of accounts payable that are usually caused by simple human errors, such as:

- Situation 1: Assume that we receive a freight bill (i.e., a bill for which we have no underlying purchase order against which to verify charges) and that on that bill a decimal point is inadvertently "slid" one place to the right. As a result, we are billed for $4,101.30 instead of for the correct amount of $410.13. Without any purchase order to compare this bill to, we may make a payment for the incorrect, larger amount.

- Situation 2: Assume that we confuse a vendor's name, perhaps 3M Co. and Minnesota Mining & Manufacturing Co. We might pay the same invoice twice not realizing that 3M and Minnesota Mining & Manufacturing are one and the same.

Although the latter mistake should be called to our attention by an honest vendor, the first error would have been made by the freight company and would not be caught by us. Even in cases where the overpayment is refunded to us, we have incurred the clerical cost of processing the payment, sending it to the vendor, and correcting the error after the fact.

APPLICATION OF THE CONTROL FRAMEWORK

In this section, we apply the control framework from Chapter 9 to the AP/CD process. Figure 13.11 presents a completed *control matrix* for the annotated systems flowchart shown in Figure 13.10 (page 494). After briefly discussing the control goals shown as column headings in the matrix, we then describe in Exhibit 13.1 (pages 498–499) each of the recommended control plans listed in the first column. As you study the control plans, be sure to see where they are located on the systems flowchart.

Control Goals

The following control goal categories are presented in the matrix. Those for the operations process are as follows:

- *Effectiveness of operations* relative to the two goals already mentioned briefly in the section on "Logical Process Description."

Figure 13.11 Control Matrix for the AP/CD Process

Recommended Control Plans	Ensure effectiveness of operations A	Ensure effectiveness of operations B	Ensure efficient employment of resources (people, computers)	Ensure security of resources (cash accounts payable master data)	For vendor invoice inputs, ensure: IV	For vendor invoice inputs, ensure: IC	For vendor invoice inputs, ensure: IA	For accounts payable master data, ensure: UC	For accounts payable master data, ensure: UA	For payment voucher inputs, ensure: IV	For payment voucher inputs, ensure: IC	For payment voucher inputs, ensure: IA	For accounts payable master data, ensure: UC	For accounts payable master data, ensure: UA
					Control Goals of the Operations Process			Control Goals of the Information Process — Control Goals of the AP/CD Business Process						
Present Controls														
P-1: Independent validation of vendor invoices				P-1	P-1		P-1							
P-2: Vendor invoice mathematical accuracy check							P-2							
P-3: Independent authorization to make payment				P-3						P-3				
P-4: Computer-generated list of vouchers due	P-4										P-4			
P-5: Calculate batch totals										P-5	P-5			
P-6: Preformatted screens			P-6									P-6		
P-7: Record disbursements			P-7											
P-8: Reconcile input-output batch totals				P-8						P-8	P-8	P-8	P-8	P-8
P-9: Digital signatures				P-9						P-9	P-9	P-9	P-9	P-9
Missing Controls														
M-1: Reconcile input-output batch totals			M-1	M-1	M-1	M-1	M-1	M-1	M-1					
M-2: Cash planning report		M-2												

Legend:

Effectiveness goals:

A = Optimize cash discounts.

B = Ensure that the amount of cash maintained in demand deposit accounts is sufficient (but not excessive) to satisfy expected cash disbursements.

IV = Input validity
IC = Input completeness
IA = Input accuracy
UC = Update completeness
UA = Update accuracy

See Exhibit 13.1 (pages 498–499) for a complete explanation of control plans and cell entries.

Exhibit 13.1 Explanation of Cell Entries for Control Matrix in Figure 13.11

P-1: *Independent validation of vendor invoices.*

Security of resources: Because cash cannot be expended in the absence of a validated, open vendor invoice, security over the cash asset is enhanced.

Vendor invoice input validity: The computerized accounts payable application, which is separate from the departments that authorized the purchase and that recorded the receipt of the goods or services, actually performs the validation of the vendor invoice. Therefore, validity of the invoice should be ensured.

P-2: *Vendor invoice mathematical accuracy check.*

Vendor invoice input accuracy: We are told that the accounts payable application program matches invoice items, quantities, prices, and terms to comparable data on the purchase order and receiving report data. Because this process is computerized, we assume that the program also checks the invoice for mathematical accuracy (extensions, footings, discount calculations, etc.). Therefore, we call this a "present" control plan as it ensures that the invoice is accurate.

P-3: *Independent authorization to make payment.*

Security of resources: Because cash cannot be expended in the absence of a validated, open vendor invoice, security over the cash asset is enhanced.

Payment voucher input validity: Records in the accounts payable master data were created by the accounts payable process. Therefore, the data gives independent authorization to the cash disbursements computer program to approve vendor invoices for payment. The validity of payment vouchers is thereby ensured.

P-4: *Computer-generated list of vouchers due.*

Effectiveness goal A: Action on this list should ensure that payments are made in a timely manner, not too early and not too late (i.e., to optimize cash discounts).

Payment voucher input completeness: Action on this list should ensure that all payments are input.

P-5: *Calculate batch totals.*

Payment voucher input validity, Payment voucher input completeness: Batch totals arise from legitimate vouchers (*input validity*). Batch totals ensure that all of the batched data is recorded (*input com-*

pleteness). The nature and extent of batch totals can vary: they can account for only the number of transactions, the number of items or lines of data, dollar amounts, and/or hash totals. As such, batch totals themselves ensure the validity and completeness of the counts and amounts they represent. However, they do not necessarily ensure input accuracy—that takes place in the reconciliation, which is discussed in control plan P-8.

P-6: *Preformatted screens.*

Efficient employment of resources: By structuring the data entry process, automatically populating fields, and preventing errors, preformatted screens simplify data input and save time, allowing a user to input more data over a period of time.

Payment voucher input accuracy: As each data field is completed on a preformatted screen, the cursor moves to the next field on the screen, thus preventing the user from omitting any required data set. The data for fields that are automatically populated need not be manually entered, thus reducing input errors. Incorrectly formatted fields are rejected.

P-7: *Record disbursements.*

Efficient employment of resources: Automatic recording of disbursement data is fast and reliable.

P-8: *Reconcile input-output batch totals (agreement of run-to-run totals).*

Security of resources, Payment voucher input validity: By determining that payments input and made reflect only those authorized by the clerk ensures the cash is not disbursed inappropriately (*security of resources*) and validity of the inputs.

Payment voucher input completeness, Payment voucher input accuracy, Update completeness, Update accuracy: By comparing totals prepared before the input to those produced after the update we ensure that all selected vouchers were input (*input completeness*), all vouchers were input correctly (*input accuracy*), all payments were updated to the master data (*update completeness*), and all payments were updated correctly to the master data (*update accuracy*).

P-9: *Digital signatures.*

Security of resources, Payment voucher input validity, Payment voucher input completeness, Payment voucher

Exhibit 13.1 Explanation of Cell Entries for Control Matrix in Figure 13.11 (*continued*)

input accuracy, Update completeness, Update accuracy: When the digital signatures are authenticated at the VAN, the VAN will know that the sender of the message has authority to send it and thus prevents the unauthorized diversion of resources (*security of resources*). This also determines that the message itself is genuine (*validity*). This will also detect if the payment message has been altered in transit, and thus is incomplete or inaccurate and does not agree with the inputs and updates that took place prior to sending the payment file.

M-1: *Reconcile input-output batch totals (agreement of run-to-run totals).*

Security of resources, Vendor invoice input validity: Determining that invoice inputs reflect only those received from an authorized vendor ensures the cash will not subsequently be disbursed inappropriately (*security of resources*) and validity of the vendor invoice inputs.

Vendor invoice input completeness, Vendor invoice input accuracy, Update completeness, Update accuracy: By comparing totals received from the VAN (or prepared before the input) to those produced after the update we ensure that all vendor invoices were input (*input completeness*), all vendor invoices were input correctly (*input accuracy*), all vendor invoices were recorded in the master data (*update completeness*), and all vendor invoices were updated correctly to the master data (*update accuracy*).

M-2: *Cash planning report.*

Effectiveness goal B: An aging of open vouchers/accounts payable records must be produced and reviewed on a regular basis in order to ensure that there is an adequate cash reserve to make required payments. Excess cash on hand should be invested.

- *Efficiency* of the accounts payable and cash disbursement processes.
- *Resource security*—note that the resources include the asset cash, and the information resources represented by the accounts payable master data.

Those for the information system are as follows:

- Input validity (IV) of input events[8]
- Input completeness (IC) and input accuracy (IA)
- Update completeness (UC) and update accuracy (UA)

Input validity for each input event type can be summarized as follows:

- *Vendor invoices.* Those that bill the company for goods that were actually ordered and actually received (i.e., the invoices are supported by proper purchase orders and receiving reports).
- *Payment vouchers.* Those that are documented by *validated*, *unpaid* vendor invoices. Note that in this case, part of ensuring validity is to prevent paying an item twice.

Recommended Control Plans

Before analyzing the plans that are germane to our AP/CD process, let's start by summarizing some plans that are *not* listed in the control matrix nor discussed in Exhibit 13.1. Certain plans simply aren't appropriate to the procedures used in the process that

---

[8] In the matrix, please note that the inputs and master data vary for each of the processes. These variations can be summarized as follows:

Process	Nature of inputs	Updated master data
payables	vendor invoice	accounts payable
cash disbursements	payment voucher	accounts payable

we are reviewing. However, you might encounter them in practice. The following are a few examples:

- Where paper documents are the basis for making disbursements, paid invoices (and the supporting purchase orders and receiving reports) are often marked "void" or "paid" to prevent their being paid a second time. In paperless systems, the computerized payable records would be "flagged" with a code to indicate they had been paid and to prevent duplicate payment.
- Where payments are by check, appropriate physical controls should exist over supplies of blank checks and signature plates that are used for check signing.
- It is not uncommon to have more than one authorized signature required on large dollar checks.
- Most companies have standing instructions with their banks not to honor checks that have been outstanding longer than a certain number of months (e.g., 3 months or 6 months).
- To prevent alteration of (or misreading of) check amounts, many businesses use check-protection machines to imprint the check amount in a distinctive color (generally a blue and red combination).

Please turn to Exhibit 13.1 and study the explanations of the cell entries appearing in the control matrix. As you know from your studies in prior chapters, understanding how the recommended control plans relate to specific control goals is the most important aspect of applying the control framework.

Summary

This chapter has covered the AP/CD process, the fourth and fifth steps in the *purchase-to-pay process* introduced in Chapter 2. Like the process in Chapter 12, the physical process implementation presented in this chapter evidences many attributes of the paperless office of the future. In addition, technologies being employed to improve the efficiency and effectiveness of the accounts payable and cash disbursements processes were introduced. Some questions in the end-of-chapter materials ask you to consider how these technologies also can help reduce the errors and frauds often found in these processes.

Review Questions

RQ 13-1 How, in your own words, would you define the AP/CD process?

RQ 13-2 What primary functions does the AP/CD process perform?

RQ 13-3 How does the AP/CD process relate to its organizational environment?

RQ 13-4 What are the fundamental responsibilities of the accounts payable department and the cashier?

RQ 13-5 What major *logical* processes does the AP/CD process perform?

RQ 13-6 What are two operations process (effectiveness) goals of the AP/CD process? Provide an example illustrating each goal.

RQ 13-7 Describe how the processing of noninvoiced disbursements is handled in (a) a "true" voucher system and (b) a non-voucher system.

RQ 13-8 Select three control plans presented in the chapter. How does each relate to the AP/CD process presented in Figure 13.10 (page 494)?

DISCUSSION QUESTIONS

DQ 13-1 Refer to effectiveness goals A and B shown in the control matrix in Figure 13.11 on page 497. For each activity (accounts payable and cash disbursements), describe goals other than the one discussed in the chapter.

DQ 13-2 Explain why ambiguities and conflicts exist among operations process (effectiveness) goals, and discuss potential ambiguities and conflicts relative to the goals you described in DQ13-1.

DQ 13-3 Without redrawing the figures, discuss how Figures 13.3, 13.4, and 13.6 (pages 481, 482, and 484) would change as a result of the following independent situations (be specific in describing the changes):

   a. Employing a voucher system that involved, among other things, establishing vouchers payable that covered several vendor invoices.

   b. Making payments twice per month, on the fifth and twenty-fifth of the month, and taking advantage of all cash discounts offered.

DQ 13-4 In terms of effectiveness and efficiency of operations, as well as of meeting the generic information system control goals of validity, completeness, and accuracy, what are the arguments for and against each of the following?

   a. Sending a copy of the vendor invoice to the purchasing department for approval of payment.

   b. Sending a copy of the vendor invoice to the requisitioning department for approval of payment.

DQ 13-5 This question relates to the nine *common business exposures* that were introduced in Chapter 7:

   a. Which exposures might an *electronic data interchange* system help *prevent*? Discuss your answer.

   b. Which exposures might an *electronic data interchange* system *cause*? For each of these situations, discuss a control or controls that might *prevent* the exposure.

DQ 13-6 In the physical implementation depicted in Figure 13.10 (page 494), the computer updated the accounts payable data upon receipt of a vendor invoice (a clerk handled any exceptions). Describe the procedures that you believe should control that process.

DQ 13-7 In the physical implementation depicted in Figure 13.10 (page 494), the payment order and the remittance advice were sent together through the banking system. We also described an option of sending the remittance advice directly to the vendor. Which is better? Discuss.

DQ 13-8 With an *electronic data interchange* system, a customer's order may be entered directly into the order entry/sales system without human intervention. Discuss your control concerns under these circumstances.

DQ 13-9 In the section on fraud in the accounts payable process, we described a fraud committed by Stanley and Phoebe and another by Veronica. For each fraud describe controls and technology that could be used to reduce the risk of those frauds occurring.

PROBLEMS

Note: As mentioned in Chapters 10 through 12, the first few problems in the business process chapters are based on the processes of specific companies. Therefore, the problem material starts with case narratives of those processes. (The purchasing and receiving portions of these two cases are in Chapter 12.)

CASE A: Speedy Grocers, Inc. (II)

Per agreement with suppliers, all payments are due within 10 days after receipt of shipped grocery stocks. When a payment is due, a screen pops up in the cash disbursement officer's computer notifying that a payment is to be made. The cash disbursements officer connects to Speedy's electronic banking system via the bank's Web site and initiates payments to all vendors via electronic transfers. A confirmation number is received from the bank instantaneously to the entering of the transaction and the cash disbursements officer enters the confirmation number into the Speedy computer and the account payable balances are updated.

CASE B: Healthy Medical Supplies (II)

Healthy Medical Supplies makes a variety of medical supplies such as test tubes, thermometers, and disposable surgical garments. Healthy employs the following procedures for accounts payable and cash disbursements.

The purchasing department receives the invoice from the vendors. The invoices are keyed into the system with reference to the purchase order number. The purchasing agent must approve any price or quantity variances that are more than 5 percent over the price or quantity quoted on the purchase order. As the invoices are entered, the computer updates the purchasing and accounts payable databases.

Every morning, the accounts payable department reviews the open invoices to determine if they should be paid. Clerks select those invoices that are to be paid and the computer prints a check in the accounts payable department and updates the accounts payable database. Accounts payable mails the check to the vendor.

P 13-1 For the company assigned by your instructor, complete the following requirements:

a. Prepare a table of entities and activities.

b. Draw a context diagram.

c. Draw a *physical* data flow diagram (DFD).

d. Prepare an annotated table of entities and activities. Indicate on this table the groupings, bubble numbers, and bubble titles to be used in preparing a level 0 logical DFD.

e. Draw a level 0 *logical* DFD.

P 13-2 For the company assigned by your instructor, complete the following requirements:

a. Draw a systems flowchart.

b. Prepare a control matrix, including explanations of how each recommended existing control plan helps to accomplish—or would accomplish in the case of missing plans—each related control goal. Your choice of recommended control plans should come from this chapter plus any controls from Chapters 9 through 12 that are germane to your company's process.

c. Annotate the flowchart prepared in part a to indicate the points where the control plans are being applied (codes P-1 . . . P-*n*) or the points where they could be applied but are not (codes M-1 . . . M-*n*).

P 13-3 The following capsule cases present short narratives of processes used by three actual organizations whose names have been changed for the purpose of this problem. You will use the cases to practice the mechanics of drawing data flow diagrams.

CAPSULE CASE 1: Rock of Gibraltar Insurance Co.

Rock of Gibraltar Insurance Co. (ROG) is one of the largest automobile insurance companies in the country. Each year, ROG receives more than 30,000 claims billings from Plexlite Glass Corp. (Plex), the country's largest auto glass replacement chain and a leading manufacturer of replacement windshields. Recently the two companies entered into an agreement to abandon paper invoices and adopt EDI for the processing of claims. The new process works as follows:

An insured party calls ROG to report glass damage. The ROG representative taking the call gives the insured an authorization number and opens a claim record (*note*: all data are stored on disk) on ROG's mainframe computer system. The insured party takes the automobile to a Plex shop to have the glass repaired, gives Plex the authorization number, and pays the deductible amount required by the insurance policy. After the Plex store replaces the glass, the store manager enters the authorization number and other data into its computer system via a point-of-sale (POS) terminal, and the data is recorded to the receivables data.

Plex's computer system collects the invoice data from the individual Plex stores and transmits the data each week to ROG in EDI format through IVANS, a value-added network owned by the insurance industry. Thus, the data is received by ROG's computer system without the need for human intervention.

After the data is checked electronically against the open claim data for proper authorization number, auto make and model, proper insurance coverage, and correct pricing by Plex, the claims invoice is written to the validated claims data, and an EDI message informs Plex which claims will be paid. Claims rejected by ROG's system are processed manually; description of the exception routines is beyond the context of this case. Once a week, ROG's treasurer accesses the validated claims data and sends a single check to Plex for all claims approved that week.

CAPSULE CASE 2: Big 2, Inc.

Big 2, Inc. (BIG), is a major manufacturer of automobiles. This narrative gives an abbreviated description of the procedures used by BIG in buying original equipment windshields from its only supplier of windshields, Akron Glass Co. (AGC). When BIG's inventory process requests the purchasing department to reorder windshields, the order information is recorded to the purchase order data (*note*: all data are stored on disk) and transmitted electronically directly from BIG's computer to AGC's computer via telephone line. AGC returns an electronic acknowledgment to BIG.

When AGC is ready to ship the order, it transmits an electronic invoice to BIG and prints a paper bill of lading that is given to the trucker who transports the goods. BIG's computer records the invoice to the pending invoices data. The receiving department at BIG keys in the goods received. The keying operation creates a receiving record in the receiving data and updates the purchase order master data to reflect the receipt. Each morning, a clerk in BIG's accounts payable department accesses the electronic invoices received from all EDI suppliers the previous day. He audits the invoice by checking it against data from the purchase order master data (e.g., descriptions, quantities, prices, and purchase terms) and from the receiving data. The clerk then enters the date to be paid and a code to authorize payment of each invoice.

The payment authorization is transmitted electronically to BIG's bank where it is stored in the authorized payments data until the specified payment date. The evening before the payment date, BIG's bank forwards the payment—with remittance data (in ANSI X12 format) electronically "attached" to it—to AGC's bank. The payment data is in encrypted, authenticated form. BIG's bank account is debited for the payment. The next morning, AGC's bank account is credited for the payment. BIG's remittance data is translated from ANSI to a standard lockbox format, is integrated with AGC's other lockbox remittances, and is reported online to AGC for automatic posting to its accounts receivable database.

For the capsule case assigned by your instructor, complete the following requirements:

a. Prepare a table of entities and activities.

b. Draw a context diagram.

c. Draw a *physical* data flow diagram (DFD).

d. Prepare an annotated table of entities and activities. Indicate on the table the groupings, bubble numbers, and bubble titles to be used in preparing a level 0 logical DFD.

e. Draw a level 0 *logical* DFD.

P 13-4 *Note*: If you were assigned DQ 13-3, consult your solution to it. Modify the DFDs in Figures 13.3, 13.4, and 13.6 (pages 481, 482, and 484), as appropriate, to reflect the following *independent* assumptions:

a. Employing a voucher system that involved, among other things, establishing vouchers payable that covered several vendor invoices.

b. Making payments twice per month, on the fifth and twenty-fifth of the month, and taking advantage of all cash discounts offered.

Note: Because the two assumptions are independent, your instructor may assign only one of them.

P 13-5 The following are 10 process failures that indicate weaknesses in control.

Process Failures

1. A cash disbursements event was posted to the wrong record in the accounts payable master data because of the data entry clerk's transposing digits in the vendor identification number.

2. Several scanned invoice documents were lost and did not get recorded.

3. The amount of a cash disbursement event was erroneous, resulting in the balance in the accounts payable master data becoming a debit balance.

4. The total shown on a vendor's invoice was greater than the sum of the invoice details, resulting in an overpayment to the vendor.

5. The vendor invoiced for goods that were never delivered. The invoice was paid in its full amount.

6. The unit prices the vendor charged were in excess of those that had been negotiated. The invoice rendered by the vendor was paid.

7. A vendor submitted an invoice in duplicate. The invoice got paid twice.

8. Because of several miscellaneous errors occurring over a number of years, the total of the outstanding vendor payable balances shows a large discrepancy from the balance reflected in the general ledger.

9. Several electronic invoices were misrouted to an organization. The invoices were received, input, and paid, but the organization had never purchased anything from the vendors that were paid.

10. Goods receipts from a certain vendor are always on time. However, the invoices from this vendor are often late or never received. As a result, the organization has lost significant amounts of money by failing to obtain cash discounts for prompt payment.

List the numbers 1 through 10 on your solution sheet. For each of the 10 process failures described, provide a two- to three-sentence description of the control plan that you believe would *best* address that deficiency. Obviously, more than one plan could exist that is germane to a particular situation. However, select *only one* plan for each of the 10 process failures and include in your description a justification of why you believe it is *best*. When in doubt, opt for the plan that is *preventive* in nature, as opposed to plans that are *detective* or *corrective*.

P 13-6 Figure 12.4 (page 448) and Figure 13.3 (page 481) show three data flows running to the general ledger (GL) for the purpose of updating the general ledger master data.

For each of the following data flows in, show the journal entry (in debit/credit journal entry format with no dollar amounts) that would result (make and state any assumptions you think are necessary).

- GL inventory received update
- GL payable update
- GL cash disbursements update

Note: Even though the debit might come from a process other than the purchasing or AP/CD processes, show *both* the debit and credit in the first entry. Also show alternative entries under each of the following assumptions:

a. Merchandise is purchased and a *periodic* inventory process is used.

b. Merchandise is purchased and a *perpetual* inventory process is used.

c. Office supplies are purchased.

d. Plant assets are purchased.

e. Legal *services* are purchased.

P 13-7 Using the following two tables as a guide, describe for each function (see Figure 13.1 on page 479):

a. A risk (an event or action that will cause the organization to fail to meet it goals/objectives).

b. A control/process or use of technology that will address the risk.

Do the same for the accounting entry.

	Function	Risks	Controls and technology
Manager	Finance		
Operations process	Accounts payable		
	Cash disbursements		

Event	Entry	Risks	Controls and technology
Record invoice	???		
	AP		
Make payment	AP		
	Cash		

P 13-8 Use the data flow diagrams in Figures 13.3, 13.4, and 13.6 (pages 481, 482, and 484) to solve this problem.

Prepare a four-column table that summarizes the AP/CD processes, inputs, and outputs. In the first column, list the two processes shown in the level 0 diagram (Figure 13.3). In the second column, list the subsidiary functions shown in the four lower-level diagrams (Figures 13.4 and 13.6). For each subsidiary process listed in column 2, list the data flow names or the data stores that are inputs to that process (column 3) or outputs of that process (column 4). (See *Note*.) The following table has been started for you to indicate the format for your solution.

Note: To simplify the solution, do not show any reject stubs in column 4.

Solution Format

**Summary of the AP/CD processes,
inputs, outputs, and data stores**

Process	Subsidiary Functions	Inputs	Outputs
1.0 Establish payable	1.1 Validate invoice	PO accounts payable notification Receiving report Vendor invoice Vendor master data	Validated vendor invoice Vendor master data
	1.2 Record payable	Validated vendor invoice Inventory master data	. . .Continue solution. . .

KEY TERMS

accounts payable/cash
   disbursements
   (AP/CD) process
vendor invoice

disbursement voucher
purchase returns and
   allowances

accounts payable master
   data
cash disbursements data

The Human Resources (HR) Management and Payroll Processes

PSS/World Medical is a medical supplies and equipment distributor in Jacksonville, Florida. The company had grown rapidly to $1.7 billion in revenue and nearly 5,000 employees. But its human resources (HR) department remained a paper-based department, processing over 85,000 HR forms annually. Three employees were dedicated full-time to handle the paperwork.

Jeff Anthony, the senior vice president for corporate development, reported that it took 6 to 7 weeks to get employee benefits-enrollment forms and information to employees and another 8 to 10 weeks to clean up what they passed in. An internal audit revealed that PSS/World Medical had overpaid more than $180,000 in administrative fees to a medical insurer because it listed the wrong number of employees. Some employees were receiving their paychecks days, or even weeks, late. Insurance coverage was denied to new employees because enrollment paperwork was delayed. Paychecks were being cut for employees who had been fired as many as five weeks earlier because proper HR forms to terminate the payments were not processed in a timely manner. One year, the company paid out approximately $600,000 in unused vacation time to departing employees because it lacked a process to track that information.

To solve this problem Anthony brought in software vendor Employease, an HR application service provider, to implement a Web-based HR self-service system. Now paychecks roll out on time and enrollments proceed smoothly in less than one hour, thanks in no small part to an employee self-service application. Employee turnover has shrunk to just 8 percent (from a high of nearly 50 percent). Anthony estimates the cost savings at $800,000 annually from reduced payroll processing costs (e.g., canceling checks, next-day air fees to expedite the delivery of late paychecks), reassigned HR employees who were no longer needed for paperwork, increased data accuracy (from 40 to 90 percent), reduced insurance penalties, and reallocated management time from HR administration to primary functions. Anthony gave himself as an example of the last benefit. He now spends more time developing, rather than hiring, personnel.[1]

Learning Objectives

- To know the definition and basic functions of the HR management and payroll processes.
- To recognize the relationship between the HR management and payroll processes and their environment.
- To comprehend the relationship between the HR management and payroll processes and management decision making.
- To understand the logical and physical characteristics of the HR management and payroll processes.
- To become familiar with some of the technology used to implement the HR management and payroll processes.
- To know some of the plans commonly used to control the payroll process.

[1] Jon Surmacz, "Automating HR," *Darwin Magazine*, http://www.darwinmag.com, October 2002; Paul Krass, "Precious Resources," *CFO.com*, http://www.cfo.com, July 23, 2003.

In this chapter, we spotlight the human resources (HR) management and payroll processes. (It will become clear later why we depict these processes with one spoke in the AIS wheel.) We will describe the various users of the HR management and payroll processes, each having their own view of the enterprise system and enterprise database. In addition, we will analyze the process controls related to the payroll process.

SYNOPSIS

Human capital management (HCM), the process of managing how people are hired, developed, assigned, motivated and retained, presumes that employees reflect a strategic investment, rather than an administrative cost. Some estimates place the value of human capital between $500,000 and $5 million per person. At the same time, the costs of such capital, including compensation, benefits, and human resources (HR), represent 43 percent of the average corporation's total operating expense.

The automation of the HR function (sometimes dubbed "e-HR") is positioned to transform HR from a lowly cost center to a highly valued, strategic, mission-critical part of the business. In addition to the changes noted at PSS/World Medical, HR automation will affect evaluation and compensation programs to reflect the changing work patterns, including graying workforce, virtual teams, telecommuters, consultants, contractors, part-timers, and temporary employees.

In this chapter we explore three themes. First, we briefly examine the importance of people to the success of any organization. Next, we describe how the HR management and payroll processes assist management in leveraging its human capital. Finally, we introduce some of the technology used to implement modern HR management and payroll processes.

INTRODUCTION

This chapter describes the basic roles played by an organization's human resources and payroll functions. The organizational structure of the HR function sets the stage for a discussion of the types of decisions HR managers face. We also look at a physical implementation of the HR management process. Next, we move to the payroll process. The organizational placement of the payroll process is followed by a detailed description of its logical and physical characteristics. Finally, control plans for the payroll process are summarized in a control matrix.

PROCESS DEFINITION AND FUNCTIONS

Any organization wishing to improve itself must start by improving its people. Recognizing people as the common denominator of progress has resulted in many organizations paying closer attention to their HR policies and practices. In the previous Synopsis section, we briefly introduced the concept of *human capital management (HCM)* and the emphasis that this process places on the value of human capital. HCM follows historically from the concept of "personnel management" and then "human resource management." Classic personnel management began with the handling of payroll and personnel administration, and evolved by adding functions to handle recruiting, employee relations, and so on. Human resource management recognized the importance of personnel in achieving organization objectives, but, like personnel management, viewed personnel as something that could be controlled.

The HCM philosophy is based on three major principles:[2]

- An individual's value to an organization is derived from his/her job-related knowledge, skills, attitude, and motivations.

- Human assets include full-time permanent employees, *plus* part-time employees, temporary employees, and independent contractors. Also, with collaborative commerce arrangements such as *supply chain management*, an organization's human assets could include employees of suppliers, sales channel partners, and customers.

- A person's relationship with an organization, from hiring through termination, must be nurtured and managed to obtain maximum lifetime value.

This last point emphasizes the importance of personnel development to maximize the benefits that each individual can provide to the organization, as well as retention of employees to ensure that important skills are not lost. It turns out that, similar to customers, retaining an employee is less expensive than replacing one. It has been estimated that it costs up to 2.5 times an employee's annual salary, plus benefits, to replace an employee. Thus, an effective HCM process is central to the achievement of an organization's objectives.

While the terms and concepts associated with HCM may represent the contemporary thinking about the HR function within an organization, most organizations still refer to their personnel-related function as human resources (HR). Therefore, in this chapter we will use HR to refer to the process whose function is to support the HCM concepts and to provide the organization with information with which to manage its personnel (i.e., its human capital).

---

[2] David A. Williams, "Why Human Capital Management?" http://www.humancapitalmanagement.biz/ArticleWhyHCM.htm, August 20, 2003.

Definition of the HR Management Process

The **human resources (HR) management process** is an interacting structure of people, equipment, methods, and controls. The primary function of the HR management process is to create information flows that support the following:

1. Repetitive work routines of the human resources department
2. Decision needs of those who manage the human resources department

The HR management process supports the work routines of the HR department and provides information for management decisions by:

- Capturing, recording, and storing data concerning HR activities.
- Generating a variety of HR forms and documents.
- Preparing management reports.
- Preparing governmental reports.

The first portion of this chapter is devoted to exploring these functions in detail.

Definition of the Payroll Process

The **payroll process** is an interacting structure of people, equipment, methods, and controls that creates information flows to support the repetitive work routines of the payroll department. To that end the payroll process maintains records containing data for payroll taxes and fringe benefits, attendance reporting, timekeeping, and paying employees for work performed. We explore these functions in detail in the second portion of this chapter.

Payroll represents an events-oriented process that has traditionally been considered separate from the HR management process. However, because of the close relationship of the two processes, we start by discussing why many companies merge the HR management and payroll processes into a single entity. Then we separate the processes so that we can analyze the distinct features of each one. In the course of this analysis, you will notice that the HR management process, more than any other information process, captures, records, and stores data that falls outside the normal accounting-oriented transaction stream. For example, data concerning an employee's health or the level of an employee's skills certainly does not fit the transaction model established by GAAP. However, from a holistic business perspective, it is important for accountants to realize the immense value of human capital and its affect on the long-term financial health of the organization.

Integration of the HR Management and Payroll Processes

Because of its labor-intensiveness and repetitiveness, the payroll function was one of the first systems within many organizations to be automated. In fact, payroll software was among the first to be commercially developed and marketed. However, the current generation of HR software has far outgrown its payroll roots. These new packages include such applications as cafeteria benefits administration, applicant tracking and processing, skills inventories, and compliance reporting. The menu for the human resources module of the SAP R/3 system is depicted in Figure 14.1 (page 512). Please examine the menu options and notice the variety of functions supported by the HR module.

Because the HR management and payroll processes share so much employee data, the integration of these functions is generally considered necessary. As you can see in

ENTERPRISE SYSTEMS

Figure 14.1 Menu Options in the Human Resources Module of SAP R/3

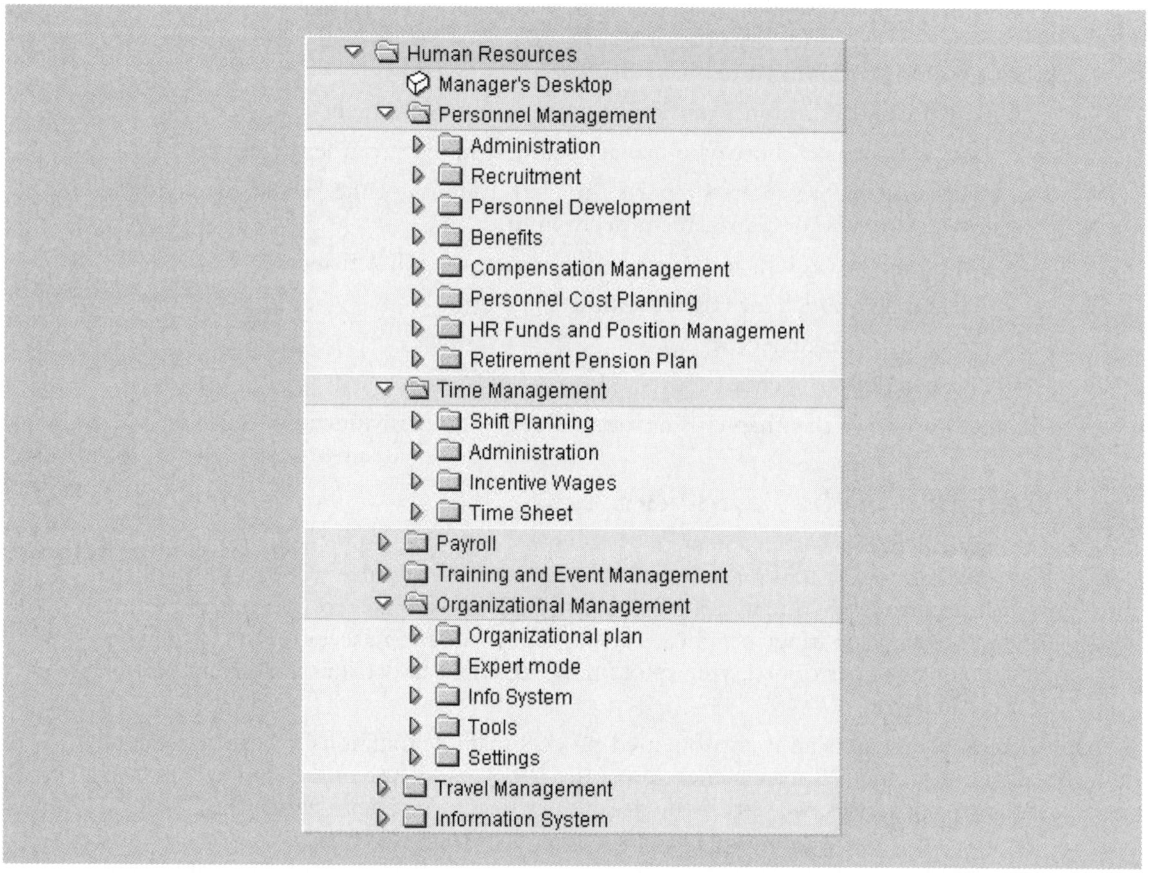

Source: Reprinted with permission from SAP.

Figure 14.1, the HR module includes options for both HR and payroll, among others. The advantages gained by allowing the two processes to share common data include:

- Creating a single source for obtaining HR information.
- Providing for faster data access.
- Minimizing data redundancy.
- Ensuring data integrity and consistency.
- Facilitating data maintenance.
- Improving data accuracy.

Having touted the advantages of integration, we'll nevertheless devote the rest of the chapter to separate discussions of the HR management and payroll processes. We do so because we believe the analysis is facilitated by differentiating between the broad HR management process and the narrower, accounting event-based payroll process. You will see how the two processes are integrated through the shared data contained in the employee/payroll master data and through certain common forms and documents used by both processes.

THE HR MANAGEMENT PROCESS

In this section, we look at the imprint of the HR function on the organization and illustrate some of the decisions HR managers must confront. Our examination will reveal that the HR and payroll functions are profoundly different in terms of their organizational significance. In some organizations, for example, the HR function is large enough to support a separate organizational unit, headed by a vice president of human resources.[3] On the other hand, the payroll function is typically housed within the controller's area and is placed at the same organizational level as the billing and accounts receivable functions.

Organizational Setting and Managerial Decision Making

Figure 14.2 identifies the key players in the HR function. For each manager shown in Figure 14.2, Table 14.1 (pages 514–515) describes the manager's key functions, types of decisions made, and some of the information needed to make those decisions. Today, the broadening scope of HR management requires decision making that directly affects an organization's internal policies and strategic plans. Table 14.1 should help you understand various informational needs of HR managers. Obviously, we can only introduce the topic here.

In addition to supporting the HR managers shown in Figure 14.2, the HR management process supports the various departmental managers (other than HR and payroll) who have direct managerial responsibility over those employees assigned to them. These responsibilities may include the assignment of tasks, the coordination of departmental activities, and the monitoring and evaluating of employee performance. Although departmental managers rely on observation and personal experience for much of their information, the HR management process supplies them with certain types of useful information. For example, the rate of absenteeism, quality of work performed, and level of skills an employee possesses represent information provided by a typical HR management process.

Figure 14.2 Organization Chart of the HR Function

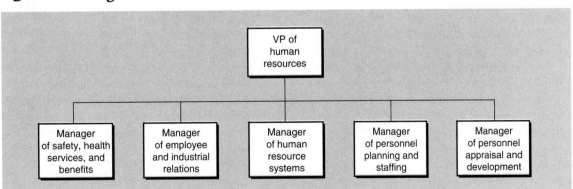

---

[3] Some organizations are not large enough to support a separate organizational unit for HR. In smaller companies, a director of HR is often housed within an organizational unit headed by a vice president of administration.

Table 14.1 HR Managers: Their Key Functions, Decisions, and Information Needs

HR Manager	Key Functions[a]	Types of Decisions Made[a]	Information Needs[a]
Manager of safety, health services, and benefits	Ensures workers' health and safety. Promotes a work environment that supports an acceptable "quality" of work life. Develops new programs for improving existing work conditions. Monitors and administers employee benefits plans.	Assesses the adequacy of employee-benefits packages. Addresses the problem of rising insurance costs. Determines ways to improve the physical work environment (e.g., should new overhead lights be installed?). Investigates ways to improve the quality of work life (e.g., should factory workers have more input into the design of new products?).	Status of existing work conditions. Employee attitudes and morale. Governmental regulations concerning worker safety, health, and benefits. Emerging trends in employee-benefits packages—features, costs, and the like. Industry and specific competitors' innovations.
Manager of employee and industrial relations	Handles employee complaints. Negotiates with organizations, such as unions, that represent employees.	Defines the nature and extent of employee influence in management's decision-making process (e.g., what role should seniority and other criteria play in deciding which employees to terminate, transfer, or promote?). Settles employee complaints and grievances (e.g., allegations of job discrimination, sexual harassment).	Current economic statistics. Outcome of grievance proceedings. Governmental laws and regulations on handling grievances.
Manager of human resource systems	Ensures that the information needs of personnel managers and staff workers are satisfied. Serves as liaison between the IT department and the personnel department.	Discovers how information technology can assist personnel managers in performing their day-to-day activities (e.g., helping managers to choose software packages). Ascertains the nature and timing of training needed for HRM users.	New and evolving HR management process technology developments. Information needs of personnel managers and staff workers. User feedback on their experience(s) in working with the HR management process.

Table 14.1 HR Managers: Their Key Functions, Decisions, and Information Needs (*continued*)

HR Manager	Key Functions[a]	Types of Decisions Made[a]	Information Needs[a]
Manager of personnel planning and staffing	Plans and forecasts an organization's short- and long-term human resource needs. Analyzes jobs to determine the skills necessary to perform them. Assists in recruiting job applicants, screening candidates, and helping new hires adjust to their work environment.	Projects an organization's future personnel needs and anticipates how to meet these needs. Decides the ways positions will be filled (i.e., outside hiring or internal promotion). Selects the means for recruiting and screening job applicants.	Labor force staffing forecasts. Job descriptions. Skills possessed by current employees. Sources of potential job candidates (e.g., college placement departments, search firms). Government laws and regulations concerning equal employment opportunity, affirmative action, and the like.
Manager of personnel appraisal and development	Assists line managers in assessing how well employees are performing. Cooperates with line managers in setting rewards for good performance. Helps line managers to provide training or take disciplinary action in cases of substandard performance. Reduces employee turnover by helping workers achieve their career goals.	Chooses the means of training and developing employees. Determines the methods for charting employees' careers.	Data on employee performance. Employee job experience, training, and salary histories. Economic statistics on general employment conditions, supply and demand of job candidates, salary levels, and so forth.

NOTE:
[a] Examples only. A complete listing is beyond the scope of this chapter.

Technology Trends and Developments

As noted in the story about PSS/World Medical at the start of this chapter, information **E-BUSINESS** technology, in particular, human resources self-service systems, have greatly improved the efficiency and effectiveness of HR management processes. Technology Summary 14.1 (page 516) describes these self-service systems. These systems are often part of a human resources portal that allows employees to access personal as well as business-related information and functions. Technology Application 14.1 (page 517) describes a

Technology Summary 14.1

Human Resources Self-Service Systems

It was not that long ago that it was pretty difficult for an employee to make changes to his human resources (HR) records. An employee might need to update his emergency contact information or change the number of payroll exemptions or the beneficiaries for his insurance policies. To do this he would need to submit a form—a hand-written form, no doubt—to his HR department to make such changes. And, it would take days, or even weeks, for those changes to take place. Performing job-related functions also was difficult. Authorizing pay raises for employees or recording performance reviews also were challenging and inefficient.

Fast forward to today and you will find that many employees can make such changes from their offices and even from the comfort of their homes. HR self-service systems, using convenient, easy-to-use Web browser interfaces, can be used to view and change HR records. These systems automate manually intensive processes and can reduce the cost of some HR processes by as much as 80 percent (see the following table).

Typically, an employee would open his Web browser and point it to his organization's HR Web site (or computer kiosk on the factory floor, for example). After inputting a user name and password, the employee would then be able to view his records and make changes. A typical self-service system might have the following features:

- HR manuals, policies, and procedures. These might include employee handbooks, codes of conduct, explanation of benefits programs, harassment policies, and procedures for travel reimbursement.
- Helpful information such as how to get a Social Security number for a new member of the family.
- Calculators for retirement income based on retirement age and investment choices.
- Personal profile containing job, payroll (e.g., check stubs), and benefits data.
- Forms for enrolling in health, retirement, and other programs.
- Places to make changes to existing programs. For example, to change payroll deductions, elections for pre-tax withholding of supplement retirement, and health care choices.
- Links to other important Web sites, such as the administrator of the 401(k) program.

Some of the changes that an employee might make will require a signature. In those cases the employee might fill out the form online and follow-up, through interoffice mail, with a signed form.

Both the employee and the employer benefit from HR self-service systems. The employee gains ready access to his records and to easily make changes to them. Employees typically view such systems as substantive and responsive. The employer gets to provide a higher level of service and increase the validity and accuracy of HR records, while reducing its own operating costs. The following table summarizes some of these cost savings.

The Lower Cost of Self-Service

Business Process/Task	Manual Cost	Self-Service Cost	Savings
Enroll in benefits	$109.48	$21.79	80%
Change contact info	$12.86	$3.39	74%
Enroll in training	$17.77	$4.87	73%
Approve a promotion	$48.64	$18.26	71%
Create job requisition	$36.89	$11.11	70%
Change salary	$44.67	$18.26	59%
Apply for a job	$21.31	$11.85	44%

Source: Peter Kraus, "Precious Resources," *CFO.Com* (July 23, 2003).

Technology Application 14.1

Self-Service Tools for Safety and Training

Docent, Inc., helps PSS/World Medical deliver compliance and safety-related information in a timely, efficient, and cost-effective manner to each employee. The Docent portion of the PSS/World Medical employee self-service system can deliver and track workplace safety and human resources-related training, including new employee orientation, workplace behavior training, and hazardous communication training. Individuals can access the employee self-service Web site or kiosks, click on their job function and branch office, and find the requirements and applicable courses for their job. Outsourcing of this function made sense because Docent ensures that the training complies with industry standards.

Source: "PSS/World Medical Uses Docent to Improve Workplace Safety and Industry Regulatory Knowledge," Docent, Inc., http://www.docent.com, August 2003.

portion of an employee self-service system that helps one organization ensure that employees receive training required for their job functions.

In addition to employee self-service systems, organizations might outsource other functions to support HR management processes. For example Technology Application 14.2 describes a Web-based collaboration that helps Shell Oil Products of Houston obtain qualified temporary labor. Technology Excerpt 14.1 (page 518) describes the outsourcing to Fidelity Investments of the management of employee benefits at General Motors. **E-BUSINESS**

In addition to the best of breed and outsourced services previously described, *enterprise systems* play a major role in implementing required HR and payroll functionality. For example, systems from vendors such as SAP (see Figure 14.1 on page 512 for the HR-related menu options within SAP R/3) include employee master data to support both HR management and payroll processes. They contain employee self-services for employees to maintain their own data and for managers to maintain and monitor data related to subordinate employees. Figure 14.3 (page 518) depicts a screen from the SAP R/3 **ENTERPRISE SYSTEMS**

Technology Application 14.2

Contingent Workforce Management Systems

Contingent workforce management systems automate management processes related to contingent labor, including labor supplier qualifications, requests for proposals, time and expense entries, and invoicing.

By implementing a Web-based workforce management system from IQNavigator, Inc., and by adopting a set of process improvements and reducing the number of labor suppliers, Shell Oil Products of Houston was able to significantly reduce (the target of 8 percent annual savings was exceeded in just two months) contingent workforce spending. For example, with these changes Shell receives volume and early payment discounts from suppliers.

Best of all, the IQNavigator system is paid for by Shell's labor suppliers. It is the norm in the industry for labor supplies to pay for contingent workforce management systems with access fees ranging from 3 to 5 percent of an invoice.

Source: Thomas Hoffman, "Managing Temporary Players," *Computerworld* (June 30, 2003): 42.

Technology Excerpt 14.1

Benefits Management: The Outsourcing of Human Resources Functions

General Motors Corp. hired Fidelity Investments to administer its health, pension, and other HR operations. Under the agreement, Fidelity will manage GM's pension plan that covers 700,000 active and retired employees and health and welfare plans that cover 1.2 million employees, retirees, and their dependents. To manage these programs, Fidelity will use many of same computer systems that it uses to manage 401(k) programs for GM and other organizations. Fidelity manages benefits programs for 15 million employees at 12,000 companies, including IBM Corp., BP PLC, and Monsanto Corp. Benefits administration amounted to a third of Fidelity's 2002 revenue of $8.9 billion.

Source: John Hechinger, "Fidelity to Handle GM's Health, Pension Plans," *The Wall Street Journal* (August 7, 2003): A2

Figure 14.3 Maintaining Employee Master Data in the SAP R/3 System

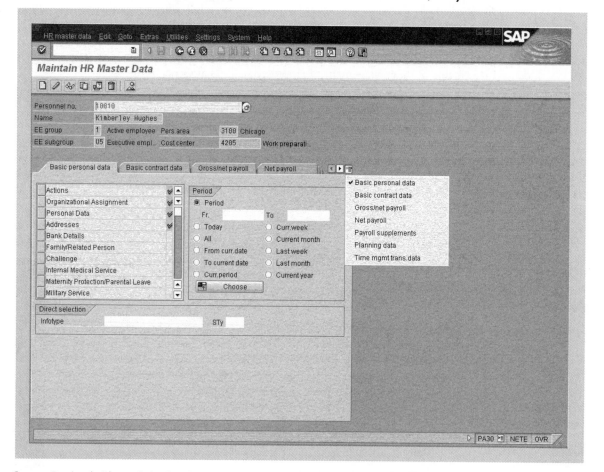

Source: Reprinted with permission from SAP.

system that is used to maintain employee data. Notice that tabs are used to access basic personal data, payroll data, organizational assignment, and personnel planning data.

When an organization chooses to implement their HR management process with an enterprise system they can recognize the benefits of integration of the HR management process with other enterprise systems modules such as financial accounting, logistics, and sales and distribution. In addition, the organizational assignment data in the HR module can join with the workflow module of the enterprise system to facilitate the routing and proper authorization of daily work. For example, this joined functionality can ensure the proper authorization of purchase requisitions, purchase orders, and payroll.

CONTROLS

Implementing the HR Management Process

This section offers a physical view of the HR management process. Using a systems flowchart as the framework for discussion, we will examine the inputs, processes, and outputs, in that order. The presentation also describes several of the operational and control aspects of a typical HR management process. The section concludes with an examination of what key data the process uses and how those data support decision making by HR managers.

Figure 14.4 (page 520) presents a systems flowchart of a typical HR management process. This physical implementation employs much of the technology previously described, including employee self-service systems, employee access to these systems via Web browsers or kiosks, and *enterprise systems* with workflow modules. Let's start by looking at the type of processing depicted. It generally is considered essential to record HR actions as soon as they are approved. A number of reasons exist for immediately recording changes affecting employees, including the need to ensure that each employee's paycheck reflects the employee's current status. As noted in the story about PSS/World Medical at the start of this chapter, paychecks that fail to reflect recent pay hikes can have a demoralizing effect on a workforce. To achieve this type of immediacy, many HR management processes use some form of *immediate mode* of processing, implemented with *online* technology. The process depicted in Figure 14.4 entails immediate recording of data, immediate updating of master data, and immediate generation of output. Let's take some time to walk through the flowchart, keeping an eye open for operational, technological, and control features.

ENTERPRISE SYSTEMS

E-BUSINESS

CONTROLS

Process Inputs. As shown in the "Various Department" column of the flowchart, actions taken by departmental managers or supervisors are captured on various online forms (i.e., enterprise system screens); these forms are discussed in more detail in the following paragraphs. In general, the HR forms in the figure capture information about three HR-related events: (1) selecting employees, (2) evaluating employees, and (3) terminating employees.

Selecting employees may be initiated in one of two ways. First, departmental supervisors and managers (outside the HR department) may initiate the process to satisfy their immediate hiring needs. The needs request screen illustrates this type of initiation. Second, the selection process may be started by the system automatically. For example, the system may be programmed to predict an organization's employment needs. In projecting this need, the program might correlate labor-force requirements (stored in the labor-force planning data) with such factors as expanding sales or production statistics.

The actual selection and hiring of employees can be accomplished by several means. First, candidates for an open or new position could be selected from the

Figure 14.4 Human Resources Management Process—Systems Flowchart

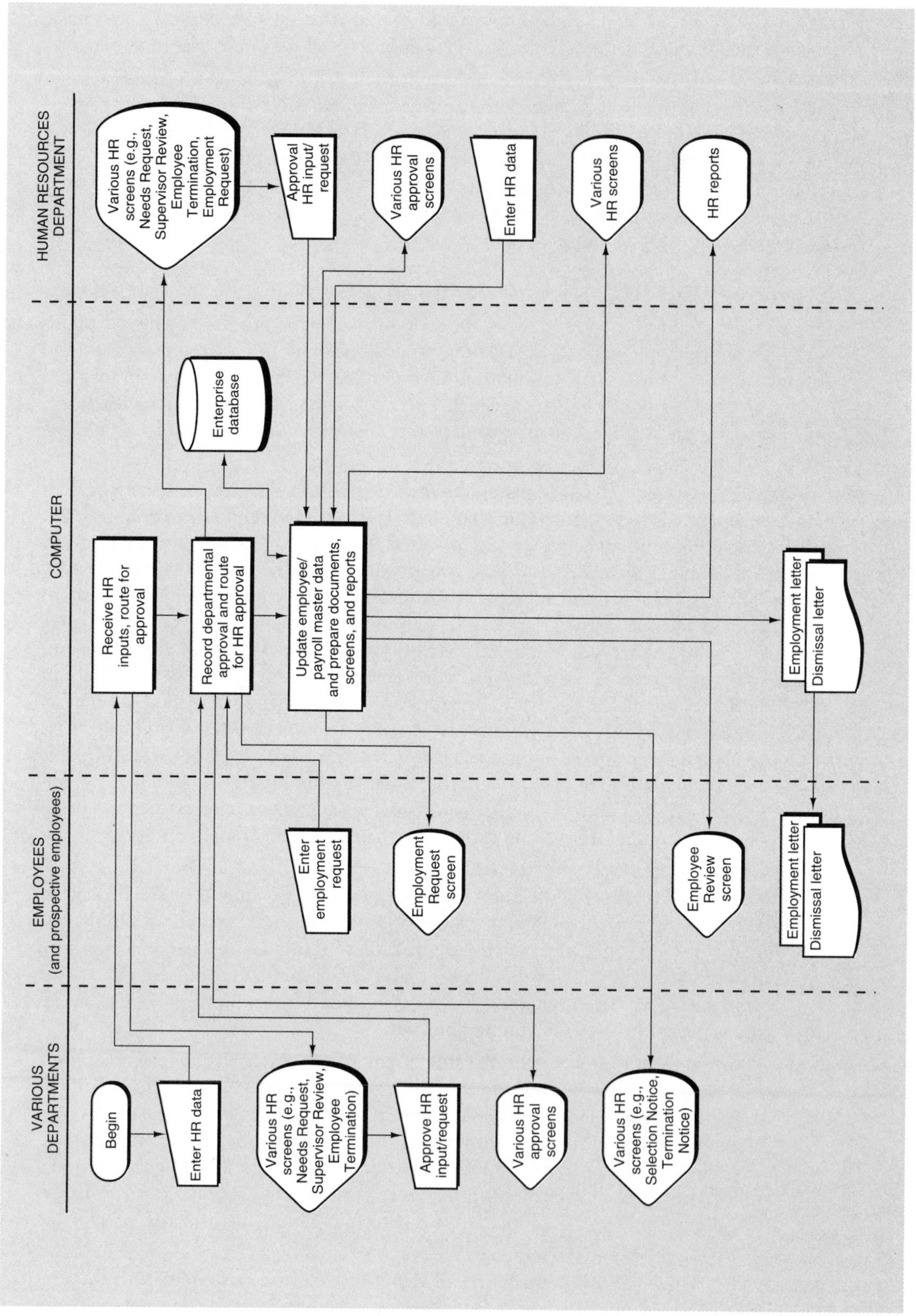

population of workers who currently are employed by the company. These candidates might be identified from (1) recommendations set forth in the needs request form, (2) recommendations based on the results of scanning the employee/payroll master data, or (3) recommendations based on the results of scanning the skills inventory data. Second, applications could be received from candidates outside the organization; the request for employment in the "Employees (and prospective employees)" column of the flowchart illustrates this interface.

Evaluating employees comprises a multitude of activities. Departmental managers and supervisors (again, outside the HR function) usually initiate actions affecting employees via the supervisor review screen shown in the flowchart. Then the manager of personnel appraisal and development (in HR) typically approves the review and implements such changes.

Terminating employees closes the employment process loop. Periodically, departmental managers and supervisors (in concert with HR managers) must make difficult decisions about the retention of employees. If a termination seems to be in order, the employee change screen is used to initiate the process of changing an employee's status from current employee to terminated employee.

The decision to terminate an employee is usually based on both qualitative and quantitative data. The HR management process assists the decision process by keeping track of certain kinds of quantitative data. For example, data concerning the number of absences during a given period, the number of times tardy, or the number of poor performance reviews an employee has received may be maintained in the employee/payroll master data. In addition, data supplied by the labor-force planning table may indicate a need to reduce the size of the workforce. In addition to termination, any other changes in the employee's status, such as changes in salary or skill levels, also are transmitted through the employee change form.

Processing Logic and Process Outputs. Let's take some time now to follow the processing logic and review the process' outputs. HR requests initiated outside of the HR department must be approved within that department and then routed to HR for their approval. Some data may be entered within HR (e.g., inputs from unions, government agencies) and may or may not need approval within HR (no such approval is shown on Figure 14.4). Once approved in HR, the employee/payroll master data, skills inventory data, and labor-force planning data within the enterprise database are updated and various reports are made available to HR and other interested parties.

As you can see from the flowchart in Figure 14.4, several outputs are also produced. In the case of a new hire, an employment letter is sent to the employee, and a selection notice is sent to the department manager or supervisor. Feedback to employees concerning their job performance is provided through an employee review form (paper, online, or both), which may be just a copy of the supervisor review form with some additional comments and notes added by the manager of personnel appraisal and development. Also, employees are notified of a dismissal action through a dismissal letter, with a termination notice being sent to the operating department manager.

In addition to the outputs shown on the flowchart, an HR management process must prepare reports for a variety of government and non-government entities. For example, the payroll process must send reports concerning employee federal, state, and local taxes. These payroll reports are discussed later in the chapter. HR-type reports might include those provided to the following:

- Unions
- Equal Employment Opportunity (EEO)
- Occupational Safety and Health Administration (OSHA)
- Department of Labor

E-BUSINESS

Also not shown in the flowchart are the numerous communications to employees of HR-related information. This information might take the form of job opening announcements, training information, phone books, benefits literature, policy and procedure manuals, and the like. Many companies have found that such materials can be disseminated effectively and efficiently through an HR portal, which serves as a central data source for such information.

Key Data Tables

CONTROLS

**ENTERPRISE
SYSTEMS**

Several tables of data are used by the HR and payroll processes. In an enterprise system these tables are included within the enterprise database. So, while these tables don't appear as separate data stores in Figure 14.4, we will discuss each next.

The *employee/payroll master data* will be defined and illustrated when we cover the payroll process. For now, let's consider how that data facilitates the HR function. Employee/payroll master data can help management determine the total cost of its workforce. It also aids in setting hiring policies in the context of providing information for compliance with affirmative action measures. Projected hiring needs may be influenced by seniority profiles. In addition, management may be given some sense of how well it is retaining employees; whether sick leave and vacation leave patterns are shifting; and, in conjunction with sales and productivity reports, how well performance matches workforce experience levels.

The **labor-force planning data** maintains data concerning an organization's short- and long-term staffing requirements. It includes data about various job specifications, with the specifications delineating the training and experience necessary to perform each job. The data also may contain statistical information regarding employee attrition by department, overall employee turnover, and so forth.

The **skills inventory data** catalogs each employee's set of relative skills. As employees gain new experience through on-the-job training or formal educational channels, the skills data is updated. When a job opening becomes available, HR managers will often consult the skills inventory data in search of qualified internal candidates. Management also may refer to this data in assigning employees to specific job tasks.

Although not discussed here, several other data stores are commonly found in an HR management process. Coverage of these data stores is beyond the scope of the chapter, but an end-of-chapter discussion question will ask you to speculate on what these data stores might be.

THE PAYROLL PROCESS

In this section, we first look at the imprint of the payroll function on the organization and then we describe the logic and data of the payroll process. We follow that with a description of a typical physical implementation of the payroll process and an analysis of the internal controls in that process.

Organizational Setting

Let's look briefly at the organizational structure of the payroll function. The discussion here is limited to an examination of *structure* only; we do not discuss the role of the controller or the other positions related to the payroll function. The organizational significance of the controller's area (where payroll resides) has been amply covered in earlier chapters.

The payroll function generally falls under the authority of the controller's office. Although the controller's office usually has line responsibility over the payroll function, it is important to note that certain activities, such as distributing paychecks, are influenced by the treasury function. Figure 14.5 is an organization chart illustrating the location of the payroll function.

Figure 14.5 Organization Chart Illustrating the Payroll Function

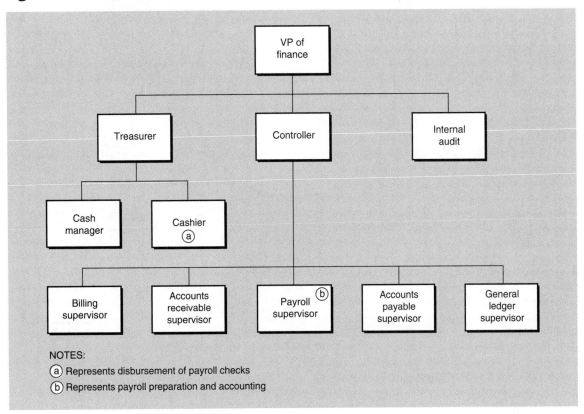

NOTES:

ⓐ Represents disbursement of payroll checks

ⓑ Represents payroll preparation and accounting

Logical Description of the Payroll Process

This section describes and illustrates the logical characteristics of a typical payroll process. Once again, we use data flow diagrams to explain the process logic. In addition, the section includes a discussion of the employee/payroll master data as it relates to the payroll process. We conclude this section by presenting the accounting events that are generated by the payroll process.

Figure 14.6 (page 524) is a context diagram of the payroll process. Study the diagram now to gain a broad overview of the process' major inputs, outputs, and interfaces. Fig-

Figure 14.6 Payroll Process—Context Diagram

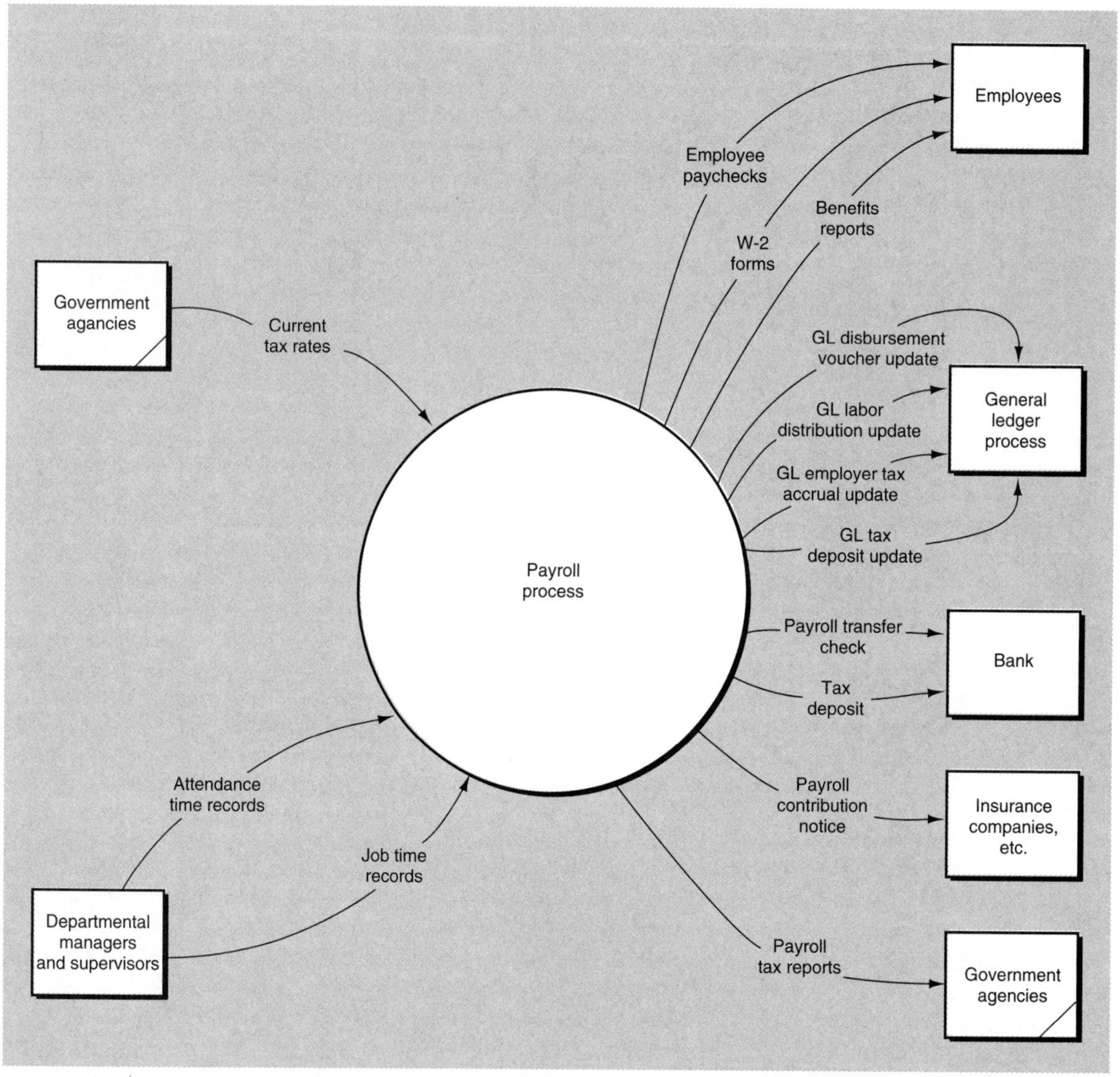

ure 14.7 presents a level 0 data flow diagram of the payroll process. This figure shows seven major activities carried out by the process; they are discussed and illustrated next.

To begin, process 1.0 periodically updates the *tax rates data* to ensure that current tax rates (federal, state, county, and city) are being used in preparing employee paychecks. Using a separate tax rates table (data store), rather than storing the rates in the employee/payroll master data, allows for easier data maintenance whenever tax rates change.

Two data flows enter the payroll process from departmental managers and supervisors: attendance time records and job time records. **Attendance time records** show the time periods that employees are in attendance at the job site and available for work. These records are used to calculate the gross amount of each employee's pay. **Job time records**, on the other hand, reflect the start and stop times on specific jobs. Their purpose is to

Figure 14.7 Payroll Process—Level 0 Diagram

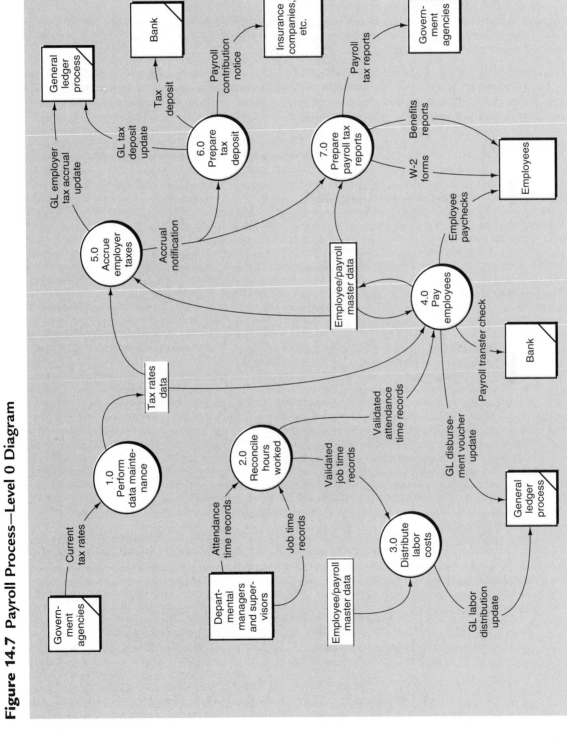

allow the distribution of payroll costs to jobs in process (or to other accounts).[4] Attendance time records are maintained near the entrance of the workplace and often take the physical form of time cards that are punched as employees come and go. Increasingly, however, employees "punch" in and out of work by swiping an employee identification card through or by a magnetic card reader. Job time records are prepared at the worksite by employees entering the time each job is started and stopped.

CONTROLS   Process 2.0 ("Reconcile hours worked") compares the total hours of each worker as shown by the attendance record with the hours reflected on the job time records for that employee. The hours should agree. This reconciliation is one of the payroll process *control* plans that is discussed in a subsequent section. Validated job time records are sent to process 3.0, which distributes labor costs to individual jobs, projects, or departments. Process 3.0 interfaces with the general ledger process to provide necessary journal entries for the distribution of labor charges.

Validated attendance time records initiate the payment to workers in process 4.0. Figure 14.8 explodes process 4.0 down to its next lower level. Let's discuss it next.

Figure 14.8 Payroll Process—Diagram 4

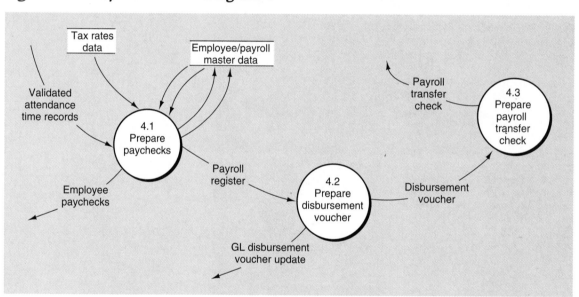

In calculating employees' gross and net pay, process 4.1 ("Prepare paychecks") retrieves data from both the employee/payroll master data and the tax rates data. Data retrieved from the employee/payroll master data includes employee identification code; employee status (active, inactive, etc.); employee name and address; employee tax status (single or married, number of exemptions, etc.); employee payment code (wage, salary, or commission employee); employee wage, salary, or commission rate; employee overtime rate; employee vacation accrual rate; and employee sick leave accrual rate. In addition, various kinds of payroll deductions, such as IRA or 401(k) deductions, union dues,

---

[4] To focus our investigation, we have limited the discussion to the preparation of paychecks for factory workers. Additional data flows would be necessary to deal with payroll for clerical, sales, and salaried employees.

and life insurance, are retrieved from the employee/payroll master data when an employee's gross and net pay is calculated.

Additions, deletions, and adjustments of various kinds to the employee/payroll master data represent another class of data necessary for processing an organization's payroll. This category of adjustments includes changes in salary or wage rates, address, department, tax exemptions, deduction authorizations, and so forth. For *control* reasons, these data items are entered in the data table by personnel in the *HR function*.

CONTROLS

Process 4.1 accumulates current, quarter-to-date, and year-to-date totals for each employee and reports this information via the data flow "Payroll register." This information also is used to update the employee/payroll master data. Finally, process 4.1 prints and distributes paychecks to employees as reflected in the "Employee paychecks" data flow.

The data flow "Payroll register" triggers process 4.2 ("Prepare disbursement voucher"). As we discussed in Chapter 13, many organizations use a disbursement voucher as documentation to recognize their payroll liability and to authorize the preparation of the payroll transfer check. Process 4.3 then prepares the transfer check and sends it to the bank to cover the organization's periodic net payroll.

Having walked through the details of process 4.0, let's now return to Figure 14.7 (page 525). Process 5.0 accrues employer-related tax liabilities, including Social Security tax (Federal Insurance Contributions Act [FICA]) and state and federal unemployment insurance taxes.[5] These accruals are reported to the general ledger process. On receipt of the accrual notification data flow, process 6.0 then prepares the tax deposit and notifies the general ledger process of the deposit.

Finally, process 7.0 provides assistance in satisfying government regulations regarding employees by preparing the following payroll tax reports:

- Form 941 (report of wages taxable under FICA)
- Form W-2 (wage and tax statement)
- Form 1099-R (annuities, pensions, or retired pay)
- Employee Retirement Income Security Act (ERISA) reports

The Employee/Payroll Master Data

The **employee/payroll master data** is the central repository of data about people who work for an organization. This data table combines data that originates in two functional areas: HR and payroll. As depicted in Figure 14.3 (page 518), each record contains employee identification data (e.g., personal data) as well as data used for the computation of employee paychecks (i.e., payroll data). The periodic preparation of the company payroll is greatly simplified by having both personal and payroll data available on each employee record. However, this situation has the potential of raising some *control* problems because staffs in two departments have the capability of making changes to the data. Furthermore, having both departments participate in the review of exception reports may result in duplication of effort and, in the case of accepting responsibility for errors, can lead to interdepartmental conflict. The solution to these problems is restricting online access for purposes of making data updates and reviewing errors so that each department can alter only those data fields over which it has predetermined authority. Such features are easily implemented with *enterprise systems* through organizational assignments in the employee/payroll master data.

ENTERPRISE SYSTEMS

CONTROLS

---

[5] Note that processes 5.0 and 6.0 also include non-tax items such as health insurance premiums, pension plan contributions, and the like.

Employee payroll records are keyed by an employee identification code, such as Social Security number or other identifier. The employee code can be designed so as to reflect certain employee attributes, such as department, factory, and position. Such code numbers can be used to provide management with labor-cost distributions.

Payroll data usually is recorded currently as well as on quarterly and year-to-date bases. This technique greatly reduces the effort necessary to meet periodic government reporting requirements and to produce ad hoc summary information for internal use. In addition, accumulating totals facilitates filing reports of amounts withheld for state and federal income taxes, unemployment insurance taxes, and Social Security taxes. At year-end, W-2 statements can be produced easily.

Accounting Entries Related to the Payroll Process

Exhibit 14.1 illustrates the four primary accounting entries recorded by the payroll process. The exhibit shows the source of each entry by cross-referencing the entry to the corresponding logical process in either Figure 14.7 or Figure 14.8. Take some time to study Exhibit 14.1. We assume you are already familiar with the entries from other accounting courses. In the section on Application of the Control Framework, we'll have more to say about the use of the "Payroll clearing" account in entries 1 and 2 of the exhibit.

Implementing the Payroll Process

This section provides a physical view of the *payroll process.* Again, we use a systems flowchart as the basis for discussion. The presentation also describes various operational and control aspects of a typical payroll process. Selected process outputs will be discussed as well.

ENTERPRISE
SYSTEMS

E-BUSINESS

CONTROLS

Figure 14.9 on page 530 shows a systems flowchart for a typical payroll process. Unlike its counterpart, Figure 14.4 (page 520), in which HR activities were processed in the *immediate mode,* Figure 14.9 shows payroll events being entered in real-time but processed in batches. In most organizations, payroll processing is generally done on a periodic basis. The process shown in Figure 14.9 reflects periodic recording of data, periodic updating of master data, and immediate generation of output.

This physical implementation employs much of the technology described earlier in this chapter, including employee self-service systems, employee access to these systems via Web browsers or kiosks, and enterprise systems with workflow modules. In addition, employee inputs to record attendance and work on specific jobs are made into an **electronic time management system**, a computer-based system that captures, stores, and reports time. Inputs to such systems are via the reading of magnetic strips on employee identification badges, *bar code* readers, and key entry. Payments to employees are made through a **payroll direct deposit system** whereby employee net pay is sent electronically through the banking system and deposited directly to the employees' bank accounts. One technology that is not utilized here is a **payroll service bureau**, a company that specializes in rendering payroll services to client companies for a fee. By using a service bureau, an organization can *outsource* much of the process depicted in Figure 14.9, including payroll calculation, paycheck preparation and direct deposit, payroll tax reporting and payments, and payments to insurance and retirement programs.[6]

Let's take some time now to follow the process logic. For now, please ignore the control annotations (P-1, P-2, etc.); we'll return to them in the section on application of

---

[6] Organizations typically employ payroll service bureaus. We depict our payroll system without one so that you can more easily see all of the steps in the payroll process.

Exhibit 14.1 Accounting Entries Related to the Payroll Process

1. PAY EMPLOYEES
    A. ESTABLISH VARIOUS PAYROLL LIABILITIES[a]
        (from process 4.2 in Figure 14.8):

Payroll clearing	XXXXX	
FIT withholdings payable		XXXXX
SIT withholdings payable		XXXXX
FICA tax withholdings payable		XXXXX
Accrued payroll		XXXXX

    B. RECORD THE DISBURSEMENT OF CASH
        (from process 4.3 in Figure 14.8):

Accrued payroll	XXXXX	
Cash		XXXXX

2. DISTRIBUTE PAYROLL TO VARIOUS ACCOUNTS
    (from process 3.0 in Figure 14.7):

Work in process (direct labor)	XXXXX	
Manufacturing overhead (indirect labor)	XXXXX	
General and administrative expense	XXXXX	
Selling expense	XXXXX	
Payroll clearing		XXXXX

3. ACCRUE EMPLOYER PAYROLL TAXES[a]
    (from process 5.0 in Figure 14.7):

Manufacturing overhead (tax on factory workers)	XXXXX	
General and administrative expense	XXXXX	
Selling expense	XXXXX	
FICA taxes payable		XXXXX
SUT taxes payable		XXXXX
FUTA taxes payable		XXXXX

4. RECORD TAX DEPOSITS[a]
    (from process 6.0 in Figure 14.7):

FIT withholdings payable	XXXXX	
SIT withholdings payable	XXXXX	
FICA tax withholdings payable	XXXXX	
FICA taxes payable	XXXXX	
SUT taxes payable	XXXXX	
FUTA taxes payable	XXXXX	
Cash		XXXXX

[a] Entries 1A, 3, and 4 would typically include deductions or accruals for non-tax items, such as health insurance premiums, pension plan contributions, and union dues.

the control framework. The process begins with factory workers recording attendance and job time in an *electronic time management system*.[7]

Periodically (i.e., weekly, bi-weekly) the time data and a batch total are downloaded from the *electronic time management system* and sent to the payroll system, where the batch totals are reconciled to ensure the integrity of the data transfer. The data are then

[7] Remember that the procedures shown in Figure 14.9 (page 530) relate to factory workers only. However, many of the steps illustrated could apply to payroll processing for many other employee categories. Generally, all employees are required to record their attendance and job time via some online time sheet.

Figure 14.9 The Payroll Process—Systems Flowchart

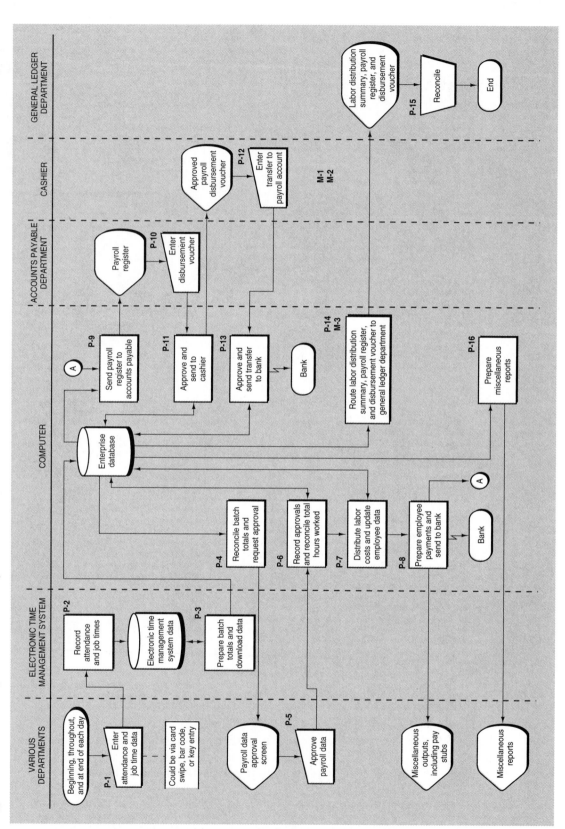

sent to appropriate supervisory personnel for approval. Once approved, the total hours worked for a pay period are reconciled (attendance time hours and job time hours). The payroll system then:

- Updates the employee/payroll master data and distributes the labor costs.
- Prepares the *employee paychecks* (i.e., electronic payments) and sends the payments to the bank for deposit into employee accounts.
- Prepares various outputs including the employee *pay stubs* that are posted to the HR portal.
- Sends the *payroll register* to the accounts payable department where a disbursement voucher is prepared for the amount of the payroll, including employee payments for taxes, insurance, and so on.

The disbursement voucher is sent to the cashier where a transfer is made for the amount of the payroll from the general checking account to the imprest payroll account. Finally, several items are sent to the general ledger department so that they might reconcile the amount to be paid (the *payroll register*), the job time incurred (the *labor distribution summary*), and amount disbursed from the bank (the *disbursement voucher*).[8]

In addition to the outputs previously discussed, many management reports can be produced for online viewing (paper outputs also may be available) from the *enterprise database* to manage and *control* the enterprise's operations. They become more meaningful and powerful if the data can be aggregated across the entire enterprise. These reports include the *deduction and benefits register,* the *state and local tax register,* the employees' *W-2 withholdings statements,* and a variety of reports and forms for government agencies. Several other reports and analyses may be generated from payroll processing. These could include reports of absenteeism and tardiness by employee and analyses of indirect labor by type of cost—supervision, materials handling, inspection, and so on. Also valuable in staff planning are certain aggregate statistics accumulated during payroll processing, such as total number of employees, total hours worked, total labor costs, average wage rate, rate of absenteeism, rate of turnover, and average cost of total fringe benefits. These statistics are most meaningful when trends in their values are analyzed and correlated with one another and with other factors. For example, useful management information may be obtained from correlating the rate of turnover with average hours worked per employee or the rate of absenteeism with the number of units that fail to pass quality control inspection.

CONTROLS

ENTERPRISE SYSTEMS

The Fraud Connection

Payroll, similar to cash disbursements, is an area ripe with fraud potential. After all, large organizations will make thousands of payments to employees for payroll and expense account reimbursements every payroll period (e.g., weekly, bi-weekly). Here are some of the types of payroll frauds, along with the median loss for each to an employer, that are committed.[9]

- *Ghost employees (median loss $275,000).* Employees who don't actually work for the company, but who receive paychecks. These can be recently departed employees or made-up persons.

---

[8] The procedures performed by accounts payable, the cashier, and the general ledger department could be automated. We show them here as manual procedures so that you might see the entire process more clearly. To simplify the flowchart, we have not shown the *exception routines* that would be needed wherever there is an approval or reconciliation.

[9] Joseph T. Wells, "Keeping Ghosts Off the Payroll," *Journal of Accountancy* (December 2002): 77–81.

- *Falsified hours and salary (median loss $30,000).* Employees exaggerate the time that they work or are able to increase the salary in their employee data.

- *Commission schemes (median loss $200,000).* Employees falsify the sales on which commissions are based or increase the commission rate in their employee data.

- *False workers' compensation claims (median loss $155,000).* Employees fake injuries to collect disability payments.

CONTROLS   Some of the procedures that can be used to prevent or detect these schemes include:

- *Segregation of duties* among personnel data creation and modification (HR), payroll preparation (payroll), disbursement (AP, and distribution [cashier]).

- *Direct deposit* of payroll to eliminate alteration, forgery, and theft of paper check. (Diversion of deposits into unauthorized accounts is not affected.)

- Check for *duplicate names, addresses,* and *Social Security* numbers in the employee data.

- Compare actual to budgeted payroll.

Other than compensation for work performed, as depicted in Figure 14.9 (page 530), employees are reimbursed for expenses incurred while conducting business for their employer. Employees may record such expenses online, in a manner similar to that used to record attendance and job times. Documentation of the expenses must then be sent to the accounts payable department so that they might verify the legitimacy of the expenses. Employee reimbursement may then take place much as it would be for regular payroll.

These reimbursements, often termed *expense accounts,* are often an area of fraud and abuse. Employee fraud schemes include:[10]

- Using legitimate documentation from personal expenses for a business expense.

- Overstating expenses by altering receipts.

- Submitting fictitious expenses by producing fake receipts.

- Obtaining multiple reimbursements for one expense by submitting copies of invoices.

CONTROLS   Such abuses can be minimized by formulating reasonable policies that compensate employees for their out-of-pocket expenses. Copies of invoices should only be accepted in extreme circumstances. Finally, expense account activities should be monitored on a regular basis to detect unusual patterns. In the next section we describe *controls* to prevent these abuses, as well as other typical payroll controls.

Application of the Control Framework

In this section, we apply the control framework to the systems flowchart presented in Figure 14.9 (page 530). Figure 14.10 (pages 533–534) presents a completed *control matrix*; Figure 14.9 is annotated to show the location of the various *control plans*. The control goals listed across the top of the matrix are derived from the framework presented in Chapter 7. Each recommended control plan listed in column 1 of the matrix is discussed in Exhibit 14.2 on pages 535–537. As you study the control plans, be sure to notice where they are located on the systems flowchart.

---

[10] Joseph T. Wells, "The Padding That Hurts," *Journal of Accountancy* (February 2003): 67–69.

Figure 14.10 The Payroll Process—Control Matrix

Recommended Control Plans	Control Goals of the Payroll Business Process									
	Control Goals of the Operations Process			Ensure efficient employment of resources (people, computers)	Ensure security of resources (cash, employee/ payroll master data)	Control Goals of the Information Process				
	Ensure effectiveness of operations					For time data inputs, ensure:			For employee/ payroll master data, ensure:	
	A	B	C			IV	IC	IA	UC	UA
Present Controls										
P-1: Enter time data close to the data's originating source	P-1			P-1			P-1	P-1		
P-2: Record input	P-2			P-2						
P-3: Calculate batch totals						P-3	P-3			
P-4: Computer agreement of batch totals									P-4	P-4
P-5: Approve attendance time data and job time data						P-5		P-5		
P-6: Reconcile attendance time data and job time data	P-6			P-6		P-6	P-6	P-6		
P-7: Distribute labor costs						P-7	P-7	P-7		
P-8: Independent paycheck distribution					P-8	P-8				
P-9: Approve payroll transfer check					P-9					
P-10: Preformatted screens	P-10			P-10				P-10		
P-11: Approve payroll transfer check					P-11					
P-12: Preformatted screens	P-12			P-12				P-12		
P-13: Approve payroll transfer check					P-13					
P-14: Accumulate payroll data for reconciliation of the payroll clearing account						P-14	P-14	P-14	P-14	P-14
P-15: Use a payroll clearing account						P-15	P-15	P-15	P-15	P-15
P-16: Prepare miscellaneous reports		P-16	P-16							

(continued)

Figure 14.10 The Payroll Process—Control Matrix (*continued*)

Recommended Control Plans	Control Goals of the Payroll Business Process									
	Control Goals of the Operations Process					Control Goals of the Information Process				
	Ensure effectiveness of operations			Ensure efficient employment of resources (people, computers)	Ensure security of resources (cash, employee/ payroll master data)	For time data inputs, ensure:			For employee/ payroll master data, ensure:	
	A	B	C			IV	IC	IA	UC	UA
Missing Controls										
M-1: Independent reconciliation of payroll bank account					M-1					
M-2: Use an imprest payroll bank account				M-2	M-2				M-2	M-2
M-3: Computer agreement of batch totals (agreement of run-to-run totals)					M-3	M-3	M-3	M-3	M-3	M-3

Legend:

Effectiveness goals:

A = Provide employees with timely paychecks.
B = Provide timely filing of tax returns and other reports to government agencies.
C = Comply with requirements of payroll and tax laws and regulations.

IV = Input validity
IC = Input completeness
IA = Input accuracy
UC = Update completeness
UA = Update accuracy

See Exhibit 14.2 (pages 535–537) for a complete explanation of control plans and cell entries.

Control Goals

The following *effectiveness* goals are shown in the matrix:

- Effectiveness of operations, within which three *representative effectiveness* goals are listed:

    A = Provide employees with timely paychecks.

    B = Provide timely filing of tax returns and other reports to government agencies.[11]

    C = Comply with the requirements of payroll tax laws and regulations.[12]

---

[11] Both effectiveness goals B and C are "compliance" goals as called for by the COSO report on internal control, which was discussed in Chapter 7. While goal B speaks to ensuring the timeliness of complying with such laws and regulations, goal C covers all other aspects of compliance, such as who must report, what wages are subject to payroll taxation, and so forth.

[12] In the interest of simplicity, we have not included goal columns in the matrix to show compliance with other laws and regulations related to the payroll process, such as compliance with Equal Employment Opportunity (EEO), Occupational Safety and Health Administration (OSHA), and Employee Retirement Income Security Act (ERISA) provisions. Many of these provisions apply more to the *HR* function than to the *payroll* function.

Exhibit 14.2 Explanation of Cell Entries for Control Matrix in Figure 14.10

P-1: *Enter time data close to the data's originating source.*

Effectiveness goal A: By having time information captured automatically, and eliminating the keying in of data, the timeliness of paycheck preparation is improved.

Efficient employment of resources: Entering time data directly into the computer system as that time is worked eliminates several payroll processing steps and the cost associated therewith, making for a more *efficient* employment of resources.

Time data input completeness: Eliminating hard copy time sheets and job time tickets removes the possibility that these documents could be lost or misplaced. As a result, real-time data capture should help to ensure input completeness.

Time data input accuracy: Because input errors can be corrected immediately, input accuracy should be improved. Additionally, automation of input entry reduces the opportunity for input errors to enter the process.

P-2: *Record input.*

Effectiveness goal A, Efficient employment of resources: Automatic recording of input event data is fast and reliable.

P-3: *Calculate batch totals.*

Input validity and input completeness: Batch totals arise from legitimate source documents (*input validity*). Batch totals ensure that all of the batched data is recorded (*input completeness*). The nature and extent of batch totals can vary: they can account for only the number of input events, the number of items or lines of data, dollar amounts, and/or hash totals. As such, batch totals themselves ensure the validity and completeness of the counts and amounts they represent. However, they do not necessarily ensure input accuracy—that takes place in the reconciliation, which is discussed in control plan P-4.

P-4: *Computer agreement of batch totals.*

Employee/payroll master data update completeness and accuracy: The attendance time data and batch totals—let's assume hash totals are used—are received from the *electronic time management system*. The computer calculates comparable hash totals for all attendance time data that were successfully updated to the employee/payroll master data. The computer-

calculated totals are then compared to the input totals and discrepancies are reconciled (the reconciliation process is not shown). Assuming that differences are promptly investigated and corrected, the control plan addresses both the goals of update completeness and update accuracy (UC and UA).

P-5: *Approve attendance time data and job time data.*

Time data input validity: Before they are forwarded to the payroll department for processing, time sheets and job time tickets are approved by operating department supervisors. These written approvals help to ensure input validity by assuring that time sheets are submitted only by bona fide employees and that these employees actually worked the time for which they will be paid.

Time sheet input accuracy: Because we assume that the supervisors also check that the hours reflected by the time sheets are correct, a cell entry is made in the input accuracy column.

P-6: *Reconcile attendance time data and job time data.*

Effectiveness goal A: By performing the reconciliation prior to undertaking further processing steps, we prevent errors from entering the process, thereby helping ensure that employee paychecks are prepared on a timely basis.

Efficient employment of resources: By performing the reconciliation, we preclude the wasted effort (inefficiency) that could result from detecting and correcting errors after the fact.

Time data input validity, completeness, and accuracy: If this control plan were not in place, discrepancies between the two data sets could result in employees being paid for work not performed. For example, if the number of hours captured on an employee's time record exceeds the total number of hours he or she has charged to various jobs throughout the week, then the company might pay this employee for services that he or she did not perform. This plan also addresses input completeness because we should have a valid attendance time record for every employee who has submitted job time tickets (and vice versa).

P-7: *Distribute labor costs.*

Time data input validity, completeness, and accuracy: See accounting entry 2 in Exhibit 14.1. This process distributes all of the labor costs to the

(continued)

Exhibit 14.2 Explanation of Cell Entries for Control Matrix in Figure 14.10 (*continued*)

appropriate expense categories. When this entry balances, as it should, we will detect and correct any discrepancies between the attendance time and job time. Therefore, in a manner similar to control P-6, this process ensures that only valid, complete, and accurate time data are input to the payroll process.

P-8: *Independent paycheck distribution.*

Security of resources: This plan entails having paychecks distributed to employees by an entity not otherwise involved in payroll processing (i.e., by an independent party such as a paymaster, a bursar, or via direct deposit to an employee's bank account). Of course, as part of this control plan, a paycheck would be released only if the employee presented proper identification. By *preventing* fraudulent payments, this plan protects the cash resource.

Time data input validity: The plan ensures that cash is expended only to employees who actually exist. In other words, this plan *detects* invalid inputs.

P-9: *Approve payroll transfer check.*

Security of resources: In order to transfer funds from the company's general account to its payroll bank account, the payroll register is sent to the accounts payable department, a disbursement voucher is prepared and *approved* in accounts payable and by the cashier, and the transfer is sent to the bank electronically. You will find the annotation, P-9, P-11, and P-13 in Figure 14.9 (page 530) to correspond to these steps. Approval of the payroll bank transfer helps to ensure that the cash asset is disbursed only for authorized expenditures.

P-10: *Preformatted screens.*

Effectiveness goal A, Efficient employment of resources: By structuring the data entry process, automatically populating fields, and preventing errors, preformatted screens simplify data input and save time (Effectiveness goal A) allowing a user to input more data over a period of time (Efficiency).

Input accuracy: As each data field is completed on a preformatted screen, the cursor moves to the next field on the screen, thus preventing the user from omitting any required data set. The data for fields that are automatically populated need not be manually entered, thus reducing input errors. Incorrectly formatted fields are rejected.

P-11: *Approve payroll transfer check.*

Security of resources: In order to transfer funds from the company's general account to its payroll bank account, the payroll register is sent to the accounts payable department, a disbursement voucher is prepared and *approved* in accounts payable and by the cashier, and the transfer is sent to the bank electronically. You will find the annotation, P-9, P-11, and P-13 in Figure 14.9 (page 530) to correspond to these steps. Approval of the payroll bank transfer helps to ensure that the cash asset is disbursed only for authorized expenditures.

P-12: *Preformatted screens.*

Effectiveness goal A, Efficient employment of resources: By structuring the data entry process, automatically populating fields, and preventing errors, preformatted screens simplify data input and save time (Effectiveness goal A) allowing a user to input more data over a period of time (Efficiency).

Input accuracy: As each data field is completed on a preformatted screen, the cursor moves to the next field on the screen, thus preventing the user from omitting any required data set. The data for fields that are automatically populated need not be manually entered, thus reducing input errors. Incorrectly formatted fields are rejected.

P-13: *Approve payroll transfer check.*

Security of resources: In order to transfer funds from the company's general account to its payroll bank account, the payroll register is sent to the accounts payable department, a disbursement voucher is prepared and *approved* in accounts payable and by the cashier, and the transfer is sent to the bank electronically. You will find the annotation, P-9, P-11, and P-13 in Figure 14.9 (page 530) to correspond to these steps. Approval of the payroll bank transfer helps to ensure that the cash asset is disbursed only for authorized expenditures.

P-14: *Accumulate payroll data for reconciliation of the payroll clearing account.*

Time data input validity, completeness, and accuracy: This plan accumulates the data from the enterprise database and presents it for reconciliation. Therefore, as described for plan P-15, matrix entries are appropriate in the input validity (IV), input completeness (IC), and input accuracy (IA).

Exhibit 14.2 Explanation of Cell Entries for Control Matrix in Figure 14.10 (*continued*)

Payroll master data update completeness and accuracy: Since plan P-15 is exercised *after* updates to the employee/payroll master data have occurred, the plan also meets the goals of update completeness (UC) and update accuracy (UA).

P-15: *Use a payroll clearing account.*

Time data input validity, completeness, and accuracy: A **payroll clearing account** is used to transfer the exact amount necessary to cover payroll checks and related expenses, such as taxes, during a given pay period. Funds are transferred into the account prior to the generation of payroll checks. The net of the transfer to the clearing account and payroll disbursements should zero out each pay period. Effectively, then, this plan does for gross labor *dollars* what plan P-6 did for labor *hours*—it reconciles the dollars that were calculated from two different input sources. Therefore, as in the case of plan P-6, matrix entries are appropriate in the input validity (IV), input completeness (IC), and input accuracy (IA).

Payroll master data update completeness, and accuracy: Since plan P-15 is exercised *after* updates to the employee/payroll master data have occurred, the plan also meets the goals of update completeness (UC) and update accuracy (UA).

P-16: *Prepare miscellaneous reports.*

Effectiveness goals B and C: Various reports can be prepared, electronically or on paper, to comply in a timely manner with tax and other government regulations. These reports can be prepared and sent automatically or by request of appropriate individuals.

M-1: *Independent reconciliation of payroll bank account.*

Security of resources: Implementation of this control plan would help ensure the safety of resources (cash) by identifying missing or unusual items entered into the account.

M-2: *Use an imprest payroll bank account.*

Efficient employment of resources: In an imprest system, or an **imprest payroll bank account**, the fund (account) is reimbursed for the *exact amount* of the disbursements made from the fund, rather than being reimbursed for round amounts. Applied to payroll, an imprest system requires that the transfer of cash from the general cash account to the payroll bank account is in the amount of the total of paychecks issued—no more, no less. The plan helps ensure efficiency of resource use because reconciling the payroll bank account is simpler when it is operated on an imprest basis.

Security of resources: Safety of the cash asset is ensured because fraudulent checks drawn on the payroll account should be readily detected. Losses due to fraudulent events would be limited to the amount of funds transferred to the account.

Time data input accuracy and employee/payroll master data update accuracy: Using an imprest payroll bank account helps check the accuracy of payroll processing (IA and UA) because the bank transfer prepared from the disbursement voucher must agree with the total net pay reflected by the payroll register.

M-3: *Computer agreement of batch totals (agreement of run-to-run totals).*

Security of resources, Input validity: By determining that updates to the employee/payroll master data reflect actual hours worked (attendance and jobs), we reduce the possibility of recording an invalid payroll event and dispensing cash for work that was not performed.

Input completeness, Input accuracy, Update completeness, Update accuracy: By comparing totals prepared before the input to those produced after the update, we would ensure that all events were input (*input completeness*), all events were input correctly (*input accuracy*), all events were updated to the master data (*update completeness*), and all events were updated correctly to the master data (*update accuracy*).

- Efficiency of payroll operations.
- Resource security. The resources of interest include cash and the information resources residing on the employee/payroll master data. Control plans should be in place to prevent unauthorized access to, or copying, changing, selling, or

destruction of, the employee/payroll master data. Equally, plans should be in place to prevent theft of, or any unauthorized use of, cash.

The five *information process* control goals, as adapted to the payroll process, are:

- Input validity (IV)[13] from the viewpoint of the payroll process, *valid* time data include those that reflect services performed by real employees.
- Input completeness (IC) and input accuracy (IA) for the time data.
- Update completeness (UC) and update accuracy (UA).

Recommended Control Plans
Take some time to study Exhibit 14.2 carefully, concentrating on understanding the relationship between each recommended control plan and the control goal(s) the plan helps to achieve. For many of the plans we discuss how it works and can assist in achieving the control goal.

SUMMARY

While not described as such in Chapters 10 through 13, the human resources management and payroll processes are an integral part of all the order-to-cash and the purchase-to-pay processes. As a member of the *purchase-to-pay process* in a merchandising organization, the HR management and payroll processes focus on business events and reports data related to employee expenses. As a member of the *order-to-cash process* in a service organization, the HR management and payroll processes assist in managing a service firm's major resource—people. In addition, the HR management and payroll processes capture employee work-related activities and use that data to bill customers for services rendered and to analyze service-related activities. As a member of the *purchase-to-pay process* in a manufacturing organization, the HR management and payroll processes capture and analyze data related to a major component of a manufactured product—employee labor.

Let's leave you with one final note about the HR management and payroll processes. We have emphasized the importance of these processes to the success of an organization and the significant resources dedicated to their operation. Here are six guidelines that should help an organization optimize the operation of these processes. At the same time these guidelines provide us some criteria to assess the *efficiency* and *effectiveness* of the operation of these processes:

1. Integrate payroll with other related processes such as HR management, electronic time and attendance recording, tax reporting, retirement, and general ledger and use the Web (i.e., HR portal) to connect these processes together.

2. Customize pay delivery by including options for paper checks, direct deposit, and payroll debit cards (pay is loaded on the card).

3. Understand each organization's culture and develop strategies to increase adoption of payroll options, such as direct deposit.

4. Consolidate related processes such as payroll, HR, and expense reimbursement, and minimize pay cycles. For example, moving from bi-weekly to monthly payroll can reduce costs by 30 to 50 percent.

---

[13] To focus our discussion, we have limited our coverage of process inputs to time data. Tax rates and job time data inputs have been ignored in the control matrix to simplify the illustration. Furthermore, neither of those two inputs is used to update the employee/payroll master data.

5. Since payroll and HR management are not key competencies, it makes sense to outsource these processes, where possible.

6. Build effective reporting and analytics. Analysis of labor costs can provide a powerful tool to improve the efficiency and effectiveness of operations.

REVIEW QUESTIONS

RQ 14-1 What is human capital management?

RQ 14-2 What is the human resources management process? What functions and activities does the process perform?

RQ 14-3 What is the payroll process? What functions and activities does the process perform?

RQ 14-4 What is the relationship between the HR process and the payroll process?

RQ 14-5 What role does each HR manager listed in Figure 14.2 (page 513) play?

RQ 14-6 What key decisions do the HR managers shown in Figure 14.2 make?

RQ 14-7 Describe an employee self-service system.

RQ 14-8 What are the principal inputs and outputs of the HR management process as reflected in the systems flowchart in Figure 14.4 (page 520)?

RQ 14-9 What data does the HR management process use? Describe the purpose of each.

RQ 14-10 What are the major logical functions the payroll process performs? Be sure to consult the logical DFDs presented in the chapter.

RQ 14-11 What are an attendance time record and a job time record? How is each used by the payroll process?

RQ 14-12 How are the tax rates data and the employee/payroll master data used by the payroll process?

RQ 14-13 What classes of general ledger journal entries are generated by the payroll process?

RQ 14-14 What is the purpose of each control plan listed in the control matrix (Figure 14.10 on pages 533–534)?

DISCUSSION QUESTIONS

DQ 14-1 In this chapter, we stated that many organizations have begun to view their human capital as an important variable in the formula of economic success. Discuss the role the HR management process plays in optimizing an organization's human capital.

DQ 14-2 Discuss the significance of having a separate organizational unit for the HR function (vice president of HR), as opposed to having the HR function housed within an administrative organizational unit (director of HR).

DQ 14-3 Examine the placement of the manager of human resource systems in the organization chart of Figure 14.2 (page 513) and review the typical functional responsibilities of this manager, decisions made, and information needs as shown in Table 14.1 (pages 514–515). Describe possible alternatives for the placement of this function in the formal organization chart and discuss the relative advantages for each placement. Consider the variables of centralized versus decentralized organizational structures.

DQ 14-4 Discuss the role unions and government agencies play in the design of procedures for the HR management process.

DQ 14-5 A number of organizations have recently instituted a position called "manager of human resource systems." Speculate about why this position may become strategically important to organizations in the future.

DQ 14-6 Discuss the significance of the employee/payroll master data in relation to the HR function and the payroll function.

DQ 14-7 Without redrawing the figures, discuss *how*, if at all, the DFDs shown in Figures 14.6 through 14.8 (pages 524, 525, and 526, respectively) would change as a result of the following *independent* situations (be specific in describing the changes):

    a. Paying a worker for vacation or sick pay, as opposed to paying her for hours actually worked.

    b. Paying some workers on a piecework basis.

    c. Paying some workers a commission based on sales.

    d. Preparing and distributing a paycheck "early" (i.e., in advance of the customary pay date).

    e. Having a work environment where all employees are salaried (i.e., none are paid hourly).

DQ 14-8 a. List several *effectiveness* goals for the HR management process.

    b. List some of the additional data stores that a typical HR management process might have.

    c. Discuss the significance of the data stores in part b in relation to achieving the effectiveness goals of the HR management process (part a).

DQ 14-9 Tax rates data is depicted in both the logical DFDs and the physical implementation systems flowchart for the payroll process in this chapter. Discuss the advantages of maintaining a separate data store versus incorporating such data into "master" data, such as the employee master data. Support your argument by constructing an analogy between the tax rates data and pay rates data (i.e., one containing hourly pay rates) for employees who are compensated for the hours actually worked.

DQ 14-10 Consult the systems flowcharts in Figures 14.4 (page 520) and 14.9 (page 530). Discuss how these processes implement the concept of segregation of duties discussed in Chapter 8. Be specific as to which entity (or entities) performs each of the four functions depicted in Table 8.2 (page 269). Limit your discussion to the process of preparing employee paychecks.

PROBLEMS

NOTE: As with the other business process chapters, the first few problems are based on the processes of specific companies. Therefore, the problem material starts with case narratives of those processes.

CASE STUDIES

CASE A: Everlast Tools

Everlast Tools is a division of a large manufacturing company. Everlast makes a variety of tools. Most employees are paid on an hourly basis. Employees receive yearly reviews to evaluate performance and to determine an appropriate pay increase. Everlast's payroll is processed by the corporate payroll department from input documents prepared by Everlast. The following *HR and payroll* procedures are related to the hourly payroll employees at Everlast.

Department supervisors initiate requests for additional employees by filling out a three-part employee requisition form. Once a requisition is filled out, the department supervisor signs it, files a copy by date, and gives the remaining two copies to the production supervisor. The production supervisor reviews and signs the copies and gives them to the HR manager. The HR manager reviews the request with the division controller. They both sign the requisition. The pay rate for the job also is determined at that time and included on the requisition. If the requisition is approved, the HR manager initiates hiring procedures by placing advertisements in local papers and announcing the opening internally. The HR manager and the supervisor interview the applicants together. They then evaluate the applicants and make a selection. The HR manager and the employee fill out the two-part wage and deduction form. The HR manager files a copy of the wage and deduction form and the personnel requisition by employee name. The remaining copies of each form are given to the division accountant.

The HR manager selects and reviews the records from the personnel file for employees who are due for their annual review. The HR manager puts some basic employee information on a three-part review form and gives it to the appropriate supervisor for his evaluation. The supervisor completes and signs the form, files a copy, and gives the remaining copies to the production supervisor, who reviews and signs the evaluation. The production supervisor returns it to the HR manager. The HR manager reviews it with the controller. They assign a new rate and sign the review form, which is given to the division accountant.

The division accountant uses the new employee information and the employee review form to prepare payroll action notices. The accountant signs the payroll action notices and files them with the other related forms by date. Each week, a clerk in the corporate payroll department retrieves the payroll forms from the division accountant, checks the signature on all payroll action notices, and processes the payroll. The forms, checks, and reports are sent back to the division accountant. He refiles the forms and gives the checks to the production supervisor, who in turn distributes them to the employees.

CASE B: Biochem Labs

Biochem Labs is an independent laboratory that performs research under contract to the government and non-government entities. The following process is used by Biochem to process weekly payroll for hourly support and service personnel. Biochem has a legacy computer system to which payroll personnel have online access from PCs located on their desks.

Each week, the computer prints time sheets using the employee/payroll master data. After receiving the time sheets from IT, the payroll department distributes them to the various department supervisors who give them to employees. The employees fill in the time sheets each day and give them to their supervisors at the end of each week. Department supervisors review and sign the time sheets and return them to the payroll department. Payroll clerks key the time sheets into the current week's payroll activity data and then file them alphabetically by department.

At the start of the weekly payroll process, the computer creates the current week's pay data, using the employee/payroll master and the current week's activity data. The following items are then printed from the pay data: checks with attached stubs, stubs for directly deposited checks, bank deposit slips for directly deposited checks (one deposit slip for each bank, which lists all the accounts to be credited), a single check for each bank receiving direct deposits, a check register, and various payroll reports. The computer operator gets the check-signing machine from the cashier and signs the checks. The checks, stubs, direct deposit slips, and check register are given to the cashier. The payroll reports are given to the payroll department.

The cashier checks the total and the number of checks against the payroll register. She sends the checks with attached stubs and the stubs for direct deposits to the department supervisors, who give them to the employees. She then mails the direct deposit slips and checks to the banks.

P 14-1 For the company assigned by your instructor, complete the following requirements:

a. Prepare a table of entities and activities.

b. Draw a context diagram.

c. Draw a *physical* data flow diagram (DFD).

d. Prepare an annotated table of entities and activities. Indicate on this table the groupings, bubble numbers, and bubble titles to be used in preparing a level 0 logical DFD.

e. Draw a level 0 *logical* DFD.

P 14-2 For the company assigned by your instructor, complete the following requirements:

a. Draw a systems flowchart.

b. Prepare a control matrix, including explanations of how each recommended existing control plan helps to accomplish—or would accomplish in the case of missing plans—each related control goal.

c. Annotate the flowchart prepared in part a to indicate the points where the control plans are being applied (codes P-1 . . . P-*n*) or the points where they could be applied but are not (codes M-1 . . . M-*n*).

P 14-3 For the company assigned by your instructor, redraw the systems flowchart assuming that the company utilizes an enterprise system, an electronic time management system, an employee self-service system, and an HR Web portal.

P 14-4 Ace Manufacturing has several large divisions. The flowchart shown in Figure 14.11 describes the termination and exit interview procedures used by each division.

Figure 14.11 Ace Manufacturing: Divisional Employee Termination/Exit Interview Procedures for Problem 14-4

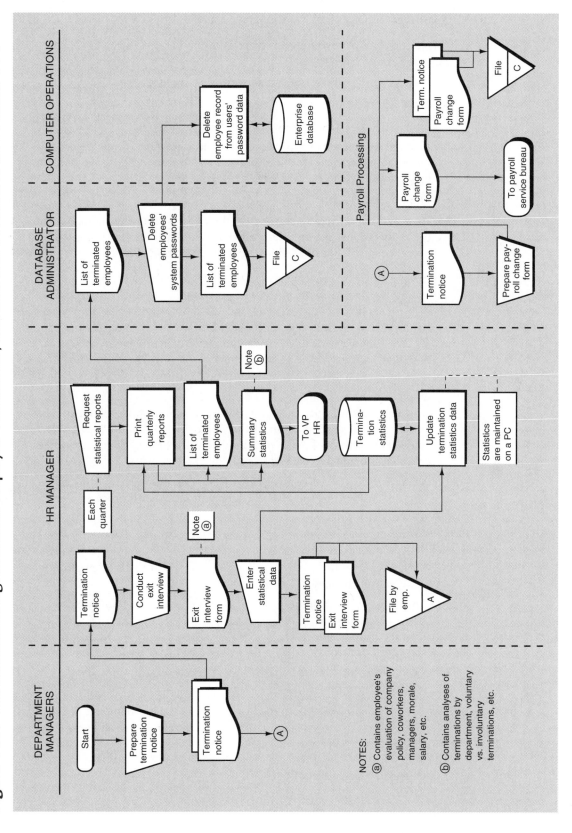

NOTES:

ⓐ Contains employee's evaluation of company policy, coworkers, managers, morale, salary, etc.

ⓑ Contains analyses of terminations by department, voluntary vs. involuntary terminations, etc.

Required:

(Make and state any assumptions that you think are necessary.) For the Ace Manufacturing process:

a. Prepare a table of entities and activities.

b. Draw a context diagram.

c. Draw a *physical* data flow diagram (DFD).

d. Prepare an annotated table of entities and activities. Indicate on this table the groupings, bubble numbers, and bubble titles to be used in preparing a level 0 logical DFD.

e. Draw a level 0 *logical* DFD.

f. Identify the principal weaknesses in the process from the standpoint of both operational effectiveness/efficiency and the generic information process control goals of validity, completeness, and accuracy.

P 14-5 Bubble 4.1 in Figure 14.8 (page 526) is called "Prepare paychecks."

Required:

a. Explode that bubble down to the next level (i.e., prepare diagram 4.1.1) to show the detailed steps involved in this process. *Hint:* Recognize that each employee paycheck also would include a pay stub. Also note, in Figure 14.8, that the data flows out of bubble 4.1 include a payroll register.

b. In your solution to part a, you should have some data flows out of data stores to process bubbles and other data flows from bubbles to data stores. For each data flow to or from data stores, *specify* the nature of the data that is being accessed or stored.

P 14-6 Following is a list of 10 control plans from this chapter (or from earlier chapters and tailored to the HR management and payroll processes of this chapter):

Control Plans

A. Specific approval of HR/payroll changes

B. One-for-one checking of hours per attendance time data and hours shown on pay stubs

C. Reconciling total hours per attendance time data with total hours per job time data

D. Imprest payroll bank account

E. Computer agreement of batch totals

F. Hash totals of employee ID numbers

G. Electronic time management system

H. Personnel termination procedures

I. Computer matching of employee ID numbers

J. Independent reconciliation of payroll bank account

Required:

Listed next are eight process failures that have control implications. Write the numbers 1 through 8 on your solution sheet. Next to each number insert *one* letter from the preceding list indicating the control plan that would *best* prevent the process failure from occurring. Also, give a brief, one- to two-sentence explanation of your choice. A letter should be used only once, with two letters left over.

Process Failures

1. A computer operator was fired for incompetence. During the two-week notice period, the operator "fired a parting shot" by destroying several computer files.

2. A novice data entry clerk had an error rate ranging from 10 to 20 percent during the first few weeks on the job. These errors resulted in several overpayments and underpayments to employees.

3. A payroll clearing account in the general ledger is debited for the gross pay amount paid to employees and is credited for the gross pay amount distributed to jobs in process or to expense categories. In theory, the clearing account should reflect a zero balance, but it consistently shows either a debit or credit balance.

4. The supervisor of an operating department prepared a fictitious attendance time record for a nonexistent employee and then deposited the bogus paycheck to her personal bank account.

5. An employee in the HR department prepared a bogus change of pay form to increase his salary by $25 per week. The form was submitted for processing and was entered into the system without being challenged.

6. Attendance time data is often not entered, not entered in a timely manner, or not accurate.

7. Each weekly pay period a check is drawn on the general cash account and deposited to the payroll bank account in an amount "estimated" to be sufficient to cover the actual total of payroll checks issued that week. As a result, the payroll account runs a balance of several thousand dollars (noninterest-bearing), a situation that the newly hired treasurer has questioned.

8. In entering attendance time data, the data entry clerk misread all 7s as 9s. Although some time data were rejected, other data were processed against wrong employees, who happened to have a 9 instead of a 7 in the comparable position in their employee ID number.

P 14-7 Following is a list of 10 control plans from this chapter (or from earlier chapters and tailored to the HR management and payroll processes of this chapter).

Control Plans

A. Fidelity bonding

B. Periodic performance reviews

C. Preformatted HR/payroll screens

D. Online data entry of HR/payroll data

E. Automatic preparation of attendance time sheets for the next pay period (i.e., turnaround documents)

F. Review of all HR changes for compliance with union and government regulations

G. Use of a skills inventory data

H. Programmed edits—reasonableness checks

I. Programmed edits—format checks

J. Computer calculations of gross pay, deductions, and so on

Required:

Listed next are eight statements describing either the achievement of a control goal (i.e., a process success) or a process deficiency (i.e., a process failure). Write the numbers 1 through 8 on your solution sheet. Next to each item insert *one* letter from the preceding list indicating the *best* control to achieve the desired goal or to address the process deficiency described. A letter should be used only once, with two letters left over.

Control Goals or Process Deficiencies

1. Should have prevented a data entry error of keying all hours worked with an extra digit (40 hours entered as 400, 45 hours as 450, etc.).

2. Helps to achieve efficiency of resource use (i.e., by reducing time needed for data entry) and accuracy of data entry.

3. Should have prevented the organization's being sanctioned for failure to abide by Equal Employment Opportunity (EEO) guidelines.

4. Should have prevented a data entry error of keying all zeroes as the letter *o* (40 entered as 4o, ID# 3062 entered as 3o62, etc.).

5. Would not have prevented employee dishonesty but would have helped the organization "recover" from such dishonesty.

6. Helps in assigning employees to particular jobs.

7. Precludes time card input errors by having certain data preprinted on the attendance time sheet.

8. Helps ensure employee job satisfaction by providing employees with appropriate feedback.

P 14-8 Use the data flow diagrams in Figures 14.7 and 14.8 (pages 525 and 526, respectively) to solve this problem.

Required:

Prepare a four-column table that summarizes the payroll processes, inputs, and outputs. In the first column, list the seven processes shown in the level 0 diagram (Figure 14.7). In the second column for bubble 4.0 only, list the subsidiary functions shown in the lower-level diagram (Figure 14.8). For bubbles *other than* 4.0, there will be no subsidiary functions shown in column 2. For *each* process shown in column 1 (or subsidiary process listed in column 2), list the data flow names or the data stores that are inputs to that process (column 3) or outputs of that process (column 4). The following table has been started for you to indicate the format for your solution.

Solution Format

Summary of the payroll processes, inputs, and outputs

Process	Subsidiary Functions	Inputs	Outputs
1.0 Perform data maintenance	None diagrammed in this chapter	Current tax rates	Tax rates data
2.0 Reconcile hours worked	None diagrammed in this chapter	Attendance time records	. . . Continue solution . . .

KEY TERMS

human capital management (HCM)

human resources (HR) management process

payroll process

labor-force planning data

skills inventory data

attendance time records

job time records

employee/payroll master data

electronic time management system

payroll direct deposit system

payroll service bureau

payroll clearing account

imprest payroll bank account

Integrated Production Processes (IPP)

In mid-1999, the Toyota Motor Corp. shook up the automotive industry when it announced it would be able to produce a custom order auto in just five days. The announcement came in an industry known for taking closer to 60 days for custom orders. Even DaimlerChrysler Corp., who was perceived to have the industry lead, was averaging over twice the Toyota-announced turnaround at 12 days. Most automotive manufacturers have been working with a goal of achieving 10 days in the future—a time that falls well short of that promised in the Toyota announcement. Toyota plans to achieve the newly announced custom order fulfillment promise with its "next generation just-in-time logistics system." This system is driven by a 15-day advanced plan "virtual production line," which forms the initial manufacturing plan. This plan generates the provisional orders for parts from its suppliers that can be revised up to five days before actual production. The process is facilitated by a complex parts delivery system that provides for parts pick-ups from suppliers and delivery to the plant on average 24 times a day. This strategy further reduces parts storage requirements by 37 percent at the plant level and reduces in-house finished goods (i.e., automobiles) inventories by 28 percent on average, helping significantly reduce inventory carrying costs. In this chapter, we explore the issues surrounding production scheduling and inventory management in greater detail and look at the role of the accountant and business advisor in improving the efficiency and effectiveness of integrated production processes.

chapter 15

Learning Objectives

- To appreciate the forces that exist in the contemporary production environment and the trends that have emerged.

- To understand the role of enterprise systems (ES) in the integration of the total manufacturing environment.

- To understand the key inputs, outputs, data, processes, and terminology included in modern integrated production processes.

- To understand the relationship between integrated production processes and other key business processes within a manufacturing organization, including human resource management, purchasing, order entry/sales, and inventory management.

- To understand the role of inventory management systems and their relationship to integrated production processes.

In this chapter, we give an overview of one business process, the integrated production process (IPP). We break down the basic steps in the IPP, highlighting the importance of enterprise systems; automation; and integration between IPP and the order entry/sales, purchasing, human resource management, and inventory management processes for success in today's complex, global manufacturing environment.

SYNOPSIS

We begin by examining the state of competition in the international manufacturing environment and the pressures that continue to increase for organizations to reduce costs, increase the global reach of their operations across the value chain, and quickly design and deliver innovative products to meet customers' ever-increasing demands. In this context, we describe how product and process innovation, supply chain management, and management accounting systems combine with IPP to manage global complexity. Then we provide an overview of the steps in the IPP, emphasizing the role of enterprise systems and management accounting information in managing this process. We also discuss inventory management and its important role in the IPP.

Our approach in this chapter is to provide a broad overview of the IPP, focusing on how they integrate with other processes you have already discussed and their importance to achieving the strategic objectives of manufacturing businesses. We use a level 0 data flow diagram to illustrate these processes. Entire books have been devoted to some individual topics in this chapter, so each process described may encompass quite a number of individual activities. Our aim is to provide you with an idea of the key goals of the processes, a basic understanding of how they work, and exposure to some of the key terminology involved. We do not present a system flowchart or control matrix for the IPP. Though controls are very important in IPP, especially for assuring a high level of operational effectiveness, the level of detail necessary to make these documents meaningful would be beyond the scope of our coverage here.

COMPETING IN A GLOBAL MANUFACTURING ENVIRONMENT

If one area in particular has been most impacted by global competition, it is clearly the manufacturing sector. Manufacturing is generally the quickest route for developing countries to increase their wealth and increase the wages of their citizens. Further, business as a whole and manufacturing in particular know no national boundaries in the rapidly growing global marketplace.

For instance, several Asian countries have become major players in the automobile industry, competing heavily in the United States, Australia/New Zealand, and European markets. Automakers (as well as manufacturers in a host of other industries) have been forced to become lean, automated, customer-focused, and efficient organizations in order to survive. Recent studies have reflected such efforts with observations of marked improvements in productivity, particularly in the United States.

Dealing with the complexity that results from mounting pressures caused by exploding globalization is key to success in the manufacturing sector. In a 2003 survey of over 392 manufacturing executives across North America and Europe, Deloitte Touche Tohamatsu identified 3 key drivers of complexity in manufacturing operations in the new millennium:[1]

- *Pressure to reduce costs throughout the value chain.* Because of global competition and the enormous buying power of "mega-retailers" like Wal-Mart, many companies have been forced to move operations across their value chains throughout the globe to reduce costs. Companies surveyed expect growth in sourcing of operations, from engineering to raw material supply to manufacturing, in other countries such as China and India, with little growth in these operations domestically.

- *Pursuit of new lucrative markets and channels.* Given the cost of developing and manufacturing products, companies continually seek to enter new markets around the globe to pursue growth and economies of scale and scope. The pursuit of new, growing markets like China also explains why these same manufacturers are sourcing more and more of their value chain operations in these countries, to better and more efficiently serve these customers.

- *The quickening pace of product innovation.* Executives surveyed reported new product innovation as the number one driver of revenue growth. Additionally, with competition and globalization come greater and greater efforts to customize products to meet local needs. Coupling this need for customization with reductions in the lifecycle for new products leads to a need to introduce more successful products more quickly than ever. Companies surveyed reported revenues from products introduced in the last three years to be 21 percent of total revenues in 1998, projecting this percentage to grow to 27 percent in 2003 and 35 percent in 2006. This is complemented by shrinking product development times from 18 months in 2000, to 16 months in 2003, and 13 months in 2006.

A Deloitte & Touche report describes the key characteristics of those companies that are successful at managing the pressures resulting from global complexity.[2]

---

[1] *The challenge of complexity in global manufacturing: Critical trends in supply chain management*, London: Deloitte Touche Tohmatsu, 2003.

[2] *Mastering complexity in global manufacturing: Powering profits and growth through value chain synchronization*, London: Deloitte & Touche LLP, 2003.

- *Improved internal business processes in the areas of customers, products, and supply chains.* These efforts include increased activities related to marketing, sales, and customer service; better innovation, engineering, and research and development for products; and improved sourcing, manufacturing, and distribution for supply chains.

- *Better use of technology to increase integration within and between these three areas (customers, products, and supply chains).* Benefits from improved operations in these three areas are further leveraged by using *enterprise systems* technologies like *customer relationship management,* as discussed in Chapter 10, to link marketing sales and service and provide information measures such as customer service and retention; *product lifecycle management* (introduced in Chapter 2 and discussed later in the chapter) to tie together the steps of product development and better manage profitability; and warehouse and transportation optimization systems to tie together suppliers, distribution, and manufacturing and develop end-to-end *supply chain management* strategies as discussed in Chapter 12.

ENTERPRISE SYSTEMS

- *Better general capabilities in the areas of collaboration, flexibility, visibility, and technology.* These capabilities, both within the company and extending out to customers and suppliers, help the best companies to integrate their efforts across customer, product, and supply chain activities to focus on overall profitability. They ensure that engineers consider the flexibility of products they design, that supply chain designers consider the future need for rapid change in supply chain processes, and that customer communication lines lead to products that better meet or exceed customer expectations.

Technology Application 15.1 (page 552) presents three different case studies illustrating how companies have demonstrated these characteristics to increase overall profitability.

Deloitte & Touche's research shows that globalization and efforts to manage it pay off. The 7 percent of survey respondents with both high value chain capabilities and high global dispersion of sourcing, manufacturing, engineering, and marketing/sales operations across their value chains were 73 percent more profitable than their counterparts with low value chain capabilities and global dispersion.

In the following sections, we further explore several of the trends in global manufacturing companies that help them achieve the level of integration described previously. In particular, we examine the following four key components of effective, integrated production processes in more depth:

1. Product innovation
2. Production process innovation
3. Supply chain management
4. Management accounting systems

Product Innovation

Designing innovative products and getting them to market quickly is key to competition in the complex global manufacturing environment. To accomplish rapid product innovation, cooperation between engineering, manufacturing, and marketing is vital. Production conventionally has been organized along functional lines. Under the functional approach to developing a product, the process is undertaken as a series of discrete, independent steps, such as design, engineering, purchasing, manufacturing, and so forth. The schism that results between the "me think" design component and the "you

---

Technology Application 15.1

Managing Global Manufacturing Complexity

Case 1: Motorola synchronizes product development

Between mid-1990 to 2002, Motorola's PCS (Personal Communications Sector) business went from owning 50 percent of the personal handset market to only 15 percent of the market, half of the share of rival Nokia. The decrease in market share was accompanied by losses of $6 billion in 2001 and 2002. The solution proposed by Motorola was to institute a "war on complexity" to simplify its supply chain. The starting point was a reengineering of its product design function, which had become highly complex with too many products and incompatible parts, leading to delays in getting new products to market. The centerpiece of the solution was a complexity index for designing, engineering, and manufacturing. The index—a compilation of information about factors like part counts, test times, assembly times, component reuse and use of industry standard parts—focused on the effect of each of these factors on key business drivers like responsiveness. Another factor in reducing complexity was a move to developing standardized model designs that are only customized for specific customer needs at the end of their lifecycle, a process called *product postponement*. This allows for maximum fit to customer needs as well as maximum standardization. The result was fewer different products; more interchangeable parts; simplified inventory management, procurement, distribution, and product support; and a return to profitability.

Case 2: GlaxoSmithKline synchronizes manufacturing plants to optimize supply chain management

GlaxoSmithKline, a UK pharmaceutical company, tackled complexity through global, rather than local optimization of its supply chain.

Prior to reengineering, plants produced for the countries or continents where they were located. The changes resulted in a drastic reduction in the number of plants, which now serve regions of the world. Plants are focused on one of three areas—flexible plants that can ramp up quickly to make new products; plants procuring large quantities of established drugs, whose volumes are more predicable; and plants dedicated to established pharmaceuticals, especially those for small markets. This strategy, which results in single plants serving larger regions around the world, helps the company optimize supply chain activities for each type of product and overcome local supply constraints that might get in the way of quickly delivering new products. The result was savings of $500 million a year.

Case 3: Samsung Electronics gets in touch with customers and markets

Samsung, a South Korean consumer electronics company and the number one maker of big-screen TVs, has grown through better customer information gathering that helps them improve sales forecasts and assure orders are fulfilled on time. To gather vital qualitative and quantitative information, Samsung hires third-party "detailers" who visit stores like Best Buy and Circuit City that stock Samsung products. These detailers monitor quality and stock levels, evaluate displays and promotions, and monitor competitor products and prices, entering data about each of these directly into Samsung's enterprise system. They also talk with customers about new product ideas at very early stages of product development. Employees from product development, sales, and marketing then use this information to make improvements to product designs, sales forecasts, and promotion strategies.

Sources: *Mastering complexity in global manufacturing: Powering profits and growth through value chain synchronization*, London: Deloitte & Touche LLP, 2003; C. Whyte, "Motorola's Battle with Supply and Demand Chain Complexity," *iSource Business*, April/May 2003.

---

do" manufacturing element has been extremely inefficient both in terms of getting products to market on time and controlling production costs.

Enterprise systems facilitate integration of all aspects of the product design, manufacturing, and marketing processes. Dramatic productivity gains have been achieved by companies that adopt a *value chain* approach that views production as a continuum, beginning with product design and running all the way through materials acquisition, manufacturing, distribution, marketing, and servicing of the product in the field. For example, with a value chain approach and effective utilization of enterprise systems, when changes are made to product design (engineering change orders), the change is automatically messaged to the production facilities and the change is incorporated in real-time. Japanese manufacturers have been particularly successful in improving product quality by fostering a close cooperation between the functions of design and manufacturing. Design engineers and manufacturing engineers coordinate their efforts to design a defect-free product. The result has been a streamlined manufacturing process that eliminates (or drastically reduces) the need to inspect the product.

ENTERPRISE SYSTEMS

More recently, companies have worked to implement *product lifecycle management (PLM)* systems, which are *ERP* modules or *enterprise systems* add-ons that organize data by product, including designs, manufacturing specifications, quality, and warranty performance. These systems allow collaborative access to this data across the organization by key suppliers and customers and increase innovation in product design, reduce design time, and improve product performance. Technology Application 15.2 (page 554) provides a description of Procter & Gamble's success in using *product lifecycle management*.

Production Process Innovation

A major contribution of the Japanese has been their managing of *throughput time*. **Throughput time** is the time it takes from when authorization is made for goods to be produced to when the goods are completed. Japanese companies have accomplished much in this area, mainly by switching from *push* to *pull* manufacturing. With **push manufacturing**, the sales forecast drives the production plan, and goods are produced in large batches. Each machine performs its operation on the batch, and then the entire job waits until the operation can be started on the next machine in the sequence.

Conversely, with **pull manufacturing**, production is initiated as individual sales orders are received. Theoretically, each job consists of a "batch" of one unit. In pacing production, an idle machine pulls the next part from the previous machine as soon as that part is available thus pulling goods through the factory only when needed to satisfy demand. As soon as machine A completes its operation on unit 1, machine B starts work on that unit, and machine A begins on unit 2.

Adopting the pull approach has several natural concomitants:

- *Short production runs.*
- *Continuous flow operations.* To approach the "ideal" batch size of one unit, plant layouts are reorganized so that goods can proceed in a continuous flow from one operation to the next.
- *Cellular manufacturing.* The modified plant layouts have led to a "cellular" arrangement of machines. In the traditional factory layout, machines are organized by departments, each containing similar types of machines. With **cellular manufacturing**, on the other hand, machines are organized in clusters or "cells" that contain all of the needed resources (machines, tools, labor) to produce a family of products. A natural extension of the cellular physical layout is a management orientation that takes a global view of overall work cell throughput rather than a narrower focus related to productivity of individual machines. In fact, it is not

Technology Application 15.2

Product Lifecycle Management at Procter & Gamble

Product lifecycle management (PLM), a subset of which is often referred to as *product data management*, provides a central storage point and sharing of information about product designs, manufacturing, and performance across the enterprise and with key suppliers and customers. The goal is to promote collaboration and learning that will speed delivery of new products and result in more efficient product designs and products that are more profitable across their lifecycles. Procter & Gamble (P&G) received *CIO Magazine's* 2004 Enterprise Value Award for their Corporate Standards PLM system, which provides a single, searchable, global repository of technical standards data for each of the 55,000 products P&G makes. The system facilitates standards access and information-sharing by P&G researchers, purchasing managers, and partners. The result is significant reductions in the cost of direct materials purchases and a 70 percent decrease in the time necessary to approve product specifications. For example, Procter & Gamble was able to reduce the cycle time and cost of package artwork design, rout-

ing, and approval by improving collaboration and workflow management with their extended supply chain partners who were helping to create designs and provide raw materials. Procter & Gamble also was able to increase responsiveness when implementing raw material, packaging, process, and equipment design changes in their plants by providing accurate, up-to-date technical drawings and documentation. In this way, plants across their network can share information and best practices and can search the database and reuse knowledge as they develop and implement new products and changes to products and processes. Ultimately, Procter & Gamble hopes to implement the PLM system with 30,000 users. Procter & Gamble has teamed with their software vendor, UGS PLM Solutions, to help build a PLM application tailored to the consumer packaged goods industry. In this way, the software was developed and deployed more quickly and better met their needs, along with being easier to support in the long term.

Sources: "And the Winners Are..." *CIO Magazine*, online edition, http://www.cio.com, February 15, 2004; "UGS PLM Solutions: Client Successes—Procter & Gamble," http://www.eds.com, October 2003; "EDS and Procter & Gamble Join Forces to Develop New Teamcenter Solution for the Consumer Packaged Goods (CPG) Industry," Procter & Gamble News Release, http://www.pg.com, December 19, 2002.

uncommon for a single worker to run several machines in a cell or for workers to be at least trained to operate multiple machines.

- *Reduced work-in-process and finished goods inventories.*
- *Reduced floor space.* This economy is a result of improved plant layout and elimination of space needed for inventory storage.

Supply Chain Management

ENTERPRISE SYSTEMS

Chapter 12 defines *supply chain management (SCM)* as the combination of processes and procedures used to ensure the delivery of goods and services to customers at the lowest cost while providing the highest value to customers. Chapter 12 Figure 12.2 (page 440) provided an overview of the many internal and external linkages that make up a modern supply chain and described these in the context of a merchandising organization. As evidenced by the prominence of supply chain management in our earlier discussion of the challenges facing manufacturers in an age of global complexity, the challenges of supply chain management discussed in Chapter 12 are further magnified in a manufacturing setting. Rather than being concerned with forecasting demand, lead times, and reorder points for finished goods, a manufacturer must forecast demand, determine lead times, monitor inventory levels for numerous raw materials, *and* plan for the manufacture of finished goods. Additionally, the time and resources necessary to manufacture key **subassemblies**, separately manufactured components used in the final product, must be considered. These subassemblies may be manufactured in the same plant as the final product, or they may be manufactured in a separate plant across the globe.

E-Business plays an increasing role in this process. Increasingly, suppliers are gaining access to the organization's production planning schedules in order to set their own production schedules and to assure an ability to fulfill orders. Similarly, the organization is opening its systems to the customer to allow the customer to view inventory and production levels before placing orders. To accomplish this in a cost-effective manner, Internet technologies are being linked to organizations' *ERP* and *supply chain management software* to provide *portals* to external organizations for safe and secure access of critical business information. In short, the simplicity of the Internet is enabling the continual growth in complexity of business processes and the underlying organizational information systems.

E-BUSINESS

Of particular interest is the enhanced capability that supply chain management software provides for *available to promise* and *capable to promise* planning. **Available to promise planning** is accumulation of the data on current inventories, sales commitments, and planned production to determine whether the production of finished goods will be sufficient to commit to additional sales orders. **Capable to promise planning** is the accumulation of the data on current inventories, sales commitments, planned production and excess production capacity, or other planned production capacity that could be quickly converted to production of the desired finished goods necessary to fulfill a sales order request. The former addresses the planned production capacity that can be used to fulfill *additional* customer orders. The latter addresses the capacity to divert production capacity from other production facilities that have not been previously planned for use on producing the product needed for an incoming customer order.

Management Accounting Systems

In this section, we would like to alert you to some changes that have already occurred (or are evolving) in cost management and cost accounting. It seems natural that many of these changes would have their origins in the developments that have transpired in the production arena and that were discussed—or alluded to—in the preceding sections. In addition, many of these changes are a result of the ability of *enterprise systems* to capture sales, product design, and production data in real-time and to share this data across the *value chain*. Table 15.1 (page 556) summarizes several key accounting changes as related to parallel changes in production processes.

ENTERPRISE SYSTEMS

Take some time to study Table 15.1. As do certain other parts of the chapter, the table assumes that you have a background in managerial/cost accounting. Probably the most important theme in Table 15.1 is the importance of increasing the accuracy and timeliness of cost information and the use of this information for strategic management of products and processes throughout the value chain from design to manufacturing to marketing and post-sales servicing.

Activity-based costing is becoming increasingly prevalent as companies seek to increase cost accuracy and usefulness. **Activity-based costing** is a costing approach where

Table 15.1 Summary of Trends in Cost Management/Cost Accounting

Development in the Production Process Environment	Related[a] Trend in Cost Management/Accounting
Shorter product lifecycles that require cost recovery over a shorter period	Emphasis on product lifecycle costing
	Shift from after-the-fact cost control reporting to reporting designed to assist strategic planning and decision making
	Increased emphasis on managing costs versus merely accounting for costs
	Attack waste as opposed to mere reporting of variances
Flexible manufacturing systems	Flexible cost systems that are also responsive to change
Factory automation	Shift in cost structure from variable costs to fixed costs
	Reduction in direct labor cost component and in the use of direct labor for applying overhead[b]
	Increase in the overhead component of total cost[c]
	Use of a fourth cost category, direct technology, in addition to the traditional direct materials, direct labor, and overhead categories
	Use of activity-based costing (ABC) systems
Automating the information system	Real-time data capture on the factory floor
	Shift away from standard cost systems back to actual cost systems
	Reduction in the administrative costs of gathering data
	Automated inventory orders via EDI without human interaction
	Collecting statistical in addition to financial data
Cellular organization of the factory	Elimination of *detail* reporting by shop order and by operation; instead, use of accounting for cell throughput time
	Use of cell throughput time instead of direct labor to apply overhead
	Trend toward process cost systems and away from job order cost systems
Reduced work-in-process and finished goods inventories	For internal purposes at least, abandonment of full-absorption costing, which loses its significance in the absence of inventories
	Accumulation of costs for decision making instead of for valuing inventories

[a] For simplicity, each cost trend has been listed only once. You should recognize that the items in the right column might very well relate to more than one development in the left column.
[b] For instance, in some high-tech companies, direct labor could account for as little as 5 percent of total cost.
[c] For some companies, manufacturing overhead may be as much as 70 percent of total cost.

detailed costs to perform activities throughout the value chain are computed and can be managed or assigned to cost objects including products. Activity-based costing recognizes that *cost drivers* (measures of the amount of activity performed) other than production volume or direct labor explain many activity costs. Cost per unit of the cost driver is computed for each activity. Costs are then assigned to products based on the amount of the cost driver used. An example of an activity that might be performed for a production facility is purchasing materials; and the cost driver might be the number of purchase orders prepared.

By using a variety of cost drivers, activity-based costs can be computed for all activities across the value chain, not just manufacturing activities. Detailed activity cost information and increasingly accurate and comprehensive product costs can be used to aid strategic decisions throughout the value chain. Information about cost drivers and activity costs can be used to improve product designs and production processes, to determine the best mix of marketing campaigns or to assess the cost of poor quality. Using activity-based costing information, product managers can estimate **lifecycle costs** or the sum of the costs to design, produce, market, deliver, and support a product throughout the product's lifecycle from conception to ultimate discontinuance, more effectively managing product profitability.

Many of the other changes identified in Table 15.1 are also aimed at more accurate identification of costs in a timely manner so that this information can be used more strategically. Many of them also stem from the importance of technology in the production process. For example, the use of a new cost category, direct technology, allows these costs, which are becoming a larger component of manufacturing costs, to be directly estimated and more effectively managed. A separate cost category for these items is possible because of *cellular manufacturing*, which devotes machines exclusively to single product lines.

INTEGRATED PRODUCTION PROCESSES

Within the backdrop of the globally complex manufacturing organization, our primary purposes in this section are to (1) acquaint you with the principal components of a modern integrated production process (IPP) and the interactions that can exist among those components and (2) arm you with basic definitions of manufacturing terms that you may encounter in your professional careers.

Figure 15.1 (page 558) provides a level 0 data flow diagram of an IPP. Consistent **ENTERPRISE** with the goal of integration across functional areas, the process actually begins at the **SYSTEMS** start of the *value chain* with the design of product and production processes (step 1.0). Based on data developed at this stage as well as information about expected or actual sales orders from the order entry/sales process and inventory levels from the inventory management process, a master production schedule is developed (step 2.0), followed by a detailed definition of needs for materials (step 3.0) and detailed production instructions (step 4.0). These steps initiate activities in the purchasing and human resource management processes to put materials and labor resources in place to complete production. Throughout these steps, and especially as resources are utilized to manufacture the goods, information about the process is continuously captured (step 5.0) so that valuable managerial information can be generated. As you can see from the number of integration points with other business processes in Figure 15.1, *enterprise systems* will play a vital part in managing the IPP. Each of these steps will be discussed in more detail in the following sections.

In practice, one key to understanding the information processes described in Figure 15.1 is understanding the underlying terminology and recognizing the acronyms used to describe the processes by engineers, manufacturing managers, and software developers. Table 15.2 (page 559) lists each of the steps in the process and provides a summary

Figure 15.1 Level 0 Data Flow Diagram of the Integrated Production Process

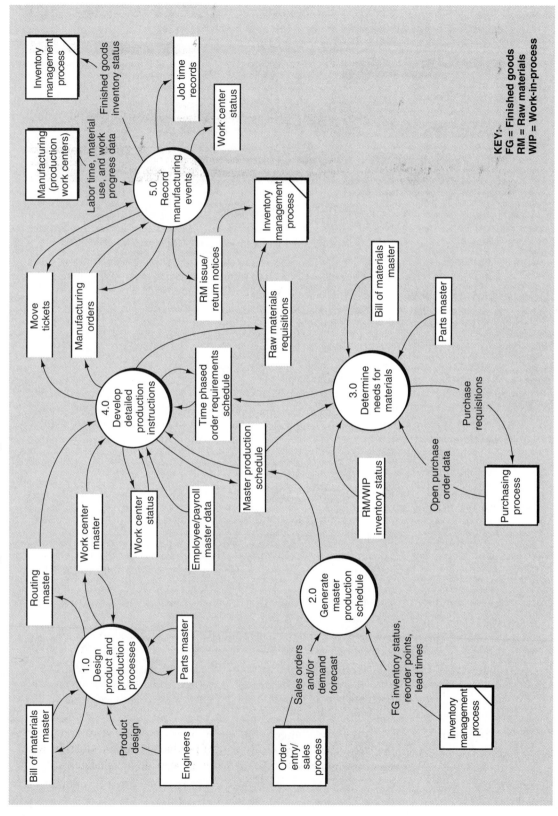

Table 15.2 Key Manufacturing Terminology in the IPP Steps

Integrated Production Process Step	Related Manufacturing Terminology
Step 1.0: Design product and production processes	*Computer-aided design/Computer-aided engineering (CAD/CAE)* is used to automate product design. *Computer-aided process planning (CAPP)* is used to generate manufacturing instructions and routings based on product requirements.
Step 2.0: Generate master production schedule	*Global inventory management* assures that production schedules consider inventory availability across the global enterprise. *Production, planning, and control* is the process of generating a schedule, determining detailed material needs, developing detailed production instructions, and tracking data during production.
Step 3.0: Determine needs for materials	*Materials requirements planning (little mrp)* is used to develop a time-phased requirements schedule for materials and subassemblies.
Step 4.0: Develop detailed production instructions	*Capacity requirements planning (CRP)* is used to develop detailed machine- and labor-utilization schedules that consider available capacity. *Manufacturing resource planning (MRP)* incorporates mrp, CRP, and planning for labor and financial capital.
Manufacturing (production work centers)	*Flexible manufacturing systems (FMS)* are automated systems used to control production that can quickly incorporate automated engineering design changes. *Computer-aided manufacturing (CAM)* is used to link machines, monitor production, and provide automatic feedback to control operations. *Automated storage and retrieval systems (AS/RS)* store and retrieve parts and tools. *Automated guided vehicle systems (AGVS)* deliver parts and tools among multiple work centers.
Step 5.0: Record manufacturing events	*Shop floor control (SFC)* is used to monitor and record the status of manufacturing orders and work centers during the manufacturing process.

of the common manufacturing terminology used at each step, which also will be discussed in the following sections.

Design Product and Production Processes

Figure 15.1, bubble 1.0. Consistent with the value chain concept, the IPP begins with design of the product and production processes. With approximately 80 percent of the future cost of producing the product locked in with decisions made during design, this step is vital to determining the profitability of new product lines. *Activity-based costing,* which provides information about the cost of production activities for existing products, can be used to develop estimates of the future cost of producing new products as well as potential cost changes from product and production process design changes.

The entire design process is automated through the use of **computer-aided design (CAD) and computer-aided engineering (CAE).** Because of their close relationships to each other, it is not uncommon to talk about CAD/CAE as a single element. CAD/ CAE is an application of computer technology that automates the product design process, including but not limited to the functions of geometric modeling, materials stress and strain analysis, drafting, storing product specifications, and mechanical simulation of a product's performance. The objectives of CAD/CAE are to:

- Improve design productivity.
- Reduce design lead time.
- Enhance design quality.
- Facilitate access to and storage of product designs.
- Make the design of multiple products more efficient by eliminating redundant design effort.
- Execute design changes almost immediately through the use of electronic messaging to notify the shop floor.

ENTERPRISE SYSTEMS With the use of *enterprise systems*, the electronic designs produced using CAD/CAE become the basis for developing detailed production schedules (step 2.0) as well as electronic control of production machines. In addition to the detailed product design, the CAD/CAE process results in several data stores of information that are used later in the IPP. These are:

- **Bill of materials**—The bill of materials is a listing of all the *subassemblies*, parts, and raw materials that go into a parent assembly showing the quantity of each required to make an assembly. Often, engineers will work to design several products with common *subassemblies*. This way, manufacturing processes are more standardized, quality can be improved, and costs are reduced. The bill of materials provides the basis for later orders of raw materials (bubble 3.0) when a finished good is to be produced.

- **Parts master**—The parts master or raw material (RM) inventory master lists the detailed specifications for each raw materials item. An engineer must specify the information for a new record in the parts master when a new part is used in a product design. Often, existing parts will be used in new products to reduce needed ordering and carrying costs for the inventory.

- **Routing master**—The routing master specifies the operations necessary to complete a subassembly or finished good and the sequence of these operations. The routing master also includes the machining tolerances; the tools, jigs, and fixtures required; and the time allowance for each operation. The routing master is vital when developing detailed production instructions (step 4.0). **Computer-aided process planning (CAPP)** is often used in developing the routing master for new products. CAPP is an automated decision support system that generates manufacturing operations instructions and routings based on information about machining requirements and machine capabilities.

- **Work center master**—The work center master describes each *work center* available for producing products, including information such as the machine available at the station, its capacity, its maintenance needs, labor needs to operate it, and so on. A **workstation** is the assigned location where a worker performs his or her job; it could be a machine or a workbench. A group of similar workstations constitutes a **work center**. When new products require new machines or production activities, a new record in the work center master must be created.

Generate Master Production Schedule

Figure 15.1, bubble 2.0. With products and production processes in place, the next step in the IPP is generating a *master production schedule (MPS)* to drive the production process. The **master production schedule (MPS)** is a statement of *specific* production goals developed from forecasts of demand, actual sales orders, and/or inventory information. It describes the specific items to be manufactured, the quantities to be produced, and the production timetable. Depending on the company's approach, the schedule may be based on information about finished goods inventory levels and re-order points, sales forecasts or actual sales orders coupled with inventory levels. Based on the master production schedule, more detailed schedules for ordering raw materials and scheduling work center operations are developed in steps 3.0 and 4.0. Figure 15.2 depicts a master production schedule including the specific items to be manufactured, the quantities to be produced, and the production timetable.

Given the increased emphasis on cost reduction for successful global competition in manufacturing, companies cannot afford to generate too much of the wrong products. **ENTERPRISE SYSTEMS**

Figure 15.2 Dynamic Production Schedule (SAP)

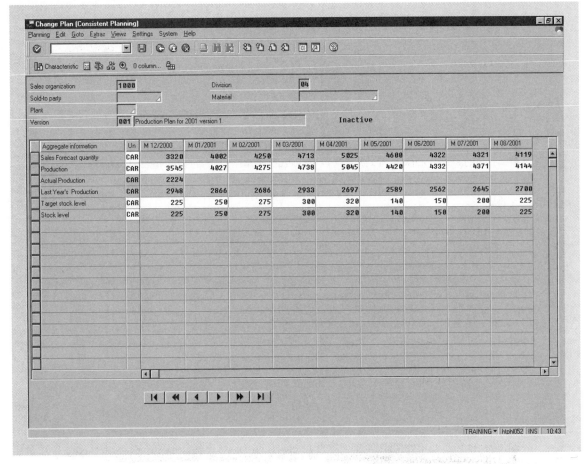

Source: Reprinted with permission from SAP.

Instead, extensive use of *enterprise systems* to gather and analyze data from past and future sales and inventory levels is used to develop a more accurate production plan. The result is minimizing unnecessary inventory investment and maximizing the likelihood that the right products will be in place at the right time.

The master production schedule is based on information from three sources. The first is actual orders from customers. Ideally, a manufacturer can cut *throughput times* to the point that they can produce goods only as customer orders are received. In this way, they minimize risk of goods not selling and maximize the likelihood that they will produce exactly the product desired by the customer.

ENTERPRISE SYSTEMS   Often, however, the time necessary to produce goods and distribute them to locations around the globe necessitates producing goods in anticipation of sales orders. In this case, a variety of techniques are used to develop sophisticated demand forecasting models that help manufacturers estimate the need for goods. These techniques can utilize the full complement of customer data available in the *enterprise system* about past sales levels and buying patterns to improve forecast accuracy. These models may take advantage of information from the *customer relationship management* system as discussed in Chapter 10, and will likely utilize some of the *data mining* techniques also described in Chapter 10 to identify important patterns and relationships in the level of demand. The importance of good forecasts is illustrated in Technology Application 15.3, which describes the impact on Nike's profits when its new sales forecasting system was not working well.

Technology Application 15.3

Nike's Sales Forecasting Woes

In June 2000, Nike went live with a new demand forecasting system designed by I2 Technologies. By February 2001, Nike had announced significant inventory write-offs because of poor demand forecasting—they had ordered $90 million of poor-selling models, while being $80 to $100 million short on popular models. This also led to added costs to expedite materials to manufacture shoes to meet orders and the cost of lost orders. Nike's stock price plummeted. While Nike blamed failures in the I2 demand forecasting software, I2 blamed Nike for not following implementation guidelines, including accelerating the recommended implementation timeline. In particular, Nike began inputting assumptions used to generate sales forecasts before the system was completely stable and nine months in advance of actual sales. Because of economic and systems changes over those nine months, those assumptions proved to be inaccurate. The result was disruption, excess inventory, delay, and excess cost throughout the value chain from sales to purchasing to manufacturing to distribution, all because of faulty demand forecasts.

Sources: Tim Wilson, "Supply Chain Debacle—Nike Faces Yearlong Inventory Problem After I2 Implementation Fails," *InternetWeek*, http://www.internetweek.com, March 1, 2001; Ben Worthen, "Future Results Not Guaranteed," *CIO Magazine*, online edition, http://www.cio.com, July 15, 2003.

ENTERPRISE SYSTEMS   Finally, the inventory management system also provides vital inputs to developing a better master production schedule. The inventory management system provides data about levels of finished goods (FG) inventory currently on hand, and also gathers data about goods scheduled to be produced. Additionally, inventory data tracked over time by the company's *enterprise system* such as lead times, optimal inventory levels, frequency of stockouts, and expected quality levels all help develop better production schedules.

One trend in inventory management facilitated by *enterprise systems* has been particularly useful in reducing inventory levels and better satisfying customer demand. This trend is *global inventory management*. **Global inventory management** is an inventory management approach where inventory needs and inventory and production capabilities are matched across the entire global enterprise, not just at a regional level. Less sophisticated inventory management systems associate specific inventory locations and manufacturing plants with specific sales regions. In this way, the South American sales region of a large electronics manufacturer would look primarily at manufacturing plants and warehouses within this same geographic region when examining the availability of inventory or production capacity to fill a large order. If insufficient capacity was available in this region, the order might be rejected, or a delivery date too far in the future might be quoted, resulting in losing the business to a competitor.

ENTERPRISE SYSTEMS

With *global inventory management*, the South American sales region can examine inventory and production capacity across the entire company's global organization when determining its ability to fill an order. Of course, if the product was to be produced in a factory across the globe in Germany, for example, the South American sales division would need to consider additional lead time to transport the goods to their customer and also the associated distribution costs, but these pieces of information would be readily available from the *enterprise database*.

Armed with information from the *enterprise system* about the sales forecast, actual sales orders, and inventory data, the *master production schedule* can be developed, as depicted in Figure 15.1, bubble 2.0. Developing the MPS along with the remaining steps in the IPP are often referred to as the production, planning, and control process. *Production, planning, and control* involves the *logistics*, or "physical" aspects of converting raw materials into finished goods. As such, **production, planning, and control** is a process that manages the orderly and timely movement of goods through the production process. It includes activities such as planning material, people, and machine requirements; scheduling; routing; and monitoring progress of goods through the factory.

ENTERPRISE SYSTEMS

Determine Needs for Materials

Figure 15.1, bubble 3.0. Once the master production schedule is determined, an important step in completing production in a timely manner is identifying, ordering, and receiving materials. At the heart of this task is the *materials requirements planning (little mrp)* process. **Materials requirements planning** is a process that uses bills of material, raw material and work-in-process (RM/WIP) inventory status data, open order data, and the master production schedule to calculate a **time-phased order requirements schedule** for materials and subassemblies. The schedule shows the time period when a *manufacturing order* or purchase order should be released so that the subassemblies and raw materials will be available when needed. The process involves working backward from the date production is to begin to determine the timing for manufacturing subassemblies and then moving back further to determine the date that orders for materials must be issued into the purchasing process. In an *enterprise system*,

ENTERPRISE SYSTEMS

this process is performed automatically using a variety of data from the enterprise database, including:

- *Bills of materials (BOM)* showing the items and quantities required as developed by engineering.
- *Parts master* data, which contains information about part number, description, unit of measure, where used, order policy, lead time, and safety stock.
- *Raw materials (RM) and work-in-process inventory status* data showing the current quantities on hand and quantities already reserved for production for the materials and subassemblies.
- *Open purchase order (PO)* data showing the existing orders for materials.

The process begins by **exploding the BOM** (shown in Figure 15.3), which involves extending a bill of material to determine the total of each component required to manufacture a given quantity of an upper-level assembly or subassembly specified in the MPS. Based on lead time data for producing and ordering, materials and subassembly requirements are output in a *time-phased order requirements schedule*, which is illustrated

Figure 15.3 Bill of Materials (SAP)

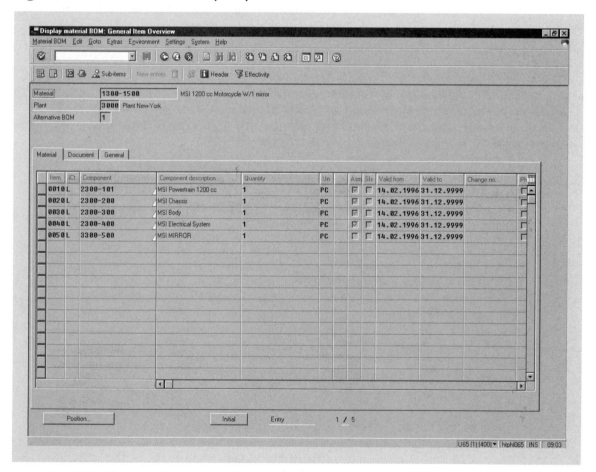

Source: Reprinted with permission from SAP.

in Figure 15.4. Based on this schedule and open purchase order data, purchase requisitions are generated and sent to purchasing.

Figure 15.4 Order Requirements Schedule (SAP)

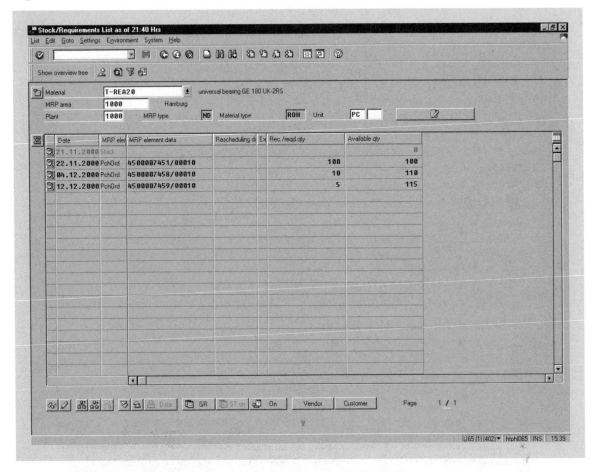

Source: Reprinted with permission from SAP.

To illustrate the "explosion" of a BOM, suppose that the BOM for one mousetrap reflects the following:

Part No.	Description	Quantity
100	Wood base (36 in.)	1
101	Coil spring	2
102	Wood screw (5/8 in.)	2
103	U-shaped wire rod (24 in.)	1
104	Cheese holder and hook	1

Note: Cheese is the customer's responsibility!

Assume that the MPS calls for making 500 mousetraps in the week ended October 4, 20XX. Exploding the BOM would result in the following materials requirements:

Part No.	Quantity	Calculation (end units times quantity per)
100	500	(500×1)
101	1,000	(500×2)
102	1,000	(500×2)
103	500	(500×1)
104	500	(500×1)

Allowing for the lead time needed to have the parts available during the week of October 4, orders would be released for 500 units of parts 100, 103, and 104, and 1,000 units of parts 101 and 102, assuming open orders were not already in process for these materials.

E-BUSINESS   *E-Business* and supply chain management may have a significant influence on the *mrp* process. With greater integration between manufacturer and vendor systems, actual orders for raw materials may be triggered by vendor systems that monitor master production schedule information and automatically ship orders at the appropriate time (i.e., *vendor managed inventory, VMI*). Even if this level of integration is not quite achieved, electronic transmission of orders may greatly reduce the necessary lead time for placing orders for raw materials.

Develop Detailed Production Instructions

Figure 15.1, bubble 4.0. Materials are not the only resources necessary for beginning production. Detailed instructions showing exactly when the goods will be processed through each necessary work center and the labor necessary to complete the work are the result of step 4.0 of the IPP. In particular, consideration of the capacity available of these resources may have a profound impact on whether the organization can ultimately achieve the master production schedule. **Capacity requirements planning (CRP)** is the process that utilizes the information from the *master production schedule* and *time-phased order requirements schedule* to develop *detailed* machine- and labor-utilization schedules that consider the feasibility of production schedules based on available capacity in the work center status records. Ultimately, this process may lead to modifications to the *master production schedule* or *time-phased inventory requirements schedule* if sufficient capacity does not exist to complete these schedules as planned. Once these adjustments are completed, CRP assigns targeted start/completion dates to operations (*workstations*) or groups of operations (*work centers*) and releases manufacturing orders and move tickets to the factory.

Manufacturing orders (MOs) convey authority for the manufacture of a specified product or subassembly in a specified quantity and describe the material, labor, and machine requirements for the job. The manufacturing order is the official trigger to begin manufacturing operations. When MOs are released, they are generally accompanied by **move tickets** (usually in the form of bar code tags) that authorize and record movement of a job from one work center to another. The move ticket contains various information for tracing work completion, such as the shop work authorization number representing the job being completed; the department, machine, operator, and time of completion; and check boxes for completion of current task and inspection of prior tasks' completion. Generally, these data are captured by scanning the bar code to expedite data entry and improve accuracy.

Additionally, *raw materials requisitions* are sent to the inventory process. A **raw materials requisition** is an authorization that identifies the type and quantity of materials to be withdrawn from the storeroom and tracks the manufacturing order being produced and the work center needing the raw materials.

Triggered by the *time-phased order requirements*, CRP used the following additional inputs from the *enterprise system* to accomplish its functions:

ENTERPRISE SYSTEMS

- The *routing master*, which shows the necessary steps and time to complete each one to produce the product. Whereas the *BOM* shows the raw material inputs required for a single unit of finished goods output, the *routing master*, illustrated in Figure 15.5, performs a similar function in respect to labor and machine requirements. The *routing master* typically shows the sequence of operations to manufacture an end item and the standard time allowance (labor hours or machine hours) for each operation. Based on the production orders, the total standard (required) labor and machine hours can be predicted by reference to the routing master. The calculations are similar to those used to explode a BOM.

Figure 15.5 Production Routing Schedule (SAP)

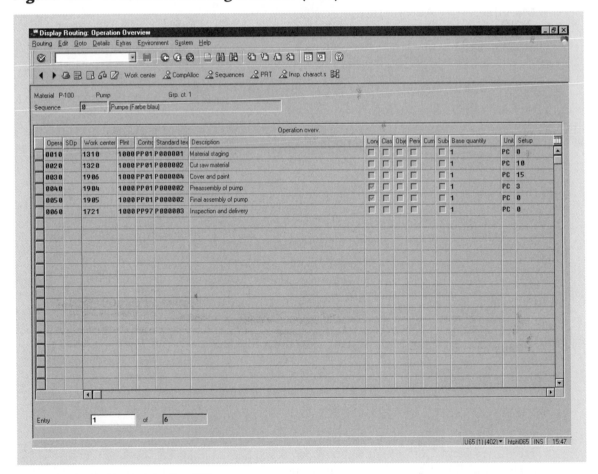

Source: Reprinted with permission from SAP.

- Resource capacity information (i.e., hours available each day/week by work center) from the *work center master data.*

- Data about the current status of work center loads from the *work center status data* (also known as *loading data*). These data can include MOs now at each work center, anticipated MOs, backlogs, and actual hours ahead or behind schedule. This data is supplemented by information from the employee/payroll master data that shows available labor capacities.

Together, mrp, CRP, and the process of planning cash flows to accommodate needs generated by the production schedule is referred to as **manufacturing resource planning (MRP)**. MRP is an integrated decision support system for planning, executing, and controlling manufacturing operations. It includes facilities for planning all manufacturing resources, including material, machines, labor, and financial capital.

Manufacturing (Production Work Centers)

The next information process shown in the DFD is collecting information about the manufacture of goods (step 5.0). However, to better understand this process, it is important to have some information about how the IPP accomplishes the manufacturing steps. First, we describe automating the production process. Then, we discuss the just-in-time aspects of manufacturing.

Manufacturing Automation

Flexible manufacturing systems (FMS) are systems used to control actual production of the goods. An *FMS* is an automated manufacturing operations system that can react quickly to product and design changes because centralized computer control provides real-time routing, load balancing, and production scheduling logic. Regardless of its components, any FMS has as its goal making the plant more flexible—that is, achieving the ability to quickly produce wide varieties of products using the same equipment.

ENTERPRISE SYSTEMS

A component of FMS, **computer-aided manufacturing (CAM)**, is intended to improve manufacturing control and reporting, coordinate material flow between machines, and facilitate rerouting. CAM is defined as the application of computer and communications technology to improve productivity by linking computer numerical control (CNC) machines, monitoring production, and providing automatic feedback to control operations. CAM systems take advantage of integration within *enterprise systems* to automatically incorporate design changes made by engineering into production processes on a nearly real-time basis, therefore decreasing the time to integrate new innovations.

Central to the *actual work performed* in an FMS environment is the use of machines that use *computer numerical control (CNC)*. These machines might be industrial robots or automated materials handling systems in the form of **automated storage and retrieval systems (AS/RS)**, which are computer-controlled machines that store and retrieve parts and tools, or **automated guided vehicle systems (AGVS)**, which are computer-based carts that are capable of delivering parts and tools among multiple work centers. Regardless of type, numerically controlled machines, in general, represent one of the earliest efforts at factory automation and have evolved in an attempt to improve worker productivity, enhance product quality and precision, and avoid the risk posed to humans by hazardous working conditions. Differences among numerically controlled machines lie mainly in the degree of process knowledge (i.e., how to operate the machine) that is transferred from the laborer to the machine (i.e., by being programmed into the machine). In some settings, a worker is still needed to load, unload, and set up the machine. Robotics and industrial parts inspection done by digital image processing machines virtually eliminate the worker and achieve productivity that is technology-paced only.

Just-In-Time Manufacturing

Many manufacturers have simplified their manufacturing operations and reduced inventories through the use of a **just-in-time (JIT)** approach to controlling activities on the shop floor. Just-in-time is a pull manufacturing philosophy or business strategy for designing production processes that are more responsive to precisely timed customer delivery requirements. Several inherent JIT objectives and the means of attaining them are summarized in Exhibits 15.1 and 15.2, respectively. JIT success stories are impressive, but you should realize that not everyone agrees that JIT is the panacea for all ills. Before proceeding, take some time to study these exhibits. JIT goes beyond production planning and control. However, JIT can have a profound impact on the production, planning, and control process. Especially in repetitive manufacturing operations where inventories of raw materials are maintained, the use of a pull approach can greatly reduce the need for capacity requirements planning and detailed materials requirements planning.

ENTERPRISE SYSTEMS

Exhibit 15.1 Just-In-Time Objectives

- *Zero defects.* Products are designed to be defect-free and to eliminate the need to inspect the product. In fact, the **total quality control (TQC)** approach to manufacturing, a subset of JIT, places responsibility for quality in the hands of the builder rather than in those of the inspector.

- *Zero setup times.* For instance, one world-class automobile manufacturer can change from one car model to another in 2.5 minutes, including complete retooling.

- *Small lot sizes.* Continuous flow operations are designed so that material does not sit idle and machine utilization is maximized (95 percent utilization is not uncommon).

- *Zero lead times.* As mentioned earlier, the goal is to eliminate the nonvalue-added (i.e., wasted in moving, waiting, and inspecting activities) portion of total lead time.

- *Zero inventories.* In successful JIT installations, a goal is to maintain only enough inventory to satisfy demand for a few hours or days.

Exhibit 15.2 Just-In-Time Implementation Features

- Arranging the factory in U-shaped work cells to optimize material flow.

- Assigning one worker to multiple machines.

- Giving production workers the responsibility and authority to stop the production line if they are running behind schedule or if they discover defective parts.

- Requiring that the daily schedule for each part or assembly remains nearly the same each day.

- Developing close working relationships with vendors to ensure that they deliver quality raw materials on the promised delivery dates. In effect, vendors are supposed to serve as extended storage facilities of the company. We alluded to these relationships when we discussed choosing a vendor and deciding when and how much to purchase in Chapter 12.

- Simplifying the process for tracking the movement of goods through the factory. JIT is often called a *kanban* process, a name taken from the Japanese word for "card." As such, the simple kanban or *move ticket* replaces the *manufacturing order* and *route sheet* of the past.

Record Manufacturing Events

Figure 15.1, bubble 5.0. As previously indicated, the process of collecting information about the manufacturing activities (step 5.0) is highly automated. The process utilized to collect this data is often called *shop floor control*. The shop floor control (SFC) process is devoted to monitoring and recording the status of manufacturing orders as they proceed through the factory. The shop floor control process also maintains work center status information showing the degree ahead or behind schedule and utilization levels. As each operation is finished, this fact is reported to SFC through a *completed move ticket,* and updates are made to the *open MO data* and the *work center status data.* When the final operation in the sequence is finished, the MO is removed from the open MO data, and the inventory process is advised to add the quantities (and costs) to its finished goods records.

Through automation, the shop floor control process is able to collect valuable real-time data that can be used for immediate feedback and control. Automated data collection might involve obtaining information by scanning a *bar code* label attached to the product, coupled with entering quality and quantity information through workstations located on the factory floor. Often, the time needed to key-enter information about the operator is greatly shortened by reading those data from an employee badge inserted in the workstation.

Information also is collected about the time worked by laborers on each production task. While old-fashioned paper time tickets may be used to enter data into the time records, more likely this process also will be automated through scanning employee badges and touching a few places on a computer touch screen to indicate the completion of manufacturing tasks. This same information becomes the necessary input for the payroll process. Finally, as additional raw materials are needed or unused raw materials are returned to the storeroom, raw materials issue and return notices will be recorded.

Generate Managerial Information

The data provided by the *integrated production process* system is vital to management of the global enterprise. Figure 15.6 shows how data collected through shop floor control, coupled with financial data available through other systems, help populate the enterprise database providing key information for both managing the IPP and also for driving other processes.

Because automation is used to collect data, it is generally available in real-time. For example, information about actual machine time used at a work center, collected once the move ticket is scanned following the operation, can be compared with standards from the routing master to give real-time information about variances from standard for that work center before the product is even completed. In this way, managers can take corrective action *before* they receive formal variance reports.

Key manufacturing decision-making outputs from the enterprise database include:

- Throughput time information derived by identifying start and completion times for manufacturing orders.
- Productivity information related to labor, machines, and materials derived by comparing standard allowance for actual production outputs to the actual levels of labor machine time and materials used.
- Quality information showing actual product quality levels achieved as well as machine and process performance.

Figure 15.6 The IPP Role in Generating Managerial Information

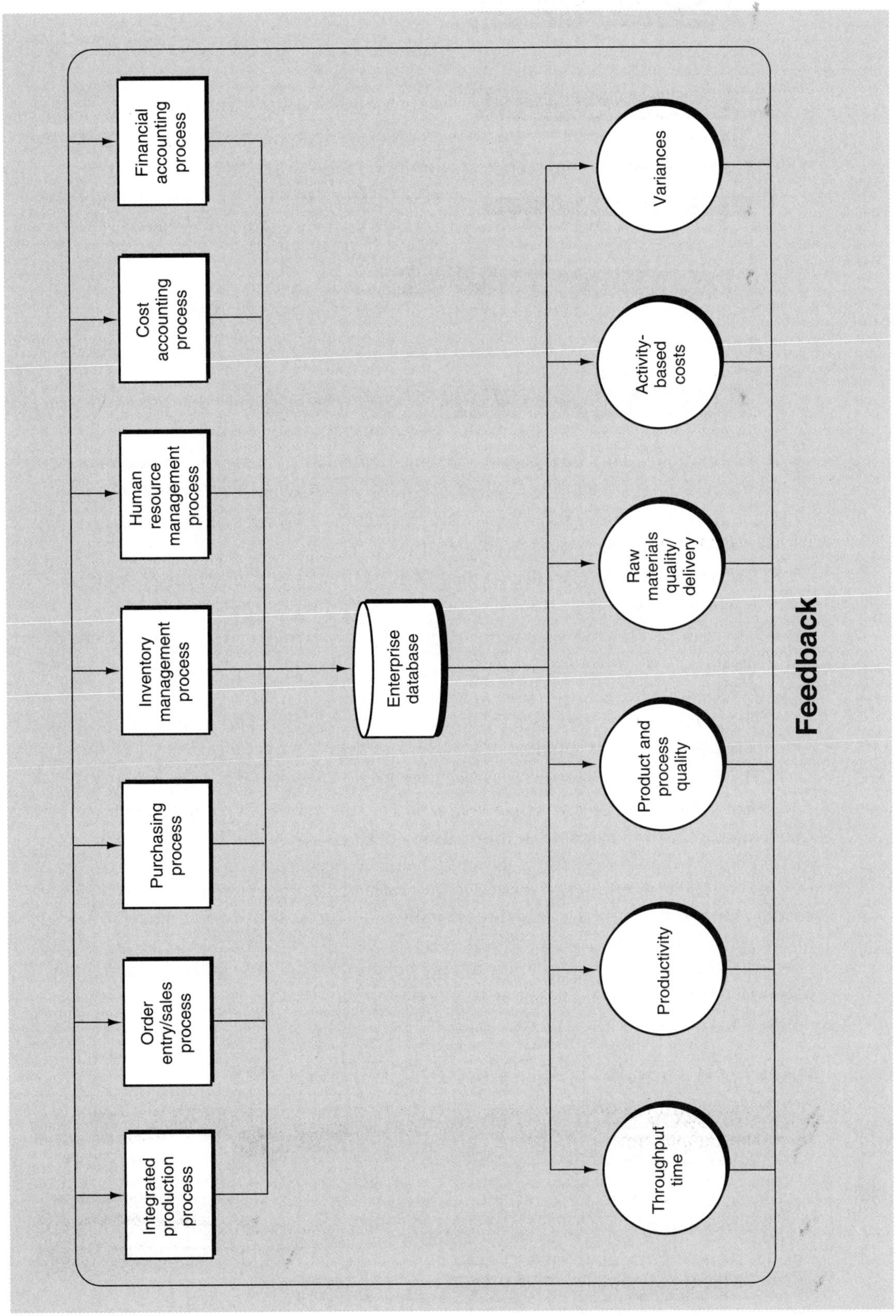

- Activity-based cost information showing the costs to perform activities at each work center as well as actual cumulative costs of producing subassemblies and final products.
- Information about raw materials including quality and on-time delivery.
- Other cost accounting information such as variances discussed in the next section.

This information provides vital feedback for improving the IPP as follows:

- Information about productivity, product quality, and activity costs can all feed back to the product and process design process to help engineers design more cost-effective products and production processes (step 1.0).
- Better information about production times can be used to develop more effective production schedules and detailed production plans (steps 2.0 and 4.0).
- Information about raw materials quality and delivery can help improve timing of RM orders (step 3.0).
- Information about machine and labor utilization levels can be used to identify, manage, and possibly eliminate unneeded capacity (step 4.0).
- Information linking quality and machine performance can be used to develop better strategies for operating machines and developing machine maintenance plans.

In addition to using this information for production decision making, the data also is used in other business processes as follows.

- The order entry/sales process utilizes information about actual throughput times to determine necessary lead times for quoting future deliveries.
- The human resources management process utilizes information about labor productivity and utilization to determine future staffing levels and specific labor needs.
- The purchasing process uses feedback about productivity and quality of raw materials inputs to assess supplier effectiveness at delivering promised levels of quality.
- The inventory process uses feedback about lead times and throughput times to revise reorder points.

One component of management information collected about the IPP is variance information used in monitoring efficiency and adherence to production plans. This information also can help companies to identify better strategies for managing tradeoffs between cost of inputs and productive use of these inputs. The process of collecting and processing variance information is described in more detail in the next section as an example of how data collected throughout the integrated production process is combined with other data in the enterprise database to produce useful decision-making information.

COST ACCOUNTING: VARIANCE ANALYSIS

ENTERPRISE SYSTEMS

CONTROLS

Variance analysis is the process of comparing actual information about input costs and usage to standards for costs and usage for manufacturing inputs. While some criticism has been leveled at the process, when used in proper context, variance analysis is an important control tool. When computed in real-time, variances help manufacturing managers monitor production processes to determine that they are performing as expected. Taking a longer-term view, variances can be monitored to assess the interplay between costs of various inputs and efficient utilization of these inputs.

The level 0 data flow diagram in Figure 15.7 (page 574) shows the steps in the process of performing *variance analysis* using a standard costing system. We choose standard instead of actual costing for our illustration in the belief that this system is more prevalent in *current* practice. Recall from Table 15.1 (page 556), however, that with ERP systems some companies are abandoning standard costing and returning to actual cost systems. Let's now examine the DFD, bubble by bubble.

Record Standard Costs

Figure 15.7, bubble 1.0 At the time that each manufacturing order is released to the factory, a record would normally be created in the *work-in-process inventory data*. At that point, the record would contain identification data (job number, end product description, quantity to be produced, start date, etc.). Think of the work-in-process inventory data as serving as a *subsidiary ledger* in support of the work-in-process inventory *control account* in the general ledger.

The standard cost master data contains quantity standards (RM quantity, DL hour, and machine hour allowances per FG unit) and price standards (standard purchase price per unit of RM, standard labor rates per hour, etc.).

The data flow "Move ticket data" entering bubble 1.0 occurs at the completion of *each* operation until the job is completed. Each completed move ticket triggers an update to the work-in-process inventory data for the standard cost of labor and overhead allowed for that particular operation. Standards are obtained from the standard cost master data.

When CRP released the MO, it sent a raw materials requisition to the inventory process. The requisition authorized the storeroom to issue the *standard* RM quantities allowed for the MO. Once the RMs have actually been issued by the storeroom, the inventory process notifies cost accounting that this has occurred (through the data flow "Standard RM issue notice"). This notification prompts an update to the work-in-process inventory data for the standard cost of the materials (i.e., standard quantities times standard prices).

Figure 15.8 (page 575) shows the raw materials that have been issued into production. In a traditional paper process, the issue notice may physically be a copy of the materials requisition, dated and signed by the storeroom clerk to signify that the goods were issued. Through the data flow "GL standard costs applied update," process 1.0 notifies the general ledger to make the appropriate entry to apply standard costs to WIP.[3]

Compute Raw Material Quantity Variance

Figure 15.7, bubble 2.0. In the discussion of bubble 1.0, you learned that RMs were first issued to production in *standard* quantities. If additional materials are later issued to complete the MO (unfavorable condition) or unused materials are returned to stock (favorable usage variance), these events are reported through the data flows "Excess RM issue notice" and "RM returned notice," respectively. The usage variance[4] is calculated

---

[3] A discussion of general ledger standard costing entries is beyond the scope of this chapter. Your managerial/cost accounting courses should cover this topic.

[4] We assume that the RM *price* variance is isolated when the materials are *purchased*. Therefore, computing the purchase price variance is a function of the *inventory process*.

Figure 15.7 Level 0 Data Flow Diagram—Cost Accounting: Variance Analysis

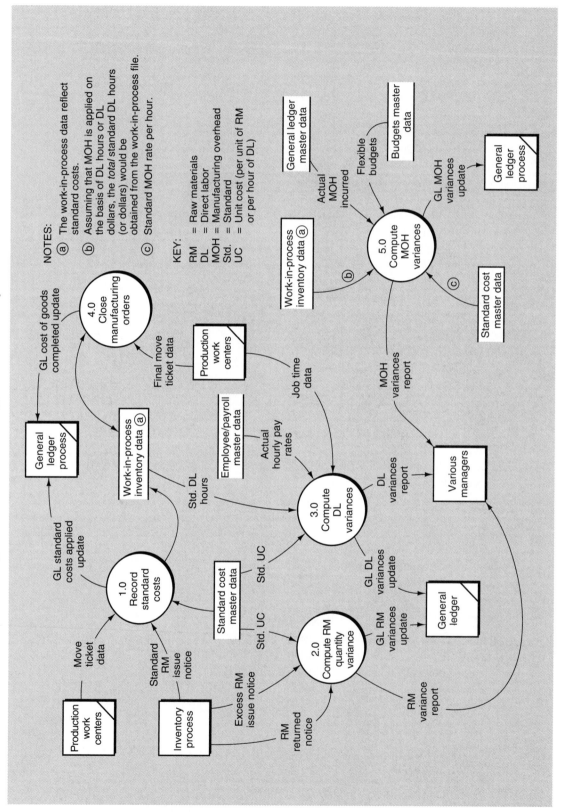

Figure 15.8 Materials Planning (SAP)

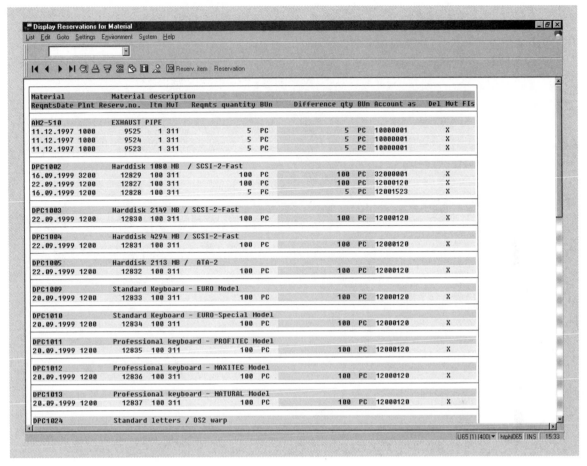

Source: Reprinted with permission from SAP.

by multiplying the quantities by standard unit costs from the standard cost master data. This variance is then reported to the general ledger and to appropriate managers.[5]

Compute Direct Labor Variances

Figure 15.7, bubble 3.0. The job time log, illustrated in Figure 15.9 (page 576), is an aggregation of entries by each factory worker of his time on a given job. It shows both the actual hours worked on specific operations of specific jobs and the budgeted labor hours. This information can largely be captured with an employee card swipe, a bar code scan of the job order, and a few simple entries.

The actual hours shown by job time data on the log constitute one of four inputs to bubble 3.0. Employee pay rates are obtained from the *employee/payroll master data* (see Chapter 14). For each operation reflected on the job time log, the standard hours charged are retrieved from the work-in-process data; the standard cost master data

[5] Reporting variances to the general ledger and to various managers is shown happening three times in Figure 15.7 (i.e., from bubbles 2.0, 3.0, and 5.0). Obviously, the three might be combined into a single update notice to the general ledger and one variance report to each manager.

Figure 15.9 Job Time Log (J.D. Edwards)

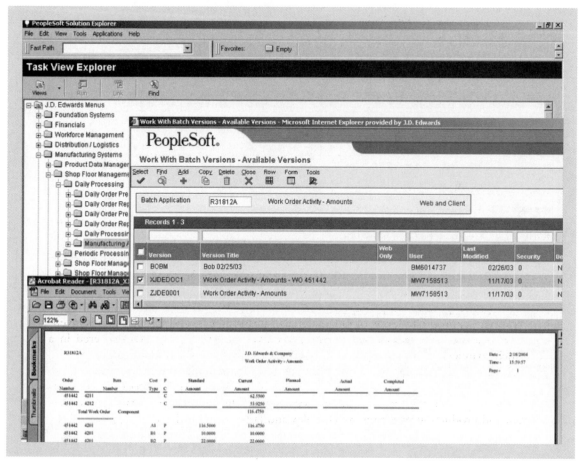

provides the standard labor rates per hour. As in the case of raw materials, the direct labor variances are reported to the general ledger and various managers.

Close Manufacturing Orders

Figure 15.7, bubble 4.0. As discussed in an earlier section, the *final move ticket data* marks the end of the conversion process and the movement of goods to the FG warehouse. Information processing activities that result from the final move ticket are:

- Close the cost record maintained in the work-in-process inventory data and compute the standard cost of the goods completed.
- Through the data flow "GL cost of goods completed update," notify the general ledger to make the appropriate entries.

Compute Manufacturing Overhead Variances

Figure 15.7, bubble 5.0. Process 5.0 is triggered by a temporal event and is performed at the end of an accounting period (e.g., each month) rather than being triggered by a specific data flow from an external entity. To compute the manufacturing overhead variances, process 5.0 would:

- Obtain the *flexible budget* from the budgets master data; the budget amount is based on the standard hours allowed to complete the actual finished goods output for the period.
- Retrieve the figures for actual MOH incurred from the general ledger master data.
- Access the work-in-process data to determine the standard hours charged to *all* jobs during the period; these hours would be multiplied by the standard MOH rate per hour from the standard cost master data.

Once again, the variances are reported to the general ledger and the appropriate managers.

INVENTORY MANAGEMENT

In addition to the management of human resources, inventory management is another major area of concern for manufacturers—particularly those that are operating in *just-in-time* environments. Manufacturers must estimate needed levels of inventory to meet customer demands, often at a moment's notice. As illustrated through our description of integrated production processes, a major challenge for the inventory manager is determining appropriate levels of raw materials, subassemblies, and finished goods inventory to assure that production can be maintained and finished goods delivered in a timely manner. Information about finished goods is an important input to the production scheduling process, while raw materials and subassemblies inventory variables play an important role in materials requirement planning. Balancing inventory levels to satisfy customer demands in this type of environment, where customer demands are uncertain and production processes are complex and fast-paced, can be a tricky business. For example, if you are a manufacturer of specialized parts for a large automaker, such as General Motors, and you cannot consistently fill orders in the desired time frame, you probably will not be a partner company for long! Similarly, companies like Compaq and IBM may require suppliers to ship orders for products like CDs within just four hours after orders are placed.

CONTROLS

The purpose of this section is to give you a better understanding of how the inventory management process supports the information needs of those responsible for managing it. The section provides a sample of the kinds of decisions made by the warehouse manager and the supervisor of the inventory control department. We also briefly discuss some of the risks associated with inventory control. We conclude this section with an exploration of the control processes for both safeguarding and efficiently using inventory.

Decision Makers and Types of Decisions

Table 15.3 (page 578) presents a *sample* of the types of decisions the warehouse manager and the supervisor of the inventory control department confront. Concentrating on the decisions presented in the table allows you to see both the opportunities and the challenges that typically face those managers. We'll discuss one of those decisions next.

Solving the first decision listed in Table 15.3, *the proper balance of inventory to achieve optimal customer service and optimal investment in inventory*, requires information from a number of sources, including customer sales and services (Chapter 10), the master

Table 15.3 Sample of Decision Making Relative to Inventory

Organizational Decision Makers	Decisions
Supervisor of inventory control department	The proper balance of inventory to achieve optimal customer service and optimal investment in inventory
	The proper models for measuring inventory performance
	The particular inventory items that require reordering
	How much inventory to reorder
	When to reorder inventory
	Who to order inventory from
Warehouse manager	Best techniques for maintaining physical control over inventory as it is received, while it is stored, and as it is shipped
	Schedules for taking physical inventory counts
	How and where inventory should be stored

production schedule (MPS), materials requirements planning (mrp), and the warehouse manager. Recall from Chapter 10 that the order entry/sales process often captures data regarding customer needs, customer satisfaction, and so forth. This information may impact production and capacity planning schedules.

From the standpoint of the production manager, inventory availability is a vital element in the ability to maintain production requirements for meeting customer demands. Consequently, this manager's inclination may be to inflate the inventory investment. However, an unwarranted increase in an organization's inventory investment can result in lowering its return on investment and decreasing its space utilization. Thus, data emanating from several functional areas must be gathered and analyzed before an organization can achieve an optimal inventory balance. An optimal inventory balance often translates to a level of inventory availability that is commensurate with some predetermined level of production capacity and upper bounds on expectations of customer orders.

Part of the responsibility of the inventory control manager is to help manage the composition of an organization's inventory investment. This responsibility may include adjusting the inventory balance so that it better fulfills flexible manufacturing needs or so that it turns over more quickly. Unfortunately, the inventory processes of many organizations may not provide the inventory control manager with the information needed to determine whether the inventory investment is out of balance. Take some time now to examine the remainder of Table 15.3.

The Fraud Connection

CONTROLS   Before we discuss internal control as it relates to the inventory process, let's first consider the topic of inventory fraud. Inventory is the number one domain for *management fraud*. While numerous cases of inventory thievery could be recited here, we elect to confine our discussion in this section to management fraud connected with inventory. That is, we will revisit a theme introduced in Chapter 7—namely, "cooking the books" by fraudulently misstating inventory in the financial statements.

The problem of inventory manipulation—both its frequency and the materiality of the financial statement misstatements—is massive. One authority states that inventory fraud has grown fourfold in five years and is one of the biggest single reasons for the proliferation of accounting scandals, and their associated lawsuits. One such case is Laribee Wire Manufacturing Co., a New York copper-wire maker. Suffering from a huge debt and declining sales, Laribee borrowed $130 million, a major portion of the loan collateral being its reported inventories of copper rod. After the firm filed for bankruptcy court protection a year later, it was discovered that much of its inventory didn't physically exist or was on the books at inflated values. It is estimated that the inventory fraud contributed $5.5 million to Laribee's before-tax profits.

While this chapter focuses on manufacturing and production processes, it should be noted that inventory control issues are similar for retailers (recall, for instance, the discussion on determining order quantities in Chapter 12). Unfortunately, retail organizations are perhaps even more susceptible to inventory fraud. One illustrative case of retail inventory fraud is that of Phar-Mor Inc., the deep-discount drugstore chain. Phar-Mor kept inventory on its books that had already been sold and created fictitious inventory at several of the chain's stores. In a suit filed against Phar-Mor's auditing firm of Coopers & Lybrand, one of its major stockholders contended that the company's balance sheet falsified and overstated inventory by more than $50 million!

In 1994 the AICPA issued *Practice Alert No. 94–2: Auditing Inventories—Physical Observations*. This *Practice Alert* includes the following examples of inventory fraud, among others:

- Including items in physical inventory counts that are not what they are claimed to be, or including nonexistent inventory. Examples are counting empty boxes, mislabeling boxes that contain only scrap or obsolete goods, and diluting inventory so that it appears to be of greater quantity than it actually is (e.g., adding water to liquid inventories).

- Counting merchandise to which the company does not have title, such as consigned goods and "billed and held" inventory.[6]

- Increasing physical inventory counts for those items that the auditors did not test count.

- Double-counting inventory that is in transit between locations, or moving inventory and counting it at two locations.

- Arranging for false confirmations of merchandise purportedly held by others, such as inventory in public warehouses or out on consignment.

- Including inventory for which the corresponding payable has not been recorded.

- Manipulating the reconciliations of inventory that was counted at other than the financial statement date. It is not uncommon to perform physical inventory taking on a "cycle" basis. That is, items are counted at staggered times throughout the year. When counts are done after the financial statement date, the counted quantities then must be reconciled to year-end quantities by adding purchases and subtracting sales made between the count date and year-end. Attempts to manipulate these reconciliations entail either overstating purchased quantities or understating

---

[6] Billed and held inventory is common in certain industries, such as the textile industry. Under the bill and hold arrangement, the seller invoices the buyer for purchased goods—thereby passing title to the buyer at the time of billing—but then holds the inventory at the seller's location until such time that the buyer issues shipping instructions.

sold quantities to make it appear that there is a greater on-hand balance at year-end than actually exists.

- Programming the computer to produce false tabulations of physical inventory quantities or priced summaries.[7]

Inventory Process Controls

CONTROLS   The criticalness of maintaining adequate inventory levels should be apparent at this point. Keep in mind, however, that we must balance the desire for high inventory levels with the need to avoid both excessive inventory carrying costs and leftover supplies of materials that are no longer required in revamped production processes. As such, inventory process controls are primarily oriented toward operational (i.e., effectiveness and efficiency) and security objectives. We focus here on three categories of control goals:

1. *Effectiveness of operations* relative to the following goals (note that these goals address the concepts discussed earlier in the chapter; namely, *optimizing* the inventory investment):

   a. to maintain a sufficient level of inventory to prevent stockouts,

   b. to maintain a sufficient level of inventory to minimize operational inefficiencies, and

   c. to minimize the cost of carrying inventory.

   Sample controls in the area categorized as effectiveness of operations might include:

   a. *Perpetual inventory records.* Maintenance of a continuous record of the physical quantities maintained in each warehouse facilitates inventory management. The receipt or shipment of each item is recorded in the inventory master data to facilitate monitoring of inventory levels and to minimize stockout risks and production interruptions. *Radio frequency identification (RFID)* tags can be attached to inventory items to track their movement throughout the warehouse, indeed, through the entire supply chain. A perpetual inventory process helps to achieve the goals by providing an up-to-date record of the status of the firm's overall inventory investment, including an account of the activity rate of each inventory item. Thus, fast-moving inventory can be identified to help prevent stockouts. Additionally, monitoring of slow-moving or excessive inventory can help minimize the cost of carrying inventory.

   b. *Just-in-time materials acquisition.* Just-in-time inventory acquisition essentially eliminates the risk of overstocks while also minimizing inventory carrying costs. Suppliers should be careful in selecting supplier partners, however, to assure they can deliver on a timely basis when demands for raw materials arise.

   c. *Internal transfer procedures.* Often, materials and finished goods inventory will be stored in multiple warehouse or plant locations. As described earlier, with *global inventory management*, needs for raw materials or finished goods orders would initially be satisfied with excess inventory available through transfers from other locations. Only when inventory needs cannot be fulfilled through internal transfers should procedures be initiated for requisitioning materials

---

[7] Division for CPA Firms—Professional Issues Task Force, *Practice Alert No. 94–2: Auditing Inventories—Physical Observations* (New York: American Institute of Certified Public Accountants, July 1994).

from suppliers or initiating increased production scheduling. Coordination between warehouses and plants helps maintain more optimal inventory levels and helps avoid inventory outages.

2. *Efficiency of process operations.* Sample controls in the area categorized as efficiency   **E-BUSINESS** might include:

    a. *Just-in-time materials acquisition.* Just-in-time inventory acquisition, when automated through *EDI* or other related approaches, can improve the efficiency of the inventory process by reducing the amount of manual labor necessary to determine when to reorder materials inventory. *Vendor managed inventory (VMI)* can shift the burden of the reordering decisions to the suppliers.

    b. *Warehouse bin location.* This plan calculates the approximate amount of space to devote to each inventory item. It also analyzes the total warehouse space available to determine *where* to locate each item to increase requisition picking efficiency.

3. *Resource security.* The resources of interest here are the raw materials, work-in-process and finished goods inventory assets, and the information resources stored in the inventory master data. Control plans should be in place to prevent unauthorized access, copying, changing, selling, or destruction of the inventory master data. Of equal importance, plans should be in place to prevent theft or unauthorized sale of merchandise inventory. Sample controls in the area categorized as resource security might include:

    a. *Periodic physical inventory counts.* Used in conjunction with a perpetual inventory process, this control plan assists in protecting materials, work-in-process, and finished goods inventory by providing the warehouse manager or the inventory control supervisor with a record of the actual (on-hand) balance of each item of inventory. This record can be compared to the corresponding perpetual records to detect any differences between the two balances. Differences between the balances may suggest the possibility of pilferage, which, in turn, exposes an organization to the risk of not achieving the control goal of resource security over its inventory. *RFID* tags can make the inventory count process more efficient and accurate.

    b. *Locked storerooms.* Locked storerooms contribute to the achievement of the operations system control goal of securing inventory. Over the years, a number of organizations have experienced a high rate of theft by employees because of inadequately secured rooms where materials and finished goods inventory are stored. As a control plan, locked storerooms limit access to an organization's inventory to authorized employees only.

One final note we should make before leaving the area of inventory control is the parallel between the processes we have discussed in this section for integrated production processes and that used in retail environments. Inventory acquisition and retail sales have been previously discussed in Chapters 10–12. However, we have not focused on retail inventory control, in part because the procedures would be redundant with the discussion presented in this section. The same concerns over operational (i.e., effectiveness and efficiency) and security risks also exist in retail environments, and similar controls to those discussed in this section should be implemented to control the receipt, storage, and distribution of retail merchandise as it is stored in or moved between various stores and warehouses.

SUMMARY

Clearly, the integrated production process represents an excellent example of the power of enterprise systems. The process integrates tightly with nearly every other process described so far, especially Order Entry/Sales, Purchasing, Human Resource Management, Payroll, and Inventory Management. With costs generated in production representing a significant portion of operating costs for manufacturing businesses and with huge pressures related to controlling product lifecycle cost, increasing innovation and decreasing time to market, the importance of enterprise systems for managing the process is paramount. Potential costs from poor information include lost sales due to stockouts; excess finished goods inventories; delays due to poor planning for labor, material, and production resources; excess raw materials due to poor forecasting; and poor reputation resulting from poor quality.

Accounting systems designers face significant challenges in meeting financial accounting needs while taking advantage of the vast array of information production capability in enterprise systems to generate more useful managerial information. In particular, they will be expected to take a lifecycle costing approach and provide valuable information in all stages of the value chain including:

- Take an active role in the early stages of product development. This role should emphasize cost reduction activities.

- Provide more advice, not only during development, but also throughout the entire manufacturing process. Some people have even suggested that cost accountants should spend most of their time on the factory floor performing value analysis to prevent variances from occurring in the first place.

- Develop non-traditional measurements that can help in managing the business, and share that information with the workers on a timely basis. Measures might include such factors as employee morale, product quality (perhaps in the form of warranty data), disaggregated production and scrap data by machine or by work center, schedule and delivery attainment, throughput time, and space devoted to value-added versus nonvalue-added activities.

- Develop new standard cost systems that will focus on quality and production as well as price and efficiency. These updated cost systems would employ input/output analysis rather than focus only on inputs as the conventional standard cost system does.

- Design new ways to evaluate investments. Traditional tools such as *return on investment (ROI)* and *net present value* analyses have proved inadequate for making decisions about major commitments of resources to enterprise systems technology, especially the important cross-functional systems such as customer relationship management, supply chain management, and product lifecycle management so critical for managing globally diverse manufacturing operations. The traditional cost justification methods must be supplemented with an analysis of intangible benefits, including items such as improved shop floor flexibility, reduced manufacturing lead time, faster delivery of product to market, improved product quality, improved product design, better customer service, and similar factors.

One final thought about how the accountant can take a leadership role in manufacturing companies concerns that of designing *simplified* processes. Much of what we have learned from the Japanese is epitomized by *KISS (keep it simple, stupid)*. Part of simplification involves making the data we capture in the information system easier to access. Another part requires that we be constantly alert to opportunities to reduce paperwork. The trend toward *paperless processes* must accelerate to keep pace with other technological changes occurring in production processes.

REVIEW QUESTIONS

RQ 15-1 How has global competition impacted the domestic manufacturing environment? How can technology help domestic companies compete?

RQ 15-2 Explain the three key drivers of complexity in manufacturing operations in the new millennium.

RQ 15-3 Describe the three key characteristics of companies that successfully manage global complexity.

RQ 15-4 What is the role of product innovation and product lifecycle management in helping manufacturing companies complete in the global arena?

RQ 15-5 What are the differences between push manufacturing and pull manufacturing?

RQ 15-6 How does supply chain management help organizations improve their competitiveness, especially in a manufacturing organization?

RQ 15-7 What important trends have occurred during the past few decades in cost management and cost accounting?

RQ 15-8 Describe the importance of both activity-based costing and product lifecycle costing for managing IPP.

RQ 15-9 What are the steps in the IPP and what happens at each step?

RQ 15-10 What is the role of the order entry/sales and inventory management processes in the IPP?

RQ 15-11 What is global inventory management and how can it be used to increase the ability of a company to deliver goods on a timely basis and manage inventories?

RQ 15-12 a. How are a bill of material (BOM) and a routing master similar? different?

b. What does "exploding a bill of material" mean?

RQ 15-13 How are materials requirements planning, detailed capacity requirements planning, and shop floor control similar? different?

RQ 15-14 What are some of the components of flexible manufacturing systems and how do they work?

RQ 15-15 What are some of the characteristics and advantages of a JIT system?

RQ 15-16 How is information generated about the IPP used for managing the IPP as well as other business processes?

RQ 15-17 What are the key processes, data, and data flows in the cost accounting system for variance analysis of a manufacturer that uses a standard cost system?

RQ 15-18 Why is inventory management and control important to the manufacturing and production processes?

DISCUSSION QUESTIONS

DQ 15-1 This chapter discusses the complexities of competing in a highly competitive global manufacturing environment. Discuss how enterprise systems can help an organization streamline its processes and become more competitive.

DQ 15-2 Discuss what you think might be the major contributing reasons for automotive manufacturers being one of the leaders in enterprise systems implementations.

DQ 15-3 Table 15.1 (page 556) presents a summary of trends in cost management and cost accounting that have occurred during the past two decades.

    a. Which trends do you consider most significant? Explain your answer.

    b. The first footnote to Table 15.1 indicates that there are additional cause-and-effect relationships that could be shown between the items in the right column and those in the left column. Give several examples (with explanations) of those other relationships.

DQ 15-4 "A company cannot implement a just-in-time (JIT) process without making a heavy investment in computer resources." Do you agree? Discuss fully.

DQ 15-5 "A company cannot implement manufacturing resource planning (MRP) without making a heavy investment in computer resources." Do you agree? Discuss fully.

DQ 15-6 "A company cannot implement a flexible manufacturing system (FMS) without making a heavy investment in computer resources." Do you agree? Discuss fully.

DQ 15-7 In your opinion, how well has your college educational experience prepared you to meet the challenges and opportunities mentioned in the chapter? What recommendations would you make, if any, to improve that experience for future accounting students at your school? Discuss fully.

DQ 15-8 Without redrawing the figure, discuss the changes that would occur in Figure 15.7 (page 574) if the company used an actual costing system instead of a standard cost system.

DQ 15-9 Discuss how the inventory control process goals support the production planning process, and the risks to the production process if such controls are not in place.

PROBLEMS

P 15-1 Refer to the level 0 data flow diagram in Figure 15.1 (page 558). Study the portion of the figure and accompanying narrative that deals with the product and production process design process *only*. Prepare a level 1 data flow diagram for the product and production process design process (bubble 1.0) *only*.

P 15-2 Refer to the level 0 data flow diagram in Figure 15.1 (page 558). Study the portion of the figure and accompanying narrative that deals with the materials requirements planning process *only*. Prepare a level 1 data flow diagram for the materials requirements planning process (bubble 3.0) *only*.

P 15-3 Refer to the level 0 data flow diagram in Figure 15.1 (page 558). Study the portion of the figure and accompanying narrative that deal with the capacity requirements planning process *only*. Prepare a level 1 data flow diagram for the capacity requirements planning process (bubble 4.0) *only*.

P 15-4 Consider all of the data stores shown in Figure 15.1 (page 558). Draw an entity-relationship diagram showing the database for the IPP based on the data stores shown in the figure. You do not need to include cardinalities.

P 15-5 Refer to the level 0 data flow diagram in Figure 15.1 (page 558). Study the portion of the figure and accompanying narrative that deal with the shop floor control process *only*. Prepare a level 1 data flow diagram for the shop floor control process (bubble 5.0) *only*.

P 15-6 Refer to the data flow diagram in Figure 15.7 (page 574). Study the portions of the figures and the accompanying narrative that deal with the cost accounting—variance analysis system *only*.

Prepare a detailed systems flowchart for the cost accounting—variance analysis system *only*.

P 15-7 Study Figure 15.7 (page 574), showing the level 0 data flow diagram of the cost accounting system. Note that the raw materials and finished goods inventory processes are *outside* the context of the system shown (i.e., the DFD covers work-in-process inventory only).

a. Draw a *context diagram* for the system as it *currently* exists.

b. Assume that both the raw materials and finished goods inventories are *within* the system context. Prepare a *context diagram* for the revised system, and redraw Figure 15.7 to reflect the revised system. Ignore the ordering of raw materials from vendors; start the raw materials process with the receipt of goods. Also ignore the issue of finished goods. Keep the assumption that the company uses standard costing for all inventories.

P 15-8 Study Figure 15.7 (page 574), the level 0 data flow diagram of the cost accounting system for a company using standard costing.

Redraw Figure 15.7 assuming that the company uses an actual cost instead of a standard cost system.

P 15-9 Figure 15.7 (page 574) shows several data flows running to the general ledger (GL) for the purpose of updating the general ledger master data.

a. For each of the following data flows in Figure 15.7, show the journal entry (in debit/credit journal entry format, with no dollar amounts) that would result (make and state any assumptions you think are necessary):
   - GL standard costs applied update
   - GL RM variances update
   - GL DL variances update
   - GL MOH variances update
   - GL cost of goods completed update

b. What other standard cost accounting entries are not included in your answer to requirement a? Show those journal entries; describe *when* they would be made and *what* event they are recording.

P 15-10 Based on the inventory control process goals discussed in the chapter, explain the impact of using a periodic inventory process instead of a perpetual process. Be sure to also discuss how you would design the process to attempt to meet the same control objectives using this periodic process.

KEY TERMS

throughput time

push manufacturing

pull manufacturing

cellular manufacturing

subassemblies

available to promise planning

capable to promise planning

activity-based costing

lifecycle costs

computer-aided design (CAD) and computer-aided engineering (CAE)

bill of materials

parts master

routing master

computer-aided process planning (CAPP)

work center master

workstation

work center

master production schedule

global inventory management

production, planning, and control

materials requirements planning

time-phased order requirements schedule

exploding the BOM

capacity requirements planning (CRP)

manufacturing orders (MOs)

move tickets

raw materials requisition

manufacturing resource planning (MRP)

flexible manufacturing systems (FMS)

computer-aided manufacturing (CAM)

automated storage and retrieval systems (AS/RS)

automated guided vehicle systems (AGVS)

just-in-time (JIT)

total quality control (TQC)

shop floor control (SFC) process

variance analysis

chapter 16

Learning Objectives

- To illustrate how the business processes feed data required for GL updates.

- To explain how the GL and business reporting capabilities support an organization's external and internal reporting functions.

- To analyze the limitations of the traditional general ledger approach in contemporary systems.

- To describe how client/server hardware and software platforms can be used to implement the GL and business reporting.

- To analyze control issues and control plans associated with client/server hardware and software used to implement the GL and related business reporting extensions.

- To evaluate potential problems encountered in operating the GL and possible solutions to those problems.

The General Ledger and Business Reporting (GL/BR) Process

What is your best excuse for turning in an assignment late? Today's students are well past "the dog ate my paper." Instead, instructors frequently hear standard excuses such as "my email was not working" or "my broadband connection was slow." With the Securities and Exchange Commission shortening filing deadlines, CFOs also may be looking for new excuses for late filings. Odds are that other CFOs will not copy the excuse Chris Dittmar, CFO of Adair International Oil and Gas Inc., provided when he recently filed a request for deadline extension with the SEC. When Dittmar arrived for his first day of work—the day after Adair shareholders fired the previous CEO and CFO, he found the financial records for the company had vanished. Not only were key computers stolen, but those left behind had relevant files deleted. Even the backup tapes were gone! Dittmar's entire staff was dismissed due to the theft. With the cooperation (and documents) from Adair's trading partners, and one former accountant, the extended deadline was met! Amazingly, considering the scope of his problem, Dittmar made his extended deadline.[1]

In this chapter we will explore the databases and information processes that must be in place to capture and store accounting and other business-related data and to produce internal and external business reports, including GAAP-based financial reports. When you have completed this chapter, we hope that you will appreciate how difficult a task Chris Dittmar faced at Adair.

[1] The source for this vignette is Alix Nyberg, "Filing Late: Excuses, Excuses," *CFO Magazine*, http://www.cfo.com, November 22, 2002.

In this chapter, we highlight our entire AIS wheel by exploring the systems that support the accumulation and presentation of information in the form of financial reports. This general ledger and business reporting system allows the external and internal use of information that was collected, stored in a database, and processed with sophisticated controls to ensure true reporting. Process controls must be in place to ensure that the data accumulation is accurate and complete, and that the underlying business processes achieve their goals. Pervasive controls must be in place to ensure these systems are secure and well documented to allow for Sarbanes-Oxley certifications required of top management. At the same time you should notice that the GL/BR process is now at the top of the wheel because it is that process that is the focus of our present discussion.

SYNOPSIS

Before you began your study of AIS, you probably would have defined the term *accounting information system* by describing the general ledger (GL) component. After all, the GL would be most familiar to you from your earlier accounting courses. Now that you have journeyed through some or all of the business processes in Chapters 10–15, you should appreciate that the GL is the repository where it all comes together, which is why this chapter appears after the related business processes were covered. Hopefully, you also have developed a realization during your coverage of these earlier chapters that more than just GL/accounting-based reports are needed. Rather, the general area of business reporting that supports an organization's decision making requires the ability to synthesize business information on operational and strategic performance derived from a multitude of sources.

As you study this chapter consider the problems faced by Chris Dittmar at Adair. He would have had *more* severe problems if Adair had lost their reporting system and not just the accounting data. As it was, they lost the GL database, but not the data in feeder systems (e.g., sales, accounts payable), not the trading partner data, and not the expertise of a former accountant. With these pieces of the general ledger and business reporting process they were able to prepare the required reports.

Topically, this chapter's organization is the same as that of the business process chapters. We will start by defining the boundaries of the GL, explaining its functions, and examining its organizational context. Then we proceed to a discussion of the *logical* system features. Sections on extended business reporting processes, technology, and controls follow. We take the opportunity in this chapter to focus on using client/server hardware and software platforms for implementing the GL and business reporting process.

SYSTEM DEFINITION AND FUNCTIONS

Similar to the business processes covered in Chapters 10 through 15, the **general ledger and business reporting (GL/BR) process** is an interacting structure of people, equipment, methods, and controls that is designed to accomplish both operations and information system functions. Unlike the other business processes, the GL/BR process has fewer *operational* functions; it focuses mainly on *information* functions. Whereas the other processes perform important functions related to their "work" of providing goods and services to customers, the *work* of the GL/BR process is the processing and communicating of information.

What are the important information services functions of the GL/BR process? This chapter emphasizes two categories: namely, general ledger activities and other business reporting.

The **general ledger (GL) process** comprises:

- Accumulating data, *classifying* data by general ledger *accounts*, and recording data in those accounts.
- Fueling the *financial reporting, business reporting,* and other reporting subsystems by providing the information needed to prepare external and internal reports. In servicing the information needs of *managerial* reporting, the GL interacts with the *budgeting* modules, as we will see in the next section.

The **business reporting process** is concerned with the following:

- Preparing *general purpose, external* financial statements (e.g., the "conventional four" that you have studied in other accounting courses: the balance sheet, income statement, statement of owner equity changes, and cash flow statement).
- Ensuring that the external financial statements conform to GAAP; therefore, among other things, the statements must contain appropriate *footnote disclosures.*
- Generating Web-based forms of key financial statement and related business reporting information for dissemination via the Internet.   **E-BUSINESS**
- Supporting the generation of both ad hoc and predetermined business reports that support operational and strategic decision making.

ORGANIZATIONAL SETTING

In this section we examine the placement of the GL/BR process in the organization and the interactions with its relevant environment. We will describe the roles of the new "players" who are involved most directly with the GL/BR process and will review the horizontal and vertical information flows within an organization.

Before we begin, we should define a term that is used in this section and throughout the chapter. A **feeder process** is any business process that accumulates *business event* data that are then communicated to and processed within the GL. Accordingly, the feeder processes include all those discussed in the earlier business process chapters. In addition, we show the treasurer as a feeder because the treasurer furnishes the GL with updates for *investing activities* and *financing activities.*

Horizontal Perspective of the General Ledger and Business Reporting Process

Like their counterparts in earlier chapters, Figure 16.1 and Table 16.1 show the placement of the business reporting function in the organization and the horizontal informa-

Figure 16.1 A Horizontal Perspective of the General Ledger and Business Reporting Process

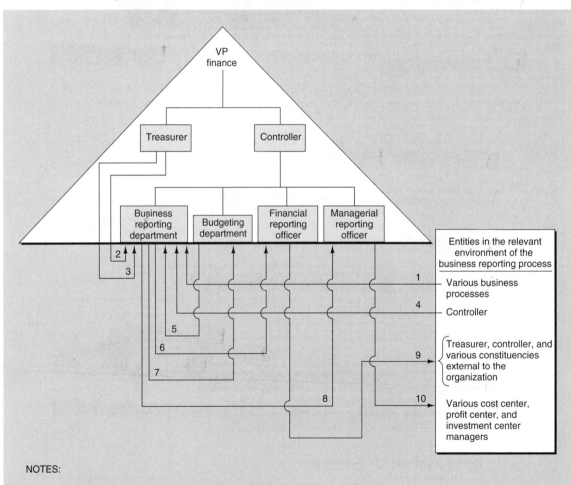

NOTES:

1. For convenience in drawing flow lines 4 and 9, the controller is shown in the external environment.

2. See Table 16.1 for a description of information flows numbered 1 through 10.

Table 16.1 Description of Information Flows

Flow No.	Description
1	Business process feeders send updates to the business reporting department.
2	Treasurer notifies the business reporting department of investing transaction activities.
3	Treasurer notifies the business reporting department of financing transaction activities.
4	Controller notifies the business reporting department of various adjusting entries.
5	Finalized budget figures are sent to the business reporting department from the budgeting department.
6	Adjusted trial balance figures are sent from the business reporting department to the financial reporting officer.
7	Actual and budget figures are sent from the business reporting department to the budgeting department; the actual results will be one of the inputs used in formulating next period's budgets.
8	Actual and budget figures are sent by the business reporting department to the managerial reporting officer.
9	The financial reporting officer sends GAAP-based financial statements to the treasurer, controller, and various external constituencies (e.g., owners, potential investors, banks, potential lenders).
10	The managerial reporting officer sends performance reports to various cost center, profit center, or investment center managers.

tion flows between the GL/BR process and other entities. Take some time now to review them before we highlight the key points.

Let's begin by examining some of the horizontal flows appearing in the figure. You should first note that flow 1 consolidates several different updates from the *feeder processes* studied in other business process chapters. However, the individual updates will be shown as separate data flows in the logical data flow diagrams (DFDs) appearing in the next section.

As we mentioned, another feeder appearing in Figure 16.1 is the treasurer. Whereas updates for *operating activities* are depicted by flow 1, the *investing* and *financing* activity updates are shown by flows 2 and 3, respectively. Moving to flow 4, we have *assumed* that all adjusting entry updates come from the controller. Obviously, such notifications could come from other sources instead. For instance, the **financial reporting officer might provide the adjustments mandated by GAAP.** Another example is depreciation adjustments, which in some companies come from a separate fixed asset system, but in many contemporary systems are simply generated automatically by the system supporting the GL. We believe the descriptions in Table 16.1 of the remaining flows in Figure 16.1 should be fairly self-explanatory.

At this point we also should consider how these information flows are affected by integrated *enterprise systems* such as ERP systems. First, for flow 1, which is the entry of data from the *feeder processes*, the ERP system *automatically* updates the database to reflect the journal entries for the GL, and to capture the information needed for other business reporting, using embedded update rules within the system. In other words, the

ENTERPRISE SYSTEMS

business reporting department does not have to enter the data—it is already entered directly by the IS component of the business processes. The flows from those processes to the GL are often labeled "GL update." Similarly, for flows 2 and 3, the ERP system sends the entries to the general ledger when personnel in the treasurer's office record investing or financing activities in the treasury module of the ERP system. For flow 5, the input again is done through the integration of the budgeting function and the general ledger in the ERP system. The output side from the ERP systems operates in much the same manner. Flows 6 through 10 are all information that can be extracted by the respective departments or constituencies using either pre-established reporting forms or through queries of the enterprise database.

Note that flow 4 is the only entry from Figure 16.1 that needs to be made directly into the general ledger. The automation of the various activities clearly reduces the number of people needed to handle the mundane accounting entry work in the business reporting department. Rather, the department can focus on the provision of more complex and interesting information that can be used to aid in the improvement of the effectiveness and efficiency of the organization's operations and strategies. We will explore some of the possibilities within this extended business reporting capability later in this chapter.

E-BUSINESS As we look to emerging capabilities, we also should consider how the external reporting model is changing. Increasingly, organizations are deciding to make their financial information available on the Internet. Currently, little standardization to this information exists between companies. Nonetheless, it should be noted that flow 9 increasingly includes the release of information to corporate Web sites.

Figure 16.2 provides a diagram that synthesizes these various information flows in what is labeled the "financial information chain." Note that the "operational data stores" are the central enterprise database or other stored business reporting system data. From the data stores, information is extracted for internal reporting (i.e., the reports on the left-hand side of the diagram) as discussed later in this chapter. Note that for external reporting, however, the information must be extracted in various formats and often reentered into various forms to service various constituents (i.e., banks, SEC, etc.). Later in this chapter, we will discuss current efforts to improve the standardization and quality of this information to improve the efficiency and effectiveness of business reporting.

Let's return to Figure 16.1 (page 590) and discuss some key points that you should observe from the organization structure within the triangle at the top of the figure. From prior chapters, you should be familiar with the typical division within the finance function between the treasurer and the controller. To emphasize differences in their functional responsibilities, we have shown four managers reporting to the controller. In some organizations, two or more of the four functions might be combined into a single job function. In others, managers might exist who are not shown in the figure, such as the manager of a tax department.

One objective of Figure 16.1 is to portray the organizational alignment of certain key entities within the finance function. However, recalling our earlier definitions of the GL/BR process, you should recognize that only the business reporting department and the financial reporting officer are technically *within* the GL/BR process as it has been defined. Therefore, when we discuss the logical system in the next section, the treasurer, controller, budgeting department, and managerial reporting officer will all be shown as external entities lying *outside* the *context* of the GL/BR process.

Before you leave Figure 16.1 (page 590), ask yourself, "What are the functions of the four managers reporting to the controller?" We already have described the functions of

Figure 16.2 Internal and External Business Reporting Flows

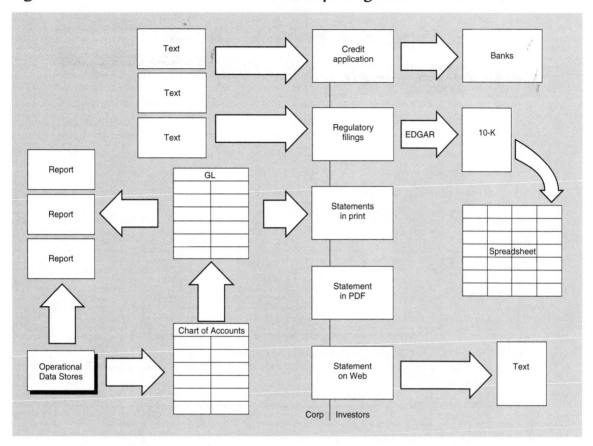

Source: Stanley Zarowin and Wayne E. Harding, "Finally, Business Talks the Same Language," *Journal of Accountancy* (August 2000): 25.

the business reporting department and the financial reporting officer in the preceding section (see the definitions of *general ledger process* and *business reporting process*, respectively). The *budgeting department advises and assists the cost center, profit center, and investment center* managers in preparing the budget.[2] The budgeting department should not actually prepare the budget estimates; it should offer technical advice to the *operating line managers* as they develop the budgets for their centers. Good participative management practice argues that the *responsibility* for budget preparation should fall to the operating center managers who later will be held *accountable* for budget variations. One final comment about the budgeting function is in order. Because the "advise and assist" role of the budgeting department cuts across all functions in the organization, it is not uncommon in practice to see the department placed much higher in the organization chart, perhaps on the same horizontal level as the president or CEO.

The **managerial reporting officer** has responsibilities similar to those of the *financial reporting officer*. The latter possesses expertise in the area of financial reporting to external parties, and the former performs a similar role in respect to preparing internal

---

[2] We assume that you understand the terms *cost center*, *profit center*, and *investment center* from your study of managerial/cost accounting.

reports to assist management decision making (this distinction may sound familiar from your earlier studies of *financial accounting* versus *managerial accounting*). Many of the reports prepared by the managerial reporting officer are called **performance reports** because they compare actual performance with budgeted expectations. Often, these reports are part of a managerial reporting system known as a **responsibility accounting/ reporting system** because it is tied to the hierarchy or chain of responsibility/authority reflected by the firm's organization chart. In such a system, as information is reported upward, the level of detail is filtered, meaning that figures are aggregated (summarized) as they are reported to successive management levels. Figure 16.3 shows a sample *performance reporting* flow for the production arm of an organization that uses a *responsibility accounting/reporting* model.

Figure 16.3 Responsibility Accounting Performance Reporting

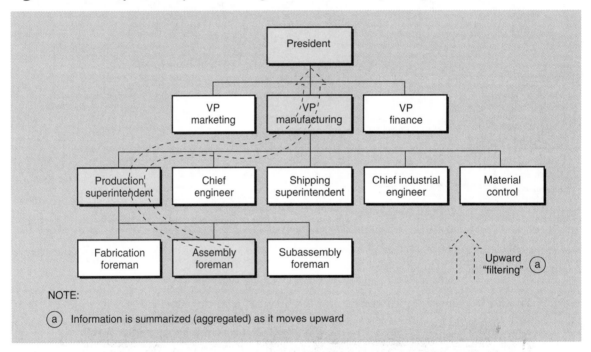

NOTE:

(a) Information is summarized (aggregated) as it moves upward

Source: Adapted with permission from James D. Wilson, "Human Relations and More Effective Reporting," *NAA Bulletin* (May 1961): 13–24.

ENTERPRISE SYSTEMS

As we will be discussing later in this chapter, the major ERP vendors are providing the additional functionality to support much of this additional business reporting demand for performance reporting. The integration of this functionality allows these reports to be easily generated from information captured by the business processes and maintained at the business event level in the enterprise database.

Horizontal and Vertical Information Flows

In Figure 1.9 (page 28), the distinction between horizontal and vertical information flows was introduced at a conceptual level. Perhaps now is a good time to review the concepts shown in Figure 1.9, and enhance that figure based on our study of AIS to date. Figure 16.4 is intended to do exactly that.

Figure 16.4 Horizontal and Vertical Information Flows

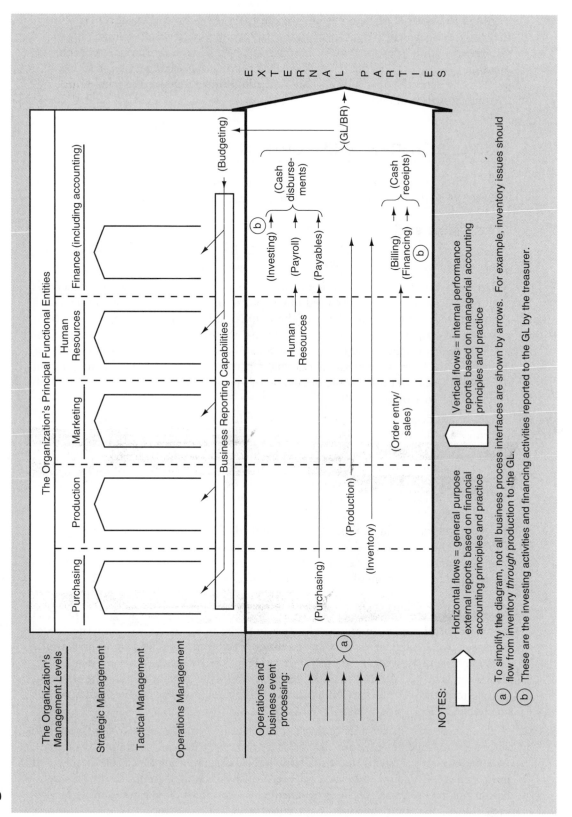

Along the bottom of Figure 16.4, we can trace the horizontal transaction flows as they progress from left to right through the various *operations systems*, culminating in the GL, and resulting in external business reporting. We also see the vertical reporting dimension (in the form of internal performance reports prepared from information supplied by the general ledger and through budgeting) flowing upward in each of the principal functional columns.

LOGICAL SYSTEM DESCRIPTION

Once again in this chapter, we use DFDs to explain the *logical* features of the GL/BR process. Study the DFDs carefully to make sure that you understand their contents.

Discussion and Illustration

We start with the highest-level view of the GL/BR process; namely, the *context diagram*, shown in Figure 16.5. Take some time now to study the figure.

Do you agree that there is nothing really new here? Note the *business event* data flows from the business processes discussed in Chapters 10 through 15. If you are uncertain about the nature and timing of any of these updates, go back to the appropriate business process chapter and review them. Note also the two types of update entries coming from the treasurer, the adjusting entry updates coming from the controller, and the finalized budget furnished by the budgeting department. Note that each system output data flow was shown earlier in the discussion of information flows (see flows 7 through 10 in Figure 16.1 on page 590).

ENTERPRISE SYSTEMS   We should define the term *journal voucher*, which appears in the data flow "Adjusting entry journal vouchers." In general terms, a **journal voucher** is an internal source document used to notify the general ledger to make an accounting entry. In addition to showing the entry's details, the journal voucher should be signed by the person(s) authorized to initiate the entry. Remember, in the case of an *enterprise system* this voucher document will likely be electronic, the person completing the adjustment will generally enter it directly into the system, and the signature will be represented through a capturing of the electronic identification of the individual making the entry. Although the DFDs use the term *journal voucher* only in connection with adjusting entry updates from the controller, you should recognize that any of the business event updates from the feeder processes might also take the *form* of a journal voucher.

Let's pursue that last point. *Logically*, each business event from a feeder process can be posted *directly*, *individually*, and *immediately* to the general ledger. As a practical matter, *physical* implementations will vary. For example, the flows from the feeder processes could comprise *summaries* of a number of business events posted *periodically* at the end of a day, week, or month. For example, the B/AR/CR process may collect the data related to sales and send the related data to the general ledger. The resulting summarized entry to the general ledger would include postings to sales and accounts receivable.

ENTERPRISE SYSTEMS   In an *enterprise system*, this business event data is recorded separately for each sale within the module designed for that business process (e.g., sales, accounts receivable). In some enterprise systems implementations this business event data could be batched during sales (or accounts receivable) processing and then used to update the GL database at one point in time. If the general ledger processing is done through this type aggregation of the source records (e.g., business events), the impact of many business

Figure 16.5 General Ledger/Business Reporting Process—Context Diagram

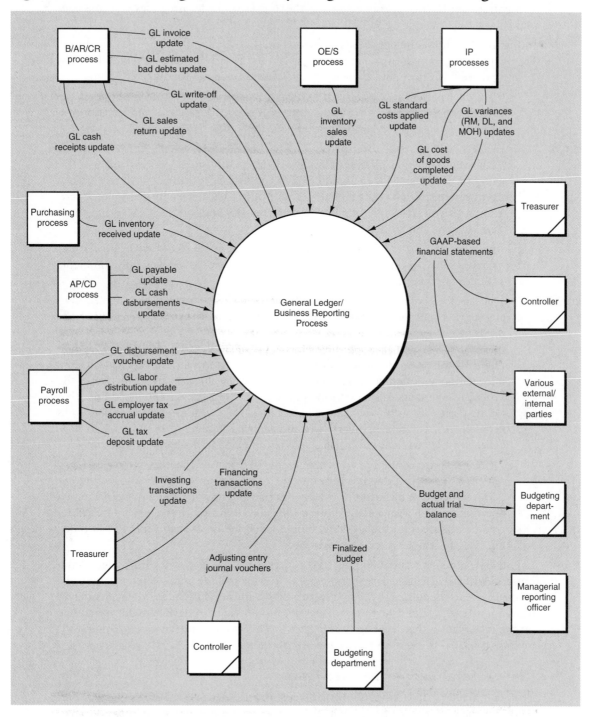

events will be posted as a batch, and the balances in the GL accounts will be adjusted accordingly. However, the enterprise system will maintain data for each individual business event in the underlying business process database, and a user can view this detail by simply drilling down on the GL balance data. At this point, however, let's continue to concentrate on the logical connections of the individual feeder processes with the general ledger.

Figure 16.6 shows the GL/BR process level 0 DFD. Again, this figure should require little explanation. Let's take a moment to talk about bubble 1.0, "Validate business event updates." What might be involved here? Some examples follow.

- We want to check business event updates to make sure that they come from the correct feeder process. Do you agree that this check addresses the information system goal of ensuring event data *input validity*?

CONTROLS
- We also want to make sure that no business event updates have been overlooked (recall the discussion of *input completeness* in each business process chapter). Finally, we verify the debit and credit equality of "halves" of entries flowing from different systems. What control goals are we trying to achieve with this kind of verification? If you answered "input completeness (IC) and input accuracy (IA)," you were right on the money.[3]

Are bubbles 2.0 through 4.0, plus 6.0, reminiscent of the *bookkeeping/accounting cycle* that you studied in earlier accounting courses? They should be! The only comments that we offer here follow.

E-BUSINESS
- You should recognize that process 4.0, "Prepare business reports," involves several steps. These steps *might* include activities such as preparing a *worksheet*, drafting financial statement footnotes, formatting the financial statements and footnotes, and compiling the financial statements into an attractive and informative reporting package. For general distribution, these financial statements and related information are often posted to the entity's Web site. Frequently, at this stage, the financial statements will be reformatted to take advantage of embedded links that can be placed into the Web page. For instance, some companies provide hot links in the financial statements directly to the financial statement footnotes to make it easier for users to tie the footnotes with specific financial statement accounts.

- Process 6.0, like some that you encountered in previous chapters, is *triggered* by a temporal event (i.e., the data flow into the process from the general ledger master data), rather than by a data flow from another process or from an external entity. Specifically, at an appropriate *point in time*, the condition of the general ledger accounts indicates that the accounts should be closed before repeating the accounting cycle for the next accounting period.

Our final comment about Figure 16.6 concerns process 5.0, "Record budget." Because GAAP-based external reports seldom, if ever, include budget information, we might have excluded process 5.0 and its related data flows. However, we included it to provide one example of how the GL/BR process can "fuel" reporting systems that rely on the information that has been aggregated in the system—in this case providing information related to both budgeted and actual results.

The General Ledger Master Data

The **general ledger master data** contains summarized information of all company event data. The main inputs to the general ledger consist of totals, extracted by event type,

---

[3] Note that this problem is alleviated in many contemporary systems as a single entry for the business event is made and the system will be programmed to execute recording to both the debit and credit account balances. This is essentially how event data entry and update is accomplished in an enterprise system environment.

Figure 16.6 General Ledger and Business Reporting Process—Level 0 Data Flow Diagram

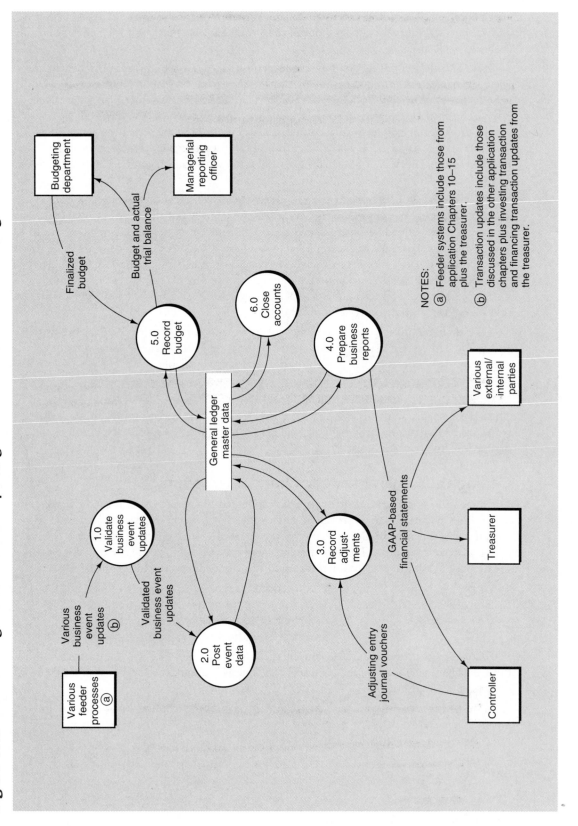

from the business event data captured in the various feeder processes discussed earlier. Adjusting entry journal vouchers, originating with the controller, are the other principal source of entries.

In traditional accounting systems, the general ledger's utility has depended largely on a well-designed and complete *chart of accounts*. The more sophisticated the *data classification and coding* scheme used for the chart of accounts (a subject discussed in the next section), the broader the range of financial reports that can be produced. For example, the first three digits in an account number might show the account's general classification. Digits in other fields then can indicate the responsibility center, project number, and so on. This way, job or plant financial statements can be generated, in addition to the consolidated statements that are made available to outside users.

CONTROLS   The source code field of each general ledger entry provides a beginning point of reference for developing a proper **audit trail**. The code gives the auditor a means of tracing back to the individual business events that have been aggregated into the general ledger balances. For instance, using a batch number, an auditor can follow an entry to the appropriate batch file. From there, the batched event data can be identified. The path then leads to the original source document. Journal vouchers can be substantiated by using the source code to locate the specific input form used by the controller (or another employee in the controller's office).

Note that in addition to storing the entries of the current period (both monthly and yearly activity are usually maintained in computer-based general ledger systems), beginning-of-period and year-to-date balances also are available.

ENTERPRISE SYSTEMS   In an *enterprise system*, since the source business event data is maintained, the user can select any beginning and ending date to accumulate information for any period of time. Thus, if a manager wants to examine sales over a two-week, three-month, or any other period, the information can be aggregated through a query to provide the manager the precise information of interest.

Coding the General Ledger Chart of Accounts

The discussion of *classifying* and *coding* data appeared in Chapter 5. You might want to review that material before proceeding. Do any of the coding systems presented in Chapter 5 seem particularly germane to the general ledger chart of accounts? What about *hierarchical coding*? To illustrate, let's suppose the number 1113 was assigned to the account "cash in bank." Moving from left to right, the hierarchy might be:

$$
\begin{array}{ll}
\text{1XXX} & = \text{ assets} \\
\text{X1XX} & = \text{ current assets} \\
\text{XX1X} & = \text{ cash accounts} \\
\text{XXX3} & = \text{ cash in bank}
\end{array}
$$

Following this "system," 1111 might mean petty cash, 1112 might mean change fund, 1121 might mean trade accounts receivable, 1122 might mean receivables from officers, and so on.

In designing a coding scheme for a chart of accounts, you should consider the following questions:

- On which financial statements, if any, must an account appear?
- In which category on a financial statement (e.g., current asset or fixed asset) should it appear?
- In what order should the accounts appear (e.g., liquidity or maturity)?

- Which accounts should be aggregated for presentation (e.g., show one cash balance)?
- Which internal reports will be required (e.g., departmental or cost center *performance reports*)?

Limitations of the General Ledger Approach

Recall in Chapter 5 the discussion regarding the limitations of traditional file processing approaches and the emerging focus on event-driven systems (you may wish to review this material before proceeding). The discussion focused on the limitations that come from disjoint stores of data for financial and non-financial information, and the elimination of source data after business event information has been added to account summaries. The traditional general ledger approach has been a primary suspect as the source of many of these problems.

If you think about the driving force in constructing a chart of accounts, the goal is to add structure to the classification of financial information. Don't get us wrong; this is a good thing. The problem is that in implementing the chart of accounts, the focus usually becomes one of "How can we classify every piece of business event data as fitting into a specific account?" And, the formation of the coding scheme (as discussed in the previous section) is based on summary aggregation requirements for creating financial reports. In reality, most general ledger systems capture the chart of accounts number and the debit or credit entry, and the remainder of the information about a business event is discarded.

While other business event information may be captured in separate systems operated by other departments, such as marketing, any such non-financial information becomes separated from the financial information. Once the end-of-period closings are completed for the general ledger, the detailed business event-level data are eventually purged from the system—the interest being only in maintaining correct current balances for each entry in the chart of accounts. It is at this point that, even if there was a link between the financial and non-financial information in the business event data, the relationships are lost. From that point on, information for decision making is limited to only that information captured in the accounts as specified by the chart of accounts. If you decide you want more detailed information than the chart of accounts provides, historical business events generally cannot be reconstructed. The information can be captured in the future only if alterations are made to the chart of accounts and the programs that use those accounts (i.e., the financial report generator).

As an example, let's take the hierarchy discussed in the preceding section and adapt it to sales. The hierarchy might start out as follows:

$$7XXX = \text{revenues}$$
$$X1XX = \text{merchandise sales}$$

After a while, one of the corporate managers decides that the system needs to capture sales by region. We could add region as a third digit, but that doesn't fit our hierarchical structure very well. Logically, the second digit needs to be region so that all types of revenues can be grouped by region. We can revise our system, but keep in mind that after we make this change, all the programs using the data also will need to be revised to recognize the new system—no small task. The new system may look as follows:

$$7XXX = \text{revenues}$$
$$X1XX = \text{sales region}$$
$$XX1X = \text{merchandise sales}$$

Just when we think we are out of the woods, the corporate sales manager decides that merchandise sales should be coded by another digit representing each of six sporting goods categories. Again, we revise our coding scheme and update applicable programs. Our scheme now looks like this:

$$7XXX = \text{revenues}$$
$$X1XX = \text{sales region}$$
$$XX1X = \text{merchandise sales}$$
$$XXX1 = \text{golf merchandise sales}$$

Now the real headaches begin. The sales manager has decided it is imperative that the coding scheme includes a digit to represent each unique salesperson. But, we don't have any digits left in the coding scheme! If we add a digit, we will have to completely revise our entire chart of accounts to a five-digit system, not just change the revenue accounts.

Changing account numbers and account structure can raise a potential information use problem: *comparability*. If a GL account number is changed, it must be changed not only in the GL, but also in every place in the accounting system that it is used, including all subsystems and historical references. If the account number is not changed in historical details, comparative information from prior periods will not be synchronized. Users may need to develop an external mapping (using a spreadsheet, for example, with column A containing the new account numbers and column B containing the old account numbers) to allow comparison of current revenue accounts (from our previous example) to the corresponding accounts from the periods prior to the account number change. Otherwise, the systems users can potentially lose the richness of comparative financial information for many years.

These are just some of the problems that charts of accounts create in limiting the flexibility of information aggregation and analysis. We already noted the limitations on other non-financial information. You will recall that in Chapters 5 and 6 we noted the push toward database-driven systems—and in particular, event-driven systems. This discussion should add to your understanding of why the rapidly expanding information needs of management are creating conflict with traditional general ledger structures. Later in this chapter, we will focus briefly on using database technology to perform our traditional financial report generation processes without having to limit the capturing of broad event data.

ENTERPRISE SYSTEMS
Before going on, we will address one issue more explicitly. When we talk about the advantages of database-driven systems, you should keep in mind that this broader range of systems has similar implications for ERP systems since they are database-driven and database-enabled. Thus, as we move toward an *enterprise system* environment, the chart of accounts becomes increasingly less important. If it exists at all it will probably be the concatenation of several fields in a database record that can be changed more easily simply through adding fields to the database to handle necessary information relationships such as the salesperson number in the previous example.

TECHNOLOGY-ENABLED INITIATIVES IN BUSINESS REPORTING

We explore a variety of topics in this section that demonstrate how technology has simplified much of the financial reporting process and enabled a far greater level of business reporting to support management decision making. We begin with three topics related to enterprise systems. The first is simply a brief look at the financial reporting module in an ERP system, while the second and third topics relate to contemporary extensions to ERP systems to accommodate contemporary business reporting interests—that is, balanced scorecard and business intelligence. The fourth topic also is related to enterprise systems in that the major vendors are currently working to build in the functionality for XBRL for business reporting via the Internet and the standardization of this reporting for all entities. The fifth topic, public databases, relates to services that are available for problem solving on issues ranging from the determination of proper accounting practices to aggregating information for benchmarking against other organizations.

ERP Financial Module Capability

Although we discussed earlier in this chapter the integration of business reporting in ERP systems (as well as integration of information from other business process activities), conceptually this integration may still be a bit foggy in your mind. For purposes of clarification, let's take a closer look at integration within the financial module.

ENTERPRISE SYSTEMS

Figure 16.7 shows the entry-level screen for J.D. Edwards' ERP software. We have exploded the menu options for the financials section to show you the wide range of options that are available in the software just for the financial module.

Figure 16.7 Financial Accounting Menu for J.D. Edwards Software

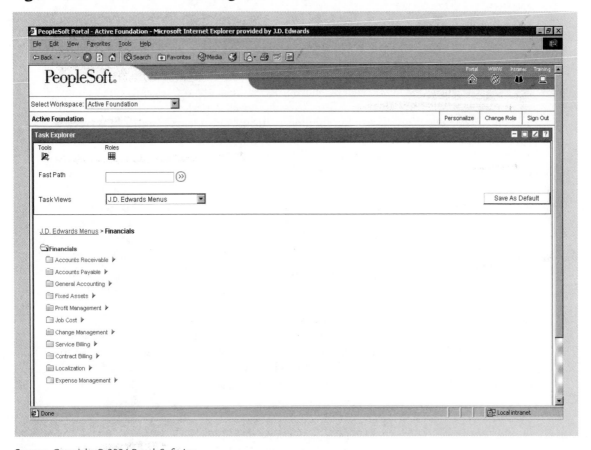

Source: Copyright © 2004 PeopleSoft, Inc.

Below the "Financials" folder, the first-level menu options for the financials module are displayed. Note that these options include information processing capabilities that are related to all the business processes we have discussed in this text. Note also that these options clearly go beyond just the general ledger-required activities to include a variety of other information processing and business reporting issues such as cost accounting, billing options, and expense reimbursements.

ENTERPRISE SYSTEMS

CONTROLS

This multitude of options should give you some feel as to the complexity and magnitude of ERP systems. You also might have thought during this discussion that all users do not need all these options. You would be correct. Indeed, for security reasons as well as ease of use, you would want to limit the access to menu items to only those needed by a given user to perform his or her responsibilities. This will mean setting up the security for an individual user to limit the menu options that appear. This becomes fairly detailed, as you may want to allow a given user to have different privilege levels for different information—that is, view access, write access, entry access, and/or change access. Sometimes users only will need to be able to view (i.e., read) information in one area of the system whereas they may need to be able to enter new event data or be able to change existing records of event data in other areas of the system. All this must be carefully specified in the user's profile to set up the system limitations for that specific user. Normally this profile is set up with the user's ID to be automatically initiated at logon.

Balanced Scorecard

Balanced scorecard is a methodology for assessing an organization's business performance via four components: (1) financial, (2) internal business processes, (3) customers, and (4) innovation and improvement activities. The financial aspect focuses on more traditional measures of business performance related to how shareholders view the organization's performance. The internal business processes relate to the organization's ability to identify its core competencies and to assess how well it performs in these identified areas of competency. The customer component focuses on identifying how customers perceive the organization in terms of the value that it is creating for them. Innovation and improvement activities are monitored to assess how the organization is continuing to improve and how it is creating additional value.

ENTERPRISE SYSTEMS

The concept of *balanced scorecard* has been around for several years, but it is only within the last few years that ERP vendors have focused on integrating this functionality and in turn making assessment a reasonable possibility. Fundamental to incorporating effective *balanced scorecard* assessment is the aggregation of varied data in a *data warehouse* (discussed in Chapter 5) that can then be analyzed using powerful analytical tools—that is, *business intelligence* tools as discussed in the next section. Since an ERP system provides the innate capability to aggregate the necessary data in its underlying database, linking this data with other data to create the necessary *data warehouse* is a logical and efficient way in which to provide *balanced scorecard* capabilities. Accordingly, all the major ERP vendors have announced, and many have included, product integration to provide the *balanced scorecard* functionality. Take a few minutes before going on to reflect on how the data captured in the various business processes could be used to support assessment in each of the four areas underlying the *balanced scorecard*.

Business Intelligence

ENTERPRISE SYSTEMS

Fundamental to providing *balanced scorecard* functionality is the development of *business intelligence* functionality within accounting and ERP systems. **Business intelligence** is the integration of statistical and analytical tools with decision support technologies to facilitate complex analyses of *data warehouses* by managers and decision makers. In short, the ideal *business intelligence* solution within an accounting and ERP system should provide the right tools, the right interface, and access to the right kind of data for effective business decision making.[4]

A typical ERP *business intelligence* module provides information details in a hierarchical form. At the top level, the user generally receives summary information on selected key performance indicators and can arrange this information into a variety of reports for analysis, performance measurement, and/or business modeling. From these summary reports (presented in electronic format), the user can subsequently drill down through further levels of detail to determine the key underlying factors driving performance. While on the surface this does not seem all that complex, the reality is that the *business intelligence* modules use highly complex analytical techniques to search for relationships in the data that will provide insight for decision making.

Extensible Business Reporting Language (XBRL)

Perhaps the most exciting technology-driven advancement in business reporting is that of *XBRL*. **eXtensible Business Reporting Language (XBRL)** is an *XML*-based language consisting of a set of tags that are used to unify the presentation of business reporting information into a single format that can be easily read by almost any software package and can be easily searched by Web browsers. As described in Chapter 10 (page 358) *XML* is a generalized system for the customized tagging of data to enable the definition, transmission, and interpretation of data over the Internet. Thus, *XBRL* is a specialized form of *XML* where the tags are predefined for multiple users to create uniformity for a set of users. In this case, *XBRL* is providing uniformity for users of financial statement and other business reporting information in order to simplify delivery of the information via the Web, enhance the searchability of the information, and to enable easy uploading and downloading of the information to other software packages for update, analysis, and so forth. Technology Summary 16.1 (pages 606–607) provides an example of XBRL tags, from a trial balance instance. This should give you a feeling of the context richness provided by using XBRL.

XBRL has been developed by an international consortium of accounting bodies and software vendors in a united effort toward uniformity of business reporting information. Participants in the consortium include many of the international professional accounting bodies, accountancy firms, Microsoft, IBM, Oracle, and SAP.

The intent is that, with a unified format, the ERP vendors (and other accounting software vendors) can add functionality that will automatically generate *XBRL*-based reports as well as any other business report. This eases the cost and complexity of delivering business information via the Web. Thus, accessibility of information should increase for external users of business reports, the information should be easier to decipher and analyze, and the information can easily be downloaded for use by other software packages such as spreadsheets, database packages, or data analysis packages. The information in Technology Excerpt 16.1 (pages 607–608) places XBRL in the context of business reporting and should give you some sense of the scope of *XBRL's* impact on the reporting, reading, and analysis of financial information.

E-BUSINESS

ENTERPRISE SYSTEMS

---

[4] Cognos, "Enterprise Reporting in an ERP Environment," *Quest Technical Journal* (Fall 1999): 27–29.

Technology Summary 16.1

An Example of XBRL

You have heard much about XBRL, but would you recognize the codes if you saw them?

The following excerpt is an example of an instance document for an XBRL-GL trial balance. The excerpt relates to the presentation of two accounts: Prepaid Expenses and Sales. As you can see, the general structure is similar to other Web-based languages such as HTML or XML. Tags (identifiers) are enclosed in brackets ("<" and ">", for example <glc:entryDetail>). The end of a specific tag includes a slash before the

identifier ("/", for example </glc:entryDetail>). There are several tags included for each data element. The excerpt for Prepaid Expenses includes GL account number: 1600; account name: Prepaid Expenses; amount: 500; date: December 31, 2001; as well as the GL category to which the item belongs: currentAssets. Also embedded in the item is the version of XBRL taxonomy that was used to create the data item and the location of that definition.

Instance of Prepaid Expenses:

```
<glc:entryDetail>
    <glc:account>
        <glc:accountMainID nonNumericContext="s1">1600</glc:accountMainID>
        <glc:accountMainDescription nonNumericContext="s1">Prepaid
        Expenses</glc:accountMainDescription>
    </glc:account>
    <glc:amount numericContext="c1">500</glc:amount>
    <glc:postingDate nonNumericContext="s1">2001-12-31</glc:postingDate>
    <glc:xbrlInfo>
        <glc:xbrlTaxonomy nonNumericContext="s1">http://www.xbrl.org/us/gaap/ci/2000-07-
        31/us-gaap-ci-2000-07-31</glc:xbrlTaxonomy>
        <glc:xbrlElement nonNumericContext="s1">currentAssets.prepaidExpenses</
        glc:xbrlElement>
    </glc:xbrlInfo>
</glc:entryDetail>
```

Instance of Sales:

```
<glc:entryDetail>
    <glc:account>
        <glc:accountMainID nonNumericContext="s1">4000</glc:accountMainID>
        <glc:accountMainDescription nonNumericContext="s1">Sales</
        glc:accountMainDescription>
    </glc:account>
    <glc:amount numericContext="c1">-82000</glc:amount>
    <glc:postingDate nonNumericContext="s1">2001-12-31</glc:postingDate>
    <glc:xbrlInfo>
        <glc:xbrlTaxonomy nonNumericContext="s1">http://www.xbrl.org/us/gaap/ci/2000-07-
        31/us-gaap-ci-2000-07-31</glc:xbrlTaxonomy>
        <glc:xbrlElement nonNumericContext="s1">salesRevenueNet.salesRevenueGross</
        glc:xbrlElement>
    </glc:xbrlInfo>
</glc:entryDetail>
```

From this example you can see the richness of information about a "number" (500 in our example) that can be included in a XBRL instance document. Decision makers can use this information, when they are trying to make comparisons between companies that support the taxonomy.

Source: For detailed information regarding XBRL, including many examples of instances and the current taxonomy, see http://www.xbrl.org. Information in the excerpt was taken from http://www.xbrl.org/gl/trialbal.xml.

Technology Excerpt 16.1

What Is XBRL?

XBRL: Transforming Business Reporting

XBRL (eXtensible Business Reporting Language) is the XML-based standard for identifying and better communicating the complex financial information in corporate business reports. XBRL makes the analysis and exchange of corporate financial information easier and more reliable.

XBRL is a royalty-free, open specification for software being developed by a non-profit consortium consisting of over 170 leading companies, associations, and government agencies around the world. Anyone interested in applying XBRL to business reporting processes can receive a license from XBRL International.

XBRL provides benefits to all members of the financial information supply chain, public and private companies, the accounting profession, regulators, analysts, the investment community, capital markets and lenders, as well as key third parties such as software developers, system integrators, consultants, and data aggregators.

How XBRL Affects Business Reporting

XBRL is a standards-based method for preparing, publishing in a variety of formats, exchanging, and analyzing financial statements and the information they contain. XBRL facilitates reporting and makes it easier for companies to expose data that is valued by investors and regulators. XBRL does not set or require changes to existing accounting rules nor require a company to disclose any additional information beyond that which they normally disclose under existing accounting standards. Instead, XBRL improves the processes of preparing, analyzing, and publishing the information in business reports.

XBRL:

- Permits the automatic exchange and reliable extraction of financial information across all software formats and technologies, including the Internet.
- Reduces the need to enter financial information more than one time, reducing the risk of data entry error and eliminating the need to manually key information for various formats, (printed financial statement, an HTML document for a company's Web site, an EDGAR filing document, a raw XML file or other specialized reporting formats such as credit reports and loan documents) thereby lowering a company's cost to prepare and distribute its financial statements while improving investor or analyst access to information.
- Leverages efficiencies of the Internet as today's primary source of financial information. Increasing numbers of companies worldwide provide some type of financial disclosure on the Internet, including 80 percent of U.S. companies, and the majority of information that investors use to make decisions comes to them via the Internet.
- XBRL meets the needs of today's investors and other users of financial information by providing accurate and reliable information for making informed decisions.

How XBRL Fits with Other Standards

Several other XML-based standards focus on financial information. These other standards include ebXML, FpML, RIXML, MDDL, FIX, FIMXL, IFX, and OFX, each of which addresses a specific aspect of financial transactions.

XBRL, on the other hand, is not designed for financial transactions, but for business reporting. This includes annual reports, SEC filings, and a variety of other reports from companies to investors, regulators, and business analysts. XBRL is for performance data rather than market data, for entities rather than investment instruments, and reported data rather than document data. XBRL defines how the numbers and facts inside a financial statement and related reports relate to one another.

Source: http://www.xbrl.org/whatisxbrl/. The copyright information for this excerpt is included at http://www.xbrl.org/copyrightinformation.asp.

Public Databases

One of the tasks facing the financial reporting officer is how to formulate the footnotes to accompany the financial statements. Take, for example, a case where the reporting officer may be having a particular problem with wording the footnote on certain litigation in which the company is a defendant, and would like to see how other companies have phrased the litigation footnote. Fortunately, her company subscribes to the **National Automated Accounting Research System (NAARS)**, an accounting research service that is one of hundreds of *public databases* (as discussed in Technology Summary 3.2 on page 83). By using a few key words linked together in a search command, she should find comparable footnotes from several companies.

The Internet, as a whole, also has become a *public database* of sorts. Through one of the many available browsers, in combination with a choice of search engines that can be found on the Web, information can be gleaned from the many varied sources available. The difficulty with the Internet is that the information is much less structured and significantly more difficult to use effectively. You should recall that in the prior section we discussed the value of *XBRL* in providing uniformity to business reporting information on the Web because of the difficulty of searching for information on the Web without such uniformity in searchable tags. Indeed, a several-hour search can leave a user virtually empty-handed unless particular sites are known in advance that can provide good links to the desired data.

Two major factors should influence the choice of using a public database versus the Internet versus some other source. The first factor to consider is cost. Public databases can be very costly for the initial connection and then for the amount of time and number of searches conducted. A half hour of searching on one of these databases can frequently lead to hundreds of dollars in access charges. The Internet is often available for free except for a monthly access charge that has already been incurred. But as the cliché goes, "There is no such thing as a free lunch."

The second factor to consider is the time required to locate the desired information. Another cliché, "Time is money," rings true here. Many wasted hours on the Internet—a problem already plaguing many companies—can be an ineffective use of human and computing resources. A public database, if an appropriate one is known and accessible, will generally allow the user to find the desired information fastest. This is primarily because such databases are generally targeted toward very specific information needs.

An increasingly important concern for management is how to control the costs of information searching—both in direct dollars and in time. The reality is that sometimes it is still cheaper to wander down the hall to the manual library and check out the resources!

IT CONTROL PROCESSES FOR NETWORKED WORKSTATIONS

This section focuses on controls in networked computer workstation environments. We approach this issue in this chapter in part because of the nature of ERP system implementations, but also in light of the many smaller accounting software packages that are run on computer workstations. We focus on ERP systems because the bulk of current implementations for ERP systems are run in a client-server environment with one or more servers connected through networks. Some ERP environments still are being run in mainframe or minicomputer environments with terminals, but these are becoming increasingly fewer as ERP vendors have started to abandon support for these versions of the software and push their clients toward client-server versions. We also should note that the new versions of ERP software are moving to Web-client environments, but these implementations are only starting to take place and conceptually the control issues are similar in most respects to that of client-server environments.

ENTERPRISE SYSTEMS

CONTROLS

As you study this section, be aware of the cumulative nature of the problems associated with computer workstation configurations. One set of control concerns is brought about by networking workstations together, and a second risk level is caused by connecting workstations to larger host computers and large-scale servers. Each risk layer leads to a corresponding group of IT control processes. Notice as you study this section that many of these controls are applications of controls first introduced in Chapter 8.

IT Control Processes for Workstation-to-Workstation Networks

The control plans for networked workstations attempt to address several questions or issues surrounding the *multiuser* environment, including:

CONTROLS

- Whereas access to computing resources in the single-user, stand-alone mode can be restricted through a number of physical controls, a critical question in the multiuser environment is whether only authorized users are allowed access to the network.
- Are all sensitive data furnished by the network file server protected from accidental or malicious destruction, disclosure, and misappropriation?
- Since failure of the network operating system could bring all applications to a halt, can we recover from a system failure? Contingency planning and backup procedures become much more critical in the network configuration.
- A common situation in networks occurs when two or more users try to access the same information resources simultaneously. For instance, user A might attempt to print a report from file Z at the same time that user B is processing business events to that same file. These situations are described as network *contention* or *concurrency*.

Now let's turn our attention to the control plans in Exhibit 16.1 (page 610). The rest of this section defines two terms appearing in the exhibit. The other items in the exhibit should be self-explanatory.

Exhibit 16.1 Controls for Workstation Networks

- Personal identification of users through passwords, magnetic ID cards, or biometrics; these controls are often built into the network operating system software.

- System access logs, including reports of invalid access attempts; review of logs by internal auditors, LAN manager, or security officer.

- Manual or automated *call-back procedures.*

- Files divided into "partitions," with access to partitions controlled by user IDs.

- Password protection at the field and record level as well as the database level.

- Different levels of authorized access (e.g., read-only, write-only, read/write).

- *Diskless workstations* and *network computers.*

- *Data encryption* and *digital signatures* (see Chapter 9).

- Physical security in the form of removable hard disks or zip drives.

- Backup facilities in the event that the network fails for any protracted length of time.

- File and record locking (usually handled through the network operating system) to resolve *contention* between two users attempting simultaneous file access.

Call-back procedures are fairly common for authenticating the identity of users who access the network from remote locations through dial-in ports. Once the user has logged on to the system and has entered his or her password and other identifiers, the connection is terminated. Either manually through an operator or automatically through security software, the user is then called back at a telephone number stored in the system for that user.

As its name implies, a **diskless workstation** contains no disk drive to enable the writing of data to floppy disks. Otherwise the unit has all the computing capabilities of any personal computer. Using diskless workstations can be an effective control procedure in applications that manipulate sensitive data.

Network computers (NCs) are restricted even further by having no storage capability. Rather, the computer contains only a processor and a connection to the server. All software and data are maintained on the server. NCs take us back toward a model more akin to the ancient history of terminals and central computers.

Take some time now to study Exhibit 16.1.

IT Control Processes for Workstation-to-Server Connections

CONTROLS   In the case of downloading data from the server, the principal concern is to prevent the unauthorized disclosure or misappropriation of the critical data that are stored on the centralized database. In situations where data also can be uploaded to the host system, an additional exposure relates to the possible accidental or intentional contamination of the database. The plans in Exhibit 16.2 address these issues.

One of those plans deserves explanation. A *front-end machine* acts as a buffer of protection between the workstation user and the central database. Only a subset of the entire database is transferred to the front-end unit. Then users work with only the data maintained by the front-end machine. Even if these data are inadvertently or maliciously damaged, the centralized database is not corrupted.

The Sarbanes-Oxley Act

In Chapter 1 we briefly introduced you to the impact that the Sarbanes-Oxley Act of 2002 has had on the accounting profession. In Chapter 7 we described how Sarbanes-

Exhibit 16.2 Controls for Workstations Connected to Centralized Servers

- Logs of all server-to-workstation file transfers; regular review of logs.
- Standardized formats to facilitate file transfers; ASCII format is fairly common.
- Read-only access to central database.

- Front-end workstations, to relieve the primary server of heavy traffic and to provide security for the server database.
- Data entry to an event data store, with later batch update to the database; instead of immediate data entry directly to the database.

Oxley has affected corporate governance. Exhibit 7.2 (page 229) outlines the 11 parts (called "Titles") of the Sarbanes-Oxley Act. In this section, we discuss a few parts of this law that pertain specifically to business and financial reporting. We should note that at the time of this writing, the law only applies to SEC registered companies, although many states are considering adopting similar legislation. Ultimately, it may apply to a wider range of organizations.

The intent of Sarbanes-Oxley, as stated in the act, is "To protect investors by improving the accuracy and reliability of corporate disclosures made pursuant to the securities laws, and for other purposes." Practically speaking, it is a new set of rules that apply to many areas, including financial reporting. Section 302 establishes who is responsible for financial reporting. It states that the CEO and CFO of an organization must certify that the statements neither contain material untrue facts nor omit material facts. The CEO and CFO also must certify that they have established and evaluated internal controls for the accounting system that produces the reports. Let's think about what this means. In earlier chapters, we discussed many controls that are necessary to ensure the proper operation of an accounting system. Historically, we made internal auditors, officers, department heads, and management throughout the organization responsible for internal controls. Sarbanes-Oxley makes top management responsible, with penalties of up to 20 years in prison and $5 million in fines for violations.

Section 401 of the act covers disclosures in financial reports. Generally accepted accounting principles (GAAP) include circumstances where certain items may or may not be disclosed in financial reports. "Off balance sheet" items are addressed in Section 401, thereby redefining GAAP for these items. The section also calls for transparent reporting of the economic effect of such transactions. This means that the report should clearly reflect, rather than obscure, the economic reality of business events.

As previously discussed, top management is responsible for internal controls. Section 404 mandates that the SEC set rules defining a report of internal controls that must be included in a company's annual report. The report must include the responsibility of management and an attestation to the control relative to internal control evaluation and reporting.

The last section of Sarbanes-Oxley we will discuss is Section 409. This section states that companies "shall disclose to the public on a rapid and current basis such additional information concerning material changes in the financial condition or operations of the issuer. . . ." This means that if anything material occurs, the SEC and the public must be notified. From this, Congress is taking us a step toward continuous or real-time reporting. If companies have in place the capability to report business events as they occur, as well as the financial impact of those events, providing key financial information to the public on a much more frequent basis than quarterly reporting is a relatively small step. We believe that this legislation will ultimately have a major effect on financial and business reporting for a multitude of organizations. As we leave this discussion, we ask that you consider the impact that these requirements will have on the GL/BR process.

Current Environment for External Financial Reporting

ENTERPRISE SYSTEMS

In the past few years, technology has created an environment where users can demand immediate information. "Overnight delivery," once the fastest way to transfer information between two entities, is frequently too slow and expensive, and is replaced by a fax (facsimile) over phone lines. The fax eliminates the one-day wait for the information. Today, many people opt for e-mail with document attachments, eliminating the need for a walk to the fax machine or the cost of a call. The same trend is occurring with respect to financial reporting. Year-end financial reports contain information that already has been released or, at a minimum, is based on events that occurred months or even over a year prior to the financial statement release. Investors want more information faster. The government is pushing for more timely reporting. In addition to the Sarbanes-Oxley Act's requirement of "rapid and current" disclosures, the SEC has shortened the time in which companies are required to file some reports, and roundtables have indicated that real-time reporting is not only feasible, but also desirable. At a recent SEC Roundtable, one of the top issues discussed is the need for information to be available in a more timely manner in the marketplace.[5] To obtain real-time reporting, *enterprise systems* must be in place so that data flows to the GL in a real-time manner. If it is feasible, and investors and regulators want it, real-time reporting is likely just over the horizon.

SUMMARY

This chapter had much to say about electronic inputs to the GL/BR process. But what about system outputs? We have been somewhat ingrained by our other accounting courses to expect hard copy documents. Will we ever see the day when business reporting will do away with paper reports and use "electronic reports"? The answer is an emphatic yes! The advent of XBRL is one clear indicator that major changes are on the way. Other projects also have existed for several years at the Internal Revenue Service (IRS) (electronic tax return filing) and at the SEC (electronic filing of annual 10-Ks). Electronic filing at the IRS has mushroomed since its inception. In fact, from 1989 to 2003, the number of electronically filed returns grew from 1.2 million to 54 million.

At the heart of the SEC's system is EDGAR (Electronic Data Gathering, Analysis, and Retrieval) and a front-end processing package called FSA—financial statement analyzer. Such a system is imperative when the filings are in a text format. If the SEC required XBRL, or some extension of XBRL for filings, the front-end processing would be greatly simplified. Although connection to EDGAR through the Internet provides easy access to the financial statements of public companies for most anyone, the SEC does not share their front-end processing with the general public. One company, EDGAR Online, Inc., has developed an online database that interprets the text-based SEC filings and provides them in a database form, complete with XBRL tagging. The service is available for a fee.[6]

Some accounting visionaries predict that within the first 10 years of the new millennium, traditional, *periodic financial reporting* will be displaced by *continuous online fi-*

---

[5] SEC: Roundtable Discussion on Financial Disclosure and Auditor Oversight, http://www.sec.gov/spotlight/roundtables/accountround030602.htm, March 6, 2002.
[6] For more information about this database and service, see http://www.edgar-online.com.

nancial reporting.[7] Part of the database reporting scenario runs along the following lines. Interested parties (i.e., all "users" who are interested in a company's financial statements) could access a company's database *at any time* through the Internet. The database would contain both financial and operating data. Through menu options, users would make different inquiries of the database, depending on their needs; a report-writing facility would allow them to tailor reports to suit those varied needs. Finally, the independent auditor's role would change from that of rendering an opinion on the fairness of periodic financial statements to one of rendering an opinion on the integrity of the database and the reliability of the systems generating the information. Does this sound a lot like the capability that XBRL is promising to provide? It should. Are you prepared to assume the auditor's revised role as information assurer? Changes are coming just about as quickly as graduation.

REVIEW QUESTIONS

RQ 16-1 What, in your own words, does business reporting entail?

RQ 16-2 What are the primary functions the GL/BR process performs?

RQ 16-3 What are the fundamental responsibilities of each of the following positions or departments: business reporting department, budgeting department, financial reporting officer, managerial reporting officer?

RQ 16-4 What, in your own words, are a performance report and the responsibility accounting/reporting model?

RQ 16-5 What major *logical* processes does the GL/BR process perform?

RQ 16-6 Why is the *hierarchical coding* system a good fit for the general ledger system?

RQ 16-7 What limitations are faced by contemporary accounting systems applying traditional general ledger account structures?

RQ 16-8 In your own words, how do ERP financial modules facilitate the GL/BR process?

RQ 16-9 In your own words, how do ERP systems facilitate *balanced scorecard* and *business intelligence*?

RQ 16-10 Why is XBRL so important to efficient Web-based business reporting?

RQ 16-11 In your own words, what are public databases?

RQ 16-12 What are several IT control processes for networked workstations, and workstations that are connected to a central server? Explain each plan.

RQ 16-13 How will the Sarbanes-Oxley Act of 2002 affect the GL/BR process?

DISCUSSION QUESTIONS

DQ 16-1 Discuss fully the difference between the "contexts" of Figure 16.1 (page 590) and Figure 16.5 (page 597).

---

[7] See Robert K. Elliott, "Assurance Services and the Audit Heritage," *AUDITING: A Journal of Practice and Theory* (Supplement 1998) and Steve G. Sutton, "The Changing Face of Accounting and the Driving Force of Advanced Information Technologies," *International Journal of Accounting Information Systems* (March 2000).

DQ 16-2 Four managers (or departments) are shown in Figure 16.1 (page 590) as reporting to the controller. Setting aside your personal career inclinations and aspirations and ignoring any work experience you have, for which position do you think your college academic studies to date have best prepared you? Discuss. Does your answer hold any implications for the curriculum design at your college? Explain.

DQ 16-3 In the real world, what problems might an organization face in performing *interim closings*? For example, the books might be left open after a December 31 closing until auditing adjusting entries are made in March or April. During the same period, interim financial statements for the new year are required. Can you suggest any solutions for those problems? Discuss fully.

DQ 16-4 This chapter assumed that the controller was the source of all *adjusting entry* journal vouchers. Mention at least one alternative source for each of the following adjustments (and explain your answers):

    a. Estimated bad debts

    b. Interest accruals

    c. Lower of cost or market adjustments for inventories

    d. Lower of cost or market adjustments for investments

    e. Depreciation adjustments

    f. Differences between physical inventory counts and perpetual inventories

DQ 16-5 The financial reporting officer in this chapter had access to an external, on-line database (NAARS) to assist her in researching how certain footnotes to the financial statements might be worded. If that database were not available, what resources might she have consulted in the "good old days"? Discuss several possibilities, some of which you may have used in prior accounting courses.

DQ 16-6 "In terms of meeting the operations system goal of security of resources, physical control plans over access to networks and personal computer hardware and software are far more important and effective than any system controls that might be designed into the software." Do you agree? Present possible arguments for and against the proposition.

DQ 16-7 Read Section 409 from the Sarbanes-Oxley Act of 2002. Do you agree that this supports "real-time" financial reporting? Research both sides of the issue and provide a conclusion based on your findings.

PROBLEMS

P 16-1 The context diagram in Figure 16.5 (page 597) shows the data flows running to the general ledger from the feeder processes studied in Chapters 10 through 14.

    a. For each data flow in Figure 16.5, show the journal entry (in debit/credit journal entry format, with no dollar amounts) that would result (make and state any assumptions that you think are necessary).

    b. Name at least two other entries that would normally come from the feeder processes that are not shown in Figure 16.5.

c. In journal form, show one *representative* entry (including an entry explanation) that the treasurer would furnish for (1) investing transaction activities and (2) financing transaction activities.

P 16-2 Refer to the level 0 data flow diagram shown in Figure 16.6 (page 599).

Draw a lower-level DFD for each of the following processes shown in Figure 16.6. Make sure that each lower-level DFD is *balanced* with its parent.

a. Process 3.0—Record adjustments

b. Process 4.0—Prepare business reports

P 16-3 In this chapter, we acknowledged the inconsistency between the "context" assumed in Figure 16.1 (page 590) and that in Figures 16.5 and 16.6 (pages 597 and 599).

Redraw the data flow diagrams in Figures 16.5 and 16.6 to make them consistent with Figure 16.1. *Hint:* Figure 16.1 includes the treasurer, controller, and certain others *within* the system.

P 16-4 Examine the *responsibility accounting performance reporting* illustration shown in Figure 16.3 (page 594).

a. Design a data coding scheme that will facilitate the aggregation of data as the data "filter" upward. Use the specific facts that appear in Figure 16.3. Make and state any assumptions you think are necessary.

b. In no more than two paragraphs, explain how your coding scheme works. Include a discussion of positions in the organization other than those in the production function.

c. In no more than three paragraphs, explain how your scheme might be handled in a database environment without the codes.

P 16-5 Find two sets of financial statements from companies within one industry. List any problems you have in doing a comparison of the balance sheets. Describe how using XBRL could help alleviate these problems.

KEY TERMS

general ledger and business reporting (GL/BR) process

general ledger (GL) process

business reporting process

feeder process

financial reporting officer

managerial reporting officer

performance reports

responsibility accounting/reporting system

journal voucher

general ledger master data

audit trail

balanced scorecard

business intelligence

eXtensible Business Reporting Language (XBRL)

XML (eXtensible Markup Language)

National Automated Accounting Research System (NAARS)

call-back procedures

diskless workstation

network computers (NCs)

Glossary

A

ABC analysis A technique used to categorize inventory items according to their importance by ranking each item based on its output (page 449).

Abstract data types Allow users to define data to be stored in an object-oriented database (page 157).

Acceptance report A formal acknowledgment that a service contract has been satisfactorily completed (page 452).

Accounting information system (AIS) A specialized subsystem of the IS whose purpose is to collect, process, and report information related to the financial aspects of business events in an integrated IS; cannot be distinguished as a separate subsystem (pages 15–16).

Accounts payable/cash disbursements (AP/CD) process A business process that includes the last two steps, invoice verification and payment processing, in the purchase-to-pay process (page 478).

Accounts payable master data A repository of all unpaid vendor invoices (page 486).

Accounts receivable adjustments data An event data store, normally keyed by date, created as sales returns, bad debt write-offs, estimated doubtful accounts, or similar adjustments are processed. In addition to date, the typical data elements include journal voucher number, customer identification, adjustment type, account(s) and amount(s) to be debited, account(s) and amount(s) to be credited, and authorization indicator (i.e., approval code, signature, or the like) (page 409).

Accounts receivable master data A repository of all unpaid invoices issued by an organization and awaiting final disposition (page 407).

Accuracy The correspondence or agreement between the information and the events or objects that the information represents (page 26).

Activity A process that originates, transforms, files, or receives data (page 119).

Activity-based costing A costing approach where detailed costs to perform activities throughout the value chain are computed and can be managed or assigned to cost objects including products (page 555).

Agents People or organizations that participate in events. They can be part of the company or they can be external to the company (page 169).

Agreement of run-to-run totals Totals, prepared before a computer process has begun, are compared, manually or by the computer, to totals prepared at the completion of the computer process (page 327).

Anomalies Errors that might occur when adding, changing, or deleting data stored in the database (page 162).

Applications approach to business event processing Under this approach, each application collects and manages its own data, generally in dedicated, separate, physically distinguishable files for each application (page 146).

Attendance time record A payroll system data flow that shows the time periods that employees are in attendance at the job site and available for work (page 524).

Attribute An item of data that characterizes an object or a relationship (page 192).

Audit trail A means of tracing back to the individual business events that have been aggregated into the general ledger balances (page 600).

Automated clearing house (ACH) A method of electronic funds transfer in which the collector's bank account is credited and the payer's account is debited for the amount of a payment (page 399).

Automated guided vehicle system (AGVS) Computer-based carts that are capable of delivering parts and tools among multiple work centers (page 568).

Automated storage and retrieval system (AS/RS) Computer-controlled machines that store and retrieve parts and tools (page 568).

Availability Relates to information being available when required by the business process now and in the future. It also concerns the safeguarding of necessary resources and associated capabilities (page 24).

Available to promise planning The accumulation of the data on current inventories, sales commitments, and planned production to determine whether the production of finished goods will be sufficient to commit to additional sales orders (page 555).

B

Balanced When two DFDs have equivalent external data flows (page 111).

Balanced scorecard A methodology for assessing an organization's business performance via four components:

(1) financial, (2) internal business processes, (3) customers, and (4) innovation and improvement activities (page 604).

Balance-only system   A system in which accounts receivable records consist of a customer's current balance due, past-due balance, and the finance charges and payments related to the account. Each month, unpaid current balances are rolled into the past-due balances (page 407).

Bar code readers   Devices that use light reflection to read differences in bar code patterns in order to identify a labeled item (page 370).

Batch control plans   Control plans used in batch processing systems to regulate information processing by calculating control totals at various points in a processing run and subsequently comparing these totals (page 323).

Batch processing   A type of data processing in which groups, or batches, of transactions are collected and processed together (page 73).

Batch sequence check   A type of batch control plan in which the serial numbers of the documents comprising a batch are checked by the computer against a sequence number range entered by the operator (page 326).

Bill of lading   A shipping document that represents a contract between the shipper and the carrier in which the carrier agrees to transport the goods to the shipper's customer (page 365).

Bill of materials   A listing of all the subassemblies, parts, and raw materials that go into a parent assembly showing the quantity of each required to make an assembly (page 560).

Billing/accounts receivable/cash receipts (B/AR/CR) process   An interacting structure of people, equipment, methods, and controls designed to create information flows and records that support the repetitive work routines of the credit department, cashier, and accounts receivable department and assist in the preparation of internal and external reports (page 394).

Blind copy   A copy of a document on which selected data are blanked out (i.e., blinded) so that persons receiving that copy will not have access to those data (page 451).

Block coding   Groups of numbers are dedicated to particular characteristics of the objects being identified (page 160).

Bubble symbol   A symbol on a DFD that depicts an entity or a process within which incoming data flows are transformed into outgoing data flows (page 109).

Business continuity planning   *See* Contingency planning.

Business event   A meaningful change in the state of the enterprise such as creating a new employee record, submit-

ting a purchase order to a vendor, receiving a payment from a customer, picking goods from the warehouse and delivering to the shipping department, and revaluing inventory (page 47).

Business event data   Data that represent the "books of original entry" used for recording most business events (page 16).

Business intelligence   The integration of statistical and analytical tools with decision support technologies to facilitate complex analyses of data warehouses by managers and decision makers (page 604).

Business interruption planning   *See* Contingency planning.

Business process control plans   Plans that relate to those controls particular to a specific process or subsystem, such as billing or cash receipts, or to a particular technology used to process the data (page 247).

Business reporting process   Comprises preparing general purpose external financial statements and internal reportss for operational and strategic decision making (page 589).

C

Call-back procedures   Procedures used for authenticating the identity of users who access a computer network from remote locations through dial-in ports. Once the user has logged on to the system and has entered his or her password and other identifiers, the connection is terminated. Either manually through an operator or automatically through security software, the user is then called back at a telephone number stored in the system for that user (page 610).

Candidate key   Any attribute that could be a primary key in a relation (page 202).

Capable to promise planning   The accumulation of the data on current inventories, sales commitments, planned production and excess production capacity, or other planned production capacity that could be quickly converted to production of the desired finished goods necessary to fulfill a sales order request (page 555).

Capacity requirements planning (CRP)   The process that translates materials requirements into detailed machine- and labor-utilization schedules, and releases purchase orders to vendors and manufacturing orders to the factory (page 566).

Cardinality   A characteristic of a relationship that shows the degree to which each entity participates in the relationship (page 169).

Cash disbursements data   An event data store that shows, in chronological sequence, the details of each cash payment made. Each record typically contains the date the payment is recorded, vendor identification (or other account to be debited), disbursement voucher number (if a voucher system is used), vendor invoice number(s) and gross invoice amount(s), cash discounts taken on each invoice, net invoice amount(s), check amount, and check number (page 486).

Cash receipts data   An event data store that contains the details of each payment received. Each record normally would show the date the payment is recorded, customer identification (or other account[s] to be credited), invoice number(s) and gross invoice amount(s), cash discount(s) taken on each invoice, net invoice amount(s), check amount, and check number (page 409).

Cellular manufacturing   A manufacturing plant layout where machines are organized in clusters or 'cells' that contain all of the needed resources (machines, tools, labor) to produce a family of products (page 553).

Centralized information systems structure   The type of organizational structure that places the information systems function under the line authority of the vice president of information systems (page 261).

Charge card (Credit card)   A method of payment whereby a third party, for a fee, removes from the collector (i.e., a retailer) the risk of noncollection of an account receivable. The retailer submits the charges to the credit card company for reimbursement. In turn, the credit card company bills the consumer (page 398).

Check digit verification   A type of programmed edit check in which an extra digit is included in the identification number of entities such as customers and vendors. Through mathematical formulae, the computer uses the check digit to verify whether the identification number is input correctly (page 314).

Child records   Records that are included in a record one level above them (page 156).

Classifying   Grouping or categorizing data according to common attributes (page 160).

Client server technology   The physical and logical division between user-oriented application programs that are run at the client level (i.e., user level) and the shared data that must be available through the server (i.e., a separate computer that handles centrally shared activities—such as databases and printing queues—between multiple users) (page 81).

Coding   The creation of substitute values, or codes (page 160).

Cold site   A recovery strategy commonly included in contingency planning. A facility usually comprising air-conditioned space with a raised floor, telephone connections, and computer ports into which a subscriber can move equipment (page 281).

Comparability   The quality of information that enables users to identify similarities and differences in two pieces of information (page 24).

Compare input data with master data   Compare input data with data that has previously been recorded to determine accuracy and validity of the input data (page 320).

Completeness   The degree to which information includes data about every relevant object or event (page 26).

Compliance   Deals with complying with those laws, regulations, and contractual obligations to which the business process is subject (i.e., externally imposed business criteria) (page 24).

Composite attribute   Attributes that consist of multiple subattributes (page 192).

Composite primary key   A primary key formed by combining two or more columns in a table (page 159).

Computer agreement of batch totals   Batch totals prepared manually before a batch is submitted for processing are entered into the computer with the batch and are compared by the computer with totals accumulated by the computer as the batch was processed (page 326).

Computer cracking   *See* Computer hacking.

Computer hacking   The intentional penetration of an organization's computer system, accomplished by bypassing the system's access security controls (page 287).

Computer virus   A program that can attach itself to other programs (i.e., "infect" those programs) and that operates to alter the programs or to destroy data (page 234).

Computer-aided design/computer-aided engineering (CAD/CAE)   An application of computer technology that automates the product design process (page 559).

Computer-aided manufacturing (CAM)   The application of computer and communications technology to improve productivity by linking computer numerical control (CNC) machines, monitoring production, and providing automatic feedback to control operations (page 568).

Computer-aided process planning (CAPP)   An automated decision support system that generates manufacturing operations instructions and routings based on information about machining requirements and machine capabilities (page 560).

Confidentiality   Concerns the protection of sensitive information from unauthorized disclosure (page 24).

Consistent   When we can compare information about the same object or event collected at two points in time, the information is consistent (page 26).

Context diagram   A top-level diagram of an information system that describes the data flows into and out of the system and into and out of the external entities (page 108).

Contingency planning (Business continuity planning, Business interruption planning, Disaster recovery planning) A process or methodology designed to provide backup facilities, equipment, and personnel that will allow an organization to survive and recover from a major calamity with a minimum disruption to its operations (page 279).

Control environment A state of control consciousness that reflects the organization's (primarily the board of directors' and management's) general awareness of and commitment to the importance of control throughout the organization (page 240).

Control goal A business process objective that an internal control system is designed to achieve (page 241).

Control matrix A tool used to analyze a systems flowchart (and related narrative) to determine the control plans appropriate to that system and to relate those plans to the system's control goals (page 301).

Control plan An information processing policy or procedure that assists in accomplishing control goals (page 247).

Corrective control plan A control plan that is designed to rectify problems that have occurred (page 248).

Credit card *See* Charge card.

Critical success factors (CSFs) Events, circumstances, conditions, and activities that are essential to the survival of the organization (page 32).

Cumulative sequence check A type of batch control plan in which document numbers are checked by the computer against a file containing all possible numbers (page 326).

Customer acknowledgment A sales order confirmation that is sent to the customer as notification that an order has been accepted and to inform the customer of the expected shipment date (page 363).

Customer master data A data store—usually indexed by a unique code number assigned to each customer—that contains data identifying the particular characteristics of each customer, such as name, address, telephone number, credit data, and other standing data (page 366).

Customer relationship management (CRM) software Software that builds and maintains an organization's customer-related data (page 42).

Customer self-service (CSS) software Software that allows an organization's customers to complete an inquiry or perform a task (including sales) without the aid of an organization's employees (page 43).

D

Data Facts or figures in raw form. Data represent the measurements or observations of objects and events (page 22).

Data encryption (Encryption) A process that employs mathematical algorithms and encryption keys to encode data (i.e., change it from plain text to a coded text form) so that it is unintelligible to the human eye and therefore useless to those who should not have access to it (page 330).

Data flow diagram (DFD) A graphical representation of a system. A DFD depicts a system's components; the data flows among the components; and the sources, destinations, and storage of data (page 108).

Data flow symbol A symbol on a DFD that represents a pathway for data (page 109).

Data independence Decoupling of data from the system applications (that is, making the data independent of the application or other users) (page 150).

Data maintenance Includes activities related to adding, deleting, or replacing the standing data portions of master data (page 17).

Data manipulation language (DML) *See* Query language.

Data marts A subset of an overall data warehouse customized for a specific department. Data marts are designed to provide detailed data for a specific set of users (page 356).

Data mining The exploration, aggregation, and analysis of large quantities of varied data from across the organization to better understand an organization's business processes, trends within these processes, and potential opportunities to improve the effectiveness and/or efficiency of the organization (page 181).

Data model Depicts user requirements for data stored in a database (page 166).

Data store symbol A symbol on a DFD that represents a place where data are stored (page 109).

Data warehousing The use of information systems facilities to focus on the collection, organization, integration, and long-term storage of entity-wide data. Data warehousing provides users with easy access to large quantities of varied data from across the organization for the sole purpose of improving decision-making capabilities (page 180).

Database approach to business processing Concept to decouple the data from the system applications (i.e., to make the data independent of the application or other users) (page 149).

Database management system (DBMS) A set of integrated programs designed to simplify the tasks of creating, accessing, and managing a database (page 150).

Debit card A form of payment authorizing the collector to transfer funds electronically from the payer's to the collector's balance (page 398).

Decision making   The process of making choices (page 27).

Decision support systems (DSS)   Information systems that assist managers with unstructured decisions by retrieving data and generating information. A DSS possesses interactive capabilities, can answer ad hoc inquiries, and provides data and modeling facilities, such as spreadsheets, to support nonrecurring, relatively unstructured decision making (page 174).

Denial of service attack   When a Web site is overwhelmed by an intentional onslaught of thousands of simultaneous messages, making it impossible for the attacked site to engage in its normal activities (page 283).

Destination   An external entity on a DFD that receives data from the system (page 109).

Detective control plan   A control plan that is designed to discover that problems have occurred (page 248).

Digital image processing systems   Computer-based system for capture, storage, retrieval, and presentation of images of real or simulated objects (page 370).

Digital signature   A technology that validates the identity of the sender and the integrity of an electronic message (page 320).

Disaster recovery planning   *See* Contingency planning.

Disbursement voucher   A business document that indicates formal approval of a voucher for payment and provides such added data as the account distribution and the amounts to be debited (page 482).

Diskless workstation   A computer workstation that contains no disk drive to enable the writing of data to floppy disks (page 610).

Distributed denial of service attack   Uses many computers that unwittingly cooperate in a denial of service attack by sending messages to the target Web sites (page 283).

Document design   A control plan in which a source document is designed in such a way as to make it easier to prepare the document initially and later to input data from the document (page 313).

Document/record count   A type of batch control total. A simple count of the number of documents entered (page 325).

Document/record hash totals   A summarization of any numeric data field within the input document or record (page 314).

Dollar total   A type of batch control total. A summation of the dollar value of items in the batch, such as the total dollar value of all remittance advices in a batch (page 325).

E

E-Business   *See* Electronic business.

Economic order quantity (EOQ)   A technique that calculates the optimum quantity of inventory to order that will minimize the total cost of acquiring and carrying particular items of inventory (page 449).

Effectiveness (a control goal)   An operations process control goal that describes a measure of success in meeting one or more goals (page 244).

Effectiveness (a quality of information)   Deals with information being relevant and pertinent to the business process as well as being delivered in a timely, correct, consistent, and usable manner (page 24).

Efficiency (a control goal)   An operations process control goal that describes a measure of the productivity of the resources applied to achieve a set of goals (page 244).

Efficiency (a quality of information)   Concerns the provision of information through the optimal (most productive and economical) use of resources (page 24).

Electronic bill presentment and payment (EBPP)   Internet-based systems for sending bills/invoices and receiving the customer payment electronically (page 400).

Electronic business (E-Business)   The application of electronic networks (including the Internet) to undertake business processes between individuals and organizations (page 69).

Electronic cash   An electronic bank note issued by a financial institution to an individual who in turn can transfer these electronic notes to make purchases or other payments (page 399).

Electronic check   Similar to a paper check, the electronic version includes the customer's name, the seller's name, the customer's financial institution, the check amount, and a digital signature (page 399).

Electronic data interchange (EDI)   Computer-to-computer exchange of business data (i.e., documents) in structured formats that allow direct processing of those electronic documents by the receiving computer system (page 85).

Electronic document management (EDM)   The capturing, storage, management, and control of electronic document images for the purpose of supporting management decision making and facilitating business event data processing (page 83).

Electronic funds transfer (EFT)   A general term used to describe a variety of procedures for transmitting cash funds between parties via electronic transmission instead of using paper checks (page 399).

Electronic lockbox   A banking service in which the lockbox bank keys the remittance advice details into its computer system from the payer's paper remittance advice and then transfers the remittance advice data electronically from the bank's computer to the collector's accounts receivable computer system (page 399).

Electronic mail (e-mail)   The electronic transmission of nonstandardized messages between two individuals who are linked via a communications network (usually an intranet or the Internet) (page 82).

Electronic store fronts   Internet-located resources for displaying goods and services for sale and for conducting related sales events (page 99).

Electronic time management system   A computer-based system that captures, stores, and reports time (page 528).

Electronic vaulting (Shadowing, Replication)   Automatically transmits events-related data or actual master data changes on a continuous basis to an off-site electronic vault (page 281).

Employee/payroll master data   The central repository of data about people who work for an organization (page 527).

Encryption   *See* Data encryption.

Enterprise application integration (EAI)   An approach to connecting together multiple pieces of an enterprise system (page 45).

Enterprise database   The central repository for all the data related to the enterprise's business activities and resources (page 30).

Enterprise information systems   *See* Enterprise systems.

Enterprise resource planning (ERP) system   Integrated software packages designed to provide complete integration of an organization's business information processing systems and all related data (page 42).

Enterprise systems   A central information resource that integrates and coordinates the business process functionality and information from all of an organization's functional areas, such as marketing and sales, cash receipts, purchasing, cash disbursements, human resources, production and logistics, and business reporting (including financial reporting). Also known as enterprise-wide information systems and enterprise information systems (page 41).

Enterprise-wide information systems   *See* Enterprise systems.

Entity   Any object, event, or agent about which data are collected (page 166).

Entity-relationship diagram (E-R diagram)   A diagram that reflects the system's key entities and the relationships

among those entities and is commonly used to represent a data model (page 166).

Entity-relationship model   A diagram of the relational model that includes entities and relationships (page 166).

Entity-relationship modeling   The most popular data modeling approach in which the designer identifies the important things (called entities) about which information will be stored and then identifies how the things are related to each other (called relationships) (page 166).

E-R diagram   *See* Entity-relationship diagram.

Error routine   *See* Exception routine.

Event-driven architecture (EDA)   An approach to designing and building enterprise systems in which business events trigger messages to be sent by middleware between independent software modules that are completely unaware of each other (page 47).

Events   Activities that occur as a result of the various business processes in which an organization engages (page 168).

Exception and summary report   A computer-generated report that reflects the events—either in detail, summary total, or both—that were accepted by the system and those that were rejected by the system (page 323).

Exception routine (Error routine)   Process for handling out-of-the-ordinary (exceptional) or erroneous transactions (page 130).

Executive information systems (EIS) (Executive support systems [ESS])   Information systems, often considered a subset of DSS, that combine information from the organization and the environment, organize and analyze the information, and present the information to the manager in a form suitable for the decision to be made (page 174).

Executive support systems (ESS)   *See* Executive information systems (EIS).

Expert system (ES)   An information system that emulates the problem-solving techniques of human experts (page 175).

Exploding the BOM   A process that involves extending a bill of material to determine the total of each component required to manufacture a given quantity of an upper-level assembly or subassembly specified in the master production schedule (page 564).

eXtensible Business Reporting Language (XBRL)   An XML-based language consisting of a set of tags that are used to unify the presentation of business reporting information into a single format that can be easily read by almost any software package and can be easily searched by Web browsers (page 605).

eXtensible Markup Language (XML)   A generalized system for the customized tagging of data to enable the definition, transmission, and interpretation of data exchanged by systems over the Internet (pages 358).

External entities   Those entities (i.e., persons, places, or things) outside the system that send data to, or receive data from, the system (page 108).

External entity symbol   A symbol on a DFD that portrays a source or a destination of data outside the system (page 109).

Extranet   A type of intranet that a company has extended to allow limited external access to its customers, vendors, and other members of its value system (page 81).

F

Feedback value   The ability of feedback information (such as past inventory shortages and overages) to improve a decision maker's capacity to predict, confirm, or correct earlier expectations (page 24). *See also* Predictive value.

Feeder process   Any business process that accumulates business event data that are then communicated to and processed within the general ledger (GL) (page 590).

Fidelity bond   A type of insurance protection that indemnifies a company in case it suffers losses from defalcations committed by its employees (page 274).

Financial reporting officer   A manager with responsibilities for reporting financial information to external parties (page 591).

First normal form (1NF)   A relation is in first normal form (1NF) if it does not contain repeating groups (page 163).

Flexible manufacturing system (FMS)   An automated manufacturing operations system that can react quickly to product and design changes because centralized computer control provides real-time routing, load balancing, and production scheduling logic (page 568).

Float   When applied to cash receipts, float is the time between the customer tendering payment and the availability of good funds (page 398).

Forced vacations   A personnel policy that requires an employee to take leave from the job and substitutes another employee in his or her place (page 274).

Forms (in DBMSs)   An element that makes up DBMSs. They are on-screen presentations of data in tables and collected by queries from one or more tables (page 158).

Fraud   A deliberate act or untruth intended to obtain unfair or unlawful gain (page 230).

Freedom from bias   *See* Neutrality.

Functionally dependent   An attribute, B, is functionally dependent on another attribute, A (or possibly a collection of attributes), if a value for A determines a single value for B at any time. If functional dependence exists, we would say that "A determines B" (page 162).

G

General ledger (GL) process   Comprises accumulating data; classifying data by general ledger accounts; recording data in those accounts; and fueling the financial reporting, business reporting, and other reporting subsystems by providing them the information needed to prepare external and internal reports (page 589).

General ledger and business reporting (GL/BR) process   An interacting structure of people, equipment, methods, and controls that is designed to accomplish both operations and information system functions including maintenance of the general ledger and preparation of internal and external reports (page 589).

General ledger master data   A data repository that contains summarized information of all company event data (page 598).

Global inventory management   An inventory management approach where inventory needs and inventory and production capabilities are matched across the entire global enterprise, not just at a regional level (page 563).

Goal   *See* Objective.

Good funds   Funds on deposit and available for use (page 398).

Group decision support systems (GDSS)   *See* Group support systems (GSS).

Group support systems (GSS) (Group decision support systems [GDSS])   Computer-based systems that support collaborative intellectual work such as idea generation, elaboration, analysis, synthesis, and decision making. GSS use technology to solve the time and place dimension problems associated with group work (page 173).

Groupware   Software identified with GSS that focuses on such functions as e-mail, group scheduling, and document sharing (page 175).

H

Hash total   A type of batch control total that is calculated for control purposes only. A summation of any numeric data existing for all documents in the batch, such as a total of customer numbers or invoice numbers in the case of remittance advices (page 325).

Hierarchical coding   Ordering of items in descending order, where each successive rank order is subordinate to (or is a subset of) the rank above it (page 161).

Hierarchical database model   A logical model for a database in which child records may have no more than one parent record. All record relationships are 1:N (page 155).

Hot site   A recovery strategy commonly included in contingency planning. A fully equipped data center, often housed in bunker-like facilities, that can accommodate many businesses and that is made available to client companies for a monthly subscriber's fee (page 281).

Human capital management (HCM)   The process of managing how people are hired, developed, assigned, motivated, and retained (page 509).

Human resources (HR) management process   An interacting structure of people, equipment, methods, and controls. The primary function of the HR management process is to create information flows that support repetitive work routines of the human resources department and decision needs of those who manage the human resources department (page 511).

I

Immediate mode   The data processing mode in which there is little or no delay between data processing steps (page 77).

Imprest payroll bank account   A payroll bank account that is reimbursed (i.e., a cash transfer is made from the general cash account to the payroll bank account) for the exact amount of the total of paychecks issued—no more, no less (page 537).

Information   Data presented in a form that is useful in a decision-making activity (page 22).

Information processing   Includes data processing functions related to economic events such as accounting events, internal operations such as manufacturing, and financial statement preparation such as adjusting entries (page 17).

Information processing activities   Activities that retrieve data from storage, transform data, or file data (page 121).

Information system (IS) (Management information systems [MIS])   A man-made system that generally consists of an integrated set of computer-based and manual components established to collect, store, and manage data and to provide output information to users (page 14).

Information systems function (ISF)   The department that develops and operates an organization's information system (page 261).

Information technology steering committee   Committee that coordinates the organizational and IT strategic planning processes and reviews and approves the strategic IT plan (page 271).

Input accuracy   An information process control goal that requires events be correctly captured and entered into a system (page 244).

Input completeness   An information process control goal that requires all valid events or objects be captured and entered into a system (page 244).

Input data   Data received by the information system from the external environment or from another area within the information system (page 16).

Input validity   An information process control goal that requires input data be appropriately approved and represent actual economic events and objects (page 244).

Instance   One specific thing of the type defined by the entity (page 192).

Integrity   Relates to the accuracy and completeness of information as well as its validity in accordance with business's values and expectations (page 24).

Intelligent agent   A software component integrated into a decision support system or other software tool that provides automated assistance and/or advice on the use of the software, factors that should be considered when using a system for decision making, or supplying of common responses by other users (page 178).

Interactive feedback check   A control plan in which the data entry program informs the user that input has been accepted and recorded (page 315).

Internal control   A system of integrated elements—people, structure, processes, and procedures—acting together to provide reasonable assurance that an organization achieves business process goals (page 237).

Internal entity   A person, place, or thing within the system that transforms data. Internal entities include accounting clerks (persons), departments (places), and computers (things) (page 110).

Internet   A massive interconnection of computer networks worldwide that enables communication between dissimilar technology platforms (page 81).

Internet assurance   A service provided for a fee to vendors in order to provide limited assurance to users of the vendor's Web site that the site is in fact reliable and event data security is reasonable (page 98).

Internet auction markets   Provide an Internet base for companies to place products up for bid or for buyers to put proposed purchases up for bid (page 100).

Internet commerce   The computer-to-computer exchange of business event data in structured or semi-structured formats via Internet communication that allows the initiation and consummation of business events (page 93).

Internet market exchanges   Bring together a variety of suppliers in a given industry with one or more buyers in the same industry to provide Internet commerce through organized markets (page 101).

Inventory master data   A repository of inventory-related data that contains a record of each inventory item that is stocked in the warehouse or is regularly ordered from a vendor (page 453).

Invoice   A business document used by a vendor to notify the customer of an obligation to pay for merchandise ordered and shipped (page 403).

Item or line count   A type of batch control total. A count of the number of items or lines of data entered, such as a count of the number of invoices being paid by all the customer remittances (page 325).

J

Job time record   A payroll system data flow that reflects the start and stop times on specific jobs (page 524).

Journal voucher   An internal source document used to notify the general ledger to make an accounting entry (page 596).

Junction tables   *See* Relationship tables.

Just-in-time (JIT)   A pull manufacturing philosophy or business strategy for designing production processes that are more responsive to precisely timed customer delivery requirements (page 569).

K

Key attribute   The attribute whose value is unique (i.e., has a different value) for every entity that will ever appear in the database and is the most meaningful such attribute for identifying each entity (page 194).

Key verification   A control plan in which documents are keyed by one individual and then rekeyed by a second individual. The data entry software compares the second keystroking against the results of the first keystroking (page 315).

Knowledge management   The process of capturing, storing, retrieving, and distributing the knowledge of the individuals in an organization for use by others in the organization to improve the quality and/or efficiency of decision making across the firm (page 180).

L

Labor-force planning data   A repository of data concerning an organization's short- and long-term staffing requirements (page 522).

Library controls   A combination of people, procedures, and computer software that restricts access to stored data, programs, and documentation to authenticated users with authorized requests (page 286).

Lifecycle costs   The sum of the costs to design, produce, market, deliver, and support a product throughout the product's lifecycle from conception to ultimate discontinuance (page 557).

Limit check   *See* Reasonableness check.

Local area network (LAN)   Communications network that links several different local user machines with printers, databases, and other shared devices (page 81).

Locations   Places or physical locations at which events occur, resources are stored, or agents participate in events (page 169).

Lockbox   A postal address, maintained by the firm's bank, that is used solely for the purpose of collecting checks (page 399).

Logical data flow diagram   A graphical representation of a system showing the system's processes and the flows of data into and out of the processes (page 111).

Logical database view   The manner in which the data appear to the user to be stored. It represents the structure that the user must interface with in order to extract data from the database (page 151).

M

Management information system (MIS)   *See* Information system (IS).

Management process   A man-made system consisting of the people, authority, organization, policies, and procedures whose objective is to plan and control the operations of the organization (page 18).

Managerial reporting officer   A manager with responsibilities for preparing internal reports to assist management decision making (page 593).

Manual reconciliation of batch totals   Batch totals are established manually before a batch is submitted for processing and reconciled against the batch totals accumulated by the computer as the batch is processed and printed or displayed at the end of processing the batch. Reconciling the batch totals means an individual must determine why the totals do not agree and make corrections as necessary to ensure the integrity of the input data (page 326).

Manufacturing orders (MOs)   Orders that convey authority for the manufacture of a specified product or subassembly in a specified quantity and describe the material, labor, and machine requirements for the job (page 566).

Manufacturing resource planning (MRP)   An integrated decision support system for planning, executing, and controlling manufacturing operations (page 568).

Master data   Repositories of relatively permanent data maintained over an extended period of time (page 17).

Master data update   An information processing activity whose function is to incorporate new master data into existing master data (page 17).

Master production schedule (MPS)   A statement of specific production goals developed from forecasts of demand, actual sales orders, and/or inventory information (page 561).

Materials requirements planning   A process that uses bills of material, raw material and work in process (RM/WIP) inventory status data, open order data, and the master production schedule to calculate a time-phased order requirements schedule for materials and subassemblies (page 563).

Mathematical accuracy checks   This edit compares calculations performed manually to those performed by the computer to determine if a document has been entered correctly (page 314).

Maximum cardinality   A measure of the highest level of participation that one entity can have in another entity (page 169).

Mirror site   A site that maintains copies of a company's primary site's programs and data. During normal processing activities master data is updated at both the primary and mirror sites (page 280).

Mnemonic coding   Coding in which some or all identifying characters are letters of the alphabet (page 161).

Move ticket   Authorizes and records movement of a job from one work center to another (page 566).

N

National Automated Accounting Research System (NAARS)   An accounting research service; a public database (page 608).

Network computer (NC)   A computer consisting of a processor and a connection to the server, but no storage capability within the machine itself (page 610).

Network database model   A logical model for a database in which child records may have more than one parent record. Record relationships may be 1:N, N:1, or 1:1 (page 157).

Network provider   Companies that provide a link to the Internet by making their directly connected networks available for access by fee-paying customers (page 94).

Neural networks (NN)   Computer-based systems of hardware and software that mimic the human brain's ability to recognize patterns or predict outcomes using less than complete information (page 177).

Neutrality (Freedom from bias)   The quality of being not biased. Bias is the tendency of information to fall more often on one side than on the other of the object or event that it represents (page 24).

Non-key attribute   An attribute that is not part of the primary key (page 164).

Non-null   A value that is not missing in a relational database. Key attributes are required to be non-null in every tuple in a relational database (page 202).

Normal forms   Rules with which the structure of relational database tables must comply. They are based on set theory, the branch of mathematics on which relational database models are based (page 162).

Null   A missing value in a relational database (page 202).

O

Objective (Goal)   An intention; a desired state or condition being sought (page 32).

Object-oriented database model   A database that allows both simple and complex objects (including such things as video, audio, and pictures) to be stored using abstract data types, inheritance, and encapsulation (page 157).

Object-relational databases   Relational DBMSs that have added the ability to store complex data types (page 158).

Offline   A computer device, such as a key-to-disk machine, that is not directly connected to the computer (page 74).

One-for-one checking   A type of application control plan that entails the detailed comparison of the individual elements of two or more data sources to determine that they agree (page 328).

Online   A computer configuration in which certain equipment is directly connected to the computer (page 75).

Online prompting   A control plan that asks the user for input or asks questions that the user must answer (page 313).

Online real-time (OLRT) systems   Systems that gather transaction data at the time of occurrence, update the master records essentially instantaneously, and provide the results arising from the transaction within a very short amount of time—i.e., real-time (page 77).

Online transaction entry (OLTE)   The use of data entry devices to allow business event data to be entered directly into the information system at the time and place that the transaction occurs (page 75).

Online transaction processing (OLTP)   A real-time system that performs all or part of the processing activities at the data entry terminal location (page 79).

Open-item system   An accounts receivable system—used in situations where the customer typically makes payments for specific invoices when those invoices are due—in which records are maintained for each open invoice. Periodic statements reflect each unpaid invoice by aging category as well as the details of payments made (page 408).

Operations process   A man-made system consisting of the people, equipment, organization, policies, and procedures whose objective is to accomplish the work of the organization (page 18).

Optical character recognition   Devices that use light reflection to read handwritten or printed characters (page 370).

Order entry/sales (OE/S) process   An interacting structure of people, equipment, methods, and controls designed to achieve certain goals; its primary function is to create information flows that support the repetitive work routines of the sales order, credit, and shipping departments and the decision needs of those who manage various sales and marketing functions (page 350).

Order-to-cash process   A process that includes the events surrounding the sale of goods to a customer, the recognition of the revenue, and the collection of the customer payment (page 59).

P

Packing slip   A shipping document—generally attached to the outside of a shipping container—that identifies the customer and the contents of the package (page 366).

Paperless system   A system that eliminates documents and forms as the medium for conducting business (page 455).

Parent records   Records that include child records and reside one level above (page 157).

Partial dependency   A problem that arises because an attribute is dependent on a portion of the primary key, *not* on the entire key (page 164).

Participation constraint   A specification of both the minimum and maximum number of occurrences of one entity that can participate in the given relationship with any one occurrence of the other entity in the relationship (page 198).

Parts master   A list of the detailed specifications for each raw materials item; also called raw materials (RM) inventory master (page 560).

Payroll clearing account   A general ledger account that should show a zero balance after both the debit for gross pay earned by workers and the credit for gross pay distributed to jobs have been posted to the account (page 537).

Payroll direct deposit system   A system where employees' net pay is sent electronically through the banking system and deposited directly to the employees' bank accounts (page 528).

Payroll process   An interacting structure of people, equipment, methods, and controls that creates information flows to support the repetitive work routines of the payroll department (page 511).

Payroll service bureau   A company that specializes in rendering payroll services to client companies for a fee (page 528).

Performance report   A managerial accounting report that compares actual performance with budgeted expectations (page 594).

Periodic mode   A data processing mode in which there is some delay between data processing steps (page 73).

Pervasive control plan   A control policy or procedure that relates to a multitude of control goals and processes; it provides a climate or set of surrounding conditions in which the various AIS processes operate (page 247).

Physical data flow diagram   A graphical representation of a system showing the system's internal and external entities, and the flows of data into and out of these entities (page 110).

Physical database storage   The manner in which data are actually physically stored on the storage medium used in the database management system. This has little relationship to how the data appear to be stored to the user (page 152).

Picking ticket   A data flow—often a sales order copy—that authorizes the warehouse to "pick" the goods from the shelf and send them to shipping (page 363).

Plan   *See* Strategy.

Populate inputs with master data   Upon entry of an entity's identification code the computer populates the input with data about that entity from existing master data (page 320).

Post-billing system   A billing system in which invoices are prepared after goods have been shipped and the sales order notification has been matched to the shipping's billing notification (page 412).

Pre-billing system   A billing system in which invoices are prepared immediately on acceptance of a customer order—that is, after inventory and credit checks have been accomplished but before the goods have been shipped. Master data are updated when the invoice is prepared, but the customer copy of the invoice is not released until the goods have been shipped (page 412).

Predictive value (Feedback value)   Improves a decision maker's capacity to predict, confirm, or correct earlier expectations (page 24).

Preformatted screen   A computer screen designed to control the entry of data by defining the acceptable format of each data field, automatically moving to the next field, requiring that certain fields be completed, and by automatically populating fields (page 313).

Preventive control plan   A control plan that is designed to stop problems from occurring (page 248).

Preventive maintenance   A hardware control plan in which all computer equipment is periodically cleaned, tested, and adjusted to ensure continued efficient and correct operation (page 288).

Primary key   Uniquely identifies any record within a file (or row within a relational table). In a normalized relation, all attributes in the relation must be functionally dependent on the primary key (page 159).

Procedures for rejected inputs   A control plan designed to ensure that erroneous data—not accepted for processing—are corrected and resubmitted for processing (page 315).

Process   A series of actions or operations leading to a particular and usually desirable result (page 236).

Production, planning, and control   A production subsystem that is concerned with the orderly and timely movement of goods through the production process and that comprises activities such as planning material, people, and machine requirements; scheduling; routing; and monitoring the progress of goods through the factory (page 563).

Product lifecycle management (PLM) software   Software that manages product data during a product's life, beginning with the design of the product, continuing through manufacture, and culminating in the disposal of the product at the end of its life (page 43).

Program change controls   Policies and procedures designed to ensure that programs that have been developed in-house or purchased externally are not surreptitiously modified. Program change controls provide assurance that all modifications to programs are authorized, tested, properly implemented, and adequately documented (page 277).

Programmed edit check   An edit that is automatically performed by data entry programs upon entry of the input data (page 314).

Public database service   A computerized database service that allows subscribers, for a fee, to access and search an external database, usually through a telephone line connection (page 83).

Pull manufacturing   An approach to manufacturing management in which an idle machine pulls the next part from the previous machine as soon as that part is available (page 553).

Purchase order (PO)   A request for the purchase of goods or services from a vendor (page 450).

Purchase order master data   A compilation of open purchase orders that includes the status of each item on order (page 453).

Purchase receipts data   An event data store with each record reflecting a receipt of goods and services (page 453).

Purchase requisition   An internal request to acquire goods and services (page 447).

Purchase requisitions master data   A compilation of the purchase requisitions, requests for goods and services from authorized personal within an organization and for inventory replenishment from automated inventory replenishment systems, such as supply chain management processes (page 453).

Purchase returns and allowances   An exception routine that occurs where purchased goods (or services) received do not conform to those ordered. The goods are either returned to the vendor or a price reduction (an allowance) is made by the vendor (page 484).

Purchase-to-pay process   A process that includes the events surrounding the purchase of goods from a vendor, the recognition of the cost of those goods, and the payment to the vendor (page 60).

Purchasing process   A business process that includes the first three steps, requirements determination, purchase order processing, and goods receipt, in the purchase-to-pay process (page 437).

Push manufacturing   An approach to manufacturing management in which the sales forecast drives the production plan, and goods are produced in large batches (or jobs) (page 553).

Q

Queries   An element that makes up DBMSs. They are tools that allow users and programmers to access the data stored in various tables (page 158).

Query language   Language used to access a database and to produce inquiry reports. Allows a nontechnical user to bypass the programmer and access the database directly (page 151).

R

Radio-frequency identification (RFID)   A chip with an antenna that can send and receive data from an RFID reader (page 458).

Raw materials requisition   An authorization that identifies the type and quantity of materials to be withdrawn from the storeroom (page 567).

Reasonableness check (Limit check)   A type of programmed edit check that tests whether the contents (e.g., values) of the data entered fall within predetermined limits (page 314).

Receiving report   The business document used to record merchandise receipts (page 451).

Record input   The process that stores the accurate, valid input data onto digital media for subsequent updating procedures in a timely manner with minimal use of resources (page 315).

Recursive relationship   A relationship between two different entities of the same entity type (page 196).

Referential integrity   A specification that for every attribute value in one relation that has been specified in order to allow reference to another relation, the tuple being referenced must remain intact (page 202).

Reject stub   A data flow assigned the label "Reject" that leaves a bubble but does not go to any other bubble or data store and indicates processing that is performed in other-than-normal situations (page 130).

Relation   A collection of data representing multiple occurrences of an object, event, or agent (page 201).

Relational database model   A logical model for a database in which data are logically organized in two-dimensional tables. Each table is referred to as a relation (page 157).

Relationships   Associations between entities (page 166).

Relationship tables (Junction tables)   Tables required to be created when implementing many-to-many relationships because relational DBMSs do not have the ability to model a many-to-many relationship directly. Each many-to-many relationship must be modeled as a pair of one-to-many relationships (page 171).

Relevance   Information capable of making a difference in a decision-making situation by reducing uncertainty or increasing knowledge for that particular decision (page 23).

Reliability of information   Relates to the provision of appropriate information for management to operate the entity and for management to exercise its financial and compliance reporting responsibilities (page 24).

Remittance advice (RA)   A business document used by the payer to notify the payee of the items being paid (page 406).

Reorder point (ROP) analysis   A technique for determining when to reorder inventory that establishes a re-order point for each inventory item based on that item's unique rate of sale or use (page 448).

Replication   *See* Electronic vaulting.

Reports   An element that makes up DBMSs. They provide printed lists and summaries of data stored in tables or collected by queries from one or more tables (page 159).

Resources   Assets (tangible or intangible) that the company owns (page 168).

Responsibility accounting/reporting system   A managerial reporting system that is tied to the hierarchy or chain of responsibility/authority reflected by the firm's organization chart (page 594).

Risk   The possibility that an event or action will cause an organization to fail to meet its objectives (or goals) (page 227).

Rotation of duties   A personnel policy that requires an employee to alternate jobs periodically (page 274).

Routing master   A data store that specifies the operations necessary to complete a subassembly or finished good and the sequence of these operations (page 560).

S

Sales event data   A file comprised of one or more invoice records, analogous to a sales journal in a manual book keeping system. Each file record normally would contain the invoice date, invoice number, customer identification, and invoice amount (page 408).

Sales force automation (SFA) software   Software that automates sales tasks such as order processing and tracking (page 43).

Sales order master data   A repository of "open" sales order records, created upon acceptance of a sales order and kept open until the order has been shipped (page 366).

Scanner   Input device that captures printed images or documents and converts them into electronic digital signals that can be stored on computer media (page 370).

Schema   A complete description of the configuration of record types and data items and the relationships among them. Defines the logical structure of the database (page 151).

Second normal form (2NF)   A relation is in second normal form (2NF) if it is in first normal form and no non-key attribute is dependent on only a portion of the primary key (page 164).

Security of resources   An operations process control goal directed toward protecting an organization's resources from loss, destruction, disclosure, copying, sale, or other misuse (page 244).

Security officer   An individual responsible for assigning passwords and performing other control-related activities directed at restricting access to an organization's resources (page 271).

Segregation of duties   An organizational control plan that consists of separating the four basic functions of event processing—authorizing events, executing events, recording events, and safeguarding resources resulting from consummating events (page 268).

Self-checking digit code   Assigns an extra digit to the code; the added digit is designed to check the accuracy with which the code is keyed into a computer system (page 161).

Semantics   The meaning of business events (page 193).

Sequence check   A type of control in the batch processing system that checks documents that are numbered sequentially—either assigned a number when the document is prepared or prepared using pre-numbered documents. Two kinds of sequence checks exist—a batch sequence check or cumulative sequence check (page 326).

Sequential coding (Serial coding) Assigns numbers to objects in chronological sequence (page 160).

Serial coding *See* Sequential coding.

Server clustering Use of clustered servers to disperse the processing load among servers so that if one fails, another can take over (page 280).

Shadowing *See* Electronic vaulting.

Shop floor control (SFC) process A process devoted to monitoring and recording the status of manufacturing orders as they proceed through the factory. It also maintains work center status information showing the degree ahead or behind schedule and utilization levels (page 570).

Significant digit coding Assigns to specific digits a meaning of their own, allowing selective inquiries of a database (page 161).

Simple Object Access Protocol (SOAP) An XML-based protocol for encoding Web Service messages (page 358).

Skills inventory data A repository of data that catalogs each employee's set of relative skills, experience, education, and training (page 522).

Source An external entity on a DFD that sends data from outside the system (page 109).

Standing data Relatively permanent portions of master data, such as the credit limit on customer master data and the selling price and warehouse location on inventory master data (page 17).

Strategic planning The process of selecting the organization's long-term objectives and of setting the strategies for achieving those objectives (page 30).

Strategy (Plan) The means (organizational structure and processes) by which an organization has chosen to achieve its objectives and critical success factors (page 32).

Structured decision One for which all three decision phases (intelligence, design, and choice) are relatively routine or repetitive (page 29).

Subassemblies Separately manufactured components used in the final product (page 555).

Subschema A description of a portion of a schema (page 151).

Subsystem A part of a system (page 13).

Supply chain The connections between an organization, including the flow of information, materials, and services, from suppliers of merchandise and raw materials through to the organization's customers (page 441).

Supply chain management (SCM) The combination of processes and procedures used to ensure the delivery of goods and services to customers at the lowest cost while providing the highest value to the customers (page 441).

Supply chain management (SCM) software Software that provides support for the planning and execution of the steps in an organization's supply chain from demand planning through selling the product (page 43).

System A set of interdependent elements that together accomplish specific objectives. A system must have organization, interrelationships, integration, and central objectives (page 13).

Systems development life cycle (SDLC) 1. A formal set of activities, or a process, used to develop and implement a new or modified information system (the systems development methodology). 2. The documentation that specifies the systems development process (the systems development standards manual). 3. The progression of information systems through the systems development process, from birth, through implementation, to ongoing use (page 275).

Systems flowchart A graphical representation of the information processes (activities, logic flows, inputs, outputs, and data storage), as well as the related operations processes (entities, physical flows, and operations activities) (page 112).

T

Tables An element that makes up DBMSs. They provide a place to store the data (page 158).

Third normal form (3NF) A relation is in third normal form (3NF) if it is in second normal form and if the only determinants it contains are candidate keys (page 166).

Throughput time The time it takes from when authorization is made for goods to be produced to when the goods are completed (page 553).

Tickler file Any file that is reviewed on a regular basis for the purpose of taking action to clear the items from that file (page 328).

Timeliness Information that is available to a decision maker before it loses its capacity to influence a decision (page 24).

Time-phased order requirements schedule Shows the time period when a manufacturing order or purchase order should be released so that the subassemblies and raw materials will be available when needed (page 563).

Top-down partitioning The successive subdividing, or "exploding," of logical DFDs that, when properly performed, leads to a set of balanced DFDs (page 111).

Total quality control (TQC)   A subset of JIT that places responsibility for quality in the hands of the builder rather than in those of the inspector (page 569).

Transitive dependency   Exists in a relational database table when a non-key attribute is functionally dependent on another non-key attribute (page 165).

Tuple   A set of data that describes an instance of an entity represented by the relation (page 202).

Turnaround document   A document—printed by the computer as an output of one process—that is then used to capture and input a subsequent transaction (page 325).

U

Understandability   Enables users to perceive the information's significance. Valued from the point of view of the user, understandable information is presented in a form that permits its application by the user in the decision-making situation at hand (page 22).

Universal Description, Discovery, and Integration (UDDI)   A protocol for registering a business in an Internet directory so that companies can find one another and carry out business over the Web (page 358).

Unnormalized table   A relation that contains repeating attributes (or fields) within each row (or record) (page 163).

Unstructured decision   One for which none of the decision phases (intelligence, design, and choice) are routine or repetitive (page 29).

Update accuracy   An information process control goal that requires that data entered into a computer are reflected correctly in their respective master data (page 244).

Update anomalies   Problems in a relational table caused by the existence of functional dependencies (page 164).

Update completeness   An information process control goal that requires that all events entered into a computer are reflected in their respective master data (page 244).

V

Validity   Information about actual events and actual objects (page 26).

Value chain   A sequence of activities performed by an organization that add value or utility to the product produced or service provided (page 46).

Value-added network (VAN)   A packet-switched network service that provides communication capabilities for organizations not wishing to obtain their own packet-switched or dedicated communication links (page 89).

Variance analysis   The process of comparing actual information about input costs and usage to standards for costs and usage for manufacturing inputs (page 572).

Vendor invoice   A business document that notifies the purchaser of an obligation to pay a vendor for goods or services that were ordered and shipped to the purchaser (page 481).

Vendor master data   A repository of data about approved vendors (page 453).

Vendor packing slip   A business document that accompanies the purchased inventory from the vendor and identifies the shipment and triggers the inventory receiving process (page 451).

Verifiability   A piece of information has verifiability when there is a high degree of consensus about the information among independent measurers using the same measurement methods (page 24).

W

Web browser   Software program designed specifically to allow users to browse various documents and data sources available on the Internet (page 81).

Web Services   A process and set of protocols for directly connecting enterprise systems over the Internet (page 358).

Web Services Description Language (WSDL)   An XML-based format for describing how one software system can connect and utilize the services of another software system over the Internet (page 358).

Wide area network (WAN)   Communications network that links distributed users and local networks into an integrated communications network (page 81).

Work center   A group of similar workstations (page 560).

Work center master   A data store that describes each work center available for producing products, including information such as the machine available at the station, its capacity, its maintenance needs, labor needs to operate it, and so on (page 560).

Workstation   The assigned location where a worker performs his or her job (page 560).

Written approval   A control plan in which a business document is checked to see that it contains an authorized signature indicating that the event has been authorized by that person (page 313).

X

XBRL   *See* eXtensible Business Reporting Language.

XML   *See* eXtensible Markup Language.